BVR/AHLA Guide to Healthcare Industry Compensation and Valuation

Timothy Smith, CPA/ABV, and
Mark O. Dietrich, CPA/ABV
Editors

What It's Worth

1000 SW Broadway, Suite 1200, Portland, OR 97205

(503) 291-7963 • www.bvresources.com

What It's Worth

Publisher: Sarah Andersen

Managing Editor: Janice Prescott

Chair and CEO: David Foster

President: Lucretia Lyons

Vice President of Sales: Lexie Gross

Customer Service Manager: Retta Dodge

ISBN: 978-1-62150-017-9

Library of Congress Control Number: 2012949852

Table of Contents

Introduction: How to Use This Guide Effectively

The BVR/AHLA Guide to Healthcare Industry Compensation and Valuation provides the first systematic presentation of the theory and practice of the newly emerging appraisal discipline of healthcare compensation valuation (CV). It includes 42 chapters and practice aids, with 24 of these presenting new material and 10 revised and streamlined chapters from prior publications. All of the contributing authors to the guide are experts in their respective areas. The guide is the first text to develop a comprehensive body of knowledge for CV practice, affording a foundation for the conceptual framework of CV as a unique discipline within the appraisal profession. At the same time, this guide delivers some of the most in-depth and penetrating analysis of the regulatory compliance issues related to healthcare valuation that has been published to date. It also seeks to educate readers about the fundamental economics of healthcare compensation arrangements and the market dynamics that drive them. These economics are analyzed further in terms of their impact on the issues and methods involved in appraising compensation arrangements in the healthcare industry.

The guide is organized to provide the reader with the analytical tools for evaluating and assessing compensation arrangements. Each section is organized as part of a progressive development of thought and analysis related to healthcare compensation arrangements and their valuation:

- *Introduction to Healthcare Compensation and Valuation:* The first section provides an introduction to CV practice, including chapters that show the common as well as distinctive areas of CV in comparison to other appraisal disciplines. It also includes chapters on adapting standard appraisal concepts to CV and developing content for CV appraisal reports.

- *Regulatory Matters in Compensation Valuation:* The regulatory section provides groundbreaking and in-depth reviews of the fundamental questions and issues involved in complying with the regulatory standards of fair market value, commercial reasonableness, and reasonable compensation for tax purposes. These chapters equip the reader to deal with the complex regulatory matters that arise in compensation valuation and consulting in the healthcare context.

- *Topics in the Economics and Analysis of Physician Services:* A separate section is devoted to a discussion of critical issues involved in the economics of physician services, ranging from physician specialties and reimbursement to quality and productivity. Practical chapters provide guidance in preparing physician productivity calculations and using benchmark data, such as MGMA.

- *Appraising Compensation Arrangements:* The chapters in this section provide general and comprehensive overviews for valuing numerous types of healthcare compensation arrangements. They use a common content outline that analyzes the key economics and market forces for the arrangement, highlights specific regulatory issues, and discusses the critical issues involved in the application of the market, cost, and income approaches.

- *Advanced Issues and Specialized Topics in Healthcare Compensation Valuation:* The final section presents unique, in-depth studies on specific areas that impact valuation methods and analysis related to compensation in healthcare. Several chapters are devoted to issues related to compensation and work relative value units (wRVUs) and to the use of physician compensation surveys in valuation and compensation-setting practices.

The guide includes material that should have appeal and application to a variety of users. It contains chapters that deal with content at a general level, providing the reader with an introduction to and comprehensive overview of the subject matter. Some chapters are highly specialized or address topics at an advanced level. Some have a practical orientation, while others deal with theoretical issues related to valuation methodology. The text includes a number of practice aids for CV appraisers to use in their daily practice. In summary, the guide provides a diversity of content, both in terms of the scope of topics and the level at which they are discussed.

One attractive and practical feature of this text is the integration of material from one chapter to the next, across an array of authors and contributors. Definitional, methodological, and regulatory matters are discussed and addressed in foundational chapters. Subsequent chapters dealing with issues and topics related to specific types of service or compensation arrangements found in the healthcare arena assume and reference material from these foundational chapters. This integration frees readers and contributors alike from the need to revisit foundational concepts and definitions when addressing the distinct issues in valuing a particular type of compensation arrangement.

To help readers use the guide effectively, each chapter begins with a table of contents that identifies the major topics in the chapter and their corresponding page numbers. We have also prepared a series of recommended readings for various audiences, beginning on page 933. These reading lists identify chapters that would be most relevant for users with varying backgrounds and information needs. One helpful list is a set of "newcomer" recommended readings that is intended for newly hired staff in professional firms or for experienced professionals who are new to healthcare or healthcare valuation. We recommend the use of this guide as part of staff training programs.

We, along with Business Valuation Resources and the American Health Lawyers Association, wish to extend our thanks and gratitude to the various contributing authors to the guide. The new material was prepared in a very short period of time, requiring significant sacrifices by very busy professionals. Moreover, we appreciate the willingness of the authors to share with the appraisal and healthcare compliance communities the insights, knowledge, and know-how that they have accumulated in their practices. The industry owes a debt of gratitude to those who are willing to spread the wealth of knowledge voluntarily for the benefit of the industry. Such broad-mindedness is the mark of a true professional! For more information about the authors, please see page 939.

Part I.
Introduction to Healthcare Compensation and Valuation

Chapter 1. An Introduction to the New Appraisal Discipline of Compensation Valuation

CONTENTS

Chapter 1. An Introduction to the New Appraisal Discipline of Compensation Valuation

By Timothy Smith, CPA/ABV

1.0 Introduction

The healthcare industry is marked by a variety of service, rental, and resource usage arrangements between various types of healthcare providers, including physicians, hospitals, health systems, or life sciences companies, such as a pharmaceutical company or medical device manufacturer. In most of these arrangements, physicians provide services to corporate healthcare providers. One may also occasionally find situations in which a hospital/health system or a life sciences company provides goods or services to a physician or physician group. These arrangements are commonly described as compensation arrangements, since the common or similar element among them is the payment of compensation over time in exchange for services, rentals, or other forms of resource utilization. Healthcare regulations generally require the compensation paid in these various arrangements to be consistent with fair market value (FMV), since physicians represent referral sources for these types of healthcare provider entities. In recent years, it has become a standard industry practice to use independent appraisers to provide valuations of these arrangements based on FMV as defined by healthcare regulations. As a result, a new appraisal discipline is emerging: compensation valuation, or CV, as it is commonly labeled by practitioners of this developing specialty.

This chapter provides a primer to the background and key topics related to this emerging form of appraisal practice. It will outline unique considerations that arise in analyzing the fundamental economics and marketplace dynamics of compensation arrangements. This material provides the groundwork for introducing readers to the critical issues involved in the practice of compensation valuation in the healthcare industry.

2.0 Overview of Compensation Arrangements

2.1 The Marketplace of Compensation Arrangements

Compensation valuation focuses on the appraisal of compensation arrangements. What is appraised in CV assignments is the compensation one party pays to another for the services or resource usage a seller provides to a buyer over a set period. While many think of CV as dealing with service arrangements only, this view is actually too narrow. The healthcare marketplace is more varied in its arrangements between healthcare providers than simply service agreements. Historically, the broad categories of arrangements in healthcare have included the following:

- Services;

- Rentals of real estate and equipment;

- Services included with the rental of real estate and/or equipment;

- Services provided together with the sale or usage of goods;

- Services provided together with rentals of real estate and/or equipment and with the sale or usage of goods; and

- Licensing of assets, such as intangible assets.

In another permutation, compensation arrangements in healthcare can involve the sale of services that require the utilization of personnel, space, equipment, goods or supplies, services, and other resources. These services are not personally provided by a healthcare professional, but by a fully operating business providing a service.

Because of their broad scope, the essence of compensation arrangements is best described as the buying and selling of services and resources over a set period. Rather than a one-time sales transaction, compensation arrangements provide periodic or ongoing sales of services or resources over the term of the arrangement. The purchase price paid in these arrangements is categorized as compensation. Thus, the term "compensation arrangement" is used to denote a broader array of arrangements than only service agreements. Compensation valuation is the discipline that appraises the value of resources provided in compensation arrangements.

A more formal definition of compensation arrangements could be constructed along the following lines:

Compensation arrangements entail the sale of resource access and usage over a set period. The resources involved in compensation arrangements primarily include services, but they may also include the usage of real property, personal property, and business property.

Compensation valuation would then be described according to the following definition:

Compensation valuation is the discipline that seeks to appraise the value of the compensation paid for resource access and usage in compensation arrangements.

2.2 The Major Types of Compensation Arrangements in Healthcare

Compensation arrangements found in the healthcare industry can be catalogued using the following general categories or types.

Physician Service Arrangements

The most prevalent form of compensation arrangement in the healthcare marketplace involves physician services. Physicians provide a variety of services to healthcare provider entities and companies. These services may be clinical, administrative, executive, management, technical, research, or educational in nature.

Rentals of Office Space and Equipment

Rentals or leases of office space and various forms of equipment leasing between healthcare industry providers and physicians are ubiquitous in the healthcare industry. The most common form of lease is between a physician and a hospital- or health system-owned medical office building for office space. So-called "timeshare" rentals are also common, whereby space, equipment, staff, and other resources are leased or licensed to other parties, frequently based on set blocks of time, as opposed to continuous exclusive use.

Clinical Procedural Services

Healthcare providers of all types occasionally sell each other various forms of clinical services. These clinical services frequently involve medical or diagnostic testing procedures, such as lab or imaging, that are commonly referred to as "technical component services." They may also involve the services of nonphysician providers, such as physician assistants or nurse practitioners, or the services of other types of healthcare professionals, including nurses and technicians.

Nonclinical Professional and Administrative Services

Healthcare companies and providers also sell each other various nonclinical-related professional or administrative services. The most common example is management services, including the operational, legal, human resources, revenue cycle, accounting, treasury, and corporate compliance functions of a company. Another frequently occurring example is employee leasing.

3.0 The Background and Emergence of Compensation Valuation

3.1 The Regulatory Origins of Compensation Valuation

As noted in Section 1.0, compensation arrangements between healthcare providers who have a referral relationship are subject to healthcare regulations. These regulations primarily stem from the federal anti-kickback statute and the physician self-referral, or Stark, law. Both sets of regulations generally mandate that transactions and arrangements between parties with referral relationships be established at pricing that is consistent with FMV. These regulations have had a profound impact on the appraisal profession. As compensation arrangements among healthcare entities proliferated in the first decade of the 21st century, the need for appraisals of the compensation paid in these arrangements grew at increasing rates. The use of independent appraisers and valuation consultants to determine FMV for regulatory compliance purposes is now a common practice within the healthcare industry. This increasing demand, coupled with seemingly endless creation and development of new forms of compensation arrangements, has given rise to the formation of a new appraisal discipline focused solely on appraising the value of compensation in these arrangements.

3.2 Emerging in the Absence of Professional Standards and an Established Body of Knowledge

As a new appraisal discipline that has not been formerly recognized and established within a profession, the practice of compensation valuation is not subject to any specific professional standards, outside of generic requirements for consulting assignments for those appraisers who belong to professional organizations, such as Certified Public Accountants, who have relatively strict requirements compared to others involved in CV. There are no professional societies or organizations dedicated to the practice of CV, nor are there any CV professional certifications or accreditations. Likewise, there is no formal established body of knowledge for this emerging discipline. The absence of professional standards and a formal body of knowledge results in a wide diversity of ideas and practices within this field of valuation. It has sometimes fostered an environment of "proprietary" thinking about methods and techniques among practitioners, although this parochialism is beginning to change. The lack of standards has also allowed for a variety of informal and ad hoc concepts, techniques, and practices to enter the CV arena. Many of these lack a systematic, formal, or intentional grounding in valuation theory and the general body of knowledge held across the appraisal disciplines. The tendency in CV practice for informal and proprietary methods and techniques has been exacerbated by the lack of clear healthcare regulatory guidance on the definition of FMV and its determination.[1] In addition, individuals with little or no formal training in the art and science of appraisal perform a significant proportion of compensation valuation work. As a result, the practice of CV has been proprietary and fragmented during this first decade of evolution.

This fragmentation has resulted in a great disparity of practice. CV practitioners who came from professional appraisal backgrounds usually had established work patterns with respect to engagement, analysis, and report writing standards and practices. They also came with the appraisal profession's long-held conceptual and theoretical framework for valuation. This framework included a developed tradition of ideas, concepts, approaches, techniques, and work standards about appraisal. It provided those with an appraisal background with a ready-made scope of work template to use in CV assignments. At the same time, many CV practitioners came from healthcare consulting or operations without formal training in the professional practice of appraisal. Their orientation and practice patterns lacked the ready-made framework and work product standards that could be crosswalked from the other appraisal disciplines, primarily from business valuation (BV). This is an almost precise replication of the circumstances that existed in the 1990s during the last healthcare consolidation with respect to business valuation in the healthcare industry.

Today, however, CV practitioners are developing a commonly held set of practices and a theoretical framework for preparing appraisals. More professional literature is being published on the subject, and there is a critical dialogue about CV principles and application emerging in the industry. The legal community has been contributing to this conversation as well. In many ways, this text, *The BVR/AHLA Guide to Healthcare Industry Compensation and Valuation*, represents the culmination of an effort within the community to establish a common theoretical framework and body of knowledge for the practice of CV.

3.3 Appraisal Disciplines Involved in Compensation Valuation

Appraisal professionals will readily recognize the fact that real estate (RE) and machinery and equipment (M&E) appraisers usually address real estate and equipment rentals, respectively. Both appraisal disciplines have traditionally valued such rentals as part of their scope of practice. The licensing of intellectual property (IP) has also been traditionally valued by appraisers in the BV discipline who also specialize in valuing IP assets. The new appraisal discipline of compensation valuation has emerged,

---

1   See Chapter 7, "Complying With the Healthcare Definition of FMV in Appraisal Practice," for a discussion of the healthcare regulatory definition of FMV.

however, to address the valuation of other types of compensation arrangements. For certain types of arrangements, CV appraisers may use and rely on the work of RE and M&E appraisers, incorporating opinions of value from these appraisal disciplines as elements in valuing the compensation for arrangements where RE and M&E rentals are part of a broader scope of resources. The practice of CV, therefore, can involve areas of overlap and collaboration with other types of appraisal professionals.

3.4 The Adaptation of the Business Valuation Body of Knowledge

Because compensation arrangements primarily involve services, BV appeared to be the most relevant of the established appraisal disciplines for adaptation to CV practice. BV afforded the concepts and techniques that were more readily adaptable to the CV context than other disciplines, such as RE or M&E appraisal. As noted previously, many compensation arrangements involve services that represent the operations of a complete business. In addition, CV generally involves analysis of economic factors and issues that are comparable to appraisal work performed in BV assignments. Thus, CV practitioners generally look to the BV body of knowledge for the conceptual and theoretical framework for this emerging discipline. They use this framework as the foundation for ideas, concepts, methods, and techniques that can be adapted in CV practice.

In addition, many CV practitioners came from the BV field and some practice in both the CV and BV disciplines. Thus, the adaption of the BV body of knowledge was a natural outgrowth of their training and experience. Since there are no established professional standards for CV, practitioners borrowed from BV to establish basic quality criteria for CV assignments. This adaptation of another appraisal discipline as a conceptual foundation for CV should not come as a surprise to professional appraisers. There is a common theoretical framework among appraisal disciplines. In the case of BV, there were many areas of commonality with CV. These areas of comparability made BV the natural starting point for the development of a CV body of knowledge.

4.0 Key Elements of Compensation Valuation Analysis

4.1 Unique Characteristics of Compensation Valuation in Appraisal Practice

The valuation of compensation arrangements gives rise to several appraisal issues that are unique to CV practice in comparison to other appraisal disciplines. First, CV does not generally address the sale or exchange of an ownership interest in real, personal, or business property as the subject transaction of the appraisal assignment. Other disciplines usually value property in use or in exchange. The subject transaction in CV typically relates to the sale of services or the usage of property over time. While compensation arrangements occasionally will include the sale of goods or supplies that are consumed as part of providing the service, ownership of property is not the primary focus of CV work. Second, the compensation in these arrangements may also be variable or contingent upon other factors, such as the level of service provided or the level of performance. In some instances, the arrangement may have multiple services or require the use of varying resources; thus, the value paid may have numerous components that may be paid for using differing terms or rates. Consequently, the compensation paid in an arrangement can have many different moving parts.

These unique characteristics of compensation arrangements, in comparison to traditional sales transactions, create new and interesting challenges for CV practitioners in terms of the scope of work and the nature of the opinion of value. For example, a CV opinion of value must be rendered to cover a specified period of the arrangement. If an arrangement has a term of multiple years, the appraiser is required to analyze whether the opinion of value for the compensation under the arrangement will be valid for the full contract term or only a portion of the term. The time question for the opinion is further complicated by the fact that clients often seek appraisals in advance of consummating an arrangement, but they may take many months to complete and sign the actual contract. There can even be a difference in the date on which an agreement is executed and when it is to become effective. As a result, the question of the duration of the valuation opinion needs to address both the arrangement term and the lead time to consummate the agreement.

Another challenging area is addressing the value of various elements in compensation arrangements. Clients usually request that appraisers opine on all the individual elements of the arrangement and on the total value of these elements taken together.[2] These elements may represent different and distinct services or resource utilization, but they may also represent the value of a single basic service that is measured using different metrics or performance outcomes. In addition, these measures may be denominated in ways that are different from the value indications that are derived from market data or various appraisal techniques, requiring the appraiser to convert or allocate the opinion of value into a different set of metrics or rates. Whereas purchase price allocation or calculations of purchase price adjustments for contractual terms may be optional assignments for BV appraisers, CV analysts are usually required to address the actual contract terms in all their complexity as part of a CV engagement.[3] So-called "stacking" opinions that address the FMV in the aggregate coming from all forms of compensation in an arrangement are becoming the norm in healthcare CV engagements.

---

2   The combining of various compensation elements is commonly referred to in CV practice as "stacking."
3   This reference to BV practice is intended generally. There are cases where BV appraisers are required to analyze contractual terms. BV appraisers should analyze post-transaction physician compensation as part of the valuation of physician practices. See Mark O. Dietrich, "What Goes Around Comes Around: *Derby vs. Commissioner,*" *The BVR/AHLA Guide to Healthcare Valuation,* Chapter 11.

4.2 Matching Compensation to the Services or Resources Provided

The fundamental key to appraising compensation arrangements is matching compensation to the services or resource usage that is provided under the arrangement. The first step in the appraisal process, therefore, is to identify the specific services and/or resources the seller will provide to the buyer. Identification requires analyzing the scope, extent, and characteristics of these services to understand the details of what is being bought and sold under the arrangement. Without a clear understanding of these details, an inaccurate assessment and valuation of the compensation may be made.

A simple illustration makes this point: What's the FMV of cell phone service? To value this service accurately, one would first have to clarify the scope of service provided. How many minutes of service will be provided each month? How many phones will be on the plan? Will the service include a data plan, text messaging, special ringtones, and other features? Does the plan include international as well as national long-distance calling? What phone hardware will be used for the service? All of these factors affect the level of service required under the cell phone plan and thereby affect the value of the service.

For service agreements, part of the process for identifying the scope of services is distinguishing among the types of services. What may appear to be a single service may actually be the combination of several different and unique services that the seller provides separately to the buyer and that are combined for purposes of compensation in the arrangement. For example, physician services can include clinical, administrative, or other types of services, but are paid for in one set amount or rate. Consequently, it is essential in CV practice to delineate the key deliverables, duties, and work requirements for each type of service. Different types and levels of service can warrant different levels of compensation because the economics and market factors related to each type of service can significantly vary.

For compensation arrangements involving resource usage, it is critical to identify all the resources that are used and included as part of the arrangement. One of the easiest pitfalls for CV appraisers is failing to identify all of the goods and services that are included in the arrangement. A nonhealthcare example can readily illustrate this point. Car rental pricing on travel websites is often initially presented without reference to taxes, gas pricing, or insurance coverage. It also doesn't include rental of GPS units or child car seats. As some of us have experienced, the final price paid can be very different from our original estimate based on website advertised pricing. To apply this illustration to valuation practice, many appraisers simply look at the value of the car rental without considering all the additional resources that may be included in the terms of the subject arrangement or worse yet, they value the full-size car rental when the contractual terms called for a compact.

4.3 Identifying Key Contractual Terms

To match compensation to the services or resources provided, a CV appraiser needs to identify and study the proposed contractual terms of the subject arrangement. The terms of the agreement detail the scope of services or resources provided by the seller to the buyer. Even when a client has not yet drafted a copy of the proposed agreement, a CV appraiser must begin to outline the key terms and provisions of the arrangement. CV, by its very nature, requires identification of these contractual elements.[4] They define what the seller provides to the buyer and how the seller will be compensated for providing the services, resources, or operating assets. A basic skill required of a CV appraiser, therefore, is the ability to read and understand contractual language and provisions. It is also important for the appraiser to have some knowledge of the types of contractual terms that are usually included in the various types of compensation arrangements found in the healthcare marketplace. In addition, the appraiser needs to evaluate and analyze these terms and provisions from an economic perspective. CV is necessarily based on a critical economic analysis of the contract terms and provisions of the subject arrangement.

4.4 Analyzing the Economics of Compensation Arrangements

Another critical reason to identify the services and resources used in compensation arrangements is that different services and resources can have very different economic drivers and be subject to highly divergent market factors. Generally, the compensation for services and resource usage varies based on the type of service or resource. Physician services, for example, are compensated differently in the healthcare marketplace, based on the type of service. As a result, services and resources can be valued differently based on consideration of different sets of factors or measures. For example, hospital call coverage arrangements are usually compensated on an hourly or shift basis, such as 24 hours. Medical directorships are also compensated on an hourly basis. But hospital call coverage services are different from medical director services. Call coverage compensation involves an element of availability or "beeper" call pay, compensation for time spent by the physician providing telephone consultations to the hospital emergency department (ED), and an allowance to offset any care provided to ED patients without health insurance or low-paying insurance. The value of these latter two elements is usually based on estimates.[5] Medical directorships, by contrast, generally involve pay for straight administrative time. They do not include multiple elements. Understanding these fundamental economics is critical to the appropriate selection of

---

4   As noted previously, BV can also require analysis of contractual elements. See "What Goes Around Comes Around: *Derby v. Commissioner.*" Ibid.

5   See Chapter 27, "Valuing Hospital Call Coverage Arrangements: An Introduction," and Chapter 28, "Valuing Hospital Call Coverage Arrangements: Appraisal Methods," for a complete discussion and analysis of hospital call coverage arrangements.

---

data sources and valuation methods to use in appraising the value of compensation arrangements.

4.5 Consideration of Both Buyer and Seller Economics

In analyzing the economics of compensation arrangements in the healthcare industry, it is frequently necessary to look at these economics from both sides of the buyer-seller equation. The reason for focusing on a "double-sided" analysis is that compensation arrangements can have very different economic and market dynamics for the buyer and the seller, even when considering the hypothetical buyer and seller that are required by the definition of FMV. These varying economics are a function of the fact that the buyer and/or seller in a healthcare compensation arrangement can be limited to only a specific type of party. For these arrangements, only one kind of seller can offer the subject services in the marketplace and/or only one kind of buyer finds utility or benefit for these services. For example, hospital call coverage arrangements or hospital medical directorships are necessarily between doctors and hospitals. By definition, other types of parties or entities cannot participate in these arrangements. Thus, the hypothetical buyer and seller in certain types of compensation arrangements are limited to specific types of entities or parties.

The reason that this structural factor matters for valuation is that each type of party has widely dissimilar operating horizons and characteristics. Thus, the economic considerations for each side of the arrangement can be quite different. The value of the service to the hypothetical buyer may be for one purpose, and the value of the service to the hypothetical seller may be for another purpose.[6] The benefits and utility derived from the services or resources under the arrangement, therefore, can vary significantly for the buyer and the seller. This difference is not a function of the individual goals and objectives of varying buyers and sellers that naturally occur in any market. Rather, it is structurally based on the types of buyers and sellers that exist for the services or resources in the healthcare marketplace, e.g., hospital call coverage.

For example, the services of the seller may represent a key element of compensation in the seller's livelihood. Indeed, the compensation may represent the totality or single source of the seller's livelihood. This point is particularly salient for physicians who sell their professional services to buyers. For the buyer, however, the services provided may be a resource that is only one input among many to general business operations or as a component of a particular service line for the entity. The buyer is expected to maximize the operations and/or economics of the enterprise in procuring the services

---

6   It should be noted that the volume or value of referrals are not being referenced in this discussion. The analysis here relates solely to the services or resources that are the subject of the arrangement.

or resources that are the subject of the arrangement. When the value of the services or resources prohibits the required enterprise maximization, the buyer will look to substitutes or alternatives in the marketplace. Similarly, the seller will look to substitutes and alternatives for enterprise or personal maximization. The critical point for CV appraisal, however, is that these substitutes or alternatives can be materially different for the buyer in contrast to the seller. The expected future benefits can also vary significantly.

This structural consideration often necessitates use of appraisal methods and techniques that analyze potential substitutions, alternatives, and future benefits from the perspective of either the buyer or seller. Since these perspectives can be very different, the appraisal methods and techniques used to value these perspectives can be diverse. In some cases, moreover, valuation analysis of both sides of the buyer-seller equation must be completed to arrive at the appropriate value of the compensation in the arrangement. For example, one may need to look at both the buyer and seller's alternatives in the marketplace for the services. The buyer may be able to replicate the service in one manner, while the seller would find different types of alternative arrangements in which to sell the services. For an exchange to take place, both alternatives may need to be considered in the appraisal analysis. In theory, there is a point of equilibrium for value in exchange within a multidimensional matrix of utility and benefits for both the buyer and seller, who may have varying substitutes, alternatives, and expected future benefits relative to the subject compensation arrangement. Finding this equilibrium value can and should require valuation methods applied to both sides of the buyer-seller equation. A single valuation method may not be able to accommodate or reflect the economics of both sides of the buyer-seller equation. This difference may also be a factor in qualitative considerations and analysis used in the valuation process.

4.6 Sources of Information and Market Data

Compensation valuation in the healthcare industry has unique and distinct sources of information and market data. Many physician compensation surveys cover different segments of the physician population as well as different types of compensation. For example, some surveys report total compensation for physicians from all services, while others focus on compensation for specific types of services, such as medical directorships or hospital call coverage. Unique measures, standards, and metrics are also used as background information or as inputs and assumptions in CV appraisal work. Examples include common procedure terminology (CPT) codes or Medicare-determined relative value units (RVUs). Other key sources of information include government reports or schedules, such as the Medicare Physician Fee Schedule that is published each year by the Centers for Medicare and Medicaid Services (CMS). CV practitioners must be familiar with and understand the characteristics of all these forms of information so that they can use them appropriately in appraisal work.

5.0 Special Issues in Compensation Valuation

5.1 The Complex Web of Regulatory Issues in Compensation Valuation

Healthcare regulations can be complicated, and the guidance provided by such regulations can be unclear and limited with regard to the determination of FMV for regulatory compliance purposes. Moreover, federal and state healthcare regulations may also affect the structure and terms of a subject compensation arrangement. Tax laws and regulations may also apply. In general, these various sets of laws and regulations establish parameters for how compensation can be structured for healthcare providers. It is important, therefore, for CV appraisers to have a working knowledge of the requirements for FMV under these laws and regulations because most CV assignments will have as their task the determination of FMV compensation for regulatory compliance purposes. An assessment of the commercial reasonableness of the compensation arrangement may also be an objective of the valuation assignment. As a result, appraisers practicing in the healthcare space need to be aware of the issues involved in FMV and commercial reasonableness for healthcare regulatory purposes.

It is also helpful for an appraiser to have a basic understanding of the parameters placed on physician compensation by these federal and state healthcare-regulatory and tax rules to navigate through potential issues and pitfalls in valuing compensation plans. While the appraiser does not provide legal, tax, and regulatory advice in a transaction, a knowledge or awareness of these regulations will increase the likelihood that the valuation is consistent with regulatory requirements. Appraisers will generally disclaim any assurance in this regard because statutory requirements for a healthcare transaction go beyond the representations an appraiser can offer, including the intent of the parties thereto. It will also allow the appraiser to identify potential issues or areas where legal or tax counsel will be needed to provide specific direction and guidance relative to the compensation structure and the scope of the valuation engagement. Appraisers must familiarize themselves with the overall framework of applicable healthcare and tax regulations.[7]

5.2 The Issue of Compensation Stacking

Compensation stacking occurs when the seller of services and/or resource usage provides a bundle of services and/or resources under a proposed compensation arrangement or provides them separately in a series of separate arrangements.[8] A critical issue in such stacking is whether an overpayment for the services and/or resources occurs when compensation amounts are added together or "stacked." An overpayment may

---

7   See Section II of this text for a variety of chapters addressing these regulations.
8   Edward Richardson, CPA/ABV, aptly coined the term "stacking" to describe this market trend.

be the result of duplicative payments for the same essential service or resource usage within an arrangement or in a series of arrangements. Arrangements involving multiple services and/or resources can sometimes overlap. An overpayment may also result when the combination of services or resources causes the level or scope to be less than the level assumed for purposes of establishing the compensation for each element. For example, a series of compensation arrangements may require work hours that are not realistic. If compensation is not based on actual hours worked, but on assumed hours that were determined separately and not in total, there is the potential for overpayment. Stacking issues can also arise when market compensation survey data are used in a uniform way that fails to recognize the combination of compensation elements that may already be present in the data. A user of the data may add compensation levels from various sources together under a market approach, when in fact one or more of the sources already included the various other elements of compensation.

The purpose of a so-called "stacking analysis" is to ensure that the potential for such duplication is eliminated. This separate evaluation of compensation looks at the cumulative total of compensation paid under all arrangements for all services and/or resources provided. The analysis identifies each service and/or resource provided and examines whether there are areas of overlap or duplication. Next, it assesses the various forms or elements of compensation in the arrangement(s) to identify any overlap or duplication in terms of payment. Finally, the stacking review procedure examines the valuation methods and techniques that were used to establish the value of the compensation under the arrangement(s). This examination also looks for areas of duplication and overlap in the valuation methods used. Because parties in the healthcare sector, particularly physicians and hospitals, commonly have multiple compensation arrangements with each other, stacking analyses are frequently part of the scope of work in CV assignments for healthcare compliance purposes. The potential for stacking issues varies by type of compensation arrangement and/or the combination of various types of arrangements.

5.3 Adapting Appraisal Opinions to the Structure of Contractual Terms

CV appraisers encounter a variety of contractual structures and terms in valuing compensation arrangements in the marketplace. These structures and terms can be complex, especially when more than one service or resource is provided. For example, different measures can be used for the utilization of various services or resources in an arrangement. Sometimes, a single service may be compensated based on a combination of multiple payment forms or measures. Furthermore, popular compensation terms and structures can be combined in what seems like an endless series of permutations. As a result, CV practice often requires the appraiser not only to value the services and/or resources provided, but also to value them under a myriad of contractual terms and structures for calculating compensation. To use an analogy relative to BV, CV assignments frequently involve not only valuation of the business enterprise, but also a purchase price allocation that must assign the value of specific assets to an array of ownership interests that are both controlling and noncontrolling. Terms make the deal and determine the specific basket of services that are being purchased or sold by the parties.

The process of converting or allocating a CV opinion into an arrangement's compensation structure can involve various steps. In general, the first step in the process is to match compensation from the opinion of value to the services and/or resources provided in terms of the proposed compensation structure. The appraiser takes each component of the compensation plan and determines what service or resource items are being paid for by the individual element. If compensation was separately calculated by type of service or resource, then the allocation of the conclusion of value can be rather straight forward. One simply takes the buildup of compensation from the valuation analysis and assigns the value of each element to the corresponding service or resource. Some compensation elements, however, may represent payment for the same services. For these cases, the appraiser assigns a portion of the FMV compensation for the service to each element.

A key part of the analysis involved in allocating the opinion of value includes taking into account what services or resources were included in the valuation methods and techniques that are used in the appraisal. In some cases, the appraiser may need to prepare an individual valuation for a specific service that is paid for separately. The individual valuation is needed when the compensation indications from valuation methods reflected total compensation from all services. To determine the FMV compensation for the separate service, the appraiser would have to apportion the total compensation using the individual valuation. In matching compensation for services or resources, moreover, the appraiser is required to think through which compensation amounts relate to which services or resources. For example, employment arrangements with physicians often include clinical as well as hospital call coverage services. The proposed agreement may pay for call coverage services separate from the clinical services. In using market data, one has to determine whether the market data already include on-call pay in total compensation. If the appraiser concludes that it does, a separate valuation for call coverage would be required and the value of the on-call pay would need to be deducted from the total compensation in the market data to arrive at the value of the clinical services.

5.4 Qualitative Analysis and Judgments of Compensation Terms
The appraisal of compensation relative to specific structures and terms in compensation arrangements can also require qualitative analysis on certain contractual terms and

requirements. These qualitative assessments focus on whether the terms are consistent with the definition of FMV, i.e., what arm's-length, independent, and well-informed parties would negotiate apart from referrals. As a corollary assessment, the appraiser may also review whether the terms and requirements of the contract are consistent with the scope of services or service requirements assumed in the valuation. These types of evaluations are not based on numerical models or mathematical techniques. Rather, they are performed on a qualitative analytical basis. The analysis may yield contractual terms or requirements that become opinion qualifications or limiting conditions on the opinion of FMV issued by the appraiser. In the informed judgment of the appraiser, the terms and requirements are needed for the compensation in the arrangement to be consistent with FMV.

5.5 Sensitivity Testing of Compensation Plans Over Varying Productivity Levels

In analyzing the value of the compensation paid under the terms of an arrangement, the appraiser may complete a sensitivity analysis to evaluate the level of compensation produced by the particular compensation model or formula over a range of service or resource utilization levels. The purpose of the analysis is to assess whether the compensation structure or formula should be adjusted at varying levels of utilization. It is possible for the economics of the services or resources to change materially at differing levels. Such changes can affect the value of the services or resources. In the sensitivity analysis, the appraiser models compensation under the contractual formula using a range of service or resource utilization and then compares the results over the same range of utilization using the valuation methods. The appraiser may recommend changes or adjustments to the FMV compensation amounts and rates based on the results of this analysis.

5.6 Evaluating the Impact of Benefits on FMV Compensation in Service Arrangements

Another recurring issue in CV practice involves evaluating the impact of benefits that accompany cash compensation for service arrangements. This is an important topic in many compensation arrangements because many arrangements in healthcare relate to professional services provided by physicians. Since many forms of compensation arrangements are based on the independent contractor status of the service provider rather than employment, benefits costs are typically included in the FMV compensation for these services. One of the challenges posed by benefits, however, is determining whether such costs are included in the various physician compensation surveys used under the market approach in CV practice. Benefit costs can also be a factor in employment-based compensation arrangements. The issue here is whether the benefits provided under the arrangement are consistent with FMV. Generally, inclusion of the value of benefits costs in CV work is not a complicated matter, but it is a recurring item in many engagements.

6.0 Concluding Notes on the Practice of Compensation Valuation

As noted in this chapter, compensation valuation is an emerging valuation discipline with many unique issues to be addressed in the valuation process. Since there are no specific professional standards to govern its practice, CV appraisers are facing the challenge of addressing these issues by using ideas and methods that are also used in other appraisal disciplines.[9] Some of these issues, however, require original thinking and application of appraisal concepts. Part of the appeal of CV appraisal practice is the opportunity to do original thought work in this new field of professional knowledge.

---

9   It should be noted that some professional organizations, such as the AICPA, have general professional standards or those covering consulting services that would be applicable to CV practice. They are not specific, however, to CV practice as such.

Chapter 2. Defining FMV and the Market, Cost, and Income Approaches in Compensation Valuation

CONTENTS

Chapter 2. Defining FMV and the Market, Cost, and Income Approaches in Compensation Valuation

By Timothy Smith, CPA/ABV

1.0 Introduction: The Need for Adapted Definitions in CV Practice

Within each appraisal discipline, standard definitions are adopted so that practitioners have a common framework for using the various approaches in valuation assignments. Uniform definitions are implemented for the various standards of value, such as fair market value (FMV) or investment value. They are also developed for the three approaches to value: the market, cost, and income approaches. Use of such standardized definitions provides for consistency, comparability, and clarity across appraisals within the discipline or area of valuation specialization. Compensation valuation (CV), as a newly emerging discipline that has not yet been recognized in a formal manner within the appraisal profession, currently lacks such uniform and standardized definitions. As a result, CV appraisal can often lack a level of consistent and clear application of appraisal ideas and concepts among practitioners in the discipline.

This irregular state of affairs needs to be remedied for the sake of clients and the development of the profession. This chapter, therefore, attempts to develop uniform definitions for FMV and the three approaches to value for use in CV assignments. Since there is not a professional organization to promulgate these definitions in an institutional manner, these definitions should be viewed as first steps toward clarification and standardization in a noninstitutional framework. Nonetheless, other chapters in this text will rely on, utilize, and assume the key definitional material of this chapter.

As discussed in Chapter 1, the appraisal discipline of business valuation (BV) has many similarities with the emerging discipline of CV. Indeed, most CV practitioners look to the BV body of knowledge as a starting point or foundation for preparing CV appraisals.

In light of this connection, the *International Glossary of Business Valuation Terms* is used as a natural starting place for developing common terminology for CV practice.[1] Since these definitions were developed for the valuation of businesses' property or interests, they need to be adapted to the relevant characteristics of valuing compensation arrangements. The development of common terminology, therefore, is essentially an adaptation of these BV definitions to CV practice.

Along with providing the development of common terminology, this chapter also looks at the key issues encountered in using and applying the three approaches to value in CV work. In addition, it presents an overview of the basic types of methods that are frequently used in CV practice under each approach to value.

As noted in Chapter 1, "Introduction to the New Appraisal Discipline of Compensation Valuation," CV deals not only with service arrangements, but also with arrangements providing for the usage of a broad spectrum of resources, including real, personal, and business property. Compensation arrangements may also include the de facto sale of personal property that is consumed as part of providing the services and/or resources. The definitions developed for CV are intended to cover the broad scope of compensation arrangements that can include both services and the usage of various types of resources.

2.0 Using Fair Market Value in CV Practice

2.1 The Adaptation of the International Glossary Definition of FMV

The definition of FMV promulgated by the *International Glossary of Business Valuation Terms* is:

> The price, expressed in terms of cash equivalents, at which property would change hands between a hypothetical willing and able buyer and a hypothetical willing and able seller, acting at arm's length in an open and unrestricted market, when neither is under compulsion to buy or sell and when both have reasonable knowledge of the relevant facts.

To adapt this definition to CV, services or resource usage can be substituted for property as the subject of the transaction or exchange. The CV definition should also reflect

---

1   The *International Glossary* was developed and adopted by the four major U.S. business appraisal professional societies (American Society of Appraisers, American Institute of Certified Public Accountants, Institute of Business Appraisal, and the National Association of Certified Valuation Analysts) along with their Canadian counterpart (Canadian Institute of Chartered Business Valuators).

the fact that the exchange happens over the term or duration of the arrangement and not at a single point. Outside of these adjustments, however, the practice of CV applies the concept of the hypothetical willing buyer and seller and their critical characteristics as articulated in the *International Glossary* definition to the appraisal definition of FMV.

Using the *International Glossary* definition, the appraisal definition of FMV for CV can be adapted in the following way:

> The price, expressed in terms of cash equivalents, at which *services and/or resources* would change hands *over a set period of time* between a hypothetical willing and able buyer and a hypothetical willing and able seller, acting at arm's length in an open and unrestricted market, when neither is under compulsion to buy or sell and when both have reasonable knowledge of the relevant facts.

Since regulatory compliance is usually the purpose of CV engagements, CV practitioners also reference the healthcare regulatory definition of FMV. It should be noted that the regulatory definition was promulgated in a form that addressed both property and service transactions and thus, needs no conceptual adjustment for CV practice. The issues associated with complying with the regulatory definition of FMV are addressed in Chapter 7, "Complying With the Healthcare Definition of FMV in Appraisal Practice."

2.2 Consideration of Both the Hypothetical Buyer and Seller

The appraisal definition of FMV focuses on both the willing and able buyer and the willing and able seller. It is important, therefore, to consider the economics and perspectives of both the hypothetical buyer and seller in determining FMV.[2] As discussed in greater detail in Chapter 1, Section 4.5, the hypothetical buyer and seller in healthcare compensation arrangements can have economics of value that are distinct from each other. It is critical, therefore, that economic and valuation factors related to both the buyer and seller are considered and analyzed in the determination of FMV. In appraisal practice in other disciplines, such as BV, there can often be an emphasis on the characteristics and perspective of the buyer only, which tends to exclude the seller. FMV requires an analysis of both, particularly in CV.

---

2   See James Hitchner, *Financial Valuation: Applications and Models*, 3rd edition (Kindle), "Application of Specific Standards of Value," Chapter 2, and Shannon P. Pratt and Alina V. Niculita, *Valuing a Business: The Analysis and Appraisal of Closely Held Companies*, 5th edition (Kindle), "Fair Market Value," Chapter 2, for discussions of the willing buyer and willing seller requirements entailed in FMV.

3.0 Defining and Using the Market, Cost, and Income Approaches in CV Practice

3.1 Developing CV Definitions for the Three Approaches to Value

A common element in the appraisal disciplines is use and application of three fundamental approaches to value, including the market, cost, and income approaches. As noted in the introduction to this chapter, standardized definitions of the three approaches are developed within an appraisal discipline to provide for consistency, comparability, and clarity among appraisals in the discipline. These standardized definitions also reflect the unique economic characteristics and factors associated with valuing the various types of property that are the subject of an appraisal discipline. Each type of property gives rise to distinct issues for appraisal practice, and thus, the three approaches have shades of meaning or application within a discipline that may not fully crosswalk from one discipline to another.[3]

The common definitions also reflect application of the three valuation principles: substitution, alternatives, and future benefits. These principles are noteworthy and are applicable to CV practice. In developing standardized definitions of the three approaches to value, it is helpful to review each of these principles.

- The principle of substitution states that a party to a transaction will pay no more for something than one would for an equally desirable substitute or for something with equal utility;

- The principle of alternatives states each party in a contemplated transaction has alternatives to consummating the transaction; and

- The principle of future benefits states that economic value is a reflection of anticipated future benefits.[4]

These three principles of valuation are not only relevant for CV appraisals, but they are also applicable to both the hypothetical buyer and the hypothetical seller in compensation arrangements. A buyer and seller may *both* consider substitutes, alternatives, and future benefits in evaluating a subject compensation arrangement.

---

3   For a summary comparison of the approaches used in real estate and business appraisal, see Pratt and Niculita, *Valuing a Business: The Analysis and Appraisal of Closely Held Companies*, 5th edition (Kindle), "Accepted Business Valuation Approaches and Methods," Chapter 3.

4   Gary R. Trugman, *Understanding Business Valuation: A Practical Guide to Valuing Small to Medium-Sized Businesses*, 2nd edition, pp. 55-56, and Robert James Cimasi and Anne P. Sharamitaro, "Valuing Physician and Executive Compensation Arrangements: Fair Compensation and Reasonableness Thresholds," *Valuation Strategies*, March/April 2010, p. 15.

The three valuation principles can be related to the approaches to value along the following lines of application:

- The market approach looks to comparable compensation arrangements in the marketplace as the basis of value using the principle of substitution;

- The cost approach seeks to replicate or reconstruct the value of the services or resources provided in a compensation arrangement though a buildup of the elements or components of the services or resources. This reproduction approach is based on the alternatives that a buyer would pursue to obtain services or resources with the same utility; and

- The income approach will look at the future benefits received by the buyer and/or the seller under compensation arrangements, apart from the volume or value of referrals between the parties.

While the applications used here correlate only one principle with an approach, one can argue that a principle can be reflected in more than one approach.[5]

3.2 General Criteria for the Use and Application of an Approach to Value

While each approach to value has unique factors and considerations relative to its application in CV assignments, general criteria are applicable to the use of all approaches to value. These criteria also apply to specific appraisal methods and techniques that are used under an approach to value. They also include certain prerequisites that are necessary for the appropriate application of valuation approaches and methods.

Identifying the Services/Resources Provided Under the Arrangement

The value of a compensation arrangement is a function of the services/resources provided. It is imperative, therefore, that the first step in the appraisal process for a compensation arrangement is identifying in detail the various elements that will be provided. Identification requires careful reading of proposed agreements or contract terms that will govern the arrangement. Unlike other forms of appraisal, where detailed review of transaction documents and terms is not always essential to the valuation of a subject property or business, careful reading of these documents or review of proposed terms is a critical requirement of CV practice.

The importance of properly identifying and analyzing the scope and level of services/resources provided under the arrangement cannot be overstressed in CV practice. Perhaps the most common pitfall in CV practice is a failure for the analyst to identify

---

5   Trugman, p. 56.

and value the actual scope proposed under an arrangement. This pitfall may also result from a client's failure to define the actual scope for the appraiser as part of the valuation process. Clients sometimes overlook key elements of the arrangement that affect the value and fail to disclose these to the appraiser. To avoid this type of pitfall, a best practice for CV assignments is to prepare a detailed summary of the contractual terms for the arrangement as part of the valuation process and include it in the report for client review.[6]

Understanding the Key Characteristics of the Subject Services/Resources

Identification of the scope of services/resources is only the first step in the process. These elements need to be analyzed and evaluated so that the CV analyst has a solid understanding of their fundamental characteristics. These characteristics can include operational, functional, and economic aspects. They can also involve study of market factors affecting the supply and demand for the services along with their impact on value. The analysis should also assess available alternatives and substitutes for both the hypothetical buyer and seller, along with an evaluation of the utility and benefits derived by both parties from buying or selling them.

Available Data

Data must be available to use an approach or method. Data availability includes not only having access to relevant data, but also that the data should be reliable and independent in terms of its source and quality. The data should also be in sufficient detail relative to the fundamental economic and market drivers of the subject arrangement so as to allow for its reasonable and appropriate use in the particular valuation method. For example, market data needs to include sufficient detail for the appraiser to assess the comparability of the underlying data to the subject arrangement for purposes of using the market approach. If the appraiser cannot establish comparability or adjust for such comparability, the data may not be accurately applied to the valuation of the subject.

Relevance to the Key Economic Drivers of the Arrangement

The approach or method used needs to address the critical economic drivers and factors of the subject compensation arrangement to be relevant and applicable to the valuation analysis. Because of the unique characteristics of various compensation arrangements in the healthcare industry, some approaches and methods may not be relevant for appraising certain types of arrangements. One needs to consider the key elements of the subject services/resources used from the perspective of both the buyer and seller and then determine whether an approach or method accounts for these elements. One may also think about relevance from a practical perspective: A method may be relevant

---

6   See Chapter 5, "Elements of a Compensation Valuation Report," for more discussion of this best practice.

in theory, but impractical to use in actual valuation practice. For example, one might have to develop numerous inputs to use in a cost or income approach. If the appraiser must make a significant number of assumptions without supportable information, the approach may simply lack credibility upon completion.

4.0 The Market Approach in Compensation Valuation

4.1 The Market Approach Defined for Use in CV Practice

The *International Glossary of Business Valuation Terms* defines the market approach as follows:

> A general way of determining a value indication of a business, business ownership interest, security, or intangible asset by using one or more methods that compare the subject to similar businesses, business ownership interests, securities, or intangible assets that have been sold.

In basic terms, the market approach uses comparable sales transactions that have occurred in the marketplace to determine the value of a subject asset or business interest. This approach illustrates the valuation principle of substitution: A buyer will not pay more for a subject asset than it would for a substitute asset that provides the equivalent economic utility.

As applied to compensation agreements, the market approach seeks to value the subject arrangement by referencing comparable arrangements in the marketplace. The *International Glossary* definition of the market approach can be adapted for CV practice along the following lines:

> A general way of determining a value indication of *the compensation paid for services and/or the usage of resources* by using one or more methods that compare the subject *arrangement to arrangements for* similar *services and/or resource usage* that have been sold.

The adapted definition reflects the focus of CV in terms of the compensation paid for services/resources provided under a compensation arrangement.

4.2 Applying the Market Approach in CV

The key to utilizing the market approach for valuing the compensation paid in service or resource usage arrangements is identifying and obtaining information on comparable agreements that can be used to establish the value of the subject arrangement. Market compensation data from arrangements with dissimilar services or resources are not relevant or applicable for valuing a subject service arrangement because they lack such comparability. It should be noted, however, that an appraiser can often use market information from arrangements that are not fully similar to the subject as long as the appraiser has sufficient information to make the appropriate adjustments to the market data and/or the subject arrangement to make them comparable for valuation purposes.

In using the market approach for compensation valuation, the task is to identify the services/resources to be provided under the subject compensation arrangement and then obtain information on comparable arrangements in the marketplace. Four elements to comparability should be considered in using the market approach in CV practice:

1. Comparability of the services/resources in the subject compensation arrangement to the market data;

2. Comparability of the market conditions for the subject arrangement and the market data for similar arrangements;

3. Comparability of past market conditions to future conditions; and

4. Comparability as demonstrated by a sufficient number of data points to establish a basis for comparison.

All of these elements are important to validating the economic comparability of the subject arrangement relative to the market data. Without such comparability, the use of market data to establish the value of a subject arrangement is questionable.

Comparability of Services/Resources

Comparability requires that the subject and market data include the same or substantially similar types of services or resources. Similarity is determined more appropriately at a comprehensive, total, or combined level, rather than on a buildup of individual elements. Using a buildup technique is better classified under a cost approach as a replication of the cost of the arrangement. A cost approach classification for a buildup method at least communicates to the user that the method attempts to re-create the compensation arrangement on a piecemeal basis. It is more common to think about comparability of market data based on the combined or bundled services.

Comparability of Market Conditions

The second criterion for comparability relates to evaluating the market conditions for the subject and the market data. Market conditions for a compensation arrangement can include the characteristics of the parties to the arrangement. There needs to be a general similarity between the characteristics of the subject parties and those of the parties in the market data because these characteristics can affect the economics of the subject services or resources as well as their scope and level in an arrangement. Another way to think about this issue of the characteristics of the parties is that different types of parties tend to provide different levels or scopes of services. For example, clinical physician services provided by physicians in an academic practice can vary in certain key respects from the clinical services provided by physicians in private practice. The patient base and reimbursement environments can be very different between the two types of practice settings. The mix and range of clinical services and the way the services are provided may also vary due to the use of medical students, residents, and fellows. Clinical services in the academic practice may focus more on possible research applications than those in a private practice.

Another example includes employed versus independent contractor physicians. The compensation paid to independent contractor physicians in compensation arrangements can include an allowance for benefits and malpractice insurance. When employed physicians are used, the compensation often includes only cash compensation, excluding benefits and malpractice. Another distinction is whether the services/resources are provided on a full-time or part-time basis. The economics and requirements of full-time versus part-time arrangements can be materially different, and thus, the compensation is not comparable between them.

A further important consideration in assessing the comparability of market conditions relates to the location of the subject in comparison to the market data. Local market dynamics, including key factors such as the supply and demand for physicians and the level of reimbursement, can have a significant impact on the compensation paid for services/resources in compensation arrangements. One of the unfortunate misnomers in healthcare is that variations in reimbursement for healthcare services, especially for physicians, do not have a material effect on the value of those services in local markets. In practice, national surveys are frequently applied to local markets without any consideration as to the applicability of national data to a local market. As discussed more completely in Chapter 37, "How Reimbursement and Physician Compensation Vary by Market," and Chapter 36, "Evaluating RVU-Based Compensation Arrangements," local market reimbursement can have a great impact on physician compensation levels, for example. Thus, one cannot simply take data from one market or a grouping of markets and apply it to a subject market without considering the potential for significant differences in markets giving rise to material variations in compensation.

Comparability of Past Market Conditions to the Future
Another factor in the comparability of a subject compensation arrangement to market data is whether transactions that have occurred in the past are relevant to current and expected market conditions during the term of the subject. Conditions in the healthcare

marketplace can change over the course of a few years or from year to year. Market data from arrangements or transaction that occurred in prior years may not reflect the current state of market conditions and dynamics or the conditions that are expected during the term of the arrangement. Reimbursement, for example, can change materially for a physician specialty. Demand for services or the mix or bundling of services or resources can also vary. As a result, market data from prior years may not be comparable to current or expected market conditions for the subject arrangement.

Comparability Defined by Sufficient Market Data

A final factor in comparability relates to the number of data points included in the market information that is available to the appraiser. If the number of comparable transactions is relatively small, there can be a question as to whether the data effectively establishes a market for comparison purposes. A small number of arrangements may not reflect market conditions, but rather outliers or transactions that reflect highly unique investment or strategic value considerations. A given data point may simply be an anomaly. Thus, a CV appraiser must assess whether the number of data points available is sufficient to reflect the overall conditions of the marketplace. It should be noted, however, that in some instances, a limited number of market comparables may be sufficient, such as when the marketplace for a given type of service is small to begin with. For example, there are certain types of highly specialized physicians for which a peer group with comparable qualifications is relatively small. Careful study and analysis should be made using market data that is limited in terms of the number of data points.

4.3 Limitations on the Use of Market Data Imposed by the Stark Regulations

The Stark regulations place limitations on the usage of certain market data from transactions between parties in a position to refer to one another for determining FMV for healthcare compliance purposes. The extent and validity of these limitations for CV appraisal practice are discussed in further detail in Chapter 8, "To Use or Not to Use: An Appraisal Analysis of the Stark Prohibition on Market Data From Parties in a Position to Refer." To summarize the key points of this chapter for the present discussion, CV practice should avoid the use of market data from parties with referral relationships to exclude any possible "noise" or impact of the referral relationships on the data used to establish value for a compensation arrangement.

4.4 Basic Types of Valuation Methods Under the Market Approach

The valuation methods available under the market approach for valuing subject compensation arrangements generally fall into two broad categories: survey-based methods and individual transaction-based methods.

Survey-Based Methods

Numerous compensation surveys are available in the healthcare industry, especially those that focus on physician compensation. There are surveys that report specific types of physician compensation, such as those on call coverage or medical directorships. Because they are publically available and some are relatively inexpensive, they are commonly used in the marketplace for benchmark data on compensation, particularly for physician compensation. In CV practice, surveys are the most frequently used source of data in valuation methods and survey-based market approach methods are frequently the norm. Survey-based valuation methods seek to establish the value of a subject compensation arrangement based on the data reported in surveys. Generally, CV appraisers will use various measures or indicators to attempt to compare the subject arrangement to the survey data to establish the market-based value of the compensation. The appraiser generally assumes or concludes that compensation levels in the survey data are a function of certain key factors or drivers. The CV analyst measures the subject arrangement in terms of these factors and then calculates a level of compensation that should correspond with these measurements.

Individual Transaction-Based Methods

The other broad category of valuation methods used under the market approach in CV practice is based on the use of data from individual transactions. Typically, the appraiser gathers this data as part of the valuation assignment. This data is contrasted with survey data. While the surveys are also based on individual transactions, the data is accumulated by the survey publisher and reported in a specific survey product that is usually available for public purchase and use. There are occasions and types of compensation arrangements where survey data is not available or is not specific enough to be comparable to the subject arrangement. In these cases, a CV appraiser may attempt to complete a separate survey or independent gathering of data on market transactions that are comparable to the subject. It should be noted, however, that obtaining market data independently can be quite difficult. Private parties may be reluctant to share such information with an appraiser. Moreover, the appraiser may not be able to obtain a sufficient number of transactions to establish a comparable basis for the marketplace for the subject type of compensation arrangement.

4.5 The Advantages of Market Approach Methods in CV Practice

There are many advantages in using the market approach for CV assignments. These areas include the following.

Availability of Compensation Surveys

As noted previously, numerous compensation surveys are available in the healthcare industry. Many of them focus on specific types of compensation, particularly for physicians. Some of them are relatively inexpensive to purchase. There are surveys that include hundreds to thousands of respondents for various forms of compensation. These surveys make a significant level of market data available for use in market-based valuation methods.

A Level of Objectivity and Real-World Support

Market data is not based on hypothetical assumptions or theoretical models of economic behavior. Rather, it is the result of real-world buyers and sellers transacting. The levels of compensation and value indicated by market data are based on these actual transactions. As such, market data has a certain level of objectivity associated with it as a basis for establishing the value of the subject arrangement.

Simplicity of Use and Application

Generally, market approach methods can be relatively simple to use in CV practice. The CV appraiser may only need a few measures of comparability to apply the market data to the valuation of the subject. Some of these measures may be relatively easy to determine. When the application techniques are simple, it is also easier for the appraiser to explain the appraisal methods used in the valuation process to clients and report users.

Wide Use and Recognition of Market Data

While not determinative of sound valuation theory and practice, one benefit of using market methods is that most users readily comprehend the notion that the value of something can be based on what others in the market are paying for it. This fact, coupled with the wide availability of surveys and the relative simplicity of market methods, make the market approach widely used and recognized in the healthcare industry.

4.6 The Limitations of Market Approach Methods in CV Practice

Various and often critical limitations are associated with the use of market approach methods and data in CV practice. These limitations can include the following:

- The surveys generally reflect *a market* comprised of those who responded to the survey, rather than a reflection of *the relevant market* for the subject compensation arrangement. This distinction is especially critical with respect to considerations of the *local market.*

- The surveys generally reflect segments of the marketplace in terms of buyer and seller characteristics. They are not based on statistical sampling methods, and the data generally reflects a bias toward the characteristics of the respondents.

- The surveys often do not report accompanying data on the key scope of service or performance measures that are needed to assess the comparability of the subject arrangement to the survey data.

- Survey data can be easily misunderstood, misused, and misapplied because of failure to understand the definitions of data and metrics reported. Respondents may also misreport data for the same reason.

- There are regulatory limitations on the use of certain market data for healthcare compliance purposes.

- There is limited available data on individual transactions in the healthcare marketplace. Moreover, gathering individual transaction data by an appraiser can be very time-consuming.

- Data that is not in the public domain or available to all appraisers does not meet the conditions of FMV. Private data is not consistent with parties acting in "an open and unrestricted market," having "reasonable knowledge of the relevant facts." Nonetheless, some appraisers may use private data as a reality check of other methods.

- Market data is a reflection of past market conditions that may not be comparable or applicable to the current or expected conditions of the subject arrangement.

- Clients and users of CV appraisals often have unrealistic expectations relative to market data. Frequently market-based "rules of thumb" become de facto valuation methods or worse yet, assumed universal and absolute indications of FMV. The median compensation per wRVU rate based on MGMA, for example, is a benchmark that has incorrectly attained universal status as FMV for every doctor in every specialty in every market in the country. A median, by definition, means that approximately half make less and half make more. Thus, the use of the median as a universal and absolute FMV rate is a self-refuting claim.

For a more in-depth and detailed analysis on the use and application of the market data in CV, see Chapter 4, "On the Informed Use of Market Data in Compensation Valuation."

5.0 The Cost Approach

5.1 The Cost Approach Defined

The cost approach is defined, according to the *International Glossary of Business Valuation Terms,* as follows:

> A general way of determining a value indication of an individual asset by quantifying the amount of money required to replace the future service capability of that asset.

The cost approach looks to the replacement cost of an asset or business interest as the basis for valuing the subject asset or interest. In business valuation, the cost approach is categorized as the asset-based or buildup approach because the appraiser attempts to re-create the value of the subject business by accumulating the values of the individual assets that comprise the subject. The appraiser attempts to re-create the business one asset at a time, building up a business enterprise value based on the value of each asset.

The cost approach also illustrates the valuation principle of alternatives: the idea that there are alternatives to acquiring the future service capacity of the subject asset or business interest. One appraisal technique often used under the cost approach is to value an asset based on its adjusted historical cost, where the adjustments to historical cost are intended to reflect the cost to replicate the asset in its current condition and in consideration of relevant marketplace factors related to the re-creation of the asset.

The cost approach as applied to compensation arrangements seeks to value the compensation for the subject arrangement by valuing alternatives in the marketplace for those services or resources included in the scope of the arrangement. An adapted version of *The International Glossary* definition of the cost approach might read as follows:

> A general way of determining a value indication of *the compensation in an arrangement for services and/or resource usage* by quantifying the amount of money required to replace the future service capability or *utility of the arrangement.*

This adapted definition redirects the focus of the cost approach to the valuation of the compensation paid for services/resources provided under a compensation arrangement.

5.2 Applying the Cost Approach in CV

Applying the cost approach in CV involves finding substitutes or alternatives for the services/resources included in the scope of the arrangement that can provide similar or comparable utility or benefit to the buyer and seller and determine their cost. The cost is used as an indication of the value of the subject arrangement. Multiple elements of cost may need to be combined to match the service capacity of the subject arrangement. The combination or bundling of various alternatives and substitutes for the subject services and resources may also require a premium or discount applied to the total cost. Other adjustments may also be necessary to make the costs or the utility received from the substitutes or alternatives be comparable to the subject arrangement.

5.3 Basic Types of Valuation Methods Under the Cost Approach

Three basic types of valuation methods are used under the cost approach in CV practice: 1) alternative cost; 2) cost buildup; and 3) adjusted historical cost. Each method has unique characteristics and factors that affect its use and application in CV practice.

Alternative Cost Methods

The first type of method seeks an alternative type of compensation arrangement to the subject that provides the same or similar services capacity or utility to the buyer or seller. There are cases in which a buyer in a compensation arrangement can obtain the same bundle of services/resources or the equivalent utility and benefit through the use of something other than that of the subject arrangement. For example, alternative ways for a hospital to obtain call coverage that are commonly utilized include employing physicians or using locum tenens physicians. A cost approach would look to the cost of these services as one method of establishing the value of hospital call coverage. It should be noted that employment and use of locums tenens physicians can introduce additional cost factors unrelated to call coverage as a distinct service. In such cases, the appraiser would filter or adjust these factors out of the analysis to arrive at the alternative cost for providing call coverage.[7]

Appraisers usually think about alternatives from the perspective of the buyer. In certain circumstances, a *seller* may have alternative arrangements in which the subject services/resources can be sold in the marketplace. Some of these alternative selling opportunities may relate to the same utility or benefit of the subject services/resources. It is conceivable that such an alternative may provide a valid indication of the value of the compensation for the subject arrangement. The theory supporting such a value indication would be based on the principle of alternatives: The seller has alternative arrangements in which compensation can be received for the same or comparable mix of services or resources and would not be induced to sell the services at a value less than what can be received for comparable alternatives. Now, a key to the use of this alternative compensation method would be the comparability of the scope of the

---

7   It should be noted that there is a cost/benefit analysis for using an appraisal method and technique that can lead an appraiser not to implement a method because it is too cumbersome, time-consuming, or not practical.

alternative arrangement to the subject. The comparability criteria would follow along the lines of those discussed in Section 4.2 above in relation to the market approach. Without comparability, the equivalence of the alternative and the subject in terms of compensation may not be appropriate.

Cost Buildup Methods

In cost buildup methods, the appraiser looks at the various elements of the services/resources and gathers market data on the cost for each element in the subject. The key to this method is the breakdown of the scope of the subject arrangement into components that can be identified and valued separately. In addition, data needs to be available for valuing these elements. In reconstructing the cost of the compensation for the subject arrangement, the appraiser also thinks about whether the sum of the parts differs from the whole. Does the buildup of costs account for the value of the combined services or resources or does the total for the buildup need an adjustment of some kind? In addition, the cost buildup should include a mark-up that reflects the cost of capital for the assets and resources involved in the arrangement. For example, capital equipment costs should include a return or interest charge that is commensurate with equipment use or leasing. Supply costs typically include a handling charge. The amount of the mark-up is based on market returns or margins for each type of resource.

Adjusted Historical Cost Methods

Another potential indication of the cost for a compensation arrangement is its historical cost, when past compensation was based on arm's-length negotiations between parties who are economically independent of each other, not having other business relationships that might influence the compensation paid under the historical arrangement. Under this analysis, the historical cost for a compensation arrangement is a reflection and indication of the value because it was negotiated at arm's length by independent parities to the arrangement. This arm's-length value may still be a valid indication of the present and future value of the services. Even when the past marketplace is not a good indication of present or future market conditions, the appraiser may be able to adjust past indications of value to reflect current or prospective conditions. The requirement for arm's-length negotiations generally precludes the use of historical compensation for parties with referral relationships. The regulatory prohibition on the use of such data is applicable to such historical compensation. The existence of the referral relationship, of course, calls into question the independence of the parties.

For this application of the cost approach, it is essential that the historical compensation was based on a comparable scope of services/resources to that required under the proposed arrangement. If the scope is dissimilar, the compensation may not be indicative of the value of the compensation in the proposed arrangement. In certain circumstances, it may be possible for the appraiser to adjust the historical compensation to place the past scope on a comparable basis with the present one. The adjustment process entails a segregation or allocation of the historical compensation to the various types of elements for which the seller received income in the past. Once the historical compensation has been allocated, the appraiser adjusts the historical compensation to be consistent with what is required under the subject arrangement. Historical compensation may also need to be adjusted to eliminate nonrecurring, one-time, or extraordinary items that are not reflective of conditions or economics of the proposed compensation arrangement.

5.4 The Advantages of Cost Approach Methods in CV Practice

There are several advantages to the use and application of cost approach methods in establishing the value of a compensation arrangement. These can include the following:

- They reflect the value of alternatives and substitutes that buyers and sellers may have in the marketplace for the subject arrangement.

- They can bring economically rational boundaries to the appraisal of a compensation arrangement by establishing a valuation floor or ceiling based on the value of alternatives and substitutes.
    - A buyer would not pay more for services/resources if an alternative arrangement would provide the same utility, but at a lower cost.
    - A seller may not enter into an arrangement to provide services or resources below their cost or if there are higher paying alternatives in the marketplace for providing them.

- Cost approach methods can introduce the framework for a "make or buy" analysis, thereby bringing resource and enterprise maximization into the valuation analysis.

- For valuation indications based on adjusted historical cost methods, the value is established based on actual performance as well as actual market and operational conditions for the arrangement between independent parties.

- In the use of cost buildup methods, it can be fairly easy to make adjustments for differences in the scope of a subject arrangement in comparison to available market data.

- Some cost approach methods may be adaptable to expected conditions for the subject arrangement based on changes to the various inputs and assumptions in the replication of costs.

- Market survey data is readily available for many of the basic services and resources provided in the healthcare industry, simplifying the data gathering process for cost buildup methods.

5.5 The Limitations of Cost Approach Methods in CV Practice

Use and application of the cost approach methods can include the following limitations and disadvantages:

- They are based on past compensation or cost outcomes that resulted from market and operating conditions that may not be indicative of future circumstances. As a result, cost approach methods may not reflect key economic factors and dynamics expected under the subject arrangement. Past compensation and cost outcomes may not determine future value.

- Some cost approach methods, particularly cost buildup methods, can require significant levels of data to be completed. Without this detailed data, the methods may lack the level of precision and accuracy that are part of their appeal. In many valuation assignments, such detailed data are not readily available to allow the appraiser to implement the methods reasonably.

- Preparing cost buildup methods can be time-consuming. In addition, they may require the use of various assumptions and estimates, making the value computation somewhat speculative in nature. The tendency for speculative analysis can also arise in looking at the value of the services/resources taken as a whole in a subject arrangement.

- Adjusted historical cost methods may not be applicable when the historical parties to an arrangement were not an independent or at arm's length. Since many types of compensation arrangements only exist between referral-related parties, adjusted historical cost methods may not be available for determining FMV for regulatory purposes. Thus, use of this method may be limited in many situations.

- When multiple services/resources are in a subject arrangement, it can be difficult to account for all the elements of value that should contribute to the compensation for the arrangement.

6.0 The Income Approach

6.1 The Income Approach Defined

The income approach is defined according to the *International Glossary of Business Valuation Terms* as follows:

> A general way of determining a value indication of a business, business ownership interest, security, or intangible asset using one or more methods that convert anticipated economic benefits into a present single amount.

The income approach is usually the most difficult of the three standard valuation approaches to apply to the valuation of compensation arrangements. This difficulty derives from the traditional definition of the income approach in the BV body of knowledge. Converting the compensation under a service or resource usage agreement to a "present single amount" may not produce an indication of value that is meaningful for a compensation arrangement. The scope of work for a CV assignment entails establishing the value of the compensation paid in an arrangement, which is not usually defined or measured in terms of a lump-sum amount. Rather, the compensation is paid out over time and can have multiple components, some of which are variable.

For valuing compensation agreements, the income approach may be adapted in terms of the valuation principle of future benefits as the basis for value, but without the conversion to a present value amount. This adaption of the *International Glossary* definition could be made along the following lines:

> A general way of determining a value indication of *the compensation in a service or resource usage arrangement* using one or more methods that *calculate and appraise* the anticipated economic benefits *of the arrangement over a set period.*

With this adaptation, the income approach can be utilized to calculate the future economic benefits to be received by one or both parties to the compensation arrangement.[8] These future benefits are then analyzed and appraised to establish a value for the services/resources provided under the arrangement.

---

8   Under this adaptation of the income approach, future economic benefits are not intended to include the value or volume of improper referrals. Rather, the appraiser looks exclusively to the revenues, expenses, resources, and investments related to the specific services and service lines provided for in the agreement.

6.2 Applying the Income Approach in CV

Under this reworking of the income approach for application to CV, the appraiser seeks to value the compensation in an arrangement for services or resources by analyzing the future benefits that a buyer or seller receives under the arrangement. A key aspect of the income approach, therefore, is that it is forward-looking. It involves forecasts and projections relative to the economics of the subject arrangement. The income approach looks to future and expected operating and market conditions to arrive at the value for the compensation in the arrangement. The analysis of future benefits can apply to either side of the buyer-seller equation. In certain circumstances, the prospective appraisal can even be applied to both the buyer and seller to the arrangement in a "double-sided" analysis that addresses the future benefits to both parties.

Future benefits under the income approach can be analyzed and evaluated in different ways. They can be assessed in terms of investment levels, resources utilized, and services provided under the arrangement in comparison to market rates of return and/or profitability for similar or comparable investments, resources, and services. In other words, the appraiser assesses the compensation that the buyer or seller receives in comparison to market returns or profit margins given the levels of investment, risk, and resource utilization attributable to either party in the arrangement. Evaluation of the future benefits can also take the form of simply assessing the total compensation received from all elements in an arrangement, given the services/resources provided.

6.3 Basic Types of Valuation Methods Under the Income Approach

Income approach valuation methods can be grouped into three basic types: 1) total compensation analysis; 2) margin or return analysis; and 3) adaptations of the discounted cash flow method. In discussing these methods, it should be noted that the volume or value of healthcare referrals are not included in the valuation analysis. When referrals may be indirectly included or appear to be included, appraisers should seek guidance from legal counsel on the use of such a method or technique.[9]

Total Compensation Analysis

In a total compensation analysis, the appraiser computes the total compensation expected under the arrangement, typically on an annual level. The appraiser then evaluates this total compensation based on relevant criteria, typically those related to productivity or the level of service provided. For example, total clinical compensation may be assessed in comparison to total wRVUs. The reason that a total compensation

---

9   For example, the net practice earnings from physician clinical services can include net earnings from technical component services. Yet, if certain criteria under the Stark regulations are met, a physician may be compensated based on these ancillary earnings. Thus, legal counsel is needed to provide guidance on how regulatory compliance should be addressed in the use of certain income approach methods.

analysis is useful in CV work is that compensation is often stated in terms of rates that are paid based on volumes or other service measures; thus, it is calculated on a variable basis. Market, cost, and other types of income approach methods can be concentrated on valuing only the specific compensation rate for the arrangement. In some cases, multiple rates may be used to pay out compensation. A total compensation analysis allows the appraiser to look at the volume-adjusted or level of service-adjusted compensation in total, rather than simply stating a rate or series of rates. Examination of compensation in the aggregate relative to the total level of services/resources provided can actually have a material bearing on the appraisal. A total compensation analysis can also serve as a "sanity" or reasonableness check. It also facilities a "stacking" analysis that evaluates the total compensation in the aggregate received from the combination of arrangements between the parties.

One variation of the total compensation analysis is the use of a sensitivity analysis technique whereby various levels or volumes of services/resources are used to project the total compensation payable under the arrangement. The various total compensation levels are then analyzed and evaluated relative to the underlying volumes or service levels. The sensitivity analysis tests the rates and the compensation formula for matching of the level or volume of services/resources to the compensation. Such an analysis can serve to indicate limits in value, the need to use tiered compensation rates, or the need to revise individual rates. The range of volumes or levels of service used in a sensitivity analysis typically include a worst case, best case, and expected case. A continuum between best and worst case can also be used.

Another form of a total compensation analysis is the stacking analysis. As discussed in more detail in Chapter 1, Section 5.2, a stacking analysis analyzes the total aggregate compensation paid under all elements of a single arrangement and/or from a combination of arrangements between a buyer and seller. It concentrates on the issue of whether compensation is duplicated for the same essential services/resources when various forms of elements or formulas of compensation are combined and paid together. A stacking analysis, therefore, is just another application of a total compensation analysis as applied to multiple compensation elements in a single arrangement or in the combination of multiple arrangements.

Margin or Return Analysis

In another application, the adapted income approach can take the form of an analysis that focuses on the rates of return on investment and/or on the economic profit margins generated for the buyer or seller under the arrangement. To use this type of method, the appraiser computes the explicit or implicit rates that the buyer or seller receives based on the levels of investment, risk, and resource utilization attributable to either party in the arrangement. The appraiser then compares these returns or margins to relevant market-level rates to assess whether the explicit or implicit rates under the arrangement are appropriate.

One variation of a margin or return analysis involves a double-sided valuation technique in which the returns or margins of both the buyer and seller are evaluated. The appraiser computes relevant returns and margins for both the buyer and seller. Now, these calculations are different. For the seller, the compensation under the arrangement represents a source of revenues for the seller's business operations. Margins or returns for the seller, therefore, are analyzed in the normal manner that they would be assessed for a business or service line. For the buyer, the compensation paid to the seller represents a cost element in the larger service line or business unit because the subject services/resources are an input to operations. The appraiser computes and evaluates the buyer's margins and returns for the service line or unit. If the margins are too low relative to market levels, the buyer would seek alternatives or substitutes or seek to reduce the cost of the services or resource usage. The theory supporting the analysis from the side of the buyer is that the hypothetical buyer will seek to maximize the business enterprise or the usage of resources. Thus, the buyer will avoid resources at pricing or costs that are not consistent with these objectives.

Another variation is based on application of a residual earnings technique or an adapted excess earnings method. As the name indicates, this technique focuses on the residual earnings associated with a compensation arrangement as a value indication for the services/resources provided. Generally, this technique is applied from the perspective of the buyer; it assesses the margin or return on the service line, including the cost of the compensation arrangement. It can be applied when the services/resources are an element of a larger service line or business unit. To use this technique, the appraiser models the service line or business unit at a given level or range of service or resource usage under the compensation arrangement. All the costs are deducted from the revenues for the service line or business unit, excluding the cost of the services/resources provided under the arrangement, to calculate the residual net earnings. The costs used for the service line or business unit should be comprehensive, including a cost of capital that entailed both a return on and return of capital for operational assets, whether tangible or intangible, used in the subject operations. The residual net earnings are then used as a valuation indication for the compensation under the arrangement.

For example, in the case of physician employment arrangements, the concept of earnings-based compensation can be used in the application of the income approach. A forecast of the practice net earnings is developed as the value indication for physician compensation under employment. For this application, practice net earnings includes the revenues and costs of the practice based on a projection of the physician's productivity.

A cost of capital is included with the practice costs, taking into account the return of and on capital used in the generation of revenues for the practice. The value indication of compensation for the physician employment arrangement is based on the level of forecasted practice net earnings. This forecast takes into account future conditions for the practice as well as the specific scope of services contemplated under employment. As a side note, BV appraisers will recognize residual net earnings models as an adaption of the excess earnings method.

Adaptations of the Discounted Cash Flow (DCF) Method

It is possible to use an adaptation of the DCF method from BV as an income approach method for CV purposes. This method is usually applicable to arrangements that are based primarily on resource usage or on a mix of services and resources and are paid on a per-use or "per-click" basis. Examples of such arrangements can include equipment leasing, technical component services, management services, or other forms of clinical or administrative services. The adaptation proceeds along the following lines. The appraiser obtains or prepares a forecast of the arrangement from the perspective of the seller. This forecast includes volume as well as cost-related projections for the arrangement. It also requires calculation of a discount rate, based on the risk profile of the arrangement for the hypothetical seller. The only item that is not estimated is the pricing of the compensation under the arrangement. The appraiser actually solves for this pricing or compensation level by finding the pricing that makes the net present value of the net cash flows from the arrangement equal the value of the investment that the seller must make to provide the service. This computation provides the indication of value at which the net cash flows from the arrangement equal the investment necessary to provide the services/resources, given the inherent level of risk present in the investment.

6.4 The Advantages of Income Approach Methods in CV Practice

The use and application of the income approach has several strong points for the valuation of compensation arrangements:

- Income approach methods are based on forecasts of future market conditions that will exist under the subject arrangement. These are fundamentally forward-looking. This feature is important because market conditions can often change quickly in healthcare.

- They are generally adaptable and adjustable for changes in volume or in the scope or level of services/resources provided under an arrangement. They provide a high level of flexibility in accommodating such variations. This flexibility includes the ability to test and analyze compensation over a range of volumes or service levels.

- They allow for detailed analysis of the economics of the arrangement, including consideration of local market factors and unique factors of the arrangement. Income approach economic modeling can be specific to the local market, while not taking into account unique properties of a specific buyer or seller. Rather, the modeling is based on the economics of the hypothetical buyer and seller in the local market.

- They allow for analysis of the economics of the arrangement considered in total and in the aggregate, including so-called stacking analysis.

- They readily lend themselves to analysis of both buyer and seller economic perspectives and dynamics.

- Income approach methods bring a level of economic rationality and efficiency to the valuation analysis by requiring fundamental economic analysis and study to the totality of compensation and to compensation as paid over a range of volume and service levels.

6.5 The Limitations of Income Approach Methods in CV Practice

There are several key limitations related to the use of income approach methods in CV practice.

- Income approach methods are not readily applicable or practically adaptable to all types of compensation arrangements. While it may be conceptually possible to apply an income approach to many types of compensation arrangements, it may not be practical to do so. For example, it is theoretically possible to use an income approach to value medical directorship services. The data, modeling, and time necessary to complete the approach, however, make it undesirable to do so. There would also be a question of the validity of the analysis, given the level of assumptions that would be needed to prepare an income approach for this type of arrangement.

- They can be data-intensive. Such data is not always available or reliable for use in a given assignment.

- Income approach methods can be complex to prepare. Completing them can be time-consuming, and reviewing and assessing them can be difficult because of the various moving parts in the analysis.

- They require forecasts and projections. Predictions and prognostications necessarily entail some level of uncertainty, even when they are well-researched and supported.

- They may occasionally appear indirectly to include healthcare service referrals, raising significant regulatory concerns. These concerns usually require review by healthcare regulatory legal counsel to determine their use in the appraisal assignment.[10] Nonetheless, given that the three approaches, if relevant and properly applied, should yield results that are in the same ballpark, this concern over referrals is present in all of the methods.

---

10 See Chapter 7, "Complying With the Healthcare Definition of FMV in Appraisal Practice," for a discussion of compliance with the regulatory definition and determination of FMV.

Chapter 3. Using Multiple Methods as a Prudent Practice in Compensation Valuation

CONTENTS

Chapter 3. Using Multiple Methods as a Prudent Practice in Compensation Valuation

By Timothy Smith, CPA/ABV

1.0 Introduction

The methodological framework of the three approaches to value does not necessitate the actual use of more than one approach or method in an appraisal assignment. This chapter will argue, however, that use and application of multiple valuation methods is a prudent and *often* best practice in valuing *some* compensation arrangements. Using more than one approach or method can, in many cases, improve the rigor and scope of the valuation analysis, providing for greater support and defense of the conclusion of value. The reasons for this increased supportability are varied. They are a function of certain unique factors and considerations in CV practice that may not be present in other appraisal disciplines. Moreover, some of these factors can be interrelated and compounding. The factors can be summarized into several general areas:

- The lack of an established body of knowledge and generally accepted appraisal methods and techniques for CV practice based on peer review;

- The dynamic economics of compensation arrangements;

- Consideration of buyer and seller differences in the utility or benefits of a compensation arrangement;

- The lack of sufficiently detailed market data and information sources; and

- The problem of appearances and uncertainty in certain single-method CV appraisals.

The following sections discuss the impact of each of these factors on CV practice. They also address how use and application of multiple approaches and methods can serve to mitigate the valuation difficulties resulting from each. Like stock portfolio diversification, one can argue that diversification of methods yields less risk in the formation of a conclusion of value. Before discussing these factors, however, a brief review of standard appraisal methodology is provided as the background for using more than one approach or method in CV practice.

2.0 Using the Standard Appraisal Methodology in CV Practice

2.1 Consideration of Three Approaches to Value as Standard Appraisal Methodology

Consideration of three approaches to value is standard practice for appraisal professionals. The major appraisal disciplines, whether they are from real estate or business valuation, begin with this methodological foundation. The reason for this commonality is that each approach provides a different, but critical, perspective on the value of a subject property or property interest. An approach will often entail relative strengths and weaknesses in valuing a subject. It should also be noted that more than one appraisal method or technique can be available under each approach to value.[1] Evaluating the use of multiple methods is also part of the framework for standard appraisal methodology. Another important note to remember is that three approaches to value are not necessarily independent of each other, but are interrelated.[2] For example, one can observe market data being used for elements of the income and cost approaches in BV practice.

The approaches can also embody the three core valuation principles of substitution, alternatives, and future benefits. For example, the market approach may take into account the valuation principle of substitution, i.e., the idea that no one will pay more for something than one would for an equally desirable substitute. The valuation principle of alternatives states that the parties to the subject transaction or arrangement have alternatives to consummating the transaction. A cost approach may utilize the principle of alternatives by valuing alternative means for re-creating the same utility. The income approach can reflect the principle of future benefits by valuing anticipated benefits under the arrangement.[3]

---

1   James R. Hitchner, "Approaches to Value," *Financial Valuation: Applications and Models*, 3rd Edition (Kindle), Chapter 1.

2   Shannon P. Pratt and Alina V. Niculita, "Interrelationship of the Three Broad Approaches," *Valuing a Business*, 5th Edition (Kindle), Chapter 3.

3   For a complete discussion of the principles of substitution, alternatives, and future benefits, see Gary R. Trugman, *Understanding Business Valuation: A Practical Guide to Valuing Small to Medium-Sized Businesses*, 2nd edition, pp. 55-56.

Considering use of the three approaches and specific methods does not mean that they all need to be applied for every type of valuation or in every valuation assignment.[4] Rather, the appraiser analyzes the fundamental economics of the subject, along with the availability of data and the purpose and scope of the engagement, and determines which approaches and methods are relevant and applicable for appraising the value of the subject.[5] An appraiser may conclude that only a single approach or method is appropriate for the valuation assignment. In the healthcare industry, for example, the most consistently utilized approach in BV is the income approach.[6] What standard appraisal methodology requires is an evaluation process to determine what approaches and methods are appropriate to the assignment. When more than one approach or method is used, the valuation conclusion is based on a reconciliation and synthesis of the value indications from each method.

2.2 Following Standard Appraisal Methodology in CV Assignments

Besides being consistent with other appraisal disciplines, there are good reasons for considering the three approaches to value and multiple valuation methods in CV assignments. Standard appraisal methodology takes into account a larger set of economic factors than only focusing on a single approach does. This broad perspective is critical: Buyers and sellers in the marketplace will frequently take into account many variables in consummating a transaction. It is consistent, therefore, with the idea of informed buyers and sellers acting at arm's length, as required in the appraisal definition of FMV.[7] In addition, a broad-based analysis is more likely to yield valuation conclusions that are more robust and comprehensive, and ultimately, more supportable and defensible. For these same reasons, one can argue that CV appraisals based on standard methodology are more likely to be consistent with the healthcare regulatory definition of FMV and commercial reasonableness. Valuation conclusions based on standard methodology yield results that can be more readily identified with *multiple* economic factors apart from referrals and are more likely to produce sustainable economic results for the parties to an arrangement.[8]

As noted previously, considering the use of available approaches and methods does not necessitate the application of them all. In fact, the selection of a single method may be

---

4   James R. Hitchner, "Approaches to Value," *Financial Valuation: Applications and Models*, 3rd Edition (Kindle), Chapter 1.

5   Shannon P. Pratt and Alina V. Niculita, "Criteria for the Selection of Valuation Approaches and Methods," *Valuing a Business*, 5th Edition (Kindle), Chapter 19.

6   I thank my co-editor, Mark O. Dietrich, for pointing out this fact to me.

7   The appraisal definition of FMV for CV is discussed in Chapter 2, "Defining FMV and the Market, Cost, and Income Approaches in Compensation Valuation."

8   Compliance with healthcare regulatory definition of FMV is discussed in Chapter 7, "Complying With the Healthcare Definition of FMV in Appraisal Practice."

the outcome of such analysis. *One should distinguish, however, between a rigorous analytic process that concludes with the selection of a single method after considering available methods and a process whose end goal is the selection of a single method. These processes are not the same, and their results will generally differ quantitatively as well as qualitatively.*

The following sections will attempt to show why this is the case in CV assignments.

3.0 Use of Multiple Valuation Methods as a Prudent Practice in CV Assignments

Beyond considering the three approaches to value, actual use of more than one method is frequently a prudent practice, and sometimes a best practice, in compensation valuation. A variety of factors that are generally unique to the world of CV assignments make using multiple methods a recommended framework for practitioners in this emerging discipline.

3.1 The Lack of Publicly Vetted Appraisal Methods in CV

One difficulty with valuation methods and techniques in CV practice is that most have not been publicly vetted within the profession through professional standards, organizations, or literature. Such public review is essential for the formation of sound methods and techniques. Critical and varied perspectives are needed to evaluate the relative strengths and weaknesses of a given valuation method or technique. Significant improvement and refinement of methods are frequently the result of independent minds making a fresh assessment of the material. While vetting a method within a firm can be a helpful first step in the review process, firm dynamics and group-oriented perspective do not generally give rise to the same level of critical evaluation that an open peer review process within the appraisal community can afford. Many methods used by CV practitioners are proprietary and unique to individual firms, making CV practice highly fragmented from a methodological consistency perspective. As a result, reliance on a single method in CV is not the same as reliance on a single approach or method in other appraisal disciplines, such as BV. Methods in BV, for example, have generally been in the public domain for some time and have been subject to formal and informal peer review in the professional and academic literature and by professional organizations. Methods in CV cannot claim any comparable level of professional scrutiny. To date, there has been little public or appraisal community-based scrutiny of CV methods and techniques.[9]

---

9   It should be noted that various editions of *The BVR/AHLA Guide to Healthcare Valuation* were the first attempt at serious publication of professional literature for CV. This text is the first attempt at a systematic body of professional literature and knowledge for the CV discipline.

3.2 The Dynamic Economics of Value in Compensation Arrangements

Compensation arrangements are necessarily complex, not only because of the mixture of services and resources that can be included in certain types of arrangements, but also in the way that compensation is paid for these services and resources. They often entail many elements that are paid for differently under the terms of the agreement. The compensation, moreover, is paid over time and can be variable, based on certain productivity or performance measures. Thus, CV assignments must address the valuation of these various payment elements over time and are frequently based on variable outcomes. These conditions add complexity to CV work because opinions must address dynamic value over time.

A single approach or method may not be able to account for all these dynamic factors and aspects of value. One method or technique may be highly applicable to one element of the arrangement, but less so for others. Another method may be useful in addressing the variable nature of the compensation over time, while another is effective at establishing value for the expected range of volume. In these situations, the full range of dynamic factors can only be addressed by multiple approaches and methods that are then reconciled and synthesized into a conclusion of value. Each method may focus on or be relatively more precise in valuing a specific element or factor in the arrangement when a single method is inadequate on a stand-alone basis.

3.3 Consideration of Both Buyer and Seller Economics

As discussed more fully in Chapter 1, Section 4.4, the economics of compensation arrangements in the healthcare industry are such that it is frequently critical to look at these economics from both sides of the buyer-seller equation. A "double-sided" analysis is used because compensation arrangements can have different substitutes, alternatives, and expected benefits for the buyer and the seller, even when considering the hypothetical buyer and seller that are required by the definition of FMV. A single valuation method may not be able to accommodate or reflect the economics of both sides of the buyer-seller equation. Using more than one method is one way to account for these varying economic and market factors for the buyer and the seller in a compensation arrangement. This unique characteristic of compensation arrangements and valuation makes consideration and use of multiple approaches and/or methods all the more salient.

To illustrate this unique buyer-seller dynamic in compensation arrangements, consider the perspectives of a hospital buyer of emergency department (ED) call coverage and a physician seller of call coverage services. Physician coverage is only one cost or resource element for a hospital's ED. The coverage itself is not generally intended to generate a separately identified and considered utility or benefit for the hospital, but is one operational input or resource to a larger service, although one that is essential. Indeed, the

ED itself is one department within a larger entity, i.e., an acute care facility. Thus, the call coverage service is not typically analyzed in terms of a specific economic return or earnings stream. Rather, the service is one cost among many associated with operating an ED. The value proposition for the hospital relates to cost management. The available substitutes for this service may be arranging for call coverage by other physicians in the marketplace. The alternatives for the hospital, however, can involve employing physicians and requiring them to provide ED call coverage or using locum tenens physicians. From a valuation perspective, valuing the alternatives would include the cost to employ physicians or the cost of locum tenens. One would not, however, generally think of these alternatives as being relevant or applicable to a seller of the service, i.e., the physician. Such options would represent sources of competition for the physician relative to the stream of income from call coverage.

On the seller side of the equation, the physician looks at the burden associated with call coverage relative to his or her substitutes, alternatives, and potential future benefits. The methods used to value these would generally relate to the value of physician services or physician compensation. These methods would focus on the value of the physician's time, work burden, and potential lost income from providing the service. Thus, the value proposition or analysis for the physician relates to compensation for the specific services provided while on call. Indeed, one potential method would be to look at the specific lost compensation that would result from providing such call coverage based on supportable evidence and real data.

As a practical matter, valuations of hospital call coverage arrangements do not frequently consider the hospital's alternatives in employment or contracting with locum tenens providers. But the fact that these alternatives relate to one side of the equation and not necessarily to the other are the salient point. Compensation arrangements can give rise to the need to value specific substitutes, alternatives, and future benefits that are generally applicable only to one side of the buyer-seller equation. In certain circumstances, FMV may need to incorporate both sides of this equation. A single method cannot always yield such incorporation. Moreover, the appraiser cannot readily assess the appropriate tradeoff between each side of the equation without completing methods for each side. By failing to value both sides, many CV analyses can produce value ranges that are one-sided and not reflective of the focus on both the willing buyer and seller under FMV. These disparate considerations for the hypothetical buyers and sellers of services as opposed to cash flows from investments or businesses are the core of the unique challenge confronted by CV appraisers.

3.4 The Lack of Reliable and Applicable Data

While physician compensation surveys abound in the healthcare industry, these surveys tend not to include all the relevant data associated with compensation levels that allows for the meaningful and precise application of such data to a subject compensation arrangement. Compensation is not reported along with data on key economic drivers and factors that affect compensation levels, such as the scope of services that gave rise to the compensation. Use and application of survey data in CV work, therefore, can be highly imprecise and general. It frequently does not allow for meaningful application to a subject compensation arrangement. The imprecision in the survey data is a point that is often missed by many CV practitioners. (See Chapter 4, "On the Informed Use of the Market Data in Compensation Valuation," for a more critical and in-depth discussion of this issue.)

For example, the surveys on call coverage do not report factors related to telephonic response and uncompensated care burdens associated with a given on-call pay rate. Thus, an appraiser cannot meaningfully apply such data to a subject arrangement. The burden of call coverage has to be matched with the compensation for such coverage. In another example, the general physician compensation surveys do not report information on the levels of technical component services, overhead, call coverage pay, medical director pay, or other forms of compensation along with the total compensation for physicians. These factors are critical to assessing the level of compensation in the market data for purposes of determining comparability to subject employment arrangement. None of the surveys reports data in a manner that allows the user to address issues related to local market dynamics. At best, data is reported at the state level.

In addition, data needed for specific inputs in cost and income approaches can also be difficult to obtain in certain types of arrangements. The appraiser may need to rely on a very small number of data sources, or alternatively, use assumptions as substitutes for data to employ various methods or techniques in the valuation process. When the key items of data to a valuation technique are imprecise, weakly sourced, limited, and speculative, those characteristics affect the indication of value from that technique. Valuation methods are dependent on the data inputs and assumptions used in their application. Thus, a single method in CV work can frequently be limited and imprecise because the underlying data is weak.

One way to mitigate the impact of data issues is to use alternative methods that take into account other data sources and different economic factors and inputs. By diversifying data sources and factors, one can dilute the impact of specific data concerns in a method on the conclusion of value. Use of multiple methods provides a data diversification strategy to offset the risk associated with a specific source.

3.5 The Problem of Appearances in Single-Method CV Appraisals

As has been argued in this chapter, CV appraisals based on critical consideration of multiple approaches and methods are more likely to reflect the FMV of a subject compensation arrangement than those based solely on the application of a single-method orientation. Because of the rigor that is produced by such valuations, it can be argued that appraisals prepared according to such consideration will have a higher probability of producing value indications that do not take into account the volume or value of referrals than those prepared using the single-method orientation. Such valuation conclusions yield results that can be more readily identified with many economic factors apart from referrals. As such, there is less ambiguity about the economic reasons and rationale for the consideration paid in a transaction. The value can be associated with a broad base of factors, all of which should exclude referrals.

Exclusion of referrals is not always apparent in compensation valuations that are based on a single method. Many times, reasonable parties can disagree about a specific input or assumption in an appraisal method or about the method itself. When such disputes happen in single-method valuations, the conclusion of value can appear questionable and controversial, leading some to wonder whether the conclusion is merely a manipulated result attempting to obfuscate payment for referrals. Moreover, a single-method orientation can easily lend itself to "cherry-picking" of potential outcomes based on the method or data selected, as noted previously. Some methods and data naturally yield higher values than others, and vice versa. These structural problems cast doubt on the objectivity and independence of the FMV opinions that are based on the single-method orientation. Incredulity can arise when opinions of value are materially dependent on debatable assumptions and methods. Compensation valuations based on single methods, where the method was selected without rigorous consideration of more than one method, naturally lend themselves to such skepticism and uncertainty.

Contrast the potential uncertainty associated with a single-method valuation to the results of a multiple-method valuation for FMV purposes. When a diversity of variables and factors are taken into account along with the approaches and methods that value them in CV practice, the resulting indication of value adds credence to the claim that the economics of the appraisal do not reflect the volume or value of referrals. The reason is that an array of factors and considerations are used to support the conclusion of value. In general, no one input or assumption can be used to impact the conclusion in a material way. Similarly, no one method can solely determine the range of value. As a result, there is less question or controversy about the objectivity and independence of the appraisal because selective use of data or methods is less likely to occur.[10] One can extend this greater level of comfort in the valuation to the question of the *commercial reasonableness* of a subject arrangement. As noted previously, such valuations are more likely to produce sustainable economic results for a buyer as a result of considering a broad array of economic factors. Sustainable results, whether from the earnings of a business or the economics of a service contract, can more readily be considered to be commercially reasonable than unsustainable results.

4.0 Final Note on the Use of Multiple Methods as a CV Prudent Practice

The combination of the factors discussed above in the unique context of valuing compensation arrangements presents a situation in which the use and application of multiple approaches and methods is a best practice for CV assignments. The benefit of this practice is that the relative weaknesses in a given approach or method should be offset by the strengths of other approaches and methods. The combination of methods, therefore, yields greater support to the conclusion of value. One might use the analogy of a rope: Each strand on its own is relatively weak compared to the full rope. If you combine the strands, the result is something that is strong and can support significant weight. This same logic can apply to CV practice. The combination of methods provides for the use and application of a broader array of factors and economic considerations in the conclusion of value. The combined result is a more robust analysis in support of the value opinion.

---

10   Certainly, it is possible to complete multiple methods and then "cherry-pick" the results in the synthesis process. It seems to me, however, that such selective use is more readily apparent to users and readers of appraisal reports. When an appraisal analysis ignores relevant and available data, assumptions, and methods, it is easy to support a particular conclusion on paper. No other consideration is given to alternative factors or issues; they can simply be ignored. An appraisal that raises a variety of considerations makes it harder to select results in a manipulative fashion because many factors are addressed in the analysis. Critical readers can readily identify dubious logic and questionable assumptions when more than a singular view is presented. One might analogize to the procedures for evidence and argumentation in a grand jury proceeding in contrast to a trial. Supposedly, a prosecutor can indict a "ham sandwich" when only one side of the evidence is presented in a grand jury proceeding. Not so, when the alleged defendant is able to present an opposing point of view.

Chapter 4. On the Informed Use of the Market Data in Compensation Valuation

CONTENTS

Chapter 4. On the Informed Use of the Market Data in Compensation Valuation

By Timothy Smith, CPA/ABV

1.0 Introduction

The prevailing paradigm for valuing compensation arrangements in the healthcare industry is to use market data and the market approach, largely due to the availability of numerous compensation surveys. The simplicity of applying survey data, coupled with the *apparent* objectivity of survey-based valuation methods, has also contributed to the predominant use of such data in CV practice. To a lesser extent, there is also a desire on the part of many in healthcare to use data from individual arrangements that have been transacted in the marketplace. Generally, the consultants valuing the arrangement gather data on these individual transactions, or the parties to the subject transaction, including their advocates, provide it. Both types of data present unique issues and considerations for CV appraisers attempting to analyze and apply survey or individual transaction data to a subject compensation arrangement. Unfortunately, many involved in the valuation process fail to recognize the critical questions that should be addressed in the use of such data for appraising compensation. The purpose of this chapter, therefore, is to identify these critical issues and discuss the criteria that can be used to evaluate such issues at a thoughtful and professional level.

2.0 General Considerations in Using Market Data for CV

2.1 Matching Market Data to the Services/Resources Provided Under the Arrangement

In using market data for compensation valuation, the task of the appraiser is to identify the service or resources elements to be provided under the subject arrangement and then obtain information on comparable arrangements in the marketplace. The first step in the application of the market data, therefore, is defining and distinguishing each type of element required under the subject agreement. Without a clear and detailed inventory of these elements, the appraiser will not be able to obtain market data that is truly comparable to the subject arrangement, resulting, of course, in an inaccurate or misleading indication of value when using this data.

Delineation of the scope of services/resources provided looks to certain key characteristics:

- Will the services be clinical, administrative, managerial, educational, scientific, or some combination thereof?

- Who will be providing these services: physicians, nonphysician providers, clinical support staff, administrative support staff, management professionals, or other types of professionals?

- Will the resources provided include real estate, equipment, medical or administrative supplies, or support services not related to specific individuals, e.g., information technology or communication services?

- Will the services or resources be provided on a full-time or continual basis or a part-time or periodic basis?

- How is the provision of services/resources measured or determined under the terms of the arrangement? What is the appropriate unit of measure?

Once an appraiser can answer these questions, he or she is ready to search for market data that is comparable. Omission or incorrect inclusion of a service or resource can have a material effect on the application of the market data in the appraisal analysis. In some cases, an appraiser may not be able to find fully comparable market data, but can adjust either the market data or the analysis of the subject arrangement to achieve comparability.

2.2 Sources of Market Data in the Healthcare Industry

The sources for market data in healthcare depend on two different sets of considerations. The first consideration relates to the type of compensation arrangement. For some types of arrangements, numerous sources of market-related information are publicly available. Examples include physician compensation surveys for clinical, academic, and administrative compensation. Market data is not readily available, however, for arrangements such as clinical co-management/service line management arrangements between physicians and hospitals or healthcare systems. Even when data is publicly available for a compensation arrangement, as in the case of the physician compensation surveys, applying it to an arrangement can be challenging. The data is not often reported with sufficient detail or with detail on key variables or metrics relative to compensation. Moreover, a detailed scope of services for the reported compensation is not included or considered in the survey data. As a result, comparability is difficult, and the data cannot always be used in a meaningful manner.

The second key consideration for market data is relevance to the local market and the characteristics of the subject arrangement. The survey data is not available by local market. Data may be reported by region or state, but this may be reflective of local market factors and dynamics.[1] Many times this data reflects certain national market tendencies or the amalgamation of the marketplaces of those who responded to a survey. It is important to note, moreover, that the surveys are not prepared using statistically valid sampling methods. Thus, bias may exist in the data in terms of the characteristics and economics of the particular respondents, the market dynamics of the particular respondents, and the position of the respondents in their markets. The surveys, moreover, tend to represent segments of the marketplace in terms of the particular types of respondents.[2] The market data may not be highly germane or applicable to a subject arrangement because the characteristics of the respondents are significantly different than those of the subject. Unfortunately, many in the healthcare industry fail to recognize the fundamental limitations of the physician compensation survey data when using it to establish FMV in compensation arrangements.

Attempts by appraisers to develop independent surveys of market transactions to remedy the lack of market data for a specific type of compensation arrangement or to obtain local market data points are not usually successful. Because these transactions are private, most parties involved in compensation arrangements are reluctant to share data. The data they do share, moreover, is often limited and partial, not providing the appraiser with sufficient detail for use in the valuation analysis. The appraiser needs specific information about the scope of services/resources provided under the agreement for the individual transaction to be useful in the valuation process. Even when such data is obtained, it is often limited to a few comparables that may not constitute a sufficient size for extrapolation to the marketplace.

---

1   See Chapter 37, "How Reimbursement and Physician Compensation Vary by Market," for a discussion of how physician compensation can vary widely by local market and within a local market.

2   See Chapter 38, "Comparing the Surveys to the Physician Marketplace: Implications for Valuation Analysis," for an in-depth discussion of whether general physician compensation is reflective of the whole or of all segments of the physician marketplace.

While data on specific types of compensation arrangements may not be available, data on some or all of the various elements or individual services or resources provided in a compensation arrangement may be available. For example, numerous surveys are available that report compensation for various types of healthcare professionals, including nonphysician providers, nurses, technicians, executives, managers, and clerical or administrative positions. Information on supply and resource costs may also be readily obtained.

2.3 Limitations on the Use of Market Data Imposed by the Stark Regulations

The Stark regulations place limitations on the usage of certain market data from transactions between parties in a position to refer to one another for determining FMV. The extent and validity of these limitations are discussed in further detail in Chapter 8, "To Use or Not to Use: An Appraisal Analysis of the Stark Prohibition on Market Data From Parties in a Position to Refer." In imposing these restrictions, regulators acknowledge that this exclusion of market data may prohibit the use of the market approach in valuing compensation arrangements. In those cases, the Stark regulations advise consideration of alternative valuation methods. While the issues surrounding the Stark limitations on the use of market data are not discussed here, suffice it to say that CV practitioners should be aware of the regulatory considerations related to the use of certain market data for establishing FMV for healthcare compliance purposes. Lack of awareness of this regulatory matter can lead to significant problems in the scope of work and the opinion of value.

2.4 The Critical Need to Understand the Details and Nuances of Market Data

Since the essence of compensation valuation is matching compensation to the services/resources provided, it is essential for the appraiser to have a thorough and studied understanding of the data sources being used in the approaches to value. Compensation arrangements in healthcare can often entail a variety of services and resources. Each service and area of resource usage may have distinct economics and market dynamics. Moreover, the combination or "stacking" of compensation arrangements between parties may result in a service or resource element being compensated twice. Such stacking of arrangements can generate compensation for services or resources not actually provided when the required elements are combined. For example, an employed physician who is paid on a compensation- per-wRVU basis does not bear any risk for providing uncompensated care as part of hospital call coverage. Any procedures performed as part of call coverage are paid at the established wRVU rate. As a result, the appraiser must be able to navigate the details and nuances of market data to identify, utilize, apply, or adjust such data. All too often, valuation consultants fail to take the time to understand market data or make unwarranted assumptions about market information without adequate research.

3.0 Critical Issues in the Use of Market Survey Data

3.1 Understanding Survey Methodology and Definitions

It is important to understand the origins of the data in the physician compensation surveys as well as the spectrum of data available in them. Unfortunately, many marketplace users of the surveys are often unaware of critical features in the methodology used to compile and report the data. Such uncritical use tends to promote misunderstandings and misapplications of the data. Thus, appraisers should complete a thorough review of the respondent profiles, survey methodology, glossary and definitions, and discussion sections of surveys before using them in valuation practice.

Many of the surveys will include a copy of the survey questionnaire and the guide to the questionnaire that were given to respondents to complete the survey. Review of such information can be extremely helpful for the appraiser in using survey data appropriately as part of the market approach. The appraiser should seek to use survey data that is comparable to the subject compensation arrangement under valuation or, when necessary, adjust for such comparability. Comparability can only be established *after* an appraiser has an understanding of what is and is not included in survey data.

One key area of the survey methodology is the criteria used for exclusion or inclusion in the data. Does the survey exclude data from respondents meeting certain profiles or criteria? For example, does the survey require a certain full-time equivalent (FTE) level for inclusion? Does the survey exclude respondents who provide only partial responses to the questionnaire? Some surveys exclude apparent anomalies or outliers in their data. Knowing such criteria can aid the appraiser in determining the comparability of the data.

Another key area is reviewing the level at which data is collected. For example, MGMA's *Physician Compensation and Production Survey* reports physician work relative value units (wRVUs) and compensation per wRVU based on the wRVUs personally performed by individual physicians. The MGMA *Cost Survey*, by contrast, reports data gathered at the group level, rather than the individual physician level. Moreover, metrics reported on a per-wRVU basis in the *Cost Survey* are based on the total wRVUs reported for a group, including both physician and nonphysician provider wRVUs.

3.2 The Importance of Understanding Definitions and Terms

Particular attention should be given to the definitions of various terms and metrics used in the physician compensation survey data. Failure to review and note these definitions can lead to the misapplication of the market approach in the appraisal process. An appraiser may assume that a given term or metric includes certain data, when in fact, the term may exclude that data. Most of the surveys provide a general glossary of terms used in the survey report, and many also provide detailed descriptions of the data. The appraiser should study the definitions prior to using the survey data. Many of the surveys also provide contact information if a user has questions about the survey data. When in doubt, an appraiser should make use of this resource to resolve questions.

Notwithstanding the guidance from a survey's glossary or questionnaire form, appraisers should be aware of the potential for respondents not to follow such guidance when completing the survey. Many experienced healthcare valuation consultants are somewhat dubious about what some groups may be reporting for certain survey metrics. This uncertainty regarding the quality of the data reported reflects the fact that many information systems used by physician practices often lack the capacities for readily calculating certain data in accordance with survey guidelines or the users of such systems lack the requisite resources or knowledge to compute the data appropriately. In summary, users of survey data should understand the complexities involved in the data gathering process for various metrics.

3.3 Evaluating Survey Data Before Using It

Often anomalies appear in the survey data. Thus, a best practice is to examine the survey data before using it. If such anomalies are observed in data from a survey, one may choose to exclude a survey or significantly reduce its impact on the valuation based on its relative weighting in the synthesis process. One could choose to exclude or reduce the weighting on a survey that the appraiser considers to be *outdated*. The surveys collect and report data from a prior year; they are published many months after the end of the data year reported. The use of noncalendar years can further influence data. In such circumstances, the current version of a survey may represent data that is nearly two years old. An appraiser may conclude that data from the survey should be excluded or be given a lower weight when current or future market conditions are thought to be materially different than they were in the year for which data is reported.

3.4 Understanding Available Survey Metrics and Data Subsets

In addition to providing data on compensation, many of the physician compensation surveys include various other relevant metrics and data categories. Many report compensation and other data based on a variety of respondent characteristics, ranging from geographic to demographic. They may also report compensation in terms of various productivity metrics or by type of practice setting, size, or other attribute.

It should be noted that the number of respondents for the various categories of data reported in the surveys varies. This variance results from the fact that not all respondents to a survey report data for all requested categories. Generally, the number of respondents for total compensation includes the greatest number of respondents because failure to report compensation is usually one criterion for exclusion from the survey. Failure to include other data items, however, may not exclude a respondent from inclusion in the survey. Thus, users of survey data should be aware of the fact that the respondent base for many categories is a subset of the total data set. This fact is important in assuming or assessing relationships between compensation and various metrics reported in the surveys.

Some of the surveys provide data based on key characteristics of the respondents. One major characteristic is geography. Most of the surveys will report selected survey data by geographic region; some will provide this data by state. Another key characteristic by which data can be segregated is physician practice ownership. Some of the surveys will separately report data for physician-owned and hospital/health system practices or owner/nonowner. Appraisers should note that nonowners *include* hospital employees in addition to employees of privately held practices. Different surveys may offer different ways to "slice and dice" the data. One example is the CD-ROM version of MGMA's *Compensation and Production Survey*. This electronic version of the survey affords multiple selection criteria for organizing and sorting the data from MGMA's flagship survey.

3.5 Comparison of Survey Respondents to the Physician Marketplace

It is important to understand the respondent base for a physician compensation survey. The surveys are generally produced by trade groups, such as MGMA or AMGA, that obtain data from their members or by survey organizations that solicit information from selected healthcare systems and physician groups. Each survey tends to reflect its members or similar types of physician practice organizations or settings. As a result, the surveys tend to represent various segments of the physician marketplace; they individually do not reflect the marketplace as a whole. For a more detailed discussion of this fact, see Chapter 38, "Comparing the Surveys to the Physician Marketplace: Implications for Valuation Analysis."

4.0 Critical Issues in the Use of Individual Transaction Data

While use of physician compensation surveys is the most common source of data for application in valuing compensation arrangements, the use of individual or specific transactions and agreements that have been consummated in the marketplace is often raised, especially by physicians who purport to have such information available to them. Typically, the appraiser must gather such data on individual transactions or the parties to an arrangement or their advisers and consultants provide it to the appraiser. The following sections provide criteria for utilizing such data in the valuation analysis of a compensation arrangement.

4.1 Accessibility of Individual Transaction Data to the Marketplace

To use market data from individual or specific transactions that have occurred in the marketplace, the data should generally be accessible to third parties. Use of proprietary data that only a specific party or limited parties can access creates a potential conflict with the appraisal definition of FMV promulgated in Revenue Ruling 59-60 and the *International Glossary of Business Valuation Terms*. In both formulations of the definition, FMV requires that the buyer and seller have "reasonable knowledge" of the relevant facts. Reliance on proprietary data that is not available to other parties raises the question of whether a hypothetical buyer and seller can have such reasonable knowledge. It also raises the question of whether another appraiser can replicate the valuation analysis. While valuation and consulting firms love the business advantages associated with proprietary data, its use does not appear to be consistent with the concept of FMV. Data monopolies are not part of "an open and unrestricted market," as required in the hypothetical conditions of FMV under the professional appraisal standards and literature. In conclusion, reliance on proprietary data that is available through an individual appraisal or consulting firm raises concerns about consistency with FMV.

4.2 Criteria for Using the Individual Transaction Data

An appraiser should consider several key criteria before attempting to use individual transaction data for establishing compensation under a subject employment arrangement:

- *Are the market transactions between parties that are in a position to refer under the Stark regulations?* From a regulatory compliance perspective, use of market transactions from parties in a position to refer is not valid support for FMV compensation in healthcare valuation practice. An appraiser may elect to present such data as part of the research prepared for the valuation.

- *Does the appraiser have actual documentation on market transactions?* Market transaction data should be based on actual transactions accompanied by an appropriate level of documentation from reliable or unbiased sources. Second-hand accounts, hearsay, and oral statements by parties with a bias toward the subject arrangement are not reliable for purposes of establishing an objective, reliable, and supportable appraisal.

- *Does the appraiser have sufficient details and information on the market transaction?* Since the key to using the market approach for compensation valuation is comparability, the appraiser should have sufficient detail on the market transactions to determine the scope of services/resources provided in these compensation arrangements. In addition, information on other key aspects of the market transactions should be available. The reason for obtaining such data is that it has a bearing on the facts and circumstances for the actual transaction. The parties can set compensation in an arrangement by considering various factors. To determine whether a market transaction is comparable, it is important to have some understanding of the factors that affected the alleged comparable transaction.

- *Is the scope of services in the market transactions comparable to the services required under the subject arrangement?* The services/resources under the market data should, of course, be comparable. The compensation in market transactions may have been "stacked," i.e., represent payment for numerous types of services or resource usage. The compensation payable to a seller providing multiple services is not comparable to a market transaction(s) where a seller provides fewer services or a reduced level of services. When sufficient information is available on the compensation for each type of service, an appraiser may be able to adjust the market data to make the scope of services and corresponding level of compensation comparable to the subject services. In addition, comparability of physician specialty or subspecialty should not be overlooked in evaluating market transaction data.

- *Are the local market conditions and the buyer-seller profiles of the transactions comparable to the subject arrangement?* Local market factors, such as the supply and demand of physicians for a given specialty, can have a significant impact on the range of compensation for physicians.[3] Commercial reimbursement dynamics can be another significant factor in the range of compensation for a given local market, as noted in the research findings of Dietrich and Anderson.[4] As discussed in Chapter 37, "How Reimbursement and Physician Compensation Vary by Market," commercial reimbursement varies widely from market to market in the United States. Moreover, commercial reimbursement can vary significantly within a market based on the relative bargaining power of a provider within the local market.[5] Thus, to assess the comparability of market transaction data, it is important to have some knowledge of these dynamics in both the markets for the subject arrangement and the market transaction data. It is also helpful to know the background on the parties in the transaction data. Different types of buyers and sellers can

---

3   See Chapter 12, "Reasonable Compensation for Income Tax Purposes."
4   Mark O. Dietrich, CPA/ABV, and Gregory D. Anderson, CPA/ABV, CVA, "Evaluating RVU-Based Compensation Arrangements," *Health Lawyers Weekly*, Nov. 14, 2008.
5   See Paul B. Ginsburg, "Wide Variation in Hospital and Physician Payment Rates Evidence of Provider Market Power," *Research Brief* No. 16, November 2010, Center for Studying Health System Change, www.hschange.org.

affect the level of compensation paid in an arrangement. Such factors may be inconsistent with the hypothetical buyer and seller required under the standard of FMV.

- *Are the subject service provider's qualifications and credentials comparable to the providers involved in the transaction data?* A provider's qualifications and credentials can affect the level of compensation in a compensation arrangement. For example, physicians recently out of residency or fellowship may not receive the same level of compensation as more experienced physicians, for which an employer may have higher productivity expectations. A physician with unique credentials or specialized training that is in high demand or has national recognition, such as robotic surgery, may receive higher compensation than others with the same specialty. If a market transaction data point includes such a physician, the transaction may not be comparable for a physician without such credentials, training, or reputation.

- *Are there sufficient points in the transaction data set to constitute a reasonable indication of the market?* An appraiser should consider whether the number of transactions for which data is available is adequate for formulating an indication of market compensation levels for comparable services. The question of the sufficiency of the data is generally a matter of judgment based on the facts and circumstances related to the subject arrangement and the data. For example, if a subject employment arrangement involves a highly unique physician specialty or subspecialty or type of services for which there is a limited number of comparable physicians or arrangements in the marketplace, a smaller data set may provide a reasonable basis for formulating an assessment of the market. A subject arrangement for a typical specialty or scope of clinical services would generally warrant a larger number of transactions to establish market trends.

4.3 Common Comparability Issues in Using Individual Transaction Data

Two key areas of comparability related to the use of data from individual transactions often arise in CV practice: independent contractor versus employee compensation and owner compensation versus compensation for services rendered.

Independent Contractor Versus Employee Compensation

Generally compensation paid to independent contractors in the marketplace includes an apparent premium more accurately described as a "gross-up" amount. This amount is intended to cover benefits or costs that an independent contractor bears but an employer would otherwise pay under an employment-based arrangement.[6] Compensation to independent contractor physicians may also include an allowance for professional liability insurance (PLI). Market transaction data for independent contractor arrangements that include a benefits and PLI allowance should be adjusted to eliminate the allowance if the data is being used for a subject employment agreement. Employers generally cover these costs. Compensation for employment arrangements is generally stated in dollar amounts that do not include the cost of employer-paid benefits and PLI. Conversely, market data from employment arrangements should generally be adjusted for benefits and PLI when being used to establish the value of an independent contractor arrangement.

Owner Compensation Versus Compensation for Services Rendered

Market transaction data for employment or other service arrangements in which physicians are both employees and owners of the business entity providing services may include compensation amounts that represent payment for services as well as a payment for owner compensation or a return on investment. In other words, the total amount of compensation received by such physicians includes a payment for the clinical services along with a payment for the owner or management services and a return on capital investment. In such cases, it is necessary to adjust the total compensation for the value of owner compensation to derive the level that relates to the clinical services the physician provided as a nonowner employee.

4.4 Benefits and Limitations of the Individual Transaction Data

When sufficient and comparable data is available, individual transaction data can be used to yield supportable market-based indications of value. The reality surrounding the use of this data, however, is that it is rarely available or accessible. Private parties are reluctant to provide detailed data on their transactions. Some attorneys and consultants may maintain proprietary databases with such data, but they are generally not willing or able to make such data widely available to third parties. There may be cases, however, where the most relevant and applicable data will be found from individual transactions in the marketplace. For subject arrangements involving highly specialized and unique physician services or physicians with highly specialized credentials or national reputations, little data may be available in the physician compensation surveys that are comparable and relevant for valuation purposes. The appraiser may need to gather transactional data independently to find truly comparable market data.

---

6   Here, we are discussing employer-paid benefit costs, not benefit costs that employees pay out of their compensation through payroll deductions.

5.0 Conclusion: Key Chapter Takeaways

The bottom line for using market data in the valuation analysis is using it intelligently. An appraiser needs to understand the characteristics of the data to apply it accurately in valuation methods. This requirement applies to data from both market surveys and individual transactions. In the case of market surveys, appraisers should have an in-depth knowledge of the respondent profiles, survey methodology, glossary and definitions, and discussion sections of surveys before using them in valuation practice. To use data from individual transactions, appraisers need to ensure that they have sufficient information on the transactions and that the data meets certain qualitative criteria. In short, "look before you leap" is the mantra for using market data in CV assignments.

Chapter 5. Elements of a Compensation Valuation Appraisal Report

CONTENTS

Chapter 5. Elements of a Compensation Valuation Appraisal Report

By Timothy Smith, CPA/ABV

1.0 Introduction

No specific professional standards govern the content and requirements for appraisal reports in compensation valuation, and there is hardly any professional literature on this topic.[1] In the absence of any professional guidance, CV appraisers have generally fallen back on business valuation reporting standards for direction in preparing valuation reports. This chapter will likewise look to the BV standards, but will also adapt and expand on these standards to address areas that are unique to CV practice and appraisal issues.

Developing templates for CV reports and exhibits that go along with them can be a daunting task for appraisers. First, report writing is not a favorite task of most appraisers; it's one of those "necessary evils," even though reports are critical to our work. We're numbers people at heart. Second, our clients are often at extremes in terms of their needs and wants in an appraisal report. At one end of the spectrum, some of our clients simply want to get that magical FMV number. They will only open the report to find the number. Once they find it, they simply file the report away somewhere, never to be seen again. At the other end of the spectrum are those clients that want to scrutinize every sentence, assumption, and number in the report. It can be hard to find a happy medium for the level of information in a report that will serve the needs of both types of client. Having two report templates may not be a good option, either. The appraisal report factory works much more efficiently with a standard template or at least

---

1 Some credentialing organizations, such as the AICPA, have standards for consulting services that would apply to CV assignments. In addition, the general code of ethics and general standards for professional responsibility would also be applicable.

a standard template for each type of compensation arrangement. In short, developing report templates for CV is no easy task.

This chapter will also discuss many practical applications and issues involved in developing CV reports. The approach taken is one of presenting "tools for the toolbox." I've written this chapter not only looking at the BV standards, but also based on personal experience, having been a client and now practicing as an appraiser. For many years, I worked in one of the nation's largest health systems that ordered appraisals by the dozens from a variety of firms. One of my duties was to develop a set of engagement and reporting standards so that various types of users within the system could have some consistency in the content and information of these reports. In the interest of full disclosure, I'll note that when I was a client, I was one of those people who went over valuation reports with a fine tooth comb, taxing the patience of many of my now colleagues in the appraisal business. Having been in the appraisal business for several years, however, I also have a feel for the appraiser's side of the equation. Appraisal reports need to be set up for efficient and timely completion. The great challenge of report writing is figuring out how to balance all of these factors. Hopefully this chapter provides you with useful information for striking that balance within your practice as you strive to meet the needs of your clients.

2.0 Key Points in Developing CV Report Content

2.1 Guidance From USPAP and BV Reporting Standards
One can observe a fair amount of consistency in the information requirements for valuation reports from the various BV standards.[2] While some of the categories or terminology may vary, the basic content elements are very similar or comparable. As noted in the introduction to this chapter, the various report elements that will be recommended for CV reports were developed from these BV standards. Not every requirement from the BV standards crosswalks to CV, however, because of certain differences in the two types of valuation work. Yet, those that do not crosswalk can usually be adapted for use in CV. These adaptations are included in the elements recommended here.

2.2 Sufficient Information on the Scope of Work
As a starting point, it may be helpful to look at the reporting requirement of the Scope of Work Rule from the Uniform Standards of Professional Appraisal Practice (USPAP). While USPAP does not apply to CV and does not govern all appraisal professionals, it is a major touchstone in the profession. The Scope of Work Rule states that an appraisal

---

2 USPAP Standard 10: Business Appraisal Reporting; SSVS1; IBA/NACVA Professional Standards.

"report must contain sufficient information to allow intended users to understand the scope of work performed." This simple and straightforward requirement is perhaps the best standard for thinking about the issue of report content for CV. A report needs to tell the user what the appraiser did to reach a conclusion of value.

2.3 The Scope of Work and the Workfile as the Foundation for the Report

While reports are critical to the valuation process, what may matter most in a valuation assignment is that the appraiser completed an adequate scope of work to arrive at a supportable conclusion of value. A great report doesn't make up for poorly conceived and implemented appraisal work. The most important and detailed record of that work is what is maintained in the appraiser's workpapers and workfile for the engagement. The report is usually going to be a summary at one level or another of the work completed, unless you want to write a really long report. Firms that have had their reports subjected to litigation will tell you that you need to have your workfiles and workpapers in order and in sufficient detail to support the conclusion of value. It is helpful, therefore, to think about valuation reports as a summarized version of the workfile. Step 1, however, is to ensure the workfile is in order.

2.4 The Level of Information in a Report

Another useful distinction found in the BV standards is the idea of a detailed or summary report.[3] Both types of reports have the same basic content requirements, but the summary report provides a more concise version of what is included in the detailed reports. This distinction makes an important point: A report is more or less the story of what we did to arrive at a conclusion of value. We can tell the short or long version of that story, as long as we make sure to include certain key parts in the plot.

USPAP's two types of BV reports, an Appraisal Report and Restricted Use Appraisal Report, appear to make a similar distinction with regard to the content and level of information in a report. The intended use and users of the report are what determine the appropriate level of information. When the intended user of a report includes only the client, a Restricted Use Appraisal Report may be used. This type of report must include the warning that "the appraiser's opinions and conclusions set forth in the report may not be understood properly without additional information in the appraiser's workfile."[4] In other words, less information is included in the Restricted Use report than in the nonrestricted version. The scope of work and the contents of the workfile, however, do not change.

---

3   See SSVS1, paragraph 48; IBA/NACVA joint Professional Standards, Section V.C.
4   Standards Rule 10-2.

3.0 Content Elements in a CV Report

The following sections outline key areas of information and content for a CV report. Each area contributes to informing the user about the scope of work completed in arriving at a conclusion of value. The level of detail included for each topic, however, is a matter of judgment for the appraiser, based on the intended use and users for the report.

3.1 Assignment Elements

Certain elements are common to valuation assignments and reports. Taken together, these elements set up the primary requirements for the scope of work in the assignment. They indicate the critical parameters that direct the appraisal work to be completed. As such, they are important topics to include in CV reports. Many of the BV standards include these elements in the report introduction requirements. Such inclusion is very logical, since they outline the engagement scope of work. These assignment elements include the following areas.[5]

Client and Intended Users of the Report

In addition to identifying the client and other intended users, CV appraisers may want to consider the possibility that their report may end up in the hands of federal and state regulators. Certainly, reports prepared under attorney-client privilege (ACP) would generally not be subject to this review. Many clients, however, do not use ACP as part of their process. One response to this possibility is simply to embrace it. Write a report with the expectation that regulators will one day scrutinize it. Your report will be that much better if you prepare it based on that expectation. Such preparation does not necessarily mean that you need to name regulators as intended users. Rather, you develop the report assuming it will one day be subject to regulatory review. You may also want to discuss this possibility with the client. If the client wants to protect the report from regulatory review, the report should be prepared under ACP.

Purpose and Use of the Valuation

In stating that the intended use of the CV report is healthcare regulatory compliance, avoid language that implies the appraisal provides regulatory or compliance advice or guidance. Appraisers do not provide regulatory opinions and advice. Our job is not compliance *per se*. That's the responsibility of the client and client's legal counsel. Certainly, use of independent appraisers is an important part of a healthcare entity's compliance program. Our task in the program, however, is simply to provide clients with conclusions of value for the subject arrangement that are consistent with the regulatory definition of FMV. A client can either choose to rely on the opinion or not.

---

5   These assignments elements are based on USPAP's Scope of Work Rule and Standard 10, the Introduction elements for a BV report in SSVS1, and the IBA/NACVA Professional Standards.

Standard of Value and Jurisdictional Exceptions

CV reports prepared for healthcare regulatory compliance purposes need to use the healthcare regulatory definition of FMV. Use and application of healthcare regulatory FMV in appraisal work, however, is a topic with many wrinkles. In certain instances, the regulatory definition of FMV may require the appraiser to depart from standard appraisal methodology. These departures are best addressed as jurisdictional exceptions. In fact, a helpful practice may be to discuss the definition of value and any jurisdictional exceptions in the same section of the report since they are interrelated. For a complete discussion of the issues involved with the regulatory definition of FMV and the use of jurisdictional exceptions, see Chapter 7, "Complying With the Healthcare Definition of FMV in Appraisal Practice."

Valuation Dates

The topic of valuation dates in CV reports is one that requires some additions and adjustments to the BV framework for CV practice. BV standards make a distinction between the valuation date and the report date. The valuation date is the effective date of the appraisal on which the conclusion of value was determined, while the report date is the date the report is issued. Because CV deals with arrangements that typically span multiple years, CV reports need to address the duration of the report: How many years of the subject arrangement are covered by the report conclusion? Another issue is the lead time between the valuation date and when the subject arrangement actually starts. Valuations are usually obtained prior to consummating a transaction and the span of time between when a valuation is completed and when an arrangement begins can be several months. As a result, a CV report typically needs to address all the following dates:

1. *Valuation date:* The date when the CV appraiser arrives at a conclusion of value. It is the date through which the appraiser has considered known and knowable conditions and circumstances that affect the conclusion.[6]

2. *Report issue date:* The date the report was issued.

3. *Length of contract covered by the valuation:* How many years of the subject arrangement are covered by the valuation opinion?

4. *Required start date for the subject arrangement:* By what date must the arrangement start for the valuation to apply or be effective?

On the question of how many years of the contract are covered by the valuation, the critical issue is how much uncertainty exists relative to future conditions for the arrangement at the time the valuation is prepared. Given an ever-changing and dynamic

---

6   See SSVS1, paragraph 43.

healthcare marketplace, two years is the standard benchmark for most appraisal firms. Some may go to three years in certain circumstances, but place special qualifications or limiting conditions on the opinion. They will say something on the order of "assuming no major changes in market conditions related to the subject arrangement."

Uncertainty of future conditions is also the central issue in determining the lead time between the valuation date and when the arrangement begins. CV practitioners frequently give three to six months of lead time. Some may go as far as one year, but again with special qualification language or limiting conditions relative to future changes in market conditions.

One needs to think about the combined period of time covered by a CV report based on the lead time and the number of years covered. A report with an effective date one year out, coupled with a three-year contract period, means the conclusion of value is applicable to a four-year span. An appraiser needs to be sure he or she thinks the conclusion is supportable over that period.

If special qualifications or limiting conditions are placed on the period covered by a CV report, it's important that such language be clear and readily apparent in the report and to the user. A client may not be comfortable relying on the report with such qualifications. For example, qualifying language related to changing future market conditions can shift the burden of the ongoing validity of the conclusion of value to the client. Someone will need to review market conditions in the future to ensure that they have not substantially changed since the valuation date of the report. Some clients will be willing to assume this responsibility; others will not.

Type of Report: Summary or Detailed
Labeling a report as "summary" or "detailed" communicates to a user what level of detail to expect in the report. It lets the reader know that there is relatively more or less information on the scope of work completed. This fact can be important for a user with questions or concerns about the valuation analysis. Most users tend to read a report at face value: What the appraiser did is what's discussed in the report. If a report leaves the user with many questions because the report is a "Cliff Notes" version of the valuation analysis, that user is likely to think the appraiser did not do adequate work. Using a label such as a "summary report" at least provides some clue to the reader that the report is merely a summary of the work, not the full account. The appraiser may have actually addressed certain issues, but failed to include details on how they were addressed in the report. The labeling, along with a brief definition of the label, can let the user know to seek additional information from the appraiser on the work completed.

Why does this matter? I have seen many summary-level reports without such labeling create negative impressions of appraisal firms within an organization. In my days as a client of valuation firms, I discussed many such reports with appraisers only to find that the negative impression was false. The report simply failed to document certain key areas of information. Not every client will be willing or able to make the effort that I did to get the rest of the story. A summary-level report that is not designated as such can mislead users about the appraisal scope of work and the appraiser's competence. I would not recommend leaving this possibility to the "face value" impressions of users.

Scope Limitations

It is imperative to identify and document scope limitations placed on the appraisal assignment, including the nature and extent of each restriction. In addition, discussing the implications of the limitations on the scope of work and conclusion of value so that the user understands them can be very important. It is also vital for the user to be aware of specific assumptions and/or limiting conditions that are included in the report to address the ramifications of certain scope limitations. When clients place scope limitations on an appraiser, they need to understand the consequences of such limitations on the appraisal.

Limitations on Access to Data

While it is a common practice to document sources of data used in a separate section of the CV report, discussing limitations on access to key data as part of the assignment elements or report introduction can serve to highlight the impact of limited data on the scope of work. This report section can include identification of the data that was not available and the circumstances surrounding the limited access to it. Users can also benefit from a discussion of the impact of the data limitations on the scope of work and the inclusion of any specific assumptions and/or limiting conditions to address the lack of pertinent data.

Reliance on the Work of Specialists

As with BV reports, documenting reliance on the work of specialists, including appraisers from other disciplines such as real estate or machinery and equipment, is essential in a CV report. Identifying the specific specialist and work that was relied on and addressing the nature, scope, and impact of this reliance on the conclusion of value are key items to include in a CV report.

Subsequent Events

SSVS1 introduces the concept of disclosing material events or changes in conditions that occur after the valuation date and that were not known or knowable at this date. Where meaningful to a user, disclosure of such subsequent events may be warranted in the report to keep users informed. Such disclosure is intended, however, only for informational purposes and should not affect the determination of value as of the valuation date. Given the span of time covered by a CV report, including both the lead time from the valuation date to the start date of the arrangement and the number of years covered by the conclusion, disclosure of subsequent events may be helpful to users. Some clients may elect not to rely on an appraisal for healthcare regulatory purposes in light of certain subsequent events. Informing clients of these events is consistent with good professional ethics and client service. For a complete discussion of this topic, see SSVS1, Paragraph 43.

3.2 Background Information and Analysis of the Subject Arrangement

Establishing the "who, what, where, when, and why" of an appraisal can be very helpful for the report user. While this information is not as important for the client contact with whom the appraiser has worked on the assignment, other users who are not familiar with the subject arrangement will appreciate an overview before having to wade through the details and critical issues of the valuation analysis. Important background information can be broken down into three key areas:

- Identification of the buyer and seller parties;

- Background and general information; and

- Analysis of the subject arrangement in the healthcare marketplace.

The content of this report section can certainly vary based on the type of arrangement being valued and specific facts and circumstances related to it. In addition, the information content can be brief and concise. A good rule of thumb is to include information that will have some bearing on the valuation analysis or at least provide a context or backdrop for it.

Identification of the Buyer and Seller Parties

While fair market value (FMV) looks to the value between the hypothetical buyer and seller, it does not preclude, and in fact requires, identification of the actual terms of the arrangement. The specific parties can point to the scope and characteristics of the services or resources provided in the subject arrangement. For example, a hospital that is a trauma center can have call coverage requirements that are distinct from a nontrauma center. A medical directorship for a new service line at a hospital may require more extensive duties and/or time demands than a directorship for a longstanding service at the facility. These types of factors, while relating to specific buyers and sellers, set the stage for the types of services provided. The key to fair market value is that it involves hypothetical transaction participants engaged in an actual transaction. That is why the specific parties, or more accurately, the specific terms contemplated, are critical to assessing fair market value.

They may also help to highlight key local market conditions. If the only neurosurgery group in town is composed of three physicians and the two hospitals in town must rely on them for hospital call coverage, it will affect the supply of available neurosurgeons in the local market for call coverage services. Another example could include a hospital located in an area with a poor payer mix and high levels of charity care. This fact can affect the level of uncompensated care that is expected for physicians providing call coverage at the facility. It could also impact the expected collections and net practice earnings from employed physicians for the hospital providing clinical services in the local community.

Discussion of such information can facilitate a full understanding of the arrangement for a user. The focus of information about the subject parties should be on service factors and market conditions. This focus provides a way to distinguish the use of such information from merging into a valuation based on investment value. The valuation analyzes the value for the hypothetical buyer and seller, given the service characteristics and local market dynamics.

Here are some potential areas of information to include in describing the parties to an arrangement:

- Hospitals or other facility-based providers:

    ○ Type of facility, including any trauma designation;

    ○ Size in terms of beds or other meaningful measures;

    ○ Location and service markets;

    ○ Service lines; and

    ○ Brief history: years in operation, past mergers (if relevant), etc.

- Physician groups:

    ◦ Number of full-time equivalent physicians and nonphysician providers (NPPs) in the group;

    ◦ Specialties and subspecialties of the physicians and NPPs;

    ◦ Locations and service markets;

    ◦ Brief history;

    ◦ Unique services offered;

    ◦ Ancillary or technical component services offered at practice locations (for employment valuations);

    ◦ Facilities at which group physicians provide call coverage (when relevant for call coverage arrangements, especially those involving concurrent call issues or limited supply of physicians in the marketplace); and

    ◦ Ownership: physician, hospital/health system, or other type of ownership.

- Individual physicians:

    ◦ Specialty;

    ◦ Board certifications;

    ◦ Specialized training, such as fellowships;

    ◦ Specialized procedures and services provided, such as robotic surgery;

    ◦ Leadership positions held, such as medical directorships;

    ◦ Presentations and publications; and

    ◦ Years in practice.

Background and General Information on the Arrangement

Two areas to address in the report are the history and service market for the arrangement. Both can have an impact on the value of the arrangement.

- A potentially important distinction is whether the arrangement is new or existing. This fact can affect the following:

  - Extent of data available on the arrangement;

  - Scope of duties: a new service may involve duties or services that would not be required after an initial start-up phase; and

  - Uncertainty regarding the economics of the arrangement: a new service can present uncertainty for the parties.

- The service market can affect the supply and demand for the subject services as well as the reimbursement and key economics. Topics to address can include:

  - Population levels and demographics;

  - Supply of providers for the service in the service market, including physicians, hospitals, and other entities; and

  - Reimbursement considerations, such as payer mix and commercial, Medicare, and Medicaid rates. These rates can vary widely across and within markets.[7]

Analysis of the Subject Arrangement in the Healthcare Marketplace

Part of analyzing the subject arrangement for valuation purposes includes an examination of the fundamental economics of the services or resources provided. One way to prepare and present this analysis in the report is to discuss the economics for the type of arrangement in a separate section. This analysis can look at four basic areas:

- *Economic and operational origins of the services:* What market forces and trends have given rise to the need for the subject services? In some cases, the origins of a service help explain the nature and extent of the services and its economics. For example, compensated call coverage has its origins in

---

7   For a complete discussion of this topic, see Chapter 37, "How Reimbursement and Physician Compensation Vary by Market."

EMTALA and various trends related to physicians. Clinical co-management arrangements arose in response to market trends in pay for performance and payment for quality.

- *Market trends and developments:* What current and expected future trends will have an impact on the nature and economics of the services? Key trends in healthcare can include the following:

    ◦ Reimbursement;

    ◦ Supply and demand for physicians;

    ◦ Pay for performance and quality outcomes;

    ◦ Healthcare reform; and

    ◦ Innovations in care, treatments, and technology.

- *Breakdown of the service/resource elements:* One way to analyze services or resources provided in a compensation arrangement is to break them down into their distinct elements or parts.

- *Analyzing key economic factors:* Identifying and discussing the key economic factors involved in an arrangement type is a critical step in CV work. Preparing a brief summary of these factors provides a foundation for the scope of work that was completed for the assignment and the conclusion of value.

3.3 Terms and Provisions of the Arrangement

Whereas BV reports describe the subject company and the characteristics of the subject ownership interest in that enterprise, CV reports need to focus on the terms of the proposed compensation arrangement. *The description and analysis of the arrangement is one of the key sections of a CV report.* The conclusion of value should be based on a set of contractual terms that affect the economics of the arrangement. Using a separate section of the report to describe, discuss, and analyze the arrangement terms and provisions gives due measure to their impact on value. Not all terms and provisions, however, affect the economics and the conclusion of value. Consequently, the CV report needs to focus on what drives the value of the compensation. The two key areas that generally determine value in a compensation arrangement are the scope of services or resources provided and the structure and terms of the compensation. The former drives the total value, while the latter affects how the compensation is specifically *paid* for the services in terms of how payments are made, e.g., hourly, base salary, per WRVU, etc., and the conditions or measures by which it is paid. In many arrangements, the total value has to be allocated among individual compensation elements. This allocation can create a second set of valuation issues that the appraiser needs to address. The focus of a CV report, therefore, needs to be on discussing these two essential aspects.

It is generally not necessary, however, to document every detail, nuance, and requirement of the contract terms related to these areas. For example, an agreement may include several specific tasks that relate to the community relations responsibilities of the medical director. It may be sufficient simply to list community relations as a duty in the description of the arrangement for a CV report. On the other hand, if the community relations tasks involved significant outreach activities and travel time was a major factor in the level of compensation or was paid at a separate rate from regular duties, including details on the outreach and travel duties would be warranted. The specific duties had an impact on the valuation.[8]

Preparing a Summary of the Arrangement

Drafting a summary of essential economic terms and provisions in a compensation arrangement is both required of the appraiser and beneficial to the appraiser for several reasons. First, the process of summarizing the terms in writing forces the appraiser to think through and analyze the arrangement. It is difficult to provide an accurate summary of something you do not understand. Second, many contracts are drafted based on legal or operational considerations that tend to overshadow the key economic elements. These elements may also be scattered throughout the document in various provisions, especially in highly complex agreements. They may appear in the document as unrelated, but economically, they are interrelated. Summarizing the terms allows the appraiser to provide a coherent economic presentation of them for the user. Third, summarizing the agreement provides a feedback mechanism or communication loop between the appraiser and the client. When an appraiser presents his or her understanding of the arrangement in summarized terms, it often highlights areas of misunderstanding. In fact, it may serve to alert the client to a misdrafting of the agreement language or to the fact that the currently negotiated terms are not what the client wants. Finally, preparing a well-written summary of the arrangement keeps the report focused, meaningful, concise, readable, and free of clutter. Cutting and pasting the actual contract language into the report can sometimes have the opposite effect. In some instances, however, it may be beneficial to include actual contract language.

Three Key Ways to Summarize and Analyze an Arrangement for the Report

An appraiser can summarize and analyze three aspects of an arrangement for purposes of the CV report.

---

8   This is a hypothetical example provided simply for illustration purposes.

1. *Description of the agreement terms.* As discussed, the report should summarize the critical economic terms related to the scope of services or resources provided and to the compensation. To do this effectively, it can be helpful to use contract summary templates that pre-establish key terms for a given type of compensation arrangement, such as hospital call coverage or physician clinical employment. The template serves as a kind of checklist with a ready-made format for summarizing the key terms. Sample templates are provided in the appendix to this chapter, "Practice Aid: Key Contractual Terms in Compensation Arrangements."

2. *Additional facts and circumstances related to the arrangement.* In some situations, relevant facts and circumstances may affect the implementation, administration, or interpretation of an arrangement. A contract may not address certain issues or areas, but the client represents that an arrangement will be handled in certain manner. Past practice or historical course of performance may also affect how contract provisions are understood between the parties. Background facts or conditions may also affect the way the arrangement is performed and administered. Various facts and circumstances may also provide additional factors related to the scope of services or resources. When such matters affect the valuation analysis, it is a prudent practice to include them in the CV report as part of the description of the arrangement. The user needs to understand that these additional facts and circumstances are an integral part of the arrangement terms that affected the conclusion of value.

3. *Observations and analysis of key terms and provisions.* It can be very helpful for an appraiser to highlight and discuss certain key contractual provisions as part of analyzing their impact on the valuation analysis. The discussion can take the form of the appraiser describing how certain terms interrelate or in pointing out the economic or compensation implications for various provisions. It could also involve the appraiser providing commentary about whether certain items are usual and customary in the marketplace or unusual and unique. Again, such commentary and analysis should focus on areas that affect the valuation analysis. In general, an appraiser should be preparing this kind of contractual analysis as part of the scope of work. It is logical, therefore, to include it in the report. Yet, not all types of arrangements need a separately discussed contractual analysis in the report, e.g., simple or straightforward hospital call coverage or medical directorships. Use of this kind of contractual analysis is best applied as needed.

Identify the Specific Legal Parties to the Arrangement

Another important point to keep in mind in providing information on the arrangement is to identify the actual legal entities or parties involved in the transaction, if known. This identification can affect the scope of the valuation analysis. Take, for example, an assignment to value call coverage for a health system-employed physician. If the scope of the arrangement is the compensation paid to the employed physician for call by the employer, the valuation needs to take into account the fact that the employer already covers benefits and professional liability insurance (PLI). The call coverage payment should not be grossed-up to include these amounts. In addition, if the employed physician is compensated based on a compensation-per-wRVU model, there is no uncompensated care risk for the physician. The employee is paid for wRVUs performed related to call. Thus, the call stipend paid to the employed physician should not include any amount related to uncompensated care. The employer, on the other hand, is at risk for uncompensated care as well as for benefits and PLI. If the subject arrangement is between a hospital and the employer practice entity, then the FMV compensation amount would need to include an allowance for benefits, PLI, and uncompensated care.

Another example would be a call coverage agreement or medical directorship with a physician group rather than an individual physician. This difference in contracting entity may mean that the practice can use any group physician or potentially independent contractors to provide the services. If the valuation analysis is built around a specific physician providing services with certain qualifications, but the arrangement is based on any physician in the group, the valuation analysis may not be applicable.

Many appraisers confuse the client with the buyer or seller entity in a transaction. If a hospital or health system engages them to prepare a physician employment valuation, they may write the report identifying the hospital as the employer, when in fact, an affiliate of the hospital will employ the physician. If the arrangement takes place in a state with the prohibition on the corporate practice of medicine, the valuation report will not only be factually incorrect, but also imply that the client is violating state law. Hospital clients may not take too kindly to this kind of factual error.

Practice Tips

Here are some suggestions that can facilitate a streamlined process for valuation and report drafting relative to the arrangement terms.

1. *Client prereview of the arrangement summary.* In certain circumstances, sending the client a copy of the arrangement summary prior to publishing the valuation can be a productive way to confirm the appraiser's understanding of it. As noted, this practice creates a feedback loop to ensure that the client and

appraiser are working off the same set of terms. This practice is generally used when dealing with complex arrangements or when a client does not provide the appraiser with a draft agreement, but represents a series of contractual terms, particularly on a piecemeal basis.

2. *When the client provides limited information on the arrangement terms.* Clients will occasionally engage an appraiser but provide very limited information on the arrangement terms. Some clients may not have even worked out the key terms of the arrangement, but they want a valuation, and they need it now! When an appraiser gets placed in this position, one tactic for moving the engagement forward is for the appraiser to assume contractual terms and provisions that are usual and customary for the subject arrangement. Some may argue that such a practice crosses the line into deal advocacy and negotiation. Yet, another way to think about this practice is that the appraiser is, in effect, articulating the assumptions and limiting conditions that are necessary to support the conclusion of value. Ultimately, however, the client has to determine the contractual terms. This tactic is only intended to jump start the client's negotiation process with the other party. Another way to work through this type of situation is to identify the key contractual areas for a client and have the client determine the terms for these areas. An appraiser may provide market information to the client on typical terms observed in the marketplace, but the client should be the decision-maker as to the terms.

3. *Documenting how terms of the arrangement were provided to the appraiser.* It is recommended practice to note in the CV report how the terms and provisions of the arrangement were communicated to the appraiser. Was a draft agreement provided? Were only selected terms and provisions communicated? Was the current agreement provided, and the client represented the same agreement form would be used? Documenting how the terms were provided can serve to protect the appraiser from claims that the valuation covered terms and provisions that were not disclosed to the appraiser as part of the valuation process.

3.4 Sources of Information

In identifying the sources of information used in the appraisal, two distinctions can be useful to make as part of a CV report. The first distinction is between the information provided by the client or the parties to the arrangement and data that was gathered independently by the appraiser. The reason this distinction is important is that the two sources of data may not be equal with respect to their quality, relevance, and independence. In addition, by separately identifying data from the client or arrangement parties, the representations of the parties with respect to the accuracy and veracity of data provided can be highlighted and tied to specific items. Alternatively, these data items could be identified in the section detailing representations made to the appraiser (see Section 3.6 below).

As noted in the inventory of assignment elements, limited access to data is an important issue to highlight in a report. It can be informative for users to know what items of data an appraiser attempted to gather, but was not successful in obtaining. Such data may include information not made available by the parties to the arrangement as well as relevant data that the appraiser could not obtain from independent sources. It could also include data that the appraiser concluded lacked credibility, independence, or sufficient detail to use in the appraisal analysis. The reason discussing such limitations can be useful is that it demonstrates the appraiser pursued an adequate scope of work relative to the assignment and maintained independence. If discussion of such data is omitted from the report, a user could conclude that the appraiser did not attempt to gather relevant data, and thu, the conclusion of value is flawed. It can also explain why the appraiser used certain assumptions, limiting conditions, and valuation approaches and methods as a result of not having access to certain data.

3.5 Assumptions and Limiting Conditions

Two meaningful distinctions can be made with regard to report assumptions and limiting conditions. The first is between those that are general in nature and those that are specific to the subject valuation assignment. General assumptions and limiting conditions can be defined as those that apply to all valuation assignments. While critical, they are essentially boilerplate to valuation reports. Assignment-specific assumptions and limiting conditions apply only to the appraisal of the subject arrangement. Reporting these separately from the general, boilerplate ones provides clients and users with very meaningful information. Because of their commonplace use and general nature, boilerplate disclaimers are often overlooked. This tendency presents a problem, however, for the appraiser. Critical and specific information relative to the conclusion of value can be contained in the assumptions and limiting conditions. Clients may need to act or respond directly to such items. If they are merely mixed in with otherwise boilerplate items, a breakdown in the communication process can occur. One way to address this situation is to separate these items out and highlight them in the report.

Another useful distinction is found in the ASA BV reporting standards. These standards distinguish between assumptions and limiting conditions relating to the data used in the valuation and to the validity of the valuation.[9] While these standards address general

---

9   ASA Business Valuation Standards, BVS-VIII Comprehensive Written Business Valuation Report, Section III.

matters, we might adopt this distinction as one way to group assignment-specific assumptions and limiting conditions. Categorizing and grouping such items can help users understand their context, meaning, and implications. A random listing of material is usually not an effective communication strategy. Use of standard BV terminology and categories for assumptions is also beneficial. The concepts of hypothetical conditions and extraordinary assumptions are applicable in CV as well as BV.

3.6 Representations of Information Provided to the Appraiser

It can be helpful to distinguish between representations to the arrangement the client made and those other parties made. This distinction is useful because it identifies the actual source of the representation. In addition, it may not be meaningful to have the client affirm a claim made by the other party. The client may not be able to ascertain the veracity or accuracy of a representation in a practical or timely manner. In addition, making the ultimate or initial source of a representation commit to it in writing is one way to screen information.

In my years of experience in negotiations and transactional development, I found information claims tended to self-correct or even disappear once a party was required to represent and affirm the claim in writing. Parties to a transaction often speak in the "heat of the moment" using overstated or fuzzy facts. A representation letter helps parties clarify their remarks.

3.7 Valuation Analysis of the Arrangement

The discussion and presentation of the valuation analysis in a CV report can readily follow along the lines of what would be found in a BV report. The topics covered can include the following:

1. Identification and definition of the approaches to value considered.

2. Identification of the approaches used and applied in the valuation, including the reasons for using the approaches and the reasons for not using other approaches.

3. Description and discussion of the valuation methods used under each approach applied, including:

   a. Data and assumptions used the method; and

   b. How the method addresses the fundamental economics of the subject arrangement.

4. Discussion of any critical issues in the analysis.

5. Support and defense of the methods, data, and assumptions used in the analysis.

3.8 Valuation Synthesis and Conclusion of Value

If multiple methods are used in the valuation analysis, the valuation synthesis section discusses how the appraiser arrived at a conclusion of value using the various indications of value from these methods. This discussion addresses the mechanics of the synthesis, but more importantly, the reasons and analysis behind the process. For conclusions of value, it is important for the CV report to relate the conclusion of value back to the compensation structure of the subject arrangement. CV report users are looking for FMV numbers that correspond to individual elements of compensation in the contract. It is helpful to present or translate the conclusion of value into these contractual components in the conclusion of value section of the report. If a separate analysis is necessary to convert or allocate the conclusion of value into the arrangement structure, a discussion of this process is usually necessary for the user to understand how the appraisal got from one set of numbers to the other. In certain situations, it may make sense to simply state the conclusion of value in terms of a statement that the proposed compensation under the subject arrangement is consistent with FMV. Even when this format is used, it is beneficial to include the proposed compensation terms and elements in the conclusion section.

3.9 Appraiser's Certification and Representations

Consistent with USPAP and BV standards, it is critical to the integrity and credibility of the CV report for the appraiser to be and represent that he or she is objective, independent, and without bias toward the subject arrangement and the valuation of it. A simple template or checklist for key representations can be found in USPAP Standards Rule 10-3.

3.10 Appendices and Exhibits

From the user's perspective, here are some thoughts to consider on the use, development, and presentation of report appendices and exhibits.

1. Users appreciate well-designed exhibits that are generally self-explanatory. They are laid out in a logical fashion with descriptive, clear labeling and notes;

2. Certain terms and acronyms may be known to the appraisal community or within a firm, but they are "Greek" to many users. It's always helpful to define terms and acronyms; and

3. If a user needs to borrow a neurosurgeon's microscopic surgery glasses to read an exhibit, you can be assured the client will not appreciate this inconvenience. Exhibits with small print that can only be read with a magnifying glass are *inconsiderate* to clients and users. It communicates that the user's ability to review the exhibit is unimportant to the appraiser.

3.11 Qualifications of the Analyst

While many CV appraisers do not include their resumes in a report, the practice is standard in BV. It can be helpful to users who are not familiar with the appraiser or firm to see the credentials of the report signatory and any contributing appraisers.

3.12 Transmittal Letter and Table of Contents

A table of contents is very helpful to users trying to find certain sections of a report. Besides incredibly small print in exhibits, nothing is more frustrating to a client than having to thumb or scroll through pages of a report to find a pertinent section, especially the page with the FMV numbers on it! A list of exhibits and appendices is also useful to users for the same reason. It also assures the user that he or she has the complete report when reviewing. Transmittal letters are mentioned in many of the BV standards. They provide information on the transmission of the report to the client.

4.0 Practical Ideas and Applications

The following sections present a series of ideas and practices that may be helpful to firms in developing reporting practices and templates for general use and with specific clients.

4.1 Use of an Executive Summary

An executive summary is a great tool for allowing a user to get right to the FMV numbers, while also being exposed to certain key elements of the report and conclusion. To be effective, its content should include these important elements, but in a highly summarized, "at-a-glance" table or bullet point format. Many of the assignment elements listed in Section 3.1 above can simply be included in an executive summary and not repeated elsewhere in the report. A sample listing of elements includes the following:

- Client and intended users of the report;

- Purpose and use of the valuation;

- Standard of value and its definition;

- Jurisdictional exceptions;

- Valuation dates:

  - Valuation date;

  - Report issue date;

  - Length of contract covered by the valuation; and

  - Required start date for the subject arrangement;

- Type of report: summary or detailed;

- Scope limitations;

- Limitations on access to data;

- Reliance on the work of a specialist;

- Summary of key arrangement terms and provisions;

- Valuation approaches/methods used;

- Conclusion of value;

- Summary of basis for the conclusion;

- Assignment-specific assumptions and limiting conditions; and

- Key representations made to the appraiser.

4.2 Standard Summaries of Contract Terms by Type of Arrangement

As discussed previously, an effective way to summarize the essential terms and provisions of the arrangement relative to the valuation analysis is to use standardized summary forms for a given type of compensation arrangement. The summary form basically outlines or lists these terms, and the appraiser simply fills in the specific provisions from the subject arrangement. The summaries provide a checklist for the appraiser and can also be used to solicit information from the client about the arrangement. They also create a useful presentation format for inclusion in the report. They can be included as tables in a report or used to establish headings, under which the terms and provisions of the contract are summarized. Sample summaries of contract terms for selected types of compensation arrangements are included in the appendix to this chapter, "Practice Aid: Key Contractual Terms in Compensation Arrangements."

4.3 Descriptive and Defensive Report Narratives

As a reader of actual and sample valuation reports over the years, I noticed that reports were often written with a focus on describing the valuation analysis, but they ignored the critical element of defending that analysis. Understanding the scope of work for an appraisal includes knowing not only what the appraiser did, but also the reasons why the appraiser did what he or she did. Report narratives, therefore, need to include both description and defense of the work completed.

4.4 Staged Deliverables for CV Reports

One process tool for addressing timing considerations in an engagement is phased deliverables of CV reports to clients. Drafting a full report can take a significant amount of time to prepare and send through an internal firm review process. Yet, submission of a full draft valuation report may not be necessary as the first communication of the valuation analysis to a client. Use of an executive summary along with supporting exhibits is one way to expedite the initial delivery of the draft valuation to the client. The benefit of the executive summary is that it includes key elements that affect the conclusion of value, such as the contractual terms and assignment-specific assumptions and limiting conditions. Including such information is preferable to simply communicating "a number" to the client. After the delivery of the executive summary report, a full report can be subsequently provided to the client within a reasonable time frame. Generally, executive summaries can be prepared in short order, much more quickly than complete reports encompassing dozens of pages of narrative and references. They should not be used, however, as a permanent substitute for a full report.

4.5 Ordering the Report for Logical Progression

In looking at designing a CV report template that is easy to use, the logical progression of information is a good criterion for ordering the content elements of the report. Sometimes appraisers will put more critical information, such as assumptions and limiting conditions, in the front sections of the report. This placement is completely understandable from the perspective of the appraiser. The appraiser wants to alert the user rather quickly to key qualifications and issues in the valuation. From a user perspective, however, this may actually have the opposite effect. Throwing critical issues at the reader before he or she even understands the details of the subject arrangement makes such issues less meaningful and understandable. The user has very limited context as to the importance of such information. Reports that follow a "storytelling" type of narrative are much easier for a user to digest. In essence, a valuation report is a story of what the appraiser was engaged to value, what the appraiser did to value the subject, and what the appraiser finally concluded was the value of the subject. Ordering the content of the report along lines of a logical buildup of information for the user will be much appreciated.

PRACTICE AID: Key Contract Terms in Compensation Arrangements

By Timothy Smith, CPA/ABV

1.0 Introduction

This practice aid provides a listing of key contractual terms and provisions in selected compensation arrangements. These terms and provisions relate to many of the essential elements in the scope of services for a given type of arrangement. By addressing these items in the valuation process, an appraiser is able to identify critical details for valuation analysis as well as for inclusion in the compensation valuation report. This practice aid is intended as a helpful tool in the appraisal process. It may not include every term or provision that may be material to the scope of services or valuation of a particular subject compensation arrangement.

2.0 Key Terms for Hospital Call Coverage Arrangements

The following list includes many of the key terms and provisions in a hospital call coverage arrangement:

1. What type of call coverage is being provided in terms of the physician specialty?

2. Is the contract with an individual physician or with a physician group?

3. How many call coverage shifts per month or year is the physician or group required to provide?

4. How many hours are included in a call coverage shift?

5. Does the call coverage include only unassigned patients from the hospital emergency department (ED) or also unassigned inpatients?

6. What is the required response time for a page or call from the hospital ED?

7. What is the required mode of response to a page or call:

   a. Telephonic response; or

   b. Present in the ED?

8. Once a physician is called into the hospital, what is the required time to present?

9. Will the physician bill separately for professional services rendered to patients from the call coverage?

10. Is the physician required to provide subsequent inpatient and outpatient care to patients initially seen while on call?

11. Will the physician be allowed to provide concurrent call with another facility while on call for the subject hospital?

12. Does the physician need to have specific certifications, credentials, or training to provide the call coverage?

13. How will the physician be compensated for call coverage:

    a. Time-based payment;

    b. Activation payment;

    c. Fee-for-service payment;

    d. Subsidy or fixed payment; or

    e. Deferred compensation structure?

14. Is the subject physician an independent contractor or employee of the hospital or health system?

3.0 Key Terms for Hospital Medical Director Arrangements

The following list includes many of the key terms and provisions in a hospital medical directorship arrangement:

1. What hospital service line or department is the medical directorship intended to cover?

2. Will a specific physician provide the medical director services or will more than one physician be able to provide the services?

3. Are there any specific qualifications, credentials, or training required of the subject physician to provide the medical directorship?

4. What specific services or tasks is the medical director required to perform?

5. Is the medical directorship a full-time or part-time position?

6. Is there a contractual minimum or maximum for the weekly, monthly, or annual hours to be provided by the medical director?

7. Will the medical director be required to complete time sheets or other documentation detailing the time spent on directorship duties or detailing the tasks completed?

8. How will the medical director be paid:

   a. Hourly rate;

   b. Monthly fixed amount; or

   c. Annual fixed amount?

9. Is the medical director an independent contractor or employee of the hospital or health system?

4.0 Key Terms for Physician Employment Arrangements

The following list includes many of the key terms and provisions in a physician employment arrangement:

1. What is the contract term in years for the subject employment agreement?

2. What are the required work duties of the physician?

3. At what locations or clinics is the physician required to work?

4. How many clinical hours per week is the physician required to work?

5. Will the physician supervise any nonphysician providers as part of the arrangement?

6. Do the work duties include providing hospital call coverage?

   a. How many shifts are required per week, month, or year?

   b. What are the requirements of the call shifts?

7. How many days of paid time off (PTO) does the physician have each year?

8. How many days is the physician given for taking continuing medical education (CME)?

9. Does the contract provide the physician with any other days of leave?

10. How will the physician be paid:

    a. Base salary;

    b. Productivity model:

        i. Compensation per wRVU;

        ii. Collections-based;

        iii. Shift- or time-based;

        iv. Encounters or surgical cases; or

        v. Earnings-based?

    c. Greater of a base amount or a productivity model?

11. Does the arrangement include other forms of compensation:

    a. Sign-on bonus;

    b. Retention payments;

    c. Relocation allowance;

    d. Other one-time payments; or

    e. Are there any payback requirements associated with these forms of compensation?

12. Is there a productivity requirement to maintain the base compensation amount?

13. What are the termination provisions in the contract:

    a. Without cause;

    b. For cause; or

    c. Do these provisions apply to both the employer and employee?

14. Is there a severance or termination payment included in the contract?

15. What employee benefits will be provided to the physician:

    a. Health and dental insurance;

    b. Retirement, such as a 401(k) or pension plan;

    c. Life insurance; or

    d. Short- and long-term disability insurance.

16. Is the physician given any allowances for CME or professional dues and licenses?

Part II.
Regulatory Matters in Compensation Valuation

Chapter 6. The Federal Statutes That Make Healthcare Valuation Unique

CONTENTS

Chapter 6. The Federal Statutes That Make Healthcare Valuation Unique

By Mark D. Folk

Editors' Note: This chapter was written at the request and direction of the editors to provide appraisers and consultants in the healthcare industry with a basic introduction to the two primary sets of federal laws that establish the regulatory framework for the industry. This introduction is not intended to be an exhaustive and fully detailed presentation of either set of laws. It was intentionally written as a nontechnical primer of the healthcare regulatory environment. Readers should use the material in this chapter accordingly. It is not intended as legal or regulatory advice.

1.0 Introduction

Two federal statutes and the regulations that implement them govern the structure of specific transactions and ongoing business relationships in the healthcare industry. Very broadly, these statutes prohibit the exchange of economic value for referrals—or stated differently, rewards for business volume—and consequently, preclude certain common practices from business arrangements in the healthcare industry. The purpose of the two statutes is to preserve the integrity of the federal Medicare and hybrid federal-state Medicaid programs and to protect them from waste, fraud, and abuse. Professional appraisers, consequently, need to have a basic knowledge of these two laws to avoid ascribing value to aspects of a transaction or ongoing business arrangement that federal law prohibits.

The purpose of this chapter is to introduce appraisers to the two federal laws that govern the structure of business arrangements in the healthcare industry. The chapter will broadly describe what the statutes and the implementing regulations prohibit, identify the penalties that attach to the prohibitions, and explain the numerous exceptions and safe harbors to each law. Due to the high-level, summary nature of the discussion in this chapter, the description of each statute and the applicable regulations is cursory and should not be construed as conveying a legal conclusion or legal advice. Additionally, many states have adopted their own versions of the two federal statutes, and in some cases, the state laws are broader than their federal counterparts. This chapter, however, does not address the impact of state healthcare laws and regulations on the structure of business transactions in the healthcare industry.

2.0 The Anti-Kickback Statute

2.1 Overview

When the Medicare statute became effective in 1965, the only prohibition on fraud and abuse was making false statements in applications for Medicare benefits.[1] When Congress expanded the Medicare program in 1972, it enacted certain low-level, misdemeanor protections against fraud by prohibiting conduct that involved a "kickback," "rebate," or "bribe."[2] By 1977, however, it had become clear to Congress that the existing protection of the Medicare program was woefully deficient; thus, Congress passed the Medicare/Medicaid Antifraud and Abuse Amendments to the Social Security Act,[3] which contained the genesis of what today is known as the anti-kickback statute.

Today's anti-kickback statute prohibits knowing and willful solicitations, receipts, offers, and payments of "any remuneration (including any kickback, bribe, or rebate) directly or indirectly, overtly or covertly, in cash or in kind," in return for a referral for any item or service that is reimbursed under a "Federal health care program" (or to induce such a referral) or in return for purchasing, leasing, ordering, or arranging for or recommending any good, facility, service, or item that is reimbursed under a federal healthcare program (or to induce such a referral).[4]

"Federal health care program" is defined broadly as any healthcare program funded, in whole or in part, by the federal or a state government other than the Federal Employee Health Benefit Program.[5] The anti-kickback statute is criminal. Violations are felonies punishable by fines of not more than $50,000 per violation, imprisonment for not more than five years (or both), and exclusion from the Medicare and Medicaid programs.

The anti-kickback statute is intent-based (i.e., "knowing and willful"); a participant to an illegal arrangement must intend that a referral for a healthcare item or service will

---

1   Pub. L. No. 89-87.
2   Pub. L. No. 92-603.
3   Pub. L. No. 95-142.
4   42 U.S.C. § 1320a-7b(b).
5   42 U.S.C. § 1320a-7b(f).

result from the provision of remuneration (or that such remuneration will induce a referral). The terms of the statute make it clear that "remuneration" is to be expansively construed. Through the years, the Office of Inspector General of the Department of Health and Human Services (OIG) and the Centers for Medicare and Medicaid Services have indicated that remuneration refers to any economic benefit (e.g., kickbacks, bribes, and above or below market rent to lease payments). The statute, however, exempts certain economic benefits from the concept of remuneration, for example:

> a discount or other reduction in price obtained by a provider of services or other entity under a Federal health care program if the reduction in price is properly disclosed and appropriately reflected in the costs claimed or charges made by the provider or entity under a Federal health care program; [and] any amount paid by an employer to an employee (who has a bona fide employment relationship with such employer) for employment in the provision of covered items or services.[6]

Through the years, the courts have provided differing interpretations of the "knowing and willful" requirement that is necessary to violate the statute. In the landmark case on the issue, the United States Court of Appeals for the Third Circuit established the "one purpose" test.[7] Under this test, "if one purpose of the payment was to induce future referrals, the Medicare statute has been violated."[8] Years later, the United States Court of Appeals for the Ninth Circuit held that the "knowing and willful" requirement of the statute is met only if persons "(1) know that [the statute] prohibits offering or paying remuneration to induce referrals, and (2) engage in prohibited conduct with the specific intent to disobey the law."[9] Although the Supreme Court has not yet ruled on the meaning of "knowing and willful" under the anti-kickback statute, the recently upheld Patient Protection and Affordable Care Act amends the anti-kickback statute to provide that actual knowledge of a statutory violation or the specific intent to violate the statute is not necessary for a conviction under the statute.[10]

Because the provisions of the anti-kickback statute are so expansive, OIG periodically has published various forms of guidance for compliance with the statute. For example, the past several years have seen an increasing amount of integration between hospital or healthcare systems and physician practices. The same sort of integration has occurred several times over the past decades, albeit for differing economic reasons. In 1992, in a letter to the Internal Revenue Service, OIG addressed its concerns with hospital purchases of physician practices.[11] OIG stated that hospitals seek to purchase

---

6   42 U.S.C. § 1320a-7(b)(3).
7   *United States v. Greber*, 760 F.2d 68 (3rd Cir. 1985), cert. denied, 474 U.S. 988 (1985).
8   Id. at 69.
9   *Hanlester Network v. Shalala*, 51 F.3d 1390, 1400 (9th Cir. 1995).
10   Pub. L. No. 111-148, § 6402(f)(2).
11   Letter from D. McCarty Thornton, Associate General Counsel, OIG to T.J. Sullivan, Technical Assistant, Office

physician practices as a means to attract new referrals and expressed concern that the remuneration a physician receives could interfere with his or her subsequent judgment regarding appropriate patient care.

According to OIG, two issues are critical to determining whether a practice acquisition violates the anti-kickback statute. First, the letter states, payment for goodwill, noncompetes, and patient records would be questionable; thus, OIG states that it may be necessary to exclude such intangibles from the valuation of a physician practice for purposes of anti-kickback analysis. Second, OIG questioned the manner in which the physician subsequently is compensated for providing services to the hospital and the legitimacy of subsequent payments to physicians even if they become hospital employees. Many of today's more advanced valuation techniques and methods used in physician practice acquisition/employment transactions evolved in response to the concerns OIG addressed in that letter.

2.2 Safe Harbors
Moreover, OIG has proposed and amended numerous "safe harbors" under the anti-kickback statute. Transactions that are structured squarely within the safe harbors are presumed not to violate the statute. Just because a transaction does not fit squarely within a safe harbor, however, does not mean that the transaction violates the statute. The regulations under the anti-kickback statute provide numerous safe harbors for economic activity within the healthcare industry;[12] business and compensation valuation analysts generally find that the bulk of their appraisal analysis centers around a handful of potential safe harbors, including the following. The description below is not intended to be exhaustive, however.

The 'Small Venture' Investment Safe Harbor
A physician's investment in a small business venture will fall within the small venture investment safe harbor if all of the following requirements are satisfied:

(a) No more than 40% of investment interests may be held in the previous fiscal year or 12-month period by investors who are in a position to refer to the entity or generate business for it;

(b) The terms on which an investment interest is offered to a passive investor who is a potential referral source must be no different than the terms offered to other passive investors and must not relate to previous or expected volume of referrals;

---

of the Associate Chief Counsel, Employee Benefits and Exempt Organizations dated Dec. 22, 1992 (available at http://oig.hhs.gov/fraud/docs/safeharborregulations/acquisition122292.htm).

12 See 42 C.F.R. § 1001.952(a)-(u).

(c) The entity does not require passive investors who are potential referral sources to make referrals to the entity;

(d) Neither the entity nor any investor may market or furnish the entity's items or services to passive investors differently than to noninvestors;

(e) No more than 40% of the gross revenue of the entity in the previous fiscal year or 12-month period may come from referrals or business otherwise generated from investors;

(f) The entity or any of its investors may not loan funds to or guarantee a loan for another investor who is a potential referral source if the investor uses any part of the loan to obtain the investment interest; and

(g) Payment to an investor as return on investment must be directly proportional to the amount of that investor's capital investment (i.e., no special distributions).[13]

Space and Equipment Rental Safe Harbors

These two safe harbors are very similar and require satisfaction of the following elements:

(a) The lease agreement must be in writing and signed, have a term of at least one year, specify all of the premises, equipment, or services to be provided, and the aggregate rental must reflect a commercially reasonable business purpose;

(b) The aggregate compensation under the lease must be specified in advance, be fair market value, and cannot take referrals into account;

(c) The aggregate space or equipment rented does not exceed that which is reasonably necessary to accomplish the commercially reasonable business purpose of the rental.[14]

The regulations note that, for purposes of the space rental safe harbor:

The term *fair market value* means the value of the rental property for general commercial purposes, but shall not be adjusted to reflect the additional value that one party (either the prospective lessee or lessor) would attribute to the property as a result of its proximity or convenience to sources of referrals or business otherwise generated for which payment may be made in whole or in part under Medicare, Medicaid and all other Federal health care programs.[15]

---

13 42 C.F.R. § 1001.952(a)(2).
14 42 C.F.R. § 1001.952(b) and (c).
15 42 C.F.R. § 1001.952(b)(6).

Similarly, the regulations for the equipment rental safe harbor provide the following:

> The term *fair market value* means that the value of the equipment when obtained from a manufacturer or professional distributor, but shall not be adjusted to reflect the additional value one party (either the prospective lessee or lessor) would attribute to the equipment as a result of its proximity or convenience to sources of referrals or business otherwise generated for which payment may be made in whole or in part under Medicare, Medicaid, or other Federal health care programs.[16]

Personal Services and Management Contracts Safe Harbor

To satisfy the personal services and management contracts safe harbor, a business arrangement must meet the following requirements:

(a) The agreement must be in writing and signed, have a term of at least one year, and specify all of the services to be provided;

(b) If the agreement is intended to provide for services on a periodic or part-time basis for the term of the agreement, it must specify exactly the schedule of such intervals, their precise length, and their exact charge;

(c) The aggregate compensation under the agreement must be specified in advance, reflect fair market value, and cannot take referrals into account; and

(d) The services to be performed under the agreement cannot involve the counseling or promotion of a business arrangement that violates any law and must not exceed those that are reasonably necessary to accomplish the commercially reasonable business purpose of the services.

Employee Safe Harbor[17]

This safe harbor allows an employer to pay an employee, who has a bona fide employment relationship with such employer, for providing covered items and services. OIG has adopted the Internal Revenue Service's definition of "employee" for purposes of the employee safe harbor. As long as a bona fide employer-employee relationship exists, the employee safe harbor protects compensation for full- and part-time employment, but it does not extend to independent contractors. Importantly, however, the employee safe harbor does not override any applicable state law "corporate practice of medicine" prohibitions.

---

16 42 C.F.R. § 1001.952(c)(6).
17 42 C.F.R. § 1001.952(i).

3.0 The Stark Law

3.1 Overview

The physician self-referral prohibitions of the Stark Law evolved through the enactment and amendment of various pieces of legislation. U.S. Representative Fortney ("Pete") Stark (R.-Cal.) introduced the original bill to Congress in 1988.[18] When the first version of the Stark Law was enacted (known colloquially as "Stark I"), the statute provided that a physician (or an immediate family member) who has a financial relationship with certain entities may not refer patients to those entities for the furnishing of clinical laboratory services for which payment may be made by Medicare.[19] Stark I also provided that an entity with which a physician has a financial relationship may not bill Medicare or a beneficiary for clinical laboratory services furnished pursuant to a prohibited referral. Stark I became effective on Jan. 1, 1992, and its final implementing regulations were published on Aug. 14, 1995.[20]

The Stark Law was expanded by Congress in 1993. In what has become known as "Stark II," the amended law expanded the referral and billing prohibitions to additional "designated health services." Thus, today, the list of designated health services includes the following:

i. Clinical laboratory services;

ii. Physical therapy, occupational therapy, and speech-language pathology services;

iii. Radiology and certain other imaging services;

iv. Radiation therapy services and supplies;

v. Durable medical equipment and supplies;

vi. Parenteral and enteral nutrients, equipment, and supplies;

vii. Prosthetics, orthotics, and prosthetic devices and supplies;

viii. Home health services;

ix. Outpatient prescription drugs; and

x. Inpatient and outpatient hospital services.[21]

---

18 H.R. 5198, 100th Cong., 2d Sess. 2(a) (1988).
19 Omnibus Budget Reconciliation Act of 1989, Pub. L. No. 101-239, § 6204, 103 Stat. 2137, 2236 (codified at 42 U.S.C. § 1395nn).
20 Physician Financial Relationships With, and Referrals to, Health Care Entities That Furnish Clinical Laboratory Services and Financial Relationship Reporting Requirements, 60 F.R. 41,914 (1995).
21 42 C.F.R. § 411.351.

Stark II became effective on Jan. 1, 1995.[22]

Despite the expansiveness of the Stark Law's referral prohibition, the statute contains many exceptions, some of which are summarized below. Establishing a violation of the Stark Law, therefore, requires the presence of three factors: a "financial relationship" between an "entity" and a physician (or an "immediate family member"), a "referral" by the physician to the entity for a "designated health service," and the absence of an exception. The keys to analyzing a healthcare business arrangement under the Stark Law are understanding its defined terms and understanding its exceptions. Importantly, however, unlike the anti-kickback statute, intent is irrelevant under the Stark Law. The Stark Law is a strict liability statute; if a "financial arrangement," "referral," and the lack of an exception are present, the law has been violated.

The penalties for violating the Stark Law can be severe. They include denial of payments, potential refund requirements, civil monetary penalties of up to $15,000 for each item provided or service rendered, and exclusion from the Medicare and Medicaid programs. Additional civil penalties may be triggered of up to $100,000 for schemes designed to circumvent the statute or of $10,000 per day for failure to meet certain reporting requirements.

3.2 Principal Definitions

Financial Relationships
There are two kinds of "financial relationships" under the Stark Law: ownership or investment interests and compensation arrangements. Ownership or investment interests can arise "through equity, debt, or other means and include an interest in an entity that holds an ownership or investment interest in any entity providing the designated health service." Compensation arrangements are any arrangement involving remuneration, direct or indirect, between a physician (or family member) and an entity other than an arrangement involving only certain very narrow categories of remuneration. "Remuneration" is defined as "any payment or other benefit made directly or indirectly, overtly or covertly, in cash or in kind" with a few limited exceptions.

Immediate Family Member
"Immediate family member or member of a physician's immediate family" is defined as a "husband or wife; birth or adoptive parent, child, or sibling; stepparent, stepchild,

---

22 CMS has issued three rounds of regulations implementing and refining the application of Stark II. Those regulations can be found at 66 *F.R.* 856 (Jan. 4, 2001), 69 *F.R.* 16,054 (March 26, 2004), and 72 *F.R.* 51012 (Sept. 5, 2007).

stepbrother, or stepsister; father-in-law, mother-in-law, son-in-law, daughter-in-law, brother-in-law, or sister-in-law; grandparent or grandchild; and spouse of a grandparent or grandchild."[23]

Referral

"Referral" is defined broadly as "the request by a physician for, or ordering of, or the certifying or recertifying of the need for, any designated health service including a request for a consultation with another physician and any test or procedure ordered by or to be performed by (or under the supervision of) that other physician, but not including any designated health service personally performed or provided by the referring physician." Alternatively, a "referral" can include "a request by a physician that includes the provision of any designated health service ... the establishment of a plan of care by a physician that includes the provision of such a designated health service ... but not including any designated health service personally performed or provided by the referring physician."[24]

Compensation Set in Advance

Certain exceptions to the Stark Law require that compensation be "set in advance." Under the Stark Law regulations, compensation is deemed to be "set in advance" if the compensation formula, but not the aggregate amount of compensation, be established upon the commencement of the business arrangement. "The formula for determining the compensation must be set forth in sufficient detail so that it can be objectively verified, and the formula may not be changed or modified during the course of the agreement in any manner that takes into account the volume or value of referrals or other business generated by the referring physician."[25]

3.3 Exceptions to the Stark Law

There are many exceptions to the Stark Law. This article will not address all of the available exceptions, but rather, will focus on the handful of exceptions that valuators likely will encounter most frequently in healthcare appraisal practice.

Bona Fide Employment Exception

Under this exception, the employment of a physician must be for identifiable services. Remuneration of the physician must be set at "fair market value" and not be determined in a manner that takes into account, either directly or indirectly, the volume or value of referrals from the employed physician (or an immediate family member). (As noted

---

23   42 C.F.R. § 411.351.
24   42 C.F.R. § 411.351.
25   42 C.F.R. § 441.354(d).

in other chapters of this manual, the Stark Law contains a definition of "fair market value"; consequently, that definition is not discussed in this chapter.) The remuneration must be made pursuant to an agreement (either oral or written) that is commercially reasonable even if no referrals were made to the employer. The Stark Law applies the common law rules used by the Internal Revenue Service in determining the existence of employment relationships (e.g., the Service's "twenty-factor" test of Revenue Ruling 87-41). Note that an employment productivity bonus is allowed if it is based on services that are personally performed by the employed physician.[26]

Personal Services Arrangement Exception

An independent contractual arrangement with a physician (e.g., for the provision of professional medical services) must be in writing, signed by the parties, and specify the services covered. Moreover, the arrangement must cover all of the services to be provided by the physician (or an immediate family member) to the entity. The aggregate services to be provided must not exceed those that are reasonable and necessary for the legitimate business purposes of the arrangement. The independent contract must be for at least one year, and compensation under the contract must be set in advance, not exceed fair market value, and not take referrals into account. The services to be performed must not encourage or promote activity that violates any state or federal law. A holdover personal services arrangement for up to six months after expiration of an agreement of at least one year (and that met all of the other Stark Law requirements) is permissible if the holdover is on the same terms and conditions as the expired agreement.[27]

Isolated Transaction Exception

This exception is most frequently invoked in the purchase or sale of property or a physician practice. According to the Stark Law regulations, remuneration that a physician receives pursuant to an isolated financial transaction must be fair market value, not be related to referrals, and must be commercially reasonable. Moreover, there cannot be any additional transactions between the parties for six months after the isolated transaction, but commercially reasonable post-closing adjustments are permitted if they do not take referrals (directly or indirectly) into account.[28] Under the Stark Law regulations, installment payments are permitted if the aggregate payment is set before the first payment is made and does not take referrals (directly or indirectly) into account. Additionally, the outstanding balance must be immediately negotiable or guaranteed by a third party or secured by a negotiable promissory note (or subject to a similar mechanism to ensure payment in the event of default by the purchasing party).[29]

---

26   42 C.F.R. § 411.357(c).
27   42 C.F.R. § 441.357(d).
28   42 C.F.R. § 441.357(f).
29   42 C.F.R. § 441.351.

The Lease Exception

Leases for office space or equipment must be in writing, signed by the parties, and specify the premises or equipment that they cover. The rented space or equipment must not exceed that which is reasonable and necessary for the legitimate business purposes of the lease and must be used exclusively by the lessee. The term of the lease must be for at least one year, and the rental charges over the term of the lease must be set in advance, must be fair market value, and may not take referrals into account. The lease must be commercially reasonable even if no referrals are made between the parties. Termination without cause during the first year of the lease is permissible as long as the parties do not enter into a new arrangement regarding the leased equipment or space within the originally established one-year period. Month-to-month holdover leases are allowed for up to six months following expiration of a lease if they continue on the same terms as the original lease and the expired lease met all of the other Stark Law requirements.[30]

The In-Office Ancillary Exception

The in-office ancillary services exception is the exception under the Stark Law that allows physician group practices to refer and perform, within the group, diagnostic services and treatments that are designated health services. To qualify for these intragroup referrals, the physicians must be constituted into a practice entity that meets the Stark Law's definition of a "group practice." Services under the in-office ancillary exception must be performed by the referring physician, another physician member of the same group practice, or someone under the "direct supervision" of the referring physician (or another physician in the group practice). (Independent contractors can qualify as supervising physicians for purposes of this exception.) The in-office ancillary services exception is subject to a "same building" test (one of three tests must be satisfied in order to meet the same building test) and a billing requirement. The exception is available for nearly all designated health services except for: (i) durable medical equipment (with carve-outs for certain infusion pumps, blood glucose monitors, and devices to assist patients in leaving a physician office, such as canes, crutches, and walkers); and (ii) parenteral and enteral nutrients, equipment, and supplies.[31]

The definition of "group practice" under the Stark Law is extremely complex. It requires two physicians or more who are organized as a legal entity. Any party, including a hospital, may organize a group practice. Each physician "member of the group" must furnish substantially the full range of medical services that he or she routinely furnishes

---

30 42 C.F.R. § 411.357(a) and (b).
31 For more information on the "same building" test, billing requirements, and scope of the in-office ancillary exception, see 42 C.F.R. § 411.355(b).

through the joint use of shared office space, facilities, equipment, and personnel (the "range of care test").

A "member of the group" practice includes physician owners, physician employees, locum tenens, and on-call physicians. As noted above, independent contractor physicians are considered "physicians in the group" to allow them to supervise ancillary services and receive profit shares and productivity bonuses, but they are not considered a "member of the group" under the Stark Law.

The group practice definition requires that substantially all of the group members' services be furnished through the group (75% of group members' total patient care services, or the "substantially all test"). Overhead expenses and income of the group practice must be distributed according to methods that have been determined in advance (i.e., prior to receipt of payments). No member of the group can receive compensation based on the volume or value of referrals, but a member may be paid a portion of the group's profits or a productivity bonus based on personally performed or "incident to" services if the bonus is not determined in a manner directly related to such physician's referrals.

Productivity bonuses can be paid to a member of the group or an independent contractor based on total personal productivity (including designated health services that the physician orders and personally performs) and any "incident to" services. Finally, members of the group personally must conduct at least 75% of the physician-patient encounters of the group (the "physician-patient encounters test").

If a valid group practice exists, physicians in the group can refer designated health services within the group if those referrals fall within the in-office ancillary services exception. Solo physician practitioners may provide designated health services only if the in-office ancillary exception is met.

4.0 Conclusion

Because the anti-kickback statute and the Stark Law (and their possible state law counterparts) are the paramount regulatory hurdles that transactions in the healthcare industry must satisfy, appraisers working in the healthcare industry need to adjust their usual and customary valuation techniques to reflect the statutory prohibitions. The general intent of each statute is similar: to prevent waste, fraud, and abuse of federally funded healthcare programs. Although both statutes focus on the primary driver of the delivery of healthcare—the referral by a physician to a hospital, by a physician to another physician, or a hospital to a physician—the two statutes analyze referrals differently. The anti-kickback statute concerns referrals for healthcare items and services generally.

Under that statute, any referral that is made with the intent to induce future business is suspect. The Stark Law, by contrast, focuses on a physician's referrals to entities in which or with which that physician has a financial incentive to profit from the referral, and the physician or entity's intent is irrelevant.

Regardless of their different focuses on referrals, the penalties for violating either statute are harsh. Professional appraisers, therefore, need to understand the differences that the two statutes create in day-to-day business practice in the healthcare industry and raise questions to their clients when a proposed business arrangement calls into question either the purview of either statute or the data sets or valuation techniques that might be used to complete a valuation assignment.

Chapter 7. Complying With the Healthcare Definition of FMV in Appraisal Practice

CONTENTS

Chapter 7. Complying With the Healthcare Definition of FMV in Appraisal Practice

By Timothy Smith, CPA/ABV

1.0 Introduction: Complying With the Healthcare Regulatory Definition of FMV

In the past decade, it has become common practice for clients, such as health systems, life sciences companies, and attorneys, to engage appraisal professionals to prepare valuations of transactions and compensation arrangements for regulatory compliance purposes. As discussed in Chapter 6, "The Federal Statutes That Make Healthcare Valuation Unique," financial relationships between parties in a position to refer healthcare services are subject to the federal anti-kickback statute (AKS) and the federal physician self-referral or Stark law and their accompanying regulations. One common requirement for both sets of regulations is that the amounts paid in such financial arrangements be consistent with fair market value (FMV).

Unlike other areas of appraisal, however, the definition of FMV used for healthcare regulatory compliance differs from the standard definitions used in other aspects of the appraisal profession. Healthcare regulations have unique definitions of FMV that are tailored to address concerns about payments for referrals. Thus, when the intended use or purpose of an appraisal is healthcare regulatory compliance, the regulatory definition of FMV should be used as the standard of value for the valuation assignment.

Use of this standard of value, however, is not straightforward. Healthcare regulations and regulatory pronouncements have indicated that compliance with the regulatory definition of FMV may require departures from standard appraisal methodology. Unlike valuations prepared for other government agencies, such as the IRS, the healthcare regulatory framework for FMV does not coincide with the body of knowledge that is common to business valuation or other appraisal disciplines. The problem for professional appraisers is that the healthcare regulations do not provide a substitute methodology. As a result, appraisers are given an elusive target when asked to provide an opinion of value based on the federal healthcare regulatory definition of FMV. This difficulty is aptly described as the "healthcare FMV conundrum."

The purpose of this chapter is to help professional appraisers navigate the murky and sometimes stormy waters of engagements when the standard of value is the healthcare regulatory definition of FMV. The chapter will argue that a key to resolving the healthcare FMV conundrum is the use of jurisdictional exceptions, a practice that is well established in appraisal professional standards.

2.0 The Conundrum of Healthcare FMV for Appraisal Professionals

2.1 The Stark Definition of FMV and FMV Methodology

The definition of FMV promulgated by the Centers for Medicare and Medicaid Services (CMS) under Stark is as follows:

> Fair market value means the value in arm's-length transactions, consistent with the general market value. "General market value" means the price that an asset would bring as the result of *bona fide* bargaining between well-informed buyers and sellers who are not otherwise in a position to generate business for the other party, or the compensation that would be included in a service agreement as the result of *bona fide* bargaining between well-informed parties to the agreement who are not otherwise in a position to generate business for the other party, on the date of acquisition of the asset or at the time of the service agreement. Usually, the fair market price is the price at which *bona fide* sales have been consummated for assets of like type, quality, and quantity in a particular market at the time of acquisition, or the compensation that has been included in *bona fide* service agreements with comparable terms at the time of the agreement, where the price or compensation has not been determined in any manner that takes into account the volume or value of anticipated or actual referrals.[1]

Several elements of this definition of FMV are worth highlighting. First, the Stark regulations define FMV in terms of arm's-length negotiations between *well-informed* buyers and sellers who do not have a relationship related to referrals. Second, FMV under the Stark regulations is established on the *date* of the transaction or service arrangement. Third, the Stark regulations further define FMV as *usually* based on comparable market transactions or arrangements, where the price or compensation is not based on the volume or value of referrals between the parties to the transaction or arrangement.

---

1   42 CFR §411.351.

The Stark regulations also provide for a highly specialized definition of FMV to be used in valuing rentals and lease payments for office space and equipment:

> With respect to rentals and leases described in § 411.357(a), (b), and (l) (as to equipment leases only), "fair market value" means the value of rental property for general commercial purposes (not taking into account its intended use). In the case of a lease of space, this value may not be adjusted to reflect the additional value the prospective lessee or lessor would attribute to the proximity or convenience to the lessor when the lessor is a potential source of patient referrals to the lessee. For purposes of this definition, a rental payment does not take into account intended use if it takes into account costs incurred by the lessor in developing or upgrading the property or maintaining the property or its improvements.[2]

While seeming unusual at first glance, this very specific definition of FMV for office and equipment rentals is intended to eliminate any allocation of value to the lease based on referral relationships between the parties to the rental arrangement.[3] This unique definition highlights what is critical to the Stark definition of FMV: The valuation excludes the volume or value of referrals for so-called designated healthcare services (DHS).[4] Consequently, the Stark definition of FMV seeks to establish a standard of value that not only excludes consideration of such referrals, but also requires that valuations be performed in a hypothetical context in which a referral relationship does not exist between the parties to a financial arrangement.

Stark indicates that FMV should be determined based on the facts and circumstances of the transaction or arrangement.[5] FMV can be determined using any method that is "commercially reasonable" and provides "evidence that the compensation is comparable to what is ordinarily paid for an item or service in the location at issue, by parties in arm's-length transactions who are not in a position to refer to one another."[6] CMS states that any range of methods can be used to determine FMV under Stark.[7] The method chosen for establishing FMV, however, depends on three key factors: 1) the nature or type of transaction; 2) the location of the transaction; and 3) other factors.[8]

---

2   42 CFR §411.351.
3   It is also consistent with the definition of FMV promulgated by the OIG under the AKS safe harbors for office and equipment rentals. See 42 CFR 1001.952(b)(6) and 42 CFR 1001.952(c)(6).
4   See Chapter 6, "The Federal Statutes That Make Healthcare Valuation Unique," for a discussion of designated healthcare services under Stark.
5   72 *F.R.* 51015-16 (Sept. 5, 2007).
6   66 *F.R.* 944 (Jan. 4, 2001) and 72 *F.R.* 51015.
7   69 *F.R.* 16107 (March 26, 2004).
8   69 *F.R.* 16107 and 72 *F.R.* 51015-16.

On the use of valuation methods, one can interpret the Stark regulations as taking the position that FMV can be determined based on consideration of a single method. The Stark regulations do not mention the traditional appraisal framework that considers three approaches to value and that can sometimes entail the use of multiple methods to determine the value of a subject. The focus of the Stark commentary on valuation methodology readily lends itself to the interpretation that a single method is always sufficient to establish FMV. The following passages seem to point to a single-method orientation or standard in Stark:

> To establish the fair market value (and general market value) of a transaction that involves compensation paid for assets or services, we intend to accept *any method* that is commercially reasonable and provides us with evidence that the compensation is comparable to what is ordinarily paid for an item or service in the location at issue, by parties in arm's-length transactions who are not in a position to refer to one another.[9] [emphasis added]

> Our Phase I discussion made clear that we will consider a range of methods of determining fair market value and that *the appropriate method* will depend on the nature of the transaction, its location, and other factors.[10] [emphasis added]

> Ultimately, *the appropriate method* for determining fair market value for purposes of the physician self-referral law will depend on the nature of the transaction, its location, and other factors.[11] [emphasis added]

> Ultimately, fair market value is determined based on facts and circumstances. *The appropriate method* will depend on the nature of the transaction, its location, and other factors.[12] [emphasis added]

Certainly, one can interpret these passages broadly and conclude that they do not establish a single-method framework for the determination of FMV. CMS is merely addressing questions related to the use of a method, not valuation methodology at a systematic level. Yet, omission of the traditional three approaches to value sets the commentary apart from other regulatory agencies, such as the IRS. Indeed, as noted later in this section, CMS passed on incorporating IRS guidelines for FMV methodology into the requirements for Stark. Some attorneys and consultants have interpreted these passages as establishing a single-method standard for healthcare valuation that ignores the traditional framework.

---

9   66 *F.R.* 944.
10   69 *F.R.* 16107.
11   72 *F.R.* 51015.
12   72 *F.R.* 51015-16.

CMS also takes the position that FMV for Stark compliance purposes may require departures from standard appraisal methodology. The specific example cited by CMS for such divergence is the prohibition on using market data based on transactions from parties in a position to refer healthcare services. The Stark regulations state:

> Moreover, the definition of "fair market value" in the statute and regulation is qualified in ways that do not necessarily comport with the usage of the term in standard valuation techniques and methodologies. For example, the methodology must exclude valuations where the parties to the transactions are at arm's length but in a position to refer to one another. [13]

The reasoning for such exclusion by CMS is that parties in such a position are not considered to be at arm's length or independent for Stark analysis purposes. As a result, the transaction pricing between such parties is not considered to be an indication of FMV. Stark instructs parties to seek other methods to determine FMV when only such related-party transactions are included in data under the market approach.[14]

CMS has provided one case study with several examples of commercially reasonable or acceptable valuation methods for determining FMV. The case study involved the rental value of office space and equipment:

> For example, a commercially reasonable method of establishing fair market value (and general market value) for the rental of office space can include providing us with a list of comparables. We would also find acceptable an appraisal that the parties have received from a qualified independent expert. Although some transactions are not subject to public scrutiny, we believe generally that there should be sufficient documentation of similar public transactions that the parties can use as a basis of comparison. In regions with inadequate direct comparables, such as rural areas, a reasonable alternative may involve comparing institutions or entities located in different, but similar, areas where property is zoned for similar use. For example, a hospital affiliated with a university in one part of the country could be comparable to other hospitals affiliated with universities that are located in similar types of communities. In other cases, all the comparables or market values may involve transactions between entities that are in a position to refer or generate other business. For example, in some markets, physician-owned equipment lessors have driven out competitive third-party lessors of similar equipment. In such situations, we would look to alternative valuation methodologies, including, but not limited to, cost plus

---

13 69 *F.R.* 16107.
14 66 *F.R.* 876-77, 941, 944.

reasonable rate of return on investment on leases of comparable medical equipment from disinterested lessors.[15]

In another passage from the Stark regulations, CMS states that a commercially reasonable method "could be as simple as consulting a price list."[16]

The commentary to the three phases of Stark regulations issued by CMS clearly indicates that healthcare industry participants were highly anxious for CMS to establish or approve specific methods for establishing FMV under Stark. CMS did develop two "safe harbor" methods for determining FMV hourly rates with its release of the Phase II Regulations in 2004. It later withdrew these methods, however, with the Phase III or final Stark regulations published in 2007 based on critical responses to the methods. CMS considered this critical feedback to be valid.[17] In general, however, CMS has resisted calls to sanction methods for determining FMV, noting that no single method could apply universally to the wide variety of arrangements, services, and markets covered by Stark.[18] The agency further argued that "because the statute covers a broad range of transactions, we cannot comment definitively on particular valuation methodologies."[19]

Nonetheless, CMS has provided some general guidance and commentary on specific matters related to valuation under Stark. Perhaps the most important guidance relates to the use of independent survey data to establish FMV. In the Phase I Stark regulations, CMS lent credence to independent surveys, while cautioning against the use of internally generated surveys:

> However, while internally generated surveys can be appropriate as a method of establishing fair market value in some circumstances, due to their susceptibility to manipulation and absent independent verification, such surveys do not have strong evidentiary value and, therefore, may be subject to more intensive scrutiny than an independent survey.[20]

The Phase II Stark regulations went on to use certain physician compensation surveys as part of one of the Stark exception hourly rate methods. In abandoning this method in the Phase III Stark regulations, CMS remained favorably disposed toward the use of

---

15   66 *F.R.* 944.
16   66 *F.R.* 944.
17   72 *F.R.* 51015.
18   69 *F.R.* 16107.
19   72 *F.R.* 51016.
20   66 *F.R.* 945.

these surveys, positing that "reference to multiple, objective, independently published salary surveys remains a prudent practice for evaluating fair market value."[21] When pressed about the use of national versus regional survey data, however, CMS responded that the appropriate use of such data would depend on the facts and circumstances of the individual case.[22]

In other noteworthy commentary, CMS addressed the use of IRS guidelines for determining FMV under Stark:

> As for using the IRS guidelines for determining fair market value that applies to tax exempt organizations, we recognize that in some cases they may not be appropriate for for-profit entities. Nonetheless, it is our view that some elements of the IRS guidelines could be applied under certain circumstances, depending upon the specifics of any particular agreement. We do not wish to either mandate their use or rule them out if they can be appropriately used to demonstrate fair market value.[23]

CMS also recognized the use of independent valuation consultants as one means for establishing FMV.[24] CMS rejected, however, the request to make independent appraisals serve as acceptable determinations of FMV for Stark compliance purposes.[25] Finally, CMS raised the issue that FMV for administrative services may be different from that for clinical services but provided no clear guidance on the difference.[26]

2.2 The OIG's Use of FMV for Compliance With the Anti-Kickback Statute

The AKS itself does not directly address the issue of FMV and contains no definition of FMV. As part of its regulations and enforcement of the statute, however, the Office of Inspector General (OIG) of the Department of Health and Human Services (HHS) promulgated the use of FMV as one of the criteria for assessing compliance with the statute. In particular, the OIG included FMV as one of the conditions for various safe harbors that provide protection from potential violations of the law. The OIG also provided commentary about FMV and its application as part of the review process for proposing and finalizing AKS-related regulations. Further commentary can be found in the OIG's compliance guidance publications to healthcare industry providers. Unfortunately, the OIG does not provide any systematic guidance on FMV and valuation methodology in any of these publications. This lack of direction, however, appears to be a function of

---

21 *72 F.R.* 51015.
22 *69 F.R.* 16107.
23 *66 F.R.* 944.
24 *66 F.R.* 945.
25 *69 F.R.* 16107.
26 *72 F.R.* 51016.

the OIG's understanding of the unique focus of the AKS and the potential for widely divergent facts and circumstances in connection with application of the statute.[27]

The safe harbors that list FMV as a condition include ownership of certain investment interests, space rentals, equipment rentals, personal services and management contracts, certain arrangements related to health plans and managed care organizations, ownership of ASCs, and ambulance replenishing.[28] In the case of rental safe harbors, the OIG has provided specific definitions for use in determining FMV under those safe harbors.

> Note that for purposes of paragraph (b) of this section, the term fair market value means the value of the rental property for general commercial purposes, but shall not be adjusted to reflect the additional value that one party (either the prospective lessee or lessor) would attribute to the property as a result of its proximity or convenience to sources of referrals or business otherwise generated for which payment may be made in whole or in part under Medicare, Medicaid and all other Federal health care programs.[29]

> Note that for purposes of paragraph (c) of this section, the term fair market value means that the value of the equipment when obtained from a manufacturer or professional distributor, but shall not be adjusted to reflect the additional value one party (either the prospective lessee or lessor) would attribute to the equipment as a result of its proximity or convenience to sources of referrals or business otherwise generated for which payment may be made in whole or in part under Medicare, Medicaid or other Federal health care programs.[30]

What is evident from these unique definitions of FMV is that the OIG is focused on eliminating any value impact related to the volume or value of referrals between the parties to leases. The OIG has concluded that the traditional definition of FMV as understood by the appraisal profession, including the definition in IRS Revenue Ruling 59-60, was not sufficient to address the unique facts and circumstances that can arise in a healthcare context between referral-related parties in space and equipment leases. The traditional definition of FMV fails to address any proximity value arising from referral relationships; the OIG's definition specifically states that proximity value may not be considered at all. Thus, the OIG definition is considerably more restrictive than the traditional and IRS definitions. As a result, the OIG promulgated a specific definition for each safe harbor.

---

27 Since it is a criminal statute, intent—scienter—is usually required, although the government has attempted to limit that standard to ease prosecution.
28 42 CFR 1001.952.
29 42 CFR 1001.952(b)(6).
30 42 CFR 1001.952(c)(6).

Indeed, the need to modify the traditional definition was made explicit in the OIG's now-famous letter to the IRS in 1992 regarding the acquisition of physician practices by hospitals, in which the OIG commented:

> When considering the question of fair market value, we would note that the traditional or common methods of economic valuation do not comport with the prescriptions of the anti-kickback statute. Items ordinarily considered in determining the fair market value may be expressly barred by the anti-kickback statute's prohibition against payments for referrals. Merely because another buyer may be willing to pay a particular price is not sufficient to render the price paid to be fair market value. The fact that a buyer in a position to benefit from referrals is willing to pay a particular price may only be a reflection of the value of the referral stream that is likely to result from the purchase.[31]

The letter cited the unique definitions of FMV for space and equipment rentals in the safe harbor regulations as a clear indication of the OIG's intent to deviate from the traditional concept of FMV.[32]

The OIG's position on traditional valuation concepts and methodology was also made clear in its commentary to the initial set of final regulations for safe harbors to the AKS in 1991. In response to commenters who sought uniformity between IRS requirements for determining FMV by tax-exempt entities and the FMV requirements under the AKS, the OIG responded:

> We do not believe that procedures for assessing the fair market value of hospital/ physician arrangements under the Internal Revenue Code are relevant to safe harbor requirements under the anti-kickback statute. The anti-kickback statute is concerned with prohibiting fraud and abuse by individuals and entities participating in the Medicare and Medicaid programs; a statute providing tax exemptions to nonprofit institutions under specified conditions does not share this focus. The requirements we have set forth for determining fair market value under the safe harbor regulation are not undermined by the fact that they do not replicate the requirements under the Internal Revenue Code.[33]

In its 2005 Supplemental Compliance Program Guidance for Hospitals, the OIG provided some additional guidance on FMV methodology. First, the OIG linked FMV with the

---

31 Letter from D. McCarty Thornton (Associate General Counsel, Inspector General Division) to T.J. Sullivan (Office of the Associate Chief Counsel, IRS) dated Dec. 22, 1992.
32 See footnote 3.
33 56 *F.R.* 35952 et seq.

idea of arm's-length transactions.[34] It also briefly commented on the use of the market approach. In an apparent echo of CMS and Stark, the OIG cautioned hospitals on the use of market data from referral-related parties.

> Is the determination of fair market value based upon a reasonable methodology that is uniformly applied and properly documented? If fair market value is based on comparables, the hospital should ensure that the market rate for the comparable services is not distorted (e.g., the market for ancillary services may be distorted if all providers of the service are controlled by physicians).[35]

The OIG also discussed the potential for payments below FMV to be a potential indication of illegal kickbacks under certain circumstances. For arrangements between hospitals and hospital-based physicians, the OIG was concerned about payments below FMV when made by the hospital to physicians, since the reduced amounts could represent a kickback from the physicians for access to the hospital's business.[36]

Like CMS and Stark, the OIG believes the critical focus of the AKS does not allow for the use of the standard FMV definition in the healthcare regulatory context. Adjustments need to be made to the traditional definition of FMV to ensure referrals are excluded. Hence, the OIG's comments suggest separate definitions of FMV by type of transaction or arrangement, an approach similar to that taken by CMS for Stark purposes. The OIG appears to be of the view that transactions or arrangements in the healthcare marketplace are such that the willing buyer and willing seller could potentially reflect referral-related activities and the value of these referrals. As a result, the OIG seeks to depart from the standard definition of FMV and from standard appraisal methodology to exclude referrals from the valuation.

Like Stark, the AKS framework for FMV seems to recognize standard appraisal methodology but is reluctant to allow standard practice to operate on its own terms in an unregulated and unspecified way. It should be noted that the OIG appears to be aware of various valuation approaches or methods, since it comments on them in various advisory opinions.[37] These opinions, however, analyze the use and application of traditional valuation methods in terms of whether the particular method directly or indirectly includes the volume or value of referrals. Additionally, like Stark, the AKS

---

34 *70 F.R. 4866-67.*
35 *70 F.R. 4867.*
36 *70 F.R. 4867.*
37 For an analysis of these opinions relative to valuation issues, see James M Pinna and Matthew D. Jenkins, *The BVR/AHLA Guide to Healthcare Valuation,* 3rd edition, "The Anti-Kickback Statute and Stark Law: Avoiding the Valuation of Referrals," Chapter 7, pp. 173-81.

calls for departure from standard appraisal methodology, but does not give substantive guidance on a replacement framework. Unfortunately, the OIG provided even less guidance in terms of valuation methodology for FMV compliance under the AKS than CMS did for Stark purposes.

2.3 The Healthcare FMV Conundrum

The difficulty for appraisal professionals in the healthcare space is that, on the one hand, the federal healthcare regulations appear to recognize standard appraisal methodology and practice. Regulators seem to be aware of different valuation approaches and methods. In the case of Stark, CMS has enough valuation knowledge to know that alternative valuation methods can be attempted if the market approach was not available due to data concerns. CMS also acknowledges the benefits of IRS guidelines on appraisal. Similarly, the OIG is able to discuss difficulties with various appraisal methods in relation to AKS compliance matters. This minimal recognition, however, does not include validation and incorporation. *In other words, aside from the use of the term "fair market value," which is decades old and well-understood, the federal healthcare regulations are ambiguous about whether the traditional appraisal body of knowledge is generally applicable for healthcare regulatory purposes.*

On the other hand, the federal healthcare regulations posit certain departures from standard appraisal methodology and practice with regard to the determination of FMV. For Stark, this departure is both explicit and implicit. Although CMS highlighted the key departure related to the market approach, it implicitly deviated from standard appraisal practice in its apparent focus on a *single* commercially reasonable method as sufficient to establish FMV. The appraisal profession, by contrast, looks to *consideration* of three approaches to establish value.[38] More importantly, an alternative valuation framework does not address or remedy the regulatory departures. The federal healthcare regulations do not provide any systematic or conceptual guidance that can serve as the basis of an alternative valuation framework or methodology for determining FMV for healthcare regulatory purposes. It is true that Stark lists three general criteria for selecting a valuation method: the nature of the transaction, its location, and "other factors." These criteria, however, are insufficient to guide appraisal work in a meaningful way.

To summarize the problem, the federal healthcare regulations promulgate distinct meanings of FMV for regulatory compliance purposes but then provide little guidance on its determination from a methodological standpoint. The question of appraisal methodology, in general, is left unresolved and uncertain. This silence with respect to appraisal methodology presents a puzzling challenge for an appraiser. Since the purpose

---

38 This issue will be discussed in greater detail later in the chapter.

of the valuation is compliance, the appraiser must look to the applicable regulations to understand the definition of value and valuation considerations that should be taken into account in the appraisal scope of work. As a result of the lack of clear guidance, an appraiser enters a kind of regulatory "no man's land." This difficulty is aptly labeled as the healthcare FMV conundrum.

3.0 FMV and Appraisal Methodology as Understood by the Appraisal Profession

3.1 Standard Appraisal Definition of FMV

In evaluating the methods and techniques, it is helpful to consider valuation methodology and the definition of FMV as understood by the appraisal profession in light of the fact that the regulatory agencies also chose the term.[39] IRS Revenue Ruling 59-60 first promulgated the standard definition of FMV for business appraisal purposes:

> The price at which the property would change hands between a willing buyer and a willing seller when the former is not under any compulsion to buy and the latter is not under any compulsion to sell, both parties having reasonable knowledge of relevant facts.

This definition was modified and enhanced slightly in the definition established in the *International Glossary of Business Valuation Terms:*[40]

> The price, expressed in terms of cash equivalents, at which property would change hands between a hypothetical willing and able buyer and a hypothetical willing and able seller, acting at arm's length in an open and unrestricted market, when neither is under compulsion to buy or sell and when both have reasonable knowledge of the relevant facts.

What is common in both definitions is the idea of a buyer and seller in a transaction who are willing parties with no compulsion to act and who both have reasonable knowledge of information that is germane to their transaction. The *International Glossary* definition goes further than Revenue Ruling 59-60 by adding the idea of arm's-length transactions

---

39 Since the backdrop for this chapter is compensation valuation, standard appraisal practice is defined relative to this new emerging appraisal discipline. Compensation valuation generally uses the definitions and framework of business valuation as its foundation. Thus, the discussion of standard appraisal practice is defined in terms of the business valuation body of knowledge.

40 The *International Glossary* was developed and adopted by the four major U.S. business appraisal professional societies (American Society of Appraisers, American Institute of Certified Public Accountants, Institute of Business Appraisal, and the National Association of Certified Valuation Analysts) along with their Canadian counterpart (Canadian Institute of Chartered Business Valuators).

in an open and unrestricted market. It also introduces the idea of the *hypothetical* buyer and seller as the touchstone parties for establishing the exchange price for the transaction. It should be noted that for compensation valuation purposes, services or resource usage are substituted for property in the definition of FMV. In other words, the seller is selling either services or the usage of resources to the buyer, and, conversely, the buyer is buying services or the usage of resources from the seller.

3.2 Focus on the Hypothetical Buyer and Seller

The business valuation definition of FMV entails the concept of a transaction by a hypothetical buyer and seller.[41] Some appraisers have applied this definition by conceptualizing the hypothetical parties as those who are typical in the marketplace for subject transaction or arrangement. Business appraisers use the idea of hypothetical parties when applying various valuation methods and techniques to a subject transaction. To the extent that such methods employ data inputs and various assumptions about the operation and the economic capacity of a subject business, the concept of a hypothetical buyer and seller limits the characteristics of these inputs and assumptions to those that are consistent with the hypothetical parties in the marketplace and do not take into account the particular attributes and resources of a specific buyer or seller. In other words, valuation inputs and assumptions are based on what the hypothetical parties could do in operating the subject business. The synergies, competitive advantages, and business opportunities (including referrals) available to the specific buyer or seller are not used in valuation models and techniques. Appraisals prepared using such characteristics are consistent with investment or synergistic value, rather than FMV. In business appraisal, investment value is the value definition that takes into account the properties of a specific buyer or seller in applying valuation methods and techniques.[42]

3.3 Standard Appraisal Methodology: Three Approaches to Value

With regard to valuation methodology, the professional practice of appraisal considers three approaches to value: cost, market, and income. The major appraisal disciplines, whether real estate or business valuation, begin with the fundamental framework of these three approaches. Consideration of the three approaches is one of the foundational concepts in the common appraisal body of knowledge in the professional practice of appraisal. The reason for this commonality is that each approach provides a different, but critical, perspective on the value of a subject entity or service contract. For example,

---

41   Editor Dietrich's Note: Fair market value contemplates a financial buyer. "Often thought of as being the same as the hypothetical buyer, the financial buyer typically comes to the transaction table with a perceived ability to complete the purchase only expecting financial returns *not impacted by any synergies or other advantages that may exist as a result of the transaction.*" (*The CPA's Role in Buying and Selling a Business*, AICPA) Prohibited referrals are a form of synergy between hospitals and physicians.

42   The *International Glossary* defines investment value as "the value to a particular investor based on individual investment requirements and expectations."

the market approach may take into account the valuation principle of substitution, or the concept that "prudent individuals will not pay more for something than they would pay for an equally desirable substitute."[43] The cost approach, by contrast, may utilize the principle of alternatives, which is defined as the idea that "in any contemplated transaction, each party has alternatives to consummating the transaction."[44] Generally, each approach will entail relative strengths and weaknesses in valuing a subject. In certain instances, application of more than one approach can serve to offset and mitigate the weaknesses of any single approach while providing for greater strength in the synthesis of multiple approaches. Within each appraisal discipline, standard definitions are formulated for each approach so that practitioners have a common framework for using the various approaches in valuation assignments.

Consideration of the three approaches does not necessitate the application and completion of each approach in a specific valuation assignment. The implementation of an approach is a function of available and relevant data as well as the capacity of the approach to address the fundamental economics of the subject transaction or arrangement. Lack of available and relevant data may limit the effective use of an approach. In various appraisal disciplines, one or two approaches may be preferred or held to be the most applicable in determining the value of certain types of property, property interests, or entities. This determination may be a function of data availability in the industry or relevance to key economics. In BV, for example, it is not common for all three approaches to be applied and used to determine the value of a subject business or business interest.[45]

In addition, an approach may not encompass or account for key economic factors in a transaction. As a result, an appraiser may not always use an approach in a given engagement after considering all of the facts and circumstances. In addition, multiple appraisal methods may be available for a given approach to value; consideration of an approach may involve use of more than one method. Evaluation of multiple data sources, such as the numerous physician compensation surveys, is another factor in the use of an approach. Similar to assessing the use of the three approaches, evaluating the application of various valuation methods and data sources is based on an analysis of the fundamental economics of a subject transaction or arrangement and the quality and extent of available data. The judgment that is exercised in selecting methods and data sources is a key aspect of an appraiser's professional practice.

---

43 Gary R. Trugman, *Understanding Business Valuation: A Practical Guide to Valuing Small to Medium-Sized Businesses*, 2nd edition, p. 55-56.
44 Ibid., p. 55.
45 James R. Hitchner, *Financial Valuation: Applications and Models*, 3rd Edition (Kindle), "Approaches to Value," Chapter 1.

In the professional practice of appraisal, when more than one method is used, the valuation process culminates in the synthesis of the various value indications arising from those methods and techniques used. The appraiser evaluates and assesses each value indication and determines the appropriate indication or range of value that is consistent with the standard of value for the appraisal assignment. In the synthesis process, the appraiser analyzes the comparative strengths and weaknesses of various valuation methods and value indications relative to the economics of the subject transaction or arrangement. Similar to selecting approaches and methods to use in an appraisal, the synthesis process is a matter of professional judgment. There is no generally accepted formula or technique for how value indications are synthesized.

4.0 Reconciling Healthcare Regulatory and Professional Appraisal FMV

Standard appraisal practice can be compared and contrasted with healthcare regulatory guidance on the determination of FMV in two key areas. The first area is in the definition of FMV. The second area relates to appraisal methodology. Review of both areas shows matters of agreement and difference between the two concepts of FMV and how to determine it.

4.1 Synthesizing the Definition of FMV

While federal healthcare regulatory pronouncements claim departure from traditional valuation practices, a comparison of the regulatory and standard appraisal definitions of FMV indicates that there are certain areas of agreement in the two standards of value. The regulatory definition focuses on the buying and selling parties' independence from each other with respect to referrals of healthcare services. In the case of the Stark definition, FMV seems to be framed in terms of the market approach with its focus on bona fide sales that have been transacted in the marketplace. By contrast, the traditional appraisal definition of FMV focuses on a broader set of economic conditions related to the parties. Both the regulatory and appraisal FMV definitions, however, refer to well-informed parties. They also both assume independent parties acting in their own self-interest at arm's length. The behavior and choices of the parties in a FMV transaction are assumed to be consistent with that of well-informed parties, not under compulsion, in bona fide negotiations. FMV under the appraisal definition adds the concept of an open and unrestricted market to the conditions for the assumed arm's-length negotiations. The fundamental question for healthcare valuation practice is whether these definitions are essentially different and incompatible or whether they share a common framework that is consistent or complementary at a core level. It is also possible that both definitions have areas of both agreement and difference.

One approach for addressing this question is to ask whether the application of the appraisal definition of FMV would yield the same or similar results that the application of the regulatory definition of FMV would. The answer to this question appears to be a function of whether the hypothetical buyer and seller in a transaction or arrangement are parties in a position to refer to each other. Is the hypothetical buyer in the marketplace a healthcare provider entity with a referral relationship to a hypothetical seller who is the source of referrals? Conversely, is the hypothetical seller a provider entity with referrals coming from the hypothetical buyer? If the answer is no to either question, then consideration of referrals would appear to be excluded from the valuation analysis under the appraisal definition of FMV.[46] Conceptually, referrals should not be taken into account in the appraisal analysis because the hypothetical parties to the transaction or arrangement are not referral-related parties. Indeed, to take such referrals into account in the valuation, when the specific parties had a referral relationship, would produce a conclusion of value more consistent with investment value, but not FMV, under the traditional appraisal body of knowledge.

When the only buyers and sellers in the marketplace for a type of arrangement are parties in a position to refer,[47] one can attempt to reconcile the regulatory and appraisal definitions of FMV by assuming that the hypothetical parties do not have a referral relationship. One analyzes value by modeling how the parties would act without regard to such referrals and exclude the volume or value of referrals from the analysis. In other words, the parties act in accordance with their interests solely with respect to the assets or services that are the subject of the proposed transaction, not including any referrals. No other potential business interests are taken into account in the appraisal analysis. The transaction or arrangement must be valued on its separate and distinct economics excluding referrals. With this one adjustment, healthcare and appraisal FMV appear to reconcile and converge.

For example, in a hospital call coverage arrangement, the hypothetical hospital buyer of call services is seeking only to procure a necessary resource for operation of the hospital's emergency department (ED). Strategic partnerships with physicians who are high admitters to the facility are not considered as a motivation or purpose of the arrangement. The *hypothetical* hospital buyer will act with economic and operational rationality, prudence, and diligence in obtaining only the level of coverage needed at the best price/value for the organization. This buyer is assumed to be indifferent about

---

46 For example, physician employment arrangements are not necessarily between hospital/health systems and physicians. Despite the trend toward hospital employment, physician-owned practices still employ physicians in the healthcare marketplace.

47 For example, in hospital call coverage or medical directorship arrangements with physicians, the marketplace parties are generally hospitals and physicians, i.e., parties in a position to refer.

the sellers who provide the services, apart from quality and value considerations. Thus, the hypothetical buyer will contract with a high admitter physician and a low admitter physician as long as the two have equal quality and value. In fact, if the low admitter physician is a better value, i.e., agrees to a lower call stipend than the higher admitter, the hypothetical hospital buyer will seek to obtain more call services from the low admitter. This buyer will treat the procurement of call coverage no differently than staffing for nurses or purchasing supplies and medical equipment. Only resources that are needed are procured based on the best quality/value combination.

Another example of the hypothetical buyer acting apart from referrals can be illustrated for medical directorships. The hypothetical buyer treats a medical directorship no differently than another administrative position in the other organization. The position needs to be justified in terms of value added to the organization and its operations based solely on the characteristics of the services provided by the position, and not based on patient referrals. The organization then looks for a qualified candidate to fill the position and selects the candidate based on the best fit for the organization in terms of experience, skills, and qualifications. The organization compensates this physician based on market norms and the resource budget and constraints of the organization.

One can similarly model the perspective and behavior of the hypothetical seller of services apart from referrals. The hypothetical physician seller of call coverage services looks at the scope and extent of the services in terms of substitutes, alternatives, and future benefits. For example, in call coverage, the seller looks at the uncompensated care arising from ED patients in comparison to compensated care that comes from the physician's practice. Why would the physician displace such compensated care to provide uncompensated care? The hypothetical seller will not. Thus, the hospital will need to provide some form of compensation for the physician to be motivated to provide call services. A similar analysis can be applied to the availability and telephonic response aspects of hospital call coverage. These aspects can interfere with a physician's normal practice and the generation of income. The hypothetical physician seller will not agree to limitations on income-producing activities without compensation.

In summary, use of hypothetical buyers and sellers in the appraisal definition of FMV, whether based on the typical parties in the marketplace or assumed parties without referral relationships, generally meets the healthcare regulatory requirements for FMV. The two definitions can be synthesized into a single concept for use in determining FMV.

4.2 Reconciling FMV Methodology
The question of FMV methodology presents a more difficult case for attempting a reconciliation or synthesis between healthcare regulations and the appraisal profession.

Technically, the healthcare regulations lack the rigor, theoretical coherence, and practical valuation experience that are found in the appraisal profession's methodological framework for valuing subject transactions. The professional framework considers appraisal methods and techniques under three fundamental approaches to value. The problem with the healthcare regulatory approach to valuation stems from its failure to address issues of methodology. In addition, Stark's standard of "any commercially reasonable method" lacks meaningful content from an economic and technical perspective. Reasonable and generally accepted valuation methods can yield a wide range of value indications. Moreover, any single method can have strengths and limitations in yielding results that encompass all the relevant factors in the value of a subject transaction. Standard appraisal methodology considers multiple approaches and methods as the way to arrive at a conclusion of value that accounts for the broadest scope of factors that can affect value. As a result, the appraisal profession across various disciplines has united on the conceptual framework of three approaches to value. Healthcare regulations lack this kind of conceptual guidance.

In fairness to CMS, the "any commercially reasonable method" approach appears to have been a response to healthcare industry players that were seeking universal formulas or safe harbors for determining FMV. The reluctance on the part of CMS to promulgate such methods is well-founded. The appraisal profession would agree that no singular formula, technique, or method can be said to yield FMV in every context. As Revenue Ruling 59-60 noted in discussing the approach to valuation:

> A determination of fair market value, being a question of fact, will depend upon the circumstances in each case. No formula can be devised that will be generally applicable to the multitude of different valuation issues arising in estate and gift tax cases. Often, an appraiser will find wide differences of opinion as to the fair market value of a particular stock. In resolving such differences, he should maintain a reasonable attitude in recognition of the fact that valuation is not an exact science. A sound valuation will be based upon all the relevant facts, but the elements of common sense, informed judgment and reasonableness must enter into the process of weighing those facts and determining their aggregate significance.

The specific facts and circumstances should be taken into consideration in each subject transaction, requiring different methods in different contexts. In this sense, the appraisal profession is consistent with the federal healthcare regulations as to the variability of methods needed to determine FMV.

Beneath another apparent divergence between healthcare regulations and standard appraisal methodology, there is yet another area of agreement. The Stark regulations' prime example of the departure of FMV under the healthcare regulations from standard appraisal practice may not be a deviation after all. While Stark's exclusion of market data from transactions between referral-related parties would appear to depart from the standard application of the market approach, a more careful study of this prohibition can lead to a different interpretation. If asked about the use of market data from transactions between family members, related parties, and affiliated or parent-subsidiary companies, most appraisers would exclude, discount, or treat cautiously the use of such data as part of the market approach. Related parties or entities would not be considered to be fully at arm's length, and, therefore, any corresponding financial arrangements may not be viewed as being truly independent, as required by the appraisal definition of FMV. Thus, it is not readily apparent that Stark's prohibition on the use of market data between parties in a position to refer healthcare services is uniformly a departure from the valuation body of knowledge. One is left to wonder whether standard appraisal practice and methodology is really significantly different from what is required to determine FMV under Stark, whether this particular example illustrates the divergence of Stark from standard practice.

4.3 The Case for Standard Appraisal Methodology in Healthcare FMV

Because they take into account a larger set of variables and economic factors, valuation conclusions based on the *consideration* of multiple approaches and methods are more robust and comprehensive and, ultimately, more supportable and defensible. They are less likely to be skewed or lopsided, producing unreasonable value indications that only take into account a narrow set of considerations. Such consideration is more likely to produce an opinion of value that is more sustainable and achievable for the buyer of a business or service because it considers a wider array of variables affecting value. As a result, valuations based on the framework of the three approaches are more likely to reflect the FMV of a subject transaction. Buyers and sellers in the marketplace will frequently take into account a variety of economic and operational factors and considerations in consummating a transaction. Use of traditional appraisal methodology reflects this wider perspective on value. It is more consistent with the idea of informed buyers and sellers acting at arm's length.

Because of the analytic rigor involved in their completion, it can be argued that appraisals prepared according to standard appraisal methodology tend to have a higher probability of producing value indications that do not appear to take into account the volume or value of referrals of healthcare services. Valuation conclusions prepared with the standard methodology yield results that can be more readily identified with multiple economic factors apart from referrals. As such, there is less ambiguity about the economic reasons and rationale for the consideration paid in a transaction. The value can be associated with a broad base of factors, none of which should include the volume or value of referrals.

Excluding the impact of referrals is not always apparent in valuations prepared without due consideration of the available approaches to value and their accompanying methods and techniques. Valuations prepared without analysis of methodology can easily lend themselves to "cherry-picking" of potential outcomes based on the method or data selected. Some methods and data naturally yield higher values than others, and vice versa. These structural problems can cast doubt on the objectivity and independence of FMV opinions that are based on single methods applied without rigorous analysis. Experienced appraisers are all too aware that indications of value can be manipulated through inputs and assumptions or by use of certain methods. A single-method orientation in valuation practice naturally lends itself to skepticism and uncertainty.

When multiple variables and factors are taken into account, the resulting indication of value adds credence to the claim that the economics of the appraisal do not reflect the volume or value of referrals that may exist between the parties to the transaction. When an array of factors and considerations is used to support the final conclusion, no one input or assumption can be used to impact the conclusion of value in a material way. Similarly, no one method can materially alter the opinion of value. As a result, there is less question or controversy about whether the valuation takes all relevant economic factors into account. In addition, the apparent objectivity and independence of the appraisal is demonstrated because of the comprehensive nature of the analysis. "Cherry-picking" of data or methods is less likely to occur.[48]

It can also be argued that appraisals based on standard methodology have a greater propensity for producing a rigorous analysis relative to the *commercial reasonableness* of a subject transaction. As noted previously, such valuations are more likely to produce sustainable economic results for a buyer as a result of considering a broad array of economic factors. Sustainable economics, whether from the earnings of a business or the economics of a service contract, can more readily be considered to be commercially reasonable than unsustainable results. A valuation based on a single variable or set of variables has a higher probability or potential to yield an unsustainable price or

---

48 Certainly, it is possible to complete multiple methods and then "cherry-pick" the results in the synthesis process. Such "cherry-picking," however, is more readily apparent to users and readers of appraisal reports. When an appraisal analysis ignores relevant and available data, assumptions, and methods, it is easy to support a particular conclusion on paper. No other consideration is given to alternative factors or issues; they can simply be ignored. An appraisal that raises a variety of considerations makes it harder to select results in a manipulative fashion because many factors are addressed in the analysis. Critical readers can readily identify dubious logic and questionable assumptions when more than a singular view is presented.

compensation level because of its narrow focus. The potential for unsustainable results can be magnified or highlighted in service agreements because of their duration over multiple years. In short, a transaction is more likely to be commercially reasonable when it is valued on the basis of the framework of the three approaches to value.

5.0 A Synthesized Approach With Jurisdictional Exceptions

5.1 The Synthesized Approach to Healthcare Valuation

The approach used by most experienced appraisal professionals specializing in healthcare valuation is to follow generally accepted practices consistent with the appraisal body of knowledge. They follow general valuation methodology consisting of the consideration of three approaches to value and a conclusion based on the synthesis of all available and relevant valuation approaches or methods. With respect to the definition of FMV, appraisers specializing in healthcare valuation begin with the traditional appraisal definition as the primary basis for FMV in the valuation process. They then adjust this definition to comport with the healthcare regulatory definition of FMV. The regulatory definition is used to supplement the appraisal definition in areas where healthcare FMV appears to conflict with appraisal FMV and where the regulatory definition has applicable content.

In addition, practitioners of healthcare valuation apply the idea that FMV entails a transaction by hypothetical buyers and sellers in the marketplace. This element of the appraisal definition of FMV is not only consistent with the healthcare regulatory definition but, in fact, helps ensure consistency with the intent of the healthcare regulations to prevent the payment for the volume or value of referrals. Taking into account the synergies and characteristics of specific physicians and healthcare provider entities to which these physicians refer not only runs the risk of including the volume or value of referrals, but also produces investment value and not FMV. Even when the hypothetical parties in the marketplace are referral-related parties, professional appraisers avoid using characteristics of such related parties in the valuation inputs and assumptions that would include referrals or give the appearance of including referrals.

While professional appraisers specializing in healthcare valuation generally apply the appraisal body of knowledge and professional standards for the determination of FMV, they make exceptions when such application could conflict with the healthcare regulations. In these cases, healthcare laws and regulations clearly supersede and have priority over standard appraisal practices and methodology. The two primary areas where such conflicts arise are: 1) including the volume or value of healthcare service referrals; and 2) use of market data derived from parties who are in a position to refer such services. In both areas, appraisal professionals avoid using such referral-laden economics or data items reflecting referral relationships.

5.2 The Use of Jurisdictional Exceptions

The practice of following standard appraisal methodology, but making departures for legal or regulatory considerations, is firmly grounded in the professional practice of appraisal. Such concessions have been given a uniform name and description in appraisal professional standards: "jurisdictional exceptions." The Uniform Standards of Professional Appraisal Practice (USPAP) even includes a separate Jurisdictional Exception Rule. This rule states that "if any applicable law or regulation precludes compliance with any part of USPAP, only that part of USPAP becomes void for that assignment."[49] The valuation standards of the American Institute of Certified Public Accountants (AICPA) provide similar guidance on jurisdictional exceptions to that found in USPAP:

> If any part of this Statement differs from published governmental, judicial, or accounting authority, or such authority specifies valuation development procedures or valuation reporting procedures, then the valuation analyst should follow the applicable published authority or stated procedures with respect to that part applicable to the valuation in which the member is engaged. The other parts of this Statement continue in full force and effect (Valuation Services Interpretation No. 1).[50]

The professional standards of the National Association of Certified Valuators and Analysts (NACVA) and the Institute of Business Appraisers (IBA) provide for similar treatment. In the event published regulatory authorities specify valuation procedures differing from the professional standards of the organization, the appraiser should follow the authority in that matter. The remaining standards continue to be in effect for the appraisal.[51]

When a jurisdictional exception is made in an appraisal assignment, USPAP calls for the appraiser to do the following:

1. Identify the law or regulation that precludes compliance with USPAP;

2. Comply with that law or regulation;

---

49 2012-2013 Edition, p. U-15, lines 437-38.

50 *Statement on Standards for Valuation Services Number 1: Valuation of a Business, Business Ownership Interest, Security, or Intangible Asset*, Section 10 (SSVS 1). See also Interpretation No. 1-01, *"Scope of Applicable Services"* of *Statement on Standards for Valuation Services Number 1: Valuation of a Business, Business Ownership Interest, Security, or Intangible Asset*, Sections 24 and 25.

51 NACVA and IBA Professional Standards (effective June 1, 2011), Section III.D, Jurisdictional Exception.

3. Clearly and conspicuously disclose in the report the part of USPAP that is voided by that law or regulation; and

4. Cite in the report the law or regulation requiring this exception to USPAP compliance.[52]

The AICPA, NACVA, and IBA standards require that jurisdictional exceptions be included in the introduction section of a report that provides information on the nature and scope of the engagement.[53, 54]

In short, there is ample precedence in valuation standards for making departures from standard appraisal methodology to adjust for the particular requirements of governmental regulations. It would be logical, therefore, to extend the use of jurisdictional exceptions to healthcare valuation, including the practice of compensation valuation, where professional standards for this emerging appraisal discipline do not exist. The concept of jurisdictional exceptions provides a helpful framework for appraisers to organize and develop their valuation work when the purpose of an assignment is healthcare regulatory compliance. In these engagements, appraisers follow standard practice as found in the appraisal body of knowledge. When following standard methodology creates a potential area that may run afoul of the healthcare regulations, appraisers simply make a jurisdictional exception in that one area so that the FMV analysis is consistent with regulatory requirements.

Whether healthcare regulators would accept this approach of using standard appraisal methodology coupled with jurisdictional exceptions is a separate question.[55] Since they have provided little practical or theoretical guidance, it is unclear what their position would be. Certainly, healthcare regulations call for departures and adjustment relative to the unique focus of healthcare FMV in terms of not paying for the volume or value of referrals. Jurisdictional exceptions that are made to exclude or avoid valuing referrals in the appraisal process are consistent with that focus. Moreover, there are important areas of consistency between healthcare FMV and appraisal FMV in terms of both the definition of FMV and methodology, as has been discussed in previous sections. There is good reason to believe that following standard appraisal practice and methodology will further compliance with healthcare FMV. Professional appraisers should also

---

52 2012-2013 edition, pg. U-15, lines 442-446.
53 See sections 52, 71, and 74 of SSVS1.
54 See section V.C.1 and 2 of the Professional Standards.
55 My co-editor, Mark O. Dietrich, has been pointing out for many years that the determination of FMV for healthcare regulatory compliance purposes involves jurisdictional exceptions. Unfortunately, professional appraisers in the healthcare marketplace have not widely acknowledged and applied this critical point. The profession would do well to begin framing the dialogue and the literature within the profession to include jurisdictional exceptions when dealing with healthcare FMV.

be confident that the decades of experience and development of standard appraisal methodology is more likely to yield reliable and supportable opinions about valuation matters, including those with unique priorities, such as healthcare FMV.

5.3 Issues in the Use and Application of Jurisdictional Exceptions

While the conceptual framework for the use of jurisdictional exceptions may be straight-forward, its application to real-world engagements is not always so easy. There are certain areas or issues where healthcare regulations related to FMV are not absolutely clear. It is important to realize that potential issues can arise from three different areas of the valuation process:

1. Specific valuation methods;

2. Data and data sources; and

3. Assumptions used in the valuation analysis, whether qualitative or quantitative.

There are also certain fact patterns in which use of a particular data source, assumption, or valuation technique may appear to be inconsistent with healthcare regulations and FMV. Many "gray" areas can involve issues related to technical component services or ancillaries included in a business being sold or in the scope of services being provided in a service contract. These areas are particularly difficult when the physician sellers of a proposed business or service are also the referral base for the business or service.

In assessing unclear or difficult issues, it is helpful for appraisers to seek regulatory guidance from the client's legal counsel. Legal, regulatory, and investment opinions and advice are not the purview of an appraiser in a transaction or compensation arrangement. The job of the appraiser is to develop a conclusion of value based on the engagement scope given by the client. Since healthcare regulatory compliance is part of that scope and since such compliance involves legal and regulatory matters, legal counsel's expertise and direction may be needed in these areas. Indeed, appraisers would be wise to avoid taking positions on valuation matters that entail significant and complex regulatory compliance questions. Appraisers are certainly competent to furnish FMV conclusions of value based on the valuation body of knowledge; they are not necessarily competent to provide legal or regulatory opinions and advice to clients.

In such cases, appraisers may be given explicit instructions by legal counsel as to the exclusion of certain data, assumptions, or valuation methods from the scope of work completed by the appraiser. *To the extent that such direction is given relative to areas of ambiguity in healthcare regulations and not about matters related to appraisal methodology per se, appraisers would be advised to follow the directions of legal counsel, while bearing in mind that independence requires that the appraiser not cede his or her judgment to a third party.* In other words, legal counsel may direct the appraiser to make a jurisdictional exception in the scope of work.

Consistent with the guidance in valuation standards, jurisdictional exceptions should be narrow in focus and selective in scope. They should relate solely to specific regulatory issues that affect the appraisal; they should not relate to the scope of work generally. The appraiser should not subordinate his or her opinion of what is required for appraising the subject transaction in terms of standard methodology and practice. Rather, the guidance should be taken as clarification of the meaning and application of healthcare regulations in particular fact patterns. To the extent such guidance causes a departure from standard appraisal methodology and practice, it should be treated as a jurisdictional exception.

Jurisdictional exceptions should be documented in the appraisal report, with discussion of its impact on the scope of work completed for the assignment.

5.4 Practical Tips for Working With Attorneys on Jurisdictional Exceptions

An important point to remember during the review process with legal counsel is that the purpose is not to discuss and debate general or technical issues in standard appraisal methodology and practice. The purpose of the review process is not for the attorney to approve the appraiser's scope of work from a general or technical standpoint. The normal selection of data sources, assumptions, approaches to value, individual methods, and synthesis considerations made by the appraiser are not subject to debate and approval by legal counsel. Appraisers need to remain objective and independent in the determination of FMV with regard to these matters. Jurisdictional exceptions only relate to a narrow set of concerns; they are focused solely on specific instances in which healthcare regulations may affect the scope of work in a particular appraisal assignment.

Effective communication between the attorney and appraiser is the key to good outcomes in using jurisdictional exceptions. Here are some practical ideas for working with attorneys on the identification and application of jurisdictional exceptions in healthcare valuation practices:

- Establish the framework for jurisdictional exceptions with the client and/ or the client's legal counsel as part of the engagement process. Include the framework in the engagement letter terms.

- Discuss major regulatory concerns and risk issues related to FMV compliance with legal counsel in the initial stages of the valuation process. Knowing counsel's "hot button" issues up-front can allow proactive addressing of issues.

- Review the appraisal work plan with legal counsel, including the details of methods and techniques, to allow for early detection of issues. Early detection and discussion can save the appraiser from investing time in valuation work that heads in the wrong direction.

- Be alert to potential issues that might arise during the valuation process.

- Provide adequate disclosure of data sources, assumptions, and methods so that legal counsel has a good understanding of the appraisal scope of work.

CHAPTER APPENDIX: Texts of Commentary on the Definition of FMV From the Phase I to III Stark Regulations

Phase I Commentary (66 F.R. 944-45, Jan. 4, 2001)

3. Fair Market Value

The term "fair market value" appears in most of the compensation related exceptions. These exceptions, among other things, require that compensation between physicians (or family members) and entities be based on the fair market value of the particular items or services that these parties are exchanging. We defined this term in the August 1995 final rule covering referrals for clinical laboratory services by using the definition that appears in section 1877(h)(3) of the Act. This provision defines fair market value as the value in arm's-length transactions, consistent with the general market value, with other specific terms for rentals or leases. In the January 1998 proposed rule, we discussed what constitutes a value that is "consistent with the general market value." We drafted the definition as follows so that it applies to any arrangements involving items or services, including, but not limited to, employment relationships, personal service arrangements, and rental agreements:

> "General market value" is the price that an asset would bring, as the result of bona fide bargaining between well-informed buyers and sellers, or the compensation that would be included in a service agreement, as the result of bona fide bargaining between well-informed parties to the agreement, on the date of acquisition of the asset or at the time of the service agreement. Usually the fair market price is the price at which bona fide sales have been consummated for assets of like type, quality, and quantity in a particular market at the time of acquisition, or the compensation that has been included in bona fide service agreements with comparable terms at the time of the agreement.

The definition of "fair market value" in the proposed rule continued to include the additional requirements in section 1877(h)(3) of the Act for rentals or leases. Among other things, the statute defines the fair market value of rental property as its value for general commercial purposes, not taking into account its intended use. Most of the comments we received addressed the question of how to establish the fair market value of an asset or agreement and how to value rental property "for general commercial purposes." We have tried to clarify these concepts in our responses.

Comment: Several commenters asked that we clarify the documentation that will suf-ficiently establish a transaction as consistent with fair market value (and general mar-ket value) for the exceptions that apply to compensation arrangements. The proposed definition of fair market value states that "usually the fair market price is the price at which bona fide sales have been consummated for assets of like type, quality, and quantity in a particular market at the time of acquisition or the compensation that has been included in bona fide service agreements with comparable terms at the time of the agreement." One commenter stated that using the word "usually" may create ambigui-ties and suggested making clear in the definition of fair market value that the standard of comparable transactions is only one potential means of establishing fair market value.

Another commenter stated that the January 1998 proposed rule is unclear about the steps that must be taken to confirm fair market value. The commenter asked that we adopt the position that a valuation from an independent person experienced in the valuation of health care operations is sufficient as one approach (but not the only approach) to establishing fair market value. However, the commenter further stated that, because sales of medical practices are private and not reported to any central database, and because there is often a lack of a representative pool upon which to draw comparisons, we should adopt the position that confirmation of fair market value does not necessarily require the finding of comparable entities for comparison. Another commenter stated that the Internal Revenue Service (IRS) guidelines for determining fair market value with respect to tax exempt organizations are too restrictive and are inappropriate for application to for-profit entities.

Response: To establish the fair market value (and general market value) of a transaction that involves compensation paid for assets or services, we intend to accept any method that is commercially reasonable and provides us with evidence that the compensa-tion is comparable to what is ordinarily paid for an item or service in the location at issue, by parties in arm's-length transactions who are not in a position to refer to one another. (As discussed in section V of this preamble, in most instances the fair market value standard is further modified by language that precludes taking into account the "volume or value" of referrals, and, in some cases, other business generated by the re-ferring physician. Depending on the circumstances, the "volume or value" restriction will preclude reliance on comparables that involve entities and physicians in a position to refer or generate business.) The amount of documentation that will be sufficient to confirm fair market value (and general market value) will vary depending on the circumstances in any given case; that is, there is no rule of thumb that will suffice for all situations. The burden of establishing the "fairness" of an agreement rests with the parties involved in the agreement. Depending on the circumstances, parties may want to consider obtaining good faith, written assurances as to fair market value from the party paying or receiving the compensation, although such written assurances are not determinative.

For example, a commercially reasonable method of establishing fair market value (and general market value) for the rental of office space can include providing us with a list of comparables. We would also find acceptable an appraisal that the parties have received from a qualified independent expert. Although some transactions are not subject to public scrutiny, we believe generally that there should be sufficient documentation of similar public transactions that the parties can use as a basis of comparison. In regions with inadequate direct comparables, such as rural areas, a reasonable alternative may involve comparing institutions or entities located in different, but similar, areas where property is zoned for similar use. For example, a hospital affiliated with a university in one part of the country could be comparable to other hospitals affiliated with universities that are located in similar types of communities. In other cases, all the comparables or market values may involve transactions between entities that are in a position to refer or generate other business. For example, in some markets, physician-owned equipment lessors have driven out competitive third-party lessors of similar equipment. In such situations, we would look to alternative valuation methodologies, including, but not limited to, cost plus reasonable rate of return on investment on leases of comparable medical equipment from disinterested lessors.

In contrast, there may be cases in which finding a commercially reasonable representation of fair market value (or general market value) could be as simple as consulting a price list. As for using the IRS guidelines for determining fair market value that applies to tax exempt organizations, we recognize that in some cases they may not be appropriate for for-profit entities. Nonetheless, it is our view that some elements of the IRS guidelines could be applied under certain circumstances, depending upon the specifics of any particular agreement. We do not wish to either mandate their use or rule them out if they can be appropriately used to demonstrate fair market value.

Comment: One commenter noted that, as part of our definition of "fair market value," we include the term "general market value," which applies to any arrangement involving items and services, including employment relationships, personal service arrangements, and rental agreements. The commenter pointed out that in the January 1998 proposed rule we do not address the specific documentation requirements necessary to verify and document that the price of an asset or the compensation for certain services actually reflects the market rate. The commenter requested that we confirm that internally generated surveys are sufficient for establishing the market rate, and that there is no requirement to use an independent valuation consultant.

Response: We agree that there is no requirement that parties use an independent valuation consultant for any given arrangement when other appropriate valuation methods are available. However, while internally generated surveys can be appropriate as a method of establishing fair market value in some circumstances, due to their susceptibility to manipulation and absent independent verification, such surveys do not have strong evidentiary value and, therefore, may be subject to more intensive scrutiny than an independent survey.

Phase II Commentary (69 F.R. 16107, March 26, 2004)

3. Fair Market Value

The definition of "fair market value" is addressed in section VIII.N.3 of the Phase I preamble (66 *FR* 944) and in the regulations in § 411.351. The following are our responses to comments to the Phase I definition.

Comment: A commenter expressed concern that the discussion of "fair market value" in the Phase I preamble does not provide sufficiently clear guidance for determining "fair market value." That commenter recommended that the regulations include a rebuttable presumption of reasonableness and "fair market value" when entities benchmark their arrangements to objective measures or when they obtain the opinion of independent third parties as to "fair market value" in a particular arrangement. The commenter suggested that the presumption be similar to that contained in the IRS's intermediate sanctions provisions.

Response: We appreciate the commenter's desire for clear "bright line" guidance. However, the statute covers such a wide range of potential transactions that it is not possible to verify and list appropriate benchmarks or objective measures for each. Moreover, the definition of "fair market value" in the statute and regulation is qualified in ways that do not necessarily comport with the usage of the term in standard valuation techniques and methodologies. For example, the methodology must exclude valuations where the parties to the transactions are at arm's length but in a position to refer to one another. In addition, the definition itself differs depending on the type of transaction: leases or rentals of space and equipment cannot take into account the intended use of the rented item; and in cases where the lessor is in a position to refer to the lessee, the valuation cannot be adjusted or reflect the value of proximity or convenience to the lessor. Our Phase I discussion made clear that we will consider a range of methods of determining fair market value and that the appropriate method will depend on the nature of the transaction, its location, and other factors. While good faith reliance on a proper valuation may be relevant to a party's intent, it does not establish the ultimate issue of the accuracy of the valuation figure itself. With respect to valuing physician services, however, we are establishing several "safe harbored" methodologies discussed in more detail in section VIII.C.

Comment: A commenter sought clarification that determinations of "fair market value" could involve comparisons of national or regional data where appropriate. By way of example, the commenter suggested that the market for physician recruitment has become national.

Response: Whether resort to national or regional data is appropriate will depend on the facts and circumstances of each case. The regulations necessarily cover a wide variety of arrangements, services, and markets, and no single means for determining "fair market value" will apply to all. For hourly physician compensation, we have added "safe harbored" methodologies for establishing fair market value that take into account national and regional data (section VIII.C of this preamble). If parties are using comparables to establish fair market value, they should take reasonable steps to ensure that the comparables are not distorted.

Phase III Commentary (72 F.R. 51015-16, Sept. 5, 2007)

C. Fair Market Value

In Phase II, we created a "safe harbor" provision in the definition of "fair market value" at § 411.351 for hourly payments to physicians for their personal services. The safe harbor consisted of two methodologies for calculating hourly rates that would be deemed "fair market value" for purposes of section 1877 of the Act. The first methodology requires that the hourly payment be less than or equal to the average hourly rate for emergency room physician services in the relevant physician market, provided there are at least three hospitals providing emergency room services in the market. The second methodology requires averaging the 50th percentile national compensation level for physicians in the same specialty, using at least four of six specified salary surveys, and dividing the result by 2,000 hours to establish an hourly rate. If the relevant physician specialty does not appear in one of the recognized surveys, the parties must use the survey's reported compensation for general practice in order to be within the safe harbor. We emphasized that use of the safe harbor was entirely voluntary and that parties may establish fair market value through other methods. We received a large number of comments questioning the new safe harbor.

Comment: Several commenters disliked the compensation survey methodology. In general, the commenters believed that the methodology was too prescriptive, and they urged more flexibility. Commenters noted that at least one of the listed surveys no longer exists, and that another is out of date. Another commenter stated that many of the survey companies will not sell their surveys to hospitals that do not participate in the surveys. According to the commenters, the available surveys are expensive. Another commenter asserted that other surveys, including the American Medical Group Association survey and *Modern Healthcare's* annual compilation of surveys, provide similar information at less expense. Several commenters objected to the use of national averages, because the national average masks significant regional differences in physician compensation.

Some commenters suggested that the compensation survey methodology be modified in other respects. One commenter urged us to expand the fair market value safe harbor to compensation that falls within the 25th to the 75th percentile of physician compensation. Commenters suggested that providers be able to use fewer than four surveys (for example, averaging the 50th percentile of any two surveys). Several commenters suggested that, where specialty-specific data is unavailable, providers should be able to use data from a similar specialty, rather than from general practitioners. According to the commenters, the compensation of physicians in one type of specialty is more similar to the compensation of physicians in other specialties than to the compensation of general practitioners. One commenter asked whether a contract could include a cost of living annual adjustment.

Response: We share the commenters' concerns regarding the availability of the surveys identified in the safe harbor. We are aware that several of the surveys are no longer available (or may not be readily available to all DHS entities and physicians), making it impractical to utilize the safe harbor. In addition, it may be infeasible to obtain information regarding hourly rates for emergency room physicians at competitor hospitals. Therefore, we are not retaining the safe harbor within the definition of "fair market value" at § 411.351. We emphasize, however, that we will continue to scrutinize the fair market value of arrangements as fair market value is an essential element of many exceptions.

Reference to multiple, objective, independently published salary surveys remains a prudent practice for evaluating fair market value. Ultimately, the appropriate method for determining fair market value for purposes of the physician self-referral law will depend on the nature of the transaction, its location, and other factors. As we explained in Phase II, although a good faith reliance on an independent valuation (such as an appraisal) may be relevant to a party's intent, it does not establish the ultimate issue of the accuracy of the valuation figure itself (69 *FR* 16107). Our views regarding fair market value are discussed further in Phase I (66 *FR* 944) and Phase II (69 *FR* 16107).

Because we are eliminating the safe harbor, it is unnecessary to address the commenters' specific suggestions for identifying permissible surveys and expanding the range of acceptable physician compensation. With respect to the inquiry regarding cost of living adjustments, we note that contracts for physician services may include an annual salary adjustment, provided that the resulting compensation is fair market value and otherwise complies with an exception.

Comment: A large number of nephrologists and groups representing nephrologists complained that the application of the safe harbor to their compensation for medical director duties at renal dialysis centers is inappropriate, especially given that the physician self-referral prohibition does not apply to dialysis services for which payment is made under the ESRD composite rate. According to the commenters, the hourly rate under the safe harbor would not adequately compensate dialysis facility medical directors for the full array of their skills and services. Several commenters expressed concern that, notwithstanding the voluntary nature of the safe harbor, the methodology would become the preferred valuation methodology to the detriment of physicians.

Response: For the reasons noted in the preceding response, we have eliminated the fair market value safe harbor in this Phase III final rule. With respect to existing arrangements, nothing in the physician self-referral regulations required use or application of the fair market value safe harbor; it was a wholly voluntary provision. Moreover, a physician's compensation arrangement with a dialysis facility implicates section 1877 of the Act only to the extent that the arrangement creates a direct or indirect financial arrangement with an entity that furnishes DHS, such as a dialysis facility that furnishes DHS not covered by the ESRD composite rate or a hospital that provides dialysis (66 FR 923–924).

Comment: A number of commenters complained that the fair market value safe harbor methodology based on local hourly rates for emergency room physician services creates significant risk under the antitrust laws.

Response: We have eliminated the fair market value safe harbor for payments to physicians.

Comment: Two commenters asked us to comment on other valuation methodologies.

Response: Nothing precludes parties from calculating fair market value using any commercially reasonable methodology that is appropriate under the circumstances and otherwise fits the definition at section 1877(h) of the Act and § 411.351. Ultimately, fair market value is determined based on facts and circumstances. The appropriate method will depend on the nature of the transaction, its location, and other factors. Because the statute covers a broad range of transactions, we cannot comment definitively on particular valuation methodologies. We refer the commenter to previous discussions in Phase I and Phase II regarding valuation methodologies (66 *FR* 944–945, 69 *FR* 16107).

Comment: One commenter wanted confirmation that a fair market value hourly rate could be used to compensate physicians for both administrative and clinical work. Another commenter asked whether the rate could be used to determine an annual salary.

Response: A fair market value hourly rate may be used to compensate physicians for both administrative and clinical work, provided that the rate paid for clinical work is fair market value for the clinical work performed and the rate paid for administrative work is fair market value for the administrative work performed. We note that the fair market value of administrative services may differ from the fair market value of clinical services. A fair market value hourly rate may be used to determine an annual salary, provided that the multiplier used to calculate the annual salary accurately reflects the number of hours actually worked by the physician.

Chapter 8. To Use or Not to Use: An Appraisal Analysis of the Stark Prohibition on Market Data From Parties in a Position to Refer

CONTENTS

Chapter 8. To Use or Not to Use: An Appraisal Analysis of the Stark Prohibition on Market Data From Parties in a Position to Refer

By Timothy Smith, CPA/ABV

1.0 Introduction

The Stark regulations place restrictions on the use of certain market data for purposes of determining FMV for regulatory compliance. The regulations exclude transactions between parties in a position to refer "designated health services" (DHS) from market comparables used for valuation purposes. Parties with healthcare referral relationships are not at arm's length; hence, transactions between these parties do not meet the criteria for FMV under the regulations. Since the intended use of nearly all compensation valuation (CV) assignments is healthcare regulatory compliance, the Stark restriction on market data is a critical issue.

Despite the explicit language in Stark, one can observe a variety of responses to the prohibition in valuation, consulting, and compensation-setting practices in the healthcare industry. Some industry participants seem to ignore the restriction as a key issue in using the market approach.[1] Others even go so far as to include referral-related parties

---

[1] See for example, William T. Carlson, Jr., *Cardiology*, "Valuation: The First Move Toward Physician-Hospital Integration," September 2009, "Principle #4: The Market Approach Is the Most Accurate, but Lack of Data Means It Is Not Helpful," p. 15, www.cardiosource.org/Practice-Management/~/media/Files/Practice%20 Management/Valuation.ashx, accessed Aug. 14, 2012. The article states, "in determining FMV, it would be helpful to know the price other cardiologists have received when they willingly sell their practice to a hospital buyer, especially when the price is a result of more than one hospital competing for that practice." The article proceeds to identify issues with the lack of relevant information on such transactions but does not mention the Stark prohibition.

as part of a "free market."[2] A second view is that the Stark prohibition applies only to equipment or space leases based on a narrow reading of the commentary in the Stark regulations. A third group of participants will use such data, but with limitations and qualifications.

For those who acknowledge and attempt to follow the prohibition on referral-related parties, a conundrum awaits. The Stark regulations call use of published physician compensation surveys a "prudent practice." Most of these surveys, however, include mixed data from both referral-related parties and those without such relationships. In recent years, hospital-employed or affiliated physicians have become the largest respondent group in all of these surveys. In addition, some specialized surveys include data solely from parties in a position to refer, based on the type of compensation arrangement covered by the survey, e.g., on-call pay and medical directorships. Reliance on survey data for valuation purposes, therefore, perplexes those practitioners who attempt to follow the valuation guidance provided by the Stark regulations.

The purpose of this chapter is to take a serious and systematic look at the Stark prohibition and its implications for CV practice. As part of CV's maturing into a professional appraisal discipline, it is important for practitioners to pursue *consistency* in key areas of practice and analysis. Users of CV appraisals are not well-served by an inconsistent approach within the CV community, especially on a topic as important as this one for healthcare regulatory compliance. This chapter, therefore, will consider four key questions in regard to the Stark prohibition on market data:

1. Does the prohibition apply to independent appraisers valuing healthcare transactions?

2. What is the scope and extent of the prohibition?

3. Does the prohibition limit the use of physician compensation survey data?

4. Does the prohibition represent a departure from standard appraisal methodology?

Our point of departure for examining these questions is a review of the Stark passages commenting on this topic.

---

2   See Douglas R. Ayres, Stephen J. Diagostino, and Thomas J. Thieme, *Valuation Strategies*, "Valuing Physician Medical Practices," May/June 2011, p. 40. The authors include health systems, along with other types of buyers, as part of the "free market" for physician practice acquisitions.

2.0 Key Passages From the Commentary on the Stark Regulations

To appreciate the issues raised by regulators and the explicit language of the Stark regulations and commentary, one should begin with the actual text of the commentary provided by the Centers for Medicare and Medicaid Services (CMS) on the use of market data between parties in a position to refer. Four passages address this issue directly. The passages are from CMS' responses to various comments on its proposed regulations for the Stark law.

2.1 Stark Phase I Commentary

Three of the four passages come from the commentary to the first phase of regulations for the Stark law, or to be precise, the amended statute that has become known as "Stark II."

Passage 1: Commentary Related to Unit-of-Service-Based Payments

The context for the first passage comes from a section titled "V. 'Volume or Value' of Referrals and 'Other Business Generated' Standards." This section dealt with the requirements for various compensation arrangements. These requirements precluded taking into account the volume or value of referrals or other business generated between the parties. CMS addressed the question of how these requirements affected unit-of-service-based payments, which led the agency to a discussion of lithotripsy lease arrangements that are paid on a per-use basis.

> Applying Phase I of this rulemaking to the lithotripter example noted above, the "per use" rental payments would be protected, even for lithotripsies performed on patients referred by the physician-owner, provided that the "per use" rental payment was at fair market value, did not vary over the lease term, and met the other requirements of the rental exception. In other words, if the "per use" payment is fair market value, we will not require a separate payment arrangement for use of the equipment on patients referred by the physician-owner. *In determining whether the initial "per use" payment is at "fair market value," we will generally look to the price a hospital would pay to rent the equipment from a company that did not have any physician ownership or investment (and thus was not in a position to generate referrals or other business—DHS or otherwise—for the hospital) in an arm's-length transaction. In some cases, all the available comparables or market values may involve transactions between entities that are in a position to refer or generate other business. In such situations, we would look to alternative valuation methodologies, including, but not limited to, cost plus reasonable rate of return on investment on leases of comparable medical equipment from disinterested lessors.* (The definition of fair market value is discussed in more detail in section VII.B of this preamble.)[3]

---

3   66 *F.R.* 876-77, emphasis added.

Passage 2: Discussion of Lithotripsy as a Hospital-Based Service

The second passage also involved lithotripsy arrangements, but addressed the issue of whether they should be included as a DHS:

> *Because the prevalence of physician ownership of lithotriptors may distort pricing in the marketplace, we believe valuation methods that look to the prices charged by persons not in a position to refer to the hospital or that consider acquisition cost and rate of return are especially appropriate.* We also are aware that some manufacturers of lithotriptors lease the machines to urologists on a "per use" basis with the urologists, in turn, leasing the lithotriptors to hospitals on a "per use" basis. In these circumstances, any disparity in the "per use" fee charged by the manufacturer to the urologists and the "per use" fee charged in turn by urologists to the hospital would call into question whether both sets of fees could be fair market value.[4]

Passage 3: Commentary on the Definition of FMV Under Stark

The final passage from the Phase I regulations includes CMS' commentary on the definition of FMV as used throughout Stark:

> Response: To establish the fair market value (and general market value) of a transaction that involves compensation paid for assets or services, we intend to accept any method that is commercially reasonable and provides us with evidence that the compensation is comparable to *what is ordinarily paid for an item or service in the location at issue, by parties in arm's-length transactions who are not in a position to refer to one another.* (As discussed in section V of this preamble, in most instances the fair market value standard is further modified by language that precludes taking into account the "volume or value" of referrals, and, in some cases, other business generated by the referring physician. *Depending on the circumstances, the "volume or value" restriction will preclude reliance on comparables that involve entities and physicians in a position to refer or generate business.*) The amount of documentation that will be sufficient to confirm fair market value (and general market value) will vary depending on the circumstances in any given case; that is, there is no rule of thumb that will suffice for all situations. The burden of establishing the "fairness" of an agreement rests with the parties involved in the agreement. Depending on the circumstances, parties may want to consider obtaining good faith, written assurances as to fair market value from the party paying or receiving the compensation, although such written assurances are not determinative.

---

4   66 *F.R.* 941, emphasis added.

For example, a commercially reasonable method of establishing fair market value (and general market value) for the rental of office space can include providing us with a list of comparables. We would also find acceptable an appraisal that the parties have received from a qualified independent expert. Although some transactions are not subject to public scrutiny, we believe generally that there should be sufficient documentation of similar public transactions that the parties can use as a basis of comparison. In regions with inadequate direct comparables, such as rural areas, a reasonable alternative may involve comparing institutions or entities located in different, but similar, areas where property is zoned for similar use. For example, a hospital affiliated with a university in one part of the country could be comparable to other hospitals affiliated with universities that are located in similar types of communities. *In other cases, all the comparables or market values may involve transactions between entities that are in a position to refer or generate other business. For example, in some markets, physician-owned equipment lessors have driven out competitive third-party lessors of similar equipment. In such situations, we would look to alternative valuation methodologies, including, but not limited to, cost plus reasonable rate of return on investment on leases of comparable medical equipment from disinterested lessors.*[5]

2.2 Stark Phase II Commentary

Phase II of the Stark regulations provided another passage that addressed the issue of market comparables between parties in a position to refer. The passage was included in CMS' commentary on the definition of FMV:

Response: We appreciate the commenter's desire for clear "bright line" guidance. However, the statute covers such a wide range of potential transactions that it is not possible to verify and list appropriate benchmarks or objective measures for each. Moreover, the definition of "fair market value" in the statute and regulation is qualified in ways that do not necessarily comport with the usage of the term in standard valuation techniques and methodologies. *For example, the methodology must exclude valuations where the parties to the transactions are at arm's length but in a position to refer to one another.* In addition, the definition itself differs depending on the type of transaction: leases or rentals of space and equipment cannot take into account the intended use of the rented item; and in cases where the lessor is in a position to refer to the lessee, the valuation cannot be adjusted or reflect the value of proximity or convenience to the lessor. Our Phase I discussion made clear that we will consider a range of methods of determining fair market value and that the appropriate method will depend on the nature of the transaction, its location, and other factors.[6]

---

5   66 *F.R.* 944, emphasis added.
6   69 *F.R.* 16107, emphasis added.

3.0 The Scope of the Prohibition

Having reviewed the relevant passages from the Stark regulations, the next task is to examine the scope of their application to appraisals prepared for purposes of healthcare regulatory compliance.

3.1 Application to the Scope of Work in Healthcare-Related Appraisals

The first key takeaway from review of the passages from the Stark regulations is that an appraisal prepared for healthcare regulatory compliance purposes needs to address the issue of the prohibition. The regulators use language that is not optional in discussing the restriction in the Phase II regulations: "the methodology must exclude valuations where the parties to the transactions are at arm's length but in a position to refer to one another." The imperative statement of the prohibition—"must exclude"—is an important point. Some marketplace participants interpreted the Phase I passages as indicating CMS' preferences, rather than a direct proscription. Since the healthcare regulatory definition of FMV is the ultimate standard of value for the assignment, the appraisal scope of work should be developed accordingly. Not following the prohibition represents a failure to understand the intended use and purpose of the valuation assignment.

Appraisers should also be aware that the Office of Inspector General (OIG) of the Department of Health and Human Services (HHS) has taken a position similar to Stark on the issue of market data from parties in a position to refer. In its 2005 Supplemental Compliance Program Guidance for Hospitals, the OIG linked FMV with the idea of arm's-length transactions.[7] It also cautioned hospitals on the use of market data from referral-related parties.

> Is the determination of fair market value based upon a reasonable methodology that is uniformly applied and properly documented? If fair market value is based on comparables, the hospital should ensure that the market rate for the comparable services is not distorted (e.g., the market for ancillary services may be distorted if all providers of the service are controlled by physicians).[8]

Thus, regulators view the use of market data from referral-related parties as not applicable for both Stark and anti-kickback statute compliance. Failure to acknowledge and address this issue in a healthcare valuation can put a client at risk for noncompliance with both sets of regulations.

---

7   70 F.R. 4866-67.
8   70 F.R. 4867.

3.2 Application to All Arrangements or Just Leases?

The next question to address is whether the prohibition should be understood broadly to include all transactions and arrangements that are subject to Stark or just certain ones, specifically those involving equipment or space leases. As noted in the introduction, some have interpreted the restriction narrowly to apply only to the lease exception under Stark. This opinion is based on the fact that the exclusion was first discussed in the context of leases in the Phase I commentary. Under this narrow interpretation, the prohibition does not apply to all of the other types of transactions and compensation arrangements that fall under the purview of Stark. Moreover, under this narrow interpretation, market data from parties in a position to refer can be used to establish FMV in physician practice acquisitions, physician employment, medical directorships, call coverage, and the like.

There are three difficulties, however, with this interpretation. The first is that the prohibition is included not only in a discussion of leases, but also in the commentary on the definition of FMV. The prohibition is stated, moreover, in general or categorical terms in both the Phase I and II commentary:

> To establish the fair market value (and general market value) of a transaction that involves compensation paid for assets or services, we intend to accept any method that is commercially reasonable and provides us with evidence that the compensation is comparable to what is ordinarily paid for an item or service in the location at issue, by parties in arm's-length transactions who are not in a position to refer to one another.[9]

> Moreover, the definition of "fair market value" in the statute and regulation is qualified in ways that do not necessarily comport with the usage of the term in standard valuation techniques and methodologies. For example, the methodology must exclude valuations where the parties to the transactions are at arm's length but in a position to refer to one another.[10]

These statements clearly are not tied to leases. Indeed, the Phase II (second) passage is rather direct and is stated in general terms relative to the definition of FMV and not to a specific exception.

Second, there is a logical difficulty with the narrow interpretation: Why would the prohibition apply only to leases and not to all transactions between parties in a position to refer? The fundamental regulatory analysis—that the parties are not at arm's

---

9   66 *F.R.* 944.
10 69 *F.R.* 16107, emphasis added.

length because of referral relationships—applies to all forms of arrangements. There is nothing unique in the nature of leases that makes them not at arm's length for purposes of that arrangement as compared to others. It the existence of the referral relationship between the parties that causes their independence to be questioned, not the type of arrangement. There is no logical or analytical reason why the prohibition would not extend to all types of transactions.

The third difficulty is that the OIG is focused on this issue and makes no apparent distinction between leases and other types of arrangements in discussing its concern with the use of market data. While CMS and the OIG can be distinguished with respect to Stark and AKS compliance, respectively, the critical point is that the OIG has adopted the logic of Stark. Parties with referral relationships are not at arm's length. Thus, market data from such parties do not reflect pricing based on independent negotiations. The enforcement wing of CMS has adopted the broad interpretation based on the logic of the referral relationship, not the characteristics of a particular arrangement.

In summary, it is highly difficult to maintain the limited view of the prohibition when looking at all the relevant commentary in Stark, the logic of the prohibition relative to a referral relationship, and the adoption of the broad interpretation by the OIG.

3.3 Application to the Use of Published Survey Data

One puzzling question is whether the prohibition precludes the use of independently published physician compensation survey data in healthcare appraisals. Data from arrangements between parties in a position to refer is included in nearly all of these surveys. The general compensation surveys include physicians who are employed by hospitals/health systems. Historically, the majority of respondents in some of these surveys have come from hospital-physician arrangements. In recent years, moreover, two of the major surveys—those published by MGMA and AMGA—have changed such that the majority of responding physicians come from hospital/health system practices. Prior to that, the majority of physicians were from physician-owned groups. As a result, nearly all the published physician compensation surveys are predominantly composed of physicians from hospital-owned practices.[11]

The reason that the use of these surveys is an issue is that the Stark regulations recommend their use in establishing FMV. Indeed, CMS developed an hourly rate method that could be used for Stark compliance purposes in the Phase II regulations. It named specific surveys that included a mixture of independent and nonindependent

---

11   See Chapter 38, "Comparing the Surveys to the Physician Marketplace: Implications for Valuation Analysis," for more discussion of this issue.

arrangements, even those where the majority of respondents have historically come from referral relationships.[12] CMS abandoned this method in the Phase III regulations, but recommended the use of independently published surveys as a prudent practice.[13] Thus, the Stark regulations recommend use of data that fails its own standard. This logical inconsistency has been perplexing to many in the industry. What is not clear is whether CMS was aware of the fact that such a significant portion of the respondents to the surveys were from arrangements between parties in a position to refer.

To add to the perplexing nature of abiding by the Stark restriction, many appraisers have found that some surveys in which the majority of respondents—or even all of them—come from referral-based relationships report compensation values that are less than those based on independent data or on other valuation methods that do not include such data. In these cases, use of the data from parties in a position to refer would actually lower the FMV conclusion. An example of the phenomenon is found in medical directorship valuations. Data from Integrated Healthcare Strategies' *Medical Director Survey* is nearly all from hospital-physician medical directorships. The hourly rates from this survey, however, are frequently less, at a material level, than rates derived by using the general compensation surveys and 2,000 or 2,080 hours per year. Rather than inflating FMV, use of this data deflates it. Such outcomes perplex appraisers who are conscientious about healthcare regulatory compliance.

Some have tried to make sense of the logical inconsistency by interpreting Stark's guidance to be that independent surveys can be used as long as the data is mixed between independent and nonindependent sources. Surveys where essentially all the data is from parties in a position to refer, on the other hand, should not be used. This approach allows the use of many of the general compensation surveys, but prohibits use of data from some of the specialized medical director or call coverage surveys, where nearly all the reporting transactions are between doctors and hospitals.

Another potential interpretation is that CMS is primarily focused on the way in which data is gathered, not so much on the characteristics of that data. In the Phase I Stark regulations, CMS favored independently published surveys, while cautioning against the use of internally generated surveys:

> However, while internally generated surveys can be appropriate as a method of establishing fair market value in some circumstances, due to their susceptibility to manipulation and absent independent verification, such surveys do not have strong

---

12   69 *F.R.* 16128.
13   72 *F.R.* 51015.

evidentiary value and, therefore, may be subject to more intensive scrutiny than an independent survey.[14]

Market surveys prepared specifically for a particular arrangement could potentially be based on selective data gathering or cherry-picking of market comparables to yield a desired outcome. The major independently published surveys, however, would not generally reflect this kind of deliberate bias in the gathering of data.[15]

Still others have attempted to make sense of the commentary on survey use by noting that the data includes hundreds or thousands of data points. They reason that large data sets may marginalize those data points when referrals were taken into account because it is unlikely that all hospital-employment deals include payments for referrals. In other words, under this view, the large number of respondents in the surveys weeds out any material impact of tainted data. No evidence of this supposition, however, is known to exist.

In thinking through a response to this logical inconsistency in Stark, one might make a case for excluding all data from hospital-affiliated physicians. Doing so would essentially preclude use of most of the surveys, since only one or two allow users to select data based on practice ownership characteristics. It also would limit the number of market data points used. Two issues arise, however, in thinking about such an endeavor. The first is whether there would be significant differences in market compensation from such narrowing of the survey data.[16] There may be no material difference in the compensation ranges or rates reported. Further analysis is needed on this issue, however. The second issue is that excluding the hospital-affiliated physicians would significantly limit the number of respondents for most specialties, resulting in a much smaller data set to use for market comparables. A potential solution is to analyze the data from hospital- and physician-owned practices and exclude data that appears to indicate a systematic bias toward higher compensation for hospital-employed physicians. When no such bias seems to be present, one can use the survey data. To the extent that such exclusion severely limits the size of the data set, an appraiser should complete other valuation methods and/or place less weight on the survey-based method in the valuation synthesis process.

---

14   66 *F.R.* 945.

15   Of course, one can cherry-pick from survey data, but that is a different issue from how the market data was compiled.

16   Preliminary research completed by the editors indicates higher compensation rates can be observed for hospital-employed physicians in various specialties. More data gathering and analysis, however, need to be completed on this topic before any formal conclusions can be presented. For example, the hospital-owned practices could come from higher reimbursement markets, resulting in higher compensation levels for physicians in those markets.

In summary, the use of surveys presents a conundrum for appraisers seeking a coherent and logically consistent approach to the use of market data under Stark. Survey data including respondents in a position to refer should logically be excluded from use in establishing FMV for healthcare regulatory purposes. Since Stark recommends use of surveys as a prudent practice, however, it is difficult to exclude their use on compliance grounds. In practice, use of the independently published general compensation surveys is nearly universal, while many practitioners exclude the more specialized surveys when the nature of the arrangements necessarily entails parties in a position to refer.

4.0 Is the Prohibition a Departure From Standard Appraisal Methodology?

Many appraisers think that the Stark prohibition is an exception to the standard appraisal application of the market approach. Indeed, CMS deemed the exclusion as a departure from standard valuation methods, as shown in the Phase II passage.[17] It can be argued, however, that the restriction is not necessarily such a departure. The definition of FMV in the *International Glossary of Business Valuation Terms* requires the value for buyer and seller who are at arm's length:

> The price, expressed in terms of cash equivalents, at which property would change hands between a hypothetical willing and able buyer and a hypothetical willing and able seller, acting *at arm's length* in an open and unrestricted market, when neither is under compulsion to buy or sell and when both have reasonable knowledge of the relevant facts. (emphasis added)

The question for the professional appraiser is whether the fundamental economics of referral-related parties allow them to be, in fact, at arm's length from a purely financial perspective, apart from the regulatory analysis. How much impact does the referral relationship between healthcare providers have on their other dealings? Can they be thought of as financially independent?

One way to think about this question is to look at other types of parties who have financial relationships and how their transactions would be used or not used for purposes of the market approach in other valuation contexts. If asked about the use of market data from transactions between family members, related parties, affiliated or parent-subsidiary companies, would most appraisers exclude, discount, treat cautiously, or exclude the use of such data as part of the market approach? The answer, most likely, is yes. These types of related parties would not be considered to be at arm's length, and, therefore, any financial arrangements would not be viewed as independent. As a result,

---

17   *69 F.R. 16107.*

they would not be consistent with the appraisal definition of FMV. While all appraisers may not follow this analysis to its logical conclusion and exclude such data, most appraisers, at minimum, would treat such data with caution and would not summarily rely on it without further analysis and consideration.

Many appraisers seem to believe that when one excludes market data from referral-related parties, it is based on the suspicion that the transaction is tainted with payments for the volume or value of referrals. They question the idea of excluding all such data because it is inconceivable that such payments are being perpetrated on a wide scale in the healthcare marketplace. The exclusion, however, need not imply that the data includes hidden payments for referrals. Rather, the exclusion is a prudent move based two factors: 1) the lack of financial independence between the parties; and 2) the idea that parties with other financial relationships may not negotiate in a way in which independent parties would negotiate. In other words, the referral relationship creates *uncertainty* with regard to the value assigned to the transaction by the parties. To account for the uncertainty, the appraiser sets aside the data in favor of other data without this uncertainty and/or in favor of other valuation methods that bypass the uncertainty altogether.

When an appraiser concludes that the prohibition is a departure from standard appraisal methodology and practice, the appropriate response is to follow the prohibition as a jurisdictional exception. Limitations placed on the appraiser based on regulatory requirements are properly characterized as jurisdictional exceptions under all the appraisal standards for business valuations. For a complete discussion of using jurisdictional exceptions, see Chapter 7, "Complying With the Healthcare Definition of FMV in Appraisal Practice."

5.0 Implications for CV Practice

Since nearly all valuation engagements in healthcare are prepared for regulatory compliance purposes, appraisers need to address the Stark prohibition in CV assignments. The following is a summary of the key points of this chapter and how an appraiser can address the prohibition in the scope of work:

1. Failure to address the restriction represents a failure to account for the intended use and purpose of the appraisal and does not meet the client's needs. Appraisers who ignore the prohibition do so at their own risk and potential peril and that of their clients. In addition, failure to address the issue indicates a lack of understanding about regulatory matters and, thus, a lack of professional expertise in healthcare valuation.

2. Due to its importance, the issue should be discussed in the report. The appraiser should disclose interpretations, analysis, and positions taken relative to the prohibition. Any regulatory guidance given by legal counsel on the issue likewise should be disclosed.

3. Taking the position that the prohibition is related to a narrow set of compensation arrangements, such as leases, is very difficult to sustain in light of the totality of regulatory guidance and a logic test of the key aspects of the prohibition. If an appraiser takes that position, however, it is highly advisable that he or she discuss it with the client and its legal counsel. A client may not wish to rely on a report that takes this interpretation. At the same time, if a client's legal counsel directs the appraiser to use the narrow interpretation and the appraiser does, disclosing this regulatory guidance from the client's legal counsel would be prudent. To use a military analogy, the narrow interpretation represents the "low ground" from a tactical position standpoint.

4. Use of survey data that includes data from parties in a position to refer presents a challenge for applying the Stark definition of FMV on a logically consistent basis. Stark prohibits use of data from referral-related parties, but then recommends the use of the surveys, which are filled with such data. Many appraisers follow the practice of using general surveys but not relying on those in which nearly all the data comes from arrangements involving parties in a position to refer. Comparing data from independent arrangements with those of nonindependent arrangements is another way to use survey data with caution and attention to the prohibition. The minimum practice for using survey-based data is not to use it without study and analysis relative to the possibility of tainted or biased data. In other words, look before you leap!

5. While the Stark regulations claim the exclusion of market comparables from parties in a position to refer is a departure from standard valuation methodology, this restriction may not be that great a deviation. The appraisal definition of FMV presumes arm's-length parties. Financial relationships outside a transaction or arrangement mitigate the independence of parties with regard to that transaction. Thus, an analysis based on the traditional definition of FMV within the appraisal profession can also call for excluding or not relying on market data from parties in a position to refer.

6. If the appraiser concludes that the prohibition is a departure from the scope of work that the appraiser otherwise would follow for the assignment, however, following the exclusion should be disclosed in the report as a jurisdictional

exception. Disagreeing with healthcare regulators about the exclusion is not a justification for ignoring the restriction in appraisal work prepared for healthcare regulatory compliance. The appraisal profession has an established tool for addressing legal or regulatory issues that require deviations from standard appraisal methodology. They are called jurisdictional exceptions and are discussed in all the professional standards for business valuation.

7. Appraisers should consult with the client and its legal counsel about the Stark prohibition as part of the scope of the engagement. The issue is too critical to most assignments to be omitted from the discussion surrounding the appraisal assignment.

Chapter 9. BV, CV, and the Relationship Between Fair Market Value and Commercial Reasonableness

CONTENTS

Chapter 9. BV, CV, and the Relationship Between Fair Market Value and Commercial Reasonableness

By Mark O. Dietrich, CPA/ABV

1.0 Introduction

The dual requirement that transactions subject to regulatory review be both at fair market value and commercially reasonable has become an increasingly important issue in both business and compensation valuations. There is much diversity in thought and practice around the issue of what is commercially reasonable, how to assess it, and who should, in fact, do the assessing. It seems that much of this diversity is caused by the failure of valuation analysts, legal counsel, and parties to the transaction to consider the meaning of the term "fair market value," in the first instance, before addressing the phrases "a sensible, prudent business agreement, from the perspective of the particular parties involved, even in the absence of any potential referrals"[1] and "an arrangement will be considered 'commercially reasonable' in the absence of referrals if the arrangement would make commercial sense if entered into by a reasonable entity of similar type and size and a reasonable physician of similar scope and specialty, even if there were no potential designated health services (DHS) referrals."[2]

Commercial reasonableness is a longstanding concept in contract law and not unique to the healthcare arena. In the context of Stark, many healthcare marketplace participants view this concept as an inquiry beyond the parameters of fair market value, perhaps even begging the question of the parties' intent in entering into the transaction. Appraisers would of necessity need to limit themselves to what is financially reasonable and perhaps, given the requisite skill set, what is operationally reasonable for a given

---

1   63 *F.R.* 1700 (Jan. 9, 1998).
2   69 *F.R.* 16054, 16093 (March 26, 2004).

healthcare enterprise when buyer and seller have "reasonable knowledge of relevant facts." It is hard to distinguish that reasonable knowledge from "commercially reasonable," which is explored throughout this chapter. Thus, many of the steps thought to be a function of a commercial reasonableness evaluation are already integral to the determination of fair market value.

Business valuation (BV) and compensation valuation (CV) go hand in hand in many of the transactions that dominate the current consolidation phase in the healthcare industry because many practices are purchased and then the purchasing hospital or system employs the physicians. In addition, the focus on the independent investor test[3] in determining reasonable compensation under Section 162 of the Internal Revenue Code—a code section tax-exempt organizations must adhere to and that requires all compensation be ordinary and necessary—generally precludes separating BV, CV, and related tax law and regulations.[4] Although discussed in detail in Chapter 12, the independent investor test focuses on whether return on assets or equity is being paid out as compensation. This is the very thing that Section 501(c)(3) precludes: the inurement or the unjust provision of any part of the tax-exempt organization's income or assets to a private party.

2.0 Fair Market Value Defined

To evaluate the need to assess commercial reasonableness, one first has to measure fair market value. To highlight this fact in the regulatory definition of fair market value, the quote below is taken from *United States of America v. Joseph Campbell, M.D.*, a case which arose out of the "community cardiologist" program at the University of Medicine and Dentistry of New Jersey (UMDNJ), where a series of no-show jobs with significant stipends were created to induce (as the court determined) referrals to the UMDNJ cardiology service line. Here, the hypothetical seller of services knew he was being paid to do nothing, which the court found failed the fair market value test.

> As the United States notes, even if Defendant Campbell believed that he was entering a legitimate employment contract he did not have to meet the requirements of that contract during his "employment." Thus, the $70,000 payment he received for the [ten] months that he held the title of Clinical Assistant Professor [CAP] with UMDNJ, *could not be considered "commercially reasonable" or the "fair market value of the services."* (Pl.'s Br. 18-19.) *Defendant Campbell relies on an expert report that supports the argument that his salary as a CAP at UMDNJ was for fair market value.* (Def.'s Opp. to Pl.

---

3 See Chapter 12 of this Guide
4 See the discussion of the *Derby* case in Chapter 12, "Reasonable Compensation for Tax Purposes."

---

1). *However, it is not just a matter of whether the salary of $75,000 annually was unreasonable for an employee who works and fulfills the obligations of a CAP. If there was no requirement to actually perform the duties of a CAP then the compensation could not be the fair market value for those services, and thus would serve some other purpose, such as compensation for patient referrals.* (emphasis added)

A determination of fair market value is not merely assigning a number to a transaction. It involves the appraiser simultaneously acting as both hypothetical buyer and seller and determining what price would be reached for the specific practice or services agreement at issue. The most commonly accepted definitions of fair market value include the one contained in Internal Revenue Service Revenue Ruling 59-60, a 1959 ruling that is the underpinning of valuation practice:

> The price at which the property would change hands between a willing buyer and a willing seller when the former is not under any compulsion to buy and the latter is not under any compulsion to sell, both parties having reasonable knowledge of relevant facts.

The ruling[5] goes on to state:

> In the final analysis, goodwill is based upon earning capacity. The presence of goodwill and its value, therefore, rests upon the excess of net earnings over and above a fair return on the net tangible assets.[6]

The other most commonly accepted definition is from the *International Glossary of Business Valuation Terms*, adopted by the various associations engaged in valuation and appraisal:

> The price, expressed in terms of cash equivalents, at which property would change hands between a hypothetical willing and able buyer and a hypothetical willing and able seller, acting at arm's length in an open and unrestricted market, when neither is under compulsion to buy or sell and when both have reasonable knowledge of the relevant facts.[7]

It is universally accepted, if sometimes conveniently ignored, that the term "fair market value" contemplates a financial buyer. This concept of the financial buyer flows from the stock market, where investors are deemed to be risk-averse and seek diversity in

---

5   Interesting—and somewhat curious—given the peculiar reliance of some in healthcare business valuation exclusively on the cost approach to value intangibles.
6   Revenue Ruling 59-60.
7   *International Glossary of Business Valuation Terms.*

their investments to minimize exposure to any one stock or business.[8] Here are some examples that are meaningful to the issue at hand:

> Financial Buyer: Often thought as being the same as the hypothetical buyer, the financial buyer typically comes to the transaction table with a perceived ability to complete the purchase only expecting financial returns not impacted by any synergies or other advantages that may exist as a result of the transaction. Financial performance expectations of the financial buyer are most typically embodied by rates of return that investors may expect by investments in publicly held corporations. Such investments in public companies are typically open to any investor with the resources to make the equity purchase.[9]

> A financial buyer will pay no more for a company than that which can be supported by the cash flow. A *strategic buyer* purchases in order to benefit from financial, operational, or market synergies to be derived from the combination of the purchase with currently owned assets.[10] (emphasis added)

Relating the concept of the financial buyer of fair market value to CV practice requires a greater focus on the principle of substitution—not paying more than an alternative of equal utility—discussed elsewhere in the guide, another key underpinning of fair market value. It emphasizes "financial returns not impacted by any synergies or other advantages that may exist as a result of the transaction."

Finally, there seems to be a failure among many to correlate the requirement of fair market value that "both parties hav[e] reasonable knowledge of relevant facts" with "fair market value" generated by valuation models. For example, one can determine a fair market rate for medical director services. If only one such individual is required based on the operational assessment that a hypothetical purchaser of such services would be expected to undertake and two are hired at the same "fair market value" rate, the transaction does meet a fair market value standard because any purchaser with "reasonable knowledge of relevant facts" would not pay twice for the same services! It is not necessary to reach a separate commercial reasonableness evaluation, although it takes you to the same place. It would seem that an operational assessment of need is a condition precedent for paying for a fair market value opinion in any event.

---

8   If the reader finds that universality expansive, a Google search of "fair market value" and "financial buyer" will turn up thousands of links relating the two.

9   *The CPA's Role in Buying and Selling a Business*, AICPA.

10 *A Primer on Business Valuation*, Fannon Valuation Group.

2.1 Stark Modifications

The Stark regulations' clarification of fair market value is well-known, but repeated here for the sake of completeness. Note that the key clarification in the definition of market value is that it not consider referrals, precisely the same requirement in commercial reasonableness.

> Fair market value means the value in arm's-length transactions consistent with general market value. "General market value" means the price that an asset would bring as the result of bona fide bargaining between well-informed buyers and sellers who are not otherwise in a position to generate business for the other party; or the compensation that would be included in a service agreement as a result of bona fide bargaining between well-informed parties to the agreement who are not otherwise in a position to generate business for the other party, on the date of acquisition or at the time of the service agreement. Usually the fair market price is the price at which bona fide sales have been consummated for assets of like type, quality, and quantity in a particular market at the time of acquisition … (420 CFR 411.351)

> Moreover, the definition of "fair market value" in the statute and regulation is qualified in ways that do not necessarily comport with the usage of the term in standard valuation techniques and methodologies. For example, the methodology must exclude valuations where the parties to the transactions are at arm's length but in a position to refer to one another. (69 *F.R.* 16053)

Of course, the Stark regulations do not adopt the Internal Revenue regulations specifically, but the term "fair market value" would have no context in appraisal practice or in the Stark law absent those regulations.[11] For example, the Stark regulations use the phrase "arm's-length transactions," a phrase virtually identical to that used in the *International Glossary of Business Valuation Terms'* definition of parties "acting at arm's length." Although the phrase does not appear in the commonly cited definition of fair market value taken from Rev. Rul. 59-60, it *does* appear later in that ruling, to wit "(g) Sales of stock of a closely held corporation should be carefully investigated to determine whether they represent transactions at arm's length." Here, again, one can readily see the connection between this 1959 ruling and the Stark regulations, whether intentional or not. The IRS is concerned that parties not at arm's length would not reach fair market value, and the Stark regulations are concerned with that as well.

---

11 For more discussion on the view of healthcare regulators toward adoption of IRS valuation requirements, see Chapter 7, "Complying With the Healthcare Definition of FMV in Appraisal Practice."

Although it is not discussed in the Stark regulations, "a sensible, prudent business agreement" conveys the same standard as "reasonable knowledge of the relevant facts," given that a transaction must meet both a fair market value and commercial reasonableness standard.

Thus, the first step in the determination of whether an agreement is commercially reasonable must of necessity be as follows: "Is the transaction value consistent with fair market value?" Any transaction that fails to be consistent with fair market value is per se commercially unreasonable. If a transaction meets a fair market value standard, it may be commercially unreasonable for reasons other than failure to meet that standard. However, to reiterate, the standard definitions of fair market value already address many of the issues thought to require a commercial reasonableness assessment.

3.0 Commercial Transactions

It is necessary to understand the concept of commercial transactions that are reasonable at the outset, before beginning to assess the fair market value of healthcare transactions, because commercial reasonableness is, in fact, inherent in measuring fair market value to begin with, not a separate undertaking. Because the requirement of a financial buyer is integral to fair market value, a simple series of examples looking at a common financial transaction is presented.

3.1 Example 1

A bank customer invests $10,000 in a certificate of deposit (CD) with a 10-year term and 3% interest. Each year, the customer expects to receive $300 of interest, or have it added to the CD balance, and at the end of the 10 years, to receive back his $10,000 plus the accumulated interest, if left on deposit. The value of the transaction under the income approach, assuming that 3% interest is the market rate for a 10-year CD, is $10,000.

Compare this example of a commercially reasonable transaction between a bank and a customer with the following transaction between a hospital and a physician.

3.2 Example 2

A hospital desires to acquire the practice of a physician located in the community but primarily associated with a competing institution. The hospital pays the physician for the tangible assets in the practice and also pays $75,000 for the trained nonphysician workforce and $100,000 for the physician workforce. The value of the practice under the income approach based on the post-transaction compensation paid to the physician is negative, i.e., the hospital will lose money.

If the physician leaves, the hospital does not recover the $100,000 physician workforce payment.

Here is the analogous situation for the bank customer.

3.3 Example 3

A bank customer invests $10,000 in a certificate of deposit with a 10-year term and 3% interest. The customer does not expect to receive $300 of interest annually, or have it added to the CD balance, and at the end of the 10 years, does not expect to receive back his $10,000. Of course, no customer with reasonable knowledge of the relevant facts of this particular CD would engage in this transaction.

It seems that Example 3 is not a commercially reasonable transaction for the customer. Example 2 is not commercially reasonable for the hospital because for the transaction to make commercial sense, the hospital would have to expect income from some source other than the physician practice's own billings and collections for services to avoid the losses. This violates the regulations' requirement that the arrangement be "commercially reasonable" in the absence of referrals; it also clearly fails to meet the financial buyer required by the fair market value standard.

It is hard to envision in the ordinary[12] course that a transaction based upon an expectation of losing money is commercially reasonable for the hospital or any entity or individual, for that matter.

4.0 Physician Workforce, Recruitment, and Retention

One of the arguments made for the commercial reasonableness of payments for the physician workforce followed by employment of the physician(s) at the same level or at levels higher than historical compensation is that a practice must be re-created, and in that process the hospital would incur costs for, among other things, recruiting and training. Leaving aside for the moment the perhaps threshold question of why a hospital would need to re-create the practice of a physician who is 1) already on its staff; and/or 2) already in its service area—something that seems to appear unreasonable on its face—consider the following regulatory standards for payments to physicians for recruitment and retention.

---

12 There are clearly exceptions, notably rural areas, safety net hospitals with poor payer mix, EMTALA-driven considerations, and others.

Phase III of the Stark regulations contains very specific rules for determining when the general prohibition against recruitment payments does not apply. One of these is a ZIP code analysis, where the physician must relocate his or her practice to the service area from which the hospital draws 75% of its inpatients.[13] Of course, if the physician is already in that service area, the exception would not apply because the regulations provide—with limited exceptions—that any physician recruited must be from *outside* the hospital's service area. As the preamble noted, even for "inactive" physicians, recruitment payments were not permitted.

> This language makes clear that the recruited physician cannot already be a member of the hospital's medical staff. We believe that the relocation requirement is insufficient to establish that a physician who is already a member of the hospital's active staff needs an incentive to move his or her practice. We are not persuaded that permitting recruitment of physicians who are not on a hospital's "active" medical staff, but who hold some type of medical staff privileges (for example, courtesy privileges), poses no risk of program or patient abuse. Moreover, defining "active" privileges is difficult, as many hospitals use different terminology to refer to different types of medical staff privileges."[14]

Given that the Stark regulations specifically preclude recruitment payments to physicians in the hospital service area, it is difficult to see how it is commercially reasonable to base a payment for the physician workforce on the cost to recruit the physician. What could be clearer than "we believe that the relocation requirement is insufficient to establish that a physician who is already a member of the hospital's active staff needs an incentive to move his or her practice?"[15] Certainly, the payment to a physician of a "trained workforce value" for himself or herself cannot rationally be distinguished from a recruitment or retention payment.

4.1 Tax-Exemption Issues Related to Commercial Reasonableness of Post-Transaction Compensation

Since a variety of citations to IRS CPE texts[16] and the Friendly Hills private letter ruling support the notion that it is appropriate to use the cost approach to value workforce in place, they are discussed here in the overall context of fair market value (the condition precedent) and commercial reasonableness. By extension, it seems, since IRS pronouncements form much of the basis for valuation practice and the definition of fair market value, sole reliance on the cost approach must represent fair market value and

---

13   With some limited modifications for ZIP code selection. 42 C.F.R. § 411.357(e)(2).
14   *72 F.R.* 171, Sept. 5, 2007.
15   Ibid.
16   Exempt Organization Continuing Education Program texts.

be commercially reasonable. These citations do not adequately consider the fact that the CPE texts clearly state that the cost approach is used to *allocate* the value determined under the income approach[17] (discounted cash flow method) and, critically, that the appraisal in support of the Friendly Hills private letter ruling included a letter from the managing partner of the physician practice that stated the following:

> It has been clearly stated to the partners that, in the past, their compensation reflected not only the value of their medical services, but also the profits attributable to their ownership of the Network; that the latter element will be replaced by a cash payment, which they can invest ... that the Medical Group's income will thereafter be derived from arm's-length contract for medical services; and that these rates will necessarily be significantly lower than the total historical income they have been receiving.[18]

Now, lest there be any doubt, what is stated here—*"The Medical Group's income will thereafter be derived from arms-length contract for medical services; and that these rates will necessarily be significantly lower than the total historical income they have been receiving"*[19]— is in stark contrast to many of the transactions[20] that take place when the physician workforce is paid for and post-transaction, the physicians receive equal or frequently higher income than they historically earned. There is simply no basis whatsoever for believing that the IRS was unaware of the interrelationship between practice valuation and physician compensation. Nor is there any basis for valuations that fail to consider the interrelationship.

Recognizing that many, if not most, dismiss the relationship between tax law and anti-referral law—this notwithstanding the interaction between the OIG Deputy Chief Counsel Thornton and the IRS's T.J. Sullivan at the outset of the hospital-physician consolidation in the early 1990s—consider this statement from the 1996 IRS CPE text:

> Thus, before any value may be assigned to covenants not to compete, it must be determined if it is unrealistic for the seller to have given a covenant the "economic reality" test. This test was first enunciated in *Schulz v. Commissioner*, 294 F.2d 52 (9th Cir. 1961), aff'g 34 T.C. 235 (1960). In this case, the court stated that a covenant "must have some independent basis in fact or some arguable relationship with business

---

17   In fact, the 1996 CPE text on valuation specifically states this: "The value of goodwill can be allocated to specific intangible assets; the value of the latter is limited to the value of the former, as calculated under the income approach."
18   Friendly Hills Appraisal Report.
19   Ibid.
20   Notably purchases of cardiology practices.

reality such that reasonable men, genuinely concerned with their economic future, might bargain for such an agreement."

This seems strikingly similar to an "arrangement [that] would make commercial sense if entered into by a reasonable entity of similar type and size."[21]

5.0 Does the Transaction Make Sense in the Absence of Referrals?

One problem that often confronts appraisers in assessing commercial reasonableness is a lack of actual experience in transaction negotiation and support as well as in the operations of an entity of the type engaged in the transaction, whether as a former employee or as a consultant. The "hypothetical" buyer and seller in the definition of fair market value do not refer to imaginary persons engaged in an imaginary transaction developed by the appraiser. In BV, they refer to investors motivated by income returns—the type of investors one would see in the stock market, from where business appraisers draw the rates of return used to determine value under the income approach and cash flow multiples (typically EBITDA) used to determine value under one method in the market approach. In CV, the buyer and seller are interested in not paying/receiving more than an alternative of equal utility. Because the requirement of "fair market value" is a condition precedent to requiring a commercial reasonableness evaluation, familiarity with real-world financial buyers as well as real-world strategic buyers[22] is invaluable in providing perspective to the appraiser.

A common example to both BV and CV when actual transactions terms are critical to achieving the correct valuation result is the presence and extent of a noncompete agreement given by the seller to the buyer. There is not a generic noncompete that an appraiser can assume for purposes of fair market value—unless that is disclosed in the report as a *hypothetical* condition. The real value of a noncompete depends on its terms, including geographic range; whether injunctive relief is available; whether there is a liquidated damages provision; and a host of other factors. An appraiser who has never been engaged in analyzing such terms and translating them to financial values is confronted with a difficult task indeed.

Another difficulty confronting the appraiser is distinguishing when "strategic value" is being used. As defined earlier, "a *strategic buyer* purchases in order to benefit from financial, operational, or market synergies to be derived from the combination of the purchase with currently owned assets." Referrals in the healthcare industry are the

---

21 69 *F.R.* 16054, 16093 (March 26, 2004).
22 Precluded, of course, under the fair market value standard.

primary example of strategic value. Thus, any valuation that assumes a strategic buyer has a very high risk of not being at fair market value and, in turn, being commercially unreasonable because it violates the stated imperative that the price paid not consider "any potential referrals."[23]

Given the prohibition against considering referrals in both the Stark regulations on fair market value and commercial reasonableness, reaching a point where investigation into where a transaction makes "commercial sense if entered into by a reasonable entity of similar type and size and a reasonable physician of similar scope and specialty" would seem to be a comparatively infrequent occurrence. Coverage arrangements for EMTALA or related purposes, maintenance of ER coverage in rural or other difficult-to-recruit areas, or staffing of unprofitable mental health departments are a few examples of where an evaluation beyond fair market value might be required. These can be deemed as "jurisdictional exceptions" to the normal requirements of fair market value, in the same manner that the Stark regulations use "general market value" to modify fair market value. On the other hand, typically profitable service lines such as cardiac care and orthopedics can more easily be addressed in the threshold question of fair market value.

5.1 Accountable Care Organization Transactions: A Different Standard

ACOs are one market change presently (post-2010) driving the consolidation of physician practices, particularly primary care, by hospitals in a pattern not dissimilar to what occurred during the managed care and capitation period of the 1990s. As was the case in the 1990s, changes in the way Medicare pays providers are spurring many buyers, while defensive buying to avoid the need to start an ACO is spurring others. Here, the appraiser should be intimately familiar with the underlying economics of the ACO and what the income opportunities are because that is what the hypothetical buyer of the fair market value standard is seeking. ACO transactions have been granted broad waivers from many of the antireferral regulations because they inherently involve referrals. Even absent those waivers, because of the potential income opportunity from formation and operation of an ACO, the requirement that it be "a sensible, prudent business agreement, from the perspective of the particular parties involved, even in the absence of any potential referrals"[24] would seem to be met for an ACO. The ACO has a legitimate business purpose, to enable it to minimize the risk it assumes by participating in a program CMS believes will reduce Medicare costs.

---

23 Editor's Note: There are some other elements of strategic value, such as a lower cost of capital for a larger entity acquiring a smaller entity, but at least for tax-exempt entities, these run afoul of 501(c)(3)'s anti-inurement requirement.

24 Ibid, 63 *F.R.* 1700.

From an appraisal or valuation standpoint, what distinguishes ACOs is the assumption of risk with respect to the amount that will ultimately be paid for the services it provides. As part of that risk assumption, significant profits can be earned or significant losses incurred,[25] thus creating the potential for "financial buyer" qualification. The fair market buyer or seller *without* "reasonable knowledge of the relevant facts" of those risks will not engage in such an ACO transaction, and it is incumbent upon the appraiser to quantify those risks for valuation purposes as well as to ascertain the parties' knowledge of the risks and rewards for a commercial reasonableness determination. ACOs may well be unique in the current market and regulatory environment in permitting rational, fair market buyers to pay values beyond tangible assets for physician practices.

6.0 Conclusion

The hypothetical buyer and seller are parties engaged in an *actual* transaction, not a hypothetical transaction. In BV, that actual transaction is the purchase/sale of a specific business or business interest, and in CV, it is the purchase/sale of specific services. Explicit in the definition of fair market value is that the transacting parties have reasonable knowledge of relevant facts. Perhaps the key difference in the current diversity of thought between appraising fair market value, where reasonable knowledge of relevant facts is *assumed* by definition, and assessing commercial reasonableness is that, for the latter, some appraisers believe it is the separate assessment of whether the *actual* transacting parties possess that reasonable knowledge.

The assumptions and limiting conditions affecting the appraiser's opinion of fair market value require clear documentation in the report as do the representations made by the client that the appraiser relied on. As the *Campbell* court suggests, however, an opinion of fair market value is of no use when the underlying assumptions are inconsistent with the parties' expectations at the time of the transaction or subsequent behavior. Appraisers need to be cautious about where they draw the line of responsibility between the requirements of fair market value and commercial reasonableness if valuation conclusions are going to meet the jurisdictional rules of fair market value.

---

25 At least in the Example 2 model.

Chapter 10. Commercial Reasonableness: Defining Practical Concepts and Determining Compliance in Healthcare Transactions for Physician Services

CONTENTS

Chapter 10. Commercial Reasonableness: Defining Practical Concepts and Determining Compliance in Healthcare Transactions for Physician Services

By Martin D. Brown, CPA/ABV,
and William Lyle Oelrich Jr., MHA, FACHE, CMPE

1.0 Introduction

Financial relationships between hospitals and physicians must be *both* commercially reasonable and at fair market value to meet certain regulatory requirements. Ensuring compliance with these requirements remains critical because failure to do so could invoke sanctions and penalties related to the Stark Law, the anti-kickback statute, the False Claims Act, and Internal Revenue Service 501(c)(3) status. As such, a thorough understanding of these requirements is necessary to ensure compliance in transactions between hospitals and physicians, as well as other parties with referral relationships within the healthcare environment. While valuators and healthcare entities have refined fair market value assessments over the past several years, the concepts and methodology for determining commercial reasonableness on its own terms has not yet been defined. However, increased government commentary underscores the need to understand and ensure that this requirement is met for all financial arrangements between parties in a position to refer.

In general terms, all business transactions (i.e., including scenarios outside of the healthcare arena) must aid organizations in accomplishing their strategic, operational, and/or financial objectives. For instance, parties at arm's length to a nonhealthcare real estate transaction would not enter into an arrangement in which they would not be awarded some benefit, such as in pricing, operational improvements, accomplishment of strategic objectives, etc. The same logic should apply to financial arrangements between referral-related parties, such as hospitals and physicians. As such, compensation arrangements for physician services, for example, must effectuate a furtherance of business objectives on the part of the healthcare entity entering into the arrangement. In this way, commercial reasonableness assesses the overall arrangement, including qualitative considerations such as strategy and operations, whereas fair market value primarily assesses the financial aspects of the arrangement (i.e., the range of dollars only).

As part of evaluating qualitative matters such as strategic and operational benefits, commercial reasonableness considers the aggregate terms of the overall arrangement and asks the question, "Does this deal make sense?" In other words, an evaluation regarding an arrangement's commercial reasonableness is broad in scope and considers the deal in the aggregate. Thus, fair market value represents a component of determining commercial reasonableness because the range of dollars represents one part of an overall contract, the entirety of which must be assessed to determine whether a transaction is commercially reasonable. Given its broader scope, including assessment of financial factors and qualitative matters (i.e., strategy, operations, etc.), one could say that commercial reasonableness observes an entire contract and represents a critically important and applied assessment to ensure that arrangements between parties in a position to refer within the healthcare environment meet regulatory requirements and thus, avert potential civil and criminal penalties.[1] As such, this chapter will clearly identify key factors that should be assessed and considered to evaluate commercial reasonableness in healthcare transactions thoroughly and practically, rather than assuming such factors to be true, as may be the case in stand-alone fair market value evaluations.

2.0 Regulatory Guidance and Definitions of Commercial Reasonableness

Several key definitions related to the standard of commercial reasonableness in healthcare agreements have been delineated in legislation and by regulatory authorities. In particular, the following definitions summarize the essential meaning of "commercial reasonableness."

The Centers for Medicare & Medicaid Services (CMS) initially defined *commercially reasonable* as:

> An arrangement which appears to be "a sensible, prudent business agreement, from the perspective of the particular parties involved, even in the absence of any potential referrals."[2]

---

1   Editor's note: This is critical. A common error in valuation practice is to treat the valuation of business assets and post-transaction compensation separately and to fail to identify income from the asset purchase that does not violate Stark, AKS, or some other statute or regulation.

2   63 *F.R.* 1700 (Jan. 9, 1998).

This definition is consistent with CMS's subsequent commentary on the Stark Law, which states that:

> An arrangement will be considered *"commercially reasonable"* in the absence of referrals if the arrangement would make commercial sense if entered into by a reasonable entity of similar type and size and a reasonable physician of similar scope and specialty, even if there were no potential designated health services ("DHS") referrals.[3]

Additionally, the Office of Inspector General (OIG) of the United States Department of Health and Human Services (HHS) also provided guidance on the meaning of commercial reasonableness:

> In order to meet the threshold of *commercial reasonableness,* compensation arrangements with physicians should be "reasonable and necessary."[4]

Note: While several definitions and regulatory citations are referenced within this chapter, a complete and thorough overview of this material can be found in the Practice Aid.

With these definitions in mind, the fundamentals for ensuring that an arrangement is commercially reasonable appear to include: (i) a sensible and prudent business agreement; (ii) commercial sense; (iii) parties contracting from a perspective of no referrals; and (iv) reasonable and necessary services.

Given these fundamentals, the standard of commercial reasonableness should be conceived as broad in scope and as requiring assessment into the overall arrangement, including its quantitative and qualitative components. As such, individuals evaluating the commercial reasonableness of proposed arrangements between parties with referral relationships should consider whether the transaction represents a prudent business decision. In other words, legitimate reasons should exist for entering into the arrangement, excluding the potential for referrals. Such reasons may vary depending upon each unique situation, but will likely include consideration of aspects inclusive of economic matters (e.g., financial gains/losses and return on investment over time), strategy (e.g., community access to care, service line development, competition for certain services, and supply/demand of physicians), and operations (e.g., recruitment/ mentoring of physicians, services management, and achievement of quality indicators).

---

3   69 *F.R.* 16093 (March 26, 2004).
4   "OIG Compliance Program for Individual and Small Group Physician Practices," Notice, 65 *F.R.* 59434 (Oct. 5, 2000); OIG Advisory Opinion No. 07-10, Sept. 20, 2007, pg. 6, 10; "OIG Supplemental Compliance Program Guidance for Hospitals," Notice, 70 *F.R.* 4858 (Jan. 31, 2005).

3.0 Guidance From Court Cases Involving Commercial Reasonableness

While assessing the relatively broad concept of commercial reasonableness requires specific fact-based assessments that are unique to each particular arrangement, the associated definitions, regulations, and evaluation criteria of certain key court rulings provide actual examples and further clarification of the concept. Accordingly, critical facts and analyses of two such cases pertaining to commercial reasonableness are outlined in the following sections.

3.1 *United States ex. rel., Kaczmarczyk v. SCCI Hospital Ventures*

The first case providing clarification involves a qui tam action in which the fair market value and commercial reasonableness of compensation paid to physician medical directors by a hospital in Texas were at issue.[5] In this matter, the United States' experts suggested a more specific test to determine whether an arrangement meets the threshold of commercial reasonableness. This test was based on two criteria: (1) the agreement is essential to the functioning of the hospital; and (2) sound business reasons exist for payment to referring physicians. To address these requirements, the government's experts relied on several factors that collectively spoke to the hospital facility, its current resources, and the oversight protocols of the hospital for assessing such arrangements.[6] In this particular instance, the government argued that: (i) the hospital's low patient census did not warrant numerous medical directors; (ii) physicians should not have been paid for certain duties that overlapped with the medical staff bylaws; (iii) the hospital needed to have coordinated protocols across its campuses to reduce waste; and (iv) the hospital did not provide adequate oversight and enforcement in terms of compliance efforts.[7] While the parties eventually entered into a settlement agreement in 2004, guidance provided in the government's arguments illustrated key factors that may lead to its determination when an arrangement is commercially *un*reasonable.[8]

3.2 *United States v. Campbell*

A second case that provides further insight into applying the commercial reasonableness threshold was decided in 2011 and involves the compensation paid to a physician at a teaching hospital in New Jersey.[9] According to the 2011 published opinion, the

---

5   Lewis Lefko, "Fair Market Value in Health Care Transactions," July 20, 2007, www.worldservicesgroup.com/publicationspf.asp?id=2086, citing *United States of America ex. rel., Darryl L. Kaczmarczyk, et al., v. SCCI Hospital Ventures, Inc. d/b/a SCCI Hospital Houston Central*, U.S. District Court, Southern District of Texas, Houston, Division, No. H-99-1031, July 14, 2004.

6   Ibid.

7   Ibid.

8   Ibid.

9   David Pursell, "Commercial Reasonableness: The New Target," *Journal of Health Care Compliance*. March-April 2011. www.huschblackwell.com/files/Publication/9c53169a-f867-48dc-8c22-aec55537117d/Presentation/PublicationAttachment/f31f106a-dcf3-426f-a68e-af78f268d327/JHCC_02-11_Pursell.pdf, citing *U.S. v. Campbell*, 2011 WL 43013, No. 08-1951 (D. N.J., Jan. 4, 2011).

---

hospital partnered with local cardiologists in private practice to increase the number of cardiothoracic patients that were referred to the hospital.[10] These cardiologists were offered part-time positions to provide principally academic services.[11] The defendant, one of the previously mentioned local cardiologists, accepted such a position and was compensated a flat annual amount to perform duties such as teaching, attending weekly conferences, and completing Medicare time studies.[12] However, according to the United States, the arrangement did not meet the commercial reasonableness threshold because the physician was not required to nor did he actually perform the majority of the duties outlined in the contract.[13] It should also be noted that the United States demonstrated that the physician had few qualifications to be a professor, including lack of teaching experience and publications.[14] Accordingly, the court reasoned the physician's title and compensation were commercially *un*reasonable, regardless of whether the compensation was at fair market value, even if the duties had been performed.[15]

4.0 Applying Guidance to Assess Commercial Reasonableness

Given the aforementioned regulatory definitions and guidance from court cases, healthcare organizations and providers should deploy several analyses to determine whether an arrangement meets the standard of commercial reasonableness. In particular, the analyses include inquiries relating to the specific terms of a proposed arrangement in relation to the transaction's: (1) business purpose; (2) provider of service; (3) appropriateness with regard to the healthcare provider's facility and patient population; (4) suitability, considering the human and capital resources of the healthcare entity; and (5) aptness related to current and proposed methods for independence and oversight. These assessments each address various aspects of potential transactions, including overall economic sense (e.g., a hospital's return on investment) and relationship to the business goals of the organization proposing to enter into a physician arrangement.[16]

---

10 *U.S. v. Campbell*, 2011 WL 43012, No. 08-1951 (D. N.J., Jan. 4, 2011).

11 Ibid.

12 Ibid.

13 Ibid. The author notes that fair market value contemplates compensation that is commensurate with the actual performance of such services. In other words, fair market value determination assumes exchange of appropriate payment for actual services rendered.

14 Ibid.

15 Ibid., see also, *U.S. v. Rogan*, 459 F. Supp. 2d at 716 (N.D. Ill. Sept. 29, 2006). See prior commentary (refer to Footnote 13) regarding substantial performance of services actually being performed in connection with fair market value determination.

16 The key questions provided for consideration in this section offer different perspectives for various types of arrangements. As such, not all inquiries will be applicable to the specific transaction being assessed for commercial reasonableness. For example, administrative time cited in the resource analysis may apply more to a medical director agreement than to a production-based clinical agreement.

4.1 Business Purpose Analysis

According to the OIG, arrangements between physicians and hospitals should be reasonably necessary to effectuate appropriate patient care and a commercially reasonable business purpose without inducing prohibited referrals and compensation arrangements.[17] In a 2007 Advisory Opinion, the OIG found a physician compensation arrangement to be reasonable despite the fact that it did not meet a safe harbor requirement of the federal anti-kickback statute. Crucial to this finding was the fact that the arrangement effectively facilitated the promotion of "an obvious public benefit" while instituting actual safeguards from prohibited referrals and improving physician performance and "overall patient satisfaction." Thus, applying a totality of the circumstances test, the OIG found the arrangement to be reasonable and stated that it would not subject the hospital to administrative sanctions.[18] While OIG opinions are merely advisory and apply only to the particular parties and specific facts involved, such determinations provide guidance as to the structure and reasonableness of other agreements, including a hypothetical proposed arrangement. Thus, if an arrangement facilitates quality patient care and is essential to the functioning of the healthcare provider, it may be presumed reasonable pending further evaluation.[19]

In addition, several key definitions and recognizable standards exist with regard to evaluating the commercially reasonable business purpose of a proposed transaction. First, as referenced above, according to an OIG Notice published in the *Federal Register*, medical services that are reasonable and necessary include those which are "for the diagnosis or treatment of an illness or injury."[20] Finally, for any business-related arrangement to be considered "reasonable," it should make sense from a general business perspective, not only fulfilling an essential need, but also effectuating and furthering the strategic and legitimate financial goals (i.e., excluding referrals) of an organization. Given this regulatory guidance, a commercial reasonableness analysis related to business purpose may include inquiries such as the following:

---

17 "Reasonable and necessary" items or services are those "for the diagnosis or treatment of illness or injury or to improve the functioning of a malformed body member." "OIG Compliance Program for Individual and Small Group Physician Practices," Notice, 65 *F.R.* 59434 (Oct. 5, 2000); OIG Advisory Opinion No. 07-10, Sept. 20, 2007, pg. 6, 10; "OIG Supplemental Compliance Program Guidance for Hospitals," Notice, 70 *F.R.* 4858 (Jan. 31, 2005) citing 42 U.S.C.1395y(a)(1)(A).

18 OIG Advisory Opinion No. 07-10, Sept. 20, 2007.

19 Lewis Lefko, "Essential to the Functioning of the Hospital" discussed in "Fair Market Value in Health Care Transactions," July 20, 2007, www.worldservicesgroup.com/publicationspf.asp?id=2086, citing *United States of America ex. rel., Darryl L. Kaczmarczyk, et al., v. SCCI Hospital Ventures, Inc. d/b/a SCCI Hospital Houston Central*, U.S. District Court, Southern District of Texas, Houston, Division, No. H-99-1031, July 14, 2004 (settled by the parties).

20 "OIG Compliance Program for Individual and Small Group Physician Practices," Notice, 65 *F.R.* 59434 (Oct. 5, 2000); OIG Advisory Opinion No. 07-10, Sept. 20, 2007, pg. 6, 10; "OIG Supplemental Compliance Program Guidance for Hospitals," Notice, 70 *F.R.* 4858 (Jan. 31, 2005) citing 42 U.S.C. 1395y(a)(1)(A).

- Does the proposed arrangement represent a reasonable necessity that is essential to the functioning of the hospital or other healthcare provider?

- Is the proposed arrangement reasonably necessary to accomplish a rational business purpose?[21]

- Is the specific purpose of the arrangement clearly identifiable and appropriately defined?

- Do the proposed services relate to the business and/or clinical plans and strategies of the healthcare provider?

- Do the proposed services contribute to the provider's profits and/or the development of a particular service line without requiring income from proscribed referrals?[22]

- Do relevant national, regional, and local economic conditions exist that may affect the appropriateness of the proposed arrangement?

4.2 Provider Analysis

In terms of ordinary business principles, arrangements characterized as unnecessary or those creating excessive waste or abuse are presumably neither reasonable nor economically sensible. As such, the government generally views arrangements involving excess waste, duplication, or abuse as commercially *un*reasonable.[23] Accordingly, hospitals and other providers must carefully consider whether *physician* services are necessary to carry out the purposes of a proposed arrangement or whether nonphysician providers can satisfactorily perform the services. Furthermore, providers must particularly contemplate whether a certain position requires the services of a physician trained in a particular specialty. For instance, if a primary care physician can successfully perform specified services, a hospital may be acting in a commercially *un*reasonable manner by paying a premium to retain the services of a specialty physician. These types of provider-specific analyses are essential to determine whether a proposed arrangement

---

21 As described in this chapter, business purposes may include strategic, operational, or other qualitative considerations given the mission and regulatory compliance matters of the particular arrangement under analysis.

22 As part of this assessment, consideration of financial losses per employed or contracted physician arrangements may require considerations specific to commercial reasonableness in addition to fair market value. Notably, a determination as to commercial reasonableness depends upon the totality of the unique facts and circumstances specific to each arrangement. As such, assessing commercial reasonableness requires a balancing of facts and findings that evaluate the arrangement in aggregate (i.e., versus one particular inquiry that may not portray the totality of the relevant circumstances).

23 Lew Lefko, "All Eyes on Physician-Hospital Arrangements," *HealthLeaders Media*. Jan, 24, 2008.

is reasonable because the medical provider will remain the central figure related to the provision of such services.

In addition to the general reasonableness of utilizing a specific provider for a specific purpose, the compensation associated with such an individual must also be commercially reasonable.[24] While an in-depth discussion related to fair market value determination is beyond the scope of this discussion pertaining to commercial reasonableness, CMS has provided guidance that speaks to commercially reasonable tactics for determining situational-specific physician compensation. In particular, according to the CMS, "reference to multiple, objective, independently published salary surveys remains a prudent practice for evaluating fair market value."[25] Additionally, CMS has stated that "ultimately, the appropriate method for determining fair market value for purposes of the physician self-referral law will depend on the nature of the transaction, its location, and other factors."[26] Again considering regulatory guidance, a commercial reasonableness analysis related to the provider of a transaction may include inquiries such as the following:

- Does the proposed arrangement require a physician to perform the services?

- Does the proposed arrangement require a physician of a certain specialty to perform the services?

- Does any specialized training and/or experience of the provider exist that should be taken into account when evaluating the proposed arrangement?

- Are the particular nature of the duties and corresponding amount of accountability associated with the proposed arrangement clearly defined and reasonable?

- Is the amount of time demanded of the physician under the proposed arrangement reasonable?

- Do any salary considerations exist that should be evaluated in relation to providers of similar specialty and experience in comparable organizations and positions?

---

24   See 42 CFR §411.357(l).
25   72 *F.R.* 51015 (Sept. 5, 2007).
26   Ibid.

4.3 Facility Analysis

As noted in the discussion of key court cases on commercial reasonableness, the size and patient population of a particular medical facility should be considered in assessing the reasonableness of a proposed arrangement to which that facility will be a party.[27] Specifically, according to the government's financial expert in one case, the arrangement should not only be essential to the functioning of the hospital, but there must also be sound business reasons for the arrangement at that particular facility. In other words, it is essential to evaluate a particular facility's size and patient population to determine whether sound business reasons exist for a specific services arrangement.[28] Therefore, in accordance with governmental guidance as outlined above, medical facilities should consider their characteristics, including size and patient population and, in turn, carefully evaluate the relevance of such factors in determining whether sound operational and/or strategic reasons exist for a proposed arrangement.

Taking into account this litigation and regulatory guidance, a commercial reasonableness analysis related to a facility may include inquiries such as the following:

- Are patient demand, the number of hospital patients, and/or the community need sufficient to justify the services?

- Are patient acuity levels such that the proposed services are necessary?

- Do patient needs dictate the necessity for a separate and distinct provider for the proposed services?

- Are the size of the hospital and the relevant department appropriate for the proposed services?

4.4 Resource Analysis

In assessing commercial reasonableness, the government also typically aims to ensure that a potential arrangement serves a necessary purpose in an efficient and effective manner. Specifically, a proposed transaction should not be duplicative of other positions and/or resources available to a particular organization.[29] Principally, the government is

---

27 Lewis Lefko, "Fair Market Value in Health Care Transactions," July 20, 2007, www.worldservicesgroup.com/publicationspf.asp?id=2086, citing *United States of America ex. rel., Darryl L. Kaczmarczyk, et al., v. SCCI Hospital Ventures, Inc. d/b/a SCCI Hospital Houston Central*, U.S. District Court, Southern District of Texas, Houston, Division H-99-1031, July 14, 2004, and Mayer Hoffman McCann and Kathy McNamara, "Fair Market Valuation of Medical Director or Program Director Services," filed with Plaintiff United States Designation of Expert Witness, July 12, 2005.
28 Ibid.
29 Ibid.

wary of situations in which an unnecessary duplication of efforts exists among professional and administrative positions entailing the involvement of a physician or physician groups. For instance, if a hospital enters into three medical directorship agreements when one such agreement would accomplish its objectives, the three agreements likely represent an unnecessary duplication of services.[30] To best adhere to this regulatory guidance, a commercial reasonableness analysis related to the resources associated with a transaction may include the following inquiries:

- Is the proposed arrangement a necessary addition to the managerial and administrative efforts already required by the medical staff bylaws?

- Have the number of committees and/or meetings that otherwise require physician attendance outside of the proposed arrangement been considered?

- If the healthcare entity is part of a larger health system, do patient care protocols and procedures exist that can be coordinated among its facilities in lieu of the proposed arrangement?

- Does the proposed arrangement lend itself to the potential for duplication or misuse?

- Does the healthcare entity maintain any features, controls, and/or safeguards to reduce or eliminate the potential for risks of duplication or misuse?

4.5 Independence and Oversight Analysis

In *U.S. v. SCCI Hospital Ventures*, the government's financial expert asserted several oversight-specific factors that are critical to a determination of commercial reasonableness related to physician services arrangements. These factors included whether: (i) the hospital performs regular evaluations of the *actual* duties performed by the physician; (ii) the hospital assesses the effectiveness of the physician's performance; and (iii) there is a sustained, bona fide need for the physician services.[31] As related to these factors, the need should be underscored for substantial performance of services to ensure that set-in-advance payments continue to result in fair market value.[32] In particular, many

---

30 Editor's note: As discussed elsewhere in the guide and assuming SSVS is applicable to FMV compensation arrangements, there is a question of whether hiring three people when one is needed meets the informed buyer requirement of the fair market value standard.

31 Lewis Lefko, "Fair Market Value in Health Care Transactions," July 20, 2007, www.worldservicesgroup.com/publicationspf.asp?id=2086, citing *United States of America ex. rel., Darryl L. Kaczmarczyk, et al., v. SCCI Hospital Ventures, Inc. d/b/a SCCI Hospital Houston Central*, U.S. District Court, Southern District of Texas, Houston, Division, No. H-99-1031, July 14, 2004.

32 Also refer to discussion and footnotes in this chapter describing *U.S. v. Campbell*.

fair market value assessments "assume" certain underlying factors (i.e., often expressly as a limiting condition). Examples of these assumptions may include that the arrangement reflects an appropriate and prudent management decision, is for a reasonable and legitimate purpose, etc. As such, from a practical standpoint, a fair market value evaluation may "assume" certain peripheral factors relevant to the overall arrangement, whereas evaluating an arrangement's commercial reasonableness entails actual "assessment" of such factors. Likewise, the OIG has suggested that internal compliance programs may effectively assure that physician services and related compensation are indeed reasonable and necessary.[33]

In fact, to successfully uphold a standard of commercial reasonableness, if a hospital discovers waste or abuse associated with a particular physician arrangement, it should either reduce the amount of time spent conducting such activities or eliminate the position altogether.[34] Additionally, according to recent rulings, if circumstances exist such that a physician does not *actually* perform services required of him or her pursuant to a particular transaction, the arrangement does not meet the standard of commercial reasonableness (and will also likely result in payments in excess of fair market value given the inherent relationship between services and payments as previously described).[35] Furthermore, the completion of time reports *alone* is insufficient to meet this obligation.[36] Finally, in keeping with numerous healthcare regulatory requirements as well as customary business standards, parties to a proposed transaction should, at a minimum, reduce the material terms of the agreement to writing to more easily facilitate a conclusion of commercial reasonableness. Given this regulatory guidance, a commercial reasonableness analysis related to the independence and oversight of a transaction may include inquiries such as the following:

- Does the provider entity currently evaluate the performance of its provider arrangements?

- Does the healthcare entity use its performance assessments to determine whether new or existing provider arrangements should be reduced (e.g., hours condensed) or eliminated?

---

33 65 *F.R.* 194 (Oct. 5, 2000); see also 70 *F.R.* 19 (Jan. 31, 2005).
34 Lew Lefko, "All Eyes on Physician-Hospital Arrangements," *HealthLeaders Media*. Jan. 24, 2008.
35 See *United States of America ex. rel. Roberts, v. Aging Care Home Health, Inc., et al.,* 474 F.Supp.2d 810, 818 (W.D. La. Feb. 16, 2007); see also *United States v. Rogan*, 459 F.Supp.2d 692 (N.D. Ill. Sept. 29, 2006). The author underscores the need for substantial performance of services to ensure that set-in-advance payments continue to result in fair market value (also refer to footnotes in this chapter describing *U.S. v. Campbell*).
36 Lew Lefko, "All Eyes on Physician-Hospital Arrangements," *HealthLeaders Media*. Jan. 24, 2008.

- Does the entity maintain a formal process for executive management and legal counsel to review and approve the proposed arrangement?

- Does the provider engage in appropriate monitoring to determine:

    - Whether services specified in similar arrangements are actually performed?

    - The total amount of funds spent for such services?

    - A verifiable outcome resulting from the arrangement?

- Will the entity engage in regular assessments of the proposed arrangement that clearly show its effectiveness and demonstrate a legitimate need for continuation and/or renewal?

- Does sufficient independence exist related to the board or committee that establishes the proposed arrangement?

- Is there a written agreement that addresses the terms of the proposed arrangement?

5.0 Contrasting Commercial Reasonableness and Fair Market Value

For many of the reasons cited herein, given its broad implications and larger scope pertaining to a transaction in its entirety, if an arrangement is not commercially reasonable, the issue of compensation may become irrelevant. In other words, if a financial arrangement is commercially *un*reasonable, a need to determine equitable payments may not exist.

However, given the intense focus on fair market value associated with various physician arrangements, hospitals and health systems may be neglecting to actually assess whether such arrangements are commercially reasonable. Fundamentally, a commercial reasonableness analysis goes beyond the determination of fair market value. In particular, while the standard of fair market value assesses the appropriateness of the range of dollars exchanged between the parties, the standard of commercial reasonableness requires that the arrangement be sensible from an overall general business (i.e., financial, operational, and strategic) perspective. As such, an arrangement could be at fair market value but yet be commercially *un*reasonable.

For example, a physician may be party to an arrangement by which he or she is compensated at an amount commensurate with his position, specialty, geographic region, and other factors. However, if the hospital compensating such a physician already has access to the same or similar services and/or compensates other physicians capable of carrying out his or her contracted duties, it may not be commercially reasonable to actually make these payments. Other such risk factors may include insufficient demand, inappropriate hospital size, inadequate patient population, lack of relationship to hospital strategic and financial goals, and inadequate oversight. For additional illustrative purposes, specific examples of potentially commercially *unreasonable* arrangements may also include the following:

- A hospital paying a cardiologist specialty compensation rates for administrative work requiring only a primary care physician;

- A health system maintaining medical director agreements at two of its facilities that contained duplicative protocols and policy responsibilities; and

- A hospital failing to maintain proper oversight of the effectiveness and necessity of its physician services arrangement.

In each of these situations, appraisers can determine fair market value rates *given the specific facts, circumstances, and assumptions provided by their clients.* However, in determining fair market value compensation, valuators are generally assessing the range of dollars and may not be appropriately questioning the overall reasonableness of the arrangement. Given the aforementioned risk factors and regulatory requirements, healthcare providers should carefully and practically determine (internally or through external assistance) whether their arrangements are actually commercially reasonable, not just whether a fair price is being paid for the services rendered.

6.0 Conclusion

As a whole, the standard of commercial reasonableness remains broad in scope and speaks to an arrangement's general business characteristics, including matters pertaining to strategy, economic factors, and operations. However, when one wants to evaluate commercial reasonableness in the healthcare setting from a practical perspective, specific terms of the proposed arrangement should be examined and analyzed in relation to the transaction's: (1) business purpose; (2) provider of service; (3) appropriateness with regard to the provider's facility and patient population; (4) suitability, considering the human and capital resources of the provider; and (5) aptness related to current and proposed methods for independence and oversight. By following such a process, commercial reasonableness analyses (based on available regulatory guidance) become more concrete and help mitigate any potential ambiguity that may exist between fair market value and commercial reasonableness.

Note: The authors of this chapter would also like to acknowledge the contributions of M. Allison Carty, JD, MBA.

PRACTICE AID: Commercial Reasonableness Assessment Tool

By Pershing Yoakley & Associates, P.C.

The following checklist represents a few of the key questions to consider in evaluating the commercial reasonableness of physician-hospital arrangements. It includes questions that a professional should assess in considering the totality of any specific arrangement. This checklist, when completed, does not convey that any particular transaction either is or is not commercially reasonable. A more thorough analysis is required to make a determination about commercial reasonableness. Judgment by a professional based on specific facts and circumstances is required to make that determination.

1.0 Business Purpose Analysis

1. Does the proposed arrangement represent a reasonable necessity that is essential to the functioning of the hospital or other healthcare provider?

2. Is the proposed arrangement reasonably necessary to accomplish a rational business purpose?

3. Is the specific purpose of the arrangement clearly identifiable and appropriately defined?

4. Do the proposed services relate to the business and/or clinical plans and strategies of the healthcare provider?

5. Do the proposed services contribute to the provider's profits and/or the development of a particular service line without requiring income from proscribed referrals?

6. Do relevant national, regional, and local economic conditions exist that may affect the appropriateness of the proposed arrangement?

2.0 Provider Analysis

1. Does the proposed arrangement require a physician to perform the services?

2. Does the proposed arrangement require a physician of a certain specialty to perform the services?

3. Does any specialized training and/or experience of the provider exist that should be taken into account when evaluating the proposed arrangement?

4. Are the particular nature of the duties and corresponding amount of accountability associated with the proposed arrangement clearly defined and reasonable?

5. Is the amount of time demanded of the physician under the proposed arrangement reasonable?

6. Do any salary considerations exist that should be evaluated in relation to providers of similar specialty and experience in comparable organizations and positions?

3.0 Facility Analysis

1. Are patient demand, the number of hospital patients, and/or the community need sufficient to justify the services?

2. Are patient acuity levels such that the proposed services are necessary?

3. Do patient needs dictate the necessity for a separate and distinct provider for the proposed services?

4. Are the size of the hospital and the relevant department appropriate for the proposed services?

4.0 Resource Analysis

1. Is the proposed arrangement a necessary addition to the managerial and administrative efforts already required by the medical staff bylaws?

2. Have the number of committees and/or meetings that otherwise require physician attendance outside of the proposed arrangement been considered?

3. If the healthcare entity is part of a larger health system, do patient care protocols and procedures exist that can be coordinated among its facilities in lieu of the proposed arrangement?

4. Does the proposed arrangement lend itself to the potential for duplication or misuse?

5. Does the healthcare entity maintain any features, controls, and/or safeguards to reduce or eliminate the potential for risks of duplication or misuse?

5.0 Independence and Oversight Analysis

1. Does the provider entity currently evaluate the performance of its provider arrangements?

2. Does the healthcare entity use its performance assessments to determine whether new or existing provider arrangements should be reduced (e.g., hours condensed) or eliminated?

3. Does the entity maintain a formal process for executive management and legal counsel to review and approve the proposed arrangement?

4. Does the provider engage in appropriate monitoring to determine:

   › Whether services specified in similar arrangements are actually performed?

   › The total amount of funds spent for such services?

   › A verifiable outcome resulting from the arrangement?

5. Will the entity engage in regular assessments of the proposed arrangement that clearly show its effectiveness and demonstrate a legitimate need for continuation and/or renewal?

6. Does sufficient independence exist related to the board or committee that establishes the proposed arrangement?

7. Is there a written agreement that addresses the terms of the proposed arrangement?

Chapter 11. Valuation Issues Affecting Tax-Exempt Healthcare Organizations

CONTENTS

Chapter 11. Valuation Issues Affecting Tax-Exempt Healthcare Organizations

By Robert F. Reilly, MBA, CPA, CMA, CFA, ASA, CBA

1.0 Introduction

This discussion focuses on the regulatory reasons why tax-exempt healthcare organizations retain valuation analysts to perform transaction valuations, reasonableness of compensation analyses, and similar fair market value analyses. This discussion will not present a "how to" explanation of valuation approaches, methods, and procedures for the valuation analyst. Such "how to" procedural explanations are presented elsewhere in this text (and in numerous principles and advanced valuation texts). Rather, this discussion will summarize the regulatory considerations that the valuation analyst (and all parties to a proposed transaction) should be aware of with respect to the valuation of a tax-exempt healthcare organization.

With regard to most tax-exempt organization transactions, the principal parties (and the valuation analyst) should be concerned with at least three potential regulatory challenges: (1) Medicare fraud and abuse challenges, (2) Internal Revenue Service private inurement issues, and (3) Stark laws compliance issues. This discussion will focus on the second potential regulatory challenge: federal income tax issues related to private inurement allegations and the related intermediate sanctions excise tax penalties. In particular, this discussion focuses on: what type of transaction price or structure may result in a private inurement, what parties are subject to the private inurement considerations, what types of transactions are encompassed in the spectrum of private inurement considerations, what the Internal Revenue Service looks for in its consideration of private inurement issues, and how the intermediate sanctions penalties work in instances of alleged private inurement.

The first half of this discussion will summarize the tax-related regulatory issues related to tax-exempt healthcare organization transactions. The valuation analyst should be generally aware of these issues in the fair market value analysis of any transaction involving (1) a tax-exempt entity and a for-profit entity or (2) a tax-exempt entity and any "disqualified person." The second half of this discussion will present a sample illustrative valuation analysis and report related as a hypothetical purchase of a tax-exempt healthcare entity by a newly formed for-profit healthcare entity. As will be presented, that hypothetical transactional valuation is prepared to provide the hypothetical transaction participants (who are created to be "disqualified persons") with professional assurance related to any private inurement aspects of the proposed transaction.

2.0 Valuation Issues

It is noteworthy that the private inurement and excess benefit issues related to tax-exempt healthcare entities encompass two types of transactions: (1) the transfer of property and (2) the transfer for services. Both of these types of tax-exempt organization transactions involve valuation issues and fair market value valuations. Both of these types of transactions are analyzed by valuation analysts who estimate a fair market value related to a proposed or consummated transaction. And the term "fair market value" is defined the same way for both types of transactions. According to Treasury Regulation Section 53.4958-(b)(1)(i):

> Fair market value is defined as the price at which property or the right to use property would change hands between a willing buyer and a willing seller, neither being under any compulsion to buy, sell, or transfer property or the right to use property and both having reasonable knowledge of relevant facts.

Many valuation analysts are more familiar with valuations related to the transfer of property-type transactions. This type of transaction occurs when the tax-exempt entity buys or sells a business, a business ownership (equity) interest, or operating assets. Some common examples exclude when the tax-exempt healthcare entity buys or sells a hospital, clinic, physicians' practice, MRI center, urgent care center, HMO, home healthcare agency, medical equipment provider, or any other healthcare delivery organization. And these transactions encompass the purchase or sale of either assets or equity interests.

Many valuation analysts may be less familiar with valuations related to the transfer of services-type transactions. This type of transaction occurs when the tax-exempt entity hires employees or contracts for professional services. Some common examples include when the tax-exempt healthcare entity compensates a chief executive officer (CEO) or other executives, pays a medical director (or other physician professionals), hires a physician group to manage the emergency room or operating room, rents office or professional space to or from staff physicians, leases equipment to or from staff physicians, provides billing or other administrative services to staff physicians, or generally enters into any joint venture or related contractual agreement with staff physicians. To analyze such services-type transactions for concerns of private inurement, valuation analysts are often asked to opine on the fair market value of the services transfer transaction.

3.0 Other Regulatory Considerations

In addition to Internal Revenue Service and taxation considerations, tax-exempt healthcare entities should comply with numerous other federal and state regulations regarding the transfers of property and services. This section provides a very brief summary of some of these other regulatory considerations that the valuation analyst should be aware of.

The Medicare fraud and abuse statutes make it illegal to pay, offer, or induce any remuneration in exchange for patient referrals. For example, a hospital cannot pay a staff physician in exchange for his or her patient referrals to that hospital. Accordingly, in a physician practice acquisition transaction, a hospital cannot pay any purchase price related to the physician's current or expected patient referrals. Therefore, tax-exempt acquirers (and any other healthcare industry acquirers) should not structure a transaction that appears to involve either (1) a "kickback" payment for physicians' patient referrals or (2) a "lockup" of physicians' patent referrals.

The Stark laws prohibit physicians with a financial relationship with an entity from referring patients to the entity for "designated health services" covered by either Medicare or Medicaid programs.

The Medicare anti-kickback laws prohibit the giving or receipt of anything of value to induce the referral of medical business reimbursed under the Medicare or Medicaid programs. Unlike the Stark laws, summarized next, the Medicare anti-kickback law is an "intent-based" statute. In addition, the Medicare anti-kickback law statutes make it clear that the healthcare entity payments for any property or services should be based on fair market value (and should not be variable, based on patient volume or patient referrals).

The Stark II statute became effective on Jan. 1, 1995. Like the Stark I statute, Stark II was intended to curb abuses inherent in physician self-referral arrangements. Like Stark I, Stark II prohibits physicians who have a financial relationship with a healthcare entity (whether tax-exempt or for-profit) from referring their patients to the entity for "designated health services" covered by either Medicare or Medicaid programs.

A financial relationship consists of an ownership or investment interest in the healthcare entity or a compensation arrangement with the healthcare entity. If the physician (1) does not own any portion of the healthcare entity and (2) does not pay the entity or receive any kind of payment from the entity for the referral or for anything else, then there is no financial relationship. Under the Stark legislation, a financial relationship can exist between a physician and a healthcare entity even if that relationship does not involve designated health services or the Medicare or Medicaid programs.

For example, a compensation arrangement is defined in the Stark II statute as any arrangement involving any remuneration between (1) a physician (or family member) and (2) a healthcare entity. This remuneration can involve payments for anything, such as payments for rent, payments for nonmedical services, or payments for housing or travel expenses. Accordingly, the Stark statutes would interpret the purchase of a physician's practice by a hospital (and the related payment to the selling physicians) as a financial arrangement.

Section 1877(e)(6) of the Stark II regulations provides that an isolated transaction, such as a one-time sale of a property or a practice, is not considered to be a compensation arrangement for purposes of the prohibition on patient referrals. This is true if the following conditions are met:

- The amount of remuneration for the one-time transaction sale is consistent with fair market value and is not determined, directly or indirectly, in a manner that takes into account the volume or the value of the physician's patient referrals;

- The remuneration is provided under an agreement that would be commercially reasonable even if no patient referrals are made to the acquirer healthcare entity; and

- The arrangements meet any other requirements the secretary may impose by regulation as needed to protect against Medicare program or patient abuse.

It is noteworthy that the term "isolated transaction" is defined as a transaction involving a single payment between two or more persons. A transaction that involves long-term or installment payments is not considered to be an isolated transaction.

To comply with the Stark laws, a healthcare entity's property or practice purchase transaction (1) should be priced at fair market value and (2) should be structured with a purchase price that is not paid in installments.

To comply with the Stark laws related to the payment for services, the healthcare entity purchase transaction should be structured as follows:

1. There should be a written agreement signed by parties that specifies the services to be covered under the arrangement;

2. The term of the agreement should be at least one year;

3. The aggregate services contracted for should not exceed those that are reasonable and necessary for the legitimate business purpose of the subject arrangement; and

4. The compensation to be paid by the healthcare entity over the term of the agreement should be:

   ○ Defined in advance.

   ○ Not in excess of fair market value.

   ○ Not determined in a manner that takes into account patient volume or the value of any patient referrals or other business generated by the parties.

4.0 Definitions

This section will summarize the definitions of certain terminology that is associated with the tax-related regulation (and valuation) of healthcare organization transactions.

4.1 Tax-Exempt Organization

First, a nonprofit entity is not the same as a tax-exempt organization, and a tax-exempt entity is not the same as a charitable institution. There are many types of tax-exempt organizations:

- Section 501(c)(4)—civic leagues and social welfare organizations;

- Section 501(c)(5)—labor, agricultural, and horticultural organizations;

- Section 501(c)(6)—business leagues; and

- Section 501(c)(7)—social and recreational clubs.

This discussion focuses on the tax regulation with regard to Section 501(c)(3), "charitable organizations." The requirements to be a Section 501(c)(3) organization include:

- The organization is organized and operated exclusively for exempt purposes;

- The net earnings of the organization do not inure to the benefit of individuals;

- The organization is without substantial lobbying activity;

- The organization is without any political activity; and

- Examples of Section 501(c)(3) organization include schools, churches, and hospitals.

Again, the focus of this discussion is on Section 501(c)(3), public charity healthcare organizations.

There are numerous advantages of Section 501(c)(3) status, including:

- Exemption from most federal and state income taxes;

- Exemption from most state sales taxes;

- Exemption from certain payroll taxes;

- State and local property tax benefits;

- Preferred U.S. postal service mailing rates;

- Charitable contribution deductions allowed for its donors; and

- Eligibility for tax-exempt bond financing.

To maintain its Section 501 (c)(3) status, the healthcare organization is required to operate "exclusively" for exempt purposes. However, the term "exclusively" doesn't mean exclusively—it means "primarily."

4.2 Disqualified Person
This term (which is also used in the private foundation tax statutes) refers to the person or persons who have a close relationship with a tax-exempt organization.

4.3 Excess Benefit Transaction

This is the type of property transfer or services transfer transaction that is at the heart of the intermediate sanctions rules. It is an impermissible transaction between (1) a tax-exempt organization and (2) a disqualified person.

4.4 Excess Benefit

An excess benefit is the impermissible aspect of a tax-exempt organization transaction that constitutes an excess benefit transaction. It is the amount that is used to compute one or more of the intermediate sanctions excise tax penalties.

4.5 Revenue-Sharing Transaction

This is a transaction between a tax-exempt organization and a disqualified person, where the benefit flowing to the disqualified person is based, in whole or in part, on the revenue flow of the tax-exempt organization.

4.6 Initial Contract Exception

This is one broad exception to the concept of the excess benefit transaction. Based on the initial contract exception, the transaction created by the initial relationship between the tax-exempt organization and the disqualified person is exempted from the intermediate sanctions excise tax penalties.

4.7 Initial Tax

This is the tax that is initially levied on an excess benefit amount. This tax is also referred to as a first-tier tax.

4.8 Additional Tax

This is the tax that can be imposed on an excess benefit amount, if the initial tax is not timely paid.

4.9 Correction

A correction is the process that is required to undo an excess benefit transaction and return the parties to the economic position they were in before the excess benefit transaction was entered into.

5.0 Tax-Exempt Organization Transactions—Private Inurement and Excess Benefits

Tax-exempt organizations are exempt from federal income tax as organizations described in Section 501(c)(3) only if they are organized and operated exclusively for charitable purposes within the meaning of the statute. However, such tax-exempt organizations are subject to certain restrictions with regard to acquisition, professional services, employee compensation, and other types of transactions.

The Internal Revenue Code (the Service) and many state attorneys general view tax-exempt organizations as charitable trusts for the benefit of the public. The regulatory scheme of Section 501(c)(3) is designed to:

1. Ensure the furtherance of public purposes; and

2. Prevent the diversion of charitable assets into private hands.

Accordingly, the tax law includes two important types of restrictions (or prohibited activities) related to tax-exempt organization transactions.

5.1 Private Inurement

The first type of restriction relates to private inurement. For Section 501(c)(3) tax-exempt organizations, no part of the net earnings may inure to the benefit of any private shareholder or individual. This means that an individual can't receive the tax-exempt organization's funds, except as reasonable payment for goods or services. There is no minimum threshold related to the private inurement restriction, and there is no de minimis exception.

The private inurement restriction applies only to "private shareholders or individuals," commonly referred to as "insiders" (i.e., those having a personal and private interest in or opportunity to influence the activities of the organization from the inside). It is noteworthy that the term "insider" does not appear in the Internal Revenue Code or regulations. However, it is widely used in the related legal, accounting, and valuation literature.

The intermediate sanctions provisions of Section 4958 were added to the Internal Revenue Code in 1996 and (as discussed below) used the terms "excess benefits transaction" and "disqualified person." The legislative history of Section 4958 states that "[t]he Committee intends that physicians will be considered disqualified persons only if they are in a position to exercise substantial influence over the affairs of an organization." The tax-exempt organization's payment of excessive or greater-than-reasonable compensation to an insider, such as a healthcare entity officer or director, is a prime example of prohibited private inurement.

5.2 Private Benefit

The second type of restriction relates to private benefit. Section 501(c)(3) tax-exempt organizations should be organized and operated to serve public rather than private interests. Unlike the private inurement transaction restrictions, the private benefit transaction restrictions are not absolute. To be a permissible transaction, a private benefit transaction should be incidental to (or a necessary concomitant of) accomplishment of the public benefits involved. Private benefit should be balanced against the public benefit. And, the Service has issued regulations that provide examples illustrating the test for serving a public rather than a private interest.

The private benefit prohibition is not limited to insiders. For example, some incidental private benefit is always present in hospital-physician relationships (e.g., when a private practice physician uses a tax-exempt hospital facilities to treat his or her paying patients).

Any private inurement or too much (i.e., other than incidental) private benefit could cause a tax-exempt hospital to lose its tax exemption. Until 1995, the revocation of the organization's tax exemption was the only sanction available to the Service. However, with regard to both private inurement and excess private benefit, the Service now relies principally on the imposition of Section 4958 intermediate sanctions excise tax penalties.

5.3 Excess Benefit

Section 4958, enacted as part of the 1996 Taxpayer Bill of Rights, allows the Service to impose penalty excise taxes on certain "excess benefits transactions" between "disqualified persons" and tax-exemption organizations described in Sections 501(c)(3) or 501(c)(4).

Excess benefit transactions include:

1. A transaction priced at other than fair market value (FMV) in which a disqualified person (a) pays less than FMV to the tax-exempt organization or (b) charges the tax-exempt organization more than FMV for a good or service;

2. An unreasonable compensation transaction, in which a disqualified person receives greater than a FMV level of compensation from the tax-exempt organization; and

3. A prohibited revenue-sharing transaction, in which a disqualified person receives payment based on the revenue of the tax-exempt organization in an arrangement specified in Section 4958 regulations that violates the inurement prohibition under current law.

6.0 Disqualified Persons

Section 4958 defines certain people to be "disqualified persons" with respect to a tax-exempt organization, including:

1. Voting members of the tax-exempt organization's governing board;

2. Persons who have or share ultimate responsibility for implementing the decisions of the governing body or for supervising management, administration, or operation of the tax-exempt organization (such as president, chief executive officer, chief operating officer, treasurer, and chief financial officer unless demonstrated otherwise); and

3. Persons with a material financial interest in a provider-sponsored organization.

The Section 4958 regulations clarify that this category of disqualified persons can include organizations such as management companies.

Section 4958 identifies other parties as not being a disqualified person:

1. All organizations described in Section 501(c)(3) (although the Pension Protection Act of 2006 appears to have created on exception for supporting organizations);

2. With respect to Section 501(c)(4) organizations, other Section 501(c)(4) organizations; and

3. Full-time or part-time employees receiving total direct and indirect economic benefits in an amount less than the amount of compensation necessary to be highly compensated, as defined in Section 414(q)(1)(B)(i) (i.e., $100,000 in 2007), who are not substantial contributors within the meaning of Section 507(d)(2) (taking into account certain adjustments) or otherwise within the definition of "disqualified person."

In all other cases, the Section 4958 regulations indicate that a "disqualified person" is (1) any person who was, at any time during the previous five years, in a position to exercise substantial influence over the affairs of the organization, (2) certain family members (lineal descendents, brothers and sisters, whether by whole or half-blood, and spouses of any of them), or (3) an entity 35% or more of which is controlled by such persons.

The legislative history of Section 4958 recognizes that a nonemployee, such as a management company or the employee of a subsidiary (even a taxable subsidiary), could be in a position to exercise substantial influence. The Section 4958 regulations provide that, in the case of multiple organizations affiliated by common control or governing documents, the determination of whether a person does or does not have substantial influence is made separately for each applicable tax-exempt organization.

The Pension Protection Act of 2006 added several new classifications of disqualified persons. Any disqualified person with respect to a Section 509(a)(3) supporting organization is a disqualified person with respect to the supported organization. Any substantial contributor to a donor-advised fund is a disqualified person with respect to the donor-advised fund. Any investment advisor to an organization sponsoring a donor-advised fund is a disqualified person with respect to the sponsoring organization.

7.0 The Initial Contract Rule

The Section 4958 regulations establish an "initial contract rule" to protect from intermediate sanctions liability certain "fixed" payments for the provision of services or the sale of property made under a binding written contract. The initial contract only applies to persons who were not disqualified persons immediately before entering into the initial contract. Fixed payments are defined to include an amount of cash or other property that is either (1) specified in the contract or (2) determined using a fixed formula specified in the initial contract. And payments that include a variable component (such as achieving certain levels of revenue or business activity) may qualify as a fixed payment as long as the components are calculated pursuant to a pre-established, objective formula.

8.0 Section 4958 Penalty Excise Taxes

Under Section 4958, a disqualified person is liable for (1) an initial 25% penalty excise tax on the amount of the excess benefit and (2) an additional penalty tax of 200% on the amount of the excess benefit if the transaction is not timely corrected. A tax-exempt organization manager who knowingly, willfully, and without reasonable cause participates in an excess benefit transaction is personally liable for a 10% penalty tax (up to a maximum of $20,000) on the amount of the excess benefit.

It is noteworthy that no Section 4958 penalties are assessed on the tax-exempt organization itself. Of course, a tax exemption revocation remains an option of the Service in extreme cases.

9.0 Intermediate Sanctions

The purpose of the intermediate sanctions tax law is to prevent wrongdoing by persons who have a special relationship with tax-exempt organizations, particularly charitable entities. Before the enactment of the intermediate sanctions laws, the Internal Revenue Service, when faced with one of these inappropriate transactions, had essentially two choices:

1. Apply the private inurement doctrine or the private benefit doctrine and revoke the tax-exempt status of the subject organization; or

2. Ignore the matter (and perhaps informally attempt to influence the behavior of the parties involved on a going-forward basis).

From the Service's standpoint, these two options were not sufficient. Accordingly, the Treasury and the Internal Revenue Service urged Congress to enact the intermediate sanctions legislation.

Revocation of an organization's tax-exempt status is a particularly harsh consequence. Moreover, the loss of the subject organization's tax-exempt status does not necessarily resolve the underlying problem—the party that obtained the inappropriate benefit still has it. Often, the only individuals truly punished in these situations are the beneficiaries of the tax-exempt organization's programs.

Intermediate sanctions are penalties imposed on the person or persons who engage in the inappropriate transaction with the tax-exempt organization. These sanctions are called "intermediate" because they fall between (1) the revocation of tax-exempt status and (2) inaction on the part of the Service. Also, the sanctions are not applied to the tax-exempt organization that was abused. Rather, the sanctions are imposed on the person or persons who improperly benefited from the subject property or services transfer transaction.

It is noteworthy that the intermediate sanctions law does not replace either (1) the private inurement doctrine or (2) the private benefit doctrine. Rather, the Service now has a range of taxpayer penalty options. The Service can impose the sanctions alone. The Service can impose both the sanctions and the private inurement doctrine or the Service can find the sanctions do not apply and nonetheless invoke the private benefit doctrine.

9.1 Intermediate Sanction Taxes
The intermediate sanctions are, in fact, federal excise taxes. These federal excise taxes are applied to the amount involved in the impermissible transaction—i.e., the excess benefit. The person who pays for intermediate sanctions tax (again, not the tax-exempt organizations) is referred to as a disqualified person.

The first intermediate sanctions tax is an "initial tax." The initial tax is 25% of the amount of the excess benefit. Also, the excess benefit property or services transaction must be reversed. This reversal or refund of the excess benefit transaction is intended to put the parties in the same economic position they were in before the excess benefit transaction was entered into. This process is referred to as correction of the transaction.

If (1) the initial tax is not timely paid and (2) the offending transaction is not timely and properly corrected, then an "additional tax" may be imposed. This intermediate sanctions tax is 200% of the amount of the excess benefit. In some instances, the trustees, directors, or officers with the tax-exempt organization may also be required to pay a tax of 10% of the amount of the excess benefit.

Under certain circumstances, the intermediate sanctions tax may be abated. Generically, the Section 4958 intermediate sanctions excise taxes are referred to as "penalties."

9.2 Intermediate Sanctions and Applicable Tax-Exempt Organizations

The Section 4958 intermediate sanctions statute and associated regulations apply with respect to public charities and tax-exempt social welfare organizations. These entities are called "applicable tax-exempt organizations" for this Section 4958 purpose.

Applicable tax-exempt organizations include any organization described in either of these two categories of tax-exempt organizations at any time during the five-year period ending on the date of the property sale or services transfer transactions. Accordingly, public charities can be:

1. Churches, integrated auxiliaries of churches, and associations and conventions of churches;

2. Colleges, universities, and schools;

3. Hospitals, other providers of healthcare, and medical research organizations;

4. Foundations supportive of governmentally operated colleges and universities;

5. Units of government;

6. Publicly supported charitable, educational, religious, scientific, and similar organizations; and

7. Organizations that are supportive of other types of public charities.

Tax-exempt social welfare organizations include entities that are: (1) civic in nature, (2) assist a community in various ways, and (3) engage in more advocacy (usually lobbying) than is allowed for charitable organizations. Therefore, an entity qualifies as an applicable tax-exempt organization if it operated as either type of tax-exempt organization at any time in the five-year period before the excess benefit transaction occurred. This five-year period rule is referred to as the "lookback rule," and this five-year period is referred to as the "lookback period."

Section 4958 provides for no exemptions from these rules (e.g., for small organizations or religious entities). That is, all domestic public charities and all social welfare organizations are applicable tax-exempt organizations. However, a foreign organization that is tax-exempt, by determination of the Service or by treaty, as a charitable or social welfare entity is not an applicable tax-exempt organization if it receives substantially all of its support from sources outside the United States.

The Section 4958 definition of the term "applicable tax-exempt organization" encompasses the concept of recognition of the entity's tax-exempt status. Most categories of tax-exempt organizations are tax exempt because they satisfy one or more federal tax law definitions of the term. However, to be recognized as tax exempt, some organizations (1) must file notice with the Service to that effect and (2) have their exempt status recognized by the Service. This recognition is accomplished by the Service's issuing of a determination letter or private ruling.

For an organization to be a tax-exempt charitable organization, it typically files a notice with, and has its tax-exempt status recognized by, the Service. Some charitable organizations, such as churches and certain other religious organizations and small organizations, are exempt from this requirement of recognition. For a charitable organization to be recognized as an applicable tax-exempt organization, it should be in compliance with the recognition requirements.

To be tax exempt, social welfare organizations do not need to have their exempt status recognized by the Service. An organization can qualify as an applicable tax-exempt organization by reason of being an exempt social welfare organization in the following four ways:

1. The organization has applied for and received recognition from the Service as an exempt social welfare organization;

2. The organization has filed an application for recognition with the Service, seeking exempt social welfare status;

3. The organization has filed an annual information return as an exempt social welfare organization; and

4. The organization has otherwise held itself out as an exempt social welfare organization.

A governmental unit or an affiliate of a governmental unit will not be recognized as an applicable tax-exempt organization if the governmental unit is (1) exempt from or not subject to taxation without regard to the general statutory basis for tax exemption or (2) relieved from the requirement of filing an annual information return. A governmental entity may be recognized as tax-exempt as an integral part of the state (1) by reason of the doctrine of intergovernmental immunity or (2) because its income is excluded from federal taxation.

An entity qualifies as a governmental unit if it is:

1. A state or local governmental unit as defined in the rules providing an exclusion from gross income for interest earned on bonds issued by these units;

2. Entitled to receive deductible charitable contributions as a unit of government; or

3. An Indian tribal government or a political subdivision of this type of government.

9.3 Intermediate Sanctions and Individual Executives and Professionals

Under the Section 4958 intermediate sanctions law, excise taxes are imposed on excess benefit transactions that occur on or after Sept. 14, 1995. The Section 4958 excise taxes do not apply to any transaction made pursuant to a written contract that was binding on Sept. 13, 1995, and continued in force through the time of the subject transaction.

An excess benefit transaction is any transaction in which a Section 501(c)(3) or 501(c)(4) organization provides an economic benefit to a disqualified person that has a greater value than what it receives from that person. An excess benefit transaction would include: (1) providing compensation to a person in excess of the value of the services rendered or (2) selling or renting property to a person for less than the property's sale or rental value. The excess benefit is measured as the difference of the fair market value of the benefit provided to the person and the fair market value of the consideration received by the tax-exempt organization.

As summarized above, there are two types of Section 4958 excise taxes. The first type of excise tax is imposed on the disqualified person who receives an excess benefit. That tax is equal to 25% of the amount of excess benefit. There is an additional excise tax equal to 200% of the amount of the excess benefit if it is not corrected before (1) the date that the Service's deficiency notice is mailed for the 25% tax or (2) the date that the 25% tax is assessed, whichever comes first. The second type of excise tax is imposed on "organizational managers" who knowingly, willfully, and without reasonable cause or participate in the excess benefit transaction. This Section 4958 excise tax is equal to 10% of the amount of the excess benefit, but no more than $20,000.

A disqualified person is defined in Section 4958 as someone who, at any time during the five years preceding an excess benefit transaction, was in a position to exercise "substantial influence" over the affairs of the tax-exempt organization. If an individual is considered to be a disqualified person, then certain related parties are also considered disqualified persons. These related parties include: spouses; brothers or sisters; spouses of brothers or sisters; direct ancestors; direct descendants and their spouses; and corporations, partnerships, and trusts in which the disqualified person has more than a 35% interest.

Certain individuals within a tax-exempt organization are automatically identified as disqualified persons. These individuals include: (1) any individual who serves as a voting member of the governing body of the tax-exempt organization, (2) any individual who has the power or responsibilities of the president, chief executive officer, or chief operating officer of the tax-exempt organization, and (3) any individual who has the power or responsibilities of treasurer or chief financial officer of the tax-exempt organization.

An employee of a tax-exempt organization is not considered a disqualified person if he or she: (1) receives less than $100,000 of direct or indirect benefits from the tax-exempt organization for the year (adjusted for inflation), (2) is not a member of a specifically included category above, and (3) is not a substantial contributor of the organization.

The Service looks at specified facts and circumstances to indicate whether a person has "substantial influence" over the subject tax-exempt organization. In particular, the Service often considers the following factors in deciding whether an individual has "substantial influence" over the tax-exempt organization:

1. The person founded the tax-exempt organization;

2. The person is a substantial contributor;

3. The person's compensation is based on the revenue derived from the activities of the tax-exempt organization;

4. The person has authority to control or determine a significant portion of the organization's capital expenditures, operating budget, or compensation for employees; or

5. The person has managerial authority or serves as a key adviser to a person with managerial authority.

The following types of facts and circumstances would indicate to the Service that a person does not have "substantial influence" over the tax-exempt organization:

1. The person has taken a bona fide vow of poverty;

2. The person is an independent contractor (e.g., an attorney) who would not benefit from a transaction aside from the receipt of professional fees; or

3. The person is a donor who receives no more preferential treatment than other donors making comparable contributions as part of a solicitation intended to attract a substantial number of contributions.

An individual can be liable for the 10% excise tax penalty on organization managers if he or she is an officer, director, or trustee of the tax-exempt organization or is a person with powers or responsibilities similar to those of officers, directors, or trustees. Attorneys, accountants, and investment advisers acting as independent contractors are typically not considered to be organizational managers. Any person who has authority merely to recommend particular administrative or policy decisions, but not to implement them without approval of a superior, is also excluded.

A tax-exempt organization's manager will be considered to have "participated" in an excess benefit transaction not only by affirmative steps, but also by silence or inaction. That would be the case when the organization's manager does not exercise a duty to speak or take action. However, the tax-exempt organization manager will not be considered to have participated in a transaction when he or she opposed it in a manner consistent with that manager's responsibilities to the tax-exempt organization.

Tax-exempt organization managers can avoid the 10% penalty if they can show that they did not act willfully or knowingly. Tax-exempt organization managers can meet this requirement if, after disclosing all facts to an attorney, they receive a reasoned written legal opinion that a transaction does not provide an excess benefit. This procedure will protect the manager even if a transaction is later determined to be an excess benefit transaction.

Compensation to an organization's management for services rendered will not be considered an excess benefit if it is an amount that would ordinarily be paid for similar services in a similar situation. For purposes of this Section 4958 excise tax, compensation includes, but is not limited to: salary, fees, bonuses, severance payments, and all forms of deferred compensation that are earned and vested, whether paid under a tax-qualified plan or not. If deferred compensation is paid to a manager in one year for services performed by the manager in two years or more, then that compensation will be allocated to the years in which the services are performed.

Compensation also includes all benefits, whether or not included in income for federal tax purposes. For example, such benefits include: medical, dental, life insurance, disability, and both taxable and nontaxable fringe benefits (other than job-related fringe benefits and fringe benefits of inconsequential value).

An economic benefit will not be treated as reasonable compensation unless the tax-exempt organization clearly indicates its intention to treat it as compensation at the time it is provided. For example, if the tax-exempt organization fails to include compensation or other payments to disqualified persons on a Form W-2 (for employees) or Form 1099 (for board members and other nonemployees) and does not treat the payments as compensation on its Form 990, then the payments will be considered an excess benefit.

A special rule applies to arrangements that compensate a disqualified person in proportion to the revenue generated by the tax-exempt organization. Such compensation may be considered an excess benefit even if it does not exceed the fair market value of the services provided. This result can occur if, at any point, the arrangement permits a person to receive additional compensation without providing proportional benefits to the tax-exempt organization. Whether such compensation is an excess benefit will depend on the facts of the individual case. The Service will consider such factors as: (1) the relationship between the size of the benefit provided and the quality and quantity of the services provided and (2) the ability of the party receiving the compensation to control the activities that generate the revenue.

To avoid the above-mentioned 200% excise tax, the excess benefit must be undone to the extent possible. In addition, other procedures may be necessary to place the tax-exempt organization in the same position that it would have been in if the excess benefits transaction was made under the highest fiduciary standards. An excess benefit can be corrected if the disqualified person repays the tax-exempt organization an amount equal to the excess benefit plus an interest element for the period the excess benefit was outstanding. A correction may also be accomplished, in some situations, by: (1) returning the transferred property to the tax-exempt organization and (2) making any additional procedures necessary to make the tax-exempt organization whole.

10.0 Excess Benefit Transaction Presumption of Reasonableness

There is an important "presumption of reasonableness" that every tax-exempt organization subject to the intermediate sanctions law may endeavor to take advantage of. That presumption is in favor of the tax-exempt organization that a compensation arrangement or property sale or rental is not an excess benefit. To qualify for this presumption of reasonableness, the tax-exempt organization must meet the following three requirements:

1. The compensation arrangement or property sale or rental must be approved by the tax-exempt organization's governing body or a committee of the governing body composed entirely of individuals who do not have a conflict of interest with respect to the subject transaction;

2. The governing body or its committee must have obtained and relied on "appropriate data" as to comparability prior to making its decision; and

3. The governing body or its committee must have "adequately documented" the basis for its decision at the time it was made.

These three presumptions of reasonableness requirements are summarized below.

10.1 Conflict of Interest

A member of a tax-exempt organization governing body or its committee will be treated as not having a conflict of interest if he or she:

1. Is not (a) the disqualified person benefiting from the subject transaction or (b) a person related to the disqualified person;

2. Is not an employee subject to the control or direction of the disqualified person;

3. Does not receive compensation or other payments subject to approval of the disqualified person;

4. Has no financial interest affected by the subject transaction; and

5. Will not receive any economic benefit from another transaction in which the disqualified person must grant approval.

10.2 Appropriate Data

The category of "appropriate data" includes such information and documents as: (1) the compensation levels actually paid by similarly situated organizations, both for-profit and tax-exempt, for similar positions, (2) independent compensation surveys compiled by independent consulting firms, (3) actual written offers from similar organizations competing for the services of the disqualified person, and (4) independent appraisals of the fair market value of the to-be-transferred property. There is a special "appropriate data" relief provision for tax-exempt organizations with annual gross receipts of less than $1 million. Such a tax-exempt organization will be automatically treated as satisfying the appropriate data requirement if it has data on the level of compensation actually paid by five comparable organizations in similar communities for similar services.

10.3 Adequate Documentation

To meet the "adequate documentation" requirement, the tax-exempt organization governing body or its committee must have written or electronic records showing (1) the terms of the transaction and the date it was approved, (2) the members of the tax-exempt organization governing body or committee who were present during debate on the transaction and the names of those who voted on it, (3) the comparability data obtained, and (4) what was done about the members who had a conflict of interest. For a decision to be documented concurrently, the records must be prepared by the next meeting of the governing body or committee occurring after the final action is taken. Also, the records must be reviewed and approved by the governing body or committee as reasonable, accurate, and complete within a reasonable time period thereafter.

For purposes of this presumption of reasonableness exclusion, a tax-exempt organization governing body is: (1) a board of directors, (2) a board of trustees, or (3) an equivalent controlling body of the tax-exempt organization. A committee of the tax-exempt organization governing body (1) may be composed of any individuals permitted under state law to serve on such a committee and (2) may act on behalf of the governing body to the extent permitted by state law. The tax-exempt organization should note that if a committee member is not on the governing board and the presumption of reasonableness is relied upon, then the committee member becomes an "organization manager" for purposes of the 10% excise tax penalty. In other words, the committee member is treated like a member of the tax-exempt organization governing body if the presumption of reasonableness relied upon is rebutted by the Service. Also, a person will not be treated as a member of the governing body or its committee if he or she (1) meets with other members only to answer questions and (2) is not present during debate and voting on the transaction.

In addition, a tax-exempt organization subject to the intermediate sanctions law should note that this presumption of reasonableness is only a presumption. The Service can rebut the presumption of reasonableness if there is information indicating that (1) the compensation was not reasonable or (2) the property transfer was not at a fair market value price. However, these three requirements should go a long way toward helping a tax-exempt organization avoid the Section 4958 intermediate sanctions penalties.

11.0 Valuation Analyst Considerations Regarding Private Inurement

This section will summarize a "top 10" list of valuation analyst considerations with regard to valuations performed for tax-exempt healthcare organizations. These valuations include both (1) fair market value appraisals of property (business interests or assets) bought and sold by the healthcare organization and (2) fair market value appraisals of the services paid for by the healthcare organization (paid as either employee compensation or vendor fees).

These considerations may not affect the valuation approaches, methods, and procedures that the valuation analyst selects and performs. And these considerations may not affect the valuation analyst's conclusions regarding the fair market value of the subject property or services. However, these are 10 factors related to the intermediate sanctions law and regulations that the valuation analyst should be aware of during the conduct of the tax-exempt healthcare organization valuation.

11.1 Tax-Exempt Healthcare Organizations

The Internal Revenue Code grants a tax exemption for nonprofit hospitals and other healthcare organizations provided that their net earnings do not inure (1) to the benefit of private shareholders or (2) to individuals with a "personal and private" interest in the healthcare entity's activities.

11.2 Criteria to Be Recognized as a Tax-Exempt Organization

To meet the statutory criteria to be recognized as a tax-exempt healthcare entity, the organization must comply with the following rules:

- Physicians cannot be "in a position to exercise substantial influence over the affairs of (the hospital)";

- The total compensation must be "reasonable" and the incentive arrangement may not be a disguised distribution of profits;

- The compensation arrangements must be negotiated or established in the context of an arm's-length relationship; and

- There is a ceiling or reasonable maximum compensation level.

11.3 No Inurement

No portion of a tax-exempt healthcare organization's income or assets may inure to the benefit of "insiders." For purposes of this consideration, the term "insiders" may be defined as someone with decision power (e.g., board members, officers, founders, selected physicians, and so on). Examples of such private inurement may include:

- Excessive employee or subcontractor compensation;

- Compensation based on the "net earnings" of the tax-exemption organization; and

- Any transfer of property or services at less than a fair market value price.

11.4 Penalty for Private Inurement

There are taxation-related penalties for any violation of this no-inurement rule. The Service may apply a broad spectrum of remedies, including:

- Revocation of the subject healthcare entity's tax-exempt status;

- Settlement of the amount of the inurement; and

- The Section 4958 intermediate sanctions excise taxes.

11.5 Purpose of Intermediate Sanctions

The objective of the Section 4958 intermediate sanctions law is to curb potential abuses by penalizing participating parties (both those that benefit from the abuse and those that knowingly authorize it). The intermediate sanctions law applies if there is an "excess benefit" transaction with a "disqualified person." An excess benefit transaction occurs when the economic benefit given in a transaction is greater than the consideration received by the healthcare tax-exempt organization. A disqualified person is any person having the ability to exercise influence over the affairs of the tax-exempt organization.

11.6 Imposition of Penalty Excise Taxes

Section 4958 imposes excise tax penalties on:

1. The disqualified person who has to correct the excess amount (i.e., pay it back to the tax-exemption healthcare organization) plus pay a penalty tax of 25%; and

2. The organization manager who has to pay a tax equal to 10% of the excess benefit amount (not to exceed $20,000 per transaction).

11.7 Rebuttable Presumption of Reasonableness

There is a rebuttable presumption of reasonableness with regard to the tax-exempt healthcare organization entering into property or services transfer transactions when:

1. The transaction is approved in advance by an independent, authorized body of the tax-exempt organization;

2. The decision was based on the appropriate comparability data; and

3. The decision is adequately and timely documented (i.e., written down by the later of the next meeting or 60 days).

11.8 Excess Benefit Transaction

An excess benefit transaction is any transaction in which an economic benefit is provided by the tax-exempt healthcare organization directly or indirectly to or for the use of any "disqualified person" if the fair market value of the benefit exceeds the fair market value of the consideration.

11.9 Disqualified Persons

For purposes of the Section 4958 intermediate sanctions rules, a "disqualified person" includes:

1. A voting member of a board of the tax-exempt organization;

2. The chief executive officer, chief operating officer, treasurer, or chief financial officer;

3. Any person, at any time during the previous five years, in a position to exercise substantial influence over the affairs of the organization;

4. Identified family members of the above; and

5. A 35% controlled entity.

11.10 Not Disqualified Person

For purposes of the Section 4958 intermediate sanctions rules, the following "persons" are not disqualified persons:

1. Organizations described in Section 501(c)(3); this exception was created by the Pension Protection Act of 2006;

2. Other Section 501(c)(4) organizations (applicable for Section 501(c)(4) organizations only); and

3. Employees receiving less than $100,000 a year in compensation.

12.0 Reasonableness of Tax-Exempt Organization Compensation

One of the current controversy areas related to the intermediate sanctions requirements relates to the reasonableness of compensation. This is particularly true with regard to healthcare industry tax-exempt organizations. This reasonableness of compensation issue appears to be the current focus of Internal Revenue Service scrutiny with regard to tax-exempt healthcare entities. To alleviate concerns regarding intermediate sanctions, the tax-exempt healthcare entity should establish that its executives and physician employees are not paid more than a fair market value-level of compensation.

Related to this reasonableness of compensation issue, many tax-exempt healthcare entities are considering the formation of a dedicated compensation committee. Such a compensation committee would:

1. Adopt a written charter;

2. Be comprised of independent directors; and

3. Be authorized to approve the organization's executive compensation.

And such a compensation committee would likely adopt a written compensation policy.

When considering the reasonableness of tax-exempt healthcare organization compensation, the Service looks at how the organization determined and documented the comparability of its executive compensation to other similarly situated organizations. In particular, the valuation analyst can assist the tax-exempt healthcare organization with the following:

1. Compensation levels paid by similarly situated organizations, both taxable and tax-exempt;

2. Independent compensation surveys compiled by independent consulting firms;

3. Actual written offers from similar institutions; and

4. Independent appraisals of the fair market value of the subject executive compensation.

The valuation analyst can assemble compensation data and prepare a compensation appraisal that considers the following:

1. Make sure that any compensation consultant relied on is independent and has no incentive to support higher pay and benefits;

2. Use data for the same or the closest functional position, and support these data in the board minutes; and

3. Use data for organizations with a similar level of annual revenue, or show that the compensation data was "normalized" to fit organizations of a similar size.

In the preparation of a fair market value compensation appraisal (i.e., a reasonableness of compensation study), the valuation analyst should note the following:

1. For-profit entity compensation data are permitted, but do not rely exclusively on for-profit entity compensation data;

2. Include compensation data related to prevalence and the value of significant employee benefits; and

3. Make sure that every element is considered and the total compensation is assessed for reasonableness (and approved by an authored body of the tax-exempt healthcare organization).

The approving body of the tax-exempt healthcare organization is protected in relying on the valuation analyst's written reasoned analysis, if the valuation analyst certifies that he or she:

1. Holds themselves out to the public as a compensation consultant;

2. Performs this type of compensation valuation regularly; and

3. Is qualified to perform such compensation valuations.

Such a written certification should be included in every type of compensation appraisal performed by the valuation analyst.

13.0 Recent Developments

Effective March 28, 2008, the Treasury issued final Section 501(c)(3) regulations regarding applicable tax-exempt organizations and excess benefit transactions. These new regulations clarify the substantive requirements for tax exemption under Section 501(c)(3). These new regulations also clarify the relationship between the substantive requirements for tax exemption under Section 501(c)(3) and the imposition of Section 4958 excise taxes on excess benefit transactions.

These new regulations discuss both (1) the imposition of the Section 4958 intermediate sanctions excise taxes and (2) the possible revocation of a tax-exempt organization's exemption status. Regulation 1.501(c)(3)-1 adds a new paragraph F that includes in part:

(ii) *Determination of whether revocation of tax-exempt status is appropriate when Section 4958 excise taxes also apply.* In determining whether to continue to recognize the tax-exempt status of an applicable tax-exempt organization (as defined in Section 4958(e) and Section 53.4958-2) described in Section 4958(c)3 that engaged in one or more excess benefit transactions (as defined in Section 4958(c) and Section 53,4958-4) that violate the prohibition on inurement under Section 501(c)(3), the Commissioner will consider all relevant facts and circumstances, including, but not limited to, the following—

(A) The size and scope of the organization's regular and ongoing activities that further exempt purposes before and after the excess benefit transaction or transactions occurred;

(B) The size and scope of the excess benefit transaction or transactions (collectively, if more than one) in relation to the size and scope of the organization's regular and ongoing activities that further exempt purposes;

(C) Whether the organization has been involved in multiple excess benefit transactions with one or more persons;

(D) Whether the organization has implemented safeguards that are reasonably calculated to prevent excess benefit transactions; and

(E) Whether the excess benefit transaction has been corrected (within the meaning of Section 4958(f)(6) and Section 53-4958-7) or the organization has made good-faith efforts to seek correction from the disqualified person(s) who benefited from the excess benefit transaction.

(iii) All factors will be considered in combination with each other.

In addition, the new regulations provide several examples regarding private inurement and the application of the Section 4958 intermediate sanctions penalty taxes. While it is not related to a healthcare industry organization, the following example is included in the March 28, 2008 regulations and is relevant to this intermediate sanctions discussion:

Example 1. (i) O was created as a museum for the purpose of exhibiting art to the general public. In Years 1 and 2, O engages in fundraising and in selecting, leasing, and preparing an appropriate facility for a museum. In Year 3, a new board of trustees is elected. All of the new trustees are local art dealers. Beginning in Year 3 and continuing to the present, O uses a substantial portion of its revenue to purchase art solely from its trustees at prices that exceed fair market value. O exhibits and offers for sale all of the art it purchases. O's Form 1023, "Application for Recognition of Exemption," did not disclose the possibility that O would purchase art from its trustees.

(ii) O's purchases of art from its trustees at more than fair market value constitute excess benefit transactions between applicable tax-exempt organizations and disqualified persons under Section 4958. Therefore, these transactions are subject to the applicable excise taxes provided in that section. In addition, O's purchase of art from its trustees at more than fair market value violate the proscription against inurement under Section 501(c)(3) and paragraph (c)(2) of this section.

The following example from the March 28, 2008 regulations is also relevant to this discussion of private inurement, excess benefits transactions, and the Section 4958 intermediate sanctions penalties:

Example 4. (i) O conducts activities that further exempt purposes. O uses several buildings in the conduct of its exempt activities. In Year 1, O sold one of the buildings to Company K for an amount that was substantially below fair market value. The sale was a significant event in relation to O's other activities. C, O's chief executive officer, owns all of the voting stock of Company K. When O's board of trustees approved the transaction with Company K, the board did not perform due diligence that could have made it aware that the price paid by Company K to acquire the building was below fair market value. Subsequently, but before the IRS commences an examination of O, O's board of trustees determines that Company K paid less than the fair market value for the building. Thus, O concludes that an excess benefit transaction occurred. After the board makes this determination, it promptly removes C as chief executive officer, terminates C's employment with O, and hires legal counsel to recover the excess benefit from Company K. In addition, O promptly adopts a conflict of interest policy and new contract review procedures designed to prevent future recurrences of this problem.

(ii) The sale of the building by O to Company K at less than fair market value constitutes an excess benefit transaction between an applicable tax-exempt organization and a disqualified person under Section 4958 in Year 1. Therefore, this transaction is subject to the applicable excise taxes provided in that section. In addition, this transaction violates the proscription against inurement under Section 501(c)(3) and paragraph (c)(2) of this section.

14.0 Revocation of Tax-Exempt Status

As indicated in the recently issued Section 501(c)(3) regulations, the Service still possesses its ultimate weapon with regard to tax-exempt healthcare organizations—i.e., the revocation of the organization's tax-exempt status. With regard to healthcare industry entities and other tax-exempt organizations, the valuation analyst should be aware that the Service may seek revocation—in addition to the provision of the Section 4958 intermediate sanctions excise taxes.

The Service has made it clear that it will consider a list of facts and circumstances in determining when the level of excess benefit transactions will jeopardize a healthcare organization's tax exemption. These factors include, but are not limited to, the following:

1. The size and scope of the tax-exempt organization's regular and ongoing activities that further exempt purposes before and after the excess benefit transaction or transactions occurred;

2. The size and scope of the excess benefit transaction or transactions (collectively, if there are more than one) in relation to the size and scope of the tax-exempt organization's regular and ongoing activities that further exempt purposes;

3. Whether the tax-exempt organization has been involved in repeated excess benefit transactions;

4. Whether the tax-exempt organization has implemented safeguards that are reasonably calculated to prevent future violations; and

5. Whether the excess benefit transaction has been corrected or the tax-exempt organization has made good-faith efforts to seek correction from the disqualified persons who benefited from it.

In other words, both the valuation analyst and the tax-exempt organization board should be aware that the imposition of the Section 4958 excise taxes are the Service's "intermediate" weapon. Revocation of the tax-exempt organization's exemption status is still the Service's ultimate weapon.

15.0 Summary and Conclusion

The valuation analyst should be aware of the Section 4958 relationship with other federal tax laws and with other federal and state regulations. There are three general sets of federal laws that are intended to achieve the same objective: prevent persons who have a close relationship with a tax-exempt healthcare organization from manipulating the flow of income or assets to them for their private benefit. These federal laws include the Stark legislation, the Medicare fraud and abuse statutes, and the tax-exempt organization provisions of the Internal Revenue Code.

All of these federal laws (and many corresponding state laws) are directly influenced by the following three legal concepts:

1. The private inurement doctrine;

2. The private benefit doctrine; and

3. The self-dealing rules.

The valuation analyst should be aware that the private inurement doctrine directly influences the Section 4958 intermediate sanctions rules. In many ways, the Section 4958 rules are a codification of the private inurement legal doctrine. The legal concepts of private inurement and excess benefit transactions are essentially identical. The same is true with respect to the legal concepts of the insider and the disqualified person. In the case of the private inurement doctrine, the ultimate sanction is the Service's revocation of tax-exempt status. The Service can apply the private inurement doctrine either (1) in lieu of the intermediate sanctions excise tax penalties or (2) in addition to the Section 4958 excise tax penalties.

The valuation analyst should be aware that the private benefit doctrine is applicable only to charitable organizations. That is, this legal doctrine is not applicable to other types of tax-exempt organizations, including social welfare organizations. The private inurement doctrine is applicable to both public charities and private foundations. In many ways, the legal concepts of private benefit and private inurement are essentially the same. That is, every transaction that is a private inurement is also a private benefit. The ultimate sanction, too, is the same: the Service's revocation of the organization's tax-exempt status.

The two principal differences between these legal doctrines are: (1) a private benefit transaction does not require an insider and (2) the tax law recognizes the idea of incidental private benefit. Therefore, the private benefit doctrine can apply even where the private inurement doctrine and the Section 4958 intermediate sanctions tax penalties cannot apply.

The valuation analyst should be aware that the rules concerning self-dealing and the Section 4958 intermediate sanctions rules do not overlap. This is because the legal rules concerning self-dealing apply to charitable organizations only with respect to private foundations. In contrast, the Section 4958 intermediate sanctions tax rules apply only with respect to public charities. Nonetheless, the self-dealing rules are still significant within the intermediate sanctions context. This is because the Section 4958 intermediate sanctions rules are patterned largely on the private foundation rules.

The valuation analyst should be aware that most healthcare industry professional advisers consider the Section 4958 intermediate sanctions rule to be a good idea. The Section

4958 provisions place the sanction—i.e., the excise tax penalties—where it should be: on the persons who inappropriately extracted a benefit from charitable and social welfare organizations and not on the tax-exempt healthcare organization itself. The intermediate sanctions rules—based on a standard of reasonableness—are an improvement over the unnecessarily stringent private foundation rules. Those rules effectively prohibit transactions with foundations and disqualified persons with respect to them.

The valuation analyst who practices in the healthcare industry should be aware of the various regulatory requirements with regard to property transfer fair market value appraisals and compensation for services fair market value appraisals. The valuation analyst should be familiar with the regulatory environment with regard to private inurement, excess benefit transactions, intermediate sanctions excise tax penalties, and other tax-exempt organization regulatory issues. The valuation analyst should be aware of these issues to provide valuation services to tax-exempt healthcare organizations that will help them address these regulatory concerns.

Chapter 12. Reasonable Compensation for Tax Purposes

CONTENTS

Chapter 12. Reasonable Compensation for Tax Purposes

By Mark O. Dietrich, CPA/ABV

1.0 Introduction

Fair market value compensation for physicians has become an increasingly important part of the healthcare delivery system as more physicians decide to become hospital or health system employees. Regulatory factors including the Stark Law and anti-kickback statute (AKS) affect the determination of fair market compensation as do inurement issues for tax-exempt organizations under section 501(c)(3) of the Internal Revenue Code. Despite the presence of significantly more tax-exempt hospitals or health systems, present appraisal practice focuses disproportionately on Stark and AKS issues and often ignores the *Derby*[1] case in its entirety, as well as general principles of tax law that are critical to the assessment of fair market compensation for those exempt entities. Stark and AKS are discussed elsewhere in this guide.

For those physicians who choose to remain independent, group practices of increasing size are part of the trend. With size come the ability and perhaps the necessity to invest in ancillary services such as imaging, laboratory, cardiac testing, and others that provide technical component (TC) net income that is distinct from the professional component income that provides compensation for physician work. Thus, private practices are faced with differentiating return on their investment in income-producing capital assets from the return on physician labor as part of the assessment of reasonable compensation, in addition to having Stark-compliant means of allocating that profit. It is arguable that the very methods of TC net income allocation allowed by Stark enhance the argument that such allocations and distributions are dividends, rather than compensation distributions for tax purposes.

---

1   Discussed later herein.

In both a hospital employment setting and private practice, the requirement that physicians supervise midlevel providers such as nurse practitioners and physician assistants can be a critical element of determining reasonable compensation. Particularly in the primary care specialties, this will become an increasingly important issue because midlevel providers will likely meet the dramatic provider shortfall in primary care. Like law firms and accounting firms (see *Mulcahy* infra), profits earned on income-producing staff pose dividend risk.

Although "reasonable compensation" is more often an issue for C corporations, where the risk that the IRS will challenge compensation payments as disguised dividends exists,[2] when the added 3.8% Medicare tax that specifically excludes from its purview pass-through income from S corporations engaged in an active business takes effect in 2013, *unreasonably* low compensation will likely become a risk issue for S shareholders. Thus, reasonable compensation will become a critical issue for both types of corporate entities for tax purposes.

In summary, appraisal professionals engaged to provide conclusions of value in healthcare-related compensation arrangements should not ignore compliance with tax regulations for reasonable compensation.

1.1 General Factors in Assessing Reasonable Compensation

Generally speaking, compensation must meet an ordinary and necessary test under section 162 of the Internal Revenue Code to be tax deductible *or* be paid by an exempt organization. The accepted definition of "reasonable compensation" under the fair market value standard is the amount required to hire a nonowner employee to perform the same function. Before proceeding to a review of factors specific to physician compensation, an overview of general factors considered in the determination of reasonable compensation is undertaken.[3]

Qualification of the Employee

"A critical factor to be considered is an employee's skill and qualifications, and where an employee's contribution is particularly impressive, compensation commensurate with such contribution is in order." *Georgia Crown Distrib. Co. v. Comr.*, 46 T.C.M. 959, 962 (1983)

---

2 See *Mulcahy* infra.
3 The author expresses his gratitude to Kevin Long, CPA, Esq., for portions of the case law citations in these factors.

Employee's Contribution to the Success of the Company

A second factor "concerns the employee's role in the taxpaying company. Relevant considerations include the position held by the employee, hours worked, and duties performed." *Elliotts, Inc. v. Comr.*, 716 F.2d 1241, 1245 (9th Cir. 1983). The court in *Elliotts, Inc.* stated that, "If *Elliotts* was performing the work of three people, the relevant comparison would be the combined salaries of those three people at another dealer."

Compensation Paid in the Industry

A third factor considered by courts is a "comparison of the employee's salary with those paid by similar companies for similar services." *Elliotts, Inc. v. Comr.*, 716 F.2d 1241 (9th Cir. 1983). However, when the business of the employer is the performance of personal services, courts have held this factor to be less useful because the best evidence of the value of the services is the profit made. See *La Mastro v. Comr.*, 72 T.C. 377, 384 (1979).

Independent Investor Standard

A fourth factor considered by the courts is the return on equity that a hypothetical inactive independent investor would consider reasonable. See *Exacto Spring Corporation, Petitioner-Appellant, v. Commissioner of Internal Revenue, Respondent-Appellee*, 196 F.3d 833 (1999); *Osteopathic Medical Oncology and Hematology*, 716 F.2d 1241, 1245 (9th Cir. 1983); and *Beiner, Inc. v. Comr.*, T.C. Memo 2004-219.

Compensation Paid to Other Employees

Finally, if appropriate, courts examine the compensation paid to other employees. However, when the services of the unrelated and nonowner employees are not comparable in scope to the responsibilities of the owner employees, the amount of compensation paid to such nonowner employees is not relevant to the reasonableness of the compensation paid to owner-employees. See *Beiner, Inc. v. Comr.*, T.C. Memo 2004-219.

1.2 Independent Investor Standard of *Exacto Springs*

Much has been written about the independent investor test used by the IRS expert in *Heitz*,[4] more or less ignored by the Tax Court and then used by the 7th Circuit in reversing in favor of the taxpayer. This test has become one of the primary standards by which the IRS and those courts that follow the 7th Circuit Court of Appeals rulings evaluate compensation paid to owner-employees. Following are the criteria:

1. The type and extent of the services rendered;

2. The scarcity of qualified employees;

---

4   TCM 1998-220, as *Exacto* was known in the Tax Court before being consolidated on appeal.

3. The qualifications and prior earnings capacity of the employee;

4. The contributions of the employee to the business venture;

5. The net earnings of the employer;

6. The prevailing compensation paid to employees with comparable jobs; and

7. The peculiar characteristics of the employer's business.

The following are extracts from the Appeals Court opinion that highlight the seven factors relevant to the independent investor test and the failures of the Tax Court's original decision in the case:

> The reasonableness of compensation is a question of fact to be answered by considering and weighing all facts and circumstances of the particular case. No single factor is determinative. In *Edwin's, Inc. v. United States*, 501 F.2d 675, 677 (7th Cir. 1974), the Court of Appeals for the Seventh Circuit, to which this case is appealable, divided these factors into seven categories: (1) The type and extent of the services rendered; (2) the scarcity of qualified employees; (3) the qualifications and prior earning capacity of the employee; (4) the contributions of the employee to the business venture; (5) the net earnings of the employer; (6) the prevailing compensation paid to employees with comparable jobs; and (7) the peculiar characteristics of the employer's business. For any given position, there will be a range, not unduly narrow, of compensation that could properly be considered "reasonable." (citations omitted) *William J. and Sandra D. Heitz, Petitioners v. Commissioner of Internal Revenue, Respondent.* (emphasis added)

> Respondent relied on an expert in the field of compensation and business valuation. In his opinion of the reasonable compensation for services rendered by Mr. Heitz to Exacto, he relied on representative data and an investor return analysis approach. Respondent's expert placed more emphasis on the investor return analysis tailored to the financial statements of Exacto. An investor return analysis compares a company's after-tax profit to its equity to determine whether an independent investor would be satisfied with the level of return. Respondent's expert indicated that the minimum required return for an investor in Exacto, given the risks associated with the industry, would be about 13 percent. Respondent's expert concluded that Exacto's after-tax profit was insufficient to support the level of compensation that was paid to Mr. Heitz and still provide the minimum required return and that reasonable compensation should, at most, be $592,500 and $621,400 for the fiscal years 1993 and 1994, respectively." (quoting *Heitz v. Commissioner*)

The failure of the Tax Court's reasoning to support its result would alone require a remand. But the problem with the court's opinion goes deeper. The test it applied does not provide adequate guidance to a rational decision. We owe no deference to the Tax Court's statutory interpretations, its relation to us being that of a district court to a court of appeals, not that of an administrative agency to a court of appeals. The federal courts of appeals, whose decisions do of course have weight as authority with us even when they are not our own decisions, have been moving toward a much simpler and more purposive test, the "independent investor" test. We applaud the trend and join it. (citations omitted) *Exacto Spring Corporation, Petitioner-Appellant, v. Commissioner of Internal Revenue, Respondent-Appellee.*

Because judges tend to downplay the element of judicial creativity in adapting law to fresh insights and changed circumstances, the cases we have just cited prefer to say (as in *Dexsil* and *Rapco*) that the "independent investor" test is the "lens" through which they view the seven (or however many) factors of the orthodox test. But that is a formality. The new test dissolves the old and returns the inquiry to basics. The Internal Revenue Code limits the amount of salary that a corporation can deduct from its income primarily in order to prevent the corporation from eluding the corporate income tax *by paying dividends but calling them salary because salary is deductible and dividends are not.* (Perhaps they should be, to avoid double taxation of corporate earnings, but that is not the law.) In the case of a publicly held company, where the salaries of the highest executives are fixed by a board of directors that those executives do not control, the danger of siphoning corporate earnings to executives in the form of salary is not acute. The danger is much greater in the case of a closely held corporation, in which ownership and management tend to coincide; unfortunately, as the opinion of the Tax Court in this case illustrates, judges are not competent to decide what business executives are worth.

The IRS's expert in *Heitz*, near as we can tell, looked at book (or tax return) after tax return and determined that 13% was a reasonable rate. However, assuming that the expert somehow developed a cost of equity of 13%, he appears to have ignored appreciation in the assets beyond book value. Any economically meaningful investor return analysis should be based upon the *fair market value* of equity and the annual changes in the value of the subject entity.

Mulcahy, which follows, examines *Exacto Spring* in the context of a professional firm.

1.3 *Mulcahy, Pauritsch, Salvador*
The recent Tax Court case *Mulcahy, Pauritsch, Salvador & Co., Ltd. v. Commissioner* (T.C. Memo. 2011-74), followed by a rapid decision on appeal by the 7th Circuit Court of

---

Appeals (No. 11-2105 (7th Cir. May 17, 2012)) highlights the increasing exposure of professional corporations operating as C corporations to challenges to their owners' compensation deductions. Because the case involves a professional firm with the same issues inherent in medical practices, it has broad implications in the determination of both deductible compensation as well as fair market compensation in the tax-exempt sector. Valuation professionals not trained in taxation often do not realize that the standards of IRC §162's "ordinary and necessary" test apply to exempt entities as well, with the added burden of meeting the inurement prohibition of §501(c)(3).

As can be seen from the extracts of the two courts' opinions that follow, the accounting firm made a critical error in shifting what were intended to be compensation deductions into "consulting" payments to shell entities for reasons that, in the opinion of the 7th Circuit, were intended to conceal the majority owners' true compensation from the rest of the firm. As the Tax Court found and the 7th Circuit upheld, that alone would have made the payments nondeductible. The courts, however, went on the find that the compensation was unreasonable under several other theories, including the independent investor standard of *Exacto Springs*, another 7th Circuit case.

The related entities that received the consulting payments performed no services:

> The related entities did not perform any services for the firm in the years at issue. The founders performed various services for the firm, including accounting, consulting, and management services. The firm's other employees (there were approximately 40 throughout the years at issue) performed both accounting and consulting services for the firm.

> Citing *Commissioner v. Natl. Alfalfa Dehydrating & Milling Co.*, 417 U.S. 134, 149 (1974), the IRS argues that the firm is bound to the form it chose for the transactions with the related entities.

> Therefore, the IRS argues, the "consulting fee" payments should be tested for deductibility as payments for the related entities' services—as opposed to payments for the founders' services. We need not reach this issue because, *even if the payments are tested for deductibility as payments for the founders' services, the firm failed to show that the payments are deductible*." (emphasis added)

> The firm concedes that no services were rendered by the related entities. Therefore, the firm is not entitled to deduct the "consulting fee" payments as payments for services rendered by the related entities.

Evaluating the payments as if they were payments for the founders' services, we find that the firm has failed to show that it is entitled to the deductions.

Return on Equity

Here is the Tax Court's discussion of what "return on equity" actually means. The accounting firm was claiming, in effect, that since such firms are typically valued on the basis of a multiple of gross revenue (which is, in fact, true), the owners were receiving their equity return each year that the revenues of the firm grew. Although this is a sound argument from a valuation standpoint, since it is well-established that return consists of both income return in the form of cash or dividend and capital appreciation, no valuation was submitted in support of either type of return. Nonetheless, this highlights why the income approach is useful in addition to a market approach, such as the rule of thumb cited by the firm purported to be.

> The firm contends that the rate of return on equity is equal to its gross revenue for one year minus its gross revenue for the prior year, divided by the gross revenue for the prior year. This definition is based on the theory that the value of the firm's equity is equal to the firm's gross revenue for one year.

> We agree with the IRS that the rate of return on the firm's equity should be calculated by reference to annual net income, not the year-to-year change in gross revenue. It is inappropriate to look to gross revenue (or to changes in gross revenue) to determine if equity investors are receiving good returns on their investment. A corporation's shareholders do not seek to maximize gross revenue. They seek to maximize profit.

> Using annual net income comports with the approach taken by the Seventh Circuit in *Exacto Spring Corp. v. Commissioner*, supra.

> But in this case, the firm reported taxable income of $11,249 for 2001, a tax loss of $53,271 for 2002, and taxable income of zero for 2003. This makes the rate of return on equity either near zero, below zero, or zero, in each respective year. Thus, the independent investor test does not create a presumption that the amounts were reasonable.

Survey Data

The firm retained Marc Rosenberg of the *Rosenberg Survey* as an expert to opine on the compensation paid to the owners. Both the Tax Court and the 7th Circuit dismissed his testimony in disparaging terms. The critical takeaway from the opinions is as follows: "Even though the $300,000 in payments [in the *Rosenberg Survey*] were nominally labeled by the company as 'salary,' the payments could in reality be a return on the owner's investment in the company." This is precisely the case with the data commonly used from the Medical Group Management Association *Physician Compensation and Production Survey* to the extent that it comes from owners of private practices! Similar anomalies exist in this and other surveys because of the reliance of various exempt institutions on compensation opinions from valuation firms to support fair market value, that are, in turn, based on private practice data that includes equity return payments to the owners! Completing the circle, these exempt institutions then submit data on their investment return-inflated compensation payments to the various surveys.

Without the aid of the presumption of reasonability, the firm has not otherwise shown that the amounts it seeks to deduct as compensation were reasonable. Generally, "reasonable and true compensation is only such amount as would ordinarily be paid for like services by like enterprises under like circumstances." Sec. 1.162-7(b)(3), Income Tax Regs. 14 The firm has not satisfied this standard because, as we explain below: (i) the firm's expert relied on irrelevant statistics regarding the amounts paid to the shareholder-employees at other companies and (ii) the firm has not shown that the other benchmarks it offered—the amounts it paid the minority shareholders and other employees—are appropriate for comparison.

Using statistics gathered from other firms, the firm's expert witness, Marc Rosenberg, opined on the reasonableness of amounts paid to each founder, which included (i) amounts designated as compensation and (ii) amounts designated as "consulting fees." The first problem with his analysis is that the statistics he gathered from other firms were irrelevant. He appears to have relied on the following statistic he gathered from each firm: (i) the sum of (a) the salaries the other firm ostensibly paid its owners for its owners' services and (b) the other firm's net income, divided by (ii) the other firm's total number of owners. This statistic does not necessarily correspond to what owners of other firms received for their services. For example, suppose that another company paid its sole owner $300,000 per year in "salary" payments that were ostensibly for services. This does not mean that the owner's services to the company were worth $300,000. Even though the company nominally labeled the $300,000 in payments as "salary," the payments could in reality be a return on the owner's investment in the company (or a repayment of the investment). Similarly, suppose that a company with a sole owner has $200,000 in net income. This does not mean that its sole owner's services were worth $200,000. The $200,000 in income could have resulted from the owner's investment in the company as opposed to the owner's services. The second problem with Rosenberg's analysis is that he opined on the wrong thing. He concluded that the payments to the founders were reasonable, not that they were reasonable compensation for services.

As discussed above, for a payment to be deductible as compensation for services under section 162(a)(1), the payer must intend to compensate for services. See supra part I.B.2.

7th Circuit Review

The 7th Circuit was, at times, almost vicious in its rejection of the accounting firm's position, with the very last sentence of the opinion capping off the attack. As the home court for *Exacto Springs*, its opinion returned to the discussion of return on equity.

> Whether the deduction that the corporation takes for the owner-employee's salary really is a dividend can usually be answered by comparing the corporation's reported income with that of similar corporations, the comparison being stated in terms of percentage return on equity, the standard measure of corporate profitability. See, e.g., *Menard, Inc. v. Comm*.

The court also distinguished a small professional firm from the subject firm, which had 40 employees and multiple offices. This is "good news" for solo medical practices or practices with few employees, no midlevel providers, and little ancillary equipment.

> But what if, as in a typical small professional services firm, the firm's only significant input is the services rendered by its owner-employees? Maybe it has no other employees except a secretary, and only trivial physical assets—a rented office and some office furniture and equipment. Such a firm isn't meaningfully distinct from its employee-owners; their income from their rendition of personal services is almost identical to the firm's income. The firm is a pane of glass between their billings, which are the firm's revenues, and their salaries, which are the firm's costs. To distinguish a return on capital from a return on labor is pointless if the amount of capital is negligible.

In one of the more pathetic aspects of the case, the 7th Circuit addressed the rationale of the firm for using the consulting payments rather than straight salary and bonus:

> They had been paid indirectly, the firm argues, in order to conceal from the firm's other employees how much of the firm's income was being appropriated by the founding shareholders. Some (maybe all) of those other employees, including employee-shareholders who are not among the founders, apparently thought that the founders were overpaying themselves.

> There is no evidence that the "consulting fees" were compensation for the founding shareholders' accounting and consulting services. If they had been that—rather than appropriations of corporate income—why the need to conceal them?"

The court also blasted legal counsel for the firm:

> Remarkably, the firm's lawyers (an accounting firm's lawyers) appear not to understand the difference between compensation for services and compensation for capital, as when their reply brief states that the founding shareholders, because they "left funds in the taxpayer over the years to fund working capital," [they] "deserved more in compensation to take that fact into account." True—but the "more" they "deserved" was not compensation "for personal services actually rendered."

The court appeared to go a little off-track, however, when addressing valuation issues as part of its decision to use a 5% capitalization rate—and calling it a discount rate—to value an accounting firm in a hypothetical example.

> The value of a firm as a going concern (rather than in liquidation) is the discounted present value of its anticipated future profits. … You cannot buy a firm that produces a $1 million profit every year for $1 million; the purchase price would be closer to $20 million (assuming a 5 percent discount rate).[5]

Finally, the court offered some backhand advice on entity structure:

> Why the firm continued as a C corporation and sought to avoid double taxation by overstating deductions for business expenses, when reorganizing as a pass-through entity would have achieved the same result without inviting a legal challenge … is a greater puzzle. But "while a taxpayer is free to organize his affairs as he chooses, nevertheless, once having done so, he must accept the tax consequences of his choice, whether contemplated or not …"

> That an accounting firm should so screw up its taxes is the most remarkable feature of the case.

From the two courts' opinions, there is no discussion of the *Norwalk* principles described in the next part of this chapter, leaving one to wonder whether the accounting firm's owners had noncompete agreements with their firm.

2.0 Who Owns the Intangible Assets?

To determine "reasonable compensation" in the context of the independent investor test, it is incumbent upon the valuation analyst to determine what underlying assets the

---

5   How excited accountants would be to receive a 20 times multiple for their practices!

independent investor is entitled to a return on.[6] Because the *Norwalk* case that follows involved a professional practice, it is an important element for determining ownership and investment return. Key takeaways from the case include the need to carefully review employment contracts and noncompete provisions. Although not specifically addressed in the case, the enforceability of noncompete agreements varies widely from state to state and thus the valuation analyst should be familiar with state law as well.

2.1 Specific Intangible Assets

Perhaps the most comprehensive source of intangible assets is derived from the regulations under IRC section 338 and the "residual method of allocation." A detailed summary is contained in Form 8594, which is a mandatory filing for buyer and seller "when there is a transfer of a group of assets that make up a trade or business (defined below) and the purchaser's basis in such assets is determined wholly by the amount paid for the assets. This applies whether the group of assets constitutes a trade or business in the hands of the seller, the purchaser, or both."[7]

Form 8594 Definitions

Classes of assets. The following definitions are the classifications for deemed or actual asset acquisitions.

> *Class I* assets are cash and general deposit accounts (including savings and checking accounts) other than certificates of deposit held in banks, savings and loan associations, and other depository institutions.

> *Class II* assets are actively traded personal property within the meaning of section 1092(d)(1) and Regulations section 1.1092(d)-1 (determined without regard to section 1092(d)(3)). In addition, Class II assets include certificates of deposit and foreign currency even if they are not actively traded personal property. Class II assets do not include stock of target affiliates, whether or not actively traded, other than actively traded stock described in section 1504(a)(4). Examples of Class II assets include U.S. government securities and publicly traded stock.

> *Class III* assets are assets that the taxpayer marks-to-market at least annually for federal income tax purposes and debt instruments (including accounts receivable). However, Class III assets do not include:

---

6   The methodology of allocating return on assets is described later.
7   Form 8594 instructions.

- Debt instruments issued by persons related at the beginning of the day following the acquisition date to the target under section 267(b) or 707;

- Contingent debt instruments subject to Regulations sections 1.1275-4 and 1.483-4, or section 988, unless the instrument is subject to the noncontingent bond method of Regulations section 1.1275-4(b) or is described in Regulations section 1.988-2(b)(2)(i)(B)(2); and

- Debt instruments convertible into the stock of the issuer or other property.

Class IV assets are stock in trade of the taxpayer or other property of a kind that would properly be included in the inventory of the taxpayer if on hand at the close of the taxable year, or property held by the taxpayer primarily for sale to customers in the ordinary course of its trade or business.

Class V assets are all assets other than Class I, II, III, IV, VI, and VII assets. Note: Furniture and fixtures, buildings, land, vehicles, and equipment, which constitute all or part of a trade or business (defined earlier), are generally Class V assets.

Class VI assets are all section 197 intangibles (as defined in section 197) except goodwill and going concern value. Section 197 intangibles include:

- Workforce in place;

- Business books and records, operating systems, or any other information base, process, design, pattern, know-how, formula, or similar item;

- Any customer-based intangible;

- Any supplier-based intangible;

- Any license, permit, or other right granted by a government unit;

- Any covenant not to compete entered into in connection with the acquisition of an interest in a trade or a business; and

- Any franchise, trademark, or trade name (however, see exception below for certain professional sports franchises).

The term "section 197 intangible" does not include any of the following:

- An interest in a corporation, partnership, trust, or estate;

- Interests under certain financial contracts;

- Interests in land;

- Certain computer software;

- Certain separately acquired interests in films, sound recordings, video tapes, books, or other similar property;

- Interests under leases of tangible property;

- Certain separately acquired rights to receive tangible property or services;

- Certain separately acquired interests in patents or copyrights;

- Interests under indebtedness;

- Professional sports franchises acquired before October 23, 2004; and

- Certain transactions costs.

Class VII assets are goodwill and going concern value (whether or not the goodwill or going concern value qualifies as a section 197 intangible).

2.2 *Norwalk vs. Commissioner*

Norwalk vs. Commissioner (TCM 1998-279) involved an assertion by the IRS of a gain on liquidation of an incorporated accounting practice.

Background

Norwalk and DeMarta formed DeMarta and Norwalk, CPAs Inc. in 1985. They each entered into employment contracts with the corporation that specified that the employee had an "absolute right to unilaterally terminate this Agreement by providing … written notice … of ninety days." The agreement also contained a restrictive covenant that forbade competing with the corporation during the term of employment, but not thereafter. Finally, a nondisclosure clause provided that the employee could not disclose the practice's clients during or after termination of employment.

In 1992, they determined that the practice should be terminated due to lack of profitability. The record indicated the earnings of the shareholder-CPAs were quite low, and in fact, they had to loan the practice money to keep it operating. Acting in their capacity as directors of the corporation, they voted to liquidate and distribute all of the assets to themselves. The assets included approximately $59,000 of fixed assets, which were contributed to another firm (Ireland) by DeMarta and Norwalk in exchange for partnership capital account balances of the same amount. Certain professional employees of the corporation established their own practices subsequent to the liquidation, taking many of their clients with them. The court noted that five years after the liquidation, the Ireland partnership still serviced only about 10% of the preliquidation clients. Ireland also leased the DeMarta and Norwalk office space for approximately 21 months after the liquidation.

During an audit of the tax return for the year of liquidation, the IRS maintained that "customer-based intangibles" were distributed to the shareholders, in addition to the fixed assets. The purported constructive distribution resulted in a taxable gain to the corporation as well as a gain to the shareholders. The IRS measured the value of the intangibles at $635,000, consisting of $266,000 for the client list and $369,000 for goodwill.

The Court's Analysis

The court noted that goodwill had previously been recognized as a "vendible asset which can be sold with a professional practice" citing, e.g., *Watson v. Commissioner* (35 TC 203 (1960)). Goodwill in an accounting firm "may include an established firm name, a general or specific location of the firm, client files and workpapers[8] ... a reputation for general or specialized services, an ongoing working relationship between the firm's personnel and clients, or accounting, auditing and tax systems used by the firm." The court went on to say "goodwill, then, is an intangible consisting of the excess earning power of a business.... [U]sually this extra value exists only because the business is a going concern. ... Goodwill may arise from: 1) the mere assembly of the various elements of a business, workers, customers, etc., 2) good reputation, customers' buying habits, 3) list of customers and their needs, 4) brand name, 5) secret processes, and 6) other intangibles affecting earnings." (*Norwalk vs. Commissioner*, ibid.)

During the presentation of expert testimony, the IRS's witness conceded that "without an effective noncompetition agreement,[9] the clients have no meaningful value." The court also noted that many of the clients had followed the corporation's nonshareholder CPAs to their own practices subsequent to the practice's dissolution. "These characteristics

---

8   Comparable to patient charts
9   A critical issue in medical practices as well

did not belong to the corporation as intangible assets, *since the accountants had no contractual obligation to continue their association with it.*" (emphasis added) The court concluded that the corporation had no goodwill that could be distributed, citing *MacDonald v. Commissioner* (3 TC 727). "We find no authority which holds that an individual's personal ability is part of the assets of a corporation by which he is employed where, as in the instant case, the corporation does not have a right by contract or otherwise to the future services of the individual."

Assessment of the Court's Opinion

It is well-established in both the business world and the courts that the transfer of the "goodwill" of a professional practice generally requires an enforceable covenant not to compete to be fully effective. Goodwill is actually a misnomer because the individual components of intangible value are frequently present and, as cited by the court, are actually identifiable, and the term "goodwill" is best left to define that portion of excess earning power not attached to any other intangible. The portion of excess earning power that attaches to the individual is commonly referred to as personal or professional goodwill, and the remainder may be referred to as practice or business goodwill.

Although the court provided an exhaustive list of the potential components of intangible value, it focused its conclusion on personal goodwill. Although not stated explicitly by the court, many of the other elements of intangible value were likely not present in this circumstance, since the practice was dissolved. For example, the intangible asset workforce-in-place was not present, since most of the firm's employees went on to competing practices. The practice ceased to function as a going concern after the liquidation, such that this asset, if present at all, was substantially diminished. DeMarta and Norwalk had to make personal loans to the practice to keep it operating; therefore, it was unlikely that any excess earnings attributable to practice goodwill were present.

On the other hand, some elements of intangible value may have been overlooked. The firm that DeMarta and Norwalk joined did continue to use the practice's office space for nearly two years, such that the intangible value associated with location might have been deemed to be transferred. The client files and work papers, cited by the court as an intangible, also seem to have been transferred, and some of these went with the shareholders and were used in their new firm. On the other hand, the court may have believed that if there was no enforceable noncompete, the shareholders were free to use these assets without regard to the corporate "ownership."

Implications

The *Norwalk* case has had significant implications and is especially relevant again in light of the spate of acquisitions of physician practices by exempt hospitals and other entities. The IRS will ultimately audit a number of these, and careful planning of such sales is critical to having an asset allocation upheld.

At the core of the court's argument is that an incorporated practice has no claim to the goodwill associated with an individual practitioner, or what is called personal/professional goodwill, in the absence of a specific contractual right: "We find no authority which holds that an individual's personal ability is part of the assets of a corporation by which he is employed where, as in the instant case, the corporation does not have a right by contract or otherwise to the future services of the individual." (*Norwalk*, citing *MacDonald*, ibid.) This has substantial tax planning implications in the sale of any incorporated professional practice taxed as a C corporation. The portion of the sale proceeds allocable to personal or professional goodwill does not belong to the corporation unless the individual is contractually bound to the corporation. This, in turn, means that such proceeds can then be paid directly to the individual and the characterization of those proceeds may be ordinary or capital, depending upon the facts and circumstances of a particular case. A valuation is required to determine precisely who owns what goodwill, and that valuation is contingent upon the specific contractual terms governing relationships between the corporation and its employees.

Valuing a physician practice in connection with a sale to an exempt hospital,[10] based upon the IRS Continuing Education Program Text on Valuation,[11] requires use of a discounted cash flow method to determine business enterprise value. Implicit in this method is the assumption that all of the intangible value reflected in the practice's earnings stream was transferable. The *Norwalk* case explicitly states that personal goodwill[12] is not transferable in the absence of a covenant not to compete. Inclusion of such a covenant between the buyer and the selling corporation and physicians is presumably the norm, but in a number of states, such as Massachusetts and Alabama, the enforceability of such a covenant is either questionable or moot.[13] Further, as noted above, the portion of the transaction consideration attributable to personal goodwill is not a corporate asset unless the corporation has a pre-existing contractual right to it.

Absent a *Norwalk*-analysis and related valuation, many practices structured as C corporations are likely to reflect as income sales proceeds properly attributed directly to their individual shareholders, who had no pre-existing noncompete. Further, reporting such proceeds as corporate income and then paying the cash as compensation to

---

10 Or perhaps a non-exempt equity buyer.
11 Discussed infra.
12 See the discussion of *Derby* also later herein.
13 This issue is discussed in-depth later in the chapter in the section "Physician Specific Factors in Assessing Reasonable Compensation, Impact of Noncompete Agreements."

shareholders may result in an unreasonable compensation attack by the IRS. If the proceeds were paid as a liquidating distribution, as argued by the IRS in the *Norwalk* case, corporate-level tax will have been unnecessarily incurred.

The case also has important implications for valuation analysts. It suggests that in valuing a professional practice, particularly one operating as a C corporation, the employment contracts and other documents of the shareholders must be reviewed to ascertain whether personal goodwill is an asset of the corporation due to the presence of a noncompete. If it is not, such goodwill should either be excluded from the valuation or separately valued and specified as a noncorporate asset.

Norwalk also appears to place a premium on separately identifying the various components of intangible value, rather than lumping them together into a single category labeled "goodwill." In a court proceeding, a valuation that measures a single quantity "goodwill" may have no probative value if it can be shown that only certain portions of the goodwill were relevant and no evidence as to the value of the individual components is presented. It seems likely that in *Norwalk*, the IRS would have had a greater chance of success if it had argued that other intangible assets had value independent of the shareholder-CPAs, as opposed to simply identifying "goodwill" and "client list."

Conclusion

A substantial portion of valuations are conducted with the tax authorities as a significant member of the likely audience. The healthcare industry has been the source of a large number of recent transactions that will now be the subject of regulatory review, as in the post-1990s era. The *Norwalk* case offers a review of the factors influencing the value and transferability of professional goodwill and potential defenses to IRS positions adverse to corporate treatment of intangible asset payments attributable to shareholders.

2.3 Larry E. Howard

Larry E. Howard and Joan M. Howard, Plaintiffs v. United States of America, Defendant, U.S. District Court, E.D. Washington, 2010-2 U.S.T.C. ¶50,542 (Jul. 30, 2010), is a recent case re-emphasizing the factors established in *Martin Ice Cream* and *Norwalk*. Howard involved the sale of an incorporated dental practice whose owner (Howard) had, perhaps inexplicably, entered into a three-year post-employment noncompete agreement with his corporate practice. The court found that the corporation, not Howard personally, owned the goodwill of the practice and that the sale proceeds attributed to that goodwill resulted in a dividend to Howard and a tax of $60,129, together with interest of $14,792.

The court stated, "In order to resolve issues of tax liability arising from legal interests, the Court must look both to state law for the determination of the legal interest and federal law for the taxation of the interest." *Analysis of state law remains a critical component of any valuation of a noncompete agreement—whether it is for tax purposes, damages purposes, or, in most circumstances, marital dissolution purposes.*

The court cited *"MacDonald v. Comm'r*, 3 T.C. 720, 726, 1944 WL 121 (1944), for the proposition that if an employee works for a corporation under contract and with a covenant not to compete with that corporation, as Dr. Howard did, then the corporation, and not the individual professional, owns the goodwill that is generated from the professional's work," a position that would conceivably have been regarded as "history" after *Martin Ice Cream*. The court also discussed that "the *Furrer* court divided an employee's goodwill as goodwill for his company, and separately, goodwill for himself, such as personal contacts." *Furrer v.Comm'r*, 566 F.2d 1115, 11171118 (9th Cir. 1977).

Citing *Norwalk*, the court observed: "In determining the value of goodwill, there is no specific rule, and each case must be considered and decided in light of its own particular facts. Moreover, in determining such value it is well established that the earning power of the business is an important factor." This reminds us that cases are very fact-specific. Finally, the *Howard* court concluded, "Bound by the covenant not to compete with Howard Corporation for a period of three years beyond when Dr. Howard no longer held Howard Corporation stock, which was until the dissolution of the Howard Corporation at the end of 2003 (see Ct. Rec. 28, Ex A at 28), Dr. Howard could not have earned income from a competitive dental practice within fifty miles of Spokane (Ct. Rec. 28, Ex F). Therefore, even if the goodwill had belonged to Dr. Howard personally, it likely would have little value, because Dr. Howard could not have practiced within a fifty mile radius from his previous practice location for at least three years beyond the date of the Howard Corporation dissolution. Those prohibitions would likely discourage patients from following Dr. Howard to a new location."

2.4 IRS Technical Advice Memo 200244009

This TAM involves the sale of a physician practice to Physician Practice Management Co. (PPMC) in a state where the corporate practice of medicine precluded it from outright ownership of practice. The IRS National Office advised that based on the documents, the physicians sold the rights and benefits of ownership in their stock to PPMC as opposed to their corporation selling intangible assets and therefore, gain was recognized at the individual level, not inside the corporation.

3.0 Specific Case Law Involving Physician Compensation

3.1 *Osteopathic Medical Oncology and Hematology, PC*

In *Osteopathic Medical Oncology and Hematology, PC v. Commissioner* (113 TC No. 26, Nov. 22, 1999), physicians scored a major victory over the Internal Revenue Service. Unlike the typical Tax Court memorandum decision heard by a single judge where the issue(s) involve determination of facts, this was a *regular* decision reviewed by the entire court involving a determination of law, "i.e., a rule of general application," quoting Judge Halpern's dissent. All of the facts of this case were stipulated (agreed to in advance) by the parties. The court was to determine whether supplying chemotherapy drugs to patients as part of an oncology practice constituted the sale of merchandise requiring inventory and the use of a hybrid accrual method of accounting. This was a "case of first impression" because the court noted that it was deciding "for the first time whether the furnishing of pharmaceuticals by a medical treatment facility as an *integral, indispensable, and inseparable part of the rendering of medical services is the sale of 'merchandise.'*" (emphasis added) Of particular significance in the timing of the decision is that the IRS had at that time completed a market segment specialization program (MSSP) audit of physician practices in the Northeast aimed at developing a new audit manual. These inventory questions were a significant issue in the audits of practices such as radiology.

Background

Osteopathic Medical Oncology and Hematology, PC is a Michigan corporation. It always utilized the cash receipts and disbursements method of accounting, deducting all of the disputed chemotherapy drugs in the year of purchase. It did not maintain a formal inventory (in this case, we mean a recorded or documented count), but typically had a two-week supply on hand. After an audit, the IRS determined that the drugs should be inventoried and, further, that the revenues associated with the sale of the drugs should be recorded on the accrual method. The remaining income from medical services could be accounted for using the cash method, thus the hybrid nature of the accounting method under the audit result. The combination of these two factors, inventory and receivables, resulted in an increase in taxable income of approximately $180,000.

Note: It is generally not recognized that it is possible for a single taxpayer to be engaged in multiple lines of business (as the IRS argued here) and to use the cash method for one line and the accrual method for another.

The Court's Analysis

The court (Judge Laro wrote the majority opinion) focused its legal analysis on the definition of "merchandise." Merchandise "is an item acquired and held for sale." The court noted that under Michigan law, only a pharmacist could legally sell drugs and Osteopathic was not licensed as a pharmacist. Further, the court noted that despite the fact that Osteopathic followed prescribed Medicare and other payer rules in billing for the chemotherapy drugs separately, this did not compel the conclusion that the drugs were being sold independent of the medical service. The reimbursement received for the drugs from payers was generally the average wholesale price (AWP) and therefore, reflected little or no profit[14] on the purported "sale." The court even noted that Medicare does not cover (outpatient) prescription drugs that can be self-administered and cited the definition of medical and health services from the Medicare statute.

The court also focused on the definition of "supplies" to contrast it with "merchandise." Citing the regulations under section 162, the court noted: "If a taxpayer carries incidental materials or supplies on hand for which no record of consumption is kept or of which physical inventories at the beginning and end of the year are not taken, it will be permissible for the taxpayer to include in his expenses and to deduct from gross income the total cost of such supplies and materials as were purchased during the taxable year." The court determined that the IRS could require Osteopathic to use the proposed hybrid method if: "1) Petitioner (the taxpayer) produced, purchased or sold merchandise, and 2) petitioner's production, purchase or sale of merchandise was an income-producing factor." The court determined that the taxpayer did not produce, purchase, or sell merchandise and therefore, did not have to make the second determination. "Petitioner's business is a quintessential service business. ... Although it furnishes chemotherapy drugs to its patients as part of its service, a person cannot obtain the drugs but for the chemotherapy treatments. ... Where, as here, the service provider dispenses the drugs as an indispensable and inseparable part of the rendering of services, the service provider is not selling 'merchandise.'" The court went on to note that "the mere fact that the chemotherapy drugs are expensive is insufficient to transmute the transaction from the sale of a service to the sale of merchandise and a service."

Implications

The IRS has broad authority to require a taxpayer to use a method of accounting that "clearly reflects income" as specified in the regulations under sections 446 (generally) and 471 (as to inventory). The IRS cannot compel a taxpayer to change its method, however, if the existing method clearly reflects income, even if the IRS method would also clearly reflect income. The court had to find that the method the taxpayer used (already) clearly reflected income to find that the one the IRS proposed constituted an

---

14   As we know from GAO reports that predated the Medicare Modernization Act of 2003, chemo drugs were often lucrative and the AWP methodology was flawed and replaced with the average sales price (ASP).

abuse of discretion. In so finding, in a decision reviewed by the entire Tax Court, a precedent of major import has been established that will alter the outcome of future conflicts between physicians and the IRS.

The emphasized quote above is perhaps the key to understanding the court's decision and applying it to other types of practices: "Where, as here, the service provider dispenses the drugs as an indispensable and inseparable part of the rendering of services, the service provider is not selling 'merchandise.'" Practitioners should focus their analysis of individual clients in various medical specialties on this criterion, without losing site of the broad purview of section 446. The examples that follow attempt to answer the inventory question for different practices where significant amounts are expended on supplies.

Radiology

Clearly, radiologists are not selling film, contrast (for MRI and CT), developer, or any other supplies consumed in the process of providing radiological services to their patients. However, global billing for radiology services consists of the professional component of interpreting the film and the technical component for the provision of equipment and supplies necessary to make the film. Clearly, the interpretation of the film covered by the professional component is a pure service. Less clear is whether the generation of the film paid for via the technical component is a pure service; the more likely conclusion is that it is primarily a payment for invested capital. Unlike the provision of chemotherapy drugs for which no separate payment beyond the average wholesale price is typically made, there is a distinct revenue stream associated with the technical component. Further, and likely more significant, it is possible for one taxable entity to provide the actual "filming" and another to do the interpretation. Another aspect of the decision that is relevant to the determination is the question of whether "the taxpayer produced, purchased or sold merchandise." Arguably, the generation of a film is a production activity, while the delivery of chemotherapy is not. If this threshold test is met, the second question, whether "the production, purchase or sale of merchandise was an income-producing factor," is easily answered yes, based upon the technical component revenue stream. Nonetheless, if the film is an "indispensable and inseparable part of the rendering of services," the taxpayer still has an argument that the accrual method is not required. It is possible that an integrated radiology practice that bills the global fee may be treated differently than a radiology facility that bills only the technical component will be.

Optometry

An optometry (or ophthalmology) practice clearly is selling merchandise in the form of eyeglasses or contact lenses, and it would seem indisputable that the inventory and accrual method would be required with respect to this activity. As is the case with radiology, a separate stream of revenue is associated with the sale of eyeglasses that is distinct from that associated with prescribing them. The possibility is raised that such a practice may use a hybrid method of accounting, reporting the service portion on the cash method and the merchandise portion on the accrual method.

Dentistry

Such a taxpayer would appear to have a better argument for the cash method after *Osteopathic*. Patients cannot obtain silver or porcelain fillings nor self-administer them, and the filling material is clearly an inseparable part of the service. Practices that do prosthetic work generally order the prosthesis from a lab and do not keep them on hand. However, here again we have risk, because the dentist is a reseller of the prosthesis, for which a separate charge would typically be made. Perhaps this indicates an accrual method, although it would have little if any impact on taxable income in the absence of inventory and receivables (and as such lessen the prospect for a general attack under section 446's "clear reflection" standard). The language of the decision seems quite strong even in this circumstance, however, since the prosthesis is an inseparable part of the service.

Laboratories of Physician Practices

If a physician practice owns, for example, a blood chemistry machine and performs its own blood tests, should this be considered the sale of merchandise? The supplies inventory consists of reagents and other items necessary to perform the tests. Automated lab tests do not have a substantial service element associated with them, unlike pathology tests that require interpretation. If the tests are provided only for the practice's own patients (and in light of licensing, insurance, and regulatory requirements, this might be expected to be the case), they would arguably be seen as an integral part of the diagnostic component of the medical service.

Plastic Surgery

The issue here would involve breast implants, collagen, and similar prosthesis or supplies. Again, since a patient cannot self-administer such things and they are an inseparable part of the service, it seems unlikely that an accrual method could be required.[15] However, those cosmetic practices that sell skin care products need to maintain inventories, and if such sales are other than for cash, they may need to reflect receivables.

---

15 Author's note: I once had a sales tax agent unsuccessfully attempt to tax breast implants and collagen being "sold" by a plastic surgeon.

Conclusion

Based on this case, tax practitioners can advise clients as to the risk associated with certain medical activities that include substantial supplies costs and whether, by extension, the profits on such supplies are properly considered compensation for services under section 162. The *Osteopathic* case offers criteria or guidelines for evaluating the risk of a challenge to the physician's method of accounting.

Ideally, no record of consumption or physical inventories of such supplies should be maintained, since the regulations at §162-3 specifically cite this as a prerequisite for deducting supplies in the year purchased, rather than when consumed.

The issue is not only limited to one of inventories under §471, but also the requirement under §446 that the accounting method must clearly reflect income. The IRS could exercise its broad authority under §446 without resorting to a requirement that inventories be accounted for, a point made by Judge Halpern in the dissent described below. Beware mismatches in the deduction of supplies expenses and the reporting of the revenue generated in the consumption of the supplies.

The ability of personal service entities to use the cash method of accounting under section 448 is not a barrier to the IRS requiring the taxpayer to use a method of accounting that clearly reflects income under §446.

Judge Halpern's Dissent and Warning

The court clearly was directly addressing only the issue of a "physician's outpatient chemotherapy facility," and practitioners should be cautious about drawing broad conclusions about other practices without carefully studying the decision. Judge Halpern's lengthy dissent (with which Judges Cohen, Whalen, and Chiechi joined) indicates that he, at least, will narrowly interpret the majority's decision when similar cases come before him. He states that the issues the IRS presented to the court are very narrow and cautions that "taxpayers not read too much into that determination." He concludes his dissent by warning that "taxpayers similarly situated to petitioner should be prepared to demonstrate that the cash method clearly reflects their income or that the hybrid method does not."

3.2 *Pediatric Surgical Associates, PC v. Commissioner,* TCM 2001-81 (2001)

This is likely the most significant compensation case for privately held medical practices, although as the discussion below indicates, it is questionable as to how broad the application of the principles therein might or should be. Key takeaways here include a need to document the allocation of expenses between owners and nonowners in the annual compensation plan determinations or in the alternative, document the rationale for the difference in pay between the two categories not pegged to productivity; the opinion alludes to what amounts to a "return on assets" approach as described in *Exacto Springs* earlier and later herein.

Background

This is a case decided by Judge Halpern, author of the dissent in *Osteopathic Medical Oncology*. Pediatric Surgical Associates is a Texas corporation. At the time of the audit, it employed four stockholders as surgeons (one who retired in the second audit year), in addition to two employee-surgeons. The initial deficiency notice disallowed $598,710 (46%) of the $1,300,231 paid to stockholders resulting in a balance due of $206,455, plus 20% §6662 penalty for calendar 1994. For 1995, $805,469 (53%) of the $1,528,125 paid to stockholders was disallowed, resulting in a balance $287,606 due, plus 20% §6662 penalty. The IRS later amended its disallowance to $140,766 and $19,450, respectively. The court ultimately disallowed $61,234 and $9,037, respectively. The average stockholder salary in each of these years was $325,058 and $382,031, respectively, certainly not anything extraordinary for pediatric surgeons with the subject's level of productivity (see, e.g., the Medical Group Management Association *Physician Compensation and Productivity Survey*). The physicians were each paid a monthly salary of $16,500 per month, plus periodic bonuses. Notable in the court's view was the fact that two of the four stockholders had countywide noncompete clauses in their employment contracts containing a penalty of $5,000 per month for 96 months. (Apparently, the two senior physicians who founded the practice did not have such provisions.)

The nonshareholder physicians had two-year employment contracts with fixed salaries of $12,000 or $12,500 per month, without bonuses. They had similar noncompete provisions with terms of 36 to 96 months and monthly penalties of $6,000 to $8,000.

The court reviewed individual surgeon productivity for each year, finding "no reliable records of collections" for 1994. The 1995 data appears in Exhibit 1 (Dr. Ellis was apparently part-time and then retired). Note that the two employee physicians generated very little of the collections:

Exhibit 1. 1995 Data		
	Collections	Salary
Ellis	$351,121	$172,896
Mann	519,396	452,969
Miller	772,752	450,485
Black	592,821	451,775
Subtotal	2,236,090	1,528,125
Vaughan	125,467	76,061
Snyder	4,339	0
Total	$2,365,896	$1,604,186

The court also noted in its opinion that (predictably) "the petitioner has never declared a dividend."

Internal Revenue Service's Position

The IRS argued in its brief that "the petitioner is entitled to deduct as wages the actual collections of the shareholder-employees, less their share of the petitioner's expenses." These expenses were apparently directly allocated where applicable, such as payroll taxes or individual fringe benefits, and then overhead items were equally allocated.

Taxpayer's Position

Counsel for the physicians (at least based upon the written opinion, as one can never be certain without a transcript) attempted to rely heavily on the fact that all of the payments to the stockholders were treated as wages and reported on W-2s.[16] Judge Halpern referred to the following quote from the physicians' counsel as "petitioner's principal argument": "In the instant case, the payments made to the shareholders surgeons were clearly compensation for services rendered and not disguised dividends. Petitioner issued W-2 forms to its shareholder surgeons and that income was duly reported on the surgeon's personal income tax returns. Moreover, the salary payments were properly deducted as such on Petitioner's tax returns." The court noted that elsewhere in the regulations under §1.162, it is stated that "any amount paid in the form of compensation, but not in fact as the purchase price of services, is not deductible." Another argument used by the petitioner was that the amounts were "reasonable" because they received less than their gross collections. It is difficult to believe that a judge (or anyone else for that matter) would have found this argument persuasive, and Judge Halpern did not.

---

16   Author's comment: Curiously, I have seen this emphasized in several prior cases by attorneys.

Issue for Decision

Curiously enough, Judge Halpern wrote: "We do not believe, however, that whether the return amounts were reasonable in amount is actually in question. The question framed by the parties' briefs is whether the remaining amounts [i.e., the disallowed amounts in question] were paid to the shareholder surgeons *purely for their services.*" (emphasis added) This is an interesting and subtle distinction.

Quantitative Approach

The court ultimately accepted, with modification, the IRS's position that the deducible compensation paid to the shareholders was *limited to their individual receipts less their allocable share of corporate expenses.* Query: Do we now have an obiter dictum version of an acceptable compensation plan?

In computing the disallowance, another problem for the judge was the lack of data for 1994. The IRS position at trial was that *the dividend received by the shareholders was equal to the profit on the nonshareholders.* To determine this profit, it was, of course, necessary to know both receipts and expenditures allocable to those nonshareholders. In the absence of data on those collections, the IRS maintained that the nonshareholder's collections should be equal to net billings ($245,597), which appears to be defined as the amount *expected to be* collected from insurers. This is a patently ridiculous position, as anyone familiar with medical billing would know, and particularly so in light of the fact that the nonshareholder physician (Dr. Snyder) had only worked for the taxpayer for one-half of the year. The taxpayer's accountant submitted an exhibit that claimed the receipts were $146,837, but the court stated this was not "supported by the evidence." Ultimately, the court used $171,918 in its calculations. Given that this taxable year generated almost all of the adverse results for the taxpayer, better data might have carried the day.

As to expenses, "both parties' allocations of expenses to Dr. Snyder's collections for 1994 and Dr. Vaughan's collections for 1995 consist of the salary paid to each plus one-tenth (one-fifth for the one-half of the audit year which each was employed) of other expenses

Exhibit 2. 1995 Expenses	
Salaries	$273,524
Repairs	8,930
Rents	57,954
Taxes	64,176
Interest	174
Contributions	5,480
Depreciation	27,592
Pension	134,917
Other	268,867
Subtotal	841,614
Officers salary	1,528,125
Total expense	$2,369,739

Exhibit 3. Final Result		
	1994	1995
Collections	$171,918	$129,806
Expenses	110,684	120,769
Profit	$61,234	$9,037

considered equally apportionable to the five surgeons during each year." There was a dispute as to whether certain expenses were at all allocable to Drs. Snyder and Vaughan. "We accept respondent's [IRS's] proposed allocation of expenses as reasonable with the following additional allocations: There should be a pro-rata (one-tenth) allocation of rent, repair and maintenance expenses, depreciation of office equipment (other than shareholder automobiles), telephone expenses, and equipment lease expenses to the nonshareholder surgeons' collections." This indicates that the IRS had not allocated *any* of these expenses against the nonshareholders, another ludicrous premise in a case that seems filled with them.

Expenses for 1995 are shown in Exhibit 2, as best as could be determined from the opinion.

The final result appears in Exhibit 3.

It was not possible from the information in the case to replicate the computation of "Expenses" because the amount and detail of "other expenses" was not disclosed. However, my analysis of 1995 indicates that the IRS must have excluded *all* of the pension contribution and most of the "other expenses" from the computation, including insurance (e.g., health and malpractice), which the opinion notes totaled $113,889. In fact, it appears that more than $187,000 of "other expenses" was excluded from the IRS's computation, and, for the most part, from the court's. (I was unable to generate a rational scenario in which there was a profit in 1995 on the nonshareholders. In fact, there appeared to be a loss in every conceivable circumstance.) Based on the court's computation of receipts of $129,806 and a salary to Dr. Vaughan of $76,061 plus the fringe benefits required, such as FICA, unemployment tax, workers' compensation, and health and malpractice insurance, to name a few, a profit seems unimaginable.

Legal Approach
Judge Halpern called attention to the corporate balance sheet and discussed likely "non-balance-sheet" assets, including "both the shareholder and nonshareholder employment contracts, petitioner's arrangement with the hospital to provide on-call services in the hospital's emergency room, and the goodwill that petitioner undoubtedly built up during its almost 20 years in business in the Fort Worth area." He goes on to say, "Together, the balance-sheet and nonbalance-sheet assets account for the in-excess-of $2 million in gross receipts that petitioner reported for each of the audit years." This seems to indicate that the judge based his decision at least in part on a "return on assets" approach. This is also significant if one compares it to the underlying rationale of Judge Ruwe in deciding the *Norwalk* case. There, the *lack* of noncompetes between

the CPA shareholder-employees and their corporation was decisive in preventing their personal goodwill from being treated as a corporate asset.

Here, it seems as though the noncompetes of the two junior physician shareholders and the employee-physicians were *corporate* assets. Unfortunately, this ignores the almost certain fact that the *senior shareholders,* who did *not* have noncompetes, possessed the bulk of the personal goodwill and had *not* assigned it to the corporation. In the real world of medical practice, a surgeon's personal reputation and skill generate referrals, not the existence of a corporation or an employment contract. Query whether the presence of a noncompete with a "profitable" employee necessitates the payment of a dividend.

The court mentions an "arrangement" with the hospital for emergency room services. If this agreement was in writing, it may have contained significant information as to the importance of the particular *individuals* covering the emergency room and highlighted the personal goodwill argument. A wiser analysis pretrial by petitioner's counsel might have addressed these issues in the brief.

Although the judge decided that the issue for resolution was "whether the remaining amounts [i.e., the disallowed amounts in question] were paid to the shareholder surgeons *purely for their services,*" this issue was based upon the positions enunciated in both parties' briefs. Perhaps the taxpayer would have won what appears to be an easily winnable case if the brief had focused on statistical evidence of reasonable compensation. Surely, if one is to retain surgeons of exceptional caliber, one will need to compensate them at salaries comparable to similar individuals. No evidence was apparent in the opinion that a comparable pay analysis was submitted, generally the most important test for reasonable compensation. Further, what administrative responsibilities the shareholder surgeons must have is not mentioned, although the judge noted specifically that the nonshareholders did not have any such responsibilities.

Conclusion

Bad presentations make for bad decisions. Given the dearth of cases on this topic and the implications for professional practices in general, this case is likely to be given far more weight than the written opinion indicates it deserves. If it is to be considered precedent, then CPA, law, architectural, consulting, and a host of other firms need to immediately re-evaluate their compensation schemes. S corporations (in particular) and LLCs taxed as partnership look extremely attractive in such an environment. Finally, the most worrisome aspect of the decision is Judge Halpern's making his decision on this issue: "The question framed by the parties' briefs is whether the remaining amounts [i.e., the disallowed amounts in question] were paid to the shareholder surgeons *purely for their services."* This would appear to expose any compensation arrangement not supported by a quantitative methodology to challenge.

4.0 Factors Specific to Tax-Exempt Entities

The federal government's grant of tax exemption to certain healthcare entities has come under increasing scrutiny due to the paling of the distinction between taxable and tax-exempt hospitals and health systems. Payments to physicians and other highly compensated individuals are at the forefront of this scrutiny, resulting in major changes to Form 990, the annual tax return filed by exempt entities, including a new Schedule J that contains detailed information about compensation payments.

4.1 Schedule J

Among the many features of Schedule J is a section in which the exempt entity is required to disclose the means it uses to establish the compensation for its CEO/executive director. An independent compensation consultant is defined for purposes of Schedule J as follows:

> Independent compensation consultant refers to a person outside the organization who advises the organization regarding the top management official's compensation package, holds himself or herself out to the public as a compensation consultant, performs valuations of nonprofit executive compensation on a regular basis, and is qualified to make valuations of the type of services provided. The consultant is independent if he or she does not have a family relationship or business relationship with the top management official, and if a majority of his or her appraisals are performed for persons other than the organization, even if the consultant's firm also provides tax, audit, and other professional services to the organization.

This mirrors the requirement for independent business valuation analysts as well.

Revenue- and Profit-Based Compensation

A number of disclosures are required with respect to revenue-based or profit-based compensation arrangements of the type that relate to common productivity-based physician compensation plans.

> Line 5. Answer "Yes" if the organization paid or accrued with respect to a listed person any compensation contingent upon and determined in whole or in part by the revenues (gross or net) of one or more activities of the organization or a related organization, or by the revenues (gross or net) of the organization or a related organization as a whole. For this purpose, net revenues means gross revenues less certain

expenses, but does not mean net income or net earnings. Describe such arrangements in Part III.

Example.

A, a listed person, is a physician employed by organization B. As part of A's compensation package, A is to be paid a bonus equal to x% of B's net revenues from a particular department operated by B for a specified period of time. This arrangement is a payment contingent on revenues of the organization, and must be reported on line 5, regardless of whether the payment is contingent on achieving a certain revenue target. However, if instead the bonus payment is a specific dollar amount (for instance, $5,000) to be paid only if a gross revenue or net revenue target of the department is achieved, the payment is not contingent on revenues of the organization for this purpose.

Line 6. Answer "Yes" if the organization paid or accrued with respect to a listed person any compensation contingent upon and determined in whole or in part by the net earnings of one or more activities of the organization or a related organization, or by the net earnings of the organization or a related organization as a whole. Describe such arrangements in Part III.

Example.

A, a listed person, is an employee of organization B. As part of A's compensation package, A is to be paid a bonus equal to x% of B's net earnings for a specified period of time. This arrangement is a payment contingent on net earnings of the organization for line 6 purposes, regardless of whether the payment is contingent on achieving a certain net earnings target. However, if instead the bonus payment is a specific dollar amount to be paid only if a net earnings target is achieved, the payment is not contingent on the net earnings of the organization for this purpose.

The Schedule J disclosure grid appears in Exhibit 4.

Exhibit 4. Schedule J Disclosure Grid

Schedule J (Form 990) 2011   Page **2**

Part II   Officers, Directors, Trustees, Key Employees, and Highest Compensated Employees. Use duplicate copies if additional space is needed.

For each individual whose compensation must be reported in Schedule J, report compensation from the organization on row (i) and from related organizations, described in the instructions, on row (ii). Do not list any individuals that are not listed on Form 990, Part VII.

Note. The sum of columns (B)(i)–(iii) for each listed individual must equal the total amount of Form 990, Part VII, Section A, line 1a, applicable column (D) and (E) amounts for that individual.

(A) Name	(B) Breakdown of W-2 and/or 1099-MISC compensation			(C) Retirement and other deferred compensation	(D) Nontaxable benefits	(E) Total of columns (B)(i)–(D)	(F) Compensation reported as deferred in prior Form 990
	(i) Base compensation	(ii) Bonus & incentive compensation	(iii) Other reportable compensation				

4.2 Excess Benefit Transaction Rules

The 1996 Taxpayer Bill of Rights established Internal Revenue Code section 4958, providing the IRS with "intermediate sanctions" for enforcing the prohibition against the private inurement of a tax-exempt entity's assets on earnings. Temporary regulations were finalized in January 2001. Section 4958 was intended to expand the IRS's enforcement tools for dealing with tax-exempt entities without resulting to the draconian measure of revoking tax-exempt status. In 2008, the Treasury issued final section 501(c)(3) regulations clarifying the application of intermediate sanctions and revocation of exempt status.

Inurement and Private Benefit

As observed in the 2004 EO CPE Text *Health Care Provider Reference Guide:*

> Treas. Reg. 1.501(c)(3)-1(d)(1)(ii) states that an organization exempt under IRC 501(c)(3) must serve
>
>> a public rather than a private interest. Thus, to meet the requirement of this subdivision, it is necessary for an organization to establish it is not organized or operated for the benefit of private interests such as designated individuals.
>
> Inurement and private benefit are often confused. Inurement is a subset of private benefit that involves unjust benefit from the income or assets of an exempt organization going to insiders. Unlike inurement, private benefit does not necessarily involve the flow of benefits to insiders. Private benefit can involve benefits to anyone.

Synopsis

In general, section 4958 and the temporary regulations impose excise taxes on excess benefit transactions between an exempt entity and a disqualified person taking place on or after Sept. 14, 1995. Simply stated, an excess benefit transaction is one in which the tax-exempt entity (or an entity it controls or deals with—an intermediary—whether it is tax-exempt or taxable) transfers (receives) assets to the disqualified person in excess of (less than) the value of goods or services it receives (provides) in the transaction. Payments of compensation and benefits to certain employees are within the purview of the law. The standard of value in making the determination is fair market value as defined in the regulations, which approximates the Revenue Ruling 59-60 definition.

Disqualified persons

Disqualified persons include any person in a position to exercise substantial influence over the affairs of the tax-exempt at any time during a five-year period ending on the date of the particular transaction subject to review. This includes, for example, the

CEO, CFO, COO, president, certain voting members of the governing body (trustees), as well as individuals whose compensation is primarily based on revenues from the tax-exempt's activities that the individual controls or who control substantial budgets or departments (collectively, organization managers). The family members of the above persons are also disqualified, as are entities in which they own 35% of the equity or more.

Note: It is generally believed (see section 53.4958-3(c)) that individuals whose compensation is tied to some portion of an exempt entity's revenue stream will be disqualified persons. As such, many physicians who are employed by hospitals whose compensation is productivity-based or who control departments could fall within this definition.

Amount of tax
The initial tax imposed on the recipient of the excess benefit is 25% of the excess amount, if the transaction is not corrected. If not repaid after the initial 25% tax, a second tax of 100% is imposed. Correction requires a payment by the disqualified person to the tax-exempt equal to "the sum of the excess benefit and interest." The interest is based upon the applicable federal rate (AFR) (as a minimum), compounded annually, for the month in which the transaction occurred.

Organization managers of the tax-exempt may be personally subject to a tax of 10% of the excess to a maximum tax of $10,000 per transaction, even though they receive no personal benefit from the transaction. The regulations provide, however, that if the manager relied upon the written opinion of a qualified professional based upon full disclosure of the facts, he or she may avoid liability for the $10,000.

Qualifications of professionals
The following professionals are among those eligible to provide opinions under the regulations: Certified Public Accountants "with expertise regarding relevant at law matters" and independent valuation experts who "hold themselves out to the public as appraisers or compensation consultants, perform the relevant valuations on a regular basis, are qualified to make valuations of the type of property or services involved and include in the written opinion a certification of those requirements."

4.3 The IRS Exempt Organization Division Continuing Professional Education Texts
The later discussion herein of the application of the independent investor test to the determination of reasonable compensation is aided by discussions in the Exempt Organization CPE Texts. These texts are nonauthoritative, but offer useful insight into the thinking of the IRS when written and a detailed explanation of valuation and reasonable compensation issues.

Valuation of Medical Practices, 1996 EO CPE Text

This text is perhaps the most significant of these documents. The IRS reconfirmed the relevance of this particular one in the 2004 CPE Text *Health Care Provider Reference Guide.* These are some of the intangible assets that can exist if generic goodwill is determined under the income approach and then allocated using the cost approach.

Goodwill in the Allocation Technique

The value of goodwill can be allocated to specific intangible assets; the value of the latter is limited to the value of the former, as calculated under the income approach. For example, if the total value of the individual intangible assets exceeds the total value of the medical practice net of the aggregate fair market value of the tangible assets, the amount of value that can be allocated among the intangible assets is more limited. Also, it is important to note that intangible value may not always be present in a medical practice.

Thus, ascribing value to intangible assets is a matter of allocating value derived using the income approach to specific intangible assets. The following example illustrates this process:

Example: The BEV of a medical practice under the income approach is $12,200,000. Medical equipment, furniture, and fixtures have a value of $2,200,000 determined under the cost approach. Buildings and real estate have a value of $6,400,000 determined under the market approach. The maximum value attributable to all intangible assets is $3,600,000.

Methods for valuing specific intangible assets commonly present in a medical practice are discussed below.

(3) Medical Records

Accurate and readily accessible medical records are an important asset of an operating medical practice. In addition, a growing market exists for the information in these records. Depending on such factors as how long the practice has operated and how many physicians it has, medical records can number in the hundreds of thousands and extend back a lifetime.

(4) Assembled Work Force

A well trained, organized, and efficient work force is a valuable asset in any business. The value of the assembled non-physician work force in a medical practice may be appraised using the cost approach, and depends on the number of full- and part-time employees, their positions, and the annual employee turnover rate (typically 15-35%). Use of the cost approach is based on the premise that for a potential buyer to re-create the particular practice, it has to hire and train a similar work force; that hiring/training process has identifiable costs—for recruitment, orientation, training, and lost salary—that form the basis of the valuation process. In general, the cost approach uses historical expenditures for these items to derive cost amounts which are multiplied by the number of employees in various job categories to derive the value of the assembled work force. Historical expenditures for the work force should be adjusted to levels in existence as of the valuation date.

Health Care Provider Reference Guide, 2004 EO CPE Text

This text contains a discussion of a variety of issues, including those related to fair market value. The portions related to reasonable compensation are described below. The reader may note many of the concepts expressed here are contained in the new Schedule J discussed supra.

Reasonable Compensation

In determining whether compensation is excessive, total compensation must be determined first. Compensation includes not only salary, but also any fringe benefits and pension plans or other deferred compensation provided. The exempt organization should provide assurance that the total compensation package provided to a physician (base salary, bonuses, and benefits) is reasonable for the physician's specialty and area. Generally, compensation is more likely to be reasonable if it is established at arm's-length by an independent board of directors or committee subject to a conflict of interest policy and is based on current compensation studies of similarly situated employees in similar geographic locales.

Revenue-Based Compensation

If compensation is based on revenues, the potential for unreasonable compensation warrants a close review of the compensation arrangement.

A fixed salary with a bonus based on a percentage of a physician's gross or net collections or billings is revenue-based. Employment contracts should be examined to determine if the amounts paid are excessive, and to ensure that the exempt organization is not using the revenue-based compensation as a vehicle for distributing the organization's profits. It may be appropriate to accept employment contracts with names and other identifying information redacted when the health care provider is concerned with confidentiality.

Compensation Plan

The compensation plan, first and foremost, must be a legitimate vehicle to compensate physicians fairly. If the health care provider cannot explain how it determines compensation is reasonable, then it needs to develop a process to ensure that its significant employment contracts will result in the payment of reasonable compensation. A process that undertakes to review compensation studies of similarly situated employees would provide an appropriate process.

4.4 The *Derby* Case

The Tax Court case *Derby et al. v. Commissioner*[17] is important for a variety of reasons, not the least of which is its instructive value as today's consolidation in the healthcare industry mirrors the one that occurred in the early and mid-1990s, when the *Derby* case originated. Key factors in the case include:

1. The use of expected post-transaction physician compensation in the discounted cash flow model based on the transaction documents *rather than* the use of some arbitrary compensation figure, such as the median for a given physician specialty;

2. Allocating enterprise or invested capital value among working capital, fixed assets, and intangible assets;

3. Carefully studying transaction documents to discern the character and extent of any intangibles being transferred or not being transferred;

4. The critical import of allocating between personal/professional goodwill and enterprise goodwill when valuing a medical practice for acquisition by a hospital;

5. The importance of any noncompete agreement in determining the value of the medical practice and the import of *Norwalk v. Commissioner*;

6. The need for "donative intent" when claiming a deduction for the value of a medical practice or other enterprise allegedly donated to a tax-exempt entity;

7. The relevance of the Friendly Hills private letter ruling and the 1994 Exempt Organizations Continuing Professional Education Technical Instruction Program manuals;

8. The citation of the anti-kickback statute (AKS); and

9. The issue of the timeliness of the valuation versus the date of the transaction.

---

17 *Charles A. and Marian L. Derby, et al., Petitioners v. Commissioner*, Respondent, T.C. Memo. 2008-45, Gale, Judge.

This is a well-written and insightful decision that highlights the typical issues in the valuation of a physician practice for sale or other transfer to a hospital, health system, or integrated delivery system. As such, Judge Gale's words are frequently quoted.

Case Summary

The case arose out of a claimed charitable deduction for the intangible value of the medical practices of more than a dozen physicians who sold their medical practices to Sutter Medical Foundation (Sutter) in 1994. The purchase agreements contained payments for fixed assets, while the selling physicians retained their accounts receivable.

The transaction took place during the period of consolidation of the healthcare industry associated with the rise of managed care and capitation on the West Coast in the early 1990s, which later spread across the country. Although restrictive managed care and capitation have fallen into disfavor and lost market share over the last six or seven years, consolidation is once again the rage in healthcare. Although some markets, such as Boston, are reconsidering the use of capitation, much of the present consolidation is driven by the more typical revenue concerns associated with fee for service medicine. Major hospital and ancillary testing revenue sources such as cardiology, orthopedics, and high-tech imaging are driving many of today's transactions.

The key decisions for the court were whether there had, in fact, been a *donative* transfer of intangible value, what the value was, and *if* the claimed value of the donation was overstated, whether the donor-physicians were subject to understatement of overvaluation penalties. As such, the valuations submitted by the taxpayers in connection with the donation received careful scrutiny from the court.

Critical in the ultimate resolution of the donation issue was a review of the history of the transaction with Sutter, which had declined to *pay* anything for intangible value, citing the anti-kickback statute (AKS) and the "famous" Thornton Letter in which the then Deputy Counsel of the Office of the Inspector General stated that a sale of goodwill by a physician to a hospital was problematic. Peter Grant, legal counsel in the seminal integrated delivery system transaction of the 1990s,[18] represented the *Derby* physicians, known as the Davis Medical Group (DMG).

> Unlike Foundation, Sutter Health was unwilling to pay anything for the intangible assets, or goodwill, that might be associated with petitioners' medical practices. ... First, and principally, because Sutter Health's management believed that doing so might constitute a crime under the Medicare and Medicaid Antikickback statute,

---

18   That being *Friendly Hills*.

42 U.S.C. sec. 1320a-7b(b), prohibiting payments for referrals of patients eligible for Medicare or Medicaid; and second, because Sutter Health's management believed, on the basis of their projections of the financial performance of the UHMG physicians' group after acquisition, that any additional payment for intangibles would have rendered the deal financially nonviable for Sutter Health.

Mr. Grant recommended that petitioners structure the transfers of the intangibles as donations because that technique had been used in connection with an acquisition of a group medical practice by a nonprofit medical foundation (*Friendly Hills Healthcare Foundation*), for which Mr. Grant had served as an adviser. Mr. Grant was familiar with the annual *Exempt Organizations Continuing Professional Education Technical Instruction Program manuals*, including the manual for 1994. (emphasis added)

Transaction Overview

The parties retained Houlihan Lokey (Houlihan), the valuation firm in the Friendly Hills[19] transaction, and arranged for an appraisal of the "business enterprise value" defined below. Note the emphasized items.

the fair market value of the aggregate assets of [the Davis Medical Group] *exclusive of any benefit or element of value conferred upon Sutter* [Health] as a consequence of its current or proposed relationship with * * * [Davis Medical Group], and *with consideration of proposed post-transaction compensation and benefits to the physician group*." Houlihan also agreed to "allocate the appraised value ... to each of its physician/shareholders" using a method to be agreed upon in consultation [physician] steering committee, but the agreed-upon method "[had to] be acceptable" to Houlihan." (emphasis added)

(Davis Medical Group later changed its name to Sutter West Medical Group (SWMG).)

SWMG entered into a professional services agreement (PSA) or employment contract with Sutter as part of the transaction.[20] The court spelled out the key economic terms of the PSA, which included a very limited noncompete—the terms of which are critical in this valuation and, for that matter, any such valuation—and a complex revenue sharing formula that included a minimum compensation guaranty. The PSA also contained what amounted to a signing bonus that the court would see as in part a payment for goodwill.

The PSA contained a noncompete provision, under which SWMG and its physician shareholder/employees were prohibited from participating in the ownership,

---

19   The first integrated delivery system ruling by IRS.
20   This is a standard feature of purchase transactions.

management, operation, or control of any business or person providing health care services within the service area covered by the agreement. However, specifically exempted from this prohibition was any SWMG physician who left the employment of SWMG. ... departing Physician may give written notice to the Departing Physician's patients named in the Departing Physician's patient list furnished to SMF on or before the ... Effective Date ... announcing the Departing Physician's separation from * * * SWMG and his or her new practice location, and offering the patient an opportunity to choose whether his or her patient records should remain with SMF or be transferred to the Departing Physician.

To provide an incentive to SWMG to form and sustain a group, SMF will pay SWMG a "Physician Access Bonus." ... The "Physician Access Bonus" was $35,000 for each of SWMG's full-time physicians.

The transaction documents stated that the seller and buyer believed the purchase price was less than the fair market value and that the difference was being donated. Significantly, the document contained a provision requiring that the appraisal be completed within 60 days—designed to avoid a "stale" valuation. Finally, a discounted cash flow model was used. All of the factors outlined in the case closely track the Friendly Hills private letter ruling and the 1994 *Exempt Organizations Continuing Professional Education Technical Instruction Program* manual.

As discussed above, the donation was to be allocated among 29 physicians who formed the group practice based on the valuation. In actuality, the donation was allocated using a formula designed by one of the physicians, which attributed "(i) 50 percent of the aggregate value on the basis of each physician's share of gross revenues generated in the year preceding the transfer to SMF; (ii) 25 percent on the basis of each physician's 'years in the community,' with up to a maximum of 5 years being counted; and (iii) 25 percent on the basis of each physician's share of the aggregate fixed assets transferred to SMF by the SWMG physicians." Although the physicians attached a Form 8283 to their tax returns, Sutter never reflected the donation in its tax return—despite the transaction documents obligating it to do so.

Taxpayers' Valuation for Trial

For healthcare industry appraisers and valuation analysts, the issues surrounding the appraisal submitted for trial are the most important. Perhaps the most significant feature of the appraisal prepared for the trial was the use of median compensation for the physician-sellers rather than the actual compensation negotiated in the transaction! This remains an item of ill-considered debate and frequently results in mistaken assumptions in physician practice and other professional practice valuation, despite being long-settled and in direct conflict with fair market value.[21] The question can be stated as follows: Would the hypothetical buyer pay a price for the practice based on a *lower* compensation than it intended to pay post-transaction, thereby paying twice to the extent of the extra compensation.[22]

> The national median for the "Western Region" for a weighted average of the medical specialties comprising SWMG, or 45.18 percent in determining the physician compensation expense for the discounted cashflow model.[23] *However, the actual negotiated compensation negotiated in the transaction "provided for compensation to SWMG equal to 57.75 percent of fee-for-service revenue, 47 to 53 percent of capitation revenue, and at least 55 percent of risk pool revenue."* (emphasis added)

The *Dutcher* appraisal contained other significant weaknesses in the view of the court. There was no allocation of any intangible value to the professional goodwill of the physicians[24] as opposed to enterprise goodwill, which the court differentiated as follows:

> No allocation of any value to the professional goodwill of the SWMG physicians despite the fact that Mr. Dutcher distinguishes, in the case of the goodwill of a professional practice, between "practice" goodwill and "professional" goodwill, the former attributable to characteristics of the practice entity such as patient records, provider contracts, and workforce in place; and the latter attributable to the personal attributes of the individual practitioner, such as charisma, skill, and reputation" and he acknowledge[d] that professional goodwill is not transferable.

Dutcher's testimony that professional goodwill is not transferable would have been one of many fatal blows to the taxpayers' position. The court went on to discuss the lack of noncompete agreements and importantly emphasized the continuing viability of *Norwalk v. Commissioner*,[25] perhaps the seminal case on the ownership and valuation of personal goodwill and noncompetes. A noncompete is the contractual basis for transferring personal or professional goodwill to an employer. The court also observed that the willing buyer would have insisted on "a significant discount" due to the lack of a noncompete!

---

21 See, e.g., "Medical Practices: A BV RX," *Journal of Accountancy*, November 2005.
22 Besides the inurement risk under the Internal Revenue Code, this error creates risk under the AKS and Stark laws.
23 The phrase "national median for the 'Western Region'" appears to be a misnomer. The data was taken from the MGMA *Physician Compensation Survey 1994 Report*, based on 1993 data.
24 "Identifying and Measuring Personal Goodwill in a Professional Practice," *CPA Expert*, Spring 2005 and Summer 2005.
25 T.C. Memo. 1998-279; See "Goodwill Requires Enforceable Covenant Not to Compete," *CPA Expert*, Spring, 1999.

There is no adjustment for the fact that the SWMG physicians were not required to execute noncompete agreements. Mr. Dutcher treated each SWMG physician as transferring an allocable share of SWMG's intangibles, including goodwill, which was not treated as diminished in any way by the physicians' not having executed noncompete agreements with respect to SWMG or SMF. However, in *Norwalk v. Commissioner*, T.C. Memo. 1998-279, we found that there is no transferable or salable goodwill where a company's business depends on its employees' personal relationships with clients and the employees have not provided covenants not to compete. ... We also believe that, under the willing buyer/willing seller standard of fair market value ... a willing buyer of SWMG on the transaction date would have insisted on a significant discount with respect to the value of the entity's intangible assets, precisely on account of the absence of noncompete agreements from the SWMG physicians.

Other problems cited by the court included the taxpayers' use of an intangible value allocation model developed by one of the taxpayers rather than one based upon sound appraisal techniques and failure to include in the valuation any consideration of the $35,000 signing bonus described above.

The Donation

There is a fundamental requirement in a charitable transfer that the contributor have "donative intent" to receive a tax deduction. Donative intent contemplates a disinterested gift to a charitable organization without the donor receiving any corresponding benefit. It remains commonplace to attempt to structure physician practice transfers as part-sale, part-donation in the current environment.

In its analysis of the transaction, the court found that the taxpayers received significant benefits from the transaction, which belied any intent to make a disinterested donation with no consideration in return. The court cited the advantages of patient retention, negotiating leverage as part of a larger system, compensation based upon a percentage of net revenue, all of which was embodied in an employment contract with "carefully delineated terms."

Conclusion

Consolidation trends are cyclical, and the wave that collapsed 10 years ago in the healthcare industry is back again. *Derby* reminds us that the old adage "those who fail to learn from history are doomed to repeat it" remains in full effect. From the standpoint of the hypothetical buyer, the court reiterated old guidance with respect to the common sense requirement that the value of the practice be based on expected post-transaction compensation. This is precisely the same issue that the Stark regulations suggest when assessing "commercial reasonableness"—the transaction must be viewed in its entirety.

Equally important, the court restated the principles espoused in the *Norwalk* case that contracts—in this case, the Purchase and Sale and Professional Services Agreement—be part of the analysis of intangible value due to the impact of (any) noncompete agreements. Thus, when valuing a medical practice for purposes of an actual transaction, the appraiser must be familiar with the terms of that transaction if the buyer and seller are to rely upon it for regulatory purposes. As the court seemed to suggest of the appraisal submitted by the taxpayers in this case, the report valued something other than that which the parties transacted. Transactional valuation requires understanding the terms of the transaction to opine on fair market value.

5.0 Physician-Specific Factors in Assessing Reasonable Compensation

Proper compensation analysis is critical to the overall quest to value a medical practice, particularly goodwill and other intangibles, because understatement of reasonable compensation will result in overstatement of goodwill. Alternatively stated, properly addressing reasonable compensation can often minimize all or a portion of the goodwill issue.

5.1 Physician Supervision of Midlevel Providers

The increasing use of midlevel providers across a broad spectrum of medical specialties has become an important part of assessing reasonable compensation versus profit. When profitable, midlevels can be a key indicator of possible enterprise value as opposed to personal goodwill. The opportunity to leverage revenue-producing as opposed to support personnel may exist in this instance and is analogous to a staff person in an accounting firm or an associate in a law firm.

Nurse practitioners (NPs) and pediatric nurse practitioners (PNPs) are graduates of nursing programs and are registered nurses (RNs) who then get an advanced degree, which includes clinical residencies. They are primarily engaged in the provision of primary care through internal medicine, family medicine, and pediatric practices, but can also be found in neonatology, mental health, geriatrics, OB/GYN practices, and in other settings.

The most advanced midlevel provider is a physician assistant (PA). The PA may be trained to perform many of the services that a physician does, including the most common procedures discussed above, such as lesion removal and new and established patient office visits. State laws vary as to the degree of independent practice a midlevel provider can engage in and the extent of physician supervision required. Similarly, Medicare and private insurers may have differing rules about how much a midlevel provider is paid for services covered by insurance. Under the so-called "incident to" billing rule used by Medicare and some insurers, a physician must be physically present in the office, although not in the exam room, supervise the midlevel, and review and sign off on all patient medical records prepared by the PA. If these requirements are met, the insurer will pay the practice the same amount as if the physician had provided the service himself or herself.

Medicare and other insurers who permit midlevels to provide services not under physician supervision—subject to state law requirements—usually reimburse for the service at a lesser amount. In the case of Medicare, it is 85% of the physician rate. This suggests that the value of physician supervision is equal to the difference or 15% and is an important element in the determination of reasonable compensation in a valuation model. The physician should be given consideration for this 15% of midlevel collected revenue as personal production in determining reasonable compensation.

5.2 Local Market Factors and Payer Rates Per RVU[26]

Relative value unit (RVU)-based compensation arrangements is increasingly popular for compensating physicians. While collected revenue-based systems—historically common in group practice, for example—reflect the individual physician's underlying payer mix, RVU systems are often payer-mix neutral. A RVU system[27] is therefore attractive to a physician employed by a hospital that treats patients regardless of their ability to pay. However, payer mix and other market conditions may taint RVU systems, which will require that the analyst understand and examine the effects of this issue when using compensation survey data to establish fair market value incentive compensation based on RVUs.

Several RVU measurement systems are associated with physician billing codes (current procedural terminology, or CPT), but the most commonly used is the resource-based relative value scale (RBRVS), which is also used by the Medicare program for establishing its physician fee schedule (MPFS). The RBRVS allocates RVUs to each procedure or service in the CPT based upon the amount of physician work, the cost of delivering the service, and the cost of malpractice insurance associated with the service. These RVUs are then multiplied by an amount known as a conversion factor and adjusted for geographic differences (the GPCI) to arrive at the fee for the service.

---

26 Gregory Anderson, CPA/ABV, contributed portions of this section; the complete chapter is included elsewhere herein.

27 It is important to note that most compensation systems focus on the physician work RVU component (wRVU), which is one component of the RBRVS and measures the total RVU values; the other two are practice expense and malpractice insurance cost. This allows for measurement of physician productivity using a measurement tool that essentially measures those areas of productivity that are under the control of the physician.

RBRVS has its weaknesses. The Medicare conversion factor suffers from a statutory construct, which attempts to peg overall Medicare physician spending to an annual limit that would seem to make that measurement unit meaningless in the present environment. Sitting at around $34 per RVU before geographic adjustment, the rate has been virtually flat for many years and does not keep pace with inflation, which the Medicare Payment Advisory Commission (MedPAC) estimates at less than 1.0% in 2012 for physician practices. Nonetheless, the vast majority of physicians continue to accept Medicare patients, suggesting, at least to government agencies such as MedPAC, that the payment rate has some relevance in assessing value. RBRVS is also subject to government manipulation that manifests itself in instability. For example, legislative intervention into the formula used to account for practice expense and statutory five-year adjustments to the physician work component of the RVU affect how RBRVS impacts physician payment.

Payment rates per RVU vary significantly from region to region, as well as from payer contract to contract. Providers and, particularly, provider-systems with negotiating strength may have payments rates per RVU well in excess of their competitors. Evaluating reasonable compensation for a physician, therefore, requires knowledge of the specific contract rates being paid for that physician's services, as well as knowledge of the underlying payer mix. Consider the example of how contract rates and payer mix impact physician compensation in Exhibit 5.

In the example, the physician is earning $190,000 per year on collected revenue of $440,000. The physician's earnings would vary from $130,000, if the practice were entirely Medicare, to $300,000, if it was entirely "market-best," a difference of 230%. The key observation to be taken from the example is that because expenses are fixed for a given volume of services in each scenario, all of the additional revenue from better contracts drops to the bottom line as physician compensation. That, in turn, suggests that "reasonable compensation" for 10,000 RVUs of services could range from $130,000 to $300,000, depending upon the mix and strength of the underlying payer contracts.

Lest that seem unrealistic on its face, consider the view from the physician working in a private practice holding only "market-best" contracts. Certainly, he or she would not be willing to work for $130,000 per year as if he or she would be seeing only Medicare patients. Similarly, a physician employed by a hospital or IDS with strong contracts for physician services would expect to be compensated at a commensurate rate, rather than have the employing institution retain the excess as profit. Similarly, it is unlikely that the managed care companies and other payers would be paying premium rates per RVU, unless market conditions warranted it and made it necessary to attract physician providers into their networks.

Exhibit 5. Example 1				
Payer mix	40.00%	10.00%	60.00%	100.00%
Payer	Medicare	Best	Non-Medicare Avg *Including* Best	Weighted Average
Total RVUs	10,000	10,000	10,000	10,000
Rate	38.00	55.00	48.00	44.00
Collections	380,000	550,000	480,000	440,000
Practice expenses	250,000	250,000	250,000	250,000
Physician income	130,000	300,000	230,000	190,000
Compensation per total RVU	13.00	30.00	23.00	19.00

Note: Payer mix weights are used to determine the weighted average rate per RVU. Each column indicates what the physician would have earned if 100% of the services provided were for each of the payer columns shown. For purposes of the example, assume that none of the total RVUs include Stark or other prohibited incentives.

The non-Medicare average value per RVU of $48 is an initial reference point for what "market" value for physician services is in this particular circumstance, assuming the weighted average conversion factor, as described in the following paragraph. The Medicare conversion factor is not negotiated, but is rather a legislatively imposed force majeure that is often disconnected from market forces. As such, it has limited worth in assessing "market" value.

The compensation reported in survey data such as that of the Medical Group Management Association will reflect the "weighted average" compensation or rate per RVU of only those entities participating in the survey. In Exhibit 5, this compensation would be $190,000. The actual rate per RVU in a given practice may be more or less than the survey result. If practices participating in the survey have a better payer and rate mix than all practices in a given area, the compensation will be higher and conversely, if the participating practices have poorer rates, the survey compensation will be less.

This type of analysis is critical to assessing the fair market value of compensation for hospitals employing physicians. In many markets, integrated provider networks that include both physicians and hospitals succeed in obtaining superior reimbursement from payers, which, in turn, results in superior compensation. The contracts may be a function of enhanced clinical quality from integration, market-based negotiating leverage, reduced administrative costs to payers due to single-signature contracting, or shifting of contract administration. Traditional analysis focusing solely on compensation surveys to determine fair market value may fall short of the market value

Exhibit 6. Example 2				
Payer mix	35.00%	30.00%	35.00%	100.00%
	Medicare	Best	Other Payers	Weighted Average
Total RVUs	3,500	3,000	3,500	10,000
Rate	38.00	55.00	48.00	46.60
Collections	133,000	165,000	168,000	466,000
Practice expenses	87,500	75,000	87,500	250,000
Physician income	45,500	90,000	80,500	216,000
Compensation per total RVU	13.00	30.00	23.00	21.60

Note: This example differs from the first in that the payer mix has been applied to the total RVUs of services performed to arrive at the actual compensation earned based upon the given payer mix.

of services based upon actual negotiated contracts for providers with a strong market position.

Returning to Exhibit 5, assume that an integrated delivery system has managed care and other payer agreements that result in the payer distribution and revenue for a physician practice shown in Exhibit 6.

In this case, the actual contracts in place generate physician compensation of $216,000 as compared to the "market" compensation described in the first example of $190,000, or about 14% greater. Solely relying on the survey result would seem to understate what is "reasonable compensation" for a physician employed in this particular provider entity. The determination of what is reasonable requires the valuation analyst and the employing provider to have keen insight into market conditions to arrive at an appropriate conclusion.[28]

An appropriate alternative to sole reliance on survey data is to measure the value of compensation per RVU based on data from the practice on revenues and RVUs produced by major payers or payer groups. Some analysts will benchmark the physician practice on a more global scale, analyzing collections per RVU to get an overall sense of favorable or unfavorable payer arrangements when the practice is compared against survey data. After this initial "litmus test" is interpreted, exploration of data by payer group, drilling down to compensation per RVU as in Exhibit 6, can give an indication as to whether and to what extent favorable or unfavorable payer contracts impact physician compensation. Thus, the use of the income-based approach in analyzing physician

---

28   See Chapter 37, "How Reimbursement and Physician Compensation Vary by Market."

compensation value essentially supplements the market-based approach conclusions derived from an interpretation of raw survey data.

What becomes clear to the analyst is that simple reliance on single survey data is not enough to yield a completely defensible conclusion of value for compensation under a RVU arrangement. Use of as many independently published surveys and as many different valuation methods as are reasonably available is certainly a prudent practice for those with the responsibility for determining compensation that must be defended as fair market value. Not only should the use of RVUs be considered, but other physician productivity benchmarks (i.e., encounters/visits for primary care, surgical cases for surgeons) may also be appropriate.

Finally, as an observation, physician practice acquisition value is often considered simultaneously with an employment decision and reasonable compensation analysis. In the practice valuation model, it is *not* appropriate to consider payer contracts held by a *particular* purchasing provider entity unless such contracts are common to the universe of potential purchasing entities in the market. This is because such an adjustment would be inconsistent with fair market value's requirement for *"any* willing buyer."

In contrast, compensation is a function of who employs you and what your services are worth at the time they are performed. From the standpoint of the hypothetical seller of services—i.e., the employed physician—being employed at a rate less than what the market is paying his or her employer currently for the physician's services would be inconsistent with the expected result in an arm's-length negotiation when reasonable knowledge is present. Thus, a physician practice may have a low value because there is little profit once the physician receives reasonable compensation for services based upon the practice's existing contracts. However, the physician may be better compensated in the future because his or her new employer holds better payer contracts.

5.3 Impact of Noncompete Agreements

Noncompete agreements are significant because they play a large part in determining who owns any goodwill that is attached to the individual physician: the practice entity or the physician himself or herself. Assume that the seller has the ability and intent to compete post-transaction absent a contractual provision precluding that competition. A hypothetical buyer would pay less for the business—if it pays anything at all—absent the noncompete, while a hypothetical seller expects to be paid for not competing in addition to being paid for the value of the other assets being sold. Thus, the noncompete has an identifiable value and two different fair market value prices would be determined for the practice based upon the terms of the deal.

The terms of the noncompete itself determine its value. Thus, a noncompete with a geographic restriction of 10 miles might be expected to have a value less than one with a geographic restriction of 25 miles, assuming that the catchment area of the medical practice extended beyond 10 miles. The sale of the practice with a 10-mile noncompete provision versus one with a 25-mile noncompete provision would have two *different* fair market values!

In addition to statutory prohibitions against physician noncompetes in some states, such as Massachusetts and Delaware, there is a line of case law around the doctrine of "contravention of public policy." In medical practices, this doctrine provides that agreements among providers, or their employing entities, should not be permitted to interfere with the physician-patient relationship. In some states, agreements found to violate this doctrine or otherwise found to be unconscionable may be thrown out in their entirety by courts. More common is a modification by the court to something reasonable. The status of a noncompete in the state in which the practice is located is a factor to consider in the risk premium, the discount for lack of control or minority discount, and the discount for lack of marketability—or as an intangible to be valued separately (see *BVR/AHLA Guide to Healthcare Valuation*, Chapter 21).

Example of a Noncompete's Impact on a Buyout Agreement

A noncompete agreement basically transfers some portion of a physician's personal goodwill to the employing entity, based upon the terms of that noncompete agreement, including duration and geographic scope. Not all goodwill in a practice will necessarily be personal, and some portion of the total goodwill may, therefore, be a corporate asset.

At least if one follows the logic of the Tax Court in the *Martin Ice Cream* and *Norwalk* cases, along with the *Howard* case, whether the stockholders have entered into a noncompete agreement with their employing entity determines to a large extent who owns the practice's goodwill. For tax purposes, the physician-stockholders selling their corporate practice can negotiate to have the buyer pay them directly for their *personal* goodwill, as properly valued, and then report it on their personal returns at favorable capital gain rates, avoiding double taxation if the practice is a C corporation. This tax/legal analysis is consistent with the underlying economics and should be considered in doing buyout and buy-in valuations and in assessing whether a payment of compensation represents a return or disguised dividend on a corporate asset.

Illustrative Cases

Here are several cases that indicate how the law in different states can influence ownership of goodwill. Before valuing a practice or determining reasonable compensation, the valuation consultant should be aware of the status of the law in the state the practice is located in. If covenants are unenforceable, certain intangible assets can be acquired, but the risk associated with maintaining them will be higher. Unenforceability of a non-compete strongly suggests that the individual physician owns the asset, and therefore, any return on that value is part of reasonable compensation.

Massachusetts: Ell Pond Medical Associates v. Lipski, MD

Massachusetts has a statute that makes unenforceable any contractual term that restricts the right of a physician to practice medicine in any geographic area after termination of employment. Several years ago, in a case called *Abisla v. Falmouth OB/GYN*, a Massachusetts trial court ruled that a financial penalty imposed on an employed physician who left a practice and opened a competing office was unenforceable. In 1998, Judge Hiller Zobel expanded the interpretation of the statute to preclude an employer from limiting a former employee-physician's solicitation of patients or suggesting that patients have their medical records transferred to the new practice.

Alabama: Michael B. Kline, MD v. Anniston Urologic Associates, PC

Alabama has a statute that voids any contractual provision that restrains the practice of a profession, citing contravention of public policy. In this case, Dr. Kline was a shareholder in Anniston Urologic (Anniston). The stock redemption agreement had two provisions that were the subject of the proceeding.

The first provision reduced the buyout price for the stock by $20,000 if the shareholder terminated employment voluntarily with less than nine months' notice. The second provision reduced the buyout price by $75,000 if the shareholder voluntarily terminated and engaged in a competing practice within a 25-mile radius of Anniston's office during the first year after termination.

The Alabama Supreme Court, on appeal, ruled that the first provision did not restrict the physician's right to practice. The second provision, however, was found to violate the statute. Noting that a similar argument was made and rejected in *Associated Surgeons, PA v. Watwood*, where Associated argued that it was not a restraint of practice, but compensation for the benefit received by *Watwood* by his having been associated with Associated, the court rejected Anniston's argument that the provision did not restrict Kline's right to practice.

Tennessee: Murfreesboro Medical Clinic, P.A. v. Udom

Although a noncompete agreement between a physician and a hospital, for example, was then enforceable in Tennessee, in the above 2005 case, the Tennessee Supreme Court banned noncompete agreements between physicians and their private physician practice employers. The court cited the right of patients to choose their physician in its decision.

The legislature followed in 2008 by almost entirely undoing the court's decision with Tenn. Code Ann. §63-1-148 and expanded the allowability of noncompetes beyond physicians to healthcare providers, such as chiropractors, dentists, optometrists, and psychologists. At that time, noncompetes effectively expired after the healthcare provider had been employed for six years. More significant from a valuation standpoint, Tenn. Code Ann. §63-1-148(a)(2) effectively exempts noncompetes in connection with a sale of a practice from the six-year term, allowing the noncompete to be enforced because it is otherwise reasonable.

In 2010, the legislature acted again to allow enforcement beyond six years, but required that the noncompete be reaffirmed with consideration, amending TCA 63-1-148(a)(2) to read:

> The healthcare provider and the employing or contracting entity may agree to an unlimited number of extensions of the six (6) year period so long as the extension is in writing, is supported by consideration, and each extension does not exceed a term of six (6) years. Any agreement to extend the six (6) year time period must be accomplished through subsequent negotiations and cannot be extended by an automatic renewal provision in an employment contract. Refusal by either party to extend or enter into a new employment contract shall not be considered grounds for terminating an existing employment contract so long as the employment term of the contract then in effect is a term longer than month-to-month.

The legislature, yet again, modified the noncompete rules on May 20, 2011, effective Jan. 1, 2012, removing the above-described limitations on enforcing a noncompete that had been in place for more than six years.

Physicians who are employed as a result of their practice being acquired are subject to a different provision than physicians who are employed without a practice acquisition. A "reasonable"[29] geographic noncompete may be imposed that cannot exceed a 10-mile radius from the primary practice site; the noncompete cannot exceed two years in length, unless the parties agree to a longer term, and that term cannot exceed five years. Further, the physician has to have the right to reacquire the practice at either the original purchase price or fair market value at the time it is repurchased. Finally, the physician need only give 30 days' notice to exercise the option to repurchase.

---

29   Tenn. Code Ann. § 63-1-148 (2011).

Texas: Valley Diagnostic Clinic, P.A. v. Dougherty

This Texas Court of Appeals case found a noncompete provision in a deferred compensation contract to be unenforceable The relevant provision contained a 50-mile radius around the practice location of Harlingen and lasted for four years. Texas law contains a covenants not to compete act (CNCA).

> Covenants not to compete are generally considered restraints of trade and are disfavored in law. See Tex. Bus. & Com. Code Ann. § 15.05(a) (Vernon Supp. 2008) ("Every contract, combination, or conspiracy in restraint of trade or commerce is unlawful."); see also *Travel Masters, Inc. v. Star Tours, Inc.,* 827 S.W.2d 830, 832 (Tex. 1991). However, the Covenants Not to Compete Act (the "CNCA") sets forth certain circumstances under which such covenants are enforceable.

> Notwithstanding Section 15.05 of this code, and subject to any applicable provision of Subsection (b), a covenant not to compete is enforceable if it is ancillary to or part of an otherwise enforceable agreement at the time the agreement is made to the extent that it contains limitations as to time, geographical area, and scope of activity to be restrained that are reasonable and do not impose a greater restraint than is necessary to protect the goodwill or other business interest of the promisee.

> Section 15.50(b) of the CNCA provides additional requirements for a covenant not to compete to be enforceable against a physician licensed by the Texas State Board of Medical Examiners. Specifically, the statute provides that:

> > (1) the covenant must:

> > > (A) not deny the physician access to a list of his patients whom he had seen or treated within one year of termination of the contract or employment;

> > > (B) provide access to medical records of the physician's patients upon authorization of the patient and any copies of medical records for a reasonable fee as established by the Texas State Board of Medical Examiners under Section 159.008, Occupations Code; and

> > > (C) provide that any access to a list of patients or to patients' medical records after termination of the contract or employment shall not require such list or records to be provided in a format different than that by which such records are maintained except by mutual consent of the parties to the contract;

> > (2) the covenant must provide for a buy out of the covenant by the physician at a reasonable price or, at the option of either party, as determined by a mutually

agreed upon arbitrator or, in the case of an inability to agree, an arbitrator of the court whose decision shall be binding on the parties; and

(3) the covenant must provide that the physician will not be prohibited from providing continuing care and treatment to a specific patient or patients during the course of an acute illness even after the contract or employment has been terminated.

To be enforceable, a covenant must comply with the terms of the statute, which require that any such covenant be "ancillary to or part of" another enforceable agreement and, as the court noted, "satisfy a two-pronged test: (1) the consideration given by the employer in the otherwise enforceable agreement must give rise to the employer's interest in restraining the employee from competing; and (2) the covenant must be designed to enforce the employee's consideration or return promise in the otherwise enforceable agreement."

The court concluded that the agreement failed to satisfy the second prong of the test:

> In order to satisfy the second prong, the forfeiture clause must have been "designed to enforce" Dr. Dougherty's "consideration or return promise" made in the deferred compensation provision. See id. Here, the only "consideration or return promise[s]" that Dr. Dougherty could be said to have provided under the deferred compensation provision were: (1) that he not compete with VDC after departing the practice, as detailed in the forfeiture provision; or (2) that he continue to practice with VDC. To the extent VDC claims that the consideration for its deferred compensation promise was a reciprocal promise by Dr. Dougherty not to compete, the forfeiture clause fails because there would be no otherwise enforceable agreement—that is, there would be no agreement that is enforceable wholly separate from the covenant not to compete.

Indiana: Central Indiana Podiatry, P.C. v. Krueger

In Indiana, noncompetition agreements may be allowed to the extent deemed reasonable. Central Indiana was a multilocation podiatry practice that employed noncompete agreements with the providers staffing its various locations.

> To be geographically reasonable, the agreement may restrict only that area in which the physician developed patient relationships using the practice group's resources.

Dr. Krueger in this case worked for Central Indiana in Clinton, Marion, Howard, Tippecanoe, and Hamilton counties at one time or another during his nine-year relationship. His noncompete clause was described as follows:

For two years after leaving CIP's employ, Krueger would be prohibited from divulging the names of patients, contacting patients to provide podiatric services, and soliciting CIP employees. Krueger also would be prohibited from practicing podiatry for two years within a geographic area defined as fourteen listed central Indiana counties and "any other county where [CIP] maintained an office during the term of this Contract or in any county adjacent to any of the foregoing counties.

The court observed that employers have a protectable interest in their customer relationships:

Indiana courts have held that "the advantageous familiarity and personal contact which employees derive from dealing with an employer's customers are elements of an employer's 'goodwill' and are a protectible interest which may justify a restraint...." E.g., Licocci, 445 N.E.2d at 561-62 (Ind. 1983) (citations omitted). CIP asserts that the noncompetition agreement serves its legitimate interest of protecting its goodwill and investment in developing its patient base.

After leaving Central Indiana, Krueger entered into an employment agreement with Meridian Health to work in Hamilton County, which was north of Marion County and subject to his noncompete clause. The court observed that:

The record does not support any inference that Krueger used CIP's resources to establish relationships throughout the approximately forty counties the agreement identifies by name or description. Because that is the area sought to be restricted by the agreement, the agreement is clearly overbroad. If a noncompetition agreement is overbroad and it is feasible to strike the unreasonable portions and leave only reasonable portions, the court may apply the blue pencil doctrine to permit enforcement of the reasonable portions.

In determining whether the geographic scope of the noncompete was reasonable, the court recorded the following analysis:

However, the geographic scope is unreasonable to the extent it reaches contiguous counties. The Nora office in northern Marion County is nearly forty miles from parts of contiguous Johnson County.... Similarly, because CIP selected entire counties as the building blocks of its agreement, even more proximate Hamilton County includes an area too broad to be reasonable.... Accordingly, the contiguous county restriction is unreasonable, and the restriction applies only to Marion, Tippecanoe, and Howard counties.

5.4 Trade Secrets and Similar Provisions

Other areas of the law can act similarly to a noncompete, and these include trade secrets, with many states having adopted the Uniform Trade Secrets Act. Nonsolicitation provisions with respect to a practice's employees, for example, may be enforceable even if a noncompete agreement is not. Rules with respect to patient medical records are discussed in the next section.

6.0 Applying the Independent Investor Test to Physician Practices

6.1 Differentiating Return on Labor From Return on Assets/Capital/Equity

As shown in Exhibit 7, the key to isolating reasonable compensation from return on the practice's capital or equity is determining what the return on the labor of the physicians is versus what the return on assets is. In some circumstances, especially when physician services are poorly paid, what would otherwise be a return on capital may be necessary to subsidize reasonable compensation. Assets can be financed with equity or debt, the combination of which is capital. The return on debt capital is paid as interest to the lender. As to who is entitled to the return on assets, the equity owners or the physician, as part of the payment for labor, ownership of "goodwill" and other intangible assets are critical. Thus, an understanding of the noncompete law in each state, the employment agreements, and cases including *Norwalk, Martin Ice Cream,* and *Howard* is required.

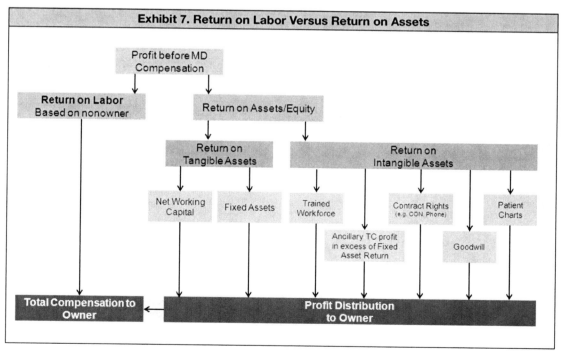

Exhibit 7. Return on Labor Versus Return on Assets

The assets in Exhibit 7 are divided into two general categories: tangible assets and intangible assets. Note that tangible assets include net working capital and fixed assets. They do *not* include trained workforce or patient charts, two common mistakes made in current valuation practice. Intangible assets can include a number of different assets besides those shown below, which include trained workforce, ancillary technical component profits in excess of a basic return on fixed asset ownership, and various contract rights, patient charts, and goodwill. *Not shown are other commonly cited intangibles, such as trade name or the allocation to any personal goodwill based on the noncompete analysis discussed above.*

Return on Equity

In a business valuation engagement, the discount rate (or, what is the same thing, the rate of return) is intended to be a measure of the risk involved in a business: the higher the risk, the higher the expected return (discount rate). The higher the rate, the lower the value of the discounted earnings. The rate developed is designed to reflect the no-risk rate of return, plus a factor for equity risk.

The return on various public stocks computed by Morningstar/Ibbotson Associates and used to compute the required rate of return for private companies is based upon two factors:

1. Income return: dividends received and taxed at established[30] rates; and

2. Capital appreciation: (often the vast majority of the return) taxed at *capital gain rates.*

In light of this, an assessment of reasonable compensation that considers the independent investor test requires the valuation analyst to be familiar with both business valuation and compensation valuation.

Practice-Specific Risk

A common mistake by valuation analysts and appraisers with little or no experience in the healthcare industry is to assume that understanding "cost of capital" can make up for their lack of understanding. Compounding that error is the frequent belief that all medical practices have a similar risk profile. Nothing could be farther from the truth or more likely to cause an incorrect practice valuation result and, therefore, a reasonable compensation analysis that is in error as well.

---

30   At least through the end of 2012, the federal rates are the same as capital gain rates.

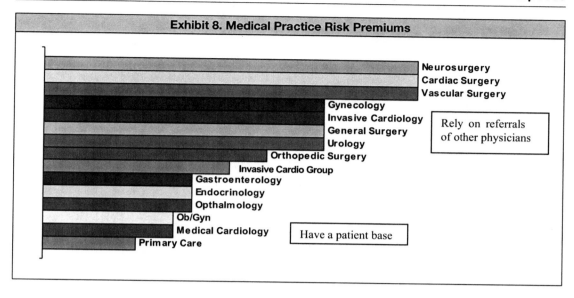

Exhibit 8. Medical Practice Risk Premiums

- Neurosurgery
- Cardiac Surgery
- Vascular Surgery
- Gynecology
- Invasive Cardiology
- General Surgery
- Urology
- Orthopedic Surgery

Rely on referrals of other physicians

- Invasive Cardio Group
- Gastroenterology
- Endocrinology
- Opthalmology
- Ob/Gyn
- Medical Cardiology

Have a patient base

- Primary Care

Exhibit 8 appeared in the article "Medical Practices: A BV Rx" in the November 2005 *Journal of Accountancy*. It clearly demonstrates that the primary care practices are the least risky, while surgical practices are increasingly risky. Among the many reasons for this risk differential is that surgeons require considerably longer training; certain physical skills, such as hand/eye coordination; and a source of personal referrals from their colleagues in the primary care and medical specialties. These factors tend to make more of the "goodwill" in a surgical practice personal rather than practice or enterprise and therefore, are critical in the assessment of reasonable compensation under the independent investor test. A similar analysis applies to medical specialists who also rely upon referrals from primary care physicians but can develop a repeat patient base for those who have chronic conditions.

Other significant practice risk factors include ancillary profits, particularly those from imaging, drug infusion and those with high utilization, expenditures, or anomalies in what one insurer pays versus another. A good source of insight into these issues is the MedPAC's Annual Report to Congress.[31]

Return on Assets

Business valuation, like accounting, has as an underlying premise that the sum of the assets equals the sum of the liabilities and equity. One notable difference is that normal trade payables and accrued expenses that are part of the computation of net working capital are moved as a negative to the left-hand or asset side of the business valuation balance sheet.

---

31 These various practice risk issues are discussed in detail in the *BVR/AHLA Guide to Healthcare Valuation* in chapters co-authored by Carol Carden and Mark O. Dietrich and authored by Mark O. Dietrich.

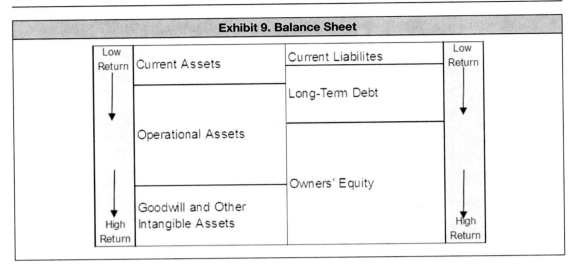

Whereas both sides of the equation must balance, the aggregate sum of the returns on the assets in a practice must be equal to the return on equity plus the return on debt, the latter, of course, being the interest paid to lenders.

As shown in Exhibit 9[32] from *Financial Valuation*, on the left-hand side of the balance sheet, risk and expected return on assets increase as one moves from current assets/working capital to operation assets (including fixed assets) and intangibles. On the right-hand side of the balance sheet, equity has a considerably greater expected return than debt.

Exhibit 10 illustrates the concept of increasing rates of return for both tangible and specific intangible assets. Assets have a risk gradient from low to high that starts with cash and working capital (accounts receivable, inventory), then moves to fixed assets (equipment, furniture), then certain intangible assets, and finally goodwill. The greater the risk, the higher the expected return.

Tangible Assets
Several accepted classes of tangible assets are discussed in the following material.

Net Working Capital
The rate of return on working capital is generally quite low. Cash balances in the current environment, for example, likely generate less than a 1% annual return if deposited in a bank. Accounts receivable return is typically evaluated in part by the ability of a business to finance them with lenders. Short-term lending rates are based on the prime rate, currently at 3.25%.

---

32 James R. Hitchner, et al., *Financial Valuation, Applications and Models.*

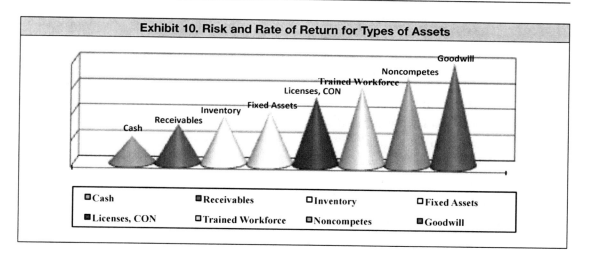

Exhibit 10. Risk and Rate of Return for Types of Assets

Fixed Assets

Fixed assets are the major source of a practice's ability to borrow money, so they are often financed with debt capital, for longer terms than the traditional short-term financing represented by the prime rate. Business valuation analysts typically consider current lender practices with respect to what portion of fixed assets can be financed with debt versus equity down payment. Use of capital leases is also common in fixed asset acquisition, and the usual lack of equity down payment is reflected in a higher interest rate.

Intangible Assets

Intangible assets vary in terms of risk and therefore, in terms of expected rate of return and are infrequently financed with debt capital. As such, the overall rate of return on intangible assets is conceptually the weighted average return of the individual intangibles.

Trained Workforce

This is one of the most controversial intangibles in the present appraisal-driven transaction market. In the overall scheme of expected return on assets and equity investment, very little of the cost of workforce would be expected to have debt capital, so it is primarily based on the cost of equity. Note: See the discussion earlier in the chapter under "Physician Supervision of Midlevel Providers" for their importance as a profit source indicating intangible, enterprise value.

Ancillary Technical Component Profits in Detail[33]

Technical component (TC) profits are crucial to the independent investor test. Many of the more common medical practice specialties require expertise in differentiating between the TC and professional component (PC) of ancillary services for practices

---

33 Kathie Wilson, CPA/ABV, contributed to this section.

such as radiology, cardiology, neurology, and others. The technical component is paid in connection with ownership of equipment, provision of a technologist to operate the equipment, supplies, and general overhead. The PC is paid to the physician specifically for interpreting the results of the test or study, e.g., an imaging study like an x-ray or MRI. Revenue from the technical component, therefore, is related to the equipment investment of the practice, not the efforts of the physician. As such, some portion of the return may be attributed to relatively low-risk equipment (fixed asset) *while the greater the overall return on TC investment, the more of the value is attributable to intangibles, including goodwill.* Thus, developing a rate of return on ancillary income requires a multistep analysis if the practice is engaged in both professional and technical component activities. In fact, it is best to consider valuing such operations within a practice separately from the professional activities, while being certain to do so on a fully allocated cost, stand-alone basis.

Definitions of Technical and Professional Component

This quote from the Centers for Medicare and Medicaid Services' Medicare Physician Fee Schedule 2010 Final Rule offers a good definition of TC and PC:

> Services with Technical Components (TCs) and Professional Components (PCs) Diagnostic services are generally comprised of two components: a professional component (PC) and a technical component (TC), both of which may be performed independently or by different providers. When services have TCs, PCs, and global components that can be billed separately, the payment for the global component equals the sum of the payment for the TC and PC. This is a result of using a weighted average of the ratio of indirect to direct costs across all the specialties that furnish the global components, TCs, and PCs; that is, we apply the same weighted average indirect percentage factor to allocate indirect expenses to the global components, PCs, and TCs for a service. (The direct PE RVUs for the TC and PC sum to the global under the bottom-up methodology.)

> Modifier. A modifier is shown if there is a technical component (modifier TC) and a professional component (PC) (modifier -26) for the service. If there is a PC and a TC for the service, Addendum B contains three entries for the code. A code for: the global values (both professional and technical); modifier -26 (PC); and, modifier TC. The global service is not designated by a modifier, and physicians must bill using the code without a modifier if the physician furnishes both the PC and the TC of the service.

As you might expect, the largest RVU element in the TC is for practice expense, whereas the largest element in the PC is typically for physician work, known as wRVUs. In some circumstances, these can be important in measuring the productivity for reasonable compensation purposes as defined later herein.

Some Common Mistakes

Most appraisers determine reasonable compensation when valuing a medical practice by reference to the physician's (or physicians' aggregate) productivity benchmarked against statistical norms, such as those from the Medical Group Management Association. The definition of collected revenue in the MGMA data is with the technical component of ancillary services *excluded*. MGMA does have some data that includes the technical component and nonphysician providers at two levels, greater than 10% or less than 10%, but that differentiation is generally not specific enough to be useful for reasonable compensation purposes. Thus, to use the data appropriately, it is necessary for the appraiser to: 1) separate the revenues associated with the professional component (related to the efforts of the physician) from those of the ancillary or technical component (related to the equipment investment); and 2) have actual experience with physician practices and the details of their compensation arrangements.

Example

When valuing a four-physician neurology practice with a single owner, the appraiser notes that the owner has collected revenue credited to him of more than twice the 90th percentile of MGMA. Upon investigation of the practice's reports of productivity by CPT (including HCPCS) code and the list of fixed assets, he determines that the practice owns an MRI unit in addition to other ancillary equipment. The technical component of the MRI services representing approximately 85% of the global (or total) collected revenue has been credited to the owner physician as well as the professional component. To determine the owner's productivity consistent with the MGMA definition, the technical component of the MRI and other ancillaries will have to be backed out. This has a dramatic effect on the reasonable compensation determination: After the appropriate modifications are made, the owner physician's collections are only at the 75th percentile of MGMA. Failure to identify and appropriately adjust for the technical component collected revenue would have resulted in a dramatic understatement of the practice's value due to an overstatement of reasonable compensation for the services of the owner physician.

Transactions

In the current transaction market, differentiating reasonable compensation along with enterprise and personal goodwill can be equally important. After a hospital acquires a physician practice, a number of employment settings are possible, including employment by the hospital, by a hospital-controlled group practice, or by the physician practice itself, if the hospital purchases the stock. The Stark laws have different permitted compensation rules depending on the nature of the employment setting, which can impact how profits from the technical component of ancillaries are handled. *This should, in turn, influence precisely what is being valued and how reasonable compensation is determined.*

Individual Market Idiosyncrasies

In some poorly reimbursed markets, it may, in fact, be necessary for the technical component income to supplement reasonable compensation for the physicians. For example, Rhode Island is notorious for the low levels of fees paid to physicians. This is due, in large part, to the fact that two insurers control nearly all of the health insurance market in that state and rates are artificially low as a result. As such, to attract and retain physicians, many practices have profitable ancillaries in place. In such a circumstance, it may be necessary to test the reasonable compensation analysis against an alternative measure of production such as compensation per RVU, work RVUs (wRVUs), or annual encounters. This is an example where the productivity data *including* technical component revenue may need to be evaluated as well. It also highlights the importance of using the various approaches to valuation described in this guide in addition to an independent investor analysis when determining reasonable compensation.

Contract Rights

The term of a contract has a significant impact on the underlying risk, and therefore, the expected rate of return. For simplicity, and because business valuation generally assumes perpetual life for the business, appraisers typically use a single expected rate of return to account for all future periods and those periods' cash returns. In fact, the nearer years have less uncertainty associated with them than do the later years: It is more difficult to forecast what will happen in five years than it is to forecast what will happen in six months, although both can be challenging. As a technical matter, this term risk can be seen by examining the yields on various United States Treasury securities. For example, Treasury bills with a 90-day term have a lower yield than Treasury bonds, which have a 30-year term at issue. In valuation, the difference between the two is known as the horizon [risk] premium. *Shorter terms have less risk than longer terms.*[34]

Patient Charts

As noted above, patient charts or medical records are *not* a tangible asset; they are an intangible asset. As described earlier herein, the IRS CPE Text from 1996 describes medical records:

> Methods for valuing specific intangible assets commonly present in a medical practice are discussed below.

---

34 There are times when the so-called "yield curve" for interest-bearing securities is inverted, leading to short-term rates being higher than long-term rates.

(3) Medical Records

Accurate and readily accessible medical records are an important asset of an operating medical practice. In addition, a growing market exists for the information in these records. Depending on such factors as how long the practice has operated and how many physicians it has, medical records can number in the hundreds of thousands and extend back a lifetime.[35]

The question often arises as to whether patient medical records have any value independent of the medical practice, e.g., as a stand-alone asset. Even before considering the rule that an asset has to have an associated cash flow to avoid economic obsolescence consideration, valuation analysts need to first look at state law and the federal HIPAA statute for the rights patients have to medical records as well as the limits on what a practice can charge for a copy. Furthermore, valuation analysts need to be aware that many provider agreements with health insurers contain specific clauses that address the right of a patient and/or subsequent provider to medical record data.

In the same manner that it is not possible to do valuation work in the healthcare industry without being aware of the Stark law and anti-kickback statute, one cannot value an alleged intangible asset without considering any laws and regulations affecting it. For example, in Vermont, the statute requires hospitals to retain medical records for a minimum of 10 years. There is, however, no specific statutory provision for physicians, but longer periods of time are usually recommended. A physician selling a practice, retiring, or relocating, therefore, needs to provide patients with the opportunity to obtain a copy of their record and to retrieve that record in the future for a patient who does not get a copy at the time the physician leaves the practice. *This creates a significant storage and retrieval obligation or* liability *that the analyst needs to measure in addition to any possible asset value.*

Another consideration is the maximum charge. Again using Vermont as an example, there is a limit on how much a physician office can charge for a medical record copy of no more than a flat $5.00 fee or $0.50 per page, whichever is greater. No charge is allowed when the request is connected to a claim for public benefits. The federal HIPAA statute allows a "reasonable charge," but specifically bars charges for searching for or reviewing the record. In Pennsylvania, 42 Pa.C.S. §§ 6152 and 6155 govern the fees that a physician can charge a patient for a medical record.[36] Any conflict between HIPAA and a state law is resolved in favor of the federal statute, of course.

---

35 Charles F. Kaiser and Amy Henchey, *Valuation of Medical Practices,* Internal Revenue Service 1996 EO CPE Text, eotopicq96.pdf, www.irs.gov/pub/irs-tege/.
36 Department of Health Amendments to Charges for Medical Records [41 Pa.B. 6453].

Massachusetts has a still more complex provision:

> Section 70E ... Every patient or resident of a facility shall have the right (g) upon request, to inspect his medical records and to receive a copy thereof in accordance with section seventy [see below], and the fee for said copy shall be determined by the rate of copying expenses, except that no fee shall be charged to any applicant, beneficiary or individual representing said applicant or beneficiary for furnishing a medical record if the record is requested for the purpose of supporting a claim or appeal under any provision of the Social Security Act or federal or state financial needs-based benefit program, and the facility shall furnish a medical record requested pursuant to a claim or appeal under any provision of the Social Security Act or any federal or state financial needs-based benefit program within thirty days of the request; provided, however, that any person for whom no fee shall be charged shall present reasonable documentation at the time of such records request that the purpose of said request is to support a claim or appeal under any provision of the Social Security Act or any federal or state financial needs-based benefit program;

> Section 70 ... and a copy shall be furnished upon the payment of a reasonable fee, which for the purposes of this section shall mean a base charge of not more than $15 for each request for a hospital or clinic medical record; a per page charge of not more than $0.50 for each of the first 100 pages of a hospital or clinic medical record that is copied per request; and not more than $0.25 per page for each page in excess of 100 pages of a hospital or clinic medical record that is copied per request.

Editor's note: Georgetown University maintains a website that summarizes patient rights to medical records at http://medicalrecordrights.georgetown.edu/records.html. Individual state medical societies and hospital websites often have more detail.

Payer Contracts

Not always identified as an intangible asset subsequent to measurement, payer contracts have become an increasingly important element and are described in more detail in the next section.

Goodwill

Goodwill, as described earlier herein in connection with the residual method of allocation, is any intangible value that is left over after all other intangibles have been identified and measured. It is simply excess earning power. Some of goodwill may be attached to the enterprise or practice, and some may be attached to the individual provider. In addition to the issues and methods discussed in this chapter, the *actual* valuation of noncompete agreements may be an important element of assessing return on investment and reasonable compensation for services.

7.0 Understanding and Documenting the Reasonable Compensation Analysis

In the event of an audit by the IRS, one of the most important things to have *already* in place is contemporaneous documentation of the historical compensation payments. Although corporate minutes, for example, in a closely held medical practice have little positive impact since they are seen as self-serving, *not* having such minutes can, in contrast, have a significantly more negative impact.

7.1 Typical Compensation Formulas[37]

Practices vary as to the nature of their compensation arrangements and the extent to which they document them. In addition to the corporate minutes discussed in the above introduction, employment contracts often contain a description of the compensation formula or a reference to a document that contains such a formula.

Productivity-Based Formulas

Productivity can be defined in terms of charges (uncommon), net revenue, collections, RVUs, or wRVUs. Payer neutrality can be introduced into any of these measures, such as assuming a uniform collection rate across all charges irrespective of the payer mix of an individual provider or paying a uniform rate per RVU or wRVU generated. Use of RVUs may create a regulatory risk if the practice has ancillary technical component income from designated health services, since the volume or value of referrals to same cannot be rewarded under a Stark-compliant group practice compensation structure.

Revenue-Based Models

If individually generated revenues are being allocated, whether based on actual collected billings or a payer-neutral system based on an overall practice collection ratio or Stark-compliant rate per RVU, it is then necessary to allocate the expenses of the practice. These are typically divided into those that are shared equally, also referred to as fixed expenses, fixed overhead expenses, and other similar terms:

Shared expenses: These would typically include the following:

- Depreciation;

- Interest expense or similar charges;

- Legal and accounting costs and retirement plan administration;

- Occupancy costs: rent, utilities, insurance, maintenance, and cleaning;

---

37   Various other chapters of the guide contain details of compensation systems.

- Certain payroll costs, such as central administration;

- Corporate dues and subscriptions;

- Compliance costs; and

- Managing partner salary.

Variable expenses: These could include the majority of the expenses of operating the practice. Included would be:

- Midlevel providers (physician extenders) and clinical assistant salaries, depending on how the associated revenue is divided in the first instance;

- Billing office and front desk staff;

- Fringe benefits of the above;

- Administrative personnel in some instances;

- Advertising;

- Data processing;

- Medical supplies;

- Office supplies;

- Postage;

- Telephone;

- Temporary help; and

- Transcription, although electronic health records have replaced transcription in many practices and make it an individual expense for physicians who continue to utilize it.

Individual or discretionary expenses: These would include all items that are discretionary with the individual physician and include:

- Automobile expense;

- Business gifts;

- Computers and software (personal);

- Continuing medical education;

- Discretionary bonuses and gifts to employees;

- Dues and subscriptions;

- Entertainment;

- Fringe benefits;

- Retirement plan benefits, such as pension and profit-sharing; and

- Travel.

As we saw in the *Pediatric Surgical* case, the way in which revenue and expense are allocated can suggest a distribution of profit or a return on investment rather than a return on labor.

wRVU Models

Conceptually, a wRVU model would be based upon what the health insurance and private pay patients paid for physician work, with the practice expenses including malpractice insurance covered by the practice expense and malpractice RVUs. In reality, the rate per wRVU actually available to physicians in the practice may be more than or less than the amounts received for physician work due to the disparities in what payers actually pay per RVU and the presence of DHS, among other factors. If ancillary net income is allocated based upon wRVUs, for example, generally, one would expect that this would be Stark-compliant, since it would only represent physician work and not any DHS TC referrals. The professional component of DHS personally performed is not a "referral."

The simplest method for using wRVUs in a productivity setting would be to take the total practice income available after paying all expenses of the practice and divide it by the total wRVUs generated by the physicians, to derive a compensation amount per wRVU. This amount or conversion factor is then multiplied by the wRVUs generated by each physician to determine compensation. Compensation would typically consist of both wages and benefits in this instance. Other methods, including hybrid methods, are available, such as dividing a portion of the available compensation equally and a portion based on productivity.[38]

---

38 The various methods are described in several chapters of this guide in more detail.

In this circumstance as well, to the extent that a portion of the value per wRVU includes ancillary TC net income, it may be seen as a distribution of profit.

Straight Salary or Fixed Compensation

This form of compensation is rarely used on a stand-alone basis by a private practice, although there may be a base salary plus bonus or incentive arrangement. To the extent that it can be shown to include a return on investment, a private practice, exempt entity, or equity owner of a practice would be at risk in the reasonable compensation area.

Equal Compensation Models

This method of determining compensation is not altogether unheard of in private practice settings, but it is uncommon because it often has the effect of allowing poor producers to benefit from the labor of higher producers. It could also pose a higher risk for low producers who may be seen as having received compensation for the labors of others. This is a risk similar to including the profit on employed physicians and MLPs in compensation.

Allocation of Midlevel Provider Profits (MLPs)

Earlier in the chapter, MLPs were described. Practices have a variety of means of supervising their MLPs and allocating the related profit earned. Some physicians have dedicated MLPs who they are solely responsible for supervising, while other practices have MLPs who are supervised by different physicians at different times. As described earlier, Medicare pays MLPs for services when they are not supervised by a physician under the "incident to" billing rules at the rate of 85% of what the physician would be paid for the service. Some commercial insurers follow Medicare. One means of measuring physician productivity is to credit the supervising physician with the 15% of collected revenue from MLPs as personal production in determining reasonable compensation.

Depending upon the compensation system, profits of MLPs may be aggregated and distributed evenly to the physicians. This methodology could pose a greater risk of appearing to be a profit distribution, all things being equal, to the extent that a physician doing less than an equal share of the supervision received an equal share of the profit.

Determination of Midlevel Profits

In light of the *Pediatric Surgical* case, the means of determining precisely what the MLP profit is should be evaluated and then documented, both in the practice's compensation plan as well as in the annual determination of compensation. Full allocation of practice expenses along with consideration of a revenue allocation for physician supervision will both reflect a more meaningful measure of true "profit" and reduce the "profit" risk in the determination of reasonable compensation.

7.2 Market Factors

The most powerful counterargument to a profit distribution attack is the need for a practice to meet market-based competitive compensation, while the greatest risk in the use of "market data"—based on the decisions by the Tax Court and 7th Circuit in the *Mulcahy* case—is that, at least with respect to the Rosenberg-type surveys, the data does not differentiate return on labor from return on investment. This is certainly true, as observed earlier, of the MGMA *Physician Compensation and Production Survey*, as demonstrated by this definition[39] from the 2011 survey:

> Total Compensation
> State the amount reported as direct compensation on a W2, 1099, or K1 (for partnerships)[40] plus all voluntary salary reductions such as 401(k), 403(b), Section 125 Tax Savings Plan, and Medical Savings Plan. The amount reported should include salary, bonus and/or incentive payments, research stipends, honoraria, *and distribution of profits*. (emphasis added)

Compensation for MGMA purposes can also include "pure" nonlabor return on investment from an ambulatory surgery center (ASC) or cardiac cath lab. The Tax Court would likely be decidedly unimpressed with MGMA data if appraised of these definitions.

> Compensation Includes Revenue from Separate Facility Fee
> Answer "Yes" if the physician received compensation that could be attributed to a separate facility fee. This could include compensation from ownership in an ASC or Cath Lab, for example.[41]

Thus, merely comparing market survey data to the actual compensation paid to owners of a medical practice or to employees of a hospital or health system is inadequate for purposes of a reasonable compensation determination.[42] It is necessary for the valuation analyst or the tax advisor for the practice to get behind the survey data and understand what local market conditions drive the competitive level of physician compensation.

Supply and Demand

In addition to the influence of rate differentials in competing network and health system contracts on physician recruitment, there is a separate but related issue of overall

---

39   Appendix F.
40   Presumably respondents would include Sub S K-1s as well.
41   MGMA *Physician Compensation and Production Survey*, 2011 on 2010.
42   Editor's note: As discussed elsewhere in the guide, failure of compensation to qualify under IRC section 162 leads to the likelihood as well that the compensation is not commercially reasonable for purposes of the Stark law.

shortages of physicians in the marketplace. The following discussion looks at the studies of physician shortages nationally and then in Massachusetts as a sample state, because it has the highest number of physicians per capita and its state medical society publishes detailed data. The valuation analyst or advisor should be familiar with such data and use it as part of the documentation of reasonable compensation.

American Association of Medical Colleges Study

A Study by the American Association of Medical Colleges (AAMC)[43] found that the number of residency (training) slots for physicians would stay status quo, even though the population is increasing. Surgery actually shows a decline in the number of active physicians over 20 years.

> Supply projections under the baseline scenario assume the status quo regarding number of new medical school graduates, number of GME slots, as well as physician hours worked and retirement patterns. This scenario also assumes the status quo in number of physicians entering residency programs: 15,500 USMDs,[44] 2,900 DOs,[45] and 6,600 IMGs[46] (for 25,000 total new residents per year). Thus the components of the projected 12% net growth in total number of active physicians from 2006 to 2025 includes an additional 28,900 USMDs (6% growth), 32,900 DOs (79% growth), and 18,900 IMGs (12% growth). There will be almost five times as many new USMDs as DOs over this time, but so many more USMDs will be leaving active practice that the net growth will be greater for DOs.

> Projected growth in FTEs varies by specialty. If specialty choice patterns remain unchanged, growth in total FTEs appears to be largest for specialties in the "medical specialties"[47] categories and declining in surgery, though these are projected to remain the two smallest specialty groups. Primary care remains the largest, though it is also projected to begin a decline prior to 2025.

The geographic distribution of physicians in the U.S. (see Exhibit 11) is by no means equal and therefore, physician shortages can vary based upon local utilization patterns as well as access to care. Generally speaking, the fewer the number of practitioners per 100,000 population, the more patients are available to a given practitioner. The Boston region, which includes all of New England, has the highest number of physicians per capita, according to the Centers for Medicare and Medicaid Services.

---

43 *The Complexities of Physician Supply and Demand: Projections Through 2025,* November 2008.
44 United States Medical Doctors.
45 Osteopaths.
46 International Medical Graduates.
47 This includes gastroenterologists.

Exhibit 11. Part B Practitioners/CMS Region		
	Active practitioners	Practitioners per 100,000 population
All regions	¹1,226,327	414
Boston	95,316	669
New York	145,680	457
Philadelphia	130,492	453
Atlanta	218,627	381
Chicago	208,189	406
Dallas	116,451	327
Kansas City	61,934	467
Denver	45,527	456
San Francisco	149,235	326
Seattle	54,876	456

¹Non-Federal physicians only. Includes limited licensed, non-physician practitioners. Unduplicated count (may include practitioners practicing in multiple sites or States). Unknown provider States distributed. NOTES: Physicians as of March 2007. Civilian population as of July 1, 2005. Resident population for outlying areas and the Virgin Islands are not available. SOURCES: CMS, ORDI, and the Bureau of the Census.

Similarly, Massachusetts is ranked first among all the states in physicians per 100,000 population, as shown in Exhibits 12 and 13. "There were 258.7 active physicians per 100,000 population in the United States, ranging from a high of 415.5 in Massachusetts to a low of 176.4 in Mississippi."[48] However, as indicated later herein, those physicians are not equally distributed throughout the state, nor are they paid at the same rate by insurers.

Massachusetts Medical Study

In September 2011, the Massachusetts Medical Society (MMS) published an update of its annual *Physician Workforce Study*. Exhibit 13, from that report, shows the dramatic differences in physician availability factors, using Boston[49] as the measuring point. The greater the value above 100%, the greater the difficulty experienced.

The data by specialty (see Exhibit 14) is also instructive as to the pressure on physician compensation in the recruitment and retention area.

Notably, the 2010 study found that community hospitals experienced considerably more difficulty recruiting physicians than did teaching hospitals or physician groups (see Exhibits 15 and 16).

---

48 *2011 State Physician Workforce Data Book,* Association of American Medical Colleges' Center for Workforce Studies, November 2011.

49 Note that Massachusetts is a very small state in geographic terms, Worcester is less than 50 miles from Boston, and New Bedford is less than 60 miles. Barnstable is on Cape Cod, which is a significantly different market from New Bedford, notwithstanding their combination in the survey.

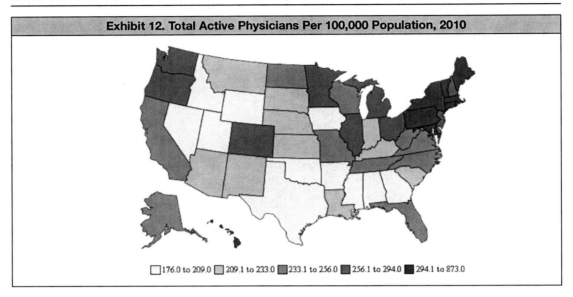

Exhibit 12. Total Active Physicians Per 100,000 Population, 2010

□ 176.0 to 209.0 ▨ 209.1 to 233.0 ▨ 233.1 to 256.0 ■ 256.1 to 294.0 ■ 294.1 to 873.0

Exhibit 13. Summary of the Composite Results of the Five Massachusetts Regional Labor Markets Indexed to the Boston Regional Market of the Nine Tight/Tightening Labor Markets Physicians Specialties

	Inadequate Pool Physicians	Yes Change Recruit Time	Yes Difficulty to Retain	Significant Difficultly Fill Vacancies	Need to Alter Services	Need to Adjust Staffing
Regional Labor Market						
Boston	100.0%	100.0%	100.0%	100.0%	100.0%	100.0%
Worcester	114.2%	126.5%	101.2%	157.5%	136.1%	129.9%
Springfield	143.9%	124.3%	97.5%	177.3%	133.2%	115.9%
New Bedford/Barnstable	122.5%	112.5%	79.1%	140.0%	102.8%	109.4%
Pittsfield/Western Mass.	147.5%	118.9%	121.9%	204.9%	142.3%	143.9%

Exhibit 14. Average Time Required for Physician Recruitment Among Practicing Physicians by Specialty

	2011 Mean in Months	2010 Mean in Months	2009 Mean in Months	2008 Mean in Months	2007 Mean in Months	2006 Mean in Months
Orthopedics	20.5	17.1	17.6	17.4	22.0	19.0
Dermatology *	17.5	19.9	28.6	26.2	---	---
Urology **	19.7	25.2	16.7	20.7	21.7	---
Family Medicine	11.8	17.9	15.5	14.5	14.3	13.6
General Surgery	14.6	16.8	13.5	19.4	17.4	14.1
Neurology *	12.7	21.7	19.2	24.1	---	---
Internal Medicine	11.5	13.1	13.8	13.4	11.4	12.7
Vascular Surgery	11.3	21.0	12.5	22.0	19.3	13.3
Psychiatry	8.7	12.8	7.9	10.0	9.3	10.2

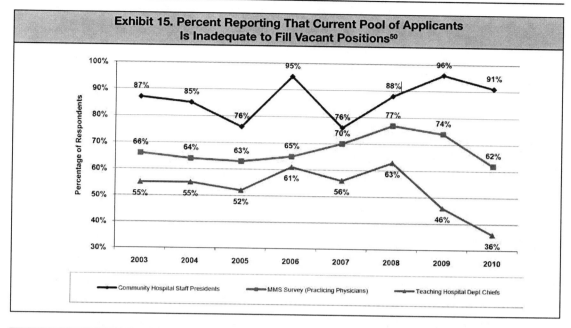

Exhibit 15. Percent Reporting That Current Pool of Applicants Is Inadequate to Fill Vacant Positions[50]

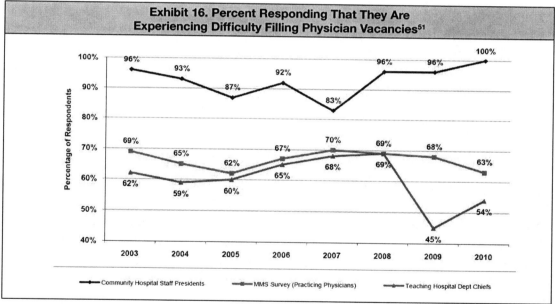

Exhibit 16. Percent Responding That They Are Experiencing Difficulty Filling Physician Vacancies[51]

Payer Contract Rates for Services

Earlier in this chapter,[52] a discussion of the influence of payer rates per RVU was undertaken. This is the most critical element missing from the typical application of the

---

50 *2010 Physician Workforce Study,* Massachusetts Medical Society.
51 Ibid.
52 Other chapters in the guide discuss this phenomenon as well.

Exhibit 17. Private Insurer Physician Payment Rates as a Percentage of Medicare

Rates for Practice (75th Percentile)								
Internal Medicine/ Family Medicine	112	117	*	89	175	128	*	169
Cardiology	155	156	*	110	223	145	*	234
Orthopedics	124	140	*	101	212	144	*	195
Anesthesiology	251	217	177	*	*	*	177	*
Radiology	166	147	*	134	238	153	*	240
Oncology - Physician Services Component	138	138	*	116	204	132	*	195

published survey-based method under the market approach for assessing reasonable compensation and should be considered in conjunction and coordination with local supply and demand analysis. Some of this failure is derived from a lack of understanding or acknowledgement of the dramatic differences in reimbursement for services within the broad regions reported in the various surveys, e.g., "East," "West," "Midwest," and "South." More importantly, there are dramatic variations intrastate and intraregion within states that are not even broken down in the surveys that are primary determinants of the competitive compensation rates required in a given market area. These differences are the subject of various studies by the Center for Studying Health System Change, as well as others, including National Public Radio.

Center for Studying Health System Change

The November 2010 study *Wide Variation in Hospital and Physician Payment Rates Evidence of Provider Market Power* found that "wide variation in private insurer payment rates to hospitals and physicians across and within local markets suggests that some providers, particularly hospitals, have significant market power to negotiate higher-than-competitive prices."[53] Exhibit 17, from that study, shows the dramatic differences based on a percentage of Medicare, with "Standard Rates" being what the typical physician would receive and the 75th percentile being what those with better contracts receive.

Massachusetts Attorney General's Report

Massachusetts Attorney General Martha Coakley released a report titled *Examination of Health Care Cost Trends and Cost Drivers* in March 2010[54] that details the vast differences in provider pay rates in that state, as well as the contracting practices between providers and insurers that led to them. For example, Exhibit 18 is based upon data contained in

---

53 *Wide Variation in Hospital and Physician Payment Rates Evidence of Provider Market Power*, Center for Studying Health System Change, Research Brief No. 16, November 2010.

54 Updated in June 2011.

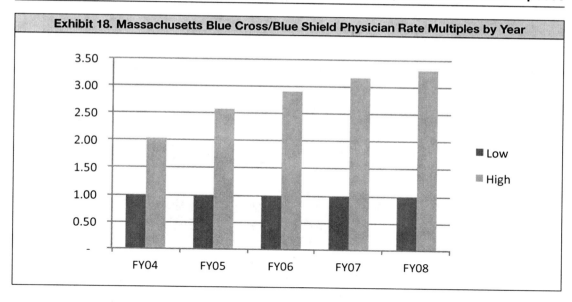

Exhibit 18. Massachusetts Blue Cross/Blue Shield Physician Rate Multiples by Year

the report and indicates that in fiscal 2008, the highest paid physicians[55] received nearly 3.5 times the generic network rates paid by Blue Cross/Blue Shield. Simply stated, a physician in the generic network would receive $100 for a service, while the best-paid physicians would receive $350 for the same service! That extra $250 would all fall through to the bottom line as compensation creating a dramatic difference.

To illustrate, if a physician provided 5,000 services per annum and 30% of them were to BC/BS insureds, those 1,500 services would result in an extra $375,000 of collected revenue and compensation at the best contract rate! That extra compensation could well exceed the median compensation for the position based on survey data. This begs the question of "reasonable compensation" for a physician employed by an entity with the negotiating strength to command such payer contracts. In addition, as we saw above in the section on the MMS study, these pay rates enhance the ability of the provider units that have them to recruit physicians at the expense of their competitors, who lack such rates. This creates an upward pressure on overall physician compensation in the marketplace and may require hospitals, for example, to subsidize from other revenue sources the compensation they pay physicians. That said, the valuation analyst or advisor may establish as a threshold condition the extent that such payer rate differentials are driving local market-based compensation to use it as a basis for expressing an opinion of fair market or reasonable compensation.

---

55   These being a teaching hospital in Boston.

7.3 Return on Labor and Return on Investment in the Final Analysis

Earlier in the chapter, Exhibit 7 was presented, highlighting the conceptual process of differentiating return on labor from return on investment. Although this analysis is critical to understanding the sources of distributable income in a practice, it is not necessarily conclusive as to whether or to what extent any return on investment represents a nondeductible dividend or other nonsalary payment. The key question to ask is to what extent are profits from ancillary services or midlevel providers necessary to subsidize physician compensation to meet market conditions.

The assessment of reasonable compensation is a complex undertaking and involves numerous elements beyond simply developing a compensation scheme, reporting the payments on a W-2 or K-1, and comparing to published surveys. The return of the independent investor test for professional practices in the *Mulcahy* test is a reminder that both tangible and intangible assets have a cash return associated with them that may be included in the compensation paid to physicians employed by a practice. For physicians who are also owners of a practice taxed as a C corporation, this raises the specter of double taxation due to the treatment of such return on investment as a dividend when it is disallowed as a compensation deduction. Perhaps surprisingly to those unfamiliar with IRC section 162, tax-exempt entities are held to the same standard as private practices where reasonable compensation is concerned, even though they have no tax deduction as such.[56] Compensation in excess of "reasonable compensation" under section 162 is likely deemed as inurement for tax-exempt entities and subject to sanctions under section 501(c)(3) or the intermediate sanctions provisions. In addition, compensation not meeting the deductibility test of section 162 is neither consistent with "fair market value" nor "commercially reasonable" for purposes of the Stark law. Purchasers of compensation opinions do well to retain appraisers with the requisite background in tax law-oriented valuation in conjunction with Stark and related valuation requirements.

The author would like to thank Kevin Yeanoplos, CPA/ABV, ASA, for his review of the technical valuation concepts in this chapter.

---

56   See §53.4958-4(b)(1)(ii).

PRACTICE AID: Checklist for Tax-Oriented Reasonable Compensation Engagements

By Mark O. Dietrich, CPA/ABV

CLIENT IDENTIFICATION

ENGAGEMENT OVERVIEW
1. Have AICPA standards for competence, independence, and related areas been addressed?

ENGAGEMENT LETTER
1. Physician specified?

2. Definition of "reasonable" or FMV specified?

3. Scope specified?

4. Signed by both parties?

5. Does this engagement involve an academic medical center, a hospital employee, a tax-exempt group practice, a for-profit practice employee, or a faculty group practice?

6. Is the engagement letter consistent with the workpapers and report?

ENTITY/ARRANGEMENT TYPE
1. Qualified group (Note: only such qualify for "incident to" and DHS profit share)

2. Employee, e.g., hospital-employed physician

3. Personal services arrangement, e.g., independent contractor

4. Other fair market value (typically a lease of other DHS)

COMPENSATION

Encounter

1. How defined? (e.g., MGMA, AMGA)

2. Does report specify the definition?

3. Is definition consistent with any external statistical sources utilized?

Net Charges, Net Revenue, Collections

1. How defined?

2. Does report specify the definition?

3. Definition exclude DHS? (prof. component personally performed is NOT DHS)

4. Is professional component of any DHS separately tracked or computed?

5. Who computes and on what basis?

6. Is computation reviewed?

Allocation of Expenses

1. What are the methods employed in allocating expense in a P&L-based compensation plan?

2. Do any of the expense allocations appear designed to avoid Stark DHS issues?

3. Are there any unsual retirement plan contributions, such as a defined benefit plan?

Incentive

1. What is the basis for the recommended incentive?

2. Has a determination been made if the compensation/incentive will generate a loss for entity?

3. If so, is the loss appropriate under FMV and other regulatory restrictions, including commercial reasonableness?

4. Have prior year reports been considered in the current year?

5. Was the employment arrangement entered into as a result of a practice purchase?

6. Has the compensation paid/recommended been compared to that used in the valuation?

7. Who did the valuation?

8. Is practice in a HPSA or MUA?

Share of Stark Designated Health Services

1. Is practice a qualified group practice under the regulations?

2. What are the method(s) used to determine and allocate DHS profits, including allocation of expenses?

3. Do the methods avoid the use of methods that would directly or indirectly be based upon referrals to the DHS?

WORK RVUs

1. How defined?

2. Does the report specify the definition?

3. Is professional component of any DHS included?

4. Who computes?

5. Is computation reviewed?

MIDLEVEL PROVIDERS

1. How are they supervised?

2. Does the practice maintain records to support "incident to" billing?

3. Are all direct and indirect costs fully allocated to midlevel revenue and cost centers?

4. How is any profit allocated to practice owners?

5. Are physicians given personal productivity credit for supervision?

6. Is computation reviewed?

7. If services are billed "incident to" the supervising physician, have the related requirements been met?

MARKET ANALYSIS

1. Are there differences in the allowed amounts for providers for a given service by a given insurer in the practice's service area?

2. Who are the major health systems, physician networks, etc.? Which are competitors?

3. How does state law treat noncompete agreements between: a) physicians and physician practices; b) physicians and hospitals or health systems; and c) physicians and private or public equity firms?

4. Is there evidence that suggests that the relative negotiating strength of practices, hospitals, and health systems and other market participants is affecting the ability of weaker particpants to recruit or retain physicians?

5. What is the number of specialist and primary care physicians per capita?

6. How does local healthcare spending per capita compare to national and regional data?

7. What percentage of the population is insured and by which insurer, e.g., Medicare, commercial, etc.?

RETURN ON INVESTMENT ANALYSIS/INDEPENDENT INVESTOR TEST

1. Does practice have signifcant income from ancillary services not related to professional component?

2. Do purchases or sales of equity interests in the practice reflect an economic basis for establishing that the physicians believe the practice has salable goodwill?

3. Do employment agreements contain noncompete or similar provisions that would have the effect of transferring personal goodwill into a practice asset?

4. Does the practice compensation plan reflect allocation of certain "profits" on a basis that tracks equity ownership as opposed to personal productivity?

5. Has the inclusion of profit distributions in survey data used for comparing compensation under the market approach been considered?

RECRUITMENT

Did physician relocate to the hospital's "geographic area" to join its medical staff?

1. Is arrangement present in file, and in writing and signed?

2. Is arrangement not conditioned on the physician referring to the hospital?

3. Is remuneration not determined based on referrals, or expected referrals, from the recruited physician or other business?

4. Is the physician allowed to establish privileges at other hospitals and refer to other facilities?

Was physician recruited to existing independent practice?

1. Existing practice must sign the recruitment agreement if it is receiving payments from the hospital;

2. All of the remuneration must remain with or pass through to the recruited physician except for "actual costs incurred" by the existing practice in recruiting the new physician;

3. In the case of income guarantees, only the "actual additional incremental costs attributable to the recruited physician" may be allocated by the existing practice to the new physician;

4. Records of the costs and passed through amounts must be kept for five years;

5. The remuneration may not be determined based on referrals, or expected referrals; the existing practice may not impose any additional practice restrictions on the recruited physician;

6. Arrangement may not violate the federal anti-kickback statute.

MEDICAL DIRECTORSHIPS

1. Is arrangement present in file, and in writing and signed?

2. Is arrangement not conditioned on the physician referring to the hospital?

3. Is remuneration not determined based on referrals, or expected referrals, from the recruited physician or other business?

4. Is the physician allowed to establish privileges at other hospitals and refer to other facilities?

5. What is the nature of the remuneration?

6. If an hourly rate, how developed?

7. Dos the engagement include review of the documentation of services provided?

8. If not, does the report specifically state so?

COMPENSATION SURVEYS UTILIZED
1. MGMA

2. AMGA

3. AMA

4. Hay Group

5. Sullivan & Cotter

6. ECS Watson Wyatt

7. Hospital/Healthcare Services

8. Mercer

9. Integrated Health Networks

COMPENSATION CONCLUSION
1. Is the conclusion consistent with the documentation in the workpapers?

2. Do the workpapers appear to have been checked for mathematical errors?

INTERMEDIATE SANCTIONS
1. Does report involve a disqualified person?

    i. Individuals whose compensation is primarily based on revenues from the tax exempt's activities that the individual controls or who control substantial budgets or departments (collectively, organization managers)

2. A family member of a disqualified person?

3. Does appraiser qualify under regulations?

REPORT

1. Terms of engagement reiterated?

    i. Physician

    ii. Objectives

    iii. Scope

    iv. Information relied upon

    v. Methodologies employed

2. Definition of FMV where required?

3. Appropriate discussion of regulatory issues

    i. AKS

    ii. Stark

    iii. Intermediate sanctions

    iv. State laws

4. Is there a statement as to independence of firm?

5. Assumptions and limiting conditions included?

6. Signed/approved?

7. CVs included?

REPRESENTATION LETTER

1. Is one present?

2. Is it signed?

3. Does it contain client reps as to

    i. Accuracy of info provided?

    ii. All info requested actually provided?

    iii. Client responsibility for comp arrangement?

Part III.
Topics in the Economics and Analysis of Physician Services

Chapter 13. An Introduction
to Physician Services and Specialties

CONTENTS

Chapter 13. An Introduction to Physician Services and Specialties

By Timothy Smith, CPA/ABV

1.0 Introduction

Since the key to valuing service agreements is matching the compensation paid for services rendered, it is essential for an appraiser to have a solid grasp and understanding of the key characteristics of the services provided by physicians. Failure to comprehend these characteristics can lead to appraisals of physician services that do not reflect the fundamental economics of the underlying services, and consequently, that are not consistent with the standard of fair market value (FMV). The following sections discuss important aspects of physician services that can affect the FMV analysis of compensation arrangements.

2.0 Types of Physician Services

Physicians provide a variety of services in the healthcare industry for which they can receive compensation. The most common type of service for a physician to provide is patient care or clinical services. Patient care or clinical services, however, can generally be broken down into two major categories: professional component services and technical component services. These services can be described as follows.

2.1 Professional Component Services

Professional component services encompass procedures generally performed directly or personally by the physician in examining, diagnosing, or treating patients. Office visits, surgical procedures, or interpretations of diagnostic imaging exams are common examples of professional services performed by physicians. The type of procedures performed by a physician will tend to vary according to specialty and practice focus.

The place of service for these services can also vary, but most services are provided in either a physician practice or facility setting, such as a hospital. One type of procedure that is common to most physician specialties is an office visit, which is a basic evaluation and management procedure performed in a physician practice. Other services that can be broadly placed under the heading of professional services are so called "incident to" services that are performed by other medical personnel, such as nonphysician providers. A physician supervises such personnel in the provision of these services, which are typically billed under and credited to the supervising physician.

2.2 Technical Component Services

Technical component services, which are also frequently referred to as ancillary services, on the other hand, are not typically provided directly or personally by the physician, but by technicians, nurses, or medical assistants working under the supervision of the physician in the physician's practice. Such services are generally provided to patients under the direction of a physician and are part of the patients' overall diagnosis and treatment. These services usually include the use of various medical technologies and may involve pharmaceuticals that are also used in the examinations or procedures. Examples of technical component or ancillary services include lab tests, diagnostic imaging procedures, immunizations, radiation therapy treatments, chemotherapy, infusion, and physical therapy. Historically, these services have been provided in the physician practice setting, with the attending physician referring the patient to undergo them as part of diagnosis or treatment. As a result, they are included in the broad categories of physician services and patient care or clinical services because of their provision to patients in the physician practice setting. In addition, technical component services generally require the supervision or oversight of a physician. In the case of diagnostic imaging and other testing procedures, a physician is also required to provide an interpretation of the results of the exam. These factors are additional reasons for including technical component services under the general category of physician services.

Physicians also provide other types of services in the healthcare marketplace. These nonclinical services may be broadly outlined as follows.

2.3 On-Call Services

Physicians provide two key forms of on-call services in the healthcare marketplace. First, physicians regularly provide hospitals and other healthcare facilities with immediate availability or access to their clinical services on an as-needed basis. Typically, the physician provides call coverage for the physician's specialty to a hospital's emergency department (ED) or to unassigned inpatients in the hospital. A second form of on-call services is provided to the patients in a physician's practice. Physicians provide their patients with access to them or their designated substitutes to address issues and questions that arise outside of general office hours at night and on weekends. Such "practice call" is generally considered part of the physician-patient relationship and should be distinguished from "hospital call." Unhappily, many in the healthcare arena fail to distinguish between practice and hospital call coverage, not recognizing the varying economics and market dynamics related to each type.

2.4 Administrative

Physicians provide various forms of administrative services to healthcare facilities and entities. While these services may be administrative in nature, they are often based on a physician's clinical expertise and knowledge and cannot be performed by nonphysicians. A prime example of physician administrative services is hospital medical directorships. Physicians may also serve in executive roles within organizations either part-time or full-time. Again, some positions may require the skills and acumen of an experienced clinician to perform the duties of the position, such as chief medical officer. For other positions, however, the physician's clinical background may play an important but not necessarily required role in the job duties of the position. Many physicians become chief executive officers or fill other executive or managerial positions within healthcare entities, where being a physician is not a requirement.

2.5 Clinical Co-Management or Service Line Management

The recent emergence of so-called clinical co-management or service line management arrangements has given rise to a new hybrid form of services that combine administrative and clinical duties and tasks. In these arrangements, physicians provide management services to healthcare organizations, using their clinical knowledge and expertise to help such entities improve clinical and operational processes to improve clinical quality or operational outcomes. The physicians are also typically participants in these processes through their practice at the facility for which they provide the services.

2.6 Educational or Academic

Educational services provided by physicians can range from teaching positions at medical schools and residency programs to specialized training programs for healthcare facilities and organizations.

2.7 Research and Development

Physicians can provide an array of research and development services to healthcare organizations, particularly in life sciences. They can also perform research as part of an academic position.

2.8 Business Management

When physicians are the owners of their practices, they often provide business management services to their practices. They make key operational and planning decisions and may be involved in the daily supervision of practice support staff. Owner-physicians may negotiate with vendors, landlords, and commercial payers. They may be directly involved in employee hiring and firing decisions and actions. While services such as these are common for physicians to provide in physician-owned groups, they should be distinguished from clinical or patient care services.

2.9 Entrepreneurial and Investor

Perhaps one of the least recognized forms of service provided by physicians are the entrepreneurial or owner services that physicians provide to their practices. In cases where physicians own their practices, they invest in their practices, often providing capital to their businesses in the form of reduced compensation that is used to finance operations and asset purchases for the practice, such as working capital, equipment, and business expansions. In essence, physician-owners provide financial services to their practices in the form of equity capital financing. Even when physicians use debt to finance capital and operating needs of their practices, the debt payments serve to reduce the earnings or cash flow available for physician compensation. In addition, physicians often give personal guarantees when borrowing money to use in their practices.

It is important to distinguish among these various forms of physician services because each type of service has its own unique characteristics and economics. More importantly, the marketplace tends to compensate for each type of service differently based on its unique characteristics and economics. Thus, the valuation tools and techniques employed to determine FMV compensation often vary by type of service. Since the key to compensation valuation for service agreements is matching the appropriate level of compensation to the services provided, valuations of physician services should be grounded in a thorough understanding of the key types of services provided by physicians and the fundamental economics of such services.

3.0 The Scope of Services for a Physician's Specialty

The nature and scope of services provided by a physician are generally a function of the physician's specialty or subspecialty. The physician's specialty denotes his or her training and clinical expertise and the types of procedures performed for clinical patient care. *The scope of services for a specialty is important because various clinical as well as other types of physician services are frequently compensated at different levels in the healthcare marketplace.* As a result, market trends and key economic factors affecting a specialty are critical considerations in the valuation process for physician services. Important trends and factors include reimbursement, physician shortages, procedural and patient care innovations, technology use and innovations, and prevailing practice paradigms for the specialty. It should also be noted that a physician's specialty can define the range of administrative, management, and education services that he or she is qualified to provide in the healthcare marketplace.

3.1 Clinical Patient-Care Services

Since most physicians receive the majority of their compensation from providing clinical patient-care services, it is essential to have a basic knowledge of the top clinical procedures for a given specialty when attempting to value these clinical services. Such knowledge is important for understanding the essential aspects of a physician's practice, including the nature and scope of services provided to patients and the revenues and costs associated with the practice. In addition, it facilitates benchmarking analysis in comparison to peer group data, such as that found in the various publicly available physician compensation and productivity surveys. Knowledge of the prevailing practice paradigm and most common procedures can illuminate the causes of variances from such data. Major procedures often define key productivity measures for a physician. Examples would include office visits for primary care physicians, certain types of surgical cases in the various surgical specialties, stents for interventional cardiology, and lesion removals for dermatology.

3.2 Technical Component Services

It is important to note that common procedures for a given specialty may include various technical component services. For certain specialties, such services represent a significant portion of the procedures performed in the practice and are important sources of practice revenue and earnings. Examples include diagnostic imaging for cardiology and orthopedic surgery, radiation therapy treatments in radiation oncology, and chemotherapy for medical oncology. Many of these ancillary procedures are technology-driven, and these technologies can be costly, with equipment ranging from tens of thousands to millions of dollars to acquire. At the same time, the reimbursement for such procedures may produce significant operating margins for the practice, affording higher levels of practice earnings that may be available for distribution to physicians as compensation. Such reimbursement may also be subject to downward market pressures, especially from Medicare and those payers whose rates are tied to Medicare reimbursement levels, making long-term returns from investments in such technology unpredictable over its useful life. Moreover, low utilization rates for such high-cost technology can create losses for physicians from technical service lines. Thus, ancillary services can be both a source of incremental or reduced earnings for a physician practice, depending upon the facts and circumstances.

3.3 Ownership in Healthcare Ventures

Another important element to consider in evaluating the prevailing practice paradigm for a given specialty is ownership in nonpractice entities, facilities, and business ventures. In certain specialties, physicians are often owners in ventures other than their practices and ownership in these ventures can represent a significant source of income to the physicians. Surgical specialists, notably orthopedic surgeons and gastroenterologists, are frequently owners in ambulatory surgical centers (ASCs), from which they receive periodic cash distributions. Many urologists have historically been owners in ventures that lease equipment or provide equipment-related services for procedures used in hospital or ASC settings for urologic patient care, such as lithotripsy. In such cases, the urologist provides the professional service for the urologic procedure, but also indirectly provides a component of the technical component or ancillary service through ownership in such leasing or service ventures. Understanding such practice paradigms for a specialty is important in evaluating total compensation data for a specialty and in matching compensation for the services provided by a physician in that specialty.[1]

4.0 Distinguishing Between Office-Based and Hospital-Based Physician Specialties

Physician specialties are typically divided into the four major specialty categories of primary care, surgical, medical, and hospital-based. These categories are widely used to denote general similarities in practice patterns among the various specialties that fall under each category. When looking at physician compensation issues, however, there is another way to categorize and think about physician specialties that can be helpful. One can group most specialties into two basic classifications based on certain operating and practice-setting characteristics and tendencies that are common to the specialties in each group. These two major categories of specialties can be labeled as office-based physicians (OBPs) and hospital-based physicians (HBPs). Examples of HBPs include anesthesiologists, hospitalists, trauma surgeons, radiologists, transplant surgeons, and critical care physicians. Examples of OBPs include primary care physicians as well as most surgical and medical specialties.[2]

The essential operating characteristics that distinguish OBPs from HBPs can include the following areas:

---

1   In the author's experience, physician ownership in ASCs and other ventures, such as those mentioned relative to urologists, is often held at the individual physician level and not by the physician practice entity. Thus, the distributions received from such entities would not flow through the physician practice. As a result, such compensation may not be necessarily included in the physician compensation survey data.
2   It should be noted that surgical specialties are included with OBPs, despite many to most procedures being performed in a facility setting. As will be shown in the subsequent discussion, surgical specialties are included with OBPs based on their key operating characteristics.

- Source of the patient base for the physician;

- Setting in which the physician provides clinical services;

- Productivity or workload measures; and

- Relationship between physician efforts and physician productivity outcomes.

For each major area, OBPs tend to work in settings and service environments that can differ materially from HBPs. While not absolutely distinguishable in all cases, recognizing these differences can be useful in identifying important operating, productivity, and economic dynamics for specialty. Such factors can also affect the structure and level of compensation afforded to physicians in the marketplace. As will be discussed in other chapters, this distinction between OBPs and HBPs can affect the methods and techniques used to value various compensation arrangements, particularly employment. In the following sections, the distinctions in each area between OBPs and HBPs are discussed and analyzed.

4.1 Source of Patient Base

For HBPs, the source of patients for the physician is generally the hospital or other healthcare facility, such as an ASC, at which the physician provides clinical services. Patients are typically admitted to such facilities based on referrals from physicians. These referrals are generally made to the facility and not to an individual HBP. In other words, the patient is typically not referred to the facility for the sole reason of being treated by a specific HBP. Rather, the referring physician generally has a relationship and practice pattern with the facility that drives the referral to a facility. Thus, HBPs are usually dependent upon referrals to the facility for patients, rather than direct referrals from other specialists. Highlighting this referral pattern does not imply that the HBPs do not have an impact on referrals to the facility. Quality patient care by HBPs at a facility can be an important factor in referrals, but HBPs are generally not the primary or specific determining factor in such referrals. Contrast this situation to that of OBPs. Patients come to the OBPs for healthcare services based on either patient selection of the physician or referrals from other specialists. Generally, choice of OBPs is based on the attributes of the individual physician or the group in which the physician practices. In other words, there is a greater relationship between the reputation, skill, and personal efforts of OBPs and their patient volumes than is found for HBPs.

4.2 Service Context

For HBPs, the primary reason the hospital or facility is the source of patients is that the physician provides services in the context of staffing a hospital or facility unit, function or service line. The physician is a resource input to a larger service. Consider, for example, the role of an anesthesiologist in an inpatient surgical procedure. An inpatient surgical procedure requires various facility and staffing resources and inputs. Facility resources include operating, recovery, and inpatient stay rooms that are appropriately equipped and maintained, while staffing includes a surgeons, an anesthesiologist, nursing staff, and other hospital support staff. While the anesthesiologist is critical to the procedure, he or she is not the only critical requirement for the total service. Each resource plays a vital role.

Another key aspect of the practice setting for HBPs is that they usually provide shift-based coverage for the facility with respect to their clinical services. Facilities often require physician coverage for certain specialties to staff their units or service lines, whether in the form of unrestricted or on-site coverage. Such coverage is tied to the facility's operating schedule and needs, which in the case of hospitals, can be continuous coverage 365 days a year.

For OBPs, physician services are usually the primary element of patient care. Patients go to OBPs primarily to obtain clinical services related to a physician's particular specialty. Even when OBPs perform the majority of their clinical services in a hospital or facility setting, such as in the case of the various surgical specialties, patients generally come to the OBP first. The OBP usually selects the facility at which to perform the procedure. In other words, the patient initially seeks physician clinical services; facility-based services are the setting in which the physician services are provided. Because physician services are the primary driver of patient care considerations for office-based specialties, the schedules of OBPs are generally centered around preset office hours or procedure days at facilities that correspond to the normal workweek cycle. In short, OBPs usually have more control over their working hours and days.

4.3 Productivity Measures

Because HBPs are generally dependent for their patient base on hospitals or facilities, the productivity of HBPs is necessarily limited by the volumes and case acuities coming into the facility. An HBP may be quite capable of handling significant patient volumes and skilled at treating high acuity cases, but if the patient base of a facility does not provide such volumes and cases, the HBP's actual productivity will not reflect his capability and skill. In addition, the professional collections of an HBP may also be dependent on the payer mix for the facility at which the physician practices. Since the HBP does not have an independent practice and referral base and works to provide coverage for a facility, she is not able to pick and choose among health plans and payers when treating patients. Even when an HBP goes "out of network" for various health plans and payers, the HBP is still affected by the essential demographics of the referral base to the facility. Patients with low reimbursement health plans may not necessarily yield better collections under out-of-network billing practices, especially when high levels of government payer, self-pay or charity are prevalent at a facility. Moreover, because HBPs often provide shift-based coverage for hospital or facility operations, they may be required to cover shifts in which there are minimal patient volumes. HBPs, therefore, tend to have less control over their day-to-day productivity levels. Outside of changing facilities, the individual efforts of HBPs may have little bearing on their productivity and on the revenues and earnings associated with their practice. In summary, HBPs have limited control over key factors that affect their compensation vis-à-vis the economics of their services.

OBPs, by contrast, have a much greater level of influence and impact on their productivity levels and the economics that relate to their compensation. The more skilled and efficient that an OBP becomes in performing procedures and providing patient care, the more patients he or she can treat within a given period of time. Moreover, the physician may be able to treat more complicated cases. The OBP may also choose to work more hours to treat higher patient volumes and case acuities. As a result, individual efforts by OBPs can directly impact productivity levels. OBPs, moreover, generally have greater flexibility with respect to the choice of health plans and payers that they will accept in their practices. They have, therefore, much more control over the economics of their services and corresponding relation to their compensation.[3]

5.0 The Impact of Physician Practice Organizational Characteristics

The scope of services provided by a physician and his or her corresponding level of compensation can be influenced by the type of practice in which the provider works. Thus, knowledge of how various practice characteristics can affect physician compensation levels is useful in establishing FMV for physician services, and especially employed physicians. Three types of practice characteristics are germane for understanding the operational and economic dynamics of the physician practice:

1. Practice size;

2. Practice specialty mix; and

3. Practice ownership.

---

3   There are certainly cases in which OBPs may have reduced control over such factors. Employed OBPs may have less control over payer mix and volumes as a result of conditions imposed by an employer. OBPs in less populated or in low payer-mix markets may also be limited. The relevant point, however, in the distinction between HBPs and OBPs for the current discussion is that the operating profile of hospital-based specialties is structurally different than that for OBPs. This structural difference generally gives rise to fundamental dissimilarities in the ways that such physicians can impact their productivity and practice economic performance.

The following sections discuss the dynamics for each characteristic that can affect the scope of services and corresponding compensation for physicians in such practices.

5.1 Practice Size

In general, larger physician practices are in a better position to offer an expanded scope of services to patients in terms of subspecialty care, access, and ancillary services. Larger practices may provide the critical mass of patients necessary for physicians within the group to develop subspecialty practices or areas of particular expertise. It may also provide for the effective use of nonphysician providers (NPPs) in the provision of patient care. Such critical mass may also allow larger practices to provide expanded levels of technical component services to patients. Unless a sufficient patient base is achieved, the acquisition cost for various forms of ancillaries is too high to justify offering such services to patients. Larger groups may also be able to achieve economies of scale with respect to various resources and costs, such as utilization of space and staff.[4] As discussed in more detail in Chapter 14, "The Economics of Physician Clinical Services and Compensation," larger groups can also have more leverage in reimbursement negotiations with commercial payers due to their size. This leverage can translate into higher reimbursement levels for the practice.

If managed properly, the economies of larger groups can increase the level of practice earnings available for physician compensation. Increase ancillary revenues, higher acuity cases, effective use of NPPs, higher reimbursement, and economized costs can all serve to increase the total earnings pool for physicians. As with all group practices, however, a critical compensation issue for the group is how these earnings are distributed to the physicians. Such distributions can be influenced by factors that may relate more to group dynamics and "politics" than to the fundamental economics of the group and the physician services it provides in the marketplace. They may not be related strictly to issues of physician productivity and contribution to net earnings. Often, larger groups experience greater levels of organizational politics in determining compensation, because the economics of multiple locations, subspecialization, and "too many cooks in the kitchen" play out within the group.

Large group practices, moreover, may actually experience diseconomies of scale relative to groups of smaller sizes. Larger practices often require more layers of middle management, more specialized support staff, and more expensive management due to complexity of managing a sizeable organization. Larger groups can be more bureaucratic,

---

4   It is possible that larger groups also achieve diseconomies of scale with respect to other costs. Solo physicians often do not provide market-level benefits to staff. Larger organizations tend to offer such benefits, thereby increasing their staffing costs.

formal, and structured, resulting in physicians being more removed from directly affecting cost-effectiveness. They may also develop compliance and other programs that add to the overhead burden. Staff benefits may also be higher as groups compete in the corporate marketplace for professional and experienced personnel.

5.2 Practice Specialty Mix

Physician group practices are either based on a single specialty or include multiple specialties. Each type of group has unique operating characteristics and economics that affect both the types of services offered and the compensation of physicians in the group. Single-specialty practices are generally organized in terms of a broadly defined specialty, such as cardiology or orthopedic surgery. Within such practices, there may be varying degrees of subspecialty physicians and services represented in group. For certain types of specialties, the physicians may implement a division-of-labor approach, in which certain physicians perform specific types of procedures to increase overall group productivity. For example, certain physicians focus on in-office or diagnostic work, while others concentrate on major procedural services. Many cardiology groups function in this manner. Noninvasive cardiologists in the group feed their invasive and invasive-interventional colleagues, allowing the latter to remain focused on cath lab-based procedures.

Multispecialty groups are generally organized in terms of primary care physicians (PCPs) and specialists. The spectrum of specialists present in a multispecialty practice can vary. An important operational feature of the multispecialty group model is the cross-referrals that occur within the group along a continuum of care that can be provided to patients on a coordinated basis within the group. Another key aspect of multispecialty groups is that they can often achieve the critical patient mass necessary for a variety of technical component services. Various specialties often utilize the same technologies for ancillary services. The concentration of such specialties under a single group generally creates the opportunity for significant diversification and support of ancillary services.

As noted previously in the discussion of group size, the distribution of group practice earnings to group physicians is a challenging area. When groups integrate their services and increase group productivity and earnings through specialized care within the group, they often implement models in which all group physicians share in the earnings from such integrated services. Such models can afford higher levels of compensation for physicians in comparison to physicians of similar specialties who practice in different settings. If the integration model is not economically efficient, however, the opposite compensation outcome may be true. In short, group practice dynamics can add new variables into the physician compensation equation.

5.3 Practice Ownership

In the current marketplace, there are two major types of ownership for physician practices: physician owned and hospital or health system owned. Practice ownership can have an impact on the operations and economics of physician practices. As a general matter in physician-owned practices, the physician-owners are at risk for the overall profitability of the practice. Since such profitability is the basis for the levels of compensation that may be paid to these physicians, physician-owned practices generally make decisions based upon considerations related to the economic viability of the practice. Decision making with respect to locations, the number of physicians, ancillary services, overhead, and other key practice variables are made from the perspective of the group and its clinical and economic optimization.

Hospital or health-system owned practices often operate out of a different planning horizon. Such practices function as part of a larger integrated delivery system (IDS) for healthcare services. Decisions related to the practice can be based on larger considerations related to the IDS and not the practice on an isolated basis. For example, a practice may be operated in a particular service market as part of meeting community need for physician services. Thus, a hospital or health system may operate a practice at a loss in this market as part of its mission to provide healthcare services in the community. Another example relates to practice costs and operational requirements. Hospitals and health systems often have greater levels of healthcare regulations that affect their operations, requiring them to implement significant compliance programs. Such programs can increase the costs of operating physician practices. As a result, physician compensation in hospital or health system owned practices may be based on considerations that are different from those affecting physician-owned practices. Indeed, such considerations may be foreign with respect to the fundamental operations and economics of the practice as a physician practice. (See Chapter 14, "The Economics of Physician Clinical Services and Compensation," for further discussion on the economics of health system owned practices.)

Chapter 14. The Economics of Physician Clinical Services and Compensation

CONTENTS

Chapter 14. The Economics of Physician Clinical Services and Compensation

By Timothy Smith, CPA/ABV

1.0 Introduction

This chapter provides an overview of the various economic and market factors that affect compensation for physician clinical services. It is essential to have a sound understanding of these factors for valuation purposes. The appropriate implementation and interpretation of various appraisal methods and techniques are contingent on the valuation analyst having a fundamental grasp of the economics related to physician services in the marketplace. Indeed, one of the most common causes of misapplications of appraisal methods in the healthcare sector arises from a lack of understanding of marketplace factors that are necessarily embedded in various data used to establish FMV compensation for physician services. To use such data appropriately, one must understand the economic dynamics that affect the characteristics and outcomes of market data as well as information sources used in the valuation process.

2.0 The Economics of Physician Clinical Services

2.1 The Key Economic Factors of Physician Clinical Services

There are two key economic factors to consider when evaluating physician services. First, physician services are generally compensated in accordance with the type of services provided. The healthcare marketplace pays physicians differently for varying kinds of services. Second, physicians generally incur costs and utilize various resources when providing these services. Thus, the revenues and fees that physicians receive for their services do not necessarily flow through as cash compensation to the physician. Rather, such revenues and fees are offset by various costs incurred by the physician in generating such cash inflows. These factors apply whether the physician is employed in a practice or is one of its owners. As a result, an appraiser should consider the impact of both revenues and expenses when evaluating the appropriate level of physician compensation for a service. The following sections outline some of the key considerations in assessing the revenues and expenses of physician services.

2.2 Clinical or Patient Care Revenues

The core revenue base for clinically practicing physicians comes from the fees generated from patient care or clinical services. As discussed above, these revenues can be further broken down into professional component and technical component services. Such services are generally detailed in terms of the specific procedures performed as denominated by current procedural terminology (CPT) or healthcare common procedure coding system (HCPCS) procedure codes. Clinical services may be paid for through a variety of reimbursement mechanisms, including fee-for-service, capitation, or episodic-care reimbursement models. Fee-for-service is by far the predominant reimbursement model in the current physician marketplace. Yet, efforts at healthcare reform are seeking to move the healthcare industry, including physicians, away from this model, toward payment for quality outcomes, patient disease management, and bundled payments for episodes of care. The extent and the speed at which the physician market migrates to these new models have yet to be determined.

It should be noted that each reimbursement mechanism has its own unique economics. Fee-for-service presents a direct correlation between revenues and services: the more services provided, the more revenue received. Capitation models, on the other hand, reflect a fixed amount of revenue for patient care. Depending on the utilization of services required by the patient base or covered lives included in the capitation payments, a practice may achieve more or less total capitation revenue. Greater levels of service per patient mean that fewer patients can be cared for on a per-physician basis. A smaller number of covered lives results in lower total capitation revenues and comparatively lower practice net earnings than could be achieved when patient care services were lower, per covered life.

Whatever the reimbursement model, the revenues received represent what the local marketplace is willing to pay for physician services on a "gross" basis, including both physician compensation and practice expense. Practice revenues may also include sales of drugs, pharmaceuticals, and durable medical equipment, some of which may be used as part of technical services for diagnostic testing, while others are provided to patients as part of treatment regimens. For some specialties such as oncology or cardiology, sales or usage of these items can represent a significant proportion of the practice's revenues. Indeed, revenues in a medical oncology practice from chemotherapy drugs can dwarf revenues from professional component services, although profitability from such drugs may be limited based on their reimbursement levels relative to cost.

One should not fail to note the potential for state-level restrictions that limit the scope of services provided by a physician practice. Maryland, for example, bars nonradiology physician practices from owning and providing MRI and CT services to patients.[1] For orthopedic surgery groups, this prohibition creates a significant limitation of the technical component services available in the practice, and thereby, on the available earnings for physician compensation. MRI services are typical in orthopedic groups of sufficient size. State certificate of need considerations as well as local market dynamics may also limit the scope of services provided by a physician practice. In addition, reimbursement and regulatory changes can also affect the scope of services. In the mid-2000s, many practices were involved in so-called under-arrangements, or block leasing of diagnostic testing facilities, until federal healthcare regulations effectively ended such practices. These restrictions point out the need for appraisers to research and understand regulatory matters as part of valuation assignments involving technical component services.

2.3 The Variability of Physician Reimbursement Across Markets

A recent study by the Center for Studying Health System Change (HSC) indicates a wide range of commercial reimbursement rates across various local markets in the United States and within those local markets.[2] The study noted that local market dynamics play a significant role in the reimbursement levels paid to physicians. Commercial payers establish a standard fee schedule, often based on the framework of the Medicare Physician Fee Schedule (MPFS) and its resource-based relative value system (RBRVS), that reflects the network goals of the insurer along with local physician supply considerations. Groups with leverage in the marketplace, however, are generally able to negotiate rates that are higher than the standard fee schedule. Small practices with little bargaining power are typically faced with accepting the standard fee schedule or not participating in the network or insurance plan.

The study selected eight markets for research because they were thought to have a wide range of payment rates, based on government studies. The exhibit below presents a summary of the study's findings for the standard fee schedule and the 75th percentile rate for specific practices in selected specialties. The data from this study show a wide variation in commercial payer rates across markets and within markets, particularly

1   See the Jan. 24, 2011, Maryland Court of Appeals ruling that the state's self-referral prohibition applies to orthopedic surgeons who refer patients for MRI and CT scans in their practices.
2   See *Wide Variation in Hospital and Physician Payment Rates Evidence of Provider Market Power*, Research Brief, No. 16, November 2010. Center for Studying Health System Change. www.hschange.org.

by specialty. The data indicate that groups with bargaining power are able to negotiate significantly higher rates than the standard fee schedule.

		75th Percentile Rates					
Market	Standard Rates	Internal Medicine / Family Medicine	Cardiology	Orthopedics	Anesthesiology	Radiology	Oncology - Physician Services
Cleveland	101%	112%	155%	124%	251%	166%	138%
Indianapolis	110	117	156	140	217	147	138
Los Angeles	92	-	-	-	177	-	-
Miami	82	89	110	101	-	134	116
Milwaukee	166	175	223	212	-	238	204
Richmond, VA	112	128	145	144	-	153	132
San Francisco	108	-	-	-	177	-	-
Rural Wisconsin	176	169	234	195	-	240	195

Commercial Rates as a Percentage of Medicare[3]

The potential impact of such variations in commercial reimbursement on local-market physician compensation should not be ignored. Revenue levels can have a significant impact on the earnings available in a practice for physician compensation. The impact of commercial reimbursement on physician compensation was first noted by Dietrich and Anderson in a groundbreaking analysis published in *Health Lawyers Weekly* in November 2008.[4] Their analysis, based on their first-hand experience in the market, showed how commercial rates can significantly affect compensation on a per-wRVU (work relative value unit) basis. For further discussion of the impact of reimbursement on physician compensation, see Chapter 37, "How Reimbursement and Physician Compensation Vary by Market."

2.4 Payer Mix Considerations in Practice Revenues

In addition to the reimbursement rates reflected in the local market, payer mix can also affect the level of revenues in a physician practice. Low or poor payers can reduce the revenues received per unit of service, e.g. patient counter, RVU, or surgical case. High payers can increase such revenues. Thus, the relative mix of low- and high-reimbursement payers can have a significant impact on the revenues of a physician practice, and thereby, on the practice's net earnings available for physician compensation. Government programs, such as Medicare and Medicaid, are generally considered to be low payers. As shown in the previous section, however, Medicare may not always be the lowest payer in all markets. Medicare pays better than commercial payers in Miami and Los

---

3   See Table 3 from study.
4   Mark O. Dietrich, CPA/ABV, and Gregory D. Anderson, CPA/ABV, CVA, "Evaluating RVU-Based Compensation Arrangements," *Health Lawyers Weekly*, Nov. 14, 2008

Angeles. Moreover, in a few states, Medicaid reimbursement exceeds that of Medicare.[5] Thus, one needs to evaluate the dynamics of a local market before determining whether a practice has a poor payer mix. High and low payers may be relative to unique factors in the market.

Another key consideration in the assessment of a practice's payer mix is whether it is reflective of the local service market or the practice's positioning within this market. In certain locales, the demographics of the service area may only lend itself to a certain payer mix; practices in this service area will not be able to achieve a different mix. Thus, one must evaluate patient volumes and physician productivity in these service markets as yielding revenues that may not be subject to improvement. Moreover, the payer mix in these service areas may not be affected by whether the practice is owned by a physician or a health system. Appraisers should be careful about summarily attributing poor-payer-mix issues to be the natural operating by-product of nonprofit health systems. The payer mix of a physician practice may be a function of the service market, not the practice's charity-care policies. On the other hand, a practice's payer mix be may the result of its marketing (or lack thereof), network participation strategy, or physician referral patterns. In such cases, an improved or more financially viable payer mix may be possible.

2.5 Other Sources of Revenue

As touched on earlier in this chapter, physicians often provide other types of services in the healthcare marketplace, such as call coverage, administrative, research, and educational services. These services often provide supplemental revenue streams and fees for physicians. The impact of revenue sources on physician compensation should not be ignored in evaluating the economics of a specific physician or practice. Stipends for hospital call coverage and medical directorships can provide a substantial amount of income for an individual physician or a physician group. Indeed, the potential impact of such revenue sources creates a difficulty for application of the market approach in valuing physician clinical services because the effect of such revenue on compensation is not gathered and reported separately in the various physician compensation surveys.

In addition, some physicians and practices provide certain types of clinical services that are indirectly provided to patients and billed to payers through another healthcare provider. Many physicians subcontract with hospitals, other facility-based healthcare providers, or other physician practices to provide professional interpretations of diagnostic testing. In such cases, the other provider or practice performs the technical component of the test, while the physician performs the professional component or

---

5   Based on the 2008 Medicaid-to-Medicare Fee Index, from www.statehealthfacts.org.

interpretation of the examination results. The other provider or practice bills the patient or payer globally for the test and then pays the physician separately for the interpretation based on a preset fee. For some physicians and practices, the revenue streams from these types of subcontracted professional services may constitute a material source of revenue.

As also discussed previously, the physician marketplace has witnessed the proliferation of so-called clinical co-management or service line management arrangements, in which physician-related entities or physicians are engaged to manage hospital or health system service lines. The physicians involved in these arrangements provide various management and quality-improvement services and functions in exchange for fees, a majority of which are usually based on performance and quality measures. The revenues generated by these arrangements can be in the hundreds of thousands to millions of dollars. Clinical co-management or service line management fees are becoming important and material sources of revenues and income for practices and individual physicians. The first versions of these arrangements were typically structured using separate legal entities in which the physicians were owners. Thus, the compensation for these arrangements was usually paid outside physician practice entities.

Some physicians and practices receive revenues from various nonoperating activities, such as space or equipment rentals, expense sharing agreements, investments, and ownership in other entities. Depending on the facts and circumstances, the revenues from these nonoperating activities can be material. The critical point to remember about these revenues is that they are not generally associated with the physician professional services. Thus, the compensation impact of such revenue streams should be excluded from the FMV analysis of a compensation for a physician's professional services.

2.6 Practice Overhead

Practice overhead represents the cost of those economic resources that are necessary to provide patient care services in a physician practice, apart from the cost of a physician's services. For office-based physicians, two key practice costs are nonphysician staffing and office space. These two resources often represent the two largest cost items in a practice's overhead structure. More importantly, they often represent the areas in which practices either run efficiently or inefficiently. For practices that benchmark relatively high for cost or overhead rates, staffing and space tend to be the culprits. Physicians will often overstaff their practices or lease more offices or square footage than is optimal for their practices. (Indeed, physicians are notorious for doing bad real estate deals.) With respect to staffing costs, benefits are an area in which practices can vary. Smaller practices often provide below-market benefits in comparison to larger groups or to corporate-owned entities. On the other hand, physician-owned groups with physicians nearing retirement may provide rich retirement benefits to support staff in order for the group to meet ERISA requirements for tax-free treatment of the practice retirement plans.

Two other key areas for costs are equipment and supplies. Some physician specialties, such as cardiology or radiation oncology, are very technology- or equipment-driven. The cost of such equipment, whether in the form of leasing or capital expenditures and the resulting depreciation expense, can run in the hundreds of thousands to millions of dollars. Drug and pharmaceutical supplies may be another area for significant overhead, especially for medical oncology practices. Finally, malpractice insurance can be another significant cost item for certain specialties, such as obstetrics and various surgical specialties.

It is also important to understand the cost behavior pattern for key resources in a practice. Some costs, such as drugs and pharmaceuticals, are variable and correlate directly with volume. Other costs do not necessarily fluctuate directly with patient or procedure volumes. Examples of such cost can often include staffing, space, and equipment. It is often assumed that these resources remain fixed over any level of patient or procedure volume. Such resources, however, are more accurately characterized as step costs, rather than fixed. Such costs can remain fixed up to a certain level of volume at which the practice must expand its facilities and staffing to accommodate the increased patient demand. Such expansion of resources may not always be achievable or practicable in the specific increment needed, e.g., hiring a 0.20 FTE or leasing an extra 500 square feet of adjacent or continuous space. Rather, resources are typically obtained in larger increments that create significant resource capacity for volume growth in the practice. Medical Group Management Association (MGMA) studies of highly productive practices over the years have frequently noted higher costs per unit of service in many of these practices, pointing to the "stair step" characteristics of many practice costs.[6]

Ultimately, resource utilization and overhead levels are an indication of the economic efficiency of the physicians in a practice vis-à-vis their volumes levels. Physicians may be highly productive from a volume or procedural standpoint, while economically inefficient because they incur excessive levels of overhead to sustain these high volume levels. Other physicians may be less productive, but more economically efficient, because they utilize lower levels of resources than their peers in generating these volumes. Such differences in economic efficiency can affect physician compensation levels in the

---

6   I am thankful to my colleague Dana Boatman, a long-time practice manager and MGMA member, for sharing this insight with me.

marketplace. All things being equal, the economically efficient physician creates a larger pool of available practice net earnings out of which physician compensation can be paid.[7]

Different specialties tend to have varying cost structures based on the manner in which they utilize resources in the provision of patient care services. Some specialties are more capital intensive than others, based on the technologies that are used in the typical bundle of services provided by practices of the specialty. Examples include cardiology and orthopedic surgery for various diagnostic imaging modalities and radiation oncology for cost of linear accelerators and other radiation therapy equipment. As a result, these specialties tend to have higher fixed cost ratios. One should not fail to include the depreciation expense on capital equipment in a practice's overhead structure. The cost of such equipment, allocated over its useful life, is necessary for the production of practice revenues and should be included in the computation of practice net earnings.

Supply-intensive specialties, on the other hand, may have significantly higher variable costs. The prime example of a supply-intensive specialty is medical oncology practice, where the revenues and costs associated with chemotherapy and other drugs are usually in the millions of dollars. Cardiology practices can have significant variable costs for the radiopharmaceuticals used in nuclear imaging, while pediatric practice may have material supply expenses for vaccines and other injectibles. By contrast, the overhead ratios of various surgical specialties may be relatively lower than other specialties because they perform a majority of their procedures in healthcare facilities. Only a limited amount of office space, support staff, and overhead are needed to support pre- and post-operative patient encounters performed in an office setting. Surgical procedures, moreover, tend to generate higher revenues per patient in comparison to other specialties, such as primary care and certain medical specialties, in which the primary procedures are office visits and exams. Primary care physicians have significant fixed costs related to support staff and space, since their key services consist of office encounters.

2.7 Cost of Capital and Practice Owner Return

Another important distinction in evaluating physician compensation is the extent to which compensation is derived from physician services versus compensation associated with ownership of the practice. When a physician provides patient care or serves as a medical director, the payment for such services should be classified as compensation for professional services. This type of compensation should be distinguished from income that a physician receives from being an owner of a business enterprise, such as a

---

7   My former HCA colleague, Ed Richardson, CPA/ABV, introduced me to this concept of the economic efficiency of a physician relative to productivity.

physician practice. As an owner in a practice, a physician is *taking risk* based on the level of investment the physician has made in the business, including working capital and other assets, such as capital equipment. He or she may also be responsible for certain liabilities of the practice, such as leases and loans. From an economic perspective, the total payment that an owner-physician receives from the practice necessarily incorporates the income (or loss) associated with his or her investment and willingness to take risk. In other words, the earnings paid to owner-physicians include payment for the cost of capital provided by the physician to the practice, in addition to compensation for physician services. Physicians may also receive owner-related compensation that derives from the profitability of other nonowner providers in the practice, such as employed physicians or mid-level providers.

2.8 The Economics of Nonphysician Providers

NPPs constitute a broad category that can include an array of various types of specialized providers, ranging from audiologists to social workers. The most common type of NPP used in the physician marketplace, however, is either a nurse practitioner (NP) or a physician assistant (PA). These types of NPPs can be used to provide a much more expansive scope of patient care services than the other types of NPPs, who tend to provide only a limited specialized set of services. Depending on state regulations, NPs and PAs can have more or less independent capacity from physicians for providing patient care services, including examinations and diagnosis, implementation of treatment plans, and prescribing of drugs and medications. In most jurisdictions, however, NPs and PAs are generally required to have some level of physician supervision.

Physician practices generally utilize NPs and PAs in two basic clinical modes or a combination of the two: as physician extenders or as practice providers. In the physician-extender mode, NPs and PAs assist physicians in patient encounters and procedures. The NPPs perform certain preparation and data-gathering activities before the patient sees the physician. The NPPs may also wrap up the office encounter with the patient, after the physician portion of the encounter is completed. If any in-office procedures are performed, the NPP is used in a similar way, including potential assistance in the procedure. This "extender" use of the NPPs increases the overall productivity of the physicians in the practice by minimizing their contact time with the patient and assigning the more routine and less clinically demanding portions of the office encounter or procedure to the NPP. The physician, therefore, is able to see more patients. NPPs may be used in a similar way for hospital patient encounters. Some practices will also use NPPs in the hospital setting as a way to minimize physician hospital call coverage response burdens. NPs or PAs placed in the hospital prescreen emergent or inpatient events for the practice to ensure that physicians are only called for clinically necessary cases. In the extender mode, NPPs do not typically generate independent procedural volume and revenue. Rather, they are used to leverage the productivity of the physicians they support in the practice.

In their use as practice providers, by contrast, NPs and PAs perform independent office encounters and procedures with patients. These encounters are not provided on a shared or "tag team" basis with physicians; patients do not see the physicians as part of the office visit or procedure. Under a typical arrangement, the physician sees the patient in the initial visit to the practice and develops a course of treatment for the patient. The NPP performs subsequent visits that are part of the treatment plan, including various pre- and post-procedural or -operative visits in certain medical and surgical specialty practices. Used as practice providers, NPPs usually create procedural volume and revenue that is separate from the physicians in the practice.

How the services of the NPP are billed to payers is a function of the payer's rules with respect to reimbursement of NPP services. Medicare affords three different billing options for the services of NPPs: incident to billing, direct billing, and shared or split encounter billing. There are specific criteria and regulations for each billing mode. Other payers besides Medicare, including Medicaid, can have different criteria and billing options for the services of NPPs. Discussing these billing criteria is beyond the scope of this chapter. Appraisers, however, should have a general understanding of these billing rules so as to understand the revenue cycle dynamics of a subject physician practice as part of a clinical services valuation assignment.

Either use of NPPs in a physician practice, whether as extender or provider, has an economic impact on the net earnings of a physician practice that are available for distribution to physicians. Used as extenders, NPPs provide for increased productivity by physicians, resulting in higher patient care revenues. These revenues come, however, at a cost equal to the compensation and benefits related to the NPP, along with any other incremental costs related to the use of the NPP. Thus, the net earnings from NPPs used as extenders would result from the increased revenues less NPP compensation, benefits, and incremental costs. Where NPPs are used as practice providers, the net earnings attributable to the use of NPPs would be equal to the collections generated by the NPP less compensation, benefits, and incremental costs. The key to incremental practice earnings from NPPs is ultimately their productivity, whether in terms of increased physician productivity or production attributable to the NPPs. It should also be noted that the utilization of NPPs may represent a lifestyle or convenience choice by physician practices. As noted earlier, physicians may use NPPs in the hospital setting as a means of limiting the burden associated with hospital call coverage.

One critical question that arises from the use of NPPs is whether the net earnings from their use should be treated as compensation for professional services or as a form of owner compensation. In reality, the net earnings may represent or include both forms of compensation. In most states, NPPs cannot practice medicine without the supervision of a physician. This supervision can include chart reviews as well as discussions between the supervising physician and the NPP. Since such supervision requires time and effort on the part of the physician, NPP supervision constitutes an administrative service provided to the practice. The value of these supervision services should not be underestimated. The success and ultimate productivity levels of NPPs can be greatly affected by the nature of this supervision relationship. In physician-owned practices, these administrative NPP supervision services may be compensated by distributing the net earnings from NPPs to their supervising physicians. Strictly speaking, however, not all of these earnings would appear to relate to supervision.

The ability of the NPP to generate net earnings is also a function of the practice's economics in terms of its capacity for attracting a patient base large enough to warrant the effective use of NPPs. Thus, some portion of these earnings would appear to accrue to the benefit of the owners of the practice. In cases of employed physicians providing such supervision, an argument can be made that supervision compensation should not be tied to net earnings from the NPP. The physician incurred time and effort supervising the other physician at the request of the employer, regardless of whether the NPP generated net earnings for the employer. Ultimately, the determination of compensation for supervision services and for ownership would need to be based on the facts and circumstances of the underlying arrangement.

2.9 The Economics of Startup and Newly Hired Physicians

It is important to understand the economics of startup and newly hired physicians because appraisers are frequently presented with a valuation assignment that involved such physicians. Startup physicians are those doctors placed in newly formed practices. Newly hired physicians are those providers that are added to an existing practice. They can be added as a replacement for a retiring or exiting physician in the practice, as an expansion of the practice, or as the addition of a new specialty or subspecialty to an existing practice. A key economic question for startup and newly hired physicians is how quickly they can "ramp up" to a normalized level of production. This normalized level will determine the expected revenues and expenses associated with the new physician. These economics are a function of the intersection of basic supply and demand as denominated in the currency of physician practices.

On the supply side of the supply-demand equation, one first considers the productive capacity of the new physician. If the physician has recently completed residency, fellowship, or other training, there is a general expectation that he or she will not ramp up as quickly to a normalized level of productivity in comparison to an experienced physician. Such "baby docs," as they are often affectionately called within the industry, are new to the practice of medicine and, thus, have a basic learning curve with respect to patient care and to the fundamentals of working in a practice. In addition, the actual level of normalized productivity for a specific newly matriculated physician is unknown. Such physicians have no track record to indicate their productive capacities. An experienced physician, on the other hand, will have a track record of historical productivity that can serve as an indication of the potential normalized level of production for which he or she is capable. For newly hired physicians coming into an established group, one should not fail to consider the typical productivity levels for physicians in the group. Generally, there can be an expectation that newly hired physicians will ramp up to a production level that is commensurate with their peers. Otherwise, the physician's continued practicing with the group may be jeopardized.

For the demand side of the equation, one must evaluate the potential for patient volumes from the four basic sources for such volumes within a local service market: 1) unmet patient demand or an underserved market, 2) increased market share or taking existing volumes from other providers in the market, 3) redistributed or "cannibalized" volumes from within the existing practice, or 4) population growth or demographic changes within a population, e.g., the aging of a population base. A new physician must draw a patient base from these four basic sources. Depending on the facts and circumstances, a new physician may have more or less favorable conditions for building a patient base. For example, a physician hired to replace a retiring physician may be more likely to have higher initial patient volumes than a physician starting up a practice in a community. A new physician in a multispecialty group can immediately benefit from group referrals, whereas a solo physician must become established in the local medical community to gain referrals from other physicians.

The cost economics of startup and newly hired physicians can also vary depending on the facts and circumstances. A solo physician is generally at risk for the fixed or step costs in a practice during the initial ramp-up period. Depending on the duration of the ramp-up period, significant startup losses can be incurred. A newly hired physician in an existing group, on the other hand, may be able to utilize excess resources or economies of scale from the existing group such that the startup losses are reduced or minimized. Typically, physicians incur startup losses during the initial one to two years of practice. Ultimately, the level of startup losses and the level of earnings available for physician compensation in a practice will be a function of the supply-and-demand curve for physician services vis-à-vis the local market demand and the physician's productivity capacity along with the dynamics of startup costs.

2.10 The Economic 'Margin' on Physician Services

One factor that should be noted in analyzing the economics of physician practices is that there is frequently little to no margin on physician services, after compensating physicians for providing those services. Physician practices contrast with other professional practices in which there tends to be billing margins on staff in the provision of professional services. In law, accounting, and consulting firms, the fees generated from the work of the professional staff are usually based on a graduated fee scale. Less experienced staff are billed at rates that are lower than more senior staff. The billing rates are intended to reflect varying levels of professional services provided to clients. Yet, professional staff who are not shareholders or partners in the firm are typically billed at rates that provide not only an allowance for overhead, but also include a margin that creates an earnings pool that is shared among the firm's owners. The higher the billing rates and the greater the economic realization and utilization of staff within such firms, the greater the compensation pool for owners.

The margin billing for junior staff is not generally present in physician practices. Physicians, whether baby docs or experienced and renowned, are paid at the same reimbursement rate for each procedure by payers. Physician professional services are compensated equally by payers under the assumption that the same level of service is provided by each physician.[8] Moreover, physicians have an expectation to be paid at rates commensurate with other physicians for their productivity. There is no graduated pay scale for physicians that is comparable to the typical graduated staffing levels and pay scales in other professional practices that are based on experience. Thus, available earnings streams in these professional practices are generally higher than those of physician practices, where there is an expectation that such earnings are paid to the physicians as compensation for professional services.[9] It should be noted that there are practices in which nonowner physicians do generate net earnings for owner physicians. In the author's experience, however, such practices are generally the exception and not the rule, primarily because physicians with sufficient productivity usually become owners in their practices. Most physicians tend to be recruited into private practice groups with an expectation that they will become owners after an initial ramp-up period. It should also be noted that there can be significant margin on NPP staffing, where such providers are highly productive. The use of NPPs reflects the general patterns for margin observed in other professional practices.

---

8   As discussed previously, commercial payers may pay certain groups or physicians more than others within a market, but this is a function of bargaining power rather than of experience per se.

9   One exception to this general trend is a practice staffed by physicians on work visas. One often observes practices staffed by nonresident physicians seeking U.S. residency who are paid at compensation rates relative to their production that generate margins. In this specific pattern, part of the consideration for services would appear to be a pathway to U.S. citizenship or residency status.

2.11 The Economics of Health System and Integrated Delivery System Practices

The ownership and operation of physician practices by hospitals, health systems, IDS, insurance plans, or other large healthcare organizations can affect the underlying services and economics of physician practices in ways that are distinct from physician-owned practices. The reason for this difference is that ownership by other types of healthcare entities can introduce business and operational considerations that are not intrinsic or related to the economic and operational efficiency or optimization of a physician practice. The larger concerns and objectives of the healthcare organization can override goals and plans that would maximize physician practice outcomes. As part of a larger healthcare organization, physician practices become one resource or service line within a larger continuum of services and product lines. Optimization of the organization takes precedence over that of the practice in terms of the healthcare entity's goals, strategies, and priorities. In addition, the practice becomes a participant in the owner healthcare entity's economics in terms of access to contracts, resources, policies, practices, and corporate culture.

Ownership by a larger healthcare organization can affect nearly every aspect of the operations and economics of physician practices in ways that are both favorable and unfavorable from the singular or solitary perspective of the practice. It can affect the revenues of the practice in many ways, including the following:

- *Participation in payer contracts:* Larger health systems or organizations may have greater leverage on commercial payers in a local market, providing a practice with higher reimbursement on commercial patients. Various studies indicate that health system power in the local market generally yields higher reimbursement for its physicians.[10] On the other hand, some health systems lack the acumen and experience in negotiating physician fee schedule rates or they may sacrifice physician rates for gains in other areas for the system. Thus, a health system may not always achieve improved reimbursement for a physician practice.

- *Centralized billing and collections:* When a practice becomes part of a larger health system, the billing and collections are often moved to a centralized office or absorbed into the hospital's billing and collection function. This move could negatively affect the practice's revenue cycle if the centralized function is inefficient or inexperienced with respect to physician practices. One of the

---

10   Robert A. Berenson, Paul B. Ginsburg, and Nicole Kemper, "Unchecked Provider Clout in California Foreshadows Challenges to Health Reform," *Health Affairs*, Vol. 29, No. 4, 2010. Ann S. O'Malley, Amelia M. Bond, and Robert A. Berenson, "Rising Hospital Employment of Physicians: Better Quality, Higher Costs?" *Issue Brief*, No. 136, August 2011, Center for Studying Health System Change, www.hschange.org.

lessons of the 1990s' wave of physician practice acquisitions and employment by hospitals was that hospital systems frequently did not understand physician billing and collection issues and performed poorly in this area in comparison to the pre-acquisition practice.

- *Payer mix:* Hospital-oriented health systems, especially those with a charitable mission, have a focus on serving community need that directs them to provide services or products in areas that may not be self-sustaining. Because these systems have access to larger resources outside of these areas, they are able to provide these services despite significant losses that occur from doing so. Physician-owned practices, by contrast, do not generally have access to such resources. Thus, they are not economically able to provide services in all areas and to all payer groups. When a physician practice is owned by a health system, it may be required to expand its payer mix to less favorable payers, thereby decreasing practice revenues on a per-unit-of-service basis.

- *Technical component and ancillary services:* The economics of technical or ancillary services in a physician practice change once the practice is owned by a health system or IDS. The health system may seek to move or consolidate such services into existing IDS facilities to maximize reimbursement. Generally, hospital or provider-based rates for certain ancillary services are higher than those for services provided in a physician practice setting. A health system or IDS may also seek to eliminate duplicative services, thereby reducing overhead and increasing the utilization of existing facilities and resources.

- *Hospital call coverage:* As will be discussed in a subsequent section, one reason that health systems are employing physicians is to ensure adequate coverage of hospital emergency departments and inpatient care. There is usually a reason that health systems are attempting to secure such coverage: Private practice physicians may be averse to such coverage for lifestyle and economic reasons. Physician practice opportunities and outcomes can be affected by such coverage.

Health system and larger healthcare organization considerations can also influence decisions related to issues such as the number of providers, the type and specialty or subspecialty of providers, and the locations of physician practices in ways that may not optimize the economies of the specific physician practice or group. These decisions can have an impact on both the revenues and overhead of a practice.

The cost and overhead structure of a practice can also be affected by health system or healthcare organization factors that may or may not benefit a physician group from the sole perspective of the practice. Such factors can include the following:

- *Corporate pay grades for support staff:* Health systems and large healthcare organizations often have formal, structured pay grades for employees. Frequently, these rates exceed those paid by smaller physician groups or solo physicians.

- *Employee benefits:* Frequently, smaller physician-owned practices do not offer benefit packages that are comparable to larger, corporate organizations in the employment marketplace. This disparity is often the result of company size: Smaller companies are usually at a competitive disadvantage in the pricing of employee benefits, such as health insurance or group life or disability policies. As noted previously, the benefits offered by physician-owned groups can also be a function of the retirement and other fringe benefit goals of the owner-physicians. Thus, ownership of a health system or healthcare organization can mean a significant change in employee benefits costs to a physician practice. For most small to medium-size physician-owned groups, this change usually entails an increase in such costs.

- *Supply and resource costs:* It is easy to assume that large organizations have bargaining power with vendors that would enable them to achieve discounts and improved pricing for supplies, equipment, and third-party services. Yet, this is not always the case. Larger organizations often have priorities in negotiating with vendors that do not always produce the cheapest pricing for goods and services. They may look at quality and delivery considerations that may create the best value, but not necessarily the least expensive cost. Large organizations with a broad spectrum of supply-chain needs may also negotiate to get reduced pricing on high-volume or high-dollar-value goods and services for the overall system, while conceding higher pricing for less used items. In the case of physician practices, many of the quality, delivery, and volume and value considerations that are considered by a health system are not applicable to the needs of the practice. Thus, health system supply and resource costs can often be higher than those experienced by a stand-alone physician practice.

- *Corporate management and support resources:* Health systems and large organizations often have multiple layers of management and support functions that are allocated to various departments and entities within the system or organization. Because of the complexity involved in managing large organizations, management and support functions may be more expensive than they would otherwise be for the effective operating of a physician practice. Larger healthcare organizations, moreover, often perceive higher levels of risk and compliance for their operations, and thus, initiate critical and extensive risk-avoidance and compliance programs. These programs, however, are not implemented without significant costs. Thus, health systems and larger healthcare organizations can have higher administrative and corporate overhead costs than physician-owned practices.

In summary, ownership of physician practices by health systems and large healthcare organizations can introduce factors and considerations that add complexity to the operations and economics of these practices. Discussion of these factors should not necessarily lead to the universal conclusion that such ownership leads to suboptimized physician practice economics in all cases. Further study and data research would be needed to establish general trends and findings. Appraisers valuing physician services, however, should be aware of the potential impact of these factors.

3.0 Physician Clinical Compensation in the Marketplace

The following sections discuss how the economics of physician services and practices can affect physician compensation.

3.1 Sources and Types of Physician Compensation

Physician compensation is a function of the services provided by the physician. The level of compensation and the factors that affect it relate to the type of service provided. Different services have varying economics and dynamics that have an impact on the compensation paid for the services. Moreover, physicians provide an array of services in the marketplace. The following list provides a summary of many of the services that physicians can provide in the healthcare marketplace:

- Patient care or clinical:

  › Professional component services performed personally by the physician,

  › Technical component services supervised by a physician, and

  › "Incident to" services supervised by a physician.

- On-call;

- Administrative;

- Educational or academic;

- Supervision of nonphysician providers;

- Clinical or service line management;

- Research and development;

- Business management;

- Entrepreneurial and investor;

- Executive; and

- Managerial.

To evaluate and analyze physician compensation, therefore, one must identify the scope of services provided by the physician and essentially compile and aggregate a series of specific compensation analyses based on the services provided. Moreover, the total earnings received by a physician from a practice or other healthcare organization should not be summarily taken as compensation for clinical services. A physician's total compensation may be the result of a variety of different services provided on an employee, independent-contractor, or business-owner basis.

Since the predominant form of services provided by physicians in the marketplace is clinical or patient care services, the remaining subsections will discuss marketplace compensation trends for clinical services. Readers may consult other chapters in this book for discussions of compensation trends and factors related to other forms of physician services.

3.2 General Market Trends and Factors for Clinical Services

There are several general market trends that affect the overall national marketplace for physician clinical or patient care services and compensation. Many of these trends will have an impact on local market dynamics for these services. Appraisers should be aware of these trends and stay informed as the physician and healthcare marketplaces evolve in the coming years. Some of the top key trends include the following:

- *Physician shortages:* The long-term outlook for the demand for physician services is that such demand will exceed the projected supply of physicians. This shortage is forecasted across nearly all specialties, and indeed, shortages among some specialties are already arising in certain markets.[11] The expected higher demand for physician services stems from the aging of the baby-boom generation as well as the increased access to health insurance through various healthcare reform initiatives. On the supply side, the limits placed on medical school entrance rates during the past two decades have served to reduce or cap the number of U.S.-trained physicians.

- *Healthcare cost containment:* While the limited supply of physicians indicates the need for rising physician compensation according to classical economic theory for supply and demand, healthcare cost containment concerns are bringing market pressures to limit physician compensation levels. The increasing cost of healthcare services, including physician services, is viewed as unsustainable economically. Thus, insurers will seek limit reimbursement for services.

- *Medicare's sustainable growth rate formula:* Beginning in the late 1990s, Medicare reimbursement was tied to a sustainable growth rate (SGR) formula that sought to limit the growth in Medicare spending for healthcare services. The SGR formula began to require reductions in Medicare reimbursement to physicians beginning in the early 2000s. Since that time, Congress and the president have intervened with a series of legislative acts that temporarily stayed the SGR reductions and replaced the cuts with modest increases. The current SGR adjustment calls for a reduction of over 25% in physician fees, which was factored into the computation of purported budget neutrality of the recently passed federal healthcare reform legislation. Odds are, however, that this reduction will not be enacted at its current level.

- *Reductions in reimbursement for technical component services:* Cost-containment efforts have also focused on the issue of ancillary services utilization by physicians, particularly in the area of diagnostic imaging. Many healthcare analysts think that overutilization of such services by physicians is one of the causes of increasing healthcare costs. Medicare recently changed the utilization assumptions for equipment in practice expense RVUs—particularly for imaging modalities—such that reimbursement declined for many technical component services. The recent Phase III Stark regulations also placed certain

---

11 Currently, there appear to be shortages as well as excesses for selected specialties in certain markets around the United States.

restrictions on the provision and billing of many technical component services that further limited physician practices for ancillaries. These reductions, as well as the potential for further reductions in technical service revenues, have placed or are expected to place limiting pressures on physician compensation levels, especially for specialties that derive a significant amount of compensation from technical component services.

- *Changes in reimbursement mechanisms:* The recent string of healthcare reform initiatives include a movement away from the current fee-for-service payment system toward other payment mechanisms. One key trend is toward pay-for-performance programs, in which payment for healthcare services is linked to quality and clinical outcomes and performance. A related trend is toward payment for disease management through medical homes and other structures, rather than for disease treatment procedures. Other reimbursement innovations include payment bundling, in which hospitals or other healthcare facilities and physicians receive a single payment for certain types of cases or episodes of care. The various providers are expected to split these payments among themselves, rather than each provider billing separately for its portion of the care related to the case or episode of care. The end goal of these various reimbursement innovations is cost containment. In other words, these initiatives will tend toward limiting or reducing reimbursement for physician services.

- *Physician employment by health systems:* For a variety of reasons, many think the recent trend toward health system employment of physicians is generally expected to sustain or provide increases to current physician compensation levels in the marketplace.

The interplay of these various market forces on physician compensation present something of an economic theory conundrum. Basic economic theory for supply and demand predicts that physician compensation for clinical services needs to rise for the supply of physicians to increase to meet the demand for services. Thus, the general market prognostication would appear to be that physician compensation will be rising in future years. Yet, cost containment efforts are seeking to limit such increases. Which forces will ultimately prevail?

3.3 Practice Ownership Factors

The ownership of a physician practice can have a critical impact on the level of physician compensation for clinical services. Physician-owned practices are necessarily limited in their total or overall compensation to the net earnings of the practice as calculated using the basic formula of revenues less expenses. In other words, total group compensation in physician-owned practices is based on the "eat what you catch" or "eat what you treat" paradigm.[12] It is true that physician-owned groups may borrow money in the short run to supplement physician incomes, but such borrowing cannot be sustained over the long run. Physician compensation for private practice groups is essentially a by-product of the revenues and expense outcomes of the physicians in the group.

Physician compensation in practices owned and operated by health systems or other healthcare organizations is not necessarily limited to the economics of practice revenues less expenses. These types of owners may be willing and able to underwrite practice losses, where physician groups provide essential services relative to the larger system or organization. The health system or organization is able to draw on funding from other sources, including the total earnings from operations within the organization.[13] In addition, the genesis of such practice losses may not necessarily relate to revenue and expense outcomes inherent to the physician practice as such, but rather to operational and economic decisions made in the context of IDS or organizational objectives. Notwithstanding such considerations, health systems and healthcare organizations can often afford to pay more for physician services, due to the earnings derived from other operations. Since the reasons and justification for such underwriting of physician compensation may not be intrinsic to the economics of physician practices, a certain level of "noise" is introduced into the physician compensation marketplace by health systems and other healthcare organizations employing physicians.

3.4 Local Service Market Factors

Physician compensation for clinical services is generally affected by a variety of local service market factors and considerations. As discussed previously, commercial, Medicare, and Medicaid reimbursement vary from market to market across the United States. Commercial reimbursement levels are the result of the supply and demand of physicians in the local market, payer objectives and goals, and available health insurance premium dollars, among other local market dynamics. Medicare reimbursement rates, on the other hand, are determined based on GPCIs related to cost of living and wage differentials in the local service area in comparison to the other service areas in the United States. Medicaid rates are set based on state budgets. These key payer reimbursement rates establish the horizon for practice revenues in the local service market and thereby, have an impact on physician compensation levels.

---

12 This paradigm is also known as "eat what you kill." For obvious reasons, this metaphor may not be the best choice for thinking about compensation for physician services.

13 The funding sources referenced here do not contemplate the volume or value of referrals, but rather the overall earnings from the health system or integrated delivery system.

The payer mix of the local service market is another factor that affects the determination of physician compensation. The demographics of the local population frame the boundaries of the payer mix that is possible in a given service area. For example, a large retirement population in a community necessarily implies a significant mix of Medicare patients for a practice in this community. Service markets that include low-income areas generally have higher levels of Medicaid patients. In general, a physician practice will have a patient base that reflects the local service market's demographics. The revenue base of the practice will necessarily be circumscribed by this payer mix, and physician compensation will also be affected.

Local population and demographic factors may also determine the level of market demand for physician services of a given specialty in the local service market. Areas with younger populations will have higher demand for pediatrics and obstetrics than retirement communities. Likewise, service markets with older populations may have greater need for cardiology, orthopedics, and geriatrics. Population size also determines the level of market demand for services. Rural areas, along with smaller cities, often cannot support a full-time physician in a given specialty, resulting in many service markets not having local access to certain types of physician services. Large population areas, by contrast, generally provide sufficient demand for a cornucopia of physician specialties, subspecialties, and highly specialized subspecialties, such as pediatric cardiovascular surgery.

The cost of resources used in a practice may also be affected by cost-of-living and wage-level factors in a local service markets. Labor costs for support staff and office rental rates are determined by the prevailing rates in a given location. These costs can vary widely across the United States and tend to be higher in large urban areas and in specific states and regions. Malpractice insurance premiums are another practice cost that is unique to state or local market dynamics. These premiums are generally tied to state insurance and malpractice considerations, but certain local markets may have claims histories and tendencies that may also affect such premiums. The cost of other resources and services used by practices can also vary based on local cost of living and expense factors. Certain practice resources, however, are not as indicative of local cost-of-living indexes. Technologically advanced equipment as well as major drugs and medical supplies are generally priced at national levels rather than varying significantly by local markets. The supply and demand for these resources is measured in national rather than local terms.

These various local market economic factors necessarily affect the total net earnings from practice operations that are available for physician compensation. They establish certain boundaries for the physician compensation pool for a practice based on the practice's fundamental economics. As discussed in the following subsection, a practice may optimize its specific operations and economics. Yet, this optimization can only occur within the horizon of what is possible in the given local service market context. For physician-owned groups, this horizon circumscribes the potential total compensation for the group. Whatever the local market economics allow is what the physician can ultimately make. This circumscription may not be as direct in the case of groups owned by health systems and other healthcare organizations. As noted previously, such organizations have a larger operational framework and pool of resources from which physician compensation levels can be established. Nonetheless, these entities are affected by local market dynamics. There is only so much in operating losses that such organizations can underwrite as part of their larger objectives and strategies.

In certain instances, local market economics are such that health systems or larger healthcare organizations tend to be the owners and operators of physician practices, at least on a significant scale. Patient demand, reimbursement rates, and payer mix in many rural areas or smaller population centers may be such that they do not afford competitive or attractive economics for physicians in private practice. For example, a rural community may only need the services of a given physician specialty at a production level equal to the 35th percentile of the major physician compensation and production surveys such as MGMA. This level of demand does not lend itself to compensation that is competitive in the physician recruiting arena. In such cases, a health system may step in and essentially subsidize or underwrite physician compensation to make practice in this smaller market competitive to potential physician candidates. Health systems are willing to make these types of funding commitments as part of their overall goals of serving community need, once the system has determined that the services of a given specialty are needed in the local community. Health systems are able to make these funding requirements for physician compensation because they have a larger pool of resources to use for such endeavors related to community need.

3.5 Practice- and Physician-Specific Factors

Within the larger framework of national and local market economic factors, physician practices and individual physicians can position themselves to optimize their compensation levels. The unique characteristics and attributes of practices and physicians determine physician compensation levels achieved within this framework. Practices and physicians can be highly productive from a volume or procedural standpoint and thereby increase their total compensation. If they have leverage in the local market, they can negotiate for reimbursement rates above the standard fee schedule with commercial payers. They can attempt to optimize their payer mix to the extent possible given the demographics of the service area. Practices can seek to improve their total revenues with the addition of technical component services, as allowed by federal and state healthcare regulations, as well as with other revenue sources, such as compensated hospital call coverage, medical directorships, diagnostic testing interpretations, and other professional services. The efficiency and effectiveness of the practice's resource utilization and overhead structure will also affect the available pool of net earnings for the practice. For physician-owned groups, these endeavors will necessarily have a direct impact on physician compensation levels, while they may have a direct or indirect effect on the compensation in nonphysician-owned practices.

3.6 Group Practice Compensation Plans

When physicians are part of a group practice, their individual compensation is generally a function of the group's compensation plan. The group compensation plan establishes the basic structure for how physicians are compensated within the group. It may also set out the specific compensation amounts or rates for particular areas or measures that are part of the basic structure. Compensation structures and specific incentive measures can vary widely from group to group.[14] A survey of the measures used by groups reporting in the MGMA and American Medical Group Association (AMGA) surveys indicates that for compensation methodologies based on productivity measures, RVUs and professional collections are the two top measures used.[15] For incentive pay and bonuses, the most frequently used incentives are based on patient satisfaction, quality, peer review, specific goals and objectives related to financial and productivity concerns, administrative duties, call coverage, and citizenship.[16] Use of base salaries is also a common structure among group practices.[17]

Group practice compensation plans can be more or less reflective of individual physician performance and outcomes. They can also be based on group performance or a combination of group and individual physician measures. Some smaller groups opt for pure egalitarian or communitarian compensation models in which group physicians share equally in group practice earnings. Other groups may elect a "silo" model in which costs are allocated individually to each physician along with the physician's professional revenues and a share of technical component service earnings. Each physician is then paid on an "eat what you catch" basis. Some groups establish a groupwide or specialty by specialty compensation per unit of productivity rate by which individual physicians are paid. In summary, individual compensation paid to physicians in groups can be based on an array of varying performance and economic factors.

---

14   Indeed, the complexity and potential permutations of various compensation plan options is evidenced by an over 500-page tome devoted to this singular topic. See Bruce A. Johnson and Deborah Walker Keegan, *Physician Compensation Plans: State-of-the-Art Strategies,* 2006, MGMA, for a comprehensive and in-depth discussion of group compensation plans.

15   See Table 17 in the *Demographics—Physician Practice* section of MGMA for the 2010 and 2011 surveys and Figure 7 in the 2010 and 2011 AMGA surveys.

16   See Table 18 in MGMA and Figure 8 in AMGA for the 2010 and 2011 surveys.

17   See Figure 8 in AMGA.

Chapter 15. An Overview
of Physician Reimbursement

CONTENTS

Chapter 15. An Overview
of Physician Reimbursement

By Richard Romero, PAHM, CHFP, AVA, and Ryan Harvey

1.0 Introduction

To analyze compensation for physician services in the marketplace, it is essential to have an understanding of the multiple factors that can affect reimbursement for services performed. This includes an understanding of the code system used to describe and bill for services, the payment systems used by Medicare and other insurers, characteristics of various types of insurers, methods used by insurers to contract with physicians for services, and how a patient visit results in revenue to a practice. This chapter will provide the reader with an overview of each area related to reimbursement for physician services.

2.0 Medicare Reimbursement

A key to understanding physician reimbursement is knowledge of how Medicare reimburses physicians for services. The Center for Medicare & Medicaid Services (CMS) website provides a wealth of information regarding reimbursement.[1]

2.1 HCPCS Background Information

CMS estimates that health insurers process 5 billion claims for payment each year. In order for insurers to process claims efficiently standardized coding systems are necessary. The Healthcare Common Procedure Coding System (HCPCS) is the standard code set used for this purpose. The HCPCS is divided into two codes sets, referred to as level I and level II of the HCPCS. Codes are designed to communicate standard information about medical services, procedures and products among physicians and

---

1   www.cms.gov.

other providers billers, coders, government organizations, and payers for benchmarking, claim submission payment, program management, fraud detection and other analytical purposes. Codes identifying physician services range from those that require significant physician time and effort, staff, equipment and supplies, to those that require little to no physician time and resources. [2]

HCPCS Level I Codes

Level I of the HCPCS is comprised of CPT (Current Procedural Terminology) codes, a numeric coding system maintained by the American Medical Association (AMA). The CPT code system is a uniform standard coding system consisting of a narrative description and numeric or alpha-numeric codes. These codes identify and communicate to users the medical services and procedures provided by physicians and other health care professionals. These health care professionals use the CPT code system to identify services and procedures for which they bill public or private health insurance programs. Decisions regarding the addition, deletion, or revision of CPT codes are made by the AMA. The CPT code system is updated January 1 of each year.[3]

The CPT code system has three categories:

- *Category I*—Physician and technical services: These are five-character numeric codes organized into six major sections:

    ○ Evaluation and management;

    ○ Anesthesia;

    ○ Surgery;

    ○ Radiology;

    ○ Pathology and laboratory; and

    ○ Medicine.

- *Category II*—Performance measurement: These supplemental codes are used for performance management. These codes are intended to gather data regarding the quality of care rendered through coding certain services and the

---

2 www.cms.gov/Medicare/Coding/MedHCPCSGenInfo/index.html?redirect=/MedHCPCSGenInfo/.
3 www.cms.gov/Medicare/Coding/MedHCPCSGenInfo/index.html?redirect=/MedHCPCSGenInfo/.

test results that support nationally established performance measures. These codes have five characters; four numeric digits followed by the letter "F."

- *Category III*—Temporary codes: These temporary codes allow data collection for emerging technology, services, and procedures. These codes have five characters; four numeric digits followed by the letter "T."

HCPCS Level II Codes

Level II of the HCPCS is a standardized coding system that is used primarily to identify products, supplies, and services not included in the CPT codes, such as ambulance services, durable medical equipment, prosthetics, orthotics, and supplies (DMEPOS) when used outside a physician's office.[4]

Level II codes are alphanumeric and are comprised of five characters; one letter followed by four numeric digits, while CPT codes are identified using five numeric digits.[5] HCPCS Level II codes are organized by the following groups:

- A—Transportation services including ambulance, medical and surgical supplies;

- B—Enteral and parenteral therapy;

- C—Reporting of pass-through payments for hospitals and items classified as new technology (temporary code);

- D—Dental procedures;

- E—Durable medical equipment;

- G—Professional procedures and services that would otherwise be coded in the CPT system but for which a CPT code does not exist or additional detail is required by CMS (temporary code);

- H—Alcohol and drug abuse treatment;

- J—Drugs administration other than by oral method;

---

4 www.cms.gov/Medicare/Coding/MedHCPCSGenInfo/index.html?redirect=/MedHCPCSGenInfo/.
5 Ibid.

- K—Used by DMERCs[6] when current permanent national codes for a medical review policy are not available (temporary code);

- L—Orthotic procedures;

- L—Prosthetic procedures;

- M—Medical services that do not qualify for CPT codes because they are either not of proven efficacy or considered obsolete modalities;

- Q—Temporary codes;

- R—Diagnostic radiology services; and

- V—Vision services, hearing services.

HCPCS Level III Codes
The CMS HCPCS—General Information website provides the following background of HCPCS Level III Codes:

> Prior to December 31, 2003, Level III HCPCS codes were developed and used by Medicaid State agencies, Medicare contractors, and private insurers in their specific programs or local areas of jurisdiction. For purposes of Medicare, level III codes were also referred to as local codes. Local codes were established when an insurer preferred that suppliers use a local code to identify a service, for which there is no level I or level II code, rather than use a "miscellaneous or not otherwise classified code." [7]

2.2 Modifiers

Modifiers are two-digit codes added to CPT and HCPCS codes to provide additional information about the procedure or service performed. This additional information can include a variety of conditions and circumstances ranging from the component of the service being performed (e.g., professional versus technical component of service), the number of procedures or services performed, when only part of the service was actually performed, when more than one surgeon was involved in the procedure, and other factors.

---

6   Durable medical equipment regional carrier.
7   www.cms.gov/Medicare/Coding/MedHCPCSGenInfo/index.html?redirect=/MedHCPCSGenInfo/.

Approximately 30 unique CPT modifiers are used for Level I (CPT) codes, and approximately 13 Level I modifiers are used for services billed by hospital outpatient departments. Modifiers applied to Level II (HCPCS) codes are far more numerous, and not all are recognized by Medicare.

It is important to note that some modifiers have a direct impact on payment. For example, for Medicare, CPT modifier -80, "Assistant Surgeon," reduces payment for codes billed with this modifier to 16% of the amount otherwise applicable for the surgery. Commercial insurers may reimburse for services differently than Medicare does. For example, Medicare reimburses CPT modifier -50, "Bilateral Procedure," at 150%, while other payers may reimburse a two-code combination: one code at 100% and a second at 50%.[8] [Note: When analyzing practice billing records, be sure to request and receive modifiers in billing records to calculate productivity and payment correctly.]

Professional and Technical Component Modifiers

As described more fully below, certain CPT codes for diagnostic testing may have a "professional" and a "technical" component of service. While some codes have both components, other codes are considered entirely professional or entirely technical. For example, an X-ray of the abdomen has both a professional and technical component. The codes for radiology treatment planning are considered entirely professional without a technical component and the codes for radiation treatment delivery are considered entirely technical without a professional component.

For these CPT codes that have both a professional and technical component, the modifier "-26" denotes the professional services component and "-TC" denotes the technical component. The identification and quantification of the professional component of services is important because this information is used in benchmarking physician productivity and professional collections.

2.3 The Resource-Based Relative Value Scale

Since Jan. 1, 1992, Medicare has paid for physician services under section 1848 of the Social Security Act (the Act) according to the physician fee schedule (PFS), or as it is commonly referred to, the Medicare Physician Fee Schedule (MPFS). The Act requires that payments under the PFS are based on national uniform relative value units (RVUs).[9] The goals underlying the creation of the PFS were to develop a system that "improved

---

8   *American Medical Group Management Association 2011 Medical Group Compensation and Financial Survey.*

9   Medicare Program; Payment Policies Under the Physician Fee Schedule, Five-Year Review of Work Relative Value Units, Clinical Laboratory Fee Schedule: Signature on Requisition, and Other Revisions to Part B for CY 2012 (2012 Final Rule).

reimbursement for primary care services, was less procedure-oriented and controlled health care costs."[10]

The resource-based relative value scale (RBRVS) assigns RVUs to services provided—evaluation and management of patients, office visits, surgeries, hospital care, procedures, anesthesia, etc.—to quantify the relative work, practice expense, and administrative costs of furnishing a given service. These RVUs allow for comparison of disparate services, such as a neurosurgery procedure with an office visit. The RBRVS can be thought of as the means by which a HCPCS code is converted to reimbursement. It is also used to determine the allowable payment for any code included in the PFS irrespective of specialty.[11] The RBRVS incorporates the three components of physician services into RVUs for service: physician work, practice expense, and professional liability insurance or malpractice expense.

"The concepts and methodology underlying the PFS were enacted as part of the Omnibus Budget Reconciliation Act of 1989 and 1990. Initially, only physician work RVUs were resource-based while practice expense and malpractice expense RVUs were based on reasonable allowable charges."[12] The data for developing original work RVUs came from a research project at the Harvard University School of Public Health conducted in the 1980s under a cooperative agreement with the Health Care Financing Administration, which his now CMS.[13] The research examined the resources and costs required to provide physician services, including "looking at the time spent before, during and after a service, as well as the intensity of the service itself."[14] Data was obtained by surveying approximately 4,000 physicians "using vignettes describing typical scenarios for each service considered."[15] The group at Harvard obtained input on its work from experts both inside and outside of the government, including physician specialty groups.[16]

Section 121 of the Social Security Act Amendments of 1994 required the development of "resource-based" practice expense (PE) relative value units for each physician service. General categories of expenses to be considered included items such as office rent and personnel wages, but medical malpractice expenses were excluded.[17] As described in the 2012 Final Rule:

---

10   *THE BASICS: Relative Value Units*, National Health Policy Forum, Feb. 12, 2009.
11   Sara E. Johnson and Warren P. Newton, "Resource-Based Relative Value Units: A Primer for Academic Family Physicians," *Journal of Family Medicine*. 2002, 34(3).
12   2012 Final Rule.
13   *Report to the Congress Medicare and the Health Care Delivery System*, Medicare Payment Advisory Commission. June 2011 (MedPAC, June 2011).
14   Sara E. Johnson and Warren P Newton, "Resource-Based Relative Value Units: A Primer for Academic Family Physicians," *Journal of Family Medicine*. 2002, 34(3).
15   MedPAC, June 2011.
16   2012 Final Rule.
17   Ibid.

This resource-based system was based on two significant sources of actual PE data: the Clinical Practice Expert Panel (CPEP) data and the AMA's Socioeconomic Monitoring System (SMS) data. The CPEP data were collected from panels of physicians, practice administrators, and nonphysician health professionals (for example, registered nurses (RN)) nominated by physician specialty societies and other groups.... The CPEP panels identified the direct inputs required for each physician's service in both the office setting and out-of-office setting.

Beginning in 2007, CMS revised the methodology for calculating PE RVUs from a "top-down" to a "bottom-up" approach. Under a bottom-up approach, the costs of providing each service (e.g., clinical staff, equipment, and supplies) is identified and summed. Resource-based payments for malpractice expenses started in 2000 based on a CMS-developed methodology using premiums paid for liability insurance.

CMS also considers local variability of the fee schedule by using a set of geographic adjustment factors called the Geographic Practice Cost Index values, or GPCIs. The GPCIs reflect the relative costs of physician work, practice expense, and malpractice costs in a given geography as they compare to national average costs for each component.[18]

These components and their relationship to the calculation of reimbursement will be explained further in the following section.

2.4 Understanding Components Used in Calculating Reimbursement

Medicare's allowable charge for a given CPT code is derived from a formula that contains seven components: three RVU values, three GPCI values, and the conversion factor. To understand more fully, the calculations can be broken down into three components: RVUs, the geographical adjustment, and the conversion factor.

Every CPT Code Has Three Sets of RVUs
The payment rate for each service or CPT code billed is based on the sum of three separate RVU components:

- Physician work RVUs;

- Practice expenses RVUs; and

- Malpractice insurance expense RVUs.

---

18   Ibid.

The following sections provide a brief discussion of each of these three components.

Physician Work RVUs

Physician work RVUs are "a scale rating the time, mental effort and judgment, technical skill and physical effort, and stress associated with providing each service" in comparison with other services.[19] Codes representing services or procedures with higher levels of any of these factors will have a greater work RVU value than codes with lesser requirements. As codes are updated each year, the work RVU value can increase or decrease from year to year.

The National Health Policy Forum developed the following illustrative example:[20]

> The work RVUs for a diagnostic colonoscopy are more than twice the work RVUs for an intermediate office visit because the colonoscopy requires more physician time and effort than the visit. A diagnostic colonoscopy is estimated to require 75 minutes of physician time, which includes 30 minutes to prepare for the procedure and 15 minutes after the procedure. The time actually spent performing the colonoscopy—termed the intra-service time—is estimated to be 30 minutes. In contrast, an intermediate office visit is estimated to take about 40 minutes of physician time. This is comprised of 5 minutes before and 10 minutes after seeing the patient, and 25 minutes of intra-service time. The intra-service time for the colonoscopy is weighted more heavily than the intra-service time for the office visit to reflect the higher skill and effort and associated stress of providing the procedure.

For an illustration of physician time required to perform selected services, see Exhibit 1.

Practice Expense RVUs

Practice expense (PE) RVUs represent the costs of operating a practice such as rent, equipment, supplies, and nonphysician staff costs. Costs are comprised of two categories, direct and indirect. The PE RVU is calculated using the aforementioned "bottom-up" methodology. Direct costs of providing a service are calculated, and indirect costs are allocated. The allocation of indirect costs is based on the direct costs specifically associated with a code and the greater of either the clinical labor costs or the physician work RVUs.[21]

---

19 MedPAC, 2011.
20 *THE BASICS, Relative Value Units*, National Health Policy Forum, Feb. 12, 2009.
21 2012 Final Rule.

Exhibit 1. Physician Time Required for Selected Services (in Minutes)				
Service Code	Total*	Pre-Service	Intra-Service	Post-Operative
X-ray - Chest (71010)	5.00	1.00	3.00	1.00
Intermediate Office Visit (99214)	40.00	5.00	25.00	10.00
Diagnostic Colonoscopy (45378)	75.00	30.00	30.00	15.00
Total Hip Replacement (27130)	478.00	90.00	135.00	30.00
Coronary Artery Bypass, Using Grafts (33510)	718.00	95.00	154.00	40.00

Source: http://www.cms.gov/Medicare/Medicare-Fee-for-Service-Payment/PhysicianFeeSched/PFS-Federal-Regulation-Notices-Items/CMS1253669.html, PhysTime_FR2012_Public.xls, 2012 Final Rule Physician Time File.

*Total Hip Replacement and Coronary Artery Bypass time includes estimate of physician time for the global period.

Malpractice RVUs

Malpractice (MP) RVUs vary depending on the relative malpractice exposure of the CPT code. As seen from a review of the Medicare RVU files, MP RVUs typically have the smallest value of the three RVU components.

Practice Expense RVUs Depend on Place of Service

Some physician services can be performed in either a facility setting, such as a hospital outpatient department, or nonfacility setting, such as a physician's office.[22] Based on the place of service (facility versus nonfacility), separate PE RVUs are calculated. When a physician performs a service in a facility, the facility bears the PE costs (e.g., supplies and staffing expenses). Facilities receive reimbursement from Medicare for its costs in providing services outside of the PFS. When services are performed in a nonfacility setting, the practice bears the PE costs. As a result, nonfacility PE RVUs are generally higher.

The National Health Policy Forum developed the following illustrative example, which was updated for 2012 based on fully transitioned PE RVUs:[23]

---

22 For a list of place of service codes and their classification as facility or nonfacility, see Chapter 26 of the Medicare Claims Processing Manual.

23 THE BASICS, *Relative Value Units*, National Health Policy Forum, Feb. 12, 2009.

For example, when chemotherapy administration by infusion (CPT 96542) is provided in the physician office, its practice expense RVUs are 2.57. This reflects the costs of 75 minutes of clinical staff time; use of equipment such as a stretcher, intravenous infusion pump, and ECG (electrocardiogram); and supplies like gowns, gloves, and syringes. When chemotherapy administration is provided in a facility, the physician practice does not incur these costs, so the practice expense RVUs are only 0.41.

"For 2012, CMS updated the indirect cost data that are used in the calculation of PE RVUs for most specialties using the American Medical Association's Physician Practice Information Survey (PPIS) data. The PPIS is a multispecialty nationally representative indirect PE survey of both physicians and non-physician practitioners. Its use is being transitioned over a four-year period which began in 2010."[24] In other words, "transitional" PE RVUs reflect the current PE payment, while "fully-implemented" PE RVUs reflect what the PE payment will be at the end of the transition period.

Every CPT Code Has Three Geographical Modifiers

As stated above, CMS adjusts for local variability of the fee schedule by using a set of geographic adjustment factors called GPCIs, which reflect the relative costs of physician work, practice expense, and malpractice costs in a given geography as they compare to the national average.

To determine payment for a given service in a given locality, CMS adjusts each of the three RVU factors by GPCI factors specific to each RVU factor. Exhibit 2 summarizes

Exhibit 2. Geographic Practice Cost Indices		
GPCI	Manhattan, NY	Muncie, IN
Work	1.062	0.969
Practice Expense	1.162	0.923
Medical Malpractice	1.271	0.613

Source: http://www.cms.gov/Medicare/Medicare-Fee-for-Service-Payment/PhysicianFeeSched/PFS-Relative-Value-Files-Items/CMS1254038.html, GPCI2012.xlsx, Addendum E Final 2012 Geographic Practice Cost Indices (GPCIs).

---

24 *Medicare Physician Fee Schedule Payment System*, Fact Sheet Series, Medicare Learning Network. December 2011.

the GPCI factors for Manhattan, N.Y., and Muncie, Ind. As illustrated, for each of the three components, operating a practice in Manhattan is considered more expensive than operating in Muncie.

For RVU Totals, Sum the Parts

To find the total RVUs for a particular CPT code, add the RVU components from the work, malpractice, and transitioned practice expense that appropriately reflect the site of service, either facility or nonfacility. Exhibit 3 illustrates a sample calculation of RVUs for selected services.

Exhibit 3. Relative Value Units for Selected Services				
Service Code	Total	Physician Work	Practice Expense*	Medical Malpractice
X-ray - Chest (71010)	0.70	0.18	0.50	0.02
Intermediate Office Visit (99214)	3.06	1.50	1.46	0.10
Diagnostic Colonoscopy (45378)	11.84	3.69	7.56	0.59
Total Hip Replacement (27130)	42.47	21.79	16.39	4.29
Coronary Artery Bypass, Using Grafts (33510)	59.19	34.98	15.80	8.41

Source: http://www.cms.gov/Medicare/Medicare-Fee-for-Service-Payment/PhysicianFeeSched/PFS-Relative-Value-Files-Items/CMS1254038.html, PPRRVU12.xlsx, 2012 National Physician Fee Schedule Relative Value File.

* PE RVUs represent transitioned non-facility PE RVUs.

Conversion Factor (CF)

To calculate payment, it is necessary to multiply the geographically adjusted RVUs by a dollar conversion factor (CF). The CF is updated annually, according to the sustainable growth rate (SGR) formula. The formula is intended to keep spending on physician services consistent with a target based on growth of the national economy.[25] "The SGR ties physician payment updates to a number of factors, including growth in input costs,

---

25 "Physician and Other Health Professionals Payment System," *Payment Basics*, MedPAC, October 2011.

growth in fee-for-service enrollment, and growth in the volume of physician services relative to growth in the national economy."[26] Congress has the ability to override the statutorily defined formula, as it has done in the past several years, to prevent declines in the CF. In 2012, the CF is $33.9764.

CMS also publishes locality-specific anesthesia conversion factors (CFs), and they are calculated from the 2012 national anesthesia CF, whose calculation is described in the final physician fee schedule regulation.

Calculating Payment—The Formula

The formula used by Medicare to calculate reimbursement is available on the CMS website. The following description has been reproduced from a page on that site: [27]

> To determine the payment rate for a particular service, each of the three separate RVUs is adjusted by the corresponding GPCI. The sum of the geographically adjusted RVUs is multiplied by the conversion factor. The CF is the dollar multiplier used to convert the RVUs to an actual dollar amount.

> The formula for calculating the Medicare fee schedule payment amount for a given service and fee schedule area can be expressed as shown in Exhibit 4.

Exhibit 4. Formula for Calculating the Medicare Fee Schedule Payment		
2012 Non-Facility Payment Amount	=	[(Work RVU * Work GPCI) +
		(Transitioned Non-Facility PE RVU * PE GPCI) +
		(MP RVU * MP GPCI)] *
		Conversion Factor
2012 Facility Payment Amount	=	[(Work RVU * Work GPCI) +
		(Transitioned Facility PE RVU * PE GPCI) +
		(MP RVU * MP GPCI)] *
		Conversion Factor

> Section 5102(b) of the Deficit Reduction Act of 2005 requires a payment cap on the technical component (TC) of certain diagnostic imaging procedures and the TC portions of the global diagnostic imaging services. This cap is based on the Outpatient Prospective Payment System (OPPS) payment. To implement this provision, the

---

26 Ibid.
27 www.cms.gov/Medicare/Medicare-Fee-for-Service-Payment/PhysicianFeeSched/PFS-Relative-Value-Files-Items/CMS1254038.html, RVUPUF12.docx, National Physician Fee Schedule Relative Value File Calendar Year 2012.

physician fee schedule amount is compared to the OPPS payment amount and the lower amount is used in the formula in Exhibit 5 to calculate payment.

Exhibit 5. Formula to Calculate Payment		
2012 OPPS Non-Facility Payment Amount	=	[(Work RVU * Work GPCI) + (OPPS Non-Facility PE RVU * PE GPCI) + (OPPS MP RVU * MP GPCI)] * Conversion Factor
2012 OPPS Facility Payment Amount	=	[(Work RVU * Work GPCI) + (OPPS Facility PE RVU * PE GPCI) + (OPPS MP RVU * MP GPCI)] * Conversion Factor

Limiting Charge

Physicians do not have to participate in the Medicare program. Those that do not participate may charge patients directly. However, charges are subject to a limit on the amount they can charge. The Medicare limiting charge is set by law at 115 percent of the payment amount for the service furnished by the nonparticipating physician. However, the law sets the payment amount for nonparticipating physicians at 95 percent of the payment for participating physicians (i.e., the fee schedule amount). Calculating 95 percent of 115 percent of an amount is equivalent to multiplying the amount by a factor of 1.0925 (or 109.25 percent). Therefore, to calculate the Medicare limiting charge for a physician service for a locality, multiply the fee schedule amount by a factor of 1.0925. The result is the Medicare limiting charge for that service for that locality to which the fee schedule amount applies.

Exhibit 6 illustrates the calculation of payment, including the impact of GPCIs on reimbursement. In this example, payment was calculated for Manhattan, N.Y., as compared to Muncie, Ind., for selected services.

2.5 Updating Payments[28]

The CMS is responsible for maintaining the PFS. Over time, the inputs used in the PFS and the manner in which reimbursement has been calculated have changed. However, CMS's methodology works to ensure that each component of providing a service (such as taking a patient history and administering an injection) is valued the same across services.[29]

---

28 "Physician and Other Health Professionals Payment System," *Payment Basics*, MedPAC, October 2011.
29 *THE BASICS, Relative Value Units*, National Health Policy Forum, Feb. 12, 2009.

Exhibit 6. Nonfacility Payment Amount Calculations

Location	Service Code	Total Payment	Physician Work RVU	Work GPCI	Practice Expense RVU*	PE GPCI	Medical Malpractice RVU	MP GPCI	Conversion Factor
Manhattan, NY	X-ray - Chest (71010)	$ 27.10	0.18	1.062	0.50	1.162	0.02	1.271	$ 33.9764
Muncie, IN	X-ray - Chest (71010)	$ 22.02	0.18	0.969	0.50	0.923	0.02	0.613	$ 33.9764
Manhattan, NY	Intermediate Office Visit (99214)	$ 116.08	1.50	1.062	1.46	1.162	0.10	1.271	$ 33.9764
Muncie, IN	Intermediate Office Visit (99214)	$ 97.25	1.50	0.969	1.46	0.923	0.10	0.613	$ 33.9764
Manhattan, NY	Diagnostic Colonoscopy (45378)	$ 457.10	3.69	1.062	7.56	1.162	0.59	1.271	$ 33.9764
Muncie, IN	Diagnostic Colonoscopy (45378)	$ 370.86	3.69	0.969	7.56	0.923	0.59	0.613	$ 33.9764
Manhattan, NY	Total Hip Replacement (27130)	$ 1,618.59	21.79	1.062	16.39	1.162	4.29	1.271	$ 33.9764
Muncie, IN	Total Hip Replacement (27130)	$ 1,320.74	21.79	0.969	16.39	0.923	4.29	0.613	$ 33.9764
Manhattan, NY	Coronary Artery Bypass, Using Grafts (33510)	$ 2,249.15	34.98	1.062	15.80	1.162	8.41	1.271	$ 33.9764
Muncie, IN	Coronary Artery Bypass, Using Grafts (33510)	$ 1,822.30	34.98	0.969	15.80	0.923	8.41	0.613	$ 33.9764

Source: http://www.cms.gov/Medicare/Medicare-Fee-for-Service-Payment/PhysicianFeeSched/PFS-Relative-Value-Files-Items/CMS1254038.html, PPRRVU12.xlsx and GPCI2012.xlsx, 2012 National Physician Fee Schedule Relative Value File and Addendum E Final 2012 Geographic Practice Cost Indices (GPCIs).
*Payment calculated using the transitioned non-facility PE WRVU.

Congress requires CMS to review the fee schedule's relative weights and update them at least every five years, although, since 2009, CMS has been reviewing the weights annually under the agency's potentially misvalued services initiative. HCPCS codes and the conversion factor are updated annually.[30]

The update of relative weights includes a review of changes in medical practice, coding changes, new data, and the addition of new services.[31] In completing its review, CMS obtains input from the AMA/Specialty Society Relative Value Scale Update Committee (RUC). The RUC is comprised of 31 members, 21 of which are appointed by national medical specialty societies.[32]

The annual updates for the CF are made according to the SGR system.[33]

---

30 "Physician and Other Health Professionals Payment System," *Payment Basics*, MedPAC, October 2011
31 Ibid.
32 www.ama-assn.org/ama/pub/physician-resources/solutions-managing-your-practice/coding-billing-insurance/medicare/the-resource-based-relative-value-scale/the-rvs-update-committee.page.
33 "Physician and Other Health Professionals Payment System," *Payment Basics*, MedPAC, October 2011

2.6 Implications of the Sustainable Growth Rate System

Since its implementation, the SGR formula has mandated reductions to physician reimbursement each year. Historically, Congress has employed legislative action to insulate physicians from the required reductions. The June 2011 *Report to the Congress: Medicare and the Health Care Delivery System*[34] provides a background as to why reductions are required each year.

> The sustainable growth rate (SGR) system is the formulaic method for annually updating fees for physician and other health professional services. Established by the Balanced Budget Act of 1997, the SGR system was designed to keep aggregate Medicare expenditures for these services on an affordable ("sustainable") trajectory, through an expenditure target approach.

> The SGR system sets an expenditure target for growth in Medicare spending on fee schedule services. This target allows for annual Medicare spending to grow at a rate consistent with the sum of four factors—namely, changes in:

> - The nation's per capita gross domestic product (GDP);
>
> - The number of beneficiaries enrolled in fee-for-service (FFS) Medicare;
>
> - Inflation in practice costs for physicians and other health professionals; and
>
> - Spending due to law and regulation.

> With respect to the first factor—per capita GDP—the SGR formula essentially allows the volume of fee schedule services to grow at the same rate as per capita GDP. Volume is tightly linked to spending because Medicare pays providers on an FFS basis. Therefore, when the SGR spending target allows for growth in the nation's per capita GDP, the formula allows for the volume of fee schedule services to grow at the same rate. Additionally, the SGR expenditure target is adjusted to account for three other factors: changes in the number of Medicare beneficiaries, changes in physician practice costs, and changes in covered services due to law and regulation. When these rates increase, so does the expenditure target, essentially allowing higher aggregate spending.

> To determine fee schedule updates under the SGR, CMS is required, annually, to compare actual cumulative Medicare spending (starting in April 1996) on fee schedule

---

34 MedPAC, 2011.

services with the target amount over the same period. If cumulative expenditures equal the cumulative target, the SGR formula sets physician fee updates to the Medicare Economic Index (MEI). However, if expenditures exceed the spending target, the update for the subsequent year is reduced, with the goal of bringing cumulative spending back in line with the target. (The reverse is also true; if cumulative expenditures are less than the target amount, then the subsequent year's update is higher.)

In the first several years of the SGR system, actual expenditures did not exceed spending targets because volume did not grow faster than per capita GDP. Therefore, updates to the physician fee schedule in the early years of the SGR system were at or above the MEI. However, beginning in 2001, actual cumulative expenditures exceeded allowed targets and the discrepancy has grown each year, resulting in a series of ever-larger cuts prescribed under the formula. With the exception of 2002, the Congress has passed a series of bills to override these reductions. The resulting updates have been fairly modest. Overrides that were implemented before 2007 contributed to the amount of dollars that need to be recouped under the SGR formula.

The primary rationale for each override of the SGR cuts has been to preserve beneficiary access to physician services. The reason why the overrides have been short term is that longer term adjustments have higher estimated costs ("scores") and thus require the Congress to find proportionately larger spending offsets.

3.0 Insurers

A number of different types of payers may insure the patients receiving services at a practice. The following is an overview of various types of insurers:

- Medicare;

- Medicaid;

- TRICARE;

- Federal Employee Health Benefit Program (FEHBP);

- Commercial; and

- Worker's compensation.

3.1 Medicare

Medicare consists of multiple parts. Part A reimburses for services such as inpatient, nursing home, home health, and hospice care. Part A is funded by payroll taxes that employers, employees, and the self-employed pay. This tax revenue is credited to a trust fund. Part B reimburses for physician-related services, some hospital outpatient services, and durable medical equipment. Beneficiaries pay a monthly premium for Part B coverage. The voluntary program is funded largely by general Treasury revenues and premiums paid by the insured. Part C is Medicare Advantage, which is managed care for Medicare. It combines Part A and Part B and covers medically needed services. Part C plans may offer extra benefits, which can include prescription drug coverage. Part D is the Medicare Prescription Drug Plan. Beneficiaries can participate through a stand-alone plan or as part of a Medicare Advantage plan.

3.2 Medicaid

Medicaid provides medical assistance for certain individuals and families with low incomes and resources. Medicaid programs are state-specific, but are funded jointly by each state and the federal government. Reimbursement from Medicaid is typically the lowest level of any insurer.

3.3 TRICARE

TRICARE, formerly known as the Civilian Health and Medical Program of the Uniform Services (CHAMPUS), is the managed care program of the U.S. military. It provides medical benefits to active-duty military and family members. TRICARE pays for coverage in facilities other than military hospitals.

3.4 Federal Employee Health Benefit Program

The Federal Employee Health Benefit Program (FEHBP) is the health insurance program for federal employees. FEHBP is the largest employer-sponsored health insurance program in the country and provides coverage for over 9 million federal employees, retirees, and their dependents through contracts with private insurance plans.

3.5 Commercial Insurers

Commercial insurers contract with providers to arrange for medical services for their beneficiaries. They collect premium dollars from participants and reimburse for services rendered to their insured beneficiaries. Commercial plans may also serve as administrative contractors to those employers who self-insure. In these circumstances, the employers bear the utilization risk and the insurer provides access to its provider network and processes claims. Plans can be for-profit or nonprofit. Reimbursement for services is typically higher than from other insurers.

3.6 Workers' Compensation

Workers' compensation insurance provides coverage for an employee who has suffered an injury or illness resulting from job-related duties. Coverage includes medical and rehabilitation costs for employees injured on the job.[35]

4.0 Physician Reimbursement Methods

Reimbursement for services provided inherently includes compensation for risk in that the amount paid to a provider varies based on utilization or cost. The various payment methodologies represent an assignment of risk for patient care between the provider and the insurer. Physician reimbursement models often include fee for service (FFS), capitation, or case rate methodologies.

4.1 Fee for Service

Under a FFS system, physicians are reimbursed based on the number and type of services provided. A price is set for each service (i.e., code billed) in advance with insurers for a set duration of time. The price can directly tie to Medicare reimbursement rates or reflect specific negotiations between insurer and physicians at rates that do not directly tie to Medicare. A benefit of the FFS model is that it encourages production by the physician provider. However, that dynamic creates a financial incentive to induce patient demand or provide services that may not be truly medically necessary. FFS fee schedules at commercial insurers are often expressed as a percentage of Medicare reimbursement rates.

4.2 Capitation

Capitation provides reimbursement to physicians based on a set monthly fee for specific services to be provided to an identified group of patients. The payment is a set monthly fee paid per member per month (PMPM). Although not exclusive to these specialties, capitation is most common in the primary care and family care specialties. The monthly amount received for each patient takes into account various characteristics that can impact health, such as age and gender. Under a capitation model, physicians have an incentive to provide effective and efficient care. However, there is also an incentive to enroll only healthy patients who are less likely to need services, thereby limiting the quantity of services and limiting costs.

4.3 Case Rate

Case rate reimbursement compensates providers based on the expected costs for a clinically defined episode of care. Case rate reimbursement is also known by other

---

35 www.sba.gov/content/what-workers-compensation-insurance.

names, such as bundled payments, global fee or global payment, and episode-of-care payment. The amount paid reflects the procedures expected to be performed during the episode of care. Under a case rate methodology, physicians have an incentive to limit costs per case, reduce the quantity and quality of services, and serve patients with lesser resources for a given episode of care.

5.0 Revenue Cycle

Physicians are paid for the resources consumed and services provided after the patient receives these benefits. The practice determines a gross charge for each CPT code, which is the same amount billed to each insurer. A bill is created and submitted to insurers for reimbursement. However, payers reimburse for services at negotiated rates, which will vary from payer to payer for the same service. The insurer processes the claim, and payment is remitted to the practice. The difference between the gross amount charged and the amount received is recorded as a contractual allowance or adjustment. The practice will also seek payment from patients for the portion of their bill for which they are responsible (i.e., office co-pays and deductibles).

Although a full discussion of the practice revenue cycle is beyond the scope of this chapter, the following provides an overview of the revenue cycle process:[36]

- *Registration*—Patient demographic information is collected.

- *Insurer verification*—Patient benefits, deductible, and co-payment amounts are verified with the insurer.

- *Patient check in*—Patient demographic and insurance information is verified. Co-payment is collected.

- *Patient visit*—Patient receives services.

- *Preauthorization*—When applicable, the practice should contact the insurer to determine any preauthorization or precertification.

- *Documentation*—The medical record is updated to reflect the services performed, the basis for the care provided, and a plan of care.

---

36 For a more detailed discussion, see the publications *Prepare That Claim, Follow That Claim,* and *Appeal That Claim* from the American Medical Association Practice Management Center.

- *Patient check out*—If not previously collected, co-payments and deductibles are collected.

- *Code selected/claim generated*—The appropriate CPT code is selected, and the claim is generated.

- *Claim submitted*—The practice submits a claim for reimbursement.

- *The insurer adjudicates the claim*—The adjudication of a claim involves several steps:

  - The insurer receives the claim.

  - The claims system processes the patient eligibility and applicable benefits for the services provided.

  - The claim is processed through a series of edits, including:

    - Pricing rules that reduce billed charges to contractually agreed-upon rates;

    - Claim edits, such as CPT guidelines, CMS payment rules, and medical society guidelines; and

    - Proprietary edits based on medical policies established by the insurer.

  - Explanation of benefit (EOB)/remittance advice (RA) is generated, explaining what was paid and denied.

  - Payment—The insurer remits payment to the practice.

- *The practice receives payment*—The practice reviews the EOB and payment received and posts payments to patient accounts.

- *Secondary insurers*—Claims are submitted to secondary insurers, if applicable.

- *Appeals*—Denied claims or claims with amounts deemed inaccurate by the practice are appealed.

- *Patient responsibility*—Amounts for which the patient is responsible are billed to and collected from the patient.

If a practice experiences inefficiency or errors in the revenue cycle, the financial performance of the practice can suffer. Understanding the steps of the revenue cycle and departures from efficient and effective methodologies can help diagnose variances between benchmark data and the subject physician or practice being analyzed.

6.0 Conclusion

Several factors can influence the financial performance of a physician and related practice. To properly analyze physician productivity for fair market value purposes, an understanding of these factors is necessary. An analyst should become familiar with the code systems used by physicians, the manner in which reimbursement is calculated, the methodology by which they are contracted with insurers, key characteristics of major insurers, and the steps necessary to obtain reimbursement from insurers. With this understanding, the analyst will be better prepared to provide an effective and supported analysis.

PRACTICE AID: Navigating Through the Medicare Physician Fee Schedule

By Richard Romero, PAHM, CHFP, AVA; Ryan Harvey;
and Timothy Smith, CPA/ABV

1.0 How to Use This Practice Aid to Navigate the Medicare Physician Fee Schedule Files

This practice aid is intended to help users work with the Medicare Physician Fee Schedule (MPFS) files that can be downloaded from the website for the Centers for Medicare & Medicaid Services (CMS). While these files come with instructions from CMS, this guidance often assumes that the user is fully familiar with many background and general matters related to the MPFS. These matters may not be readily apparent to appraisers and consultants who are relatively new to healthcare practice. The purpose of this practice aid, therefore, is to "back fill" background information on the MPFS for the reader. The practice aid does not attempt to reproduce all the details or instructions in the MPFS files, but rather to supplement them. This practice aid should be used in tandem with the instructions and information already provided by CMS with the MPFS.

The CMS website is located at www.cms.gov.

This practice aid also assumes the reader is generally familiar with how to calculate Medicare reimbursement. Information on Medicare reimbursement is included in Chapter 15, "An Overview of Physician Reimbursement."

2.0 Introduction to the Medicare Physician Fee Schedule

2.1 The Medicare Physician Fee Schedule Overview

First of all, it is important to understand what the MPFS is. The MPFS is a listing of the fees used by Medicare to pay physicians or other providers/suppliers. It contains current information for the more than 10,000 physician services that are covered by the fee schedule and indicates the maximum amount that Medicare will reimburse a physician and/or other providers on a fee-for-service basis.

The MPFS provides the relative value units (RVUs) used to calculate payment, a fee schedule status indicator, and various payment policy indicators needed for payment adjustment (i.e., payment of assistant at surgery, team surgery, bilateral surgery, etc.).

The fee schedule also includes information necessary for payment adjustments to reflect the variation in practice costs between different geographic localities across the country. To make this adjustment, CMS established a Geographic Practice Cost Index (GPCI) for every Medicare payment locality for each of the three components of a procedure's relative value unit (i.e., the RVUs for work, practice expense, and malpractice expense).

CMS also developed fee schedules for physicians, ambulance services, clinical laboratory services, and durable medical equipment, prosthetics, orthotics, and supplies.[1]

2.2 Resources Available to Calculate Payment

Payment rates for an individual service are based on the following three components: (i) the RVUs; (ii) the GPCIs; and (iii) the conversion factor (CF). The inputs for each of these components, as well as information relating to the various payment policy indicators needed for payment adjustment, are included in the MPFS. The following resources are available from CMS to help users calculate payment for services.

CMS Physician Fee Schedule Look-Up[2]

Current information for services covered by the MPFS is available online at the CMS Physician Fee Schedule Look-Up website. This website takes users through various selection steps prior to the display of the pricing information. The site allows users to:

- Search pricing amounts, various payment policy indicators, RVUs, and GPCIs by a single procedure code, a range of procedure codes, or a list of procedure codes; and

- Search for the national payment amount, a specific carrier/Medicare administrative contractor (MAC) or a specific carrier/MAC locality.[3]

CMS Relative Value Database Files[4]

CMS publishes a downloadable version of the fee schedule. These files include current information for services covered by the MPFS and allow users to calculate reimbursement amounts on their own. The MPFS Relative Value File database file is available for download for the forthcoming calendar year upon publication of the Final Rule of the MPFS in the *Federal Register*. This usually occurs in early November each year. This file

---

1   www.cms.gov/Medicare/Medicare-Fee-for-Service-Payment/FeeScheduleGenInfo/index.html?redirect=/ FeeScheduleGenInfo/.
2   www.cms.gov/apps/physician-fee-schedule/overview.aspx.
3   See "The Geographic Practice Cost Index (GPCI) File" in this chapter.
4   www.cms.gov/Medicare/Medicare-Fee-for-Service-Payment/PhysicianFeeSched/PFS-Relative-Value-Files-Items/CMS1254038.html, RVUPUF12.docx, National Physician Fee Schedule Relative Value File Calendar Year 2012, accessed June 26, 2012.

is updated each April 1, July 1, and October 1 to incorporate midyear changes. Six files comprise the Relative Value File:

- A Word document containing the file's record layout and file documentation (MPFS Instruction Sheet);

- A file containing the RVUs and various indicators that affect the calculation of reimbursement under the MPFS;

- A file providing each GPCI component for each carrier/locality for the year;

- A file containing the locality/county crosswalk (this file details which counties in a given state are included in a defined locality);

- A file containing the separate anesthesia conversion factors for the year; and

- A file containing the payment amounts after the application of the Outpatient Prospective Payment System (OPPS)-based payment caps.[5]

Note: CMS provides these files in a zip file that can be downloaded from the CMS website. Each of the five information files noted above come in three formats: Excel worksheet, Excel comma separated values (CSV), and text/PRN.

3.0 The Relative Value File

Medicare payments are based on the relative value units assigned to each physician service included in the MPFS. The National Physician Fee Schedule Relative Value File, however, contains 37 columns of data, listing various RVUs and other information that factor into the RVU component of the payment calculation.[6] It is important, therefore, to understand the file's contents to know which of the RVU figures CMS uses to determine payment. The following section provides supplemental information on the contents of the different columns included in the Relative Value File. A summary of the various columns is presented in Exhibit 1.

Column 1: HCPCS

HCPCS stands for Healthcare Common Procedure Coding System. HCPCS includes not only the CPT codes promulgated by the AMA, but also an additional series of codes

---

5   See "The Outpatient Prospective Payment System (OPPS) Payment File" in this chapter.
6   The total RVU amount is then multiplied by a dollar conversion factor to calculate payment.

Exhibit 1. The National Physician Fee Schedule Relative Value File

1	2	3	4	5	6	7	8	9	10	11	12	13	14
HCPCS	MOD	DESCRIPTION	STATUS CODE	NOT USED FOR MEDICARE PAYMENT	WORK RVU	TRANSITIONED NON-FAC PE RVU	TRANSITIONED NON-FAC NA INDICATOR	FULLY IMPLEMENTED NON-FAC PE RVU	FULLY IMPLEMENTED NON-FAC NA INDICATOR	TRANSITIONED FACILITY PE RVU	TRANSITIONED FACILITY NA INDICATOR	FULLY IMPLEMENTED FACILITY PE RVU	FULLY IMPLEMENTED FACILITY NA INDICATOR
Procedure Code	Modifier	Procedure Description	Status Code Indicators		Work RVU	Practice Expense RVU							

15	16	17	18	19	20	21	22	23	24	25	26	27	28	29	30
MP RVU	TRANSITIONED NON-FACILITY TOTAL	FULLY IMPLEMENTED NON-FACILITY TOTAL	TRANSITIONED FACILITY TOTAL	FULLY IMPLEMENTED FACILITY TOTAL	PCTC IND	GLOB DAYS	PRE OP	INTRA OP	POST OP	MULT PROC	BILAT SURG	ASST SURG	CO-SURG	TEAM SURG	ENDO BASE
Malpractice RVU	Total RVUs				PC/TC Indicator	Surgical Procedure Indicators									

31	32	33	34	35	36	37
CONV FACTOR	PHYSICIAN SUPERVISION OF DIAGNOSTIC PROCEDURES	CALCULATION FLAG	DIAGNOSTIC IMAGING FAMILY INDICATOR	NON-FACILITY PE USED FOR OPPS PAYMENT AMOUNT	FACILITY PE USED FOR OPPS PAYMENT AMOUNT	MP USED FOR OPPS PAYMENT AMOUNT
Conversion Factor	Physician Supervision Indicator	Calculation Flag Indicator	Diagnostic Imaging Family Indicator	OPPS Payment Cap		

Source: http://www.cms.gov/Medicare/Medicare-Fee-for-Service-Payment/PhysicianFeeSched/PFS-Relative-Value-Files-Items/CMS1254038.html, PPRRVU12.xlsx, 2012 National Physician Fee Schedule Relative Value File.

called HCPCS Level II codes. (Level I codes are the CPT codes.) These codes relate to additional procedures or services paid by Medicare that are not included in CPT codes. Level II codes are five-digit and alphanumeric.

Column 2: MOD

This column is primarily used to denote the professional and technical component codes of certain global diagnostic testing procedures. It indicates these codes by use of the "-26" and "-TC" modifiers. The -26 modifier is used for the professional component of the code, while the -TC modifier is used for the technical component. The version of the CPT code that is shown without a -26 or -TC is the global version of the code. The only other modifier included in this column is -53, relating to a discontinued service.

Column 3: Description

This column provides a description of the HCPCS code.

Column 4: Status Code

Columns 4 provides information relating to the status of a service or CPT code. A value in this column indicates the status of a procedure (i.e., whether the code is in the fee schedule or whether it is separately payable if the service is covered). While there are 16 different status codes (ranging from A to X), only RVUs associated with status codes of "A," "R," or "T" are used for Medicare payment. A status code "C" indicates that the carrier determines the level of reimbursement, based on documentation provided by the provider. Exhibit 2 provides the description of the A, R, and T codes from the MPFS Instruction Sheet. For information on all the status codes, see the MPFS Instruction Sheet.

	Exhibit 2. Status Codes, 2012	
Status Code	Code Name	Description
A	Active Code	These codes are paid separately under the physician fee schedule, if covered. There will be RVUs for codes with this status. The presence of an "A" indicator does not mean that Medicare has made a national coverage determination regarding the service; carriers remain responsible for coverage decisions in the absence of a national Medicare policy.
R	Restricted Coverage	Special coverage instructions apply. If no RVUs are shown, the service is carrier priced. (NOTE: The majority of codes to which this indicator will be assigned are the alpha-numeric dental codes, which begin with "D". We are assigning the indicator to a limited number of CPT codes which represent services that are covered only in unusual circumstances.)
T	Injections	There are RVUS and payment amounts for these services, but they are only paid if there are no other services payable under the physician fee schedule billed on the same date by the same provider. If any other services payable under the physician fee schedule are billed on the same date by the same provider, these services are bundled into the physician services for which payment is made. (NOTE: This is a change from the previous definition, which states that injection services are bundled into <u>any</u> other services billed on the same date.)

Source: http://www.cms.gov/Medicare/Medicare-Fee-for-Service-Payment/PhysicianFeeSched/PFS-Relative-Value-Files-Items/CMS1254038.html, RVUPUF12.docx, National Physician Fee Schedule Relative Value File Calendar Year 2012.

Columns 7 and 11: Transitioned Non-Facility and Facility PE RVU

In looking at which PE RVUs to use for current reimbursement, the "transitioned" values should be used (columns 7 and 11) rather than the "fully implemented" ones (columns 9 and 13). In 2010, CMS updated the way it calculates the indirect cost portion of the PE RVUs. This updated methodology is being transitioned over a four-year period. The "transitioned" PE RVU value represents the current PE RVU value and the "fully-implemented" value represents what the PE RVU value will be at the end of the transition. To calculate the correct payment, the user should include the transitioned PE RVU value.

The costs of providing a given service varies depending on whether they are provided in a "facility" setting, such as a hospital, or in a "nonfacility" setting, such as a free-standing physician's office. It is important to identify the correct setting for the service when choosing the value for the PE RVU component. To determine the correct setting (facility or nonfacility), see the Medicare Claims Processing Manual, Chapter 26—Completing and Processing Form CMS-1500 Data Set, Section 10.5—Place of Service Codes (POS) and Definitions.

Columns 8, 10, 12, 14: Facility vs. Non-Facility NA Indicator

The "NA Indicator" columns indicate whether a given service is: (i) rarely or never performed in a nonfacility setting; or (ii) rarely or never performed or not paid under the MPFS in the facility setting.

It is important to note that there are a few exceptions. Nonfacility fees are applicable to therapy procedures regardless of whether they are furnished in facility or nonfacility settings. Occasionally, institutions such as hospitals are under the MPFS. When this occurs, they are paid at the nonfacility (higher) rate. Although the terminology might seem confusing at first, the higher payment makes sense because here, the facility is responsible for the cost of providing the staff and supplies.[7]

Columns 16 to 19: Total Columns

Columns 16 through 19 are the total RVU columns and represent the sum of the work, the facility or nonfacility practice expense, and the malpractice expense RVUs.

Column 20: PC/TC Indicator Code

The values in Column 20 range from 0 to 9 and provide additional information about the services or CPT codes billed. These codes indicate the type of service provided in the procedure. Exhibit 3 provides the description of the PC/TC indicator codes given in the 2012 MPFS Instruction Sheet.

Columns 21 to 30: Various Information Columns Related to Surgical Procedures

Columns 21 through 30 relate to surgical procedures. They provide information on adjustments made to reimbursement for various aspects of the surgical procedures to which they apply.

- The "Global Days" column, Column 21, provides time frames that apply to each surgical procedure from preoperative through postoperative;

- Columns 22 through 24, the preoperative, intraoperative and postoperative percentage columns, indicate the percentage of the global package that relates to each portion of the surgery;

- The values in Column 25, multiple procedure indicators, range from 0 to 5 or 9 and denote which payment adjustment rule applies to services with multiple procedures. Exhibit 4 provides a description of the multiple procedure indicators; and

- The remaining columns, 26 through 30, denote payment adjustments necessary for bilateral surgery, services where an assistant at surgery may be paid,

---

7   www.cms.gov/Outreach-and-Education/Medicare-Learning-Network-MLN/MLNProducts/downloads/
MedcrePhysFeeSchedfctsht.pdf.

services for which two surgeons (co-surgeons) each in a different specialty may be paid, services for which team surgeons may be paid, and codes that identify an endoscopic base code for each code with a multiple surgery indicator of "3."

	Exhibit 3. PC/TC Indicators, 2012	
Indicator	Code Name	Description
0	Physician Services Codes	Identifies codes that describe physician services. Examples include visits, consultations, and surgical procedures. The concept of PC/TC does not apply since physician services cannot be split into professional and technical components. Modifiers 26 and TC cannot be used with these codes. The RVUS include values for physician work, practice expense and malpractice expense. There are some codes with no work RVUs.
1	Diagnostic Tests for Radiology Services	Identifies codes that describe diagnostic tests. Examples are pulmonary function tests or therapeutic radiology procedures, e.g., radiation therapy. These codes have both a professional and technical component. Modifiers 26 and TC can be used with these codes. The total RVUs for codes reported with a 26 modifier include values for physician work, practice expense, and malpractice expense. The total RVUs for codes reported with a TC modifier include values for practice expense and malpractice expense only. The total RVUs for codes reported without a modifier include values for physician work, practice expense, and malpractice expense.
2	Professional Component Only Codes	This indicator identifies stand-alone codes that describe the physician work portion of selected diagnostic tests for which there is an associated code that describes the technical component of the diagnostic test only and another associated code that describes the global test. An example of a professional component only code is CPT code **93010--Electrocardiogram**; Interpretation and Report. Modifiers 26 and TC cannot be used with these codes. The total RVUs for professional component only codes include values for physician work, practice expense, and malpractice expense.
3	Technical Component Only Codes	This indicator identifies stand-alone codes that describe the technical component (i.e., staff and equipment costs) of selected diagnostic tests for which there is an associated code that describes the professional component of the diagnostic test only. An example of a technical component only code is CPT code **93005-- Electrocardiogram**; Tracing Only, **without interpretation and report**. It also identifies codes that are covered only as diagnostic tests and therefore do not have a related professional code. Modifiers 26 and TC cannot be used with these codes. The total RVUs for technical component only codes include values for practice expense and malpractice expense only.
4	Global Test Only Codes	This indicator identifies stand-alone codes that describe selected diagnostic tests for which there are associated codes that describe (a) the professional component of the test only, and (b) the technical component of the test only. Modifiers 26 and TC cannot be used with these codes. The total RVUs for global procedure only codes include values for physician work, practice expense, and malpractice expense. The total RVUs for global procedure only codes equals the sum of the total RVUs for the professional and technical components only codes combined.
5	Incident To Codes	This indicator identifies codes that describe services covered incident to a physician's service when they are provided by auxiliary personnel employed by the physician and working under his or her direct personal supervision. Payment may not be made by carriers for these services when they are provided to hospital inpatients or patients in a hospital outpatient department. Modifiers 26 and TC cannot be used with these codes.
6	Laboratory Physician Interpretation Codes	This indicator identifies clinical laboratory codes for which separate payment for interpretations by laboratory physicians may be made. Actual performance of the tests is paid for under the lab fee schedule. Modifier TC cannot be used for these codes. The total RVUs for laboratory physician interpretation codes include values for physician work, practice expense, and malpractice expense.
7	Physical Therapy Services, For Which Payment May Not Be Made	Payment may not be made if the service is provided to either a patient in a hospital outpatient department or to an inpatient of the hospital by an independently practicing physical or occupational therapist.
8	Physician Interpretation Codes	This indicator identifies the professional component of clinical laboratory codes for which separate payment may be made only if the physician interprets an abnormal smear for hospital inpatient. This applies to CPT codes 88141, 85060 and HCPCS code P3001-26. No TC billing is recognized because payment for the underlying clinical laboratory test is made to the hospital, generally through the PPS rate.
9	Not Applicable	No payment is recognized for CPT codes 88141, 85060 or HCPCS code P3001-26 furnished to hospital outpatients or non-hospital patients. The physician interpretation is paid through the clinical laboratory fee schedule payment for the clinical laboratory test. Concept of a professional/technical component does not apply.

Source: http://www.cms.gov/Medicare/Medicare-Fee-for-Service-Payment/PhysicianFeeSched/PFS-Relative-Value-Files-Items/CMS1254038.html, RVUPUF12.docx, National Physician Fee Schedule Relative Value File Calendar Year 2012.

Column 25: Multiple Procedure

The multiple procedure adjustment applies not only to surgical procedures, but also to diagnostic testing procedures. Exhibit 4, which is copied from the 2012 MPFS Instruction Sheet, presents the payment adjustments made for each indicator code included in this column.

Column 32: Physician Supervision of Diagnostic Procedures

The value in Column 32 is used to identify the physician supervision requirements for diagnostic procedures, including whether physician supervision is required (i.e., personal supervision of a physician, direct supervision of a physician, or general supervision of a physician, etc.) or whether a physician must perform a procedure.

Column 33: Calculation Flag

The calculation flag value in Column 33 indicates adjustments to be made to the fee schedule payment amount for certain codes. *Notwithstanding the normal formula for calculating Medicare reimbursement, an additional adjustment may be required based on the codes in this column.*

Exhibit 4. Multiple Procedure Indicators, 2012	
Indicator	Description
0	No payment adjustment rules for multiple procedures apply. If procedure is reported on the same day as another procedure, base payment on the lower of: (a) the actual charge or (b) the fee schedule amount for the procedure.
1	Standard payment adjustment rules in effect before January 1, 1996, for multiple procedures apply. In the 1996 MPFSDB, this indicator only applies to codes with procedure status of "D." If a procedure is reported on the same day as another procedure with an indicator of 1,2, or 3, rank the procedures by fee schedule amount and apply the appropriate reduction to this code (100 percent, 50 percent, 25 percent, 25 percent, 25 percent, and by report). Base payment on the lower of: (a) the actual charge or (b) the fee schedule amount reduced by the appropriate percentage.
2	Standard payment adjustment rules for multiple procedures apply. If procedure is reported on the same day as another procedure with an indicator of 1, 2, or 3, rank the procedures by fee schedule amount and apply the appropriate reduction to this code (100 percent, 50 percent, 50 percent, 50 percent, 50 percent, and by report). Base payment on the lower of: (a) the actual charge or (b) the fee schedule amount reduced by the appropriate percentage.
3	Special rules for multiple endoscopic procedures apply if procedure is billed with another endoscopy in the same family (i.e., another endoscopy that has the same base procedure). The base procedure for each code with this indicator is identified in field 31G.
	Apply the multiple endoscopy rules to a family before ranking the family with other procedures performed on the same day (for example, if multiple endoscopies in the same family are reported on the same day as endoscopies in another family or on the same day as a non-endoscopic procedure).
	If an endoscopic procedure is reported with only its base procedure, do not pay separately for the base procedure. Payment for the base procedure is included in the payment for the other endoscopy.
4	Subject to 25% reduction of the TC diagnostic imaging (effective for services January 1, 2006 through June 30, 2010). Subject to 50% reduction of the TC diagnostic imaging (effective for services July 1, 2010 and after).
5	Subject to 25% of the practice expense component for certain therapy services (effective for services January 1, 2011 and after).
9	Concept does not apply.

Source: http://www.cms.gov/Medicare/Medicare-Fee-for-Service-Payment/PhysicianFeeSched/PFS-Relative-Value-Files-Items/CMS1254038.html, RVUPUF12.docx, National Physician Fee Schedule Relative Value File Calendar Year 2012.

Column 34: Diagnostic Imaging Family Indicator

The value in Column 34 is used to identify the applicable diagnostic service family that is based on the modality (e.g., ultrasound, CT, and MRI) and body area. These service families are used in the calculation of the multiple procedure adjustments discussed above.

Columns 35 to 37: OPPS Payment RVU Amounts

The last three columns indicate the PE and MP RVU values that apply in the calculation of payment for services affected by the OPPS payment cap. The services affected by the cap are detailed in the OPPS file, which is described later in this practice aid.

4.0 The Geographic Practice Cost Index (GPCI) File

Once the user identifies and calculates the correct RVUs for a given service or CPT code, it is necessary to account for the geographic differences in the cost of the practices across the country. This is done by making adjustments to each of the three RVU values. The GPCI file contains the locality-specific information that factors into the adjustment to each value. It is important to identify the applicable GPCI factor to correctly calculate the maximum payment for the provider's location. The file includes the carrier and locality numbers for 90 unique GPCI payment localities and their associated GPCI factors. Exhibit 5 illustrates the carrier number and locality information as well as the corresponding GPCI factors for California.

A carrier or Medicare administrative contractor (MAC) is a company contracted by the government to serve as the primary point of contact for Medicare providers. The MAC is typically a regional company that oversees the administration and processing of Medicare policies. Indicating a specific carrier allows searches for information by a specific geographic area. Larger states, such as California, have more than one MAC, while smaller states, such as South Carolina, have only one. For example, Southern California is represented by "01192" and Northern California is represented by "01102," while South Carolina is represented by "11202."

A locality is a region defined by CMS as having a particular cost structure (i.e., a major metropolitan area). Larger states with many metropolitan areas, such as California, will have more than one locality. For example, San Francisco starts with the Northern California carrier number, "01102," followed by the locality-specific number "05." For some states, such as South Carolina, pricing is statewide. In this case, the "11202" carrier number followed by the locality specific number "01" represents all of South Carolina.

Exhibit 5. Geographic Practice Cost Indices (GPCIs), 2012					
Carrier or Contractor	Locality	Locality name	Work GPCI	PE GPCI	MP GPCI
01192	26	Anaheim/Santa Ana, CA	1.044	1.218	0.676
01192	18	Los Angeles, CA	1.036	1.154	0.642
01102	03	Marin/Napa/Solano, CA	1.051	1.248	0.456
01102	07	Oakland/Berkeley, CA	1.058	1.254	0.516
01102	99	Rest of California	1.024	1.085	0.547
01192	99	Rest of California	1.024	1.085	0.547
01102	05	San Francisco, CA	1.072	1.360	0.516
01102	06	San Mateo, CA	1.072	1.354	0.516
01102	09	Santa Clara, CA	1.077	1.337	0.516
01192	17	Ventura, CA	1.034	1.193	0.605

Source: http://www.cms.gov/Medicare/Medicare-Fee-for-Service-Payment/PhysicianFeeSched/PFS-Relative-Value-Files-Items/CMS1254038.html, GPCI2012.xlsx, Addendum E Final 2012 Geographic Practice Cost Indices (GPCIs).

5.0 The Locality/County Crosswalk File

CMS provides two resources to help users determine the correct locality. The locality/county crosswalk file details which counties in a given state are included in a defined locality. CMS also publishes a file on its website called the ZIP Code to Carrier Locality File. This file is primarily intended to map ZIP codes to CMS carriers and localities.[8]

6.0 The Anesthesia Conversion Factor File

Medicare has specific billing guidelines and a separate payment system for anesthesia services. For these services, payment is calculated using a different set of locality-specific conversion factors (CF). To calculate the correct payment for these services, it is important to use the CFs published in the Anesthesia Conversion Factor File, rather than those published in the Relative Value File for other services. *Exhibit 6 illustrates the conversion factors for California.*

7.0 The Outpatient Prospective Payment System (OPPS) Payment File

Section 5102(b) of the Deficit Reduction Act of 2005 requires a payment cap on the TC of certain diagnostic imaging procedures and the TC portions of global diagnostic imaging services. This cap is based on the OPPS payment. The OPPS file indicates the

---

8   www.cms.gov/Medicare/Medicare-Fee-for-Service-Payment/FeeScheduleGenInfo/index.html?redirect=/FeeScheduleGenInfo/.

Exhibit 6. Anesthesia Conversion Factors, 2012			
Carrier or Contractor	Locality	Locality name	CF
01192	26	Anaheim/Santa Ana, CA	22.33
01192	18	Los Angeles, CA	21.93
01102	03	Marin/Napa/Solano, CA	22.12
01102	07	Oakland/Berkeley, CA	22.37
01102	99	Rest of California	21.33
01192	99	Rest of California	21.33
01102	05	San Francisco, CA	22.94
01102	06	San Mateo, CA	22.92
01102	09	Santa Clara, CA	22.95
01192	17	Ventura, CA	21.95

Source: http://www.cms.gov/Medicare/Medicare-Fee-for-Service-Payment/PhysicianFeeSched/PFS-Relative-Value-Files-Items/CMS1254038.html, GPCI2012.xlsx and ANES2012.xlsx, Addendum E Final 2012 Geographic Practice Cost Indices (GPCIs) and Anesthesia Conversion Factors.

services affected by the cap and illustrates the facility/nonfacility cap on these services. To implement this provision, the physician fee schedule amount is compared to the OPPS payment amount and the lower amount is used to calculate payment.

8.0 Examples of How to Use the MPFS to Calculate Payment[9]

Example 1

In the example presented in Exhibit 7, "11202" represents South Carolina, and "01," as the last two digits, indicates the desired locality. As explained above, South Carolina's pricing is statewide; therefore, "01" represents pricing for the entire state. Exhibit 8 illustrates the difference in payment for a nonfacility over a facility. The nonfacility price is $98.00 for "99214" and $131.85 for "99215," and the facility price is $72.63 for "99214" and $102.14 for "99215." Remember: This is because when physicians perform a procedure in a nonfacility setting, such as a free-standing practice, they incur the costs of clinical personnel, equipment, and supplies that physicians in a facility, such as a hospital, would not.

Nonparticipating healthcare professionals and suppliers who enroll in Medicare but have decided not to sign the Form CMS-460 are subject to what is called the limiting

---

9   www.cms.gov/Outreach-and-Education/Medicare-Learning-Network-MLN/MLNProducts/downloads/MedcrePhysFeeSchedfctsht.pdf.

Exhibit 7. Payment Calculations With Modifiers

HCPCS Code	Modifier	Carrier Locality	Non-Facility Fee Schedule Amount	Facility Fee Schedule Amount	Non-Facility Limiting Charge	Facility Limiting Charge	Conversion Factor
Diagnostic Mammography (77057)	26	1120201	$ 32.89	$ 32.89	$ 35.93	$ 107.06	$ 34.0376
Diagnostic Mammography (77057)	TC	1120201	$ 42.57	NA	$ 46.50	NA	$ 34.0376
Diagnostic Mammography (77057)		1120201	$ 75.45	NA	$ 82.43	NA	$ 34.0376

Source: http://cms.hhs.gov/Outreach-and-Education/Medicare-Learning-Network-MLN/MLNProducts/downloads/How_to_MPFS_Booklet_ICN901344.pdf

Exhibit 8. Facility and Nonfacility Payment Calculation

HCPCS Code	Modifier	Carrier Locality	Non-Facility Fee Schedule Amount	Facility Fee Schedule Amount	Non-Facility Limiting Charge	Facility Limiting Charge	Conversion Factor
Intermediate Office Visit (99214)		1120201	$ 98.00	$ 72.63	$ 107.06	$ 79.35	$ 34.0376
Intermediate Office Visit (99215)		1120201	$ 131.85	$ 102.14	$ 144.04	$ 111.59	$ 34.0376

Source: http://cms.hhs.gov/Outreach-and-Education/Medicare-Learning-Network-MLN/MLNProducts/downloads/How_to_MPFS_Booklet_ICN901344.pdf

charge. These professionals and suppliers accept assignment on a case-by-case basis. For services paid under the MPFS, there is a 5% reduction in the Medicare-approved amounts for nonparticipants and there is a limit on what the healthcare professional/supplier may charge the beneficiary (limiting charge). The limiting charge equals 115% of the fee schedule amount and is the maximum the nonparticipant may charge a beneficiary. Calculating 95% of 115% is equivalent to multiplying the payment amount by a factor of 1.0925 of (109.25%). Therefore, the nonfacility limiting charge is $107.06 for "99214" and $144.04 for "99215." The facility limiting charge is $79.35 for "99214" and $111.59 for "99215."

Example 2

Exhibit 7 illustrates additional pricing information that displays codes that may be billed globally or with a professional/technical component.

The first row provides information for CPT code 77057 (Diagnostic Mammography) submitted with modifier -26, which should be used when only the professional component of the procedure was performed (i.e., the interpretation of the mammography only). In this row, prices are listed in each column, with $32.89 in the two pricing columns and $35.93 in the two limiting charge columns. The professional component relates to the billable services provided by physicians.

The second row displays the results if CPT code 77057 is billed with modifier -TC, which represents only the technical component. "-TC" indicates the claim was billed for the performance of the mammography only, not for the interpretation. "$42.57" is displayed under nonfacility price as the Medicare-allowed amount for this code with a -TC modifier, and $46.50 is the maximum amount a nonparticipating professional may charge a beneficiary as the nonfacility limiting charge. "NA" (not applicable) is shown under facility price and facility limiting charge because the facility does not receive payment for the technical component under the MPFS.

The third row is blank in the modifier column. When a provider does not use a modifier with this code, it means this provider has performed both the technical and professional components of the procedure (i.e., the performance of the mammography and the interpretation, respectively) and is billing globally. The global pricing includes one payment for both the professional and technical component and in this example, is $75.45 for the nonfacility price and $82.43 for the nonfacility limiting charge. These amounts equal the sum of the amounts in the two other rows under these columns. Because the facility does not receive payment for the technical component under the MPFS, there is an "NA" shown under the facility price and facility limiting charge columns.

Chapter 16. The Devil's in the Details: Navigating Key Issues in the Calculation of wRVUs and Professional Collections

CONTENTS

Chapter 16. The Devil's in the Details: Navigating Key Issues in the Calculation of wRVUs and Professional Collections

By Timothy Smith, CPA/ABV

1.0 Introduction

Physician productivity metrics such as work relative value units (wRVUs) and professional collections are essential to the benchmarking and analysis of physicians in both business and compensation valuation. For valuing clinical services, most market-based valuation methods utilize these metrics to establish fair market value (FMV) compensation levels for physicians. As a result, they are critical for valuation work.

Unfortunately, calculating these productivity metrics correctly from data provided by physician practices can be a difficult task. Not only can there be issues with obtaining accurate and usable data, but also various caveats are entailed in calculating and benchmarking physician productivity. Many appraisers and healthcare consultants are not aware of some of the issues. Furthermore, there is a lack of standardization and documentation at a detailed level to guide practitioners through the maze of minutiae and the stacks of numbers, rates, codes, and the like.

The purpose of this chapter, therefore, is to discuss various issues and nuances in computing productivity. The chapter identifies areas of concerns, while providing helpful suggestions for dealing with data and surveys. It does not attempt to resolve all issues or establish industry standards. Rather, the chapter seeks to educate industry participants to important considerations in the calculations.

Author's note: Readers should be generally familiar with the Medicare Physician Fee Schedule (MPFS) and how to calculate RVUs and Medicare reimbursement to use and reference this chapter. For those without such familiarity, see the following chapters in this guide:

1. Chapter 15, "An Overview of Physician Reimbursement."

2. Appendix to Chapter 15, Practice Aid, "Navigating Through the Medicare Physician Fee Schedule."

2.0 The Data Sources for wRVUs and Professional Collections

Before discussing issues related to the calculations of productivity, it is helpful to highlight some important features of the data sources used to determine wRVUs and professional collections.

2.1 The Primary Source of Physician Productivity Data—Billing System Information

The calculation of wRVUs and professional collections is based on the volumes, charges, and collections for services rendered by the subject physician and/or physician practice. This data is contained in the practice's billing system. It should be included in the billing system by CPT/HCPCS code for each provider or physician. The level of information and the reporting capabilities of billing systems, however, can vary. How these systems are used can also be different from practice to practice. As a result, the data that can be provided from billing systems is not uniform across the industry.

2.2 Key Data Items in a Billing System

Some data fields in a billing system are essential for gathering the information necessary to calculate wRVUs and professional collections at a fully accurate level. Knowing about these items can facilitate the data request process with a practice. Key fields include the following:

- *Date of service:* Date on which the service was performed;

- *Date of entry:* Date on which a service or receipt was entered into the billing system;

- *Date of receipt:* Date on which payment was physically received by the practice;

- *Service or rendering provider:* Physician or nonphysician provider (NPP)[1] who physically performed the procedure or service for the patient; and

---

1   Nonphysician providers, also known as midlevels, include nurse practitioners, physician assistants, optometrists, etc.

- *Billing provider:* Physician or provider (midlevels can bill directly in some cases) in whose name the procedure or service was billed to a payer and/or patient.

Some practices or systems do not separately track the service or rendering provider. All service information is entered or maintained in the billing system based on the billing provider. This distinction is important because productivity needs to be calculated based on those services personally performed by the provider. When this information is not available, estimates will need to be used for the productivity calculations, resulting in less accuracy.

2.3 Billing and Collections

Practices generally bill for services rendered to patients based on a standard charge for each CPT/HCPCS procedure code. Typically, this charge is based on a uniform percentage of the Medicare reimbursement rate that is applied to all codes. Practices often set the percentage well in excess of Medicare, for example, in the 250%-to-300% range. They set charge rates well above Medicare because many commercial payers will reimburse at the lesser of the standard fee rate or the billed charge.[2] When payments are received, most systems allow posting of the payment against the specific claim billed. Practices are thereby able to track unpaid claims as part of their revenue cycle management. Different payers will reimburse for services rendered at different rates. The collections received as a percentage of billed or gross charges will vary based on payer as well as by procedure code, as described later in Section 4.5, "Gathering Information on Collections for Calculating Professional Collections."[3]

2.4 Common Data Gathering Issues Related to Billing System Information

Many issues can arise that create obstacles in getting the right data needed from a practice. These can range from billing system limitations to lack of user knowledge on the part of practice staff to billing practices by the practice. These issues can prevent a practice from providing data to an appraiser with the right level of detail or in a usable format. Moreover, while many practices may be able to provide the right data, they may not be able to provide it in usable formats.

Sometimes the issue is not getting the right data out of the system, but that the wrong data went into the system from the start. Appraisers should be aware that some practices, including large ones and those owned by health systems, can have significant revenue

---

2 Surprisingly, many commercial payers will not publish their standard fee schedule to physicians. Thus, practices set very high charge rates to ensure they receive the maximum reimbursement.

3 For more information on reimbursement, see Chapter 15, "An Overview of Physician Reimbursement."

cycle problems in areas such as coding, claims billing, accurate use of systems, and collection practices. Common issues can include the following:

1. Failure to use accurate coding, including modifiers, resulting in high levels of claim denials.

2. Incorrectly handling claim denials and resubmissions in the billing system, resulting in duplicative or inaccurate volumes and procedural information.

3. Failing to distinguish between rendering/service provider and billing provider, thereby eliminating a source of precise data on procedures personally performed by a provider.

4. Misapplication of payments, resulting in inaccuracies in collections and accounts receivable.

The basic concept of "garbage in/garbage out" should not be forgotten when gathering data from billing systems. It can be helpful to talk with a physician group about its revenue cycle practices before requesting data, so as to identify problem areas up front. The data request can be tailored to the data available from the practice's system.

2.5 The Productivity of Nonphysician Providers in an Extender Model

When a supervising physician uses an NPP under an "extender model," both providers are involved in a patient encounter, whether in an office setting on in the hospital. Under this model, the NPP completes many of the lower-level clinical tasks in the encounter, allowing the physician to have reduced patient contact time. The idea is that the physician leverages the NPP to increase his or her total productivity. This model should be distinguished from incident-to and direct billing models for the use of NPPs in a practice.[4]

The extender model naturally creates a question as to how to count the productivity related to the patient encounter. Should some portion of the productivity be assigned to the NPP? To do so would require an allocation, which would then require various estimates and assumptions. Many appraisers alternatively choose to assign the productivity to the physician but adjust the compensation level for the physician by deducting the compensation, benefits, and other costs of the NPP from that of the physician as part of the fair market value (FMV) analysis. This deduction is made either by reducing the FMV compensation level or by insisting that the compensation formula for the physician include a deduction for NPP costs. This approach bypasses the difficulties in

---

4   For a description of these models, see Chapter 14, "The Economics of Physician Clinical Services and Compensation."

allocating productivity, while adjusting FMV compensation to reflect the fact that the NPP is helping the physician achieve higher levels of productivity.

2.6 Lack of Standardized Definitions and Formulas for Calculation

Another problem area in the calculation of wRVUs and professional collections includes the formulas for computing them. There is no standardized set of instructions that is sufficiently detailed for industry participants to follow with complete precision and accuracy. It is true that the physician compensation surveys, such as MGMA and AMGA, provide directions for determining these metrics. These directions, however, are often highly general and lack specificity. In addition, the variability of reimbursement rates and adjustments across payers creates inconsistencies in how RVUs are paid for in the physician marketplace. Medicare, for example, has some highly complex adjustments to RVUs and reimbursement related to the use of certain modifiers, as will be discussed in detail later in this chapter. Commercial payers, however, may not follow these rules. To compound matters, a survey may give instructions on how to compute RVUs that do not follow the Medicare adjustment rules, such as AMGA's modifier adjustment table. As a result, the calculation of wRVUs and professional collections can lack uniformity at a detailed level and can be confusing for those trying to sort through these various sources of information.

3.0 Calculating and Benchmarking wRVUs

3.1 Using the Medicare Physician Fee Schedule for Basic wRVU Rates

One area for which there appears to be general consensus in the industry is the use of the MPFS rates or RBRVS for calculating RVUs. MGMA and AMGA, for example, both use MPFS RVU rates. Nonetheless, there are alternative sources for RVUs. These sources, for example, may take into account RVUs based on commercial payer rates. Some practices may use sources such as Ingenix[5] to supplement the rates in the MPFS. In addition, MGMA provides guidance on how to develop RVU rates for procedures with no CPT code or with a zero RVU value.[6] In general, however, the industry has established the MPFS as the standard for RVU rates. An important requirement of this standard is *not* adjusting RVU levels for the Geographic Practice Cost Indexes (GPCIs) included in the MPFS. The RVU GPCIs relate to how Medicare will reimburse the provider based on location. They are not part of the basic measurement of productivity, however. In fact, use of a GPCI distorts the productivity level.

---

5   A subsidiary of insurer United Health, somewhat famous for Governor Cuomo of New York's investigation into the methods in which it established so-called "usual and customary" fees for use by health insurance companies.

6   See the instructions for Column 29 in the survey questionnaire guide, p. 321.

Since RVU rates change from year to year, one needs to use rates that correspond to the year for the data from the subject. It is preferable to use the latest or last version of the MPFS published by CMS so that you get the version that has been updated and corrected. This advice, however, differs from MGMA instructions. MGMA directs respondents to the rates published in the *Federal Register* just prior to the beginning of the year or the first release of the MPFS. You can follow that guidance, but you may not get the revised version that will be more reflective of reimbursement and the corrected rates.

For more information on the MPFS, see the Appendix to Chapter 15, "Practice Aid: Navigating the Medicare Physician Fee Schedule."

Some practical tips for using wRVU rates in the MPFS schedule include the following:

1. The wRVU rates are given by CPT/HCPCS code. Some codes do not have wRVUs because there is no physician work associated with the code.

2. In prior years, some wRVU rates were not included with the global version of the procedure code, but could be found in the professional version of the global that includes the "-26" modifier.

3.2 Overview of Adjustments for Modifiers

Finding the right wRVU adjustment factors for CPT/HCPCS code modifiers is probably the least standardized area of productivity calculations. The following section presents some key issues in dealing with modifiers.

Overview of Modifiers

Modifiers provide additional information about the circumstances of each procedure as applied to a patient. There are two sets of modifiers. The American Medical Association (AMA) defines CPT code-related modifiers. The CPT code modifiers are two-digit numerical codes. CMS defines HCPCS Level II modifiers, which are alphabetic.[7]

Only Some Modifiers Impact RVUs Based on Reimbursement

Only some modifiers will result in adjustments to the reimbursement level paid for the procedure. Other modifiers are used for informational purposes. Conceptually, the adjustments to reimbursement are the best standard for the adjustments to RVUs. Matching modifier adjustment rates with reimbursement allows the adjusted RVU levels to mirror how the marketplace values the variation in service, as indicated by

---

7 Deborah J. Grider, *Coding With Modifiers: A Guide to Correct CPT and HCPCS Level II Modifier Usage*, 3rd edition. American Medical Association, 2007, p. 13.

the modifier. Otherwise, there's no special magic to modifier adjustments. Adjustments for modifiers primarily impact surgical specialties, and this impact is usually material to the total level of wRVUs by provider. Thus, if a practice is not able to provide CPT/HCPCS code data with modifiers, the full accuracy of the wRVUs for the providers in that practice will usually be compromised.

The Lack of Uniform Adjustment Factors for Modifiers

The MPFS and the Medicare Claims Processing Manual (MCPM) specify the adjustments for the modifiers that affect reimbursement. Some of the adjustment calculations can have several moving parts. In addition, the Medicare carriers determine some adjustments based on the documentation submitted with the claim.[8] The commercial plans, moreover, may follow the MPFS in how commercial reimbursement is adjusted for certain modifiers. Furthermore, information on modifier adjustment factors used by commercial payers is not always available. In its survey directions, AMGA provides a table showing various adjustment factors for certain modifiers. These factors, however, do not fully correspond to the MPFS adjustments. AMGA appears to have simplified and streamlined the calculation of wRVU computations for the participants in its survey. MGMA, however, does not include specific instructions in its survey for modifier adjustments. In summary, a variety of modifier adjustment rates are available in the marketplace, and these rates are not always consistent.

3.3 MPFS Adjustments for Specific Modifiers

Since the MPFS is the industry-accepted standard for the basic RVU rates, the following section provides information on the adjustments for selected modifiers from the MPFS. The modifiers presented here correspond to those identified in AMGA's survey instructions. Readers can compare the MPFS adjustments to those indicated by AMGA for comparison purposes as an illustration of the diversity of guidance available in the industry for calculating modifier adjustment factors.

Modifier -22

Modifier	Description[9]	RVU Adjustment
22	Increased Procedural Services	Adjustment determined by the carrier.

The *Medicare Claims Processing Manual* (MCPM) states the following with respect to modifier -22:[10]

---

8   Medicare carriers are the third-party contractors who act as intermediaries between providers and Medicare. They pay claims on behalf of Medicare.

9   Descriptions taken from *Current Procedural Coding Expert: 2011*, Ingenix, 2010, pp. 449-52.

10   *Medicare Claims Processing Manual*, Chapter 12, Physicians/Nonphysician Practitioners (Rev. 2354, 11-18-11) (Rev. 2373, 121-21-11).

20.4.6 - Payment Due to Unusual Circumstances (Modifiers "-22" and "-52")
(Rev. 1, 10-01-03)
B3-15028

The fees for services represent the average work effort and practice expenses required to provide a service. For any given procedure code, there could typically be a range of work effort or practice expense required to provide the service. Thus, carriers may increase or decrease the payment for a service only under very unusual circumstances based upon review of medical records and other documentation.

Modifier -50

Modifier	Description	RVU Adjustment
50	Bilateral Procedure	150%—but may not apply to all codes.

The MPFS includes several different codes (0, 1, 2, 3, and 9) in the column for Bilateral Surgery in the RVU file. These codes indicate whether the adjustment applies for a specific CPT/HCPCS code. See MPFS Instruction Sheet for Bilateral Surgery (modifier -50) for more information on the specific amounts for the adjustments.[11]

Modifier -51

Modifier	Description	RVU Adjustment
51	Multiple Procedures	50%, applied to the lower paying procedures included in the bundle of procedures. Subject to special rules.

Modifier -51 is used when the same provider performs multiple procedures, other than evaluation and management (E&M) services, in the same patient care session. The primary procedure or service can be reported without the modifier. The additional procedures, however, may be identified by including the "-51" modifier with the CPT/HCPCS codes for the other procedures.[12]

Like modifier -50, the MPFS includes several codes (0, 1, 2, 3, 4, 5, and 9) in the column for Multiple Procedures in the RVU file. These codes indicate whether the 50% adjustment applies and how it applies to a given bundle of procedures. See the MPFS Instruction Sheet for Multiple Procedure for the specific computations and adjustments.

---

11 See document titled "National Physician Fee Schedule Relative Value File Calendar Year 2012," Word file included with MPFS download from CMS website (MPFS Instruction Sheet).
12 *Current Procedural Coding Expert: 2011,* p. 449.

> *Data Tip: Many payers and claims processors have edit functions that analyze claims for multiple procedures. Even when a practice fails to include the "-51" modifier in the billing, the processor can still adjust the payment based on these edits. Such adjustments, made in the absence of the "-51" modifier, can cause a material disconnect between RVUs and collections in the data for a practice. The lack of modifiers in the data can overstate RVUs, while the collections reflect the application of the 50% reduction. As a result, appraisers should be careful when significant variances are found in RVUs and collections that cannot be explained by payer mix or local market reimbursement factors.*

Modifier -52

Modifier	Description	RVU Adjustment
52	Reduced Services	Adjustment determined by the carrier.

The MCPM states:

20.4.6 - Payment Due to Unusual Circumstances (Modifiers "-22" and "-52")
(Rev. 1, 10-01-03)
B3-15028
The fees for services represent the average work effort and practice expenses required to provide a service. For any given procedure code, there could typically be a range of work effort or practice expense required to provide the service. Thus, carriers may increase or decrease the payment for a service only under very unusual circumstances based upon review of medical records and other documentation.

Modifier -53

Modifier	Description	RVU Adjustment
53	Discontinued Procedure	Specific RVUs are given for the modifier's use with 45378, G0105 and G0121. Use with other codes is carrier determined.

The MPFS Instruction Sheet includes the following guidance on modifier -53:

The presence of CPT modifier -53 indicates that separate RVUs and a fee schedule amount have been established for procedures which the physician terminated before completion. This modifier is used only with colonoscopy CPT code 45378, or with G0105 and G0121. Any other codes billed with modifier -53 are subject to carrier medical review and priced by individual consideration.[13]

---

13   See the discussion of the "Modifier" column.

Modifier -54

Modifier	Description	RVU Adjustment
54	Surgical Care Only	Varies by procedure. See the Intraoperative Percentage column in the MPFS RVU file for the applicable percentage.

The "Intraoperative Percentage" column in the MPFS RVU file indicates the percentage of the global fee paid for the surgical care or intraoperative portion of the surgical procedure. The RVUs should be reduced to the level equivalent to this percentage relative to the total RVUs for the procedure.[14]

Modifier -55

Modifier	Description	RVU Adjustment
55	Postoperative Management Only	Varies by procedure. See the Postoperative Percentage column in the MPFS RVU file for the applicable percentage.

The "Postoperative Percentage" column in the MPFS RVU file indicates the percentage of the global fee paid for the postoperative portion of the surgical procedure. The RVUs should be reduced to the level equivalent to this percentage relative to the total RVUs for the procedure.[15]

Modifier -56

Modifier	Description	RVU Adjustment
56	Preoperative Management Only	Varies by procedure. See the Preoperative Percentage column in the MPFS RVU file for the applicable percentage.

The "Preoperative Percentage" column in the MPFS RVU file indicates the percentage of the global fee paid for the preoperative portion of the surgical procedure. The RVUs should be reduced to the level equivalent to this percentage relative to the total RVUs for the procedure.[16]

Modifier -62

Modifier	Description	RVU Adjustment
62	Two Surgeons	RVUs adjusted to 62.5% of MPFS rates, where two surgeons are allowed.[17]

---

14 See MCPM, 40.4—Adjudication of Claims for Global Surgeries (Rev. 1, 10-01-03), B3-4824, B3-4825, B3-7100-7120.7, B. Claims From Physicians Who Furnish Less Than the Global Package (Split Global Care), and MPFS Instruction Sheet for Intraoperative Percentage column.

15 Ibid.

16 Ibid.

17 See MCPM, 40.8. Claims for Co-Surgeons and Team Surgeons (Rev. 1, 10-01-03), B3-4828, B3-15046.

Two surgeons may be allowed for certain surgical procedures. Allowance is indicated by several codes (0, 1, 2, and 9) in the column for co-surgeons in the RVU file.[18]

Modifier -74

Modifier	Description	RVU Adjustment
74	Discontinued Outpatient Hospital/ ASC Procedure After Administration of Anesthesia	Not applicable. Should not be used for physician services. Modifier -53 should be used.[19]

Modifier -74 is used for hospital and not physician reporting.[20]

Modifier -76

Modifier	Description	RVU Adjustment
76	Repeat Procedure of Service by Same Physician or Other Qualified Healthcare Professional	None. Carriers may not make adjustments in fee schedule amounts provided by CMS for the -76 modifier.[21]

Modifier -78

Modifier	Description	RVU Adjustment
78	Unplanned Return to the Operating/ Procedure Room by the Physician or Other Qualified Healthcare Professional Following Initial Procedure for a Related Procedure During the Postoperative Period	RVUs adjustment is based on the procedure to which it applies.

The MCPM states:

C. Payment for Return Trips to the Operating Room for Treatment of Complications
When a CPT code billed with modifier "-78" describes the additional services involving a return trip to the operating room to deal with complications, carriers pay the value of the intra-operative services of the code that describes the treatment of the complications. Refer to Field 18 of the MFSDB to determine the percentage of the global package for the intra-operative services. The fee schedule amount (Field 34 or 35 of the MFSDB) is multiplied by this percentage and rounded to the nearest cent.

When a procedure with a "000" global period is billed with a modifier "-78," representing a return trip to the operating room to deal with complications, carriers pay the full value for the procedure, since these codes have no pre-, post-, or intra-operative values.[22]

---

18 See MPFS Instruction Sheet for Co-Surgeons (Modifier -62).
19 *Coding with Modifiers: A Guide to Correct CPT and HCPCS Level II Modifier Usage*, pp. 360-63.
20 Ibid.
21 MCPM, 20.5—No Adjustments in Fee Schedule Amounts (Rev. 1, 10-01-03), B3-15054.
22 40.4—Adjudication of Claims for Global Surgeries (Rev. 1, 10-01-03), B3-4824, B3-4825, B3-7100-7120.7, C.

This section continues with additional adjustments based on other factors.

Modifier -80

Modifier	Description	RVU Adjustment
80	Assistant Surgeon	Reduce to 16% of the stated RVU amounts.

The MCPM states:

20.4.3 - Assistant at Surgery Services

For assistant at surgery services performed by physicians, the fee schedule amount equals 16 percent of the amount otherwise applicable for the global surgery.

Carriers may not pay assistants at surgery for surgical procedures in which a physician is used as an assistant at surgery in fewer than five percent of the cases for that procedure nationally. This is determined through manual reviews.

In addition to the assistant at surgery modifiers "-80," "-81," or "-82" any procedures submitted with modifier AS are subject to the assistant surgeon's policy enunciated in the Medicare physician fee schedule database (MPFSDB). Accordingly, pay claims for procedures with these modifiers only if the services of an assistant surgeon are authorized.[23]

Modifier -81

Modifier	Description	RVU Adjustment
81	Minimum Assistant Surgeon	Reduce to 16% of the stated RVU amounts.[24]

Modifier -82[25]

Modifier	Description	RVU Adjustment
82	Assistant Surgeon (when qualified resident surgeon not available)	Reduce to 16% of the stated RVU amounts.[25]

Modifier -AS[26]

Modifier	Description	RVU Adjustment
AS	Physician assistant, nurse practitioner, or clinical nurse specialist for assistant at surgery	Reduce to 10.4% of the stated RVU amounts.[26]

Payment for Return Trips to the Operating Room for Treatment of Complications.

23 MCPM, 20.4.3—Assistant at Surgery Services (Rev. 1, 10-01-03), B3-15044.
24 Ibid.
25 Ibid.
26 MCPM, 110.1—Limitations for Assistant-at-Surgery Services (Rev. 1, 10-01-03), B3-16001.

Physician assistant services are paid at 85% of the 16% of the physician fee schedule amount.[27]

3.4 What Modifier Adjustment Rates Should be Used to Calculate wRVUs?

Since there are multiple scales for how RVUs should be adjusted for the use of modifiers, a critical question is: What scale should be used? The answer to that question is: It depends. For example, if one is benchmarking against the AMGA survey data, then clearly the AMGA adjustments would be the most appropriate. If one is trying to prepare reimbursement analysis, the MPFS rates would allow for greater precision in matching reimbursement with RVU levels.[28] Regardless of the scale adopted, there will most likely be some level of imprecision in benchmarking against survey data due to the lack of consistency in the marketplace. Unfortunately, this is one of those areas in which the industry needs to adopt a uniform scale.

3.5 Using Service or Rendering Provider for Calculating wRVUs

Since wRVUs are intended to reflect the personally performed productivity of the individual physician or nonphysician provider (NPP), the data used for wRVU calculations needs to be prepared based on the service or rendering provider. The service or rendering provider, therefore, should be used for computing wRVU productivity, and not the billing provider. When NPPs are used on an incident-to basis, their services are billed under the supervising physician. Data based on billing provider will not properly separate productivity data based on who performed the procedure. Thus, the data needs to be based on service or rendering provider.

Unfortunately, some practices do not have systems or capture procedures based on service or rendering provider. They enter patient care services based solely on billing provider or they use IT systems that don't have the capacity for recording both providers. In these cases, the data will not reflect the actual work of the individual provider. Estimates will have to be made and used for the wRVUs of each individual provider. Unfortunately, this makes the resulting wRVU levels by provider less accurate.

3.6 Changes in wRVU Rates From Year to Year

The RVU rates in the MFPS are not static from year to year; they change. Some of these revisions can be material. Revisions or changes in how CPT/HCPCS codes relate to specific procedures can also affect rates from one year to the next. The AMA or CMS often split out or consolidate the codes involved in a given procedure or service. It's important, therefore, to analyze the higher volume codes in a data set for changes in RVU

---

27 Ibid.
28 The precision of this analysis, however, would also depend on the extent to which commercial payers made comparable adjustments to Medicare.

rates. If there are material changes, one needs to interpret benchmarking and trending outcomes accordingly. Trending patterns can be affected by rate changes in addition to volumes and service mix considerations. Annual rate changes that are material can also affect benchmarking. Since the surveys report data for a given year, the respondents should have used the MPFS RVU rates for that year to calculate the productivity numbers. If you are using data from years other than that of the survey and there was a material change for key codes, benchmarking for those other years will not be fully accurate. The rate changes will account for some of the specific ranking, rather than actual productivity considerations.

4.0 Calculating and Benchmarking Professional Collections

4.1 Why Use Professional Collections for Assessing Physician Productivity?

Some in the physician marketplace question the use of professional collections for analyzing physician productivity. They think that collections as a metric relates to the effectiveness of back-office management functions in a physician practice, not to physician productivity. This view is partially correct. Collections is dependent on effective revenue cycle efforts. When collections is normalized for the practice's patient base in the local market, however, professional collections provides a critical piece of information. It indicates the value of physician productivity in the local marketplace. As noted in Chapter 37, "How Physician Reimbursement and Compensation Vary by Market," reimbursement can vary significantly from market to market and within a local marketplace. Reimbursement rates can affect physician compensation at a material level. Thus, professional collections is actually a more useful productivity metric because it measures the market value of physician productivity. RVU-based productivity only measures the productivity at the pure procedural or clinical service mix level, apart from their market value. Thus, it is difficult to make the leap that wRVUs in and of themselves represent fair market value.

4.2 The Two Critical Elements of Professional Collections

There are two parts in the calculation of professional collections. The first is identifying those services and procedures that should be classified as professional. The range of items encompassed in the CPT/HCPCS codes covers professional services, technical component services, global diagnostic testing services, incident-to services, drugs and pharmaceuticals, miscellaneous services, dental services, and a variety of goods and products. As a result, one has to sort through all the various codes to determine what should be classified as professional services personally performed by a provider.

The second element is determining the collections received for the professional services. Calculating collections can have many twists and turns, depending on the level of data available in a billing system and how this information can be reported. More importantly, the level of data that is available for collections can have a material impact on the accuracy of the professional collections computation. Unfortunately, there are a few misnomers and imprecise practices in the appraisal and consulting worlds that can result in significantly imprecise calculations of this metric. Computing and interpreting collections information, therefore, are critical tasks.

4.3 Identifying Professional Services

In general, professional services are readily identified in the MPFS based on the "PC/TC Indicator" field in the RVU file. This file includes the entire range of CPT/HCPCS codes, and a PC/TC indicator is assigned to each procedure code. The MPFS Instruction Sheet provides definitions for each indicator code. Exhibit 1 summarizes this information.

Exhibit 1. PC/TC Indicator Codes	
PC/TC Indicator Code	**Basic Code Description[29]**
0	Physician service codes
1	Diagnostic tests for radiology services
2	Professional component-only codes
3	Technical component-only codes
4	Global test-only codes
5	Incident-to codes
6	Laboratory physician interpretation codes
7	Physical therapy service, for which payment may not be made
8	Physician interpretation codes
9	Not applicable—concept of a professional/technical component does not apply

Using these indicator codes, one can readily identify procedures that relate to physician services as follows:

1. Codes 0, 2, 6, 7, and 8; and

2. Codes 1 with a -26 modifier.

One nuance, however, is that CMS classified certain HCPCS Level II codes as professional services (indicator code 0), but a review of these codes indicates they may not be professional services in the sense used for physician productivity. These codes include A4641, A4642, and A4890 as well as the range of A9500 to A9699.[30]

---

29 See the MPFS Instruction Sheet for the full description of each code.
30 Based on the 2012 MPFS.

For incident-to codes (indicator code 5), some of these services may qualify as professional when wRVUs for the procedure code are shown in the MPFS. These codes can relate to the administration of chemotherapy and immunizations. MGMA includes these administration-related procedures in its definition of "Collections for Professional Charges."[31]

Certain HCPCS Level II codes that have wRVUs associated with them are classified as "Not Applicable" by CMS (indicator code 9). As a result, one may consider these for inclusion in professional services, depending on the characteristics of the code and the rendering provider. Examples of such codes are included in Exhibit 2.

HCPCS	DESCRIPTION	STATUS CODE	WORK RVU	NON-FAC PE RVU	FACILITY PE RVU	MP RVU	PCTC IND
92625	Tinnitus assessment	A	1.15	0.76	0.58	0.05	9
92626	Eval aud rehab status	A	1.40	1.11	0.78	0.07	9
92627	Eval aud status rehab add-on	A	0.33	0.30	0.19	0.01	9
92640	Aud brainstem implt programg	A	1.76	1.20	0.78	0.37	9

Exhibit 2. HCPCS Level II Codes Classified as 'Not Applicable' by CMS

It is a prudent practice to review the PC/TC Indicator Code classifications of CPT/HCPCS procedures in each year's MPFS before using them for calculating professional collections. This review should look for data anomalies such as the ones noted above.

4.4 Determining the Professional Component of Global Diagnostic Testing Services

There are two types of codes for which the professional services component needs to be broken out of the total charges or collections for the procedure code. These include CPT/HCPCS codes for diagnostic radiology test services (indicator code 1) and global test codes (indicator code 4). These global procedure codes include both a professional and technical component.

---

31   See the instructions for Column 19: Collections for Professional Charges, p. 316, 2012 survey.

One common misnomer in the MPFS is that the professional and technical components of CPT/HCPCS codes are only identified by codes denoted with the -26 and -TC modifiers. This statement is only partially true. Procedure codes with a PC/TC Indicator Code of 2, 3, and 4 can also represent the professional component, technical component, and global version of various diagnostic testing procedures. Both types of procedure codes encompass global procedures for which there are both professional and technical components. Examples are included in Exhibit 3.

HCPCS	DESCRIPTION	Work RVU	PE RVU	MP RVU	PCTC IND
	Exhibit 3. Procedure Codes That Encompass Global Procedures for Which There Are Both Professional and Technical Components				
93040	Rhythm ECG with report	0.15	0.21	0.02	4
93041	Rhythm ECG tracing	0.00	0.16	0.01	3
93042	Rhythm ECG report	0.15	0.05	0.01	2
93000	Electrocardiogram complete	0.17	0.37	0.37	4
93005	Electrocardiogram tracing	0.00	0.30	0.30	3
93010	Electrocardiogram report	0.17	0.07	0.07	2

When the global version of these testing procedure codes is used, the professional component of the services needs to be broken out. To do this, the common practice is to allocate the global charge or collected amount based on the professional component version of the service. The ratio of total RVUs for the professional component version of the code to the global version of the code (or the Medicare allowable for the professional component to the global version) is used to allocate the global charge or collected amount to the professional service portion.

Another common misnomer is that global codes and global splits only relate to procedures involving professional and technical component services. In the MPFS, global codes can also refer to global surgical procedures where the procedure code reflects the full array of services included in the episode of care, including pre- and post-operative services along with the actual surgery itself. A global split in this context can refer to allocations among pre-, intra-, and post-operative services. The concept of a global procedure for an episode of care also applies to other types of procedures, such as baby deliveries or "co-management" of cataract surgery cases between ophthalmologists and optometrists. Thus, the term "global" can have different meanings relative to the type of service being discussed.

4.5 Understanding Charge and Collections Data

Charges for services provided are usually reported on a date-of-service basis, although some billing systems allow reporting on a date-of-entry basis. Collections, however, tend to be reported based on date of entry, posting, or receipt. In other words, 2012 collections represent what was collected in 2012. There is a timing difference between charges and collections that relates to the collecting process. This difference creates a wrinkle in using collections data for analysis and benchmarking purposes. If one uses collections data based on date of entry or receipt, the productivity measured by this data will include some services performed in the prior year. This inclusion may not be significant and not matter.

There are cases, however, when this inclusion creates "noise" in the collections data. These cases would include those where a practice has a lengthy collection cycle and there were material differences in reimbursement, collection efforts, or volumes from the prior year to the subject year. Such noise can distort comparative analysis of RVUs and collections for the subject year or collections-based productivity trending from year to year.

Another key point relates to situations in which professional collections are calculated based on collection rates determined as a percentage of gross charges. The nuance here is that commercial and other non-Medicare reimbursement levels can vary from one CPT/HCPCS service code to another relative to Medicare rates. For example, many commercial payers may reimburse for E&M codes at levels well in excess of what Medicare reimburses, but then pay below what Medicare pays for diagnostic tests. Some surgical or medical procedures may be reimbursed at rates relatively less than E&M codes. Medicare does not reimburse some HCPCS Level II codes for drugs and pharmaceuticals based on RVUs, but on average sales price to the provider or national pricing.

- Since a practice's gross charge rates are often set based on a uniform percentage of the Medicare allowable, collection rates determined as a percentage of gross charges can vary from code to code. *The average collection rate for a physician or a practice in the aggregate based on total collections and charges can be very different from the effective collection rate for a specific service or procedure.* Since professional collections relate only to certain codes, noise can be introduced into the computation of professional collections by use of aggregate collection rates rather than collection rates for a procedure code.

4.6 Gathering Information on Collections for Calculating Professional Collections

In requesting information from a practice for purposes of computing profession collections, it can be preferable to obtain collections data as follows:

By Rendering or Service Provider

Since the individual provider who performed the services needs to measure productivity, the data needs to be segregated by rendering or service provider. As noted with wRVUs, if a practice can only provide information by billing provider, estimates will need to be used, and the productivity needs to be treated as lacking in full accuracy and precision. In addition, the providers in a practice can often have different payer mixes. Collections by provider will reflect these payer mix differences.

By CPT/HCPCS Code

Obtaining collections by CPT/HCPCS code addresses the differences in reimbursement levels by type of service. It allows for a much more accurate analysis of professional collections than simply obtaining total collections for a provider.

Based on Date of Service Rather Than Date of Entry or Receipt

Again, greater accuracy and precision can be achieved in the overall analysis when collections are matched with procedures based on date of service. Volumes, RVUs, and the actual collections on those volumes and RVUs can be better evaluated. Such matching allows for more precise study of revenue cycle concerns as well as for volume trending from year to year.

Two nuances can arise, however, in using collections relating to date of service. The first is that you need to be about 60 days out or more from the period end through which you request data to have truly matching collections data. Thus, if you are requesting year-end data for 2012, that data will not fully reflect the collections on 2012 volumes and charges until after February 2013, for a typical practice (this can vary from practice to practice). Second, use of collections based on date of service may not be consistent with MGMA, which appears to be based on date of receipt, but would appear to be consistent with AMGA, who report "collected charges," where charges appear to be based on date of service.

Some practices will not be able to provide data at this level of detail. Their billing systems or their knowledge of these systems does not provide for access to such data. In such cases, appraisers and consultants have to make the best of what data is available. Yet, knowing the nuances and importance of some of data selection criteria listed above can nonetheless facilitate better interpretation and application of data that is not provided according to these criteria.

5.0 Conclusion

Calculating wRVUs and professional collections is a critical task in benchmarking physician productivity as well as in establishing compensation for a subject physician. While there is consistent guidance on how these metrics should be determined at a general level, there are many nuances and caveats to their accurate computation. Available data also plays a significant role in the level of accuracy and precision that can be achieved in these calculations. Appraisers, consultants, and practices preparing productivity calculations and using them for benchmarking and compensation-setting purposes need to be aware of the wrinkles and noise involved in the process.

Chapter 17. Critical Condition—A Coding Analysis for a Physician Practice Valuation

CONTENTS

Chapter 17. Critical Condition—A Coding Analysis for a Physician Practice Valuation

By Mark O. Dietrich, CPA/ABV, and Frank Cohen, CMPA

1.0 Introduction

At the outset, we should emphasize that a coding analysis is not always feasible. In a number of circumstances, the data may not be available because of poor information systems or a refusal to provide the data. Depending upon the nature of the engagement, the analyst may want to consider the implications of the lack of availability or a refusal to supply data. That said, this article focuses on the significance of a coding analysis. Basic coding analysis is within the reach of the valuation analyst using the approaches and tools described herein.

2.0 Established Patient Office Visits

The most commonly used codes in the Medicare database are the established patient office visits, which are designated 99211 through 99215. The codes are copyrighted by the American Medical Association (AMA). Of these five codes, 99212, 99213, and 99214 are the most frequently used; 99214 pays about 60% more than a 99213 and more than 220% of 99212. Clearly, incorrect or improper coding can dramatically affect the normalized revenues of a practice. For this reason alone, a coding analysis is critical.

In the last five years, there has been a steady, rightward shift of the historical bell curve coding pattern, with a decrease in 99212 codes and an increase in the 99214 codes. (See Exhibit 1.)

This shift has not gone unnoticed. The Department of Health and Human Services (DHHS), Office of Inspector General (OIG) produced Medicare fee for service (FFS)

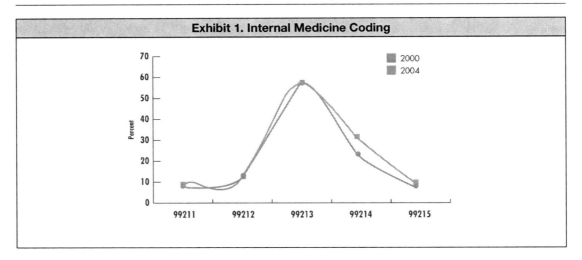

Exhibit 1. Internal Medicine Coding

error rates from 1996 to 2002. This process, known as the comprehensive error rate testing (CERT) program revealed that payers were reimbursing practices erroneously for procedures that were not documented properly and did not meet medical necessity tests. A focus of this study has been a select group of procedure codes that have historically had very high levels of improper payment, the least of which has been the aforementioned code 99214. Medical reviews of 4,436 lines for the period between Jan. 1, 2004, and Dec. 31, 2004, disclosed that 648 lines, or 14.6%, were in error. Based on the application of these results, Centers for Medicare & Medicaid Services (CMS) estimates that improper payments of $234,489,004 were made to physicians for this code alone. For medical practices, this means that these codes are under greater scrutiny from payers and other outside investigative agencies.

Evaluation and management (EM) coding in particular is dependent on a series of guidelines that require the physician to consider 1,600 unique decision points during a typical patient visit. In determining the code to be assigned, there are two major players with respect to validating the use of the EM code, namely, documentation and medical necessity.

Documentation is simply the process of recording or writing down a detailed summary of the visit, including the chief complaint, past family and social history, results of the physical exam, and information that would indicate the level of complexity of decision making during the examination. This process is analogous to the working papers of the valuation analyst or certified public accountant (CPA).

Medical necessity is a process used by Medicare and private payers to determine whether they should pay for goods or services billed by the physician. Medical necessity is defined as including that which is reasonable and necessary to diagnose or treat illness or injury or improve the function of a malformed body member. Medicare has a number of policies, including national coverage determinations (NCDs) and local medical review policy (LMRP), also known as local coverage determinations (LCDs), that outline what is and is not covered. In a small number of cases, Medicare may even determine whether a method of treating a patient should be covered on a case-by-case basis. Even if a service is accepted as reasonable and necessary, coverage may be limited if the service is provided more frequently than allowed under standard policies or standards of care.

In almost every case, these two tests dominate the decision to reimburse the provider for the procedure submitted on the claim. It is a complicated process because there is no effective relationship between documentation and medical necessity even though both medical necessity and documentation are tied to the procedure code. Submitting a claim for a service or procedure binds the practice to a highly complex and complicated series of laws, policies, rules, and regulations, any violation of which could result in substantial civil and criminal penalties.

3.0 Other Examples

Many medical specialists, such as cardiologists, infectious disease specialists, and pulmonologists, earn a substantial amount of their income from consultations. A consultation is specifically defined as a request from another physician. The AMA's current procedural terminology defines a consultation as "a type of service provided by a physician whose opinion or advice regarding evaluation and management of a specific problem is requested by another physician or other appropriate source." There are four parts to a consultation, namely, a request for review and an opinion; the rendering of the opinion; the documentation in the patient's chart; and the report provided to the referring physician. A recent OIG study suggests that billions of dollars in improper consultations were being billed to Medicare, placing these procedures, along with established office visits and subsequent hospital visits, high on the OIG's hit list.

4.0 Sources Of Data

Certain data can be downloaded from the CMS Web site, at www.cms.hhs.gov/PhysicianFeeSched/01_Overview.asp#TopOfPage.

Copies of the CERT report, updated definitional information on consults, the physician fee schedule database (PFSDB), and other files related to this article may be downloaded for free by going to www.cpahealth.com and clicking on the download tab.

5.0 Identifying Problematic Coding

A major area of utilization analysis involves the use of the EM codes. This kind of analysis involves looking at the use of codes within specific categories and between specific categories and comparing the utilization of each category to the global use of EM codes. Performing a complete EM utilization analysis can be complex and time-consuming; however, it is the category that most frequently accounts for the resource utilization and financial revenue of the practice. The use of EM codes is under considerable scrutiny from outside reviewers and special attention should be paid to this area.

In the valuation practice of Mark Dietrich, one of the co-authors of this article, the top 50 code spreadsheets by specialty are used extensively to identify potential issues that warrant further inquiry. (See Exhibit 2.) These data are extracted from the Medicare master database and summarized by CPT code and frequency of use. A complete set of tables for all specialties can be purchased by contacting info@cpahealth.com.

		Exhibit 2. Ranking of Codes Within Top 50		
Rank in Top 50	**CPT Code**	**Service Description**	**Count**	**Percent of Inpatient Consults**
7	99254	Initial inpatient consult	337,300	52.31%
13	99255	Initial inpatient consult	204,283	31.68%
21	99253	Initial inpatient consult	103,218	16.01%
				100.00%
Rank in Top 50	**CPT Code**	**Service Description**	**Count**	**Percent of Top 50**
35	99291	Critical care, first hour	37,849	0.68%
45	99238	Hospital discharge day	24,241	0.44%
26	99262	Followup inpatient consult	61,413	1.11%
34	99263	Followup inpatient consult	39,668	0.71%
39	99223	Initial hospital care	26,367	0.48%
7	99254	Initial inpatient consult	337,300	6.08%
13	99255	Initial inpatient consult	204,283	3.68%
21	99253	Initial inpatient consult	103,218	1.86%
33	99312	Nursing fac care, subsequent	40,830	0.74%
43	99311	Nursing fac care, subsequent	24,467	0.44%
46	99244	Office consultation	22,299	0.40%
6	99213	Office/outpatient visit, established	339,957	6.13%
10	99214	Office/outpatient visit, established	247,192	4.45%
24	99212	Office/outpatient visit, established	67,810	1.22%
29	99215	Office/outpatient visit, established	49,383	0.89%
31	99211	Office/outpatient visit, established	47,594	0.86%
2	99232	Subsequent hospital care	2,367,869	42.67%
3	99231	Subsequent hospital care	840,012	15.14%
4	99233	Subsequent hospital care	704,910	12.70%
			5,586,662	100.00%

For example, the spreadsheet for infectious disease (ID) indicates that the most frequently billed consult code is 99254, initial inpatient consult, which is 52% of all inpatient consults. The most frequently billed code is 99232, subsequent hospital care. The ratio of all consultations (both office and hospital) to all patient visits is 12%.

Note that the remaining Top 50 services in this subspecialty represent injections or tests. In reviewing the coding of an infectious diseases (ID) practice as part of a valuation, the Medicare data can easily be compared to those of the practice.

Another benchmark is to statistically analyze the incidence of related procedures, such as office visits and outpatient consults. In performing this intercategory analysis, we could take the total number of outpatient consults (99241 to 99245) compared to the total volume of new office visits (99201 to 99205). For example, the ratio of office consults to new office visits for cardiology is 4.3-to-1, meaning that for every new patient office visit, the average cardiovascular (CV) doctor or cardiologist reports about four consults. In our example, let's say that, for the practice, the ratio was 2-to-1. This might indicate that the practice is shifting what should be consults to new office visits. These kinds of aberrant practices could result in financial and compliance problems.

For example, significant excessive numbers of consults, no matter how they are measured, can help frame the interview questions used to assess whether there is something particular to the practice. The interview of an ID doctor might take place as follows:

Analyst:
Dr. Smith, I noted in my review of your coding data that the volume of office consultations you report is significantly higher than that of your peer group. I generally see physicians in your specialty seeing consults in the hospital. Can you tell me about the unique aspects of your practice that might explain the difference?

Dr. Smith:
Answer A: Since my office is here on campus, many patients simply come here rather than wait for me to see them in the hospital.

Answer B: You'll note that many of my patients have communicable diseases, and, in this area, I receive most of the referrals to confirm or rule out a particular diagnosis.

Answer C: I didn't realize there was a difference.

Answer D: When I see patients for the first time, I charge for a consult. It pays more than a new patient visit.

6.0 Analysis

Answer A would require the analyst to know whether a particular medical condition typically requires hospitalization before an ID consult. Answer B might be a perfectly acceptable answer if, for example, Dr. Smith practices in an inner city, where tuberculosis is often a public health problem. Answer D is a red flag and a tacit admission of incorrect coding. Obviously, Answer C is of no assistance to the analyst.

7.0 Modifiers

The same sort of analysis applies to the use of modifiers. Over- or underuse of certain modifiers may raise a flag with carriers, payers, and other outside reviewing agencies. For example, if modifier 25 (used to describe *separate, distinctly identifiable* services from other services or procedures rendered during the same visit) is used at a level greater than 10% of a particular EM category, it may cause a carrier to perform a review of the practice's billing and coding patterns. These flags are most often the source of focused reviews and audits. Most recently, OIG published two separate reports, one on modifier 59 and one on modifier 25. According to the reports, violations in the way these codes are reported by providers resulted in hundreds of millions of dollars in inappropriate payments. These reports are also available at www.cpahealth.com by clicking on the download tab.

8.0 Utilization of Tests

One process is the ranking of procedure codes within the practice compared to national averages. For example, we might rank the codes within our practice by frequency and dollar volume, and compare this result with the top 50 codes for that specific specialty based upon the national average. This analysis identifies areas in which there may be patterns of over- or underuse. A subset of this analysis is the utilization of tests in the physician's office, and many of the top 50 CPT codes consist of such tests. Some of this variation can be traced to the ancillary capabilities of the practice, such as whether it has a blood chemistry lab, X-ray, or other imaging technology. Comparisons between the practices with and without this equipment are not possible; therefore, it is important to ascertain the practice's capabilities before attempting a utilization analysis.

9.0 Surgical Practices

For surgical practices, the utilization of procedure codes is more complex and can involve a number of different kinds of analysis, many of which are likely beyond the purview of the valuation analyst. However, certain simple analyses can rule out or identify common problems. It may also be helpful to identify the revenue potential associated with procedures that are not being provided by the practice but that are being performed or reported by other practices within the same specialty. In specialty practices, such as ophthalmology, physicians trained in the most recently developed surgical techniques may have greater earning power than the current practitioners, who are relying on less-advanced techniques.

Another utilization issue concerns the use and reporting of the post-operative code 99024. Medicare pays for all surgery on the basis of a global fee that includes *both* pre-operative and post-operative care. For example, a practice reports 5,250 global surgical procedures that have either a 10- or 90-day follow-up period. In performing a utilization analysis, it is found that they reported the 99024 code (surgical follow-up) 1,025 times. The resulting ratio of 0.195-to-1 indicates that only one in five surgical procedures was followed! This conclusion could raise troubling questions about the quality of care, as well as compliance and *the potential for reimbursement*. Even though the relevant codes are considered bundled codes for Medicare, it is important to ensure that all post-operative visits that fall within the global period, i.e., are recorded for reasons relating to the global procedure, and accurately documented as such. For each global surgical code, there is a preservice, intraservice, and post-service component that represents both the resource consumption and fee allocation for that procedure. For example, for procedure code 28190 (the removal of a foreign body from the foot), the preoperative portion is 10%, the surgical portion is 80%, and the post-operative portion is 10%. If adequate follow-up is not reported, the insurer could reduce the post-service payment portion (by 10%), indicating that the follow-up portion was not satisfied based upon the utilization statistics.

The use of global fees for surgery is a critical consideration in valuation or litigation. For example, assume a surgeon has left the group practice and the geographic area and is seeking additional compensation or other benefits. The group practice has the responsibility and lost revenue associated with providing post-operative care, including the repair of complications, for any patients of that departed surgeon. This must be considered in any damages calculation.

10.0 Beware Changes in the Value of Codes

For example, in June 2006, CMS announced its intent to increase the relative values of EM services in 2007, following closely on the heels of a suggestion by MedPAC in its March 2006 report that these services had declined in value, in large part to the benefit of high-tech imaging services.

The work component for RVUs [Relative Value Units] associated with an intermediate office visit [99213], the most commonly billed physician's service, will increase by 37%. The work component for RVUs for an office visit requiring moderately complex decisionmaking and for a hospital visit also requiring moderately complex decisionmaking will increase by 29% and 31%, respectively. Both of these services rank in the top 10 most frequently billed physicians' services out of more than 7,000 types of services paid under the physician fee schedule.

The 99213 code presently has a fully implemented work RVU value of 0.67. Under this proposal, the value would rise to approximately 0.92 RVUs. With a conversion factor of $37.90, this would represent an increase in the fee of nearly $10, or 18%, to about $62.15 from the present level of $52.68 on the National Physician Fee Schedule.

Significantly, because of the budget-neutrality provisions of the existing Part B system, the increased cost associated with the increased RVUs has to come from a reduction in the value of other services and CMS proposes "to establish a budget-neutrality adjustor that would reduce all work RVUs by an estimated 10% to meet the budget-neutrality provisions." For example, CMS estimated that the proposed changes would increase reimbursement for internal medicine by 5% in 2007 while decreasing the reimbursement for radiologists by the same amount. The *Federal Register* notice contains the details of estimated changes for all specialties.

CMS is also proposing changes to the practice expense component of the RVUs to be phased in over four years through 2010, which will result in further revenue shifts.

11.0 Conclusion

Valuation analysts are not coding consultants. Nevertheless, given regulatory issues and the impact of coding on the future cash flow being valued, it is necessary that analysts have some basic knowledge of the subject and conduct a basic review. Relatively simple processes can be implemented using readily available data from the Internet or vendors such as MIT Solutions Inc. (www.mitsi.org) to incorporate a basic assessment of coding into the valuation process. This results in a valuation conclusion that reflects the risk, if any, of unusual coding patterns and may identify potential lost revenues available to a hypothetical or other owner of the practice. In the latter instance, the analyst can bring additional value to the valuation.

This article first appeared in the Fall 2006 Edition of CPA Expert. Reprinted with permission.

Chapter 18. Understanding and Using the Technical and Professional Component of Ancillary Revenue When Valuing Medical Practices

CONTENTS

Chapter 18. Understanding and Using the Technical and Professional Component of Ancillary Revenue When Valuing Medical Practices

By Mark O. Dietrich, CPA/ABV, and Kathie L. Wilson, CPA, CVA

1.0 Introduction

Valuing any business requires an understanding of how revenue is generated: what products or services are sold, how much revenue comes from each, competing products or services, and competing sellers. Valuing a medical practice is no different in that regard. It is important to understand that services sold by medical practices are commonly specified by current procedural terminology (CPT) codes and healthcare common coding procedure system (HCPCS or "Hickpicks") codes. For example, CPT code 99213 is a Level 3 office visit for an established patient. HCPCS codes can denote "products" such as certain injectable drugs or chemotherapy that are specified by J codes or services and procedures that are specified by G codes. The HCPCS codes are alphanumeric and start with a letter. For example, J0133 is the code for an acyclovir injection; G0202 is the code for screening mammography. Thus, considerable background is required by an appraiser to understand the revenue lines in the variety of medical practice specialties.

Many of the more common specialties require more expertise than simply being familiar with the codes for seeing patients in the office. Of particular note is the differentiation between the technical component and professional component of ancillary services for practices such as radiology, cardiology, neurology, and others. The technical component is paid in connection with ownership of equipment, provision of a technologist to operate the equipment, supplies, and general overhead. The professional component is paid to the physician specifically for interpreting the results of the test or study, e.g., an imaging study such as an X-ray or MRI. Revenue from the technical component, therefore, is related to the equipment investment of the practice, not the efforts of the physician.

This can be seen in the following quotes from the Centers for Medicare and Medicaid Services' Medicare Physician Fee Schedule 2010 Final Rule:[1]

> Services with technical components (TCs) and professional components (PCs). Diagnostic services are generally comprised of two components: a professional component (PC) and a technical component (TC), both of which may be performed independently or by different providers. When services have TCs, PCs, and global components that can be billed separately, the payment for the global component equals the sum of the payment for the TC and PC. This is a result of using a weighted average of the ratio of indirect to direct costs across all the specialties that furnish the global components, TCs, and PCs; that is, we apply the same weighted average indirect percentage factor to allocate indirect expenses to the global components, PCs, and TCs for a service. (The direct PE RVUs for the TC and PC sum to the global under the bottom-up methodology.)

> Modifier. A modifier is shown if there is a technical component (modifier TC) and a professional component (PC) (modifier -26) for the service. If there is a PC and a TC for the service, Addendum B contains three entries for the code. A code for: the global values (both professional and technical); modifier -26 (PC); and, modifier TC. The global service is not designated by a modifier, and physicians must bill using the code without a modifier if the physician furnishes both the PC and the TC of the service.

Within the relative value unit (RVU) allocations are components for physician work, practice expense, and malpractice insurance. As you might expect, the largest element in the TC is for practice expense, whereas the largest element in the PC is typically for physician work, known as wRVUs. In some circumstances, these can be important in measuring the productivity for reasonable compensation purposes as defined later herein.[2]

2.0 Some Common Mistakes

Most appraisers determine reasonable compensation when valuing a medical practice by reference to the physician's (or physicians' aggregate) productivity benchmarked against statistical norms such as those from the Medical Group Management Association (MGMA). The definition of collected revenue in the MGMA data is with the technical

---

1   CMS-1413-FC.
2   Not all, or even many, practices track wRVUs, however.

component of ancillary services excluded! MGMA does have some data that include the technical component and nonphysician providers at two levels, greater than 10% or less than 10%, but that differentiation is generally not specific enough to be useful for reasonable compensation purposes.[3] Thus, to use the data appropriately, it is necessary for the appraiser to separate the revenues associated with the professional component (related to the efforts of the physician) from those of the ancillary or technical component (related to the equipment investment).

2.1 Example

While valuing a four-physician neurology practice with a single owner, the appraiser notes that the owner has collected revenue credited to him of more than twice the 90th percentile of MGMA. Upon investigation of the practice's reports of productivity by CPT (including HCPCS) code and the list of fixed assets, he determines that the practice owns an MRI unit in addition to other ancillary equipment. The technical component of the MRI services representing approximately 85% of the global (or total) collected revenue has been credited to the owner-physician as well as the professional component. To determine the owner's productivity consistent with the MGMA definition, the technical component of the MRI and other ancillaries will have to be backed out. This has a dramatic effect on the reasonable compensation determination: After the appropriate modifications are made, the owner-physician's collections are only at the 75th percentile of MGMA. Failure to identify and appropriately adjust for the technical component collected revenue would have resulted in a dramatic understatement of the practice's value due to an overstatement of reasonable compensation for the services of the owner-physician.

3.0 Jurisdictional Issues

Aside from the obvious effect on the reasonable compensation determination, the source of profit in a practice can be quite significant from a jurisdictional standpoint. For example, in marital dissolution valuation, many jurisdictions distinguish between personal goodwill and enterprise goodwill. In many circumstances, the revenue, profit, and value resulting from the technical component of ancillary services may be included in enterprise goodwill and therefore, considered marital property subject to division, again, because it is not related to the personal efforts of the physician, but to the investment in the equipment of the practice. In other circumstances, even the technical component element may be considered nondivisible if a noncompete agreement is required from the seller to maintain the related revenue and profit in the hands of a buyer. Absent a jurisdictional rule, that portion of the practice value connected to

---

3 See the Rhode Island example later herein for an important exception.

technical component revenue that would be present absent the seller is perhaps the clearest element of enterprise goodwill.

4.0 Transactions

In the current transaction market, differentiating reasonable compensation along with enterprise and personal goodwill can be equally important. After a physician practice is acquired by a hospital, a number of employment settings are possible, including employment by the hospital, a hospital-controlled group practice, or the physician practice itself, if the hospital purchases the stock. The Stark laws have different permitted compensation rules depending on the nature of the employment setting, which can impact how profits from the technical component of ancillaries are handled. This should, in turn, influence precisely what is being valued and how reasonable compensation is determined.

One of the most important practice types from a valuation and transaction standpoint in the present market is cardiology. Cardiologists employ a variety of ancillary testing equipment including single photon emission computed tomography (SPECT),[4] used for myocardial perfusion, ultrasound (echocardiogram as distinct from an electrocardiogram, or EKG), coronary computed tomography angiogram, and cardiac MRI. Despite some fairly dramatic cuts for SPECT and other nuclear medicine in the 2010 Medicare Physician Fee Schedule, these practices remain attractive for the technical component of tests as well as for the highly profitable admissions they generate for hospitals.

4.1 Example

CPT code 78465,[5] heart image (3rd) multiple, is a SPECT code for myocardial infusion and represented a staggering 10.3% ($2,072,176,147) of charges for cardiovascular physicians billing Medicare in 2007, the highest single code in terms of charges as well as frequency of billing. CPT code 78465 also represented 10.4% ($2,017,599,660) of charges in 2006 and 10.4% ($1,863,154,763) of charges in 2005. Exhibits 1 and 2 are taken from the indicated proposed and final rules and show the global, technical, and professional component breakdown by RVU.

Exhibit 3 is sample data from a cardiology group practice with numerous subspecialties (service codes in addition to those for SPECT also shown). Net revenue (expected

---

4   Due to its ability to generate true three-dimensional images, it is gradually replacing traditional gamma (ray) cameras.

5   Codes are Copyright, American Medical Association. This code was "cross-walked," or changed to 78452 in the period between the 2010 proposed and final rules. This illustrates one more complication that emphasizes the import of understanding CPT codes.

Exhibit 1. 2010 Final Rule

CPT[1]/ HCPCS	Mod	Status	Description	Physi-cian Work RVUs[2,3,4]	Fully Imple-mented Non-Facility PE RVUs[2,4]	Year 2010 Transi-tional Non-Facility PE RVUs[2,4]	Fully Imple-mented Facility PE RVUs[2,4]	Year 2010 Transi-tional Facility PE RVUs[2,4]	Mal-Practice RVUs[2,4]	CPT[1]/ HCPCS
78452		A	Ht muscle image spect, mult	1.62	8.84	8.84	NA	NA	0.06	XXX
78452	TC	A	Ht muscle image spect, mult	0.00	8.32	8.32	NA	NA	0.01	XXX
78452	26	A	Ht muscle image spect, mult	1.62	0.52	0.52	0.52	0.52	0.05	XXX

Exhibit 2. 2009 Final Rule

CPT[1]/ HCPCS	Mod	Status	Description	Physi-cian Work RVUs[2]	Fully Imple-mented Non-Facility PE RVUs[2]	Year 2009 Transi-tional Non-Facility PE RVUs[2]	Fully Imple-mented Facility PE RVUs[2]	Year 2009 Transi-tional Facility PE RVUs[2]	Mal-Practice RVUs[2]	Global
78465		A	Heart image (3d), multiple	1.46	10.96	11.32	NA	NA	0.67	XXX
78465	TC	A	Heart image (3d), multiple	0.00	10.23	10.64	NA	NA	0.62	XXX
78465	26	A	Heart image (3d), multiple	1.46	0.73	0.68	0.73	0.68	0.05	XXX

Exhibit 3. Sample Data From a Cardiology Group Practice With Numerous Subspecialties

STRESS LAB (P-K counted once)		UNITS	PERCENT	NET REVENUE	PERCENT
SPECT MYOCARDIAL PERF	78465	1,353	5.82%	1,488,000	24.00%
MYOCARDIAL PERFUSION	78478	1,143	4.92%	248,000	4.00%
MYOCARDIAL PERFUSION	78480-78481	517	2.22%	310,000	5.00%
MYOCARDIAL PERFUSION	78483	860	3.70%	744,000	12.00%
GENERATION AUTODATA-P	78490	1,240	5.33%	248,000	4.00%
INFUSION	90765	559	2.40%	248,000	4.00%
STRESS	93015	1,488	6.40%	372,000	6.00%
OTHER		4,960	21.33%	248,000	4.00%
SUBTOTAL		12,119	52.12%	3,906,000	63.00%

collections) from SPECT nuclear medicine tests is $2.8 million. Assuming for the sake of illustration that all payers use an 85% TC and 15% PC split, nearly $2.4 million of net revenue has to be excluded from individual physician production to be comparable to MGMA data.

In some practices the professional component and technical component may be billed separately either because of payer rules or because the practice, in fact, only provides one or the other. In this case, a modifier is used for billing and should appear in the billing system reports: "26" is the modifier used for the professional component only and "TC" is the modifier used for the technical component only. If the billing is global (has no modifier), it is necessary to separate the professional component and technical component. The accompanying checklist provides detail on how to accomplish this.

5.0 Individual Market Idiosyncrasies

In some poorly reimbursed markets, it may, in fact, be necessary for the technical component income to supplement reasonable compensation for the physicians. For example,

---

Professional and Technical Component Analysis Checklist

1. What is the practice's specialty?

    Note: Certain specialties may include technical component revenue (neurology, cardiology), while other specialties (family practice, pediatrics) would probably not include technical component revenue.

2. Does the practice own ancillary equipment that has a technical component?

    Note: Look through the depreciation schedule for expensive pieces of equipment. Technical equipment purchases typically stand out from the routine office equipment and furnishings.

3. Identify expected technical component CPT codes for equipment identified in Step 2.

    Discuss with provider and billing staff. Inquire as to whether ancillary revenues are billed globally separately for professional and technical component, or both; this may be payer-specific.

    Some practices may bill globally for in-office ancillary services and professional only for hospital-based services when the hospital owns the equipment. This is common for cardiology practices where the physician may interpret the result of hospital-based stress tests, for example.

4. Request production data by provider and CPT code for your period of analysis. If available, request both charges and receipts by CPT code.

    Review services by CPT code; professional component only income is denoted with a "26"; technical component income is typically denoted with "TC," but other acronyms may be used. Global is typically not specified, but assumed by default if no modifier is present.

5. Calculate production, by provider, preferably using receipts, excluding technical component receipts

    Receipts are used because best MGMA data is based upon collections. Because payment rates are set by insurers, the amount a practice charges has little significance except to an uninsured patient or noncontracted insurer.

    For globally billed ancillary tests, it is necessary to separate out the professional component. Download the Medicare Physician Fee Schedule for the years the data related to, state, and region in which the practice is located. www.cms.hhs.gov/PhysicianFeeSched/PFSCSF/list.asp#TopOfPage

---

Rhode Island is notorious for the low levels of fees paid to physicians. This is due in large part to the fact that two insurers control nearly all of the health insurance market in that state and rates are artificially low as a result. As such, to attract and retain

For example, these are codes for certain imaging procedures from the Massachusetts Medicare fee schedule, with the modifier:

Codes for Imaging Procedures From Massachusetts Medicare Fee Schedule

CPT Code	Modifier	Fee Nonfacility	Fee Facility	Percent
70490		$309.59	$309.59	100.0%
70490	26	70.80	70.80	22.9
70490	TC	238.79	238.79	77.1
70491		373.21	373.21	100.0
70491	26	76.19	76.19	20.4
70491	TC	297.02	297.02	79.6

Not all payers use the same split between professional and technical component, so make inquiries of the practice.

Consider alternative measures of productivity including wRVUs or collections including TC revenue depending upon data available from client.

For forecasting purposes, the values of CPT codes may change dramatically from year to year, particularly when ancillary testing is involved. You may want to look at the subsequent year's fee schedule, for example, if using 2009 data as a basis for forecasting 2010 results.

6. Compare calculated production to applicable statistical data to determine reasonable compensation.

   Subtract reasonable compensation from the practice's precompensation profit to determine cash flow to capital and equity.

   (Alternatively, add difference between actual compensation and reasonable compensation to the practice profit and loss.)

7. Isolate the cash flow attributable to the technical component production. Be sure to identify expenses associated with technical equipment.

   Note: Examples include billing and collection, technician wages and benefits, insurance, maintenance contracts, certifications, and so on.

8. Compare the cash flow profit in Step 7 to the practice's profit in Step 6.

   Consider Jurisdictional rules as to determination of personal and enterprise goodwill.

   E.g., if a noncompete agreement is nondivisible in a marital dissolution, calculate the impact on TC profit due to a noncompete.

physicians, many practices have profitable ancillaries in place. In such a circumstance, it may be necessary to test the reasonable compensation analysis against an alternative measure of production, such as compensation per RVU, wRVUs, or annual encounters. This is an example where the productivity data *including* technical component revenue may need to be evaluated as well.

6.0 Conclusion

Valuing medical practices requires an in-depth understanding of the individual practice and the healthcare industry. This article highlights just one aspect of a myriad of issues unique to medical practice valuation and the determination of reasonable compensation (see sidebar, What Is "Incident to" Billing?). The environment that physicians work in,

---

What Is 'Incident to' Billing?

Many medical practices increase revenue through the use of nonphysician providers (NPPs). These are employees who provide separately billable services to patients, but are not physicians. Physician assistants (PAs), nurse practitioners (NPs) and midwives are examples of NPPs.

Although they provide separately billable services, there are options for how to bill these services. The services can be billed directly and, because they are not physicians, the reimbursement for these services is a portion of the physician's fee schedule (Medicare sets the rate for many services at 85% of the rate for a physician; non-Medicare payers may have different rules). Another option is to bill the services as "incident to" the services of a physician. If the requirements for incident to billing are met, the services are billed under the physician's provider number and reimbursement is at the full physician's fee schedule. The physician is required to participate in the services provided by the NPP (e.g., supervision, chart review, physical presence in the office suite when the services are provided, among others), but the bulk of the effort is provided by the NPP.

This becomes an issue in valuation because, like the technical component billing, the productivity related to the nonphysician providers' services could be included in the physician's productivity. Without identifying and segregating the production unrelated to the efforts of the physician from the productivity related to the efforts of the physician, the valuation analyst can end up with an inconsistent reasonable compensation calculation.

In addition to understanding technical component revenue, understanding the use of nonphysician providers and the methodology for billing their services is important to developing reasoned valuation conclusions.

---

dominated by the Medicare system, changes frequently. Some of these changes can be anticipated, such as the annual Medicare fee schedule modifications. Other changes are less predictable but can have a far greater impact, such as legislation. As any other highly regulated industry, it is critical that valuators remain current. The goal is always to have your valuation upheld, be it in court or in a settlement conference. Failure to understand the industry and its related terminology can undermine your authority as a valuation analyst and reduce the value of your opinion.

Chapter 19. Quality Performance and Valuation: What's the Connection?

CONTENTS

Chapter 19. Quality Performance and Valuation: What's the Connection?

By Alice G. Gosfield, Esq.

1.0 Introduction

When the Institute of Medicine (IOM) published *Crossing the Quality Chasm* in 2001,[1] a new era in health care was launched. With no less a goal than the promulgation of a blueprint to drive healthcare delivery in the 21st century, the report announced and explicated those values intended to determine how care is purchased, provided, and evaluated for the foreseeable future. Later characterized as the STEEEP values, the IOM called for care to meet six explicit standards. Care should be:

- Safe—delivered in a manner that avoids injuries;

- Timely—explicitly organized to reduce waits and harmful delays;

- Effective—based on scientific knowledge avoiding underuse and overuse;

- Efficient—avoiding waste of equipment, supplies, ideas, and energies and although not articulated, economically efficient;

- Equitable—not variable in quality because of gender, ethnicity, location, and socioeconomic status; and

- Patient-centered—respectful and responsive to patient preferences, needs, and values and therefore, subject to patient choice, which itself implies a more transparent and publicly reported healthcare system.

---

1   Corrigan, et al., National Academy Press, Washington, D.C.

The report called for new payment models that would enhance the ability to render care in concordance with the values.

Quality problems in health care had long been identified as overuse, misuse, and underuse.[2] Overuse occurs when the patient gets too much of the proper treatment. Misuse is when the patient gets the wrong treatment. Underuse occurs when the patient does not get all the services he or she needs. All three have been found to be endemic in American healthcare. Overuse has led payers to impose blunt force control measures, such as prior authorization of provider services, post-payment review, and recoupment for medically unnecessary services. Misuse has gotten little attention in payment policy, but most of the pay-for-performance (P4P) programs, which are burgeoning throughout the country, are focused on underuse because they pay physicians to do things they have not been doing enough of,[3] in part in response to studies that have demonstrated that Americans are receiving only about 55% of the services that evidence says should be used to treat them.[4]

2.0 Pay for Performance

With the call for better quality performance, we have seen a proliferation of P4P programs: initiatives primarily sponsored by health plans to pay mostly physicians, but sometimes hospitals as well, additional monies on top of the capitation, fee for service, or DRG payments they are already being paid, for performance as measured in enunciated metrics. The explosion of more measures themselves[5] has also been part of this changed environment with the National Quality Forum—a public-private partnership of multiple stakeholders (www.nqf.org)—providing consensus approval of measures created by others, to be applied nationally for a plethora of clinical conditions and services.

The data so far available about P4P programs, which began to appear around 2003, are neither robust nor compelling.[6] Many of these programs did not start with a threshold of performance against which to measure improved performance. There remain many

---

2   Galvin Chassin and The National Roundtable for Health Care, "The Urgent Need to Improve Health Care Quality," *JAMA*, Sept 16, 1998; 280; pp.1000-1005.

3   Gosfield, "Pay for Performance: Transitional at Best," *Managed Care* (Jan. 2005). www.managedcaremag.com/archives/0501/0501.p4p_gosfield.html.

4   McGlynn, et al., "The Quality of Health Care Delivered to Adults in the United States," 548 NEJM 2635, Jan. 16, 2003.

5   Gosfield, "The Performance Measures Ball: Too Many Tunes, Too Many Dancers?," *Health Law Handbook* (Gosfield. ed.), 2005 Edition, WestGroup a Thomson Company, pp. 227-283, www.gosfield.com/PDF/Ch4Gosfield.pdf.

6   See Gosfield, "Physician Compensation for Quality: Behind the Group's Green Door," *Health Law Handbook* (Gosfield, ed.), 2008 edition, pp. 3-7.

questions about the extent to which they are improving the quality of health care services; yet there is a sense of inevitability about them, and they are proliferating throughout the country.

All of them have added more money on top of the already existing payment systems. Sometimes these payments are a percentage of a shared pool of money (CMS-Premier Hospital program), an enhancement to the capitation rates (the most typical model), or a fixed stipend (the Bridges to Excellence model).[7] Most of them pay for physicians to do something they were not doing before—perform more tests, prescribe more drugs—to get better scores.

While the commercial payers have led the way in the development of these programs, Medicare is squarely in this business as well, with its demonstration projects,[8] reduced payment to hospitals that do not report their quality results,[9] and an incipient program for physicians, which pays them merely for reporting information, not for achieving specific scores.[10] The quality-payment nexus is more tightly joined with the refusal of payers, including Medicare, to pay hospitals at all for "never events"—errors and patient safety failures that never should have occurred in the first place, such as wrong-site surgery, bed sores, and hospital-acquired pneumonia.[11]

3.0 Efficiency

The obverse of this pay-for-performance (or no pay for no performance) phenomenon is the parallel expansion of efficiency-based measurement, primarily in the form of tiered networks that exclude more expensive providers from eligibility to render care, when the health plan deems them too expensive.[12] Highly controversial, they have been characterized as "networks of the cheapest" by some,[13] with allegations of defamatory and misguided characterization of the providers reported. Tensions have run so high that on one hand, the New York State Attorney General has investigated the operation of these programs,[14] while on the other, a voluntary agreement among health plans and providers emerged regarding how these programs will be unfurled.[15] Still, the issue of

---

7   www.hci3.org.
8   www.cms.gov/HospitalQualityInits/35_HospitalPremier.asp#TopOfPage; http://innovations.cms.gov/initiatives/index.html.
9   www.cms.gov/HospitalQualityInits/15_HospitalQualityAlliance.asp#TopOfPage.
10   www.cms.gov/PQRI.
11   Gabriel, "Medicare: Uncle Sam's New Scrutiny," *Physicians' Practice* (May 2008) www.physicianspractice.com/index/fuseaction/articles.details/articleID/1159.htm.
12   See, Shay, "Transparency and the Law," *Health Law Handbook* (Gosfield, ed.), 2008 edition, pp. 77-121.
13   uft-a.com/latest_issues/issues.htm#netcheapest.
14   www.americanbar.org/newsletter/publications/aba_health_esource_home/King.html.
15   healthcaredisclosure.org/docs/files/PatientCharterDisclosureRelease040108.pdf.

the efficiency of healthcare delivery is also in high relief as the quality mandates are also emphasized.

Crystallizing one side of the government's interest in performance, quality has now been cited by the Office of the Inspector General (OIG) as grounds for fraud and abuse enforcement.[16] Similarly the Department of Justice is paying attention to quality and its failures as the basis for enforcement.[17] Where providers exercise so much budgetary constraint that patients do not get appropriate care, criminal penalties have been imposed and false claims have been assessed in still other contexts.

So the extent to which quality and payment are linked and made the basis for regulatory accountability is increasing. What does this quality-payment connection have to do with a book on valuation? As the implications of these connections are emerging, placing a value on what quality is will be an increasingly important challenge in a variety of ventures going forward.

4.0 The Legal Nexus With Valuation

Framed in terms that speak to the quality problems of overuse, misuse, and underuse, the Stark statute is about overuse. The law was enacted because of data in the early 1990s that showed that physicians will refer patients to a provider entity in which they are invested, sometimes when those services are not medically necessary. The Stark statute[18] is a strict liability statute—no intent is required to find a violation. It affects physician referrals only for a specified hit list of "designated health services" (DHS) and prohibits both the referral of Medicare patients to entities with which they have financial relationships for those services and the entity's submission of claims pursuant to a tainted referral, unless the relationship complies with an exception.[19] Violations entail $15,000 civil money penalties for each claim submitted as a result of an improper referral, as well as the payment being deemed an overpayment.

There are many exceptions, including for personal services and rental of space and equipment. Many of them are particularly important for transactions between physicians and the hospitals to which they refer, because all inpatient and outpatient hospital services are DHS. There are a number of exceptions that require that payment reflect fair

---

16   Co-authored with the American Health Lawyers Association, "Corporate Responsibility and Health Care Quality," oig.hhs.gov/fraud/docs/complianceguidance/CorporateResponsibilityFinal%209-4-07.pdf.

17   www.gosfield.com/newissues.htm#pptjgs.

18   42 USC 1395nn.

19   For more information on the Stark statute, see, Gosfield, *Medicare and Medicaid Fraud and Abuse*, 2008 ed., WestGroup, a Thomson Company, Chapter 3, and www.gosfield.com/publications.htm.

---

market value and others that no payment directly reflects the volume or value of referrals of DHS. In addition, because of the effort to forestall improper referrals whenever they might arise, the statute establishes that some of its exceptions are only available for application by a medical group that meets specific standards, among which are standards regarding how the physicians in the group are compensated.[20]

An older, broader, but less rigid statute is often, today, included by nonlawyers under the rubric of Stark, but the anti-kickback statute (AKS) is entirely different and not even in the same title of the Social Security Act.[21] The AKS sweeps into its ambit all federal health payment programs and all parties to a violating transaction. Whoever solicits, pays, offers, or receives any remuneration, in cash or in kind, covertly or overtly, directly or indirectly, for the referral, to induce the referral, or for ordering, providing, leasing, furnishing, recommending, or arranging for the provision of any service, item, or good payable under a federal program can be found to have violated the law. Penalties are criminal—up to $25,000 fine, up to five years in jail, or both—but also can be punished by a $50,000 civil money penalty for each violation.

Unlike Stark, though, the AKS has an intent requirement. To violate it, one must knowingly and willfully engage in improper behavior. The AKS can also be said to reflect a desire to curb overuse of services that can result from a desire to realize the financial opportunities in business relationships involving patients whose care is paid for by the government. Unlike the regulations under Stark, which provide refinement to the strict prohibitions in the statute, the safe harbor regulations[22] under the AKS report only what is explicitly safe. Arrangements that do not comply do not necessarily violate the statute but will be evaluated on their facts and circumstances as reviewed with prosecutorial discretion. Like the Stark statute, the AKS also focuses heavily on the fair market value of the financial relationships involved.

While Stark targets leases of real estate and equipment for a discussion of payment for quality, the fair market value of *services* is far more relevant. The definition of "fair market value" for Stark purposes turns on "general market value."

> *Fair market value* means the value in arm's-length transactions, consistent with the general market value. "General market value" means the price an asset would bring as the result of *bona fide* bargaining between well-informed parties to the agreement

---

20 Gosfield, "Physician Compensation for Quality: Behind the Group's Green Door," *Health Law Handbook* (Gosfield, ed.), 2008 edition, WestGroup, a Thomson Company pp. 1-44, gosfield.com/PDF/gosfield.2008%20 HLH.articlewithcoverpage.122807.pdf.
21 42 USC 1320a-7b(b)(1) and (2).
22 42 CFR §1001.952 et seq.

who are not otherwise in a position to generate business for the other party on the date of acquisition of the asset or at the time of the service agreement. Usually the fair market price is the price at which *bona fide* sales have been consummated for assets of like type, quality, and quantity in a particular market at the time of acquisition or the compensation that has been included in *bona fide* service agreements with comparable terms at the time of the agreement, where the price or compensation has not been determined in any manner that takes into account the volume or value of anticipated or actual referrals.[23]

This definition was streamlined from an earlier version that created a safe harbor for hourly payments to physicians for services rendered. Payments for medical directorships, for example, were traditionally compensated on the basis of an hourly payment with documentation of time spent. The Stark regulations had taken this further, with a safe harbor for hourly payments reflecting an average of the 50th percentile of four out of six compensation surveys or the 50th percentile of what emergency department physicians were paid in the community as with at least three emergency departments. With the publication of the Stark III regulations, that aspect of the definition was removed, thereby enhancing the flexibility of the definition and opening the door to more creative ways of quantifying the value of physicians' personal services.

Although there is a similar definition of "fair market value" in the space and equipment lease safe harbor, there is none generally for AKS purposes or in the personal services and management contract exception, which is far more relevant to quality-based payments. The payment terms state that:

> The aggregate compensation paid … over the term of the agreement is set in advance, is consistent with fair market value in arms-length transactions, and is not calculated in a manner that takes into account the volume or value of any referrals or business otherwise generated between the parties for which payment may be made in whole or in part under Medicare or under a state health care program.[24]

5.0 Valuing Quality

Against this background of performance measurement, payment change, and fraud and abuse regulations, a range of initiatives is now emerging, particularly where hospitals and physicians relate to each other, that is intended to improve quality of care. Because much of what occurs in a hospital is ultimately derivative of a physician order

---

23   42 USC §411.351 (72 F.R. 51081, Sept 5, 2007).
24   42 CFR §1001.952(d)(5).

(even though a lot of what is being scored in hospital pay-for-performance programs involves teamwork in the institution among nurses, technicians, and others), for many scores, the collaboration between hospitals and physicians is essential for hospitals to succeed.[25] To pay physicians for their help, some measure of value becomes essential, especially in light of the impact of Stark and the AKS on these relationships.

As hospitals seek to improve their quality scores, for which they are at risk of reduced Medicare payments for reporting failures, they increasingly seek to engage physicians with them.[26] Paying the physicians for their activities in support of improvement can fall under the "personal services arrangement" exception under the Stark regulations, but the payment must be based on fair market value. Some commentators now argue that lost opportunity time is a reasonable measure of fair market value when the job being performed by the physicians requires their special expertise.[27] Different specialties would be paid differently under this analysis. The types of activities for which this type of payment is relevant can include selection of clinical practice guidelines, pathways, protocols, or other approaches to standardization of care, as well as medical staff leadership and service on medical staff committees, since the whole raison d'etre of the medical staff organization is to monitor and assure the quality of care in the institution and provide recommendations to the board about privileges, credentialing, and corrective action.

Another approach to improving quality and efficiency has been through implementation of the modern versions of gainsharing that the OIG has approved. Gainsharing has been a basis for fraud enforcement against hospitals since 1983, when diagnosis-related groups (DRGs) were introduced. When gainsharing re-emerged as a potential approach to bonding with physicians and saving money for the hospital in July 1999, the OIG published a very critical statement that it would not approve programs that paid physicians to reduce services, even if they were from a baseline of overuse.[28] With six favorable opinions in 2005[29] and more in subsequent years, the OIG approved a revamped, time-limited, surgical- and procedure-focused approach to gainsharing,

---

25   Gosfield, "In Common Cause for Quality," *Health Law Handbook* (Gosfield ed.), 2006 edition, WestGroup, a Thomson Company, pp. 177-222, www.gosfield.com/PDF/commoncausequalityCh5.pdf; Reinertsen, Gosfield, Rupp and Whittington, "*Engaging Physicians in a Shared Quality Agenda.*" IHI Innovation Series white paper. Cambridge, MA: Institute for Healthcare Improvement; 2007. www.gosfield.com/PDF/IHIEngagingPhysicians WhitePaper2007.pdf and www.uft-a.com.

26   Gosfield and Reinertsen, "Sharing The Quality Agenda with Physicians," *Trustee* (Oct. 2007) pp. 12-17.

27   Johnson, "Fair Market Value Support Required, " ALHA, *Health Law Weekly* (May 2008), www.healthlawyers. org/Template.cfm?Section=HLW_Archive&template=/ahlatestcode/google/g_articlelayout.cfm&ContentID=5 5890&IssueDate=2008-05-30%2000%3A00%3A00.

28   oig.hhs.gov/fraud/docs/alertsandbulletins/gainsh.htm.

29   Advisory Opinions 05-01 through 05-06, oig.hhs.gov/reports-and-publications/archives/advisory-opinions/ index.asp.

which turned in part on the valuation and payment methodologies. Under the gain-sharing programs, which are intended to save money by standardizing supplies used, those that are explicitly approved do so because they have safeguards that prevent reduction of clinical services to patients. All of them are time-limited to one year. They pay physicians half of the savings over thresholds currently achieved, so they reward actual improvement. The cost savings are calculated by subtracting the actual costs for the year of the supplies from historic costs associated with a set of recommended practices during specified procedures rendered. From these results are subtracted any inappropriate reductions that would run afoul of the prohibition on a hospital paying physicians to reduce their services.[30]

While the OIG was clear that the arrangements implicated the prohibition on payment to reduce services, the safeguards cited as supporting approval included, among the eight reasons cited: transparency and disclosure to patients; credible medical support that the arrangement wouldn't adversely affect patient care; all surgeries were included and not just those paid for by federal programs; the cost savings reflected actual costs and "not an accounting convention"; using clinical benchmarks of historical and current performance, any undue inducement to restrict care was mitigated.

Those reasons motivated the government to believe civil money penalties for reduction of services was inappropriate. In addition, addressing the compensation under the anti-kickback statute because the program was limited to surgeons already on staff, the additional payment from the program, the OIG said, would not induce others to join the staff to get the money. Because only surgeons would benefit, referrals from other physicians, such as cardiologists, would not be stimulated by the program. The payment reflected additional risk to the surgeons from changing their behaviors, which the OIG regarded as potentially not much more than "simple common sense," but a change in operating room practice based on standardized rules nonetheless. As a result of the analysis, in quality terms, the OIG postulated that the risks of underuse had been avoided by the safeguards against reduction of services, while the risks of overuse had been avoided by not encouraging additional referrals to obtain the additional, time-limited money the program would make available. While many would regard the analysis as purely financial, in fact, at its core, it reflects quality concerns.

Yet another tantalizing opportunity to improve quality was raised with the publication of the Stark III regulations. The regulators said compensation related to patient satis-faction goals or other quality measures unrelated to the volume or value of business generated by the referring physician and unrelated to reducing or limiting services

---

30 Advisory Opinion 07-21.

would be permitted under the personal service arrangements exception.[31] This relatively open-ended recognition of the changing environment offers the opportunity to pay physicians not on a time basis, but on a value-of-contribution basis, now that the definition of fair market value no longer drives toward hourly payments. Of course, the protection would only pertain provided that all requirements of the exception are satisfied. The regulators have cited as a legitimate example compensation to reward physicians for providing appropriate preventive care services when the arrangement is otherwise structured to satisfy the requirements of the exception.

How physicians have contributed to improved performance could be valued by looking at each quality metric with a financial impact and assessing the ratio of their contribution to their accomplishment, as distinct from the contributions of nurses, technicians, pharmacists, and others. Similarly, payments that recognize physician contributions to commercial pay-for-performance enhancements to hospital reimbursement would also be permitted under this acknowledgement.

What likely is *not* proper under the definition is looking at hospital payment on the DRG and subtracting from it the fair market value of the hospital contributions (e.g., heat, light, staff, building, and license) and paying the remainder to the physicians.

In its co-authored guidance to hospital boards regarding trustee responsibilities for quality with the American Health Lawyers Association, the OIG cited as a risk area the ways that incentive pools will be developed when otherwise independent providers seek to collaborate to achieve both improved efficiency and higher quality scores.[32] To set a value on the services rendered and results achieved, as contributed by each participant in an incentive pool, will present additional challenges to providers and those assisting them in constructing their arrangements within the boundaries of the law. Some have looked to commercial disease management companies as the analogues for valuation of the services rendered. These companies typically are paid performance bonuses for achieving specific targets or benchmarks. Given the definition of fair market value under the Stark regulations, this is one general market source of comparison to support the legitimacy of the compensation that might be earned.

Selecting targets that do not reflect a shift to reduced services to patients is also important to avoid the potential for civil money penalties. Reduced length-of-stay measures would not be a good choice. Those measures that reflect correction of underuse—use of

---

31   72 *F.R.* 51046 (Sept 5, 2007).
32   oig.hhs.gov/fraud/docs/complianceguidance/CorporateResponsibilityFinal%209-4-07.pdf.

beta blockers after heart attack, door to balloon time in providing angioplasty, timely administration of drugs—are less problematic.

While Medicare now pays for improved hospital mortality scores, paying physicians or hospitals or giving them bonuses for killing fewer of their patients is not an ideal page one story, if characterized inappropriately. So valuation in this delicate arena may have public relations implications if the underpinnings of the financial model are made public. Worse yet are the risks from discovery requests and potential application in a lawsuit where a patient is harmed.

The likelihood that quality performance measures, particularly in combination with financial benefits to the participants, will become integral to malpractice actions is very high.[33]

6.0 Conclusion
With the highly increased attention to quality performance in health care generally, business relationships where financial value attaches to that performance are proliferating. The law establishes significant restrictions on what is legitimate to take into account in valuations that support these new relationships, but it also offers new opportunities to connect the financial implications of improved quality of care with financial consequences.

---

33 Gosfield and Reinertsen, "The 100,000 Lives Campaign: Crystallizing Standards of Care for Hospitals", *Health Affairs* (Nov. 2005), pp. 1560-1570.

Chapter 20. Physician Compensation and Financial Statement Benchmarks: Using MGMA Data

CONTENTS

Chapter 20. Physician Compensation and Financial Statement Benchmarks: Using MGMA Data

By David Fein, MBA

1.0 Introduction

Valuation of a medical practice, as with any valuation, consists of quantifying earnings and risk. The drivers of earnings and risk in a medical practice, however, are unique. There is a tremendous amount of diversity in medical practices, with over 700,000 physicians in the United States and over 470,000 working in over 40,000 group practices. There are single-specialty, multispecialty, hospital-affiliated, non-hospital-affiliated, for-profit, not-for-profit, and academic practices. Specifically, on the revenue side of a medical practice, the valuator must understand how encounters, procedures, and surgeries (physician production per RVUs) drive gross charges and billings and how the collection process (which can be complicated in a medical practice) drives gross revenue. In addition, many medical practices operate on a cash basis and pay out dollars to physician-owners before year-end earnings.

On the expenses side, a medical practice has significant physician and staff (e.g., business, front office, clinical, ancillary, contracted, and so on) costs as well as a number of unique general operating costs (e.g., medical supply, drug supply, lab, radiology and imaging, and so on). It's also very important to evaluate physician compensation in relationship to production, whereas in most businesses, the relationship between compensation and production is disregarded. A medical practice can be managed by physician owners, a hospital, a health maintenance organization (HMO) or management service organization (MSO). Medical practices also exist within a complex regulatory environment that must also be evaluated in relationship to revenue and risk.

Exhibit 1 shows some of the revenue and expense drivers in a medical practice.

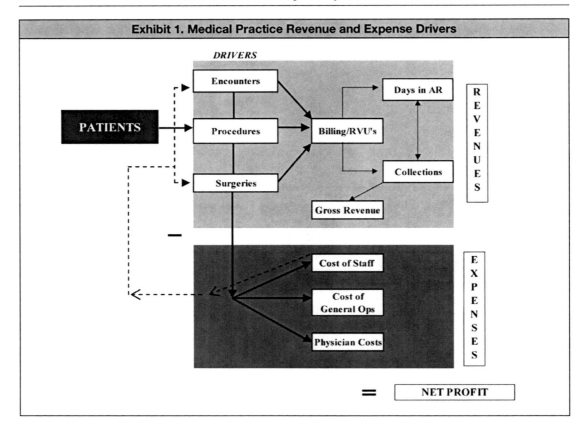

Exhibit 1. Medical Practice Revenue and Expense Drivers

To accurately value a medical practice, the valuator must understand these distinct characteristics. Medical Group Management Association's (MGMA) data provide excellent information professional valuators rely on to normalize physician compensation and benchmark financial performance. It is also important to understand that valuation of physician compensation arrangements (particularly when paid by tax-exempt hospitals) is becoming an increasing focus of the Internal Revenue Service (IRS) and the Office of Inspector General scrutiny.

Founded in 1926, MGMA has nearly 21,000 members who manage and lead 12,500 practice organizations, representing 270,000 physicians. MGMA's survey *Interactive Reports* provides the valuator with statistically robust data, as well as sophisticated, easy-to-use tools.

The MGMA is a premier source of benchmarking data, but valuators should consider other sources, as well. You can find benchmarking data from the following:

- MGMA offers a number of benchmarking tools as well as the comparative data;

- The Centers for Medicare & Medicaid Services (CMS) and state governments can provide some external data, but they may be limited;

- Some specialty groups offer data, but they also may be limited;

- Physician Compensation and Production Survey reports that can be used include:

  - ᵒ Medical Group Management Association's *Physician Compensation and Production Survey Report;*

  - ᵒ Sullivan-Cotter & Associates' *Physician Compensation and Productivity Survey Report;*

  - ᵒ Hay Group's *Physician's Compensation Survey Report;*

  - ᵒ Hospital and Healthcare Compensation Services' *Physician Salary Survey Report;*

  - ᵒ ECS Watson Wyatt's *Hospital and Health Care Management Compensation Report;*

  - ᵒ American Medical Group Association's *Medical Group Compensation & Financial Survey; and*

  - ᵒ American Medical Association's publications on physician statistics.

MGMA data are specifically useful for valuators because:

- MGMA has conducted physician practice surveys for over 50 years;

- Data are derived from group practices of all sizes, types, and specialties (with major reporting categories separately portrayed);

- The *2007 Report on Physician Compensation* observes more than 50,000 providers;

- Distinguishes private and academic physicians;

- The *2007 Cost Survey* observes more than 1,200 single- and multispecialty practices;

- Cost surveys are individualized for some of the larger specialties;

- Both tools use a census-style approach; and

- Built-in benchmarking tools are provided.

As with any data, MGMA data have limitations you should understand. One limitation is the data may not be representative of all practices. Because participation in MGMA surveys is voluntary and all practices do not complete and return the survey questionnaires, respondents represent only a sample of medical practices. It's difficult, therefore, to determine whether a sample is biased. Bias could occur if more professionally managed practices participate, with differences in region and size, with a lack of responses, and other characteristics.

It's important to use statistics correctly and understand both their strengths and weaknesses. There are a number of things to keep in mind when using statistics, including MGMA's:

- *Benjamin Disraeli* once said, *"Lies, damn lies, and statistics."* It's important to understand the data, how they were collected, what they truly represent, their strengths, limitations, and appropriate application to avoid both misusing and misinterpreting statistics.

- Understand medians versus means. Means include every data point; the median is the middle data point. Medians remove the impact of outliers and are a better representation of the midpoint than the mean.

- *Skewness.* The shape (or skewness) of sample can have a large impact on how you interpret the data. Understand not only the specific data points, but also the overall response curve, as well. The shape of the curve is represented by the standard deviation, but having a good visual picture of what this represents can be very useful.

- Exercise your judgment. Understand the limitations of the data and do not read more into them than is warranted.

- Talk to your peers. They can validate your thinking, and you can learn from them.

- Know the practice! Understand that MGMA data may not represent a particular practice due to specific characteristics of the practice.

- Consult other sources of information, such as specialty societies.

2.0 The Three Ps of Benchmarking

Before delving into the specifics of MGMA data, it's important to have a general feel for the kind of data the survey represents. MGMA data are best understood as a function of the three "Ps" of medical practice benchmarking. The three "Ps" are based on what the survey is observing or the "unit of observation." MGMA develops its survey products by sending out questionnaires to its members and asks questions about various aspects of physician and medical practice performance. The three major areas the surveys observe are the physician, the practice, and the procedure. MGMA produces surveys covering each of these areas.

The first "P" is for "physician." Individual physicians are the focus of MGMA's *Physician Compensation and Production Survey*, which has over 50,000 responses from more than 100 specialties. This survey includes compensation and productivity (compensation; relative value units, or RVUs; collections; gross charges; and so on). This survey, in other words, revolves around what the physician is paid and what he or she produces. As a valuator, it's crucial to understand the relationship between physician compensation and production and to normalize physician compensation in relationship to both of these metrics.

The second "P" represents the practice. Based on the entire practice, the MGMA *Cost Survey* measures more than 700 practicewide variables, such as revenue, costs, staffing, and accounts receivable (AR).

The third "P" is procedures. This survey is based on measuring individual procedures. Physicians can perform more than 10,000 procedures, and each has a unique current procedural terminology (CPT) code. Think of procedures as the unique (mostly billable) tasks a physician performs when he or she sees a patient. The CPT procedure codes are the basis for all medical practice billing and also are the basis for computing physician work RVUs (more information RVUs to follow). Although you can perform a great number of complex analyses using procedure-based data, one of the most useful is understanding how physicians are coding (i.e., what CPT code they assign) office visits (CPT codes 99201 to 99205 and 99211 to 99215). Although this advanced benchmarking topic will not be covered in this chapter, it's a very useful analysis we encourage valuators to understand. The survey pertaining to procedures is the MGMA *Coding Profiles Sourcebook*.

The data we are going to examine in this chapter come from two following MGMA interactive reports:

- *Physician Compensation and Production Survey*; and

- *Cost Survey.*

This chapter will cover both compensation normalization and financial statement benchmarking, and how each of the interactive reports data and tools can be used effectively. The chapter is organized around some of the important steps in the valuation process and concepts unique to medical practice valuation. As these topics are discussed, I will explain more about the available data and relevant tools that provide the valuator a strong quantitative approach.

3.0 Benchmarking Basics

It's important to understand benchmarking basics to best use the MGMA interactive reports. Benchmarking means comparing the data from a practice to either internal or external standards. Internal standards can be based on either comparing to physicians within the practice or comparing to data from a different period (i.e., this quarter versus last quarter). This chapter will focus on external benchmarking using the MGMA data as the external standard.

3.1 Benchmarking Checklist

To understand the general concepts and steps in benchmarking, let's review the benchmarking checklist from Consulting Training Institute's "Health Care Boot Camp." This checklist applies to both the interactive reports as well as the printed reports. The checklist takes you step by step through the benchmarking process:

Step 1: Determine what you are benchmarking (i.e., RVUs, compensation, A/R aging, cost per full-time equivalent—FTE—and so on).

Step 2: Determine what the benchmark is (i.e., the specific number you are benchmarking against). For example, median RVUs for family practice would be 4,073).

Step 3: What is the practice data? (If you are benchmarking RVUs, determine the physician's RVU data.)

Step 4: Determine how you compare to the benchmark.

- Is your performance better than the benchmark? ❑ Yes ❑ No

- Is your performance in an acceptable range? ❑ Yes ❑ No

- Is your performance worse than the benchmark? ❑ Yes ❑ No

- Is there any action we need to take? ❑ Yes ❑ No (This step can be ignored for valuation.)

Step 5: If the benchmark is not acceptable, estimate the economic benefit derived if the benchmark were achievable and quantify best-case potential. (This is a very valuable step for valuators to take.)

Note: Steps 6 to 9 can be ignored for valuation but are included to provide the full benchmarking process.

Step 6: Assess potential changes if action needs to be taken.

Step 7: Quantify potential cost and estimate potential cost benefit of action and changes.

Step 8: What are the action items and responsibilities for the above action?

Step 9: How often will you review this benchmark and what progress do you expect?

Exhibit 2 is a diagram of the full benchmarking process. For the purposes of valuation, focus on the "assess" phase of the process. If you consult with medical practices as well, you can provide a tremendous service to your clients by understanding and using the full benchmarking process.

3.2 How MGMA Interactive Reports Can Help You Benchmark More Precisely

One important concept to understand is the difference between benchmarking against medians and using rankings. Medians (also called the 50th percentile) represent the midpoint of the data and are commonly used as the key measure to benchmark against. For example, the median compensation for a family practice physician (without obstetrics) is $164,000. If the physician you are benchmarking is making $185,000, you would determine the difference as a percentage and use that as your benchmark. In this case, $185,000 is 13% greater than the median. If you have access to the entire curve of responses as you do in the interactive reports, however, you can quickly determine that $185,000 represents the 64th percentile. In other words, the compensation of $185,000 is larger than 64% of what the survey respondents reported as their compensation.

Determining that your physician ranks at the 64th percentile is more precise than saying their compensation is 13% greater than the median.

Since response curves can have small or large standard deviations (i.e., be steep or shallow), it's difficult to quickly determine whether the magnitude of the variation from the median is significant. MGMA interactive reports allow you to easily understand the shape of the response curve and exactly where your data is ranked.

Exhibit 3 shows two different response curves: one with a standard deviation of one and the other with a standard deviation of two. You can see that the number "2" on

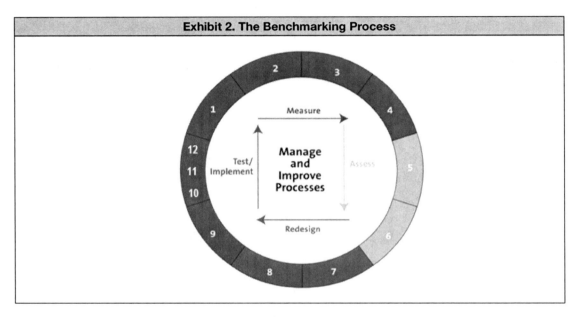

Exhibit 2. The Benchmarking Process

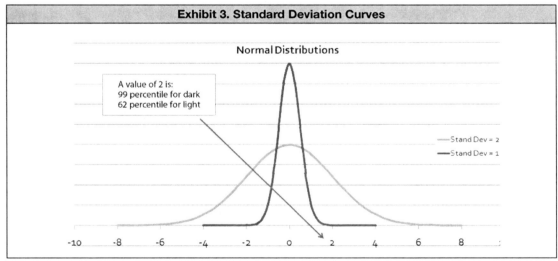

Exhibit 3. Standard Deviation Curves

the x-axis represents the 99th percentile for the curve with a standard deviation of one and the 62nd percentile for the curve with a standard deviation of two. The numerical difference from the median of zero is two for both curves, but this really represents vastly different situations. For the steeper curve, the data point 2 is extremely high, but for the flatter curve, the data point represents being slightly higher than the median.

3.3 Normalizing Physician Compensation

MGMA's *Physician Compensation and Production Survey* interactive report provides a wide variety of data and tools to assist you in normalizing physician compensation for a medical practice valuation. The goal in normalizing physician compensation is to determine what is fair compensation for all owner-shareholder physicians and make an adjustment (normalize) for the excess compensation. For example, three owner physicians are in a family practice with each of them receiving more than fair compensation, you would make the following adjustments as shown in Exhibit 4.

This example is simplified to show the concept of making adjustments for each physician based on fair compensation. However, in reality, each physician's "fair compensation" will probably be different based on a number of factors, including years in specialty, production, and so on.

Your task in normalizing compensation is to develop a practicewide compensation adjustment that will normalize the physician's compensation; it represents what owners would be earning if they were paid as nonowners. This means looking at each owner in a practice and determining the fair market compensation for each of them. To accomplish this, you will have to look at each individual physician, taking into account all the various conditions that impact fair compensation, including specialty, years in the practice, production levels, and so on.

It is possible to develop a practicewide compensation adjustment by using metrics, such as overall compensation, as a percentage of revenue or average compensation on

Exhibit 4. Compensation Normalization Example			
	Actual Compensation	Fair Compensation	Adjustment
Physician 1	190,000	174,000	16,000
Physician 2	209,000	174,000	35,000
Physician 3	234,000	174,000	60,000
Total	633,000	522,000	111,000

a per-FTE basis. Using these practicewide adjustments, however, is just an approximation and not nearly as accurate as evaluating each physician and making individual adjustments. It is recommended you develop normalization adjustments for each individual physician.

To understand physician compensation, you have to understand physician production. To understand production, you have to understand specific production metrics, including:

- **RVUs:** relative value units, the value the Centers for Medicare and Medicaid Services (CMS) assigns to physician procedures;

- **Encounters:** number of patients the physician treats;

- **Procedures:** number of procedures the physician performs;

- **Gross charges:** how much the physician bills;

- **Collections:** how much the physician actually collects; and

- **Hours worked:** how many hours per week the physician works.

Many valuators feel RVUs are the most appropriate measure for gauging production, but collections and charges are commonly used, as well. When using something other than RVUs as a productivity measure, you should compare RVU productivity to the measure being used. If both measures lead to the same conclusion about productivity, you can be more confident in the productivity measure. On the other hand, if RVUs provide a different productivity benchmark, you need to understand why. Collections can be used as a productivity measure, but a practice's billing procedures, payer mix, and other variables make it more challenging to isolate physician production from collections data. Encounters are a very weak indicator of production because they measure how many patients a doctor sees, rather than how much work they are performing. Therefore, attempting to gauge the amount of "work" a physician does based on encounters is not feasible. Gross charges can be a useful measure of productivity, but because there is wide variation in fee schedules, it's once again difficult to isolate physician productivity from the data.

The relationship between compensation and production is an area where medical practice valuation is significantly different from general business valuation. In general business valuation, there is no standardized method to gauge "productivity," therefore, compensation is analyzed without regard to productivity. An easy way to think about this is to consider physician compensation as based on the amount of work performed. The more work a physician performs, the more he or she is compensated. A physician who is making 50% more than another physician may be fairly compensated if he or she is working twice as hard (however you measure "work"). That is why only looking at compensation data without considering production data is not recommended for normalizing physician compensation.

3.4 What Is an RVU?

Now that we understand that an RVU is a good measure of physician productivity, let us review what an RVU is and how it is calculated. There are a number of complexities in understanding RVUs, but this chapter will provide only the basics so you can use them as productivity measures to normalize physician compensation. For a fuller understanding of RVUs, we recommend *RVUs: Applications for Medical Practice Success*, 2nd edition, by Kathryn P. Glass, MBA, MSHA, PMP, available through the MGMA store.

CMS developed RVUs to provide a standardized method to measure the work performed by physicians, as well as provide the basis to reimburse physicians. RVUs were constructed to represent the relative intensity of resources required to care for a broad range of diseases and conditions and are associated with CPT codes. An RVU contains three components: malpractice, physician work (work RVU, or wRVU), and practice expenses. For our purposes, we will only use wRVUs.

3.5 How Are RVUs and CPT Codes Related?

When a physician provides any type of service to a patient, he or she must provide a billing code associated with that service to get paid. There are over 10,000 different CPT codes representing every possible service a physician can provide, from an office visit to brain surgery. Each CPT code has a corresponding RVU assigned to it; these values are the basis to determine how many RVUs a physician produces in a period of time.

Let's look at an example to see how this works. The CPT for a new patient office visit is 99201; the associated work RVU is 0.45. The CPT code for removal of a brain lesion (brain surgery) is 61510; the associated work RVU is 28.41. This makes sense, because brain surgery requires more "work" from a physician than an office visit. The beauty of the RVU system is that for most specialties, it is a very reliable indicator of how hard a physician is working. However, if you are working with radiologists, anesthesiologists, pathologists, or emergency room physicians, you will need to find a different productivity measure than RVUs, because they do not accurately reflect the amount of work physicians in these specialties are performing.

For our neurosurgeon, let us take a very simple example calculating his RVU production for the year. We will assume he does only two procedures (new patient office visits and brain surgery). We need to determine how many of each of these procedures he performs, and then calculate his total work RVU number for the year, shown in Exhibit 5.

Exhibit 5. Calculating RVU Production				
CPT Code	Frequency	Description	RVU Value	Total
99201	500	New patient office visit	0.45	225
61510	100	Removal of brain lesion	28.41	2,841
Total				3,066

Although this is a simplified example, the concept is exactly how you would calculate a physician's total wRVUs for a period of time. Take every procedure (i.e., CPT code) he or she performs, how many times he or she performs the procedure, and multiply that frequency by the wRVU value. Do this for every procedure, add them up, and you have calculated the total number of work RVUs for the physician.

Remember, the MGMA data is based on annual data, so make sure your data also represents a full year. The MGMA data also represents a full-time physician, so make sure you normalize your physician data to one FTE. For example, if you have a physician that is working half-time (i.e., 0.5 FTE), you will need to multiply his or her wRVUs by two, to calculate a one FTE equivalent.

Luckily, most practice management systems have a built-in report that computes RVUs; just ask someone in the practice for the wRVU report. Make certain you specify "work RVUs" or you may get total RVUs, making your benchmarks meaningless because you will be comparing apples to oranges.

4.0 Using the Physician Compensation and Production Survey Interactive Report

The Physician Compensation and Production Survey interactive report provides access to both data and tools to assist you in developing reasonable and defendable normalization adjustments for physician compensation. It also offers a wealth of data on more than 100 specialties and breaks the data down into a number of categories, including:

- By all providers;

- Group type;

- Region of the country;

- Method of compensation; and

- Ownership.

The metrics the survey reports on are in Exhibit 6.

The interactive report also includes data based on individual characteristics:

- Specialty;

- Years of experience;

- Gender; and

- Partner or shareholder status.

And organizational characteristics:

- Ownership;

- Geographic location;

- Percentage of capitation contracts;

- Compensation method; and

- Group type.

Exhibit 6. Metrics of Survey Reports	
Compensation	Total compensation Retirement contribution
Productivity	Collections Gross charges Work RVUs Total RVUs Encounters Surgical cases Hours worked per week Weeks worked per year
Relationship of compensation to productivity	Compensation per $ of collections Compensation per $ of gross charges Compensation per work RVU Compensation per total RVU

The interactive reports will be used for two basic tasks: opening tables and using the built-in benchmarking tools. When the interactive report starts, you'll see this startup dialog box in Exhibit 7.

From this dialog, you can perform all the major functions of the interactive report. We encourage you to read the MGMA documentation, particularly the Survey Data Definitions, for a clear understanding of each metric in the survey. When you are collecting data from a practice, it is crucial you explain exactly what you are looking for.

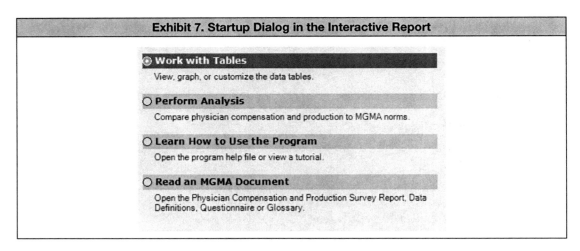

Exhibit 7. Startup Dialog in the Interactive Report

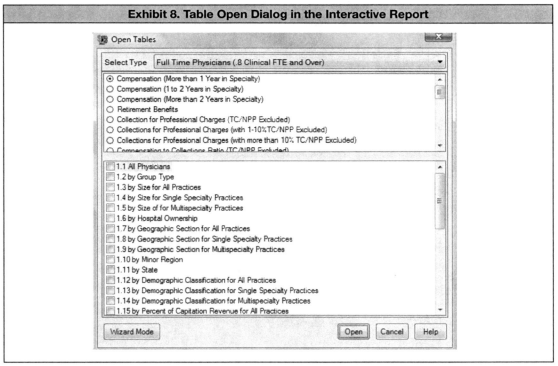

Exhibit 8. Table Open Dialog in the Interactive Report

Otherwise, you may be provided data that does not match the MGMA definitions and your comparisons will be meaningless. For example, if you are seeking encounters, be sure the practice is not providing procedures.

To open a table, select the "Work with Tables" option or the "Open Tables" toolbar button from the main menu. You will see the following dialog (advanced mode is shown) in Exhibit 8.

This dialog allows you to open any table on the interactive report. Note that for every metric (compensation, retirement benefits, collections, and so on), a number of tables are available to view. Select the metric, then choose the table to open. For example, the Compensation for All Physicians appears in Exhibit 9.

Specialties are displayed on the left, with statistics shown in the columns. Be aware the interactive report will not display data unless there are at least 10 providers (physicians) and three unique practices. If you see blanks or stars in the data, it means there are insufficient physicians or practices.

Since the interactive report contains every percentile from 10 to 90, you can customize the display to show more of the data. This is helpful to get a feel for what the entire MGMA curve looks like. The same table expanded to show deciles appears as below in Exhibit 10.

You can set the program defaults to always show more data so you do not have to customize each table. The interactive report allows you to open many tables at the same time to view multiple metrics or slices of the same table. All of the tables can be easily exported to Excel for custom analysis and charting. You also can chart any table by selecting the chart toolbar buttons.

Exhibit 9. Compensation for All Physicians

Specialty	Providers	Practices	Mean	Std. Dev.	25th %tile	Median	75th %tile	90th %tile
Allergy/Immunology	175	85	$295,873	$136,255	$208,263	$267,688	$340,967	$539,160
Anesthesiology	3,903	184						
Anesthesiology: Pain Management	191	62						
Anesthesiology: Pediatric	105	10						
Cardiology: Electrophysiology	203	96						
Cardiology: Invasive	528	139						
Cardiology: Inv-Intvl	627	161						
Cardiology: Noninvasive	516	138						
Critical Care: Intensivist	97	20						
Dentistry	58	18						

Exhibit 10. Table Expanded to Show Deciles

Specialty	Providers	Practices	Mean	Std. Dev.	10th %tile	20th %tile	30th %tile	40th %tile	Median	60th %tile	70th %tile	80th %tile	90th %tile
Allergy/Immunology	175	85	$295,873	$136,255	$161,674	$196,748	$218,262	$239,055	$267,688	$284,239	$320,976	$374,534	$539,160
Anesthesiology	3,903	184											
Anesthesiology: Pain Management	191	62											
Anesthesiology: Pediatric	105	10											
Cardiology: Electrophysiology	203	96											
Cardiology: Invasive	526	139											
Cardiology: Inv-Intvl	627	161											
Cardiology: Noninvasive	516	138											
Critical Care: Intensivist	97	20											
Dentistry	58	18											
Dermatology	361	128											

5.0 Benchmarking Tools in the Physician Compensation and Production Survey Interactive Report

One of the most important functions of the Physician Compensation and Production Survey interactive report is the seven built-in benchmarking tools, which allow you to input data from a practice and have the benchmarks performed automatically.

5.1 Physician Benchmarking Tool

This comprehensive benchmarking tool provides both internal (i.e., physician against physician) and external (i.e., against MGMA norms) benchmarking. You can input data monthly, quarterly, or annually. It provides a ranking report both in table and graphic formats. You can automatically load data from a practice's IT system into this tool, without having to manually input data. This tool also produces a number of tables and charts, including the ranking report below in Exhibit 11, which you can export to Excel for custom analysis. Note each physician is ranked for each metric benchmarked; the rankings show exactly where the physician lies on the curve.

5.2 Physician Compensation Analysis Tool

This tool offers a quick method to determine compensation based on data from a number of tables. The output (see Exhibit 12) is a weighted average compensation that allows you to change the default weights and recalculate the weighted average compensation level.

5.3 Physician Compensation Estimator Tool

This tool provides a predictive statistical model based on the most significant compensation drivers. *Note: This tool should not be used to normalize physician compensation.*

5.4 Physician Pay-to-Production Plotter Tool

This is the single best (and statistically valid) method to get a comprehensive picture of how physician compensation and production (RVUs and collections) are related. You can input the compensation and production values for your physicians, and they are plotted against the MGMA data. This is the only tool that allows you to see individual MGMA responses rather than statistics based on the responses. The Pay-to-Production Plotter Tool offers a significant advantage to using compensation and production tables

Exhibit 11. Ranking Report Section of the Physician Benchmarking Tool

	MGMA	Tyler Jones	Michael Cane	Sample Practice
	Physician Ranking			
	Compared to MGMA Data for Specialty Cardiology: Invasive			
Compensation	Median	3 to 7 years in Specialty	8 to 17 years in Specialty	Practice Average
Physician Compensation	$431,533	<10th %tile	68th %tile	30th %tile
Physician Retirement Benefits	$29,500	18th %tile	70th %tile	32nd %tile
Production				
Physician Collection for Professional Charges	$629,195	42nd %tile	45th %tile	42nd %tile
Physician Gross Charges	$1,497,479	13th %tile	58th %tile	34th %tile
Physician Total RVUs	18,419	12th %tile	31st %tile	20th %tile
Physician Work RVUs	9,256	27th %tile	48th %tile	38th %tile
Physician Ambulatory Encounters	2,257	31st %tile	43rd %tile	36th %tile
Physician Hospital Encounters	1,264	34th %tile	52nd %tile	43rd %tile
Physician Surgery/Anesthesia Cases	82	61st %tile	82nd %tile	71st %tile
Physician Clinical Hours Worked per Week	40	54th %tile	23th %tile	53rd %tile
Physician Weeks Worked per Year	46	11th %tile	11th %tile	11th %tile

Exhibit 12. Compensation Analysis Tool

Data Source	Compensation	Weight
Physician Compensation by All Physicians		
All Physicians	187,393	1
By Years in Specialty:		
1 to 2 years	-	0
By Method of Compensation:		
1-99% prod less allocated overhead	-	0
By Group Type:		
Single Specialty	187,396	1
By Geographic Location:		
Midwest	251,518	1
By Gender:		
Male	201,148	1
By Size of Practice:		
10 FTE or fewer	212,785	1
Weighted Average Compensation Level	$ 208,048	

to correlate compensation and production, because the data is based on a sample population that responded to both the compensation and production questions. In this case, RVUs are along the x-axis, with compensation along the y-axis. You will see your physicians plotted as diamonds against the MGMA data (circles) in Exhibit 13.

5.5 Physician Dashboard Report Tool

This tool provides a 50,000-foot view of physician compensation and production in a dashboard format. The dashboard gauges provide rankings for compensation, charges, collections, RVUs, ambulatory encounters, and hospital encounters. Because the dashboard presents the data in an easy-to-understand, green-yellow-red gauge format, the "benchmarking story" the gauges tell can be communicated to those who do not understand statistics, benchmarks, or MGMA data. Exhibit 14 shows the dashboard.

5.6 Management Summary Analysis Tables Tool

Provides summary tables for the management data that are included in an expanded version of the *Physician Compensation* and Production Survey interactive report.

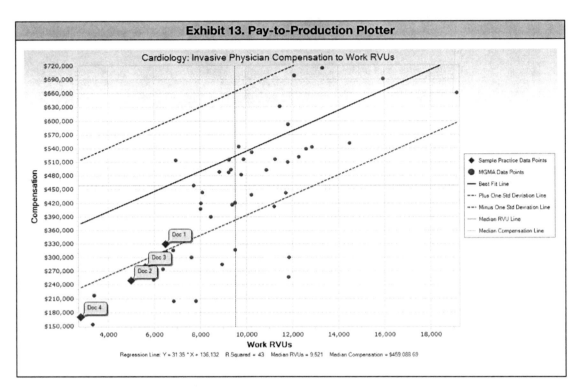

Exhibit 13. Pay-to-Production Plotter

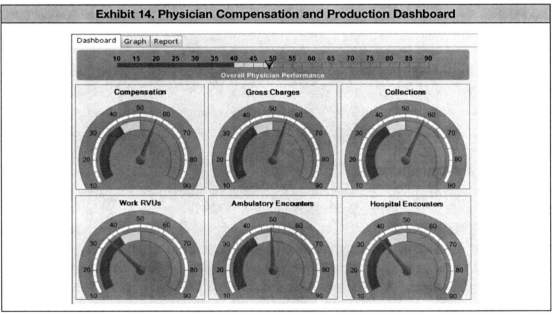

Exhibit 14. Physician Compensation and Production Dashboard

6.0 Financial Statement Benchmarking

In the normal course of valuing a company, a financial statement benchmark often is performed to better understand how the company performs against industry norms. Performing this analysis assists the valuator in assessing ongoing cash flows, company risk, and sustainable growth. One of the challenges of financial statement benchmarking, however, is there is no direct correlation between the results of benchmarking and drivers of business value (cash flows, risk, and growth). In other words, no accepted valuation standard allows the valuator to apply a formula or method to translate the results of financial statement benchmarking into something directly related to company value. Financial statement benchmarking will provide you a better understanding of the practice's financial and operational dynamics and give you a quantitative approach to assist you in developing and defending your assumptions relating to value drivers.

6.1 Finding Financial Statement Benchmarking Data

In looking for financial statement benchmarking data for medical practices, the industry has relied on sources such as Risk Management Association (RMA), Integra, and other general sources of benchmarking data. Although this general data provide some insight into how a medical practice is performing, a medical practice is substantially different from a general business. For example, in RMA data, you'll find common size statements and general financial ratios for physician practices, but the underlying financial and operational drivers that are unique to a medical practice are ignored.

This is where the MGMA provides a far superior set of data and tools to benchmark a medical practice. RMA provides approximately 45 metrics (i.e., data points); MGMA's *Cost Survey* has more than 700.

6.2 Medical Practice Benchmarking Basics

To understand financial statement benchmarking for medical practices, you have to understand some of the value drivers in the practice. To understand these drivers, you have to understand the fundamental categories of group practice metrics including:

- **AR:** Accounts receivable should be broken down per physician, as well as a percentage of total medical revenue. You should also review a standard AR aging.

- **Gross charges by payer type:** A practice's revenue can be significantly impacted by its payer mix (i.e., insurance companies).

- **Charges and revenue:** Physician charges and revenue should be broken down per physician and as a percentage of total medical revenue.

- **Operating cost:** General operating costs should be broken down per physician, as well as a percentage of total medical revenue.

- **Provider cost:** Provider costs (i.e., cost for anyone providing billable services, including physicians, physician's assistants, registered nurses, and so on) should be broken down per physician, per provider along with as a percentage of total medical revenue.

- **Staff FTE levels and costs:** Staff costs should be broken down by FTE (i.e., how many FTEs per position) and their associated costs. The data should be also broken down on a per-FTE basis as well as a percentage of total medical revenue.

- **Procedures:** Procedures are broken down on a per-FTE basis.

This data, as you can see, delve deeper into the dynamics of value in a medical practice than a general data set such as RMA. As with the *Physician Compensation* data, it's important to understand the exact definition of each metric you use to obtain and interpret the data correctly. The *Cost Interactive Report* includes a definitions document we strongly encourage you read to be sure you are collecting data based on the same definitions that MGMA uses to collect it. There also are a number of complex formulas that go into calculating some of these metrics. By using the benchmarking tools in the interactive report, you are assured the calculations are performed correctly.

7.0 Using the Cost Survey Interactive Report
The Cost Survey interactive report is based on observing organizations, not individuals. The data is presented in 30 tables that cover the 700-plus metrics. Each "slice" of data contains the exact same 30 tables. The 30 tables include the following:

7.1 Staffing and Practice Data
- AR data, collection percentages, and financial ratios;

- Breakout of total gross charges by type of payer;

- Staffing, RVUs, patients, procedures, and square footage per FTE physician;

- Charges and revenue per FTE physician;

- Operating cost per FTE physician;

- Provider cost per FTE physician;

- Net income or loss per FTE physician;

- Charges and revenue as a percentage of total medical revenue;

- Operating cost as a percentage of total medical revenue;

- Provider cost as a percentage of total medical revenue;

- Net income or loss as a percentage of total medical revenue;

- Staffing, RVUs, patients, procedures, and square footage per FTE provider;

- Charges, revenue, and cost per FTE provider;

- Staffing, RVUs, patients, and procedures per 10,000 square foot;

- Charges, revenue, and cost per square feet;

- Staffing, patients, procedures and square footage per 10,000 total RVU;

- Charges, revenue, and cost per total RVUs;

- Staffing, patients, procedures, and square footage per 10,000 wRVU;

- Charges, revenue, and cost per wRVUs;

- Staffing, patients, procedures, and square footage per 10,000 patients;

- Charges, revenue, and cost per patient;

- Activity charges to total gross charges ratios;

- Medical procedure data (inside the practice);

- Medical procedure data (outside the practice);

- Surgery and anesthesia procedure data (inside the practice);

- Surgery and anesthesia procedure data (outside the practice);

- Clinical laboratory and pathology procedure data;

- Diagnostic radiology and imaging procedure data; and

- Nonprocedural gross charge data.

The data is broken down by:

- Per FTE physician;

- Per FTE provider;

- Expense as a percentage of total medical revenue;

- Per square foot;

- Per total RVU;

- Per wRVU; and

- Per patient.

The key indicators for medical group are included in Exhibit 15.

Depending on the nature of the engagement, you may have to understand and review one or more of these areas. The interactive report provides a robust benchmarking tool that allows you to quickly and easily perform a financial and operational benchmark.

Exhibit 15. Key Indicators for Medical Group Practices	
Financial	**Revenue** - Medical revenue, ancillaries, other revenue **Expense** - Support staff, general operating and provider expense
Operational	**Staffing** **Process efficiency and quality** **Resource utilization** **Contracting** **Relationship management** – referrals/marketing
Clinical	**Profile** **Quality** – outcomes, adverse events **Patient satisfaction** **Compliance**
Individual	**Productivity** – work effort **Income/Cost** **Clinical Profile** – quality, procedure mix **Job Performance**
Environmental	**Population** **Other Medical Groups** – partners/competitors **Payer Market** **Hospital Market** **Vendors**

The two basic tasks you will use the interactive report for are opening tables and using the built-in benchmarking tools. When the interactive report begins, you'll see the startup dialog box in Exhibit 16.

To open a table, select the "Work with Tables" option or the "Open Tables" toolbar button from the main menu. You will see the dialog (advanced mode is shown) in Exhibit 17.

The interactive report consists of both multispecialty and single-specialty tables. In each of these categories, you may select from a number of different data "slices," including

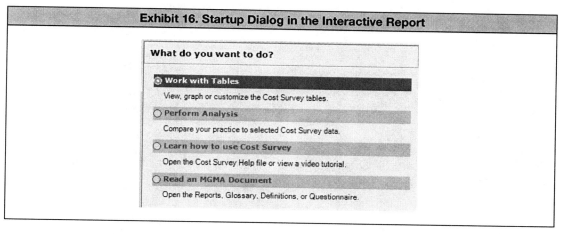

Exhibit 16. Startup Dialog in the Interactive Report

What do you want to do?

Work with Tables
View, graph or customize the Cost Survey tables.

○ **Perform Analysis**
Compare your practice to selected Cost Survey data.

○ **Learn how to use Cost Survey**
Open the Cost Survey Help file or view a video tutorial.

○ **Read an MGMA Document**
Open the Reports, Glossary, Definitions, or Questionnaire.

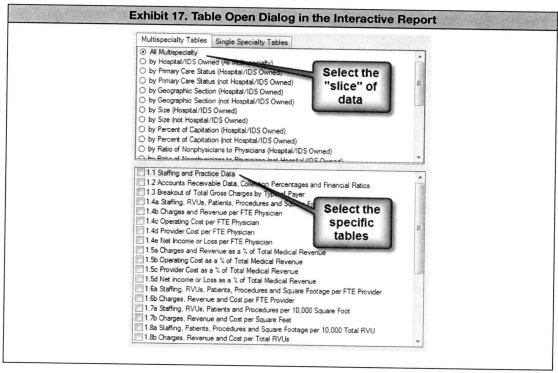

Exhibit 17. Table Open Dialog in the Interactive Report

Multispecialty Tables | Single Specialty Tables

⊙ All Multispecialty
○ by Hospital/IDS Owned (All Multispecialty)
○ by Primary Care Status (Hospital/IDS Owned)
○ by Primary Care Status (not Hospital/IDS Owned)
○ by Geographic Section (Hospital/IDS Owned)
○ by Geographic Section (not Hospital/IDS Owned)
○ by Size (Hospital/IDS Owned)
○ by Size (not Hospital/IDS Owned)
○ by Percent of Capitation (Hospital/IDS Owned)
○ by Percent of Capitation (not Hospital/IDS Owned)
○ by Ratio of Nonphysicians to Physicians (Hospital/IDS Owned)
○ by Ratio of Nonphysicians to Physicians (not Hospital/IDS Owned)

Select the "slice" of data

☐ 1.1 Staffing and Practice Data
☐ 1.2 Accounts Receivable Data, Collection Percentages and Financial Ratios
☐ 1.3 Breakout of Total Gross Charges by Type of Payer
☐ 1.4a Staffing, RVUs, Patients, Procedures and Square Footage
☐ 1.4b Charges and Revenue per FTE Physician
☐ 1.4c Operating Cost per FTE Physician
☐ 1.4d Provider Cost per FTE Physician
☐ 1.4e Net Income or Loss per FTE Physician
☐ 1.5a Charges and Revenue as a % of Total Medical Revenue
☐ 1.5b Operating Cost as a % of Total Medical Revenue
☐ 1.5c Provider Cost as a % of Total Medical Revenue
☐ 1.5d Net Income or Loss as a % of Total Medical Revenue
☐ 1.6a Staffing, RVUs, Patients, Procedures and Square Footage per FTE Provider
☐ 1.6b Charges, Revenue and Cost per FTE Provider
☐ 1.7a Staffing, RVUs, Patients and Procedures per 10,000 Square Foot
☐ 1.7b Charges, Revenue and Cost per Square Feet
☐ 1.8a Staffing, Patients, Procedures and Square Footage per 10,000 Total RVU
☐ 1.8b Charges, Revenue and Cost per Total RVUs

Select the specific tables

Exhibit 18. Table 1.1

Staffing and Practice Data	Practice Type							
	All Multispecialty							
	Count	Mean	Std. Dev.	10th %tile	25th %tile	Median	75th %tile	90th %tile
Total provider FTE	282	69.76	86.47	9.45	18.37	45.51	89.79	160.93
Total physician FTE	325	52.90						
Total nonphysician provider FTE	283	13.95						
Total support staff FTE	325	257.65						
Number of branch clinics	315	8.95						
Square footage of all facilities	279	110,946						

Exhibit 19. Table 1.1 Expanded to Show Deciles

Staffing and Practice Data	Practice Type											
	All Multispecialty											
	Count	Mean	Std. Dev.	10th %tile	20th %tile	30th %tile	40th %tile	Median	60th %tile	70th %tile	80th %tile	90th %tile
Total provider FTE	282	69.76	86.47	9.45	15.84	21.95	29.12	45.51	55.48	71.42	102.78	160.93
Total physician FTE	325	52.90										
Total nonphysician provider FTE	283	13.95										
Total support staff FTE	325	257.65										
Number of branch clinics	315	8.95										
Square footage of all facilities	279	110,946										

all, hospital-owned, geographic section, and so on. The next step is to pick one of the tables to display the specific data you are interested in. For all multispecialty, staffing, and practice data, the table appears in Exhibit 18.

Metrics are on the left; statistics are shown in the columns. As with the *Physician Compensation and Production Survey* interactive report, the program will not show data unless there are at least 10 providers (physicians) and three unique practices. If there are blanks or stars in the data, it means there are insufficient physicians or practices.

Since the interactive report contains every percentile from 10 to 90, you can customize the display to show more data. This is helpful to get a feel for what the entire MGMA curve looks like. The same table expanded to show deciles appears in Exhibit 19.

In the Cost Survey interactive report, data is available for multispecialty and 18 single-specialty practices. If your specialty is not provided, you will either have to use the multispecialty data or select a single specialty you feel is representative of the specialty.

8.0 Benchmarking Tools in the Cost Survey Interactive Report

One of the most important functions of the Cost Survey interactive report is three built-in benchmarking tools, which allow you to input practice data and have the benchmarks performed automatically.

8.1 Dashboard Report Tool

This tool provides a 50,000-foot view of a medical group in a dashboard format. The dashboard gauges provide rankings for total medical revenue per physician, total AR per physician, total operating cost per physician, total general operating cost per physician, total support staff cost per physician, and total medical revenue after operating cost per physician. Once again, because the dashboard presents the data in an easy-to-understand, green-yellow-red gauge format, the "benchmarking story" can be communicated to those who do not understand statistics, benchmarks, or MGMA data. The following screen shows the dashboard in Exhibit 20.

8.2 Practice Performance Report Tool

This is the tool you want to use if you are a valuator. Once data is collected, you can perform a comprehensive income statement, staffing, AR, and ratio analysis in under an hour. As with all benchmarking tools, select the areas you want to benchmark and ignore the rest. Unless you have the background to interpret staffing data (FTEs and costs), stick with the other sections of this tool. Staffing levels and costs, however, are a significant driver of value in a medical practice; we encourage you to learn how this area impacts both financial performance and value. This tool is Excel-based, so you can export the entire tool to perform detailed analysis, roll-ups, and other custom analyses. It is also possible to prepopulate the tool with data, so you do not have to type in each engagement's data. Exhibit 21 shows the first input screen from the tool.

Once you input data, the tool performs the rest of the calculations and benchmarks, including a ranking report. The following schedule shows the revenue and cost as a

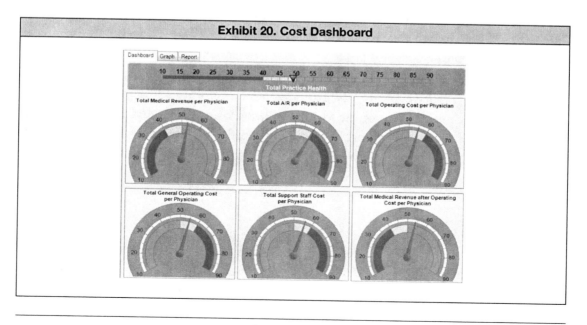

Exhibit 20. Cost Dashboard

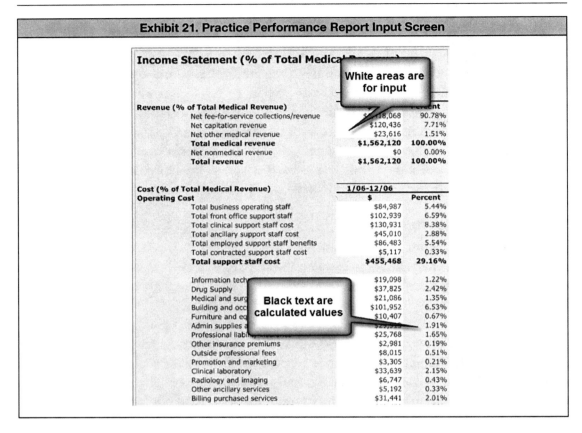

Exhibit 21. Practice Performance Report Input Screen

percentage of total medical revenue, which is calculated based on the input screen. The last three columns show MGMA data, the differences between the practice and MGMA data, and the ranking of the practice. The ranking gives you a precise picture of how your practice compares to MGMA data, shown in Exhibit 22.

8.3 Advanced Benchmarking Report Tool

The practice performance report provides an easy-to-input financial statement format benchmark report. However, it only provides benchmarking for a subset of the *Cost Survey*'s 700-plus metrics. If you need to benchmark anything that is not contained in the practice performance report, use the advanced benchmarking report. This tool will allow you to customize the report for exactly the metrics you are interested in benchmarking.

9.0 Summary

Since medical practices are unique, using MGMA and other medically based data will help you understand the unique drivers of value in a medical practice. This chapter was developed as a brief look at using MGMA data for valuing a medical practice; it does

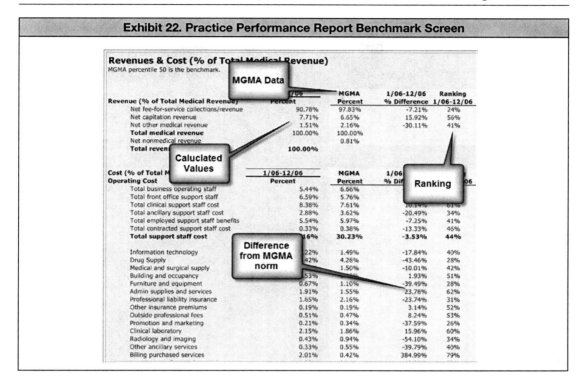

Exhibit 22. Practice Performance Report Benchmark Screen

not provide a comprehensive discussion of these topics. If you are interested in getting more detailed information, we encourage you to check out the following resources:

- Join the MGMA (www.mgma.com);

- MGMA *Physicians Compensation and Production Survey* interactive report;

- MGMA *Cost Survey* interactive report;

- *RVUs: Applications for Medical Practice Success*, 2nd edition by Kathryn P. Glass, MBA, MSHA, PMP;

- *Benchmarking Success: The Essential Guide for Group Practices* by Gregory Feltenberger, MBA, FACMPE, FACHE, CPHIMS, and David Gans, MHSA, FACMPE;

- Arrange a custom training session with ValuSource on these topics. You can reach ValuSource at 800-825-8763 or email sales@valusourcesoftware.com or visit its Web site at www.valusourcesoftware.com;

- Participate in the Consulting Training Institute's (CTI) five-day healthcare boot camp (www.nacva.com); and

- Read books and take webinars on these topics.

Thanks

I would like to thank the MGMA, Laurie Foote, Bill Sipes, and Robert Cimasi for their time, numerous conversations, and outstanding comments and suggestions regarding material in this chapter.

Chapter 21. Benchmarking Practice Performance

CONTENTS

Chapter 21. Benchmarking Practice Performance

By Gregory S. Feltenberger, MBA, FACMPE, FACHE, CPHIMS,
and David N. Gans, MSHA, FACMPE

1.0 Introduction

Why benchmark? There are many reasons for benchmarking, and most are related to a specific purpose (usually improvement). For example, a practice may want to determine how the billing office performance or physician productivity compares to other like practices. But in general, practices benchmark to gain a deeper understanding of where they are, where they want to go, and how to get there.

However, benchmarking when used in conjunction with trending—comparison to a standard over time—can be a powerful tool for assessing the past and present. And although the past cannot predict the future, it can be used to "suggest" the future. Therefore, benchmarking and trending can provide numerical insights into the past, present, and future "value" of an organization. And since the current state of healthcare—constantly changing and growing in complexity—dictates more elaborate and accurate methods of measurement, analysis, comparison, and improvement, long-term success has become directly related to a practice's ability to identify, predict, and adjust for changes.

Two key principles of benchmarking are: (1) If you don't measure it, you can't manage it and (2) if you don't value it, you won't change it. These principles have been applied to nonhealthcare industries for many years and are ideally suited for use in healthcare. It has been said that healthcare is the only service industry that doesn't treat itself like one. And although the healthcare industry appears to have gone to great lengths to separate itself from other business sectors, there are many more similarities than differences.

1.1 If You Don't Measure It, You Can't Manage It

To manage something, it's necessary to know what it is (description), where it is (comparison), and how it got there (context). This can be accomplished through measurement and benchmarking. Proper practice management requires the use of subjective and objective measurement, analysis, comparison, and improvement.

1.2 If You Don't Value It, You Won't Change It

Driving change in a practice will affect every member of the organization and many will resist; therefore, the value (benefit) of instituting a change must outweigh the status quo, or leaving things as is. Measurement and benchmarking are not the final step in the process—they simply enable the process to evolve toward action. It is completely appropriate to measure and benchmark; however, this activity is in vain if something isn't done with the findings. Ideally, the results should be used to support change; however, they may be used to validate past changes or support the current status. And once a benchmarking process is finished, the practice can pick and choose the areas in which to focus its efforts, create buy-in (sell the change), and start the process of improvement (or repeat the entire benchmarking exercise—that is, continuous process improvement).

What can be done with the findings? There are many options: (1) drive and support change, (2) educate staff, (3) validate the past, (4) build buy-in, (5) conduct performance reviews, and (6) plan for the future.

When using the key benchmarking principles—"if you don't measure it, you can't manage it" and "if you don't value it, you won't change it," it is imperative to understand the interrelationship. First, proper management requires some degree of measurement to ensure the attribute of interest if fully understood (for example, is a full-time equivalent (FTE) clearly defined?). Second, once measurement has taken place, management must decide whether the value of pursuing change is worth disrupting the practice in the quest for improvement. And third, if management feels the measures dictate a need to change and value can be realized by making the change, the most important step is to instill a sense of value in making the change with physicians and staff—without buy-in, the value (benefit) of change will never be fully realized.

Of special note, processes can easily be changed, but it's only with the support and buy-in of physicians and staff that real improvement can be achieved. It has been said, "If you take care of your people, your people will take care of you, but if you don't take care of your people, your people will take care of you."

What is benchmarking? Simply put, benchmarking is measurement and comparison for the purpose of improvement. In particular, medical practice benchmarking is a systematic, logical, and common-sense approach to measurement, analysis, comparison, and improvement (see Exhibit 1). Therefore, benchmarking is comparison to a standard. Benchmarking improves understanding of processes and clinical and administrative characteristics at a single point in time (snapshot) or over time (trend).[1] In addition, benchmarking is the continuous process of measuring and comparing performance internally (over time) and externally (against other organizations and industries). And finally, benchmarking is determining how the best-in-class achieve their performance levels. This consists of analyzing and comparing best practices to uncover what they did, how they did it, and what must be done to adopt it for your practice (process benchmarking).

Exhibit 1. What Is Benchmarking?

- A systematic, logical, and common-sense approach to measurement, comparison, and improvement.
- Copying the best, closing gaps and differences, and achieving superiority.
- "A positive, proactive process to change operations in a structured fashion to achieve superior performance. The purpose is to gain a competitive advantage."
- Comparing organizational performance to the performance of other organizations.
- Continuous process of comparison with the best or "the toughest competitors or companies renowned as leaders."
- A method for identifying processes to new goals with full support of management.

2.0 The 'Value' of Benchmarking

Proper benchmarking consists of more than simple comparison of two numbers. The true value of benchmarking lies in the numbers and through an understanding of the current state of the practice, calculation of a difference between the current state and a new value or benchmark, knowing the context and background of the practice values when interpreting the results, deciding on a course of action and goal, and determining when the goal is achieved. For example, a comparison of average number of procedures per patient visit per physician to a known benchmark will only permit a mathematical analysis. However, what if one physician in the practice has been focusing on patients with simple medical issues that don't generate multiple procedures? The numbers alone would indicate this physician is underperforming and is below the others in procedural productivity; whereas, knowing the background, context, or other measures permit for a more detailed analysis. Perhaps this physician's focus is on acute care services and his or her average number of patient encounters per day is almost twice that of other physicians in the practice?

---

1   E.W. Woodcock, "Practice Benchmarking," in *Physician Practice Management: Essential Operations and Financial Knowledge.* Jones and Bartlett Publishers, 2005.

3.0 How to Benchmark

There are several methods of benchmarking. A simple 10-step process might consist of the following:

1. Determine what is critical to your organization's success;

2. Identify metrics that measure the critical factors;

3. Identify a source for internal and external benchmarking data;

4. Measure your practice's performance;

5. Compare your practice's performance to the benchmark;

6. Determine whether action is necessary based on the comparison;

7. If action is needed, identify the best practice and process used to implement it;

8. Adapt the process used by others in the context of your practice;

9. Implement new process, reassess objectives, evaluate benchmarking standards, and recalibrate measures; and

10. Do it again—benchmarking is an ongoing process and tracking over time allows for continuous improvement.

4.0 Standardizing Data for Comparison

Since the primary purpose of benchmarking is comparison, it is necessary to standardize data so organizations of different sizes can be compared. A common method for standardizing data is to convert measures to percentages, per unit of input, or per unit of output. For example, per unit of input can be presented as per FTE physician, per FTE provider, or per square foot, whereas per unit of output can be presented on a per-patient, per-RBRVS unit, or per-procedure level.

5.0 What's Our Baseline?

Benchmarking, like any activity involving comparison, requires an understanding of "where you are"—this is known as your baseline. The baseline represents where you are today or where you've been and provides a point of origin or starting point. In addition, a baseline is an initial state that forms a logical basis for comparison. For example, to determine whether physicians have increased the average number of procedures per patient visit, it is necessary to have two measurements: the old value or baseline and the new value. To calculate the delta (or difference) between the two values, a simple formula can be used: new value minus old value. Without the baseline, it would not be possible to perform this or many other calculations like percentage change.

6.0 How Are We Doing?

This question can be answered by asking the question, "What is the difference between the baseline and current state (or where we are today)?" The baseline can be an internal benchmark (historical measure) from inside the practice, a benchmark across like practices from a Medical Group Management Association (MGMA) *Survey Report*, or a benchmark from outside the industries such as Disney or Wal-Mart. Additional insights can also be assessed by calculating the difference between current state and an established benchmark or industry average or median. To determine the difference, there are several methods and statistical tools. For instance, the mathematical difference, or delta, consists of subtracting the baseline value from the current value, whereas percentage change is a method for assessing changes over time or the proportion of one value in comparison to another. In addition to these methods, there are more statistically intense methods to determine difference that can be generalized across a group (see Exhibit 2).

Exhibit 2. What Is the Difference?
• Mathematical difference (delta) • New value minus old value • Current state minus Initial state • Benchmark and industry value minus current state • Percentage change • Difference between three or more average

Interpretation of the difference is dependent on the method used. When using the delta, the difference will be a raw number, since the method consists of simple subtraction. Determining whether the difference is good or bad depends on the context, background, and what the values represent. For example, if medical revenue after operating cost per FTE family practice physician is $145,000 and the MGMA benchmark indicates a median of $214,377, then the delta is $69,377 ($214,377 minus $145,000). A delta of $69,377 may suggest poor practice performance, reduced physician productivity, a capital investment, or other practice deficiencies or large expenses, whereas the percentage change method indicates this practice is only generating 67% of the median for similar types of practices (see Exhibit 3). Therefore, the result is different between delta and percentage change, and the interpretation may also be different.

Exhibit 3. Difference Between Delta and Percentage Change		
Is the result positive or negative?	Delta	Percentage Change
Positive value	New value (or benchmark) is greater than the old value. For example, $214,377 minus $145,000 equals a delta of $69,377	New value has increased. For example, $145,000 divided by $214,377 equals 0.67. This when multiplied by 100 equals 67%.
Negative value	New value is less.	New value has decreased.

7.0 Methods and Checklists

Failing to plan, it has been said, is planning to fail. Therefore, an integral component of the benchmarking process is the proper use of systematic methods, checklists, scales, and comparable measures. Systematic methods consist of formulas and ratios as found in this chapter. Checklists are a planning tool to ensure all variables and methods are used and considered—checklists ensure attention to detail and minimize the chance of missing steps in a process (see Exhibit 4). Scales provide the measuring stick—meaning they indicate whether your measures are high or low, good or bad, or where they are in comparison to others. And comparable measures are key to the heart and soul of benchmarking and provide a means for determining how your practice compares to others.

Exhibit 4. Example Checklist[2]
The following checklist items can be used to increase the likelihood that a claim will be processed and paid when first submitted: ❏ Patient information is complete. ❏ Patient's name and address matches the insurer's records. ❏ Patient's group number and subscriber number is correct. ❏ Physician's Social Security number, provider number, or tax identification number is completed and correct. ❏ Claim is signed by the physician. ❏ All necessary dates are completed. ❏ Dates for care given are chronological and correct—for example, is the discharge date listed as before the admission date? ❏ Dates for care given are in agreement with the claims information from other providers, such as the hospital, etc. ❏ Diagnosis is complete. ❏ Diagnosis is correct for the services or procedures provided. ❏ Diagnostic codes are correct for the services or procedures provided. ❏ CPT and ICD-9 codes are accurate. ❏ Diagnosis is coded using ICD-9-CM to the highest level of specificity. ❏ Fee column is itemized and totaled. ❏ All necessary information about prescription drugs or durable medical equipment prescribed by the physician is included. ❏ The claim is legible.

---

2   DecisionHealth, "A/R Benchmarks," Part B News 20, no. 40 (Oct. 16, 2006).

8.0 Small and Solo Practices

8.1 Small and Solo Practice Benchmarking

Small and solo practices share many similarities with their larger counterparts; however, the benefits and risks associated with the differences can have significant impact on a small practice's longevity and financial success.

8.2 Similarities With Larger Practices

Small and solo practices share many similarities with larger organizations. For instance, all medical practices must operate in the same healthcare environment and deal with the same healthcare legislation, malpractice insurance, payers, collection challenges, patient needs and expectations, delivery and standards of care, and processes—just to name a few.

Also, the benchmarking methods used by large organizations are identical to those used by small and solo practices (see Exhibit 5). And the use of normalized metrics permits comparison regardless of organizational size. Common examples available in most benchmarking datasets consist of measures per FTE physician or provider, per square foot, per patient, per procedure, and per RVU.

Exhibit 5. Similarities Regardless of Size or Type[3]
• Legislation can change payment (for example, Medicare and Medicaid reimbursement rates are determined through legislation).   • Costs are increasing greater than inflation (for example, medical supplies and equipment costs are increasing at a greater percentage than reimbursement rates).   • Expenses change.   • Increases in physician compensation are from production (for example, much of physician compensation is based on physician production or the number of patients seen and the procedures performed).   • Health savings accounts will change patient behavior (for example, patients will treat medical care more like a product or service they pay for using the funds in their account).   • Hospitals are purchasing physician practices (again).   • Advances in medical care are changing care delivery.   • Physicians are publicly rated for quality and outcomes.   • Physicians are publicly rated for patient satisfaction.

8.3 What's the Difference?

Small and solo practices are different from larger groups in several ways, some of which are beneficial, while others are not. For instance, smaller organizations are generally more flexible, can adapt or change quickly and in general, tend to be more efficient. However, small and solo practices are more sensitive to the risks associated with costly

---

3   E.J. Pavlock, *Financial Management for Medical Groups*, 2nd ed. MGMA, 2000.

mistakes, lack of alternative revenue-generating methods, and the absence of (or antiquated condition of) robust information systems. For example, with only one or two physicians in a practice, what impact would a poor decision or loss of a physician (due to sickness or some other unforeseen event) have on the practice? Can a small practice afford to retain adequate earnings for contingencies? Does the existing information system compliment and add to the efficiency of the practice? And does it interface (communicate) with the information systems used by payers, hospitals, and other medical practices such as referring practices and physicians?

Ultimately, the goals of smaller practices mirror those of larger groups—to have more satisfied patients, more fulfilling work environments for physicians and staff, and better economic outcomes. However, the additional sensitivities of small and solo practices must be considered to ensure surprise events don't adversely impact the practice.

9.0 Practice Measurement

Measurement is the collection and organization of data. In many cases, measurement is a method of converting an array, group, list, or set of data into a single variable that describes the entire dataset. A mean or average is a calculation that summarizes the central tendency or mathematical center of many data points, provided all data are of the same unit of measurement. In general, an average is the most common calculation used to analyze and compare data. It's the most common, since most people understand the concept of an average and how to calculate it. For example, if we count the number of patients seen per month for the last 10 months for an eight-provider family medical practice located in the suburbs, we have an array of data with 10 data points—one data point for each month (see Exhibit 6). If we also have a list with the number of patients seen per month for the last 10 months for an eight-provider family medical practice located in a rural community, how can we easily compare these two practices? We can line up and organize the data points in ascending order, but what does this tell us? We might conclude the suburban practice sees a greater number of patients per month, but we can't accurately describe the difference or make a comparison. All we've done so far is arrange the data and guessed there was a difference by looking at or "eyeballing" the data—not the most accurate method. However, by calculating the average number of patients seen per month for the last 10 months for each practice, a single and accurate measure can be used to describe and compare the two groups.

Exhibit 6. Example of Measurement: Number of Patients Seen Per Month		
Month	Suburban Practice	Rural Practice
January	2,620	2,650
February	2,231	2,660
March	2,264	2,266
April	2,650	2,067
May	2,657	1,687
June	2,670	3,690
July	3,067	3,070
August	2,690	2,071
September	3,171	2,731
October	3,710	3,730
Sum of patients seen	27,730	26,622
Number of data points (months)	10	10
Average patients seen per month	2,773	2,662

Comparing these practices, the suburban practice, on average, sees more patients per month than the rural practice—111 more (average number of patients seen per month in the suburban practice minus average number of patients seen per month in the rural practice; 2,773 minus 2,662 equals 111).

10.0 Art and Science of Benchmarking

Benchmarking, as it's related to measurement, is the art and science of comparison. The "art" takes place during the data gathering and interpretation phases and requires a method with some common sense, whereas the "science" is the systematic and logical process of analysis. Once interpretation and analysis have occurred, data are considered transformed into information that can be used for comparison and decision making. That is, it is possible to determine whether the data are similar or different and by how much. Exhibit 7 represents several examples of metrics and associated benchmarks.

Exhibit 7. Examples of Benchmarks					
Encounters per FTE* physician	Mean	3,006	4,759	5,891	7,612	9,159
Total procedures per FTE physician	6,341	3,006	4,759	5,891	7,612	9,159
Physician work RVUs per FTE physician	4,751	4,412	7,506	5,123	5,622	6,809
Physician compensation	$4,751	$1,426	$3,684	$5,123	$5,622	$6,809

Other topics associated with benchmarking are: (1) continuous improvement and (2) evaluation and assessment. Continuous improvement refers to the need for repeated analysis using the same measures over time (trend). An evaluation is a subjective, personal judgment of the value (or worth) of something, whereas an assessment is objective and quantifiable (or assigned a numeric value).

11.0 Benchmarking Methods

Effective benchmarking consists of a systematic process; therefore, several methods have been developed to ensure the process is efficient (see Exhibit 8).

Proper measurement begins with selecting the right practice attribute, characteristic, property, dimension, or variable to be assessed. In other words, what do we want to measure? For example, encounters per FTE physician, total procedures per FTE physician, and physician work RVUs per FTE physician are common examples of benchmarks and practice measures. This book presents many practice attributes that have been operationally defined, that is, the attribute and measurement process have been clearly described in practice and literature as generally accepted. However, there may be practice attributes that are not typically measured or found in the literature. In these cases, it would be necessary to fully explore the characteristic before moving to the next step—this type of attribute could be called "homegrown." Of note, there are probably few instances when "homegrown" attributes are needed since the healthcare management field is sufficiently mature to have identified most, if not all, key practice characteristics.

Once a practice variable is selected, the next step is to decide on the appropriate method of measurement (or what metric should be used) and the intended purpose. There are two general categories of metrics: (1) informational and (2) actionable. Informational metrics provide a simple description and unlike actionable metrics, they don't clearly suggest ways of affecting change. For example, if we decide to measure the average number of patients seen per month in a suburban practice as a metric to describe monthly practice productivity, then this metric simply tells us the arithmetic mean—it doesn't suggest anything more, whereas, actionable metrics are usually more complex, require an understanding of the context, and are compared to a benchmark or baseline. For instance, the formula to calculate average number of patients seen per month (for the last 10 months) per provider for an eight-provider family medical practice is the sum of the number of patients seen per month for the last 10 months divided by the number of months divided by the number of providers. If we use this formula as a metric to assess monthly practice productivity per provider and want to improve productivity per provider, then this metric used in this context suggests, for example, we can affect change by working with individual providers whose average is below the practice's overall average to increase the number of patients seen per month by the provider of interest.

Exhibit 8. Methods of Benchmarking			
Transfer Model	**Five Stages of Benchmarking**	**5 Steps of Benchmarking**	**10 Steps to Benchmarking**
1. Identification and documentation of best practices. 2. Validation and consensus of what to focus on and what are true best practices. 3. Transfer and develop buy-in; sell ideas to management and get commitment to performance assessments, identify priorities, and establish a plan. 4. Implementation using team champions, selection of critical practices to support strategic initiatives.	1. Planning, selecting the processes to benchmark, and identifying customer expectations and critical success factors. 2. Form the benchmarking team from across the organization. 3. Collect the data from best practice organizations and identify own processes. 4. Analyze data for gaps. 5. Take action, identify what needs to be done to match best practice, and implement change.	1. Planning what to benchmark and what organization to benchmark against. 2. Analyze performance gaps and project future performance. 3. Set targets for change and communicate to all levels. 4. Develop action plans, implement plans, and adjust as necessary. 5. Achieve a state of maturity by integrating best practices into organization.	1. Determine what is critical to your organization's success. 2. Identify metrics that measure the critical factors. 3. Identify a source for internal and external benchmarking data. 4. Measure your practice's performance. 5. Compare your practice's performance to the benchmark. 6. Determine whether action is necessary based on the comparison. 7. If action is needed, identify the best practice and process to use to implement it. 8. Adapt the process used by others in the context of your practice. 9. Implement new process, reassess objectives, evaluate benchmarking standards, and recalibrate measures 10. Do it again—benchmarking is an ongoing process and tracking over time allows for continuous improvement.

Several questions should be asked as part of preliminary measurement steps. For instance, what do you want to measure? Is it a generally accepted practice characteristic (typical practice factor) or is it a homegrown practice attribute (custom or self-defined factor or metric)? What metric should be used? What is the appropriate method for measurement? And finally, what type of metric do you want to use and what is your intended purpose (information or action)?

12.0 Interpretation Pitfalls

Reliability is defined as repeatability and consistency. If given the same dataset and using the same measure, someone else should be able to calculate, describe, and compare the data in the same way. For instance, if given the number of patients seen per month for the last 10 months in a suburban and rural practice and asked for the average number of patients seen per month for both practices, you would find the same average with the same comparison for each practice. Note that the same unit of measurement must be used, that is, all the data in your data set or data array should be the same unit of measurement (in the example above, all numbers are based on number of patients seen). Reliability cannot be achieved if the unit of measurement is different in any of the data used in the measurement. For example, you cannot calculate an average using 2,650 patients seen in January, 2,264 seen in February, 3,265 seen in March, 2,166 seen in April, 3,167 seen in May, 1,869 seen in June, 2,771 seen in July, and 3,171 appointments booked in August without first changing appointments booked to the number of patients seen in August.

Validity is meaningfulness within a generally accepted theoretical basis (see Exhibit 9). Or simply stated, does it really mean what it's expected to mean or is it being interpreted accurately? How you interpret your data and measurements are as important as ensuring you have used a highly reliable method. Understanding what a particular measure is meant to describe is paramount to using data properly to support good decisions. For instance, averages (means) represent the mathematical center of an array of data or central tendency, whereas the median is the 'actual' center of the array. In some cases, the average and median can be the same, but often, there is a difference. Therefore, knowing how a measure is used, collected, and calculated will assist in supporting your decisions, that is, your conclusions and analysis will be more valid and meaningful. This is particularly important when presenting your findings to others since the better you understand the measures, why you selected them, and how to explain them to others, the value and usefulness of your results will add significant credibility to your recommendations and decisions.

Exhibit 9. Example of Meaningfulness

It is important to understand the formulas used for measurement and how the measurement is collected and calculated. Using the data array from the previous example of number of patients seen per month [suburban practice: 2,620 (January), 2,231 (February), 2,264 (March), 2,650 (April), 2,657 (May), 2,670 (June), 3,067 (July), 2,690 (August), 3,171 (September), 3,710 (October)]:

- Average (mean) = Sum of all data divided by the number of data points
- Sum of all data = 27,730
- Number of data points = 10
- Average = 2,773
- Median = The data point in the center of the array (when arranged in order)
- Data array = 2,231, 2,264, 2,620, 2,650, 2,657, 2,670, 2,690, 3,067, 3,171, 3,710
- Center of array are two data points = 2,657 and 2,670
- Median = 2,657 + 2,670 divided by 2 = 2,664
- Note: If the data array consisted of an odd number of data points, the median would be the true center data point.

Another pitfall to avoid that is a common mistake is averaging averages, for example, which presents a danger during measurement. Since any array of data points can be averaged (or measured using other methods), it's important to understand the limitations or implications of measuring calculated measures. The validity of the interpretation may be suspect.

The extremely low and high values in all the practices are minimized or diluted (their effect is almost eliminated). The effects of the low- and high-productivity practices almost eliminate one another, which is why the average of the averages is near the average of the more balanced array (Family Practice 1).

Strength is related to validity and is the power, magnitude, or accuracy of your interpretation or how confident you are in your interpretation. For instance, if you want to describe the number of patients seen per month for three months (2,231, 2,264, and 2,620), a mean is an ideal descriptive statistic (mean = 2,372). This figure is somewhat descriptive of the lower months of 2,231 and 2,264, but a mean of 2,372 is not descriptive of the higher months when 2,620 patients were seen. Therefore, your confidence in a mean of 2,372 patients seen per month provides a less accurate description of the average number of patients seen per month. However, if this array consisted of a large number of months, that is, a large dataset with many data points, the accuracy of this metric and your confidence in the descriptive power of the mean is much higher.

A final interpretation issue is related to the mutually exclusive and exhaustive nature of data. Mutually exclusive refers to a data point fitting into only one category. For example, we decide months with 3,600 patients or more are categorized as high productivity, months with between 2,401 and 3,599 patients are medium or normal, and months with 2,400 patients or less are low. Therefore, each month fits into only one category—that's mutually exclusive—a single month cannot be categorized as "high" and "medium." If a single month could be assigned to multiple categories, it would be difficult to accurately describe each month or interpret your findings. Exhaustive refers to the description of the attribute, that is, does the definition encompass all collected attributes? For example, since all the measurements taken consisted of the number of patients seen per month, this attribute was defined to be actual patient encounters with a provider and all collected measures were based on this definition. That is, patients seen only by a nurse were not included since these encounters didn't fit the definition (or criteria).

Management can use numbers to diagnose and treat practice deficiencies, plan improvements, and examine practice activities and processes. And because numbers are less susceptible to the effects of human variation (feelings and emotions), they are more appropriate for decision making. The beauty of numbers comes from their brevity, clarity, and precision. For example, using the example array (list) that shows the number of no-shows per day from last month, it is possible to quickly summarize the week or entire month regarding no-show activity. These averages and totals provide a brief, clear, and precise picture describing no-show activity during each week or the entire month. There's little room for misinterpretation or confusion, provided a no-show is clearly defined, that is, a no-show is a patient who fails to show up within 15 minutes of an appointment, rather than someone who fails to cancel 24 hours prior to his or her appointment.

Organizing a group of numbers is the cornerstone in the benchmarking process. An array or group of numbers only becomes valuable once it is organized, whereas statistical methods and proper interpretation of the findings are necessary to uncover the useful information behind the numbers. A systematic approach is necessary and has been established through the use of averages (or means), medians, standard deviations, percentiles, quartiles, and percentage change. These techniques can be used to measure and benchmark all practice attributes. In addition, these methods are easy to use, understand, and communicate—most people are familiar with some, if not all methods.

There are a handful of key financial performance indicators understood and used by the majority of practices to measure financial operations. Many of these formulas are presented in this chapter as a comprehensive "starter set" of key performance indicators and financial metrics for benchmarking.

13.0 Key Financial Indicators
Benchmarks for many of the following formulas are available in the MGMA *Cost Survey and Performance and Practices of Successful Medical Groups* reports.

13.1 Total net collections
Net fee-for-service revenue + capitation revenue – provision for bad debt

13.2 Gross (unadjusted) collection ratio
Definition: Indicates how much of what is being charged is actually collected.

Goal: The higher, the better

$$\frac{\text{Total net collections}}{\text{Total gross charges}}$$

Note: In general, the goal of this measure is "the higher, the better"; however, this metric will vary significantly depending on the fee schedule of the practice. For instance, a practice with a high fee schedule will have a lower gross collection ratio than a practice with a low fee schedule (setting a fee schedule too low can have a negative effect on net revenue). This metric is often used to measure billing office performance.

13.3 Gross collection ratio

Definition: Indicates a ratio of the amount of revenue "actually" collected over the amount charged.

Goal: The higher, the better

$$\frac{\text{Net FFS revenue or collections}}{\text{Gross FFS charges}}$$

13.4 Adjusted (net) collection ratio

Definition: Indicates how much of what is being charged (gross FFS charges) is actually collected after total adjustments to charges; does not include funds the practice should not receive (e.g., contractual allowances) and funds it will not receive (e.g., bad debt).

Goal: The higher, the better

$$\frac{\text{Net fee-for-service collections}}{\text{Net fee-for-service charges}}$$

13.5 Average adjusted revenue per day

Definition: Indicates the average amount of revenue generated per business day.

Goal: The higher, the better

$$\frac{\text{Adjusted charges for the last three months}}{\text{Number of business days for the same time period}}$$

Note: It isn't required that the time period be three months; rather, it should be a recent period of time.

13.6 Days revenue outstanding

Definition: Indicates how long it takes before claims and charges are paid.

Goal: The lower, the better

Step 1: Calculate "days revenue"

$$\frac{\text{Total revenue for the last three months}}{\text{Number of business days in the last three months}}$$

Step 2: Calculate "days revenue outstanding"

$$\frac{\text{Outstanding net AR}}{\text{Days revenue}}$$

13.7 Days in AR

Definition: Indicates how long it takes before claims and charges are paid.

Goal: A net collection ratio (NCR) of 96% to 99% and 40 to 50 days in AR (a days in AR of 45 or less is ideal) indicate your practice is functioning efficiently and doing very well. If NCR is 93% to 95% and 50 to 60 days in AR, there is some (little) room for improvement. And if 92% or less and 70 days or more in AR, there is significant room for improvement in billing operations.

$$\frac{\text{Outstanding AR}}{(\text{Average monthly charge}/30)}$$

Note: Include at least the last three months to calculate the average monthly charges

13.8 Days in AR (alternate calculation)

Definition: Indicates how long it takes before claims and charges are paid.

Goal: The lower, the better

$$\frac{\text{Outstanding net AR}}{\text{Average adjusted revenue per day}}$$

13.9 Months revenue in AR

Definition: Indicates the average number of months charges are outstanding for collection.

Goal: The lower, the better

$$\frac{\text{Total AR}}{(\text{Annual adjusted FFS charges} * 1/12)}$$

13.10 Expense to earnings

Definition: Indicates the ratio of overhead (expenses) to revenue (collections).

Goal: The lower, the better

$$\frac{\text{Total operating expenses}}{\text{Total collections}}$$

13.11 Average revenue per patient

Definition: Indicates the average amount of revenue generated per patient seen. In addition, it can be used to determine the number of patients that must be treated to receive a predetermined amount of revenue (collections).

Goal: The higher, the better

$$\frac{\text{Total monthly collections for last month}}{\text{Total patient visits last month}}$$

13.12 Average cost per patient

Definition: Indicates the average cost of providing treatment per patient visit.

Goal: The lower, the better

$$\frac{\text{Total operating expenses}}{\text{Total patient visits}}$$

13.13 Departmental or service ratio

Definition: Indicates the expenses to revenues ratio for a specific department or service.

Goal: The lower, the better

$$\frac{\text{Total expenses for ancillary service for the last three months}}{\text{Total net charges for all CPT codes related to ancillary service}}$$

13.14 Collections rate by payer

Definition: Indicates different rates of reimbursement by payer.

Goal: Depends on many practice factors; should be proportional to the percentage of patients covered by each payer.

$$\frac{\text{Net collections by payer}}{\text{Total gross charges by payer}}$$

Note: Reimbursement received from a payer is based on the specific fee schedule established with a payer and is on a per-procedure basis. Net collections is the sum of all reimbursement received from a payer, whereas gross charges is what the practice billed the payer.

13.15 Volume and reimbursement by service line

Definition: Indicates workload volume and revenue generated by service line; provides a method for identifying the relative contribution of each service line.

Goal: Depends on many practice factors; in most cases, volume should be directly related to revenue generated by service line.

Volume by service line:

$$\frac{\text{Volume measurement (encounters/visits, RVUs, etc.) by service line}}{\text{Volume measurement for total practice}}$$

Reimbursement by service line:

$$\frac{\text{Revenue by service line}}{\text{Total practice revenue}}$$

13.16 Surgical yield

Definition: Indicates relative contribution of revenue generated from surgical or procedural workload to total practice revenue.

Goal: Depends on many practice factors; in most cases, volume should be directly related to revenue generated by service line.

$$\frac{\text{Revenue derived from surgeries or procedures}}{\text{Total practice revenue}}$$

13.17 Reimbursement per procedure code

Definition: Indicates average amount of revenue generated from procedures provided to patients.

Goal: Depends on many practice factors; in general, it will be higher if the procedures provided to patients are higher RVU procedures.

$$\frac{\text{Net collections}}{\text{Total number of procedures}}$$

Note: This metric can be adapted to show average reimbursement per procedure by payer using net collections by payer divided by total number of procedures charged to a payer.

In conclusion, benchmarking provides a means to measure performance in relation to a standard like the odometer (total mileage) in a car is used as one of many measures to assess value (future performance). For example, a car with 100,000 miles is probably worth less than the same type of car with 50,000 miles. And this can be determined by comparison (benchmarking) against a standard like the Kelly Blue Book values for a car or the MGMA surveys for medical practice performance. Trending, as it's related to benchmarking, can be used to compare practice measures against a standard over a period of time—this increases the "value" benchmarking by displaying past and present performance. And once benchmarks are complimented with trended data, it is possible to extend the measures into the future, thereby predicting the future. However, like any measure of a complex system or organization, a single measure studied in a vacuum only provides a narrow view that's prone to error. Therefore, multiple benchmarks and trends should be evaluated to gain a richer, fuller, and more rewarding picture of the performance landscape and associated value of the organization.

Part IV.
Appraising Compensation Arrangements

Chapter 22. Valuing Physician Employment Arrangements for Clinical Services: An Introduction

CONTENTS

Chapter 22. Valuing Physician Employment Arrangements for Clinical Services: An Introduction

By Timothy Smith, CPA/ABV

1.0 Introduction

The employment of physicians by nonphysician-owned healthcare entities, particularly hospitals and health systems, is becoming more commonplace in today's healthcare marketplace. Many believe that physician employment by hospitals and health systems will become the prevailing physician practice paradigm within the next 10 years or less. Yet, such employment by hospitals and health systems is subject to various healthcare regulations, including the requirement that the compensation paid under such arrangements be consistent with fair market value (FMV). As a result, these employers generally pursue various programs or approaches for ensuring that employed physicians are paid FMV compensation for their services. Typical FMV compliance efforts include internal review processes, use of survey data, and engaging outside consultants to determine FMV compensation.

From the standpoint of the professional practice of appraisal, the key to valuing services of any kind, including those provided under employment agreements, is matching the appropriate compensation with the services provided under the terms of the arrangement. It is essential, therefore, that the valuation of physician employment arrangements be based on a sound understanding of the economics and market dynamics of physician services. Yet, a broad array of complex factors affects the value of physician services in the marketplace and thereby in employment arrangements. Valuation analysts appraising the compensation in physician employment arrangements for clinical services need to be fully aware of these factors. To that end, two key chapters in this guide should be read as prerequisites for understanding the economic and marketplace dynamics of physician clinical services. They include the following:

1. Chapter 13, "An Introduction to Physician Services and Specialties"; and

2. Chapter 14, "The Economics of Physician Clinical Services and Compensation."

The remainder of this chapter provides an introduction to the market trends toward employment of physicians by health systems and the typical terms included in these arrangements. Key regulatory and valuation matters are also highlighted to provide an overview of critical areas related to the valuation of physician employment arrangements for clinical services.

2.0 Recent Trends Toward Physician Employment

2.1 Typical Employers in the Marketplace

There are a number of different types of healthcare organizations employing physicians to provide clinical services in the current marketplace. They include:

- Physician-owned groups;

- Hospitals and health systems;

- Physician practice management companies;

- Health plans; and

- Government agencies or departments.

Excluding employment by governmental entities, the vast majority of physicians are employed either by hospitals and health systems or by physician-owned groups. Since most physicians in physician-owned groups are actually employee-owners, hospitals and health systems are by far the predominant employers of physicians in true private practice employment arrangements in the United States. Various market forces are converging to accelerate this current market trend.

2.2 Hospital Employment: Wave of the Future?

In the past several years, employment of physicians has been increasing. Two recent studies noted that the proportion of physicians with ownership in their practices has declined from 61.6% in 1996-97 to 56.3% in 2008.[1] Employment by hospital or health

---

1   "Physicians Moving to Mid-Sized, Single-Specialty Practices," Center for Studying Health System Change, *Tracking Report* No. 18, August 2007. "A Snapshot of U.S. Physicians: Key Findings From the 2008 Health Tracking Physician Survey," Center for Studying Health System Change, *Data Bulletin* No. 35, September 2009. www.hschange.com.

systems has been a major contributor to this market shift, which has been accelerated in the past few years. Indeed, the president and chief executive officer (CEO) of the Medical Group Management Association (MGMA) recently predicted that within five years, the majority of physicians will work for hospitals.[2] A Health Management Academy reports that 88% of responding health system CEOs and chief marketing offiers (CMOs) believe physician employment will become the dominant and permanent model for medical staff relationships.[3] This recent trend in physician employment is especially common with specialists. In April 2010, a spokesperson for the American College of Cardiology indicated that roughly half of all cardiology practices had migrated to health system employment.[4] This percentage has surely risen since that time. Cardiology, primary care, neurosurgery, and orthopedics comprise the top specialties pursued by hospital-health systems for employment.[5]

A convergence of various market forces has created the context in which hospital or health systems and physicians are increasingly seeking to align through an employment relationship.[6]

For hospital or health systems, the motivations for employing physicians are varied, but systemic in relation to developments in the healthcare arena:

- Hospital competition and expansion into a new markets.

- Staffing profitable service lines and providing for physician-leaders to "brand" the service.

- Ensuring hospital call coverage and inpatient care.

- Filling shortages of particular specialties in the service area of a facility.

- Gaining cooperation with quality improvement efforts as part of pay-for-performance and public reporting programs.

2   Kenneth J. Terry, "Become a Partner or Remain an Employee?" May 19, 2009. Medscape Business of Medicine: www.medscape.com/viewarticle/702784_print, accessed June 4, 2009.
3   "Physician Alignment in Health Systems: Building Infrastructure," *The Academy*, December 2008, hmacademy. com/latestIssue.html, accessed Oct. 30, 2011.
4   Barbara Kircheimer, "Independent Medical Practice: Does Healthcare Reform Mark the Beginning of the End?" *Becker's ASC Review*, April 22, 2010. www.beckersasc.com, accessed June 21, 2010.
5   Catlin LeValley and Lindsey Dunn, "3 Medical Specialties Most Pursued for Employment by Hospitals," *Becker's Hospital Review*, Sept. 27, 2010. www.beckershospitalreview.com, accessed Oct. 1, 2010.
6   The following section is a summary of salient points from various articles and studies on recent employment trends in the healthcare marketplace. The specific articles and studies are cited in the bibliography for this part.

- Increasing acceptance by hospitals and physicians of the employment model.

- Disappointing results from other, less-integrated models of physician-hospital alignment.

- Seeking the potential benefits of actualized integration: better quality, coordination of care, and increased efficiency; anticipation of bundled payment approaches.

- Healthcare regulatory climate that favors employment over other types of physician arrangements.

For physicians, the motivations for employment also stem from major healthcare trends, but also from changes in the lifestyle attitudes of younger physicians:

- Declining physician incomes resulting from downward reimbursement trends, high malpractice costs, and restrictions on income from under arrangements, specialty hospitals, and similar arrangements.

- Complexity of running a physician practice.

- Uncertainty in the healthcare arena.

- Gaining more regular work hours.

- Reducing call coverage responsibilities.

- Aligning with one or another hospital or health system in a highly consolidated market.

The meeting of these forces has created a strong trend toward employment of physicians, especially specialists, by hospital or health systems.

One consequence of the trend toward health system employment by physician is the loss of technical component services, or in-office ancillaries, within physician practices. Many hospital and health systems are transferring or converting the ancillary services formerly provided by physician practices to hospital-based outpatient department (HOPD) or provider-based status. As a result, the net earnings from these technical component services are moved out of the legal entity housing the physician practice and over to the hospital. The reason for this transference or conversion is that these services receive a higher level of reimbursement when provided as part of an HOPD rather than a physician practice. Hospital and health systems can increase overall system earnings by making this conversion.

3.0 Employment Structures and Terms

3.1 Physician Services Included in Employment Arrangements

Physicians provide and are involved in a variety of services in the healthcare industry for which they can receive compensation. Many employment arrangements will include duties and tasks that go beyond clinical-related services. These services can include the following:

1. Professional component services;

2. Technical component services;

3. Call coverage services, including hospital call and practice call;

4. Administrative, executive, and managerial;

5. Clinical co-management or service line management;

6. Academic, educational, and research.

It is important to distinguish among these various forms of physician services because each type of service has its own unique characteristics and economics. More importantly, the marketplace tends to compensate for each type of service differently based on its unique characteristics and economics. Thus, the valuation tools and techniques used to determine fair market value (FMV) compensation often vary by type of service. Since the key to valuing service agreements is matching the compensation paid for services rendered, it is essential for an appraiser to have a solid grasp and understanding of the key characteristics of the services provided by physicians. Failure to comprehend these characteristics can lead to appraisals of physician services that do not reflect the fundamental economics of the underlying services and, consequently, that are not consistent with the standard of FMV.

3.2 Overview of Physician Employment Structures

Physicians can be employed through a variety of contractual structures. The most common employment arrangements are those in which the employer entity is a subsidiary or affiliate of a hospital in the larger corporate entity structure of a health system. This employer entity is generally a physician practice entity that employs other physicians as well. Some hospitals and health systems will employ physicians of the same or similar specialties in a single group; others will employ physicians in a single multispecialty group. Employer entity practices may also be denominated by locations or by affiliation with particular hospitals. In some cases, physicians are employed directly by hospital entities. Generally, state laws and billing considerations, such as the so-called 72-hour rule related to what pre-hospital admission outpatient services can be billed separately from hospital services to Medicare, can affect the legal organization of physician practice entities within a larger hospital or health system.

3.3 Arrangements in States Prohibiting the Corporate Practice of Medicine

Some states prohibit the so-called corporate practice of medicine by barring non-physician-owned entities from employing physicians. Thus, hospitals or health systems are proscribed from direct employment of physicians by subsidiaries or affiliates. In some of these states, corporate entities are allowed exceptions to these prohibitions through use of certain nonprofit legal entities or foundations. The two notable exceptions are Texas and California.[7]

Texas '501a' Entities:

Texas allows physicians to be employed by so-called 501a entities that meet certain requirements. These requirements include, without limitation, that the entity have a board of directors comprised of physicians and be nonprofit. These entities are allowed to have corporate members who retain certain reserve powers over key decisions of the 501a entity.

California Foundation Model:

California affords a narrow exception to its corporate practice prohibition through use of a so-called foundation model. A charitable foundation is permitted to enter into an independent-contractor arrangement with a physician practice to provide professional services to its clinical patients, subject to certain specific conditions. Among these requirements, the foundation must be a nonprofit entity organized for the purpose of providing both medical care and research, and the physician practice must meet certain size, specialty, and full-time practice requirements for its physicians.

Other states with the corporate practice prohibition may have similar exceptions that allow indirect employment or professional services contracting with physicians or physician groups by health systems.

---

7 The discussion of the Texas and California exceptions is intended to be general summaries of the requirements for each. Readers should consult alternative materials or legal counsel for the precise statutory requirements for each exception.

3.4 The Synthetic Employment/Foundational Model/Professional Services Agreement Model

Recently, a new market model has emerged that is a variation or adaptation of the foundation model. Often called "synthetic employment," this model is based on the professional services agreement, rather than employment, as the contractual vehicle for obtaining physician clinical services. The structure of the model can be described as follows:

- Physicians remain in their current group entity (Group) as owners or employees.

- Group entity sells or leases its assets to the health system's (HS) new practice entity (HS Practice).

- HS Practice hires Group's support staff as employees (or leases from Group).

- HS Practice assumes leases and operations of the practice.

- HS Practice contracts with payers and bills and collects for all patient care provided by practice.

- HS Practice enters into a professional services agreement with Group to provide clinical patient care services.

- HS Practice compensates Group for services based on a compensation model that includes an allowance for benefits and professional liability insurance (PLI) of Group's physicians.

- Group determines how compensation received from HS Practice is paid to physicians within the group.

- Group determines and pays for the benefits provided to its physicians and nonphysician providers.

- Group maintains and pays for its PLI.

- Group manages its own internal affairs.

This new foundation or synthetic employment model has benefits for both physician groups and hospital and health systems. From the physician side, this model allows the physicians to retain a certain level of internal autonomy in terms of compensation and benefits. Physician groups determine how the compensation paid by the health system practice is distributed among the group's providers, provided such allocations are within the bounds of applicable healthcare regulations. Physician groups may also determine the level of benefits provided and paid for by the group, and since only physicians or providers are employees of the group, many of the Employee Retirement Income Security Act (ERISA) and nondiscrimination requirements related to benefits for highly compensated employees may be avoided.[8]

This autonomy feature is also a key benefit for the health systems in managing their practices. They can avoid the "herding cats" issues commonly associated with employing physicians, especially with respect to individual physician compensation and benefit issues. Synthetic employment can also represent an intermediate pathway to hospital-physician integration that allows for clinical integration, but organizational independence with respect to group practice matters among the physicians. Some physicians and health systems find the foundation model attractive for its exit strategy implications. If the relationship does not work out, the arrangement can more easily unwind with the physician group remaining intact and ready for business on its own. One might metaphorically say that synthetic employment is the "live-together-before-getting-married" approach to hospital-physician integration.

3.5 Popular Compensation Plans Under Employment

Typical compensation plans offered under hospital and health system employment include a variety of structures and characteristics. In today's market, most tend to be productivity-based. By far, the most popular plan is the compensation per work relative value unit (wRVU) model. The following provides an overview of this model as well as other commonly used compensation plans observed in the current physician employment marketplace.

Compensation per wRVU:
Under this model, the physician or group is paid a set rate of compensation per wRVU generated by the physician or group. The compensation rate may be set as single amount or based on a graduated scale.

---

8 Editor's note. This is a complex area of the tax law that involves the affiliated service group provisions of IRC §414(m) and the leased employee provisions of §414(n). The Patient Protection and Affordable Care Act (PPACA) introduced nondiscrimination requirements in the provision of health insurance under §105, although implementing regulations have been deferred by the IRS. The "Copperweld Doctrine" may also apply to permit otherwise related entities to stand alone and not be treated as an integrated entity for fringe benefit purposes.

Base Salary and Incentive and Productivity Bonus:

It is common for physicians in startup practices or in new positions to receive a base level of compensation during the initial years of an employment arrangement. Frequently, these salaries are coupled with productivity bonuses or incentive compensation based on a variety of measures. One popular formula includes compensation based on the greater of a base compensation level or compensation per wRVU.

Percentage of Revenue:

While not as common, some employers may compensate physicians based on the collections or revenues generated in the practice. There are various healthcare regulations that must be satisfied to compensate physicians legally based on practice collections or revenues, particularly those relating to the prohibition on being compensated for the volume or value of referrals for technical component services.

Percentage of Practice Precompensation Earnings:

Precompensation earnings (PCE) are defined as practice revenues less expenses, excluding physician compensation. Often thought of as the "Phycor" model because of its relation to the former physician practice management giant of the 1990s, the PCE model compensates physicians based on a percentage of the practice PCE. This model also must meet certain healthcare regulatory requirements because it involves the earnings from ancillary services.

Hybrid and Mix-and-Match Models:

Many hospital and health systems are developing hybrid compensation models that address various organizational or transactional objectives for the physician employment arrangement. For example, one variation on the compensation per wRVU model places a portion of the wRVU compensation rate into a quality or clinical outcomes pool. Physicians must reach various quality targets to receive a graduated percentage of this pool. In a similar move, a portion of the compensation per wRVU rate may be placed into a retention bonus pool. Monies from this pool are paid to physicians based on their tenure with the employer. Sign-on bonuses are also common in physician employment arrangements.

3.6 Compensation Stacking for Multiple Services

Another frequently observed compensation trend is so-called compensation "stacking," in which physicians are required to provide multiple levels or types of services under employment. Commonly observed stacking services include medical directorships, extensive hospital call coverage, or clinical or service line management of hospital service lines or departments. These services are required of a physician *in addition to* his or her clinical services that are provided to practice patients. Consequently, a physician is paid incrementally for these services *over and above* the compensation for clinical patient care services. So-called stacking arrangements can yield significant levels of additional compensation such that, when aggregated with clinical compensation, the physician's total compensation benchmarks in the upper percentiles of survey data. The potential difficulties or issues that can arise in so-called stacking arrangements include whether a physician is 1) being overpaid in the aggregate for the totality of services, 2) being compensated twice for the same work, or 3) realistically capable of providing the totality of services.

3.7 Level for Applying a Compensation Plan

Physician compensation models under employment are often applied at the individual physician level. They are also applied at the specialty or group level in some employment arrangements. In the group or specialty level models, a compensation pool is determined first at a collective level based on group or specialty performance and productivity. Individual physicians are then paid a pro rata share of this group or specialty compensation pools based on various criteria or measures.

3.8 Typical Benefits Packages for Employed Physicians

It should be noted that most hospital or health system employment arrangements will include the typical basket of employee benefits that one observes in corporate and larger organizations. Frequently, the employee benefits offered under employment will exceed the benefits physicians were receiving in their own practices, especially when the physician practiced on a solo basis or with a small to medium-size group. The one exception may be where a group was comprised of physicians nearing retirement and who had implemented a rich retirement plan. Most market-based retirement plans will not match the retirement benefits that physicians could pay themselves under various tax-free retirement benefit plans. Finally, physicians under employment are not able to expense or have reimbursed various "perks" that commonly run through the expenses of a physician-owned practice.

4.0 Healthcare Regulatory Requirements

4.1 Key Requirements of Healthcare and Tax Regulations

There are a series of healthcare and tax laws and regulations that have a bearing on physician compensation and particularly on physician compensation in the employment setting. Appraisers working in the discipline of healthcare compensation valuations should have general familiarity with these laws and regulations. They establish parameters for how compensation can be structured for physicians, but more importantly, they promulgate requirements for physician compensation. In general, these laws and regulations mandate that physician compensation:

- Not include compensation for the volume or value of referrals for certain healthcare services.

- Be consistent with fair market value (FMV).

- Be consistent with reasonable compensation.

- Be commercially reasonable.

It is also helpful for an appraiser to have a basic understanding of the parameters placed on physician compensation by these healthcare regulatory and tax rules to navigate through potential issues and pitfalls in valuing compensation plans. While the appraiser does not provide legal, tax, and regulatory advice in a transaction, a working knowledge of these rules will help ensure that the valuation is generally consistent with regulatory requirements. Thus, appraisers should seek to familiarize themselves with the overall framework of applicable healthcare and tax regulations. The following subsections provide an overview of the key regulatory matters. An in-depth analysis of these areas is beyond the scope of this chapter.

4.2 The Federal Anti-Kickback Statute and Stark Regulations

Two key sets of regulatory requirements are the federal anti-kickback statute (AKS) and the so-called Stark laws and regulations (Stark). Both AKS and Stark have highly specific requirements and related compliances issues that are not discussed here. There are, however, common elements between the two sets of regulations. First, AKS and Stark proscribe payment for the referral of certain healthcare services. Second, they require that transactions between parties with referral relationships should include remuneration that is consistent with FMV. Third, AKS and Stark specifically address physician employment arrangements where the employer is a provider of healthcare services referred by the employed physician. As part of its regulations for "in-office ancillaries" and the definition of a "group practice," Stark has an array of specific requirements related to how physicians may be compensated for technical component services that are generated within practices.

4.3 Tax Law Issues for Physician Compensation and Employment Arrangements

The tax considerations that can affect physician compensation in employment arrangements relate to the legal form and status of the employer entity. First, the legal form of the employer entity can raise the issue of how compensation paid to physicians is characterized for tax purposes. Specifically, C and S corporations are subject to rules related to whether amounts paid to physician-owners should be classified as compensation for services provided as employees or as ownership distributions or dividends in the case of C corporations. These classification issues affect the taxation of the amounts distributed. Second, tax-exempt organizations face a series of requirements related to compensation paid to employees. In particular, such compensation is subject to the standard of reasonable compensation as defined by tax regulations. It must also be based on methods that are consistent with the mission of the exempt organization.

4.4 State Laws and Regulations

Many states have their own so-called "mini" Stark laws and regulations addressing the referrals of healthcare services. As discussed previously, some states have prohibitions on the "corporate practice of medicine" that bar non-physician-owned entities from employing physicians to provide clinical and patient care services. States may also prohibit physician practices from providing certain types of ancillary services or have certificate-of-need requirements for such services. An overview and discussion of the myriad of state laws and regulations in these areas is clearly beyond the scope of this chapter, but appraisers should be aware that such regulations may have a bearing on their engagements to value physician employment arrangements. It is advisable for appraisers to inquire with clients and legal counsel involved in transactions as to whether any such laws and regulations are applicable to the subject arrangement.

5.0 Key Issues in Valuing Physician Employment Arrangements

5.1 Matching Compensation to Employment Services Provided

Since the key to the valuation of service arrangements is matching compensation to the services provided, it is essential to delineate the services being provided by the physician under a proposed employment arrangement. Compensation should be set in accordance with the services rendered to the employer by the employed physician. The first step in the valuation process for an employment agreement, therefore, is to identify the specific scope of services that the physician will provide. The scope of services can include clinical, administrative, or other types of services. Part of the process for identifying the scope of services is not only distinguishing among the types of services, but also the work requirements for each type of service. Key duties and work requirements can include the following, without limitation:

- Weekly required clinical hours;

- Required weeks worked per year;

- For physicians who are providing shift coverage (such as hospital-based physicians), shifts worked per week, month, and the required hours per shift;

- Required hospital call coverage, including type of coverage (restricted or unrestricted), shifts worked per month, and duration of shifts;

- Administrative duties, such as a medical directorship, including the specific duties and the required or estimated hours for performing these duties; and

- Supervision duties, including supervision of NPPs and technical component services.

The next step in the appraisal process is to determine the appraisal methods and techniques that are relevant and applicable to the valuation of the specific services. Since physician services are usually compensated based on the economic characteristics of the service, different valuation methods may need to be applied to each of service. The data sources for each type of service may also vary. Engagement planning, therefore, is built around an evaluation of the scope of services under employment and the economics characteristics of each service. A comprehensive assessment of total compensation may also be required as part of the valuation assignment. Many clients seek valuation opinions that address the total compensation paid for all services under an employment arrangement, not just the clinical services. When appraisal of the total compensation is included in the assignment, an appraiser will also need to prepare a "stacking" or total compensation analysis that assesses whether there is any overlap in compensation for the same service provided by the physician.

5.2 Using Surveys or Earnings as the Basis for Clinical Services Compensation

From a "big picture" perspective, generally two essential pathways for valuing clinical services are provided under physician employment arrangements. The first is based on application of the various published physician compensation surveys. For this approach, the valuation analyst gathers data on physician compensation from the surveys and develops criteria for comparability between the subject physician employment arrangement and the compensation levels reported in the surveys. The comparability measure is then used to determine a compensation level for the subject that is derived from the survey data. Since clinical services are the focus of the arrangement, the comparability measures used are generally based on various productivity measures, such as physician work relative value units (wRVUs) or professional collections. Methods that use the surveys are generally considered under the market approach.

The second way to approach the valuation of physician clinical services is using earnings-based compensation. This concept of compensation is based on the idea that the net earnings received by a professional are an economic measure of the value for these professional services. It applies not only to physicians, but also to other professionals, such as lawyers, accountants, consultants, and appraisers. Professionals such as these provide services in the marketplace to customers, whether in the form of patients or clients. The revenues received for services less the cost of providing the services (i.e., the net earnings from professional services) represent the value or compensation for the services in the marketplace. In general, earnings-based compensation as applied to physicians as professionals looks to the revenues generated by physician services less the cost of providing those services for the value of the services rendered. It includes the revenues, fees, and income generated by the physician in providing the specific scope of services contemplated in the subject service arrangement. These services can include clinical, administrative, hospital call coverage, and other professional services. The cost and expense of providing these various services are then deducted from the revenues or income streams for the services to arrive at a level of net earnings from the professional services rendered. These net earnings are considered the value of the physician's services. The concept of earnings-based compensation is usually reflected in valuation methods used under the cost and income approaches.

5.3 The Complexity in Valuing Physician Employment Arrangements for Clinical Services

On the surface, valuing physician employment arrangements for clinical services may appear more straightforward than it is. Because of the widespread use of physician compensation surveys to set compensation levels for employed physicians, some might think it is simply a matter of pulling numbers out of a book to establish market-based compensation for a subject physician. However, a professional appraisal of an employment arrangement under the healthcare regulatory definition of FMV is not a simple task. It involves so much more than merely pulling numbers out of a survey. As will be discussed in the accompanying chapters to this introduction, the valuation of physician employment arrangements for clinical services requires a high level of sophistication and rigor in dealing with market data, economic analysis, and appraisal reasoning. Multiple approaches and valuation methods should be considered and generally applied in valuing these arrangements. Consequently, employment valuations are one of the more complicated forms of compensation valuation in the healthcare arena.

6.0 Bibliography

Works Cited for Marketplace Trends in Physician Employment
Darves, Bonnie. "Physician Employment and Compensation Outlook for '07," April 2007. *New England Journal of Medicine*, Career Center Web site: www.nejmjobs.org/career-resources/physician-compensation-trends.aspx, accessed June 15, 2009.

Casalino, Lawrence P., Elizabeth A. November, Robert A. Berenson and Hoangmai H. Pham, "Hospital-Physician Relations: Two Tracks and the Decline of the Voluntary Medical Staff Model." *Health Affairs*, 27, no. 5 (2008): 1305-1314.

Hamilton, James, "Is the Future of Physician Practice Management Changing? Market Indicators Would Say Yes!" Somerset CPAs, Health Care commentaries Web site: www .somersetcpas.com/Newsletters/2007NovemberHCC/HCCarticle3.Print.htm, accessed on May 21, 2009.

Kennedy, Dennis, Clay, Scott, and Kolb Collier, Deborah, "Factors Driving Physician Employment Trend." *hfm Magazine*, April 2009: www.hfma.org/Templates/Print. aspx?id=1757, accessed May 21, 2009.

Liebhaber, Allison and Joy M. Grossman, "Physicians Moving to Mid-Sized, Single-Specialty Practices." Center for Studying Health System Change, *Tracking Report No. 18*, August 2007: www.hschange.com/CONTENT/941/, accessed June 15, 2009.

Merritt Hawkins & Associates, "2008 Review of Physician and CRNA Recruiting Incentives." Physician Salary, Compensation and Practice Surveys: www.merritthawkins. com/pdf/mha-2008-incentive-survey.pdf, accessed June 15, 2009.

Terry, Kenneth J., "Become a Partner or Remain an Employee?" May 5, 2009, Medscape Business of Medicine: www.medscape.com/viewarticle/702784_print, accessed June 4, 2009.

Chapter 23. Valuing Physician Employment Arrangements for Clinical Services: Market-Based Valuation Methods

CONTENTS

Chapter 23. Valuing Physician Employment Arrangements for Clinical Services: Market-Based Valuation Methods

By Timothy Smith, CPA/ABV

1.0 Introduction

The key to utilizing the market approach for valuing the compensation paid in service agreements is identifying and obtaining information on comparable agreements that can be used to establish the value of the subject contract. An appraiser can employ a variety of individual methods or techniques to establish a FMV guideline compensation level for the professional services of a physician using market data. The key to all these techniques is that they attempt, in one manner or another, to establish criteria for comparability between the market data and the subject physician or practice. The key to using such criteria in market approach methods is identifying those factors that affect compensation in the physician marketplace. In developing individual valuation techniques, the appraiser utilizes the criteria and information available in the data to derive relationships between compensation levels and these key factors. The appraiser then evaluates the subject physician or practice according to these criteria and determines an appropriate level or range of compensation using the data. Market-based methods are predicated on the concept that physician compensation in the marketplace is not random, but related to key factors that stem from the fundamental economics of physician services and from the market for physician services.

2.0 Sources of Market Data

2.1 Matching Market Data to the Services Provided

For valuations of employment agreements, use of the market approach begins with the identification of the scope of services to be provided under employment:

- Will the services be clinical, administrative, academic, or some combination thereof?

- Will the services be provided part time or full time?

- What scope of duties is required in the subject employment arrangement?

The appraiser should be able to enumerate and differentiate the types of services required under the employment contract as the first step in application of the market approach. Delineating the scope of services allows the appraiser to seek market data that is comparable to the subject arrangement. Market compensation data from arrangements with dissimilar services is not relevant or applicable for valuing a subject service arrangement because it lacks such comparability. It should be noted, however, that an appraiser can often use market information from service arrangements that are not fully similar to the subject arrangement, as long as the appraiser has sufficient information to make the appropriate adjustments to the market data and the subject arrangement to make them comparable for valuation purposes.

2.2 Qualitative Analysis and Criteria for Using Market Data in Valuation Methods

Since the essence of compensation valuation is matching compensation to the services provided, it is essential for the appraiser to have a thorough and studied understanding of the data sources being used for the market approach. Physician service arrangements under employment can often entail a variety of services. Each service may have distinct economics and market dynamics. Moreover, the combination or "stacking" of services may yield the possibility of duplicative payment for the same service or compensation for services or burdens not actually provided by the physician. As a result, the appraiser must be able to navigate through the details and nuances of market data to identify, utilize, apply, or adjust such data for use in valuing a subject employment arrangement. All too often, valuation consultants fail to take the time to understand market data or make unwarranted assumptions about market information without adequate research. Unhappily, their valuation work reflects uncritical and unstudied misapplication of market data.

Chapter 4, "On the Informed Use of Market Data in Compensation Valuation," provides a comprehensive discussion of criteria and qualitative analysis tools for assessing survey as well as individual transaction data in CV practice.

Another important criterion for the CV analyst to consider is the limitation placed by healthcare regulations on the use of market data for determining fair market value (FMV). See Chapter 8, "To Use or Not To Use: An Appraisal Analysis of the Stark Prohibition on Market Data from Parties in a Position to Refer," for an in-depth discussion of the restrictions.

2.3 Market Data From the Physician Compensation Surveys

The most widely available and accessible information sources on physician service arrangements are the various physician compensation surveys. These surveys are readily available to the public and can encompass thousands of responding practices and physicians from around the country. They include data from practices in which physicians are employees of health-system owned and operated practices as well as those that are physician-owned. Many of the surveys also include relevant data on physician productivity and other physician characteristics that can be useful in establishing comparability between the subject physician employment arrangement and the market data. Finally, some of the surveys contain data on administrative as well as clinical compensation. There are also surveys that report compensation for specialized types of services such as hospital call coverage and medical directorships. For these reasons, the physician compensation surveys have become a touchstone for establishing market levels of compensation for physicians in employment arrangements.

The following list presents *some* of the major surveys.

- Major surveys for clinical and total compensation:

  - Medical Group Management Association (MGMA), *Physician Compensation and Production Survey*

  - MGMA, *Cost Survey*

  - Sullivan, Cotter and Associates Inc. (SCA), *Physician Compensation and Productivity Survey Report*

  - Hospital & Healthcare Compensation Service, *Physician Salary Survey Report*

> ○ American Medical Group Association (AMGA), *Medical Group Compensation and Financial Survey*

> ○ Towers Watson Data Services, *Survey Report on Health Care Clinical & Professional Personnel Compensation*

- Survey data for newly hired physicians:

> ○ MGMA, *Physician Placement Starting Salary Survey*

> ○ AMGA, *Medical Group Compensation and Financial Survey*

- Major surveys for academic compensation:

> ○ SCA, *Physician Compensation and Productivity Survey Report*

> ○ MGMA, *Academic Practice Compensation and Production Survey for Faculty and Management*

> ○ Association of American Medical Colleges, *Report on Medical School Faculty Salaries*

- Surveys for executive compensation:

> ○ Cejka Search and the American College of Physician Executives, *Physician Executive Compensation Survey*

As noted, this list is not intended to be exhaustive. Other surveys and compensation data are available from various trade groups, medical specialty groups, and publishers. In addition, surveys are available for specific types of compensation, such as call coverage and medical directorships. Appraisers in the healthcare industry should keep abreast of the available survey data.

2.4 Market Data From Individual Transactions

In contrast to the physician compensation surveys, information on individual employment arrangements in the marketplace is generally difficult to obtain in sufficient detail for use in the valuation analysis. Nonetheless, an appraiser may be able to gather data on specific employment arrangements that are comparable to the subject arrangement or that can be adjusted for comparability to the subject. Where this is possible, the information gathered on the market comparable employment arrangements should be based on data that are accessible to appraisers generally. Use of proprietary data that only a specific appraiser or limited parties can access creates a conflict with the appraisal definition of FMV promulgated in Revenue Ruling 59-60 and the *International Glossary of Business Valuation Terms*. In both formulations of the definition, FMV requires that the buyer and seller have "reasonable knowledge" of the relevant facts. Reliance on proprietary data that are not available to other appraisers or parties raises the question of whether a hypothetical buyer and seller can have such reasonable knowledge. It also raises the question of whether another appraiser or outside parties can replicate the valuation analysis.

3.0 Productivity as the Measure of Comparability for Clinical Services

3.1 Relevant Criteria for Comparability

Various criteria can be used to place a subject physician on a comparable basis with market data, including the physician compensation surveys. Such criteria are considered to have an impact on physician compensation in the marketplace. They can and often vary based on the type and scope of physician services involved in the subject employment arrangement. Most physician employment valuations will focus on physicians who practice full-time or nearly full-time in a clinical setting providing patient care services. Since the nature of the services in this setting is clinical, the criteria used for relating the services should also be clinical in nature. Many potential criteria could be considered by an appraiser in evaluating clinical services. Factors such as training, experience, board certifications, and quality outcomes can affect the type and scope of clinical services provided by a physician.

The most common measure of clinical services used in the marketplace, however, is productivity. Multiple measures of physician productivity abound in the marketplace, and many of the physician compensation surveys include such productivity data. Since the predominant reimbursement mechanism in the current healthcare marketplace is based on fee-for-service, physician productivity is necessarily an important consideration in physician compensation.[1] As a result, physician productivity measures are widely used criteria for applying market compensation data to subject physicians in employment arrangements.

---

1   It should be noted that quality outcomes may become another critical factor as the healthcare industry focuses more on the quality of services, rather than the mere quantity of services. This pivot to payment for quality, however, appears to be a few years in the making and is not the current paradigm for reimbursement.

3.2 The Concept of Productivity-Matched Compensation

For clinical physician services, the prevailing techniques for applying market data for physician compensation to subject physicians are predicated on the concept of productivity-matched compensation. Simply stated, the concept seeks to match compensation with productivity: the higher the level of productivity, the higher the level of compensation, and vice versa. Productivity-based compensation presupposes that there is an inherent relationship between compensation and productivity in the survey data, i.e., that compensation correlates with compensation in a fairly consistent fashion. Because of its simplicity and apparent objectivity as a formula for determining physician pay, productivity-based compensation is a widely used concept in valuing compensation for physicians in the healthcare marketplace.

Productivity-matched compensation valuation techniques are generally based on two approaches for applying market data to a subject physician. In the first approach, a subject physician's productivity can be benchmarked relative to his or her peers in the survey data[2] using productivity metrics. A corresponding level of reasonable compensation can then be determined using the compensation data from the survey. A second approach applies compensation rates per unit of productivity from the surveys to the historical or forecasted level of productivity for the physician and thereby establishes a guideline compensation amount.

The use of productivity measures to apply physician compensation survey data to a subject physician in an employment valuation is analogous and comparable to the guideline public company method in business valuation. Under this business valuation method, various pricing multiples or ratios are derived from the equity markets for publicly traded companies. These multiples or ratios are applied to the subject company being appraised to establish the value or range of value for the subject. Such ratios as price to earnings, price to revenue, or other common-sizing metrics based on market data are considered to reflect a reasonable economic relationship to value in the marketplace. By applying these ratios to key operating metrics of a subject company, a market value can be established. Physician productivity measures are used similarly in valuing physician compensation for clinical service arrangements. Ratios and relationships are derived from the survey data for compensation and productivity. These guidelines are then applied to the subject physician's productivity levels to establish a market-based level of compensation.

---

2   Since the most readily available and extensive sources of market data for physicians are the various surveys, this chapter will focus on the use and application of survey market data. The methods discussed here, however, could also be applied to data from individual market transactions.

3.3 Selecting Productivity Measures

Several key factors should be considered in selecting productivity measures to serve as the basis for productivity-matched compensation valuation techniques for individual physicians:

1. The measures should be a reflection of an individual physician's productivity and work efforts. Hence, they should generally reflect personally performed services by the physician.

2. Data on the productivity measures need to be available in the survey data, or alternatively, the appraiser should be able to estimate the measure on a reasonable basis relative to the survey data.

3. The measures should have a substantial relationship to the fundamental economics of the clinical services being valued.

4. The measures need to be readily accessible and determinable from the information available in a physician practice. Otherwise, use of a measure may be impracticable for valuation purposes.

5. It is advisable to use measures that are widely accepted or used in physician practices, where such measures meet the other criteria. Obscure or foreign measures may unduly complicate and obfuscate use of the valuation by the parties to the arrangement.

In the following subsections, several commonly used productivity measures are discussed.

3.4 Physician Work RVUs

Physician work relative value units (wRVUs) are perhaps the most popular measure of physician productivity in the marketplace today. This popularity is not without reason. Physician wRVUs represent a universal scale by which all physicians can be measured because they are calculated using publicly available rates established each year in the Medicare Physician Fee Schedule (MPFS) by CPT and HCPCS procedure code. Thus, wRVUs can be calculated in a consistent and uniform manner from provider to provider. As a result, they provide a highly relevant measure of provider productivity.

There are several important points, however, that appraisers should take into account in using wRVUs as the measure of productivity for physicians:

1. *Personally performed procedures:* As noted previously, the wRVUs used for a provider, whether a physician or a nonphysician provider, should be based on the procedures personally performed by the provider. For physicians, any procedures performed by nonphysician providers that are billed "incident-to" under a supervising physician should not be counted in the calculation of wRVUs for the subject physician.

2. *Modifier adjustments:* The calculation of wRVUs may include an adjustment when procedures are performed subject to the use of certain CPT code modifiers. When these modifier codes are used, adjustment factors should be applied to the wRVU calculations. Each of the relevant modifiers has a separate adjustment factor. Some modifiers reduce the number of wRVUs, while others increase the wRVUs allotted to the procedure. To adjust the wRVUs for the use of modifiers, the adjustment factor for the modifier is multiplied by the wRVU rate for the procedure code and then by the number of procedures performed subject to the use of the modifier. The product of this computation is the adjusted wRVUs for those procedures performed subject to the modifier.[3]

3. *No GPCI adjustment:* Medicare GPCIs should not be used in calculating the wRVUs for physician benchmarking and valuation purposes. The GPCI rates are intended for use in computing Medicare reimbursement for the local market. They are not part of the universal scale for determining how many wRVUs a physician has generated.

4. *Annual wRVU scale:* We note that the surveys report wRVUs for responding physicians based on the data from the prior year, e.g., a 2011 report based on 2010 data. Thus, the survey data are based on the wRVU rates from the MPFS for the year of data provided. MPFS wRVUs rates may change from year to year, however, creating potential "noise" for multiyear benchmarking of physicians when using the most recently available survey. To reduce the potential impact of changes in wRVU rates per procedure code when using historical data in comparison to survey data, it is advisable to review the changes in wRVU rates for the relevant years used in benchmarking. An appraiser may need to adjust for any material changes, on a volume-weighted basis, in wRVU rates for the historical years reviewed and the rates used in the reference survey data.

---

3   The reason for this adjustment is that the procedure was performed under circumstances that have a bearing on reimbursement, and thereby, on the RVUs associated with the procedure. It should be noted that there are numerous modifiers related to CPT and HCPCS codes. Not all modifiers will affect the computation of wRVUs.

Appraisers should also note the advantages and disadvantages of using wRVUs for measuring an individual physician's productivity level. The advantages of using wRVUs include the fact that they provide a universal and common scale for measuring the productivity of physicians in the same practicing specialty. They are widely used in the healthcare industry for compensation and productivity benchmarking purposes and data for wRVUs is available in many of the surveys. The main disadvantages of using wRVUs as a productivity measure for compensation valuation purposes is that they take into account only one factor that can affect compensation in the physician marketplace. Other key economic factors such as reimbursement in the local market, technical service mix, and cost considerations are not encapsulated in wRVU data.

3.5 Professional Collections

Professional collections are the collections received from professional component services and the professional component of global diagnostic testing services provided to patients. The professional component of a global diagnostic testing service represents that portion of a service or procedure that is performed by a physician, which is typically the interpretation of the exam. It is distinguished from the technical component of a global procedure or service, which usually entails the technological aspects of the exam.

Since professional collections are based on the collection efforts of the practice support staff or third-party vendors, one may question why this metric would be used for measuring the individual productivity of a physician. *The critical reason for using professional collections is that they can reflect what the local market is paying for a physician's productivity.* As discussed in Chapter 37, "How Reimbursement and Physician Compensation Vary by Market," both Medicare and commercial payers reimburse physician services at varying rates. There is wide variability in commercial reimbursement from market to market within the United States and within a market. Moreover, professional collections may reflect local market payer mix conditions that also affect what is paid for a physician's productivity in the local market. Thus, professional collections are a key indicator of the revenue streams generated by a physician's productivity that will ultimately have a significant impact on the level of compensation that can be afforded and sustained by the practice. Professional collections, therefore, adds a local market dynamic to the determination of provider productivity.

Professional collections also reflect the effectiveness of a practice's revenue cycle efforts. Where the billing and collection operations of a practice are reasonable and well-operated, professional collections can provide a window into the revenue value of profession services in the local market. Where a practice has revenue cycle issues, however, the appraiser may need to normalize the collections to reflect what a reasonable operator, or the typical employer (who one would assume is a reasonable operator), would collect for professional services. Normalizing professional collections removes the one aspect of this measure that is not related to the physician's productivity.

The use of professional collections along with wRVUs can provide an appraiser with differing and yet complementary information about a physician's productivity. While wRVUs provide a uniform scale for measuring the productivity across all markets, the amount of professional collections serves as an indication of productivity as measured by local market reimbursement factors. Reimbursement can be a key factor in determining the range of market-based compensation for physicians. Use of professional collections for productivity benchmarking purposes can reflect this market variability and thereby affords an added informational element beyond the uniform productivity scale afforded by using wRVUs. Use of professional collections can provide a more localized indicator of the value of physician compensation in the local market context because they reflect the market reimbursement level for physician services.

3.6 Other Measures of Physician Productivity

Other measures can be relevant for assessing the productivity of certain types of physician specialties. For example, patient encounters are a useful productivity measure for primary care physicians, whose main form of clinical services tend to be office and hospital visits. Surgical cases are clearly a relevant measure for surgical physician specialties. Both metrics, however, may not be as informative as wRVUs in that the complexity and level of service may vary by patient encounter or surgical case. Anesthesiologists have created their own RVU-type scale using American Society of Anesthesiologists (ASA) units. These ASA units are based on measures of time established for each anesthesia procedure. In evaluating the use of other measures, the appraiser should consider the utility of such measures based on the previously discussed criteria for evaluating productivity measures.

Some of the surveys report professional charges or gross charge information. While such information may be helpful in certain areas, charge data are not always meaningful for productivity comparison and benchmarking purposes. The difficulty with charges relates to the fact that physician practices establish gross charge levels based on varying formulas. Many practices, for example, set their gross charge rate by procedure based on a percentage of Medicare, but the percentage of Medicare can vary from practice to practice. Thus, comparison of charges across physician practices may not be based on a uniform and standard scale. Gross charges by physician can be relatively higher or lower from practice to practice based solely on varying calculations for establishing gross charge rates. This lack of uniformity in the measuring scale makes the use of gross charges a less meaningful tool for productivity measurement.

3.7 Productivity Measures for Hospital-Based Physicians

As noted in Chapter 13, "An Introduction to Physician Services and Specialties," the fundamental economics and service-setting of hospital-based physicians can be significantly different than their office-based peers. These differences may necessitate the use of alternative productivity measures for hospital-based physicians. Moreover, the work requirements and productivity expectations for hospital-based physicians in employment and professional service arrangements often revolve around definitions that are not focused on volumes or maintenance of a weekly office schedule. The workload of hospital-based physicians is commonly denominated in terms of shifts covered at a facility. Often, these shifts are distinguished in terms of the time of day, the day of the week, and the time of year, i.e., holidays. Shifts may be also differentiated in terms of the types of cases that will be covered during the shift. Recognition may be given to the relative workload for a specific shift time or at a given facility. For example, the patient volumes for the emergency department (ED) at one hospital may be substantially higher than the volumes at another facility a few miles away. Similarly, the weekend night shifts for an ED may be busier and more acute when the ED is in close proximity to bars and clubs with histories of closing-time violence. As a result, pay for such shifts may be paid at a premium.

Productivity for hospital-based physicians, therefore, may be better defined or primarily defined in terms of annual hours in comparison to procedure volumes or collections in many circumstances. Annual hours provide a means of converting annuals shifts worked by a physician into a common scale because shift hours and shifts worked per month can vary from facility to facility. One difficulty, however, in attempting to use annual hours as a measure of productivity is that survey data for this metric is not readily available at the level that other productivity measures are. MGMA and SCA had been reporting some data in this area, but in the past couple of years, they have stopped doing so.

3.8 Productivity Measures for Physician Practices

An appraiser may want to assess a physician practice's overall productivity in terms of both professional and technical services and thereby look at compensation at the practice level. Such productivity assessment can be helpful in operational evaluations of a practice and in evaluating aggregate or overall compensation at the practice level. Two key productivity metrics that can be used for such measurement are total relative value units (tRVUs) and total revenues.[4] Like wRVUs, tRVUs provide a productivity

---

4   Use of these measures for individual physicians is ill-advised, given the prohibitions on payments for referrals under the Stark regulations. Group-level use of these metrics, however, can be appropriate, where the criteria for sharing in ancillary earnings under Stark are met by the subject arrangement.

measurement for professional and technical services using a universal scale. Total revenues represent the revenues from both professional and technical services. It may also include other forms of professional service revenues, such as compensated call coverage, medical directorships, special services contracts, and the like. Similar to professional collections, total revenue can provide an indication of the value of a practice's total services in the local marketplace. Since these practice-level measures include technical component services, appraisers should be aware of any potential Stark implications of valuing these services.

4.0 Market-Based Valuation Methods Based on Productivity

While there may be a variety of techniques that individual appraisers or appraisal firms have developed over the years, the following section discusses some of the more commonly used or noteworthy methods. In general, the various techniques using market survey data all attempt to relate such data to the subject physician to establish a market-based level of compensation for the subject. They focus on making the subject physician or employment arrangement comparable to the survey data. Each method necessarily has relative strengths and weaknesses and may or may not be applicable to a particular physician or employment arrangement. It is the task of the appraiser using sound valuation thinking and professional judgment to determine what methods are applicable and supportable based on the facts and circumstances. Indeed, such thinking and judgment are the real value-added element that trained and skilled appraisers bring to the healthcare industry in the determination of FMV compensation.

4.1 Percentile Matching Technique

The percentile matching technique calculates a compensation level that corresponds to a physician's benchmarked level of productivity based on the reported percentiles of productivity and compensation in the survey data for the subject physician's specialty. For example, a physician who benchmarks at the 65th percentile for productivity is assigned 65th-percentile compensation as a market-based guideline for compensation. In benchmarking a physician's productivity and matching level of compensation, appraisers generally utilize a linear interpolation computation to determine benchmarked productivity percentile and the corresponding compensation amount. As a result, this technique is also known as the linear interpolation method.[5]

---

5   The linear interpolation method is perhaps the more widely used name for this valuation technique. While this label is descriptive of the mathematical calculations involved in the method, it fails to describe the basic concept and logic entailed in the method. I have therefore relabeled this method in a manner that is more descriptive and user-friendly to the variety of users of valuation reports found in the healthcare market. The invocation of "linear interpolation" unnecessarily complicates the method for the typical user: Most users would rather forget the statistics courses they took in college or graduate school, much less think about how an appraiser applied linear interpolation to survey data.

By far, the percentile matching technique is one of the most commonly used methods for appropriating physician compensation survey data and applying them to a subject physician. Its common use is not without reason. First, the method is readily understood and accepted by players in the healthcare marketplace because it directly relates compensation to productivity in a proportional manner. Second, the method is objective in the sense that it is formulaic and applied consistently from physician to physician and from specialty to specialty. Third, the method can be readily replicated by another appraiser using the same input data to the valuation process. Finally, the method appears to be "elegant" in that it provides a simple formula for common-sizing physicians and compensation survey data vis-à-vis productivity.

Users of the technique should be aware, however, of the assumptions inherent in the method as well as its fundamental limitations. The percentile matching technique assumes a one-to-one or directly corresponding relationship between compensation and productivity. Users should note that this is an *assumption* that is not necessarily validated by the underlying data. To use the technique, the user has to reference two sets of data tables, one for compensation and the other for productivity. Generally, the data presented in these tables are not fully consistent. The data set for productivity is usually a subset of the data for compensation. The difference results from the fact that the primary criterion for inclusion in the reported survey data is providing compensation information. Many respondents do not report productivity. Thus, the data set for respondents reporting productivity measures is usually much lower than the number reporting compensation.

In correlating the data set with its subset, the percentile matching technique necessarily assumes that the range and dispersion of productivity for those respondents who reported compensation but not productivity is comparable to those who did report the productivity. Stated alternatively, the respondents who did report productivity are representative of the entire respondent base included in the compensation table. In positing this assumption, the use of a data set and a subset of these data to correlate two variables is not considered to be a fundamental objection to the technique.

A more critical issue related to the percentile matching technique is that the underlying data for compensation and productivity do not generally correspond in the direct relationship presupposed by the method. Conceptually for the technique to hold true, nearly all physicians in the data set would need to be compensated on a productivity basis that is directly variable with the productivity measure and paid at the same effective rate relative to the measure. The reality of the physician marketplace is that physicians are compensated based on a variety of factors, including productivity- and non-productivity-based factors. Moreover, the variability in market reimbursement, payer mix, service mix, and cost structures in physician practices does not readily lend itself to uniform rates of compensation per unit of productivity.

Moreover, examination of the underlying data from MGMA does not indicate a strong correlation between a productivity measure and compensation. Regression line analysis using compensation and wRVUs as well as compensation and professional collections as variables is discussed in Chapter 39, "An Analysis of the Relationship Between Productivity and Compensation in the MGMA Data and Its Implications for Valuation and Compensation-Setting Practices." As shown in this chapter, the regression analysis does not show a correlation between compensation and each productivity variable at levels whereby a single productivity metric alone explains compensation levels. *What this regression line analysis may also indicate is that a single productivity measure is insufficient to account for a physician's compensation level.* A multiplicity of productivity factors as well as considerations related to service mix and cost may also affect physician compensation levels. Other noneconomic factors may play a role as well.

Moreover, MGMA has recently starting analyzing the compensation per wRVU rate for physicians in each quartile of productivity based on wRVUs. Their analysis, as detailed in the introductory section of the survey for the past few years, shows that the compensation per wRVU rate is greatest for physicians in the first quartile of production, i.e., up to the 25th percentile. The compensation per wRVU rate is the lowest for physicians in the fourth quartile of production, i.e., for physicians above the 75th percentile. The MGMA data, therefore, appear to present a more complex and less direct relationship between compensation and productivity than is implied through the percentile matching technique. For more information on this issue, see Chapter 40, "An Analysis of MGMA's Compensation by Quartile of Production Data: Compensation Rates Decline as Production Increases."

The author notes, however, that the percentile matching technique often yields results that tend to display effective compensation rates consistent with MGMA's compensation by quartile of production data. The author frequently observes that the effective or calculated compensation rate yielded by dividing compensation reported at each major percentile, i.e., 25th, median, 75th, and 90th, by the productivity level at each corresponding percentile frequently declines from the 25th to the 90th percentile. This indicates the effective compensation per unit of productivity rate implied in the percentile matching technique also declines, when one observes this decline in the calculated rates. In short, the percentile matching technique, despite its statistical inadequacies, may yield results that parallel more statistically valid computations in certain cases. The author notes that further study would be needed to determine the overall frequency of this pattern and its relation to actual data.

Observing fundamental conceptual and statistical limitations of the percentile matching technique is not necessarily grounds for rejection of the method. Productivity clearly affects the level of revenue coming into a physician practice, and thereby, the level of net earnings available for physician compensation. Moreover, respondents to the surveys indicate that productivity is one of the key factors in establishing compensation for physicians.[6] In addition, statistical analysis of the MGMA data does show some level of correlation between productivity and compensation. Thus, there is support for the method. The precision and finality of its application to a subject physician, however, should not be viewed in an unqualified or uncritical manner. Recognition of its qualified validity as a method of applying physician compensation survey data to a subject employment arrangement should serve as a governor of uncritical deployment of the method in compensation valuation. Such recognition should also point appraisers away from overreliance or sole use of the method, where other techniques and the required data for these methods are available to the appraiser.

4.2 Median Rate Technique

The median rate technique (MRT) uses the median compensation rate per unit of productivity from the physician compensation surveys and a physician's historical productivity level to establish a market-based level of compensation. To compute the guideline compensation level, the median compensation rate for a productivity measure is multiplied by the historical level of productivity. The median rate is used for two reasons. First, the median, as the middle value in a data set, can be viewed as a reasonable or representative proxy for a typical rate within the data set. In addition, some appraisers have observed that the median rate is often fairly consistent with the calculated compensation per unit of productivity rate each reported percentile in the survey data. In other words, compensation at a given percentile divided by the reported productivity level at the same percentile frequently approximates the median rate or is within a reasonable range of the median.[7] The median rate, in such cases, can be viewed as the most explanatory rate for the reported range of compensation and productivity in the survey. Thus, use of the median compensation rate per unit of productivity for a given productivity metric is often employed as technique for establishing market-based compensation guidelines.

Use of the median rate, particularly the median compensation per wRVU rate, has unhappily become a valuation "rule of thumb" for employment compensation. Physician expectations are frequently set for compensation purposes at the median rate from the

---

6   See the respondent profile sections of MGMA, AMGA, and SCA, where methods for compensated physicians are discussed.

7   For further discussion and analysis of calculated compensation per wRVU rates, see Chapter 41, "Analyzing Physician Compensation per wRVU: Why Benchmark Data Is Only the Beginning."

survey data, especially MGMA. For many in the physician marketplace, the median compensation per wRVU is a categorical imperative: All physicians should receive compensation consistent with their historical productivity multiplied by the median rate. Unfortunately, this market expectation is misinformed.

Statistically speaking, the median rate represents the middle rate from the data set. Thus, approximately half of the respondents in the data received less than the median, and approximately half received more than the median rate. The claim that every physician should make at least the median compensation per wRVU is just not grounded in sound statistical reasoning and analytics.

MGMA's recent analysis and reporting of the compensation per wRVU rate by quartile production also provides a reality check on the categorical and unqualified use of the median compensation per wRVU rate to establish FMV compensation for employment arrangements. As noted previously and as will be discussed in more detail in the following section, MGMA has presented data indicating that the compensation per wRVU rate declines as the productivity level of wRVUs increases, and vice versa. The reported median, therefore, may have limited validity at the upper and lower ends of the productivity scale.

Like the percentile matching technique, recognizing the limits and weaknesses of the median rate technique do not necessarily serve as reasons for wholesale jettisoning of the technique. Rather, such acknowledgment can serve to circumscribe, qualify, and limit the use of and reliance on the technique for establishing FMV compensation. Given the availability of survey data and the simplicity of calculation, the median rate technique can be easily calculated when valuing physician employment compensation and used for comparison purposes. Appraisers should be wary, however, of sole reliance, overreliance, and unqualified reliance on the method. As a practical matter, use of the median rate may be the most supportable when a physician's productivity approximates the median level of productivity.

4.3 Compensation by Quartile of Production Technique

A new and noteworthy valuation technique has emerged with the publication of certain studies in MGMA that examines the compensation per wRVU rate of physicians by quartile of wRVU production.[8] The compensation by quartile of production technique (CQPT) uses certain median compensation to productivity rates by quartile of production for a given physician specialty to determine a guideline compensation level. The technique is applied as follows. First a physician's productivity level is benchmarked

---

8   These studies are published in the introductory sections of MGMA.

into the appropriate quartile of production based on the survey data for the relevant productivity measure. Next, the applicable median compensation to productivity rate for the quartile of production is multiplied by the physician's productivity level to compute a guideline level of compensation. In general, physician wRVU and professional collections are used as the measure of productivity for this technique.

MGMA is currently the only survey providing these data, and it is available by special order. MGMA has, however, presented limited data from a specialty or two for compensation per wRVU in the "Key Findings" section of its survey in last few years. It has also discussed the implications of these data, noting that the compensation per wRVU generally decreases as productivity increases. Thus, physicians in the fourth or top quartile of productivity generally make less per unit of productivity than those in lower quartiles, although their total compensation is higher. For an in-depth discussion of this data, see Chapter 40, "An Analysis of MGMA's Compensation by Quartile of Production Data: Compensation Rates Decline as Production Increases."

The appeal and strength of the compensation by quartile of production technique is that it is based on the actual correlation of compensation and productivity within the data. To calculate the median by quartile of production, MGMA segregates individual respondents into quartiles based on their production and then computes the compensation to productivity rate for the respondents in each quartile to derive a median for the quartile. Unlike the percentile matching technique, which assumes that the compensation at a given percentile correlates with the production at the same percentile, these data are based on the actual compensation of respondents within a quartile of production.

In evaluating the CQPT, one should not fail to understand the nature of the data used in the method. *The CQPT uses a median for the quartile; the method does not indicate that there are physicians not making more or less than the median for the quartile.* Thus, the CQPT should not be taken as a precise value applicable to any physician in the quartile. Once again, there is wider variability in the rates for all respondents within a quartile of production than is indicated by sole consideration of the median rate. A single compensation rate per unit of productivity measure appears to be inadequate to explain the full range of compensation outcomes for physicians. While the CQPT may have more statistical validity and afford greater applicability to varying ranges of productivity, it is not intended to produce an exact and precise determination of market-based compensation. Rather, it provides an indication based on the median for the quartile.

4.4 Workload and Hourly Techniques

Another technique for applying physician compensation survey data to a subject employment arrangement focuses on the workload associated with the arrangement in terms of hours worked or on a comparable FTE level. In general, workload and hourly rate techniques use survey data and estimates of annual hours to derive guideline hourly rates. These guideline hourly rates are then applied to shifts or annual hours required by the terms of a subject physician employment arrangement to determine an appropriate level of compensation for the arrangement. As discussed previously, this method is highly relevant when valuing employment arrangements for hospital-based physicians in which shifts or annual hours worked may be the primary or critical definition of productivity.

Workload techniques may also be used to assess or adjust salary or base compensation levels when the work requirements of the subject arrangement appear to be above or below market norms for a given specialty. For example, an employment arrangement may provide a physician with eight weeks of leave, including continuing medical education (CME) days. If survey or other market data indicate that the norm for the specialty is five weeks of leave, the appraiser may conclude that the subject arrangement requires a reduced workload in comparison to the market data. As a result, the appraiser will reduce the compensation for the arrangement, when market data from physicians with five weeks of leave or less are used to establish the level of pay for the position. Likewise, a proposed employment agreement requiring 2,400 annual working hours may represent an above-market level of hours for a specialty. The appraiser may increase the compensation level, where the survey data are based on physicians working annual hours substantially below the subject arrangement.

The key factor or analysis point in applying a workload valuation technique is the selection of the annual hours or weeks worked per year that is applied or correlated with survey data to establish an hourly pay rate or the number of weeks of worked expected for a given compensation level. The difficulty for the appraiser in selecting these inputs to the valuation process is the dearth of available survey data on annual work hours and weeks worked per year. Up until the last couple of survey years, MGMA and SCA reported some data that could be used to make such estimates. SCA had been reporting annual hours by specialty, while MGMA reported weeks worked per year and hours worked per week by specialty. The only metric appearing in the current surveys is MGMA's weeks worked per year.[9]

The exhibit illustrates the potential range of annual hours that can be worked by physicians, based on varying weeks worked and hours worked per week. The level of assumed

---

9   Based on the 2010 MGMA and SCA surveys as well as the 2011 MGMA survey. It should be noted that these data was often reported with few respondents and may not have been meaningful. The frequent use of 40 hours per week or 2,000 hours per year across numerous specialties seemed to indicate respondents were reporting such hours on a pro forma basis.

Annual Hours Worked					
Weeks Worked per Year	Weekly Work Hours				
	35	40	45	50	55
50	1,750	2,000	2,250	2,500	2,750
49	1,715	1,960	2,205	2,450	2,695
48	1,680	1,920	2,160	2,400	2,640
47	1,645	1,880	2,115	2,350	2,585
46	1,610	1,840	2,070	2,300	2,530
45	1,575	1,800	2,025	2,250	2,475
44	1,540	1,760	1,980	2,200	2,420

annual hours is not without consequence for the valuation analysis, since the lower the annual hours, the higher the hourly rate and vice versa.

A second challenge in applying workload appraisal techniques is how estimates of annual hours or weeks worked per year should be related to compensation levels reported at the various percentiles in the surveys. Should a normalized or constant number of annual hours or weeks worked per year be used as the divisor for all reported percentiles or should varying levels be used? For example, an appraiser may attempt to rationalize or normalize the compensation data and estimates of annual hours by assuming that compensation levels tend to increase with higher annual hours. Such an assumption can be reflective of certain market realities, where physicians in a fee-for-service reimbursement environment or in productivity-based compensation models can earn more by working longer hours and performing more procedures. To implement this approach, the appraiser associates higher estimated annual hours with higher levels of compensation in the surveys and vice versa. Yet, one cannot be assured of such correlation in the data or meaningful outcomes in utilizing this approach.[10] Another potential assumption is that hourly rates are a function of physician productivity and efficiency within a normalized working year. Higher hourly rates should reflect greater productivity and efficiency achieved per working hour. To utilize this assumption, the appraiser selects a normalized workload of annual hours and divides it into selected compensation levels to derive a range of hourly rates.

---

10   The author recounts his attempt at such correlation using the formerly available workload data. The results did not appear to be meaningful. The use of increasing annual hours divided into reported percentiles of compensation resulted in a wide array of randomly fluctuating hourly rates from percentile to percentile.

In summary, application of workload-based valuation techniques will require appraisers to make estimates, judgments, and assumptions about workload levels and their relation to reported compensation levels in the survey data. Unfortunately, minimal market survey data are available for physician workloads, and even less data showing the relationship between compensation levels and annual hours worked. Given this lack of data and the need for hourly compensation rates in the marketplace, appraisers should strive to make the most of any data that are available and utilize the most supportable estimates and assumptions possible.

5.0 Non-Productivity-Based Methods and Independent Criteria Techniques

In certain circumstances, an appraiser may need to develop criteria independently of the survey data that are then used to apply survey compensation data to a subject physician. The criteria are independent of the survey data in that such criteria are not included in the various reported metrics of the surveys. They are developed and assessed by the appraiser using informed, but subjective judgment. In some cases, alternative data sources may be found to support the criteria as important factors in the determination of physician compensation. Yet, the correlation of these factors with specific percentiles or ranges from the survey data is based on informed but nonetheless subjective judgment on the part of the appraiser. These criteria may include comparability factors unrelated to physician productivity measures, such as those related to qualifications.

Because they involve subjective judgment, the use of such methods should only be used when necessitated by a valuation engagement where more objective techniques are not available due to data limitations or unique facts and circumstances rendering alternative methods less relevant and applicable to the subject arrangement. The appraiser should make a concerted effort to document and support the assumptions, estimates, judgments, and reasoning entailed in such subjective techniques. Use of scoring or ratings for various factors used in the judgment process can be a productive way to apply and relate the survey data to the subject arrangement. Such scorings or ratings do not necessarily need to result in a mathematic outcome; they can be used merely to document and present the thought process informing the judgment of the appraiser.

The use of independent criteria techniques based on subjective professional judgments may be analogous to the development of specific company risk premiums in the cost of capital calculation in business valuation. In preparing a cost of capital rate, the appraiser formulates a series of factors that can affect the subject company's risk profile relative to the market and industry and then evaluates the subject using these criteria. The process results in a specific risk premium based on the informed, but subjective judgment of the appraiser. Some appraisers will actually create a scoring formula that assigns a certain number of basis points to the specific company risk premium. Whatever approach is used, the appraiser is expected to support and defend the specific risk premium, notwithstanding the fact that it is ultimately based on professional and informed, but subjective judgment.

Appraisers, who by necessity, utilize subjective valuation techniques in applying the physician compensation survey data to subject employment arrangements should likewise be able to support and defend such methods. The methods should be grounded, to the extent possible, in facts, evidence, research, sound valuation reasoning, and a rigorous understanding of the physician marketplace and the fundamental economics of physician practices. The mere assertion of criteria or relationships between factors and the survey data without clearly articulated support and defense does not constitute the professional practice of appraisal. Users of valuation services should not accept work product that does not meet such professional standards.

6.0 Key Terms and Metrics to Define in Using Survey Data

There are certain terms and metrics in the physician compensation surveys whose definitions must be carefully understood for appropriate use of the survey data. An appraiser should ensure that he or she has adequately reviewed the definitions of these terms to ensure that the survey data is not used erroneously. The reason such background research is necessary is that many commonly used terms related to physician services and practices can have highly specific definitions and uses in the surveys. Moreover, surveys may not use certain terms consistently from survey to survey. Finally, there are often data nuances to what may or may not be included in a given metric. The following is a listing of many of the key terms and metrics for which appraisers should ensure a correct understanding.

6.1 Compensation

The key compensation measures in the surveys generally report total cash compensation from all sources. Some surveys, however, do report data on selected forms of compensation, such as base salary or signing bonuses. To use compensation data in the market approach appropriately, it is essential to use data that are comparable to the compensation for the subject agreement. Thus, use of market data based on total cash compensation for valuing one compensation element in an employment arrangement, such as base compensation, may represent a misapplication of the data, depending on the nature of the other elements. Appraisers should review and be clear on the definitions used for various compensation metrics in the survey data.

6.2 Physician Specialty

Another critical area for establishing comparability in using market survey data relates to the selection of the relevant physician specialty or subspecialty. To the consternation of many users, the physician compensation surveys do not always use clear or consistent terminology with respect to all physician specialties or subspecialties. Special attention, therefore, should be given to the definitions and terminology used in the surveys. Moreover, appraisers should be aware of the distinction between a physician's training and board certifications and his or her primary practice patterns with respect to specialty or subspecialty designation. Training and board certifications may not always be indicative of a physician's primary clinical focus. Thus, appraisers should not only evaluate the survey definitions and terminology, but also a subject physician's credentials and practice patterns to ensure that the appropriate, comparable specialty in the market data is applied. MGMA, for example, bases specialty classification on the where the physician spends 50% of more of his or her time in providing clinical services.

6.3 Relative Value Units

Many of the physician compensation surveys provide productivity and other data, including various metrics related to wRVUs and tRVUs. There are nuances, however, in how such data are reported in the surveys. Most of the surveys report physician wRVUs based on those personally performed by physicians and excluding those performed by nonphysician providers but credited to and billed under physicians. The reason for this exclusion is that the surveys seek to report the personal productivity of physicians. When gathering productivity data on a subject physician, appraisers should ensure that such data are provided on a basis that is consistent with the surveys for accurate comparison purposes. A helpful distinction to make in gathering such data is between rendering or service provider and billing provider. The former represents the provider who actually performed the services, while the latter indicates the provider under which the services were billed to payers.

One exception to this general definition for wRVUs is the MGMA *Cost Survey*. The "physician wRVUs" reported in this survey include all wRVUs for a reporting practice, regardless of the type of provider who performed the services. Thus, they include both physician and nonphysician provider wRVUs.

Total RVUs (tRVUs) is another metric where close attention should be given to the definition in the surveys. The metric of tRVUs in the MGMA *Physician Compensation and Production Survey* includes only RVUs associated with the professional services, excluding the technical component of clinical services. The *Cost Survey*, by contrast, includes RVUs from technical component services.

Another key to the definition of RVUs in the surveys is that they generally exclude any adjustments for the geographic practice cost index (GPCI) under Medicare or for weightings based on conversion factors. In addition, RVUs are typically determined based on the Medicare Physician Fee Schedule (MPFS) rates. Where rates are not available for a procedure, the surveys often provide guidance on how to compute RVUs for such services.

6.4 Professional Charges and Collections

In addition to RVUs, professional charges and collections are frequently reported productivity metrics in the surveys. Like RVUs, these metrics can have precise definitions in the surveys. They generally exclude services performed by nonphysician providers, but billed incident-to a physician. They also exclude technical component services. Other exclusions may also apply in a survey. MGMA, for example, provides specific inclusions and exclusions for professional charges and collections from professional charges as part of the questionnaire guide for respondents completing its survey.

7.0 Critical Considerations in Using the Physician Compensation Surveys

The market approach and the use of the physician compensation surveys are, by far, the most commonly used approaches for establishing physician compensation in employment arrangements. For many involved in physician employment deals, they are the only approaches considered. Other approaches, such as the cost and income, are considered foreign and irrelevant to the valuation process. The fundamental question for professional appraisers is whether this sole reliance on the market approach is consistent with the valuation body of knowledge and sound valuation practice. The answer to that question, from a methodological standpoint, is fairly clear: The valuation body of knowledge does not summarily privilege the market approach over and against the other approaches. Rather, it calls for consideration of all three approaches and for the application of methods that are relevant to the valuation of the subject transaction and for which there are reliable and available data. The following sections probe some of the implicit assumptions made about the market data and the market approach in the current healthcare marketplace. The question for professional appraisers is whether these assumptions are valid enough to warrant the market-approach-only orientation that is ubiquitous in the physician employment marketplace.

7.1 Understanding the Implications of Using Total Cash Compensation

Many players in the healthcare marketplace commonly mistake the physician compensation surveys to reflect the compensation for clinical patient care services only. As discussed previously, the reality is that the physician compensation surveys generally define physician compensation as total cash compensation from all sources. This definition, therefore, can encompass compensation received not only from clinical patient care services, but also from other types of services as well. It would include compensation from call coverage, medical directorships, clinical co-management arrangements, research, expert witness fees, and other such sources. Compensation may also include net profits earned from nonphysician providers or preferential distributions paid to senior physicians in a group. Earnings from technical services may also be included. As discussed in Part I, a portion of the compensation earned by shareholders or owner-physicians in physician-owned groups can represent owner compensation or a return on investment in the practice.

Recognition of the diversity of sources or types of services contributing to compensation reported in total cash compensation can affect the comparability of survey compensation data under the market approach for employment agreements. To determine comparability, the appraiser must match the services included in the scope of the subject employment arrangement to the scope of services entailed in the survey data. Yet, compensation by type of service or income source is not detailed in the compensation survey data. Thus, the appraiser may not be assured of full or exact comparability between the scope of services included in the subject arrangement and the scope of services provided by the respondents reporting compensation in the surveys. *The inability to fully determine the comparability of a subject arrangement and the survey data in terms of the scope of services represents a notable limitation and weakness in using the market survey data for valuing physician employment.*

One might argue that this limitation on ascertaining the comparability of services only relates to marginal services. The level of compensation for various nonclinical services is not material relative to the total compensation received for patient-care services, given the number of respondents for a specialty in the survey data. In effect, the impact of additional services provided over and above patient care services is diluted with large respondent sizes. Thus, the issue of comparability is merely theoretical, and not a realistic or substantial consideration. This objection certainly has credibility with respect to certain forms of compensation. For example, paid medical directorships at hospitals are common in the healthcare marketplace, but the number of physicians providing these services as a percentage of total physicians is generally small. Expert witness fees or honoraria are also infrequent in the typical physician practice.

There are other nonclinical services, however, where the frequency of such services is not so easily determined, given current market trends. Compensated hospital call coverage is becoming more common in the marketplace and may represent the prevailing staffing model for hospital coverage in many markets. For certain physician specialties, compensation from hospital call coverage can be material relative to the compensation from clinical services. MGMA reports that roughly 75% of the physicians reported in the 2010 and 2011 surveys had on-call duties.[11] Unfortunately, MGMA did not indicate whether such duties were compensated or not. In the 2010 survey, however, MGMA reported significantly higher compensation for specialty care physicians with on-call duties.[12]

The impact of owner compensation may be a diminishing factor in future surveys as the trend toward hospital and health system employment continues in the current round of the healthcare provider consolidation. The percentage of physicians from physician-owned groups has been declining in MGMA and AGMA over the past few years. In addition, owner compensation is often most significant for specialties that are technology-driven or capital-intensive, such as cardiology or radiation oncology. Thus, owner compensation may not warrant significant consideration for all specialties in all cases.

One form of compensation to watch in the next few years is compensation from clinical co-management or service line management agreements. The compensation from such arrangements can be significant. Since compensation for such services was paid through separate or joint venture entities in the initial market iterations of co-management models, such compensation was most likely paid to individual physicians outside of physician practices. Thus, its impact on compensation in the surveys may have been negligible. Trends in co-management agreements, however, are heading toward inclusion of such services as part of physician employment arrangements with hospitals under the new nomenclature of service line management services. This trend may have a significant impact on compensation in the future.

Since the compensation surveys do not report compensation by source or service, the appraiser may be put in the position of making informed judgments or assumptions about what is and is not included in market compensation data or to what extent it is included. For making such determinations, it is essential to know practice norms and trends for a specialty in terms of the expected mix of services and sources for compensation. While one can point to the potential compensation impact of various types of prevalent nonclinical services, quantifying and adjusting the survey data for such compensation can be a highly difficult task. Many variables would need to be determined to attempt to parse the compensation survey data or to adjust it. Thus, it may not be practicable to attempt such quantification and adjustment.

---

11   See Table 26. "On-Call Duties" from the "Demographics—Medical Practice" section.
12   Page 9 of "Key Findings" section.

Despite the difficulties in quantitative analysis relative to the issue of compensation from nonclinical services, an appraiser should be aware of such sources of compensation when applying the physician compensation survey data to a subject employment arrangement. This recognition should be factored into the interpretation and analysis of indications of value derived from market approach techniques and in the broader valuation synthesis of the cost, market, and income approaches for a subject employment arrangement. In summary, a qualitative assessment should be included in the valuation process to account for the various forms of compensation included in the survey data.

7.2 How Comparable Is the Subject Arrangement to the Survey Data?

Users of the physician compensation surveys tend to assume that national or regional market survey data is readily applicable or comparable to the subject physician employment arrangement. Indeed, the penchant for using the median compensation per wRVU as a universal benchmark for FMV physician compensation implies the notion that local market conditions, and indeed, specific physician practice patterns and habits, have no material effect on physician compensation. The reality, however, is that the survey data may not be readily comparable to the subject arrangement. The surveys tend to reflect segments of the physician marketplace, and they are not reported in a manner that allows for informed application to a specific local market. This latter point is critical: variations in conditions across and within markets can be significant. As a result, summarily using the survey data without consideration of differences in local market reimbursement and compensation can lead to misapplication of survey data.

For an in-depth discussion of this issues, see Chapter 38, "Comparing the Surveys to the Physician Marketplace: Implications for Valuation Analysis."

7.3 Evaluating the Relationship Between Productivity and Compensation

A central assumption underlying the exclusive use of the market approach for employment compensation is the belief that productivity is or should be the central, if not *the* critical, factor in establishing FMV physician compensation for clinical services. This belief, moreover, has tended to hold wRVUs as the definitive measure of physician productivity. These assumptions are implicit in one of the most popular methods of establishing market compensation: matching compensation to benchmarked wRVUs. The critical question for the appraiser is: How valid are these assumptions?

From the analysis dealing with the impact of market reimbursement rates on compensation in Chapter 38, "Comparing the Surveys to the Physician Marketplace: Implications for Valuation Analysis," it should be readily apparent that professional collections are the preferable or more meaningful market indicator for compensation. Professional collections, when such collections are normalized, reflect the dollar value paid for physician productivity. Thus, such payments can indicate key aspects of the local market's dynamics for physician services. Since there is a critical link between the professional component of clinical procedures and wRVUs, professional collections contain information about the physician's work efforts coupled with the local value placed on those efforts. They surpass wRVUs in terms of accounting for a broader mix of compensation factors.

As discussed in Chapter 39, "An Analysis of the Relationship Between Productivity and Compensation in the MGMA Data and Its Implications for Valuation and Compensation-Setting Practices," compensation and productivity, defined in terms of wRVUs and PCs, have a weak level of correlation in the MGMA data using regression analysis. Use of these productivity measures, especially wRVUs on a solitary basis, seems overly simplistic for addressing all the fundamental economic variables in a physician practice. Physician productivity measures do not address three key factors in generating available earnings for physician compensation in a doctor practice:

1. Level of ancillary services or technical component earnings for the practice.

2. Level of other services provided by the practice, such as compensated call coverage, medical directorships, research, interpretation services for other healthcare providers, and clinical co-management agreements.

3. Cost structure and overhead levels for the practice.

All physicians of a given specialty are not created equal with respect to these factors, nor do they practice equally with respect to these areas. Physician practices can vary widely with regard to each other. One inherent limitation of the physician compensation surveys is that data on these key factors are generally not collected and reported.[13] As a result, use of the compensation surveys under the market approach does not account for all key variables in the economic productivity of a physician or practice, viewed from a comprehensive perspective. The scope of data in the physician compensation surveys lead to a narrow and limited analysis of physician compensation for employment services from a comprehensive economic and valuation perspective.

---

13 The MGMA *Cost Survey* does report information on many of these additional factors. It, however, does not report compensation and productivity data on individual physicians. It reports all data at the collective group practice level, combining productivity from physicians and nonphysician providers. Such collective reporting of data limits the use of the *Cost Survey* for valuing many physician compensation arrangements.

8.0 Determining FMV Compensation Under the Market Approach

8.1 Using Multiple Methods, Surveys, and Matching Criteria as a Best Practice

As discussed above, multiple valuation techniques and multiple survey data sources are available to appraisers for determining market-based employment compensation. The case for using multiple methods in the market approach is based on the recognition that each method has its relative strengths and weakness. No single appraisal technique is perfect. Often, a valuation method takes into account a single factor relative to the issue of comparability between the market data and the subject. A singular criterion or consideration, however, is often not fully indicative of the complexity of the physician marketplace relative to compensation. One approach for mitigating the limitations of individual techniques is to use multiple methods and productivity measures. By doing so, a variety of factors and relationships between the subject and the market data are considered in the valuation process. The result of using multiple methods and measures is generally a more balanced and supportable appraisal analysis. One might use this analogy: Each strand of a rope, on its own, may be relatively weak, but bound together, the various strands create strength. This same logic applies to the use of multiple valuation methods as well as multiple criteria or productivity measures for determining comparability.

The use of multiple surveys can also yield a more balanced and supportable analysis. First, use of multiple surveys affords a larger number of reference points in the marketplace. Second, use of multiple surveys can expand the market spectrum considered with respect to the characteristics of the respondents in the data. Wider geographic coverage and diversity of practice types and settings can result from this practice. As has been discussed previously, each survey tends to represent a segment of the physician marketplace. Using more than one survey is one way to include more market segments in the analysis. It should be noted, however, that the inclusion of more segments may not create a total market data reference set that is reflective of the total physician marketplace or of the relevant marketplace for the subject. Third, use of multiple surveys can serve to dilute or mitigate against anomalies that can sometimes arise in a survey for a particular specialty.

8.2 Evaluating the Use of Specific Appraisal Tools and Resources

That the use of multiple methods, surveys, and comparability measures is a best practice does not mean that an appraiser should summarily use every possible tool and resource in a valuation assignment. Consideration of the relevance and applicability of each tool is still a critical part of the appraisal process. For both practical as well as sound methodologically reasons, an appraiser should go through a systematic process of evaluating the potential tools available for determining FMV compensation for a subject employment arrangement. Based on this assessment, specific methods, surveys, and comparability measures are selected for application in the valuation.

The selection of the relevant and applicable tools for an employment valuation should be based on consideration of various factors related to the subject and the available tools. As noted earlier, employment arrangements should be distinguished between clinical, academic, administrative, and executive services. Different surveys and measures of comparability are relevant for each type of service. When evaluating employment arrangements for clinical services, there are several key factors and criteria one should consider in the selection process. Evaluating these factors relative to valuation resources is often a dynamic process in which the appraiser selects a specific combination of tools based on their combined applicability to the subject. The following subsections outline many of the key considerations in selecting tools.

Productivity Data

As discussed in Chapter 13, "An Introduction to Physician Services and Specialties," the operating environment and fundamental economics of office-based physicians and hospital-based physicians can be quite different. Hence, the relevant comparability measures, i.e., the definitions of productivity, are often different for physicians in each practice-setting type. The productivity measures used generally determine the available valuation techniques. They can also affect the selection of relevant surveys. For example, some of the surveys do not include physician productivity data on wRVUs or professional collections. Thus, these surveys cannot be readily used for the percentile matching technique based on these metrics. On the other hand, if one is using annual hours as the definition of productivity and assuming 2,000 or 2,080 annual hours as an assumption derived independently of the survey data, one could use all the physician compensation surveys in determining FMV hourly rates. In this case, a survey is not excluded by virtue of not having relevant data for the productivity measure. This measure was independently derived and is applied on a normalizing basis to all market data.

Practice Profile and Characteristics

An assignment to value a large multispecialty group may warrant exclusive use of MGMA and AMGA because such surveys are representative of large groups. For valuing compensation in an academic-affiliated group, it may be advisable to exclude MGMA and AMGA and use SCA and other more academically represented surveys.

Compensation Structure

Valuation assignments to appraise group-level compensation plans may allow consideration of the MGMA *Cost Survey* data. The group-level compensation formula may be consistent with various compensation-related metrics reported in this survey. AMGA also provides group-level metrics that may be applicable for group-level models in multispecialty groups. It should be noted that the contractual use of a specific metric for compensation in a subject arrangement, such as compensation per wRVU, does not preclude the use of other metrics in applying the market approach. As will be discussed later in Part V, the outcomes of valuation methods can be converted into various compensation formulas and structures. Thus, the contractual compensation formula does not necessarily determine the productivity or comparability measures used in the market approach. For example, if the employment agreement calls for compensation based on a set rate per wRVU, it does not preclude the appraisers from using professional collections as the measure of productivity for application of a given valuation technique. Rather, the valuation indications from methods based on professional collections can be used to establish a compensation per wRVU rate.

Data Concerns

Occasionally, one observes anomalies in the survey data. Thus, a best practice is to examine the survey data before using them. If such anomalies are observed, one may choose to exclude a survey or significantly reduce its impact on the valuation based on its relative weighting in the valuation synthesis process. One might also elect to exclude or reduce the weighting on a survey that the appraiser considers to be outdated. As noted previously, the surveys represent data from a prior year; they are published several months after the end of the data year reported. Sometimes, certain surveys are not published for nearly a year after the year for which they publish data. In such circumstances, the current version of a survey may represent data that are nearly two years old. An appraiser may conclude that data from the survey should be excluded or weighted lower when current or future market conditions are thought to be materially different than the year for which data are reported.

Available and Relevant Data Considerations

In certain circumstances, data for a subject physician or employment arrangement may not be available. Moreover, available data may not be particularly meaningful or applicable relative to the subject employment arrangement. Examples of such circumstances may include the following, although this listing should not be construed as comprehensive:

- A physician seeking to exit a current employment or work situation may not be able to provide historical productivity data.

- Physicians coming out of residency, fellowship, or other training programs may not have productivity data or productivity data that is relevant or meaningful for a full-time private practice physician.

- A physician coming out of an academic setting may be in a similar position with respect to historical data.

- The historical productivity of a physician moving out of one service market into another may not be indicative of the physician's future productivity. If the physician was in a small, rural market with limited demand for services, the historical productivity may not reflect the physician's skill. In addition, professional collections in one market may not be indicative of productivity in another market.

In circumstances such as these, the appraiser is necessarily limited in terms of the productivity measures, valuation methods, and relevant surveys applicable to the subject physician and arrangement. The appraiser is left with implementing those methods that are available, given the data.

There is one practice tendency in valuation assignments of this type that appraisers should reconsider and view with a critical eye. As discussed previously, there is a tendency to use the median from the surveys representing full-time clinically practicing physicians as the universal benchmark for FMV compensation. The median is often considered to be the best estimate of what a newly hired physician would receive or expect in the marketplace. Essentially, the median compensation level has become a valuation "rule of thumb" for hiring physicians and is essentially treated as a valuation floor for compensation. Examination of the actual recruiting data, however, does not necessarily validate this assumption. A more supportable position with respect to establishing compensation for physicians with little available data is to reference the placement surveys as part of the valuation process.[14] In addition, appraisers should be careful in using a "rule of thumb" as an actual valuation method, as frequently noted in the business valuation body knowledge.

8.3 Benchmarking Multiple Metrics as an Indispensable Tool for the Market Approach

As noted in this chapter, questions regarding the comparability of the market survey data to the broad spectrum of physician practices and physicians have been raised in a general manner. One tool for assessing individual comparability between the subject practice or physician and the survey data is the benchmarking of key metrics for the subject against the survey data. By observing benchmarking outcomes and, more importantly, examining such outcomes in tandem, an appraiser can begin to formulate a

---

14 It is acknowledged that the placement surveys often have a limited number of respondents. Referencing such data in the valuation process, however, is preferable to relying on the median "rule of thumb" as a valuation technique. The median is the middle value in the data set. By definition, it is not a floor.

clearer picture of the comparability of the subject to the data. Once such comparability is examined, the appraiser is in a better position to evaluate the outcomes of the various survey-based valuation techniques under the market approach.

The metrics selected for benchmarking should relate to fundamental productivity and compensation indices. When using MGMA, AGMA, and SCA, the following metrics can be essential to the benchmarking analysis:

1. Productivity: wRVUs, professional collections, and professional collections per wRVU.[15]

2. Compensation: compensation, compensation per wRVU, and the compensation-to-professional-collections ratio.

The benchmarking analysis consists of comparing the subject physician's historical data against the survey data by calculating the subject's approximate percentile ranking for each metric in a given survey. Next, the appraiser compares the percentile rankings across all metrics to examine the relationships among the benchmarking outcomes, looking for variances in productivity and compensation rankings. Such variances can reflect areas in which the subject is and is not comparable to the surveys. For example, do wRVUs and professional collections benchmark differently? Does the benchmarking of professional collections per wRVU help explain this difference? Which productivity measure benchmarks more closely with the percentile ranking of the subject's historical compensation? Examination of such questions can aid the appraiser in assessing comparability of the subject to the survey data and in evaluating the various valuation methods that are based on this data.

The MGMA, AMGA, and SCA surveys do not include relevant data with regard to certain key factors that can materially affect physician compensation. Overhead levels, ancillary earnings, and other service revenues are data categories that are not collected or reported by these surveys at the physician-specialty level.[16] In many ways, these missing categories of data impede the level of benchmarking that is needed to determine comparability comprehensively. Such supplemental data would also help appraisers better understand the economics of the respondents to whom the subject is being compared and whose compensation levels are being used to establish market-based compensation. Physicians and physician practices are not all equal with respect to these factors.

---

15   Unfortunately, AMGA does not currently report professional collections per wRVU.
16   AMGA does provide some data relative to these categories at the group level. MGMA provides an overview of the level of ancillary revenues for all respondents in its introductory practice profile section.

Use of the MGMA *Cost Survey* can be helpful for benchmarking analysis. Cost, benefits, total revenue, and tRVU metrics can provide useful measures for comparison, along with wRVUs and compensation. Payer mix and staffing ratio benchmarking is also helpful. Even when the *Cost Survey* is not used in a valuation method, benchmarking an array of metrics for the subject physician or practice using it can be useful as part of the valuation process. Such analysis is also useful in applying the cost and income approaches (discussed further in Part IV).

8.4 Critical Use of the Physician Compensation Surveys

Critical issues and considerations have been raised in the foregoing analysis and discussion of market approach valuation techniques using the physician compensation surveys. These considerations have been raised as part of an examination of the sole use of the market approach using the surveys in valuation practice. What should be apparent from the above discussion of the issue is that exclusive and uncritical use of the market surveys for valuation purposes is beset with imprecision, difficulties, and fundamental limitations. These difficulties and limitations relate to the issue of the comparability of the survey data to specific subject physicians and proposed employment arrangements as well as to the question of the correlation between compensation and physician productivity measures, narrowly defined.

The identification and examination of the relative limitations of the market approach for valuing physician employment compensation is not necessarily an impediment to the use of the approach. Rather, such considerations serve as a cautionary finding relative to the *exclusive* and *uncritical* use of market survey data in establishing physician compensation. In addition, recognition of these issues should affect the interpretation, assessment, and weighting of the outcomes from valuation techniques that rely on the compensation survey market data. It also signals the need for serious consideration of the cost and income approaches in the valuation process. Comparing the indications of value under the market approach with the results of cost and income approaches mitigates the inherent imprecision that arises from use of the market data for establishing physician compensation in employment arrangements. Finally, identifying and critically evaluating relative strengths and weaknesses of valuation data and methods represent the essence of the trade and practice of appraisal! Such evaluation is the kind of professional diligence and analysis that should be expected of trained and skilled appraisal professionals.

Practical considerations should also be noted relative to the market approach and physician compensation survey data. One reason for continuing to use market survey data, however imperfect or unrepresentative such data are relative to the entirety of the physician marketplace, is that the physician compensation surveys are the only readily and publicly available source of market data to use in the valuation process. Practically speaking, the market approach would not be available to appraisers in most cases were it not for the market survey data. It should also be noted that, in certain cases, no other methods and data may be available to an appraiser, save the market approach based on the compensation surveys. When used, however, the market approach should be applied with circumspection and awareness relative to its limitations. Moreover, it should also be noted that areas of potential imprecision and difficulty in the market survey data may not be applicable in every valuation assignment. The critical objections to the application of the survey data should not be taken as categorical. Rather, the claim is that general trends and tendencies of the survey data can make their application to specific employment arrangements and physicians limited and qualified. One should therefore use the market approach based on the surveys, but not to the exclusion of other approaches.

Chapter 24. Valuing Physician Employment Arrangements for Clinical Services: Cost- and Income-Based Valuation Methods

CONTENTS

Chapter 24. Valuing Physician Employment Arrangements for Clinical Services: Cost- and Income-Based Valuation Methods

By Timothy Smith, CPA/ABV

1.0 Introduction

Whereas productivity-matched compensation was a key concept in the application of the market approach to valuing physician employment arrangements for clinical services, the concept of earnings-based compensation is fundamental to the cost and income approaches for these services. This chapter begins, therefore, with an in-depth discussion of the concept before addressing the use and application of various cost-based and income-based valuation methods. It will detail the various factors involved in earnings-based compensation for physician clinical services. The chapter will then apply the framework of earnings-based compensation in various cost and income approach methods. There will also be a discussion of two cost-based valuation methods that do not utilize this concept: the cost to recruit method and the locum tenens cost method.

2.0 Earnings-Based Compensation for Professional Practices

2.1 The Concept of Earnings-Based Compensation

The concept of earnings-based compensation is that the net earnings received by a professional are an economic measure of the value for these professional services. It applies not only to physicians, but also to other professionals, such as lawyers, accountants, consultants, and appraisers. Professionals such as these provide services in the marketplace to customers, whether in the form of patients or clients. The revenues received for services less the cost of providing the services (i.e., the net earnings from professional services) represent the value or compensation for the services in the marketplace.

Earnings-based compensation for professional services is grounded in the business valuation body of knowledge with respect to the issue of the value of services provided by owners in closely held and small businesses. In their text, *Reasonable Compensation: Application and Analysis for Appraisal, Tax, and Management Purposes*, Kevin Yeanoplos and Ron Seigneur posit that:

> Professional practices, regardless of the form of organization, primarily do one thing. They provide services that are largely the result of the personal services rendered by the professionals within the enterprise. It is logical to conclude that the net earnings of the professional practice represent the reasonable compensation to those professionals, after an allowance for other ordinary, necessary, and reasonable operating expenses.[1]

They argue that each professional's contribution and corresponding compensation is a function of the excess of what each individual is capable of producing over the cost of production.[2]

Earnings-based compensation is also grounded in various tax court cases that have established the idea that net earnings from services provided by a professional can be considered as reasonable compensation for services rendered.[3] One of these cases dealt directly with the determination of physician compensation. In the 2001 *Pediatric Surgical Associates* case,[4] the court concluded that the value of the services performed by shareholder physicians was related to the earnings from those services only. The distributions the shareholder-physicians received from the net earnings of nonshareholder-physicians in the group were not considered to be reasonable compensation for the services rendered by shareholders.[5] In this case, the court made a distinction between compensation for providing professional services and owner compensation accruing to the ownership of a business.

---

1   Kevin Yeanoplos and Ron Seigneur, *Reasonable Compensation: Application and Analysis for Appraisal, Tax, and Management Purposes*. Business Valuation Resources, LLC (BVR), 2010, p. 8.
2   Yeanoplos and Seigneur, p. 8.
3   Yeanoplos and Seigneur, pp. 7-10.
4   Editor's note: This case warrants a careful reading as to the IRS position, the taxpayer's response, and the court's ultimate decision. The court's changes were comparatively minor compared to the IRS audit results.
5   Yeanoplos and Seigneur, pp. 9-10. The tax issue in this case was the amount of the compensation claimed as a deduction in a C corporation for the shareholder physicians. The IRS claimed some of this compensation should have been treated as dividend income, rather than compensation for services.

In general, earnings-based compensation as applied to physicians as professionals looks to the revenues generated by physician services less the cost of providing those services for the value of the services rendered. It includes the revenues, fees, and income generated by the physician in providing the specific scope of services contemplated in the subject service arrangement. These services can include clinical, administrative, hospital call coverage, and other professional services. The cost and expense of providing these various services are then deducted from the revenues or income streams for the services to arrive at a level of net earnings from the professional services rendered. These net earnings are considered the value of the physician's services.

Earnings-based compensation for physician services as a methodology has several conceptual and practical advantages for valuation purposes.

Use of Historical and Forecasted Net Earnings

The net earnings used for valuing compensation can be based on both historical and future periods. This ability to use multiple periods affords the appraiser with significant capacity for addressing a broad array of relevant factors related to the appraisal of the services. Expected changes in the marketplace or in the economics of services can be factored into the analysis alongside of the historical economics, thereby allowing the appraiser to assess the impact of trends and forecasts for the services. It also allows the appraiser to evaluate the reasonableness and risk factors associated with projected net earnings.

Use of Local Market Conditions and Factors

The net earnings from professional services are generally representative of the local market conditions and factors affecting the value of such services. The revenues for such services necessarily reflect the local marketplace in terms of what the subject physician or practice has been able to achieve in the market. While the revenues may not be optimized to the extent possible within this local-market context, they are certainly indicative of it with a level of precision that is not available using physician compensation survey data. As discussed in Chapter 37, "How Reimbursement and Physician Compensation Vary by Market," local reimbursement levels have a tremendous impact on the net earnings available for compensation in a physician practice. Use of net earnings, therefore, gives a realistic initial picture of local market conditions with respect to reimbursement and payer-mix factors. It may also provide an indication of the demand level for physician services in the local service market. The local cost of resources can also be revealed using net earnings. Critical cost components of a medical practice, such as office rental rates and wage levels, are used in the calculation of net earnings. Such expenses may need to be adjusted or optimized (as discussed in subsequent sections in this chapter), but once revised, they can appropriately reflect the prevailing cost levels in the local market.

Use of Practice- or Physician-Specific Patterns and Factors

Medical practices and physicians are not created equal in their clinical practice patterns, patient bases, and utilization of resources. Medical groups and individual doctors can vary in terms of the demographics and diversity of ailments of their patient populations. They may have relatively different service mixes in terms of the specific professional component and technical component services they regularly perform in treating patients. For example, some physicians may elect to limit their inpatient work or may focus on certain types of procedures at a level that is distinguished from their peers within a group or in other practices. Clinical judgments and the case acuity of patient populations can affect the level of ancillary utilization in the practice. These varying clinical practice patterns have different overhead and cost-utilization structures. Moreover, groups and physicians diverge in terms of their economic efficiency in using resources to provide services. Some physicians and practices have lower overhead structures than their peers even though they may have equal or greater productivity levels. Using net earnings from services takes these actual practice patterns and resource-utilization levels into account in valuing these services.

Use of Specific Scope-of-Service Adjustments

Earnings-based compensation allows the appraiser to value the specific scope of services contemplated under a proposed arrangement. The revenues and expenses from individual services can be directly included or excluded and calculated in detail as part of determining net earnings. This methodology also provides the appraiser with the ability to analyze so-called "stacking" issues related to duplication of payment for the same service or to overpayments in total compensation for the totality of services provided. Such issues can be evaluated with greater precision, since the particular economics of a service are readily identifiable and quantifiable in the net earnings analysis.

Use of Normalization and Optimization Adjustments

As part of the conceptual framework of earnings-based compensation, adjustments can be made to the net earnings from physician services. These adjustments can represent certain normalizations to the net earnings or optimize the net earnings consistent with the hypothetical-typical employer operating a practice on a reasonable basis. (These adjustments will be discussed in greater detail in subsequent sections.) The ability to apply such adjustments affords a greater level of precision or specificity in valuing physician services.

Use of Specific Facts and Circumstances Adjustments

Similar to normalization and optimization adjustments, use of net earnings allows the appraiser to make other adjustments that reflect unique facts and circumstances related to the subject arrangement. Such adjustments, however, should only be made consistent with changes or service terms and operations reflective of the typical employer entity. Adjustments made that are unique to a specific employer should move the valuation analysis toward investment value rather than fair market value. (A complete discussion of this issue is provided in a subsequent section.)

These adaptive features and advantages of earnings-based compensation give the cost and income approaches a level of precision that is not available under the various market approach methods and techniques for valuing physician services. As noted in Part III, the market approach is limited and qualified in terms of its precision with respect to various economic aspects of physician services. Generally, the market approach is less effective and exact in accounting for key physician practice economic factors such as local market reimbursement, service mix, clinical practice patterns, resource utilization, and scope of services. Since market data are based on prior periods, the market approach is also limited in its capacity to include actual and anticipated changes in the marketplace that occurred or will occur after publication of survey data. Fundamentally, earnings-based compensation is more precise and exacting than productivity-based compensation, which tends to homogenize physician compensation according to one or two measures of productivity. Earnings-based compensation generally takes into account the whole array of economic factors that can affect physician compensation in the marketplace. Consequently, consideration of earnings-based compensation methods is a critical feature in valuing physician services.

2.2 Critical Issues in Earnings-Based Compensation

When applying the concept of earnings-based compensation to physicians, there can be several critical issues to consider in the application of the methodology. These issues generally revolve around what revenue or net earnings streams are included in the computation of net earnings from professional services. The central issue is whether these revenues or net earnings relate to the professional services of a physician such that they should be considered as a component of physician compensation. Three primary sources of net earnings that can raise challenging issues in the appraisal process are practice ownership, other practice providers, and technical component services. Another source of critical issues can arise from questions related to what costs should be included in the calculation of net earnings. These critical issues may not arise in every context; they tend to become concerns in certain fact patterns. The following sections provide an introduction and evaluation of these issues. These issues arise due to the nature of physician services and medical practices.

2.3 Exclusion of Owner Compensation From Net Earnings

The net earnings from owning and operating a business are distinguished from the net earnings from providing professional services. This distinction may seem misguided, at first glance, because both types of compensation are computed using revenues less expenses. Moreover, professionals tend to own and operate their practices. How, then, are the net earnings from professional services different from the net earnings from owning a professional practice? The difference in the two forms of compensation is found in whether the net earnings are the result of services provided by the professional or from the economics of owning and operating a business. The difference may be stated in the following terms: net earnings from owning a professional practice are what results after deducting the value of professional services from the net earnings from services rendered (see the exhibit). Yet, the question remains: How does one distinguish between the two? What portion of the net earnings from services rendered should be allocated to professional services and what portion relates to ownership?

This very same question has arisen in business valuation in the context of determining reasonable compensation for closely held or small businesses. In such entities, owners typically provide functional or operational services to the business that are comparable to those provided by employees of the business. For example, a business-owner may perform functions that would otherwise be provided by managers, accountants, human resource personnel, sales, and the like. The reason that determining compensation for such services is important is that a deduction for the value of such services is critical in the use of the income approach for valuing the business. The net earnings available to the business owner are those remaining after paying for the labor associated with

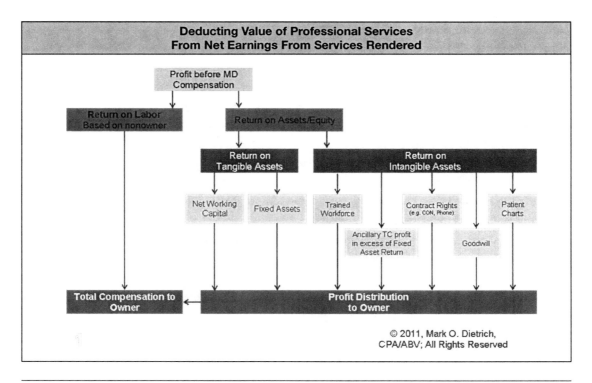

© 2011, Mark O. Dietrich, CPA/ABV; All Rights Reserved

the services necessary to operate the business. Many techniques have been developed to value these services, including use of market survey data for various types of management and executive services. These techniques are comparable to market-approach methods used to value physician services.

One alternative technique that has been developed in the framework of business valuation, and also in tax matters related to compensation, is the so-called independent-investor test or method. In the independent-investor test, the value of operational services provided by an owner-employee is determined based on the net earnings in the business after providing for an appropriate return on investment in the business. The conceptual framework supporting this method is that owner-employee's compensation for employment-related services is presumed to be reasonable as long as the business owner receives acceptable returns on his or her investment in the enterprise.[6]

As applied to compensation for professional services, the independent investor test would indicate that the value of professional services is the net earnings from those services, where net earnings include a return on assets or investment in the professional services firm. Stated in alternative terms, the net earnings from professional services should include a deduction for the cost of capital necessary to provide the professional services. By adjusting net earnings for the cost of capital, the resulting net earnings should reflect only the value of the professional services rendered. The cost of capital represents the compensation for providing capital to the professional practice and for taking risk on this investment. For medical practices, the net earnings from physician services can be determined by deducting a cost of capital for the investment in assets necessary for the operation of the practice.

2.4 Inclusion or Exclusion of Net Earnings From Other Practice Providers

One specific issue that arises in the determination of net earnings from professional services is whether to include or exclude net earnings from other providers in a medical practice. Generally, there are two key types of providers from which physicians can receive earnings distributions as part of a practice:

Other Physicians

As shareholders or owners of medical practices, physicians can sometimes receive distributions from the excess net earnings of nonshareholder-physicians practicing in the group.[7] Such distributions should generally be classified as ownership earnings

---

6   Ronald L. Seigneur, *Closely Held Owner-Employee Compensation*, slide 16-6, AICPA National Business Valuation Conference, Nov. 16, 2009.

7   As noted in Part I, significant or long-term margins from nonshareholder-physicians are not common in the author's experience with medical practices or are not the prevailing practice paradigm.

---

rather than net earnings from physician services. Margins made from nonshareholder-physicians in a group do not relate to the services provided to patients and other healthcare providers by shareholder-physicians. Rather, they relate to being owners in a medical practice, whereby the owners have sufficient patient volume and market position to employ or contract with physicians at compensation levels that generate net earnings or profits for shareholders. In many cases, these net earnings may be temporary because nonshareholder-physicians subsequently become shareholders themselves. These profits may also be returns of and on the underwriting of startup losses by shareholder-physicians during the ramp-up phase of newly hired physicians.[8] At any rate, such margins do not relate to the provision of physician services by the shareholder-physician.

Net Earnings From Nonphysician Providers

As discussed in Part I, the issue of how to classify the net earnings from nonphysician providers (NPPs) is a matter to analyze on the basis of the facts and circumstances. Net earnings from NPPs arise from the difference in the revenues generated by the patient procedures personally performed by NPPs and the compensation, benefits, and incremental overhead for the NPPs. Conceptually, NPP net earnings would appear to accrue to the benefit of the employer entity and would not be part of compensation for physician services. There are additional considerations, however, that may lead an appraiser to treat or apportion such net earnings differently in certain circumstances. NPPs in most states require physician supervision, including physician review of patient charts. Such supervision and chart review require the physician's time, which could otherwise be used for personally performed productivity. Some of the net earnings from an NPP, therefore, could be allocable as compensation for supervision services provided by the supervising physician. The amount would depend on the facts and circumstances related to the arrangement.

One such method for apportioning NPP net earnings to physician supervision pay is based on a "subcontractor" model. Under this model, physicians are credited with the work of NPPs that they supervise under an incident-to billing model for purposes of a production bonus or production-based compensation. While a discussion of the various requirements for incident-to billing are beyond the scope of this chapter, it should be noted that the services provided under an incident-to billing model are reimbursed at a higher rate than under a direct billing model. NPP services provided under direct billing are reimbursed at 85% of the level paid to physicians or as incident-to physician services under Medicare. *It should also be noted that certain regulatory requirements must be met for use of this subcontractor model, including those related to Stark.*

---

8   See Part I for further discussion of the economics of this issue.

In the subcontractor model under employment, the compensation, benefits, and incremental costs of the NPP are deducted from the physician's compensation. Thus, the physician is at risk in these models for the productivity level of the NPP. At lower production levels for the NPP, the physician's compensation can be significantly reduced because the costs for the NPP are greater than the compensation credited to the physician for the production level of the NPP. If the NPP ramps ups, however, the physician is able to retain the net earnings from the NPP as supervision compensation. The conceptual support for such arrangements is that the physician is required to manage the overall productivity of the physician-NPP duo in providing patient care. The physician has downside risk and upside compensation for the NPP's productivity. The physician, in effect, becomes a business owner for compensation purposes relative to the NPP.

In addition, the compensation formula is structured such that the employer makes money from the very first amount of production generated by the NPP because the revenues generated by the NPP exceed the amount credited or paid to the physician for purposes of a production-bonus or productivity-based compensation. (*To use this model, the revenues from the NPP must exceed the amounts credited or paid to the physician.*) Thus, an owner return to the employer is generated by the NPP as part of the structure. A typical example of this structure is where the wRVUs of an NPP are credited to the supervising physician for purposes of calculating compensation based on a compensation-per-wRVU formula. The costs of the NPP, however, are deducted from such compensation as part of the formula. In addition, the collections per wRVU from the NPP's services exceed the compensation-per-wRVU amount that is paid to the physician.

It is possible, therefore, for the net earnings of an NPP to be included in the net earnings from physician services under certain circumstances in terms of supervision pay. Whether such earnings should be included and the amount that should be included requires a specific analysis of the economics of the compensation structure and supervision services provided by the physician. *In addition, Stark issues and requirements may need to be met for such arrangements.* Appraisers should work with legal counsel in such instances to ensure that the valuation is prepared consistent with applicable healthcare regulations.

2.5 Inclusion or Exclusion of Net Earnings From Technical Component Services

In determining the net earnings derived from physician services, one key question that comes to the fore is whether the net earnings from technical component services *provided in a physician practice setting* (TCS) should be included in the computation of earnings from physician services. Are the net earnings from TCS part of the professional clinical services provided by a physician or are they part of a technical service line offered by a medical practice that accrues to the benefit of the practice owners? From the standpoint of who performs the services, the answer is rather straightforward. TCS are not directly part of physician services because they are not personally provided by a physician. The net earnings from TCS (TCSNE), therefore, would appear to relate to practice ownership rather than physician services. Hence, they should not be included in the calculation of physician compensation for professional services. Yet, an analysis of the historical, economic, and regulatory issues surrounding the provision of TCS in physician practices can give rise to an alternative perspective on including TCSNE in physician compensation.

In thinking about TCSNE and physician compensation, several factors should be considered:

1. TCS generally require the supervision of a physician; they are not procedures that can be performed without some level of general oversight and responsibility by a physician. These oversight requirements may not necessarily entail direct visual observation and immediate, over-the-shoulder supervision of the technicians or nursing staff performing the TCS. Nonetheless, some level of physician supervision is required. As a result, TCS cannot be fully removed from the overall context of physician services.

2. Certain types of TCS have historically been provided as part of the scope of clinical patient care services found in medical practices for selected specialties. For example, diagnostic testing through echocardiograms, EKGs, and nuclear camera studies are routinely provided in cardiology practices are part of the continuum of patient care services. Imaging modalities, such as MRI and CT, are frequently offered in orthopedic groups, while chemotherapy is part of most medical oncology practices. Primary care practices frequently provide basic lab and radiology (X-ray) services to patients. Most ob/gyn practices provide ultrasound services as part of prenatal care.

3. TCSNE have been part of the historical compensation levels received by physicians in specialties where these services have been provided customarily within a physician practice setting. As a result, such TCSNE are generally included or "baked into" market expectations for physician compensation levels for a given specialty. Moreover, it is highly likely that such TCSNE are included in the compensation amounts reported in the physician compensation surveys. Up until the last couple of years, the majority of respondents to MGMA and AMGA have been from physician-owned practices. Thus, the compensation from these practices would generally include TCSNE. Compensation for hospital and health system-employed physicians is commonly established using such survey data, whether through

internal valuation efforts or the use of appraisers or valuation consultants. The referencing of such data by hospital and health systems in establishing compensation for employed physicians is likely to have utilized and perpetuated compensation based on the inclusion of TCSNE.[9] Thus, historical compensation levels, market expectations, and much of the survey data would appear to be inclusive of TCSNE for certain types of TCS in selected specialties.

4. As long as the referring physicians and groups meet various federal and state regulatory requirements, such as the AKS and Stark, they can include certain TCSNE in the computation of physician compensation. Thus, physicians are readily able to refer TCS and be compensated from TCSNE as part of their professional practices and in providing patient care services as long as they are within the bounds of regulatory compliance. (Another condition is that they are not subject to restrictive covenants with respect to TCS that were agreed to as part of acquisition transactions.) The economic reality of this ability is that physicians can readily move their TCS referrals from one practice to another, apart from such restrictive covenants.

5. When the physicians had sold their TCS line to a buyer-employer entity as part of a larger physician practice acquisition and employment transaction, TCSNE necessarily accrue to the benefit of the buyer and would not be included in the resulting compensation for the physicians employed by the buyer. The structure of the acquisition transaction necessarily created a reduction in future compensation to the physicians. In essence, this purchase of the TCS line of the practice is comparable to acquisition patterns in the 1990s, in which physicians gave up future compensation to receive up-front value for their practices.

6. Exclusion of TCSNE may not be consistent with the idea of fair market value (FMV) in the appraisal body of knowledge from the perspective of the typical seller of physician services, i.e., the prospective employee physician. FMV as defined by the appraisal profession looks to what the hypothetical buyer and seller would do, given arm's-length negotiations and full knowledge of the facts. The FMV definition, therefore, poses this fundamental question: Why would a physician become an employee if a material portion of his or her

---

9   The argument that utilization of the market approach allows the appraiser to avoid the issue of TCSNE is somewhat uncritical and superficial. To make such an argument plausible, one would have to make the case that TCSNE were not a factor in establishing historical physician compensation levels and that use of the surveys to establish compensation for hospital and health system physicians was not a prevalent practice in the industry.

compensation were reduced without a commensurate reduction in the services provided under employment? In short, physicians would not be incentivized to become employees of employers who reduced their compensation for TCSNE, apart from the sale of their practice that contemplated the sale of TCSNE in the purchase price, as discussed above. They would simply remain in their current practices where such net earnings are part of the compensation formula. This analysis from the perspective of the physician, i.e., the seller of physician services, would apply regardless of the potential employer. Whether the potential employer is a hospital or health system, physician-owned practice, physician practice management company, insurance company, or other employer type, the physician would look at his or her alternatives in the marketplace when faced with a significant reduction in compensation. Where alternatives exist in which a physician's compensation includes TCSNE, it is doubtful that a physician acting in accordance with the standard of FMV would choose an arrangement were TCSNE were excluded. Only where other sufficient factors, considerations, and incentives were present would a physician generally make such a choice to forego TCSNE.

In light of these considerations, it is possible to make an economic and valuation argument for the inclusion of certain TCSNE in physician compensation. TCS may not be personally performed professional services, but inclusion of the net earnings from certain types of TCS has become part of the expected compensation for physicians in selected specialties. In addition, such physicians may have marketplace alternatives in which they can readily gain access to TCSNE, as long a regulatory requirements are met. It is hard to contemplate, apart from a separate acquisition of TCS or unique factors specific to a physician, that physicians acting at arm's length would be ready to part with such compensation in employment arrangements. Based on this line of reasoning, a case can be made for the inclusion of TCSNE in physician compensation under a FMV analysis.

On the other hand, TCS falls within the purview of the healthcare services that are the subject of the federal anti-kickback statute (AKS) and the Stark regulations. Thus, a series of healthcare regulatory concerns are raised in the process of examining the inclusion of TCSNE in the compensation of referring physicians. These concerns may have implications for determining the FMV of physician compensation from a regulatory compliance perspective. Since appraisals are generally obtained for healthcare compliance purposes, the appraiser cannot afford to ignore the potential regulatory implications and issues that can arise as part of a valuation assignment. Guidance of legal counsel as to the impact of such regulations can be an important part of addressing the issues entailed in including TCSNE in physician compensation for valuation purposes.

Since appraisers do not provide legal, regulatory, or investment advice, they would be prudent to seek regulatory guidance from the legal counsel involved in a proposed employment arrangement. As discussed in Chapter 7, "Complying With the Healthcare Definition of FMV in Appraisal Practice," such regulatory guidance is not intended to subordinate or supplant the FMV opinion of the appraiser. Rather, regulatory guidance is intended to clarify the definition of FMV for purposes of valuation for the appraiser. Such clarification is appropriate because regulatory compliance is usually the impetus for engagement of the independent appraiser. The healthcare regulatory definition of FMV, moreover, can involve issues and considerations that are legal in nature and beyond the scope of the appraiser's area of expertise and body of knowledge. Legal guidance relative to the standard of value for an engagement is usual and customary in divorce and damages litigation. Legal guidance relative to the healthcare standard of value is similar and comparable to these other areas of appraisal practice.

2.6 Scope of Service Adjustments

In applying the concept of earnings-based compensation, the appraiser needs to identify the scope of services contemplated under the proposed employment arrangement in terms of the types of services provided. The proposed scope of services can potentially include any of the following:

- Clinical or patient care services, including professional and technical component services;

- Hospital call coverage;

- Other professional services;

- Administrative services;

- NPP supervision services;

- Research services; and

- Other services.

Once the scope of services has been identified, the appraiser uses the revenues and fees earned or collected by the physician or practice for these same services to establish the revenues earned from the services provided. This analysis of revenues from a comparable scope of service eliminates revenues and fees for services or activities that are not part of proposed employment services provided by the practice or physician. For example, fees from a medical directorship that will not be part of the services provided under employment would be excluded. Income from rents, interest, and other nonoperating and nonservice-related items would also be removed from the computation of historical practice net earnings. Next, the appraiser obtains information on the costs and expenses required to produce these same scope of services. The costs associated with the production of the services should be considered comprehensively, including the depreciation or amortization cost of assets such as furniture and equipment, as well as an allowance for a cost of capital on all practice assets. Physician benefits are also included as costs of the practice.

These revenues and expenses are then used to compute the practice net earnings for a physician group or an individual physician. As will be discussed in subsequent sections, the revenues and expenses from services can be based on historical amounts under the cost approach or on projected amounts under the income approach. Use of the earnings-based compensation framework can be applied to historical or expected amounts, thereby providing indications of value that reflect both historical and future operating factors and contexts. The appraiser considers each indication of value derived from the physician's or medical group's practice net earnings—whether based on the past or on the future—in the synthesis process for establishing FMV compensation.

Scope of service adjustments should also look at the services provided at a more granular level to ensure that services are matched in terms of relevant measures for the services. For example, clinical hours worked per week, weeks worked per year, call shifts provided per month, medical director hours, and the like should be established for the subject employment arrangement. Revenues and expenses associated with these services are adjusted so that the quantity or relative measure of the services is consistent between the practice net earnings computation and what will be required under employment. For example, if historical practice net earnings are used, the appraiser should ensure that the annual working hours under the proposed employment arrangement are consistent with the historical working hours. *If historical hours are higher than the required hours under employment, it may not be reasonable to expect a comparable level of practice net earnings to be generated by the physician under employment as in prior years.*[10]

2.7 Normalization Adjustments

In determining the amount of practice net earnings, the appraiser may need to make a series of adjustments to the reported or historical revenues and expenses of the subject physician or practice. These adjustments seek to normalize revenues and expenses consistent with what would be expected under the employment arrangement. For revenues, the appraiser considers to what extent historical revenues may reflect volumes and collections that are one-time occurrences, nonrecurring, and not reflective of current

---

10 Editor's Note: This is a simple fact that is often overlooked in appraisal and was one of the things that led to the failure of the last physician-hospital consolidation in the 1900s.

productivity levels. Adjustments may be made to historical revenues for such items in an effort to determine a normalized level of historical revenues. Another technique for establishing a normalized level of revenue is to use and evaluate multiple historical periods to determine a normalized base year amount. The adjusted historical revenues are then used as the basis for projecting future revenues from the physician or practice.

For expenses, there are several areas and items for the appraiser to review as part of the normalization of costs for providing professional services.

Nonbusiness-Related Expenses

Physician practice expenses often include the costs of items that do not relate to the operation of the practice or to provision of physician services. Some of these items may represent perquisites that are not consistent with typical employment arrangements. In general, such nonbusiness-related expenses should be adjusted out of expenses for purposes of determining practice net earnings.

Nonrecurring and Nonoperating Expenses

One time, extraordinary, or nonrecurring expenses should also be removed from historical practice net earnings since they can overstate the normalized costs necessary for the production of physician services. Nonoperating expense should be removed for similar reasons.

Related-Party Resource Costs

The cost of resources provided by parties related to the subject physicians may not be reflective of typical or FMV costs for such resources. Examples of such items include rents from physician-owned buildings and the salaries of physician family members. Such costs may be higher or lower than one could obtain for these resources in the local marketplace. To establish historical practice net earnings that are consistent with FMV, such costs should be normalized using current market rates for such resources.

Physician Benefits

The historical level of benefits afforded to a physician in private practice may not be reflective of a market-based level of benefits typically provided in an employment arrangement. Historical benefits may be higher or lower than normalized or market-based benefits. To ensure that practice net earnings are comparable to the compensation to be received under employment, benefits should be adjusted for consistency with market levels. Such benefits can include the following:[11]

---

[11] A best practice for categorizing physician benefits is to use the definition found in the MGMA *Cost Survey*.

- Payroll-related taxes, including FICA, FUTA, SUTA, and workers' compensation;

- Health, dental, life, and disability insurance coverages;

- Employer retirement plan contributions;

- Continuing medical education (CME) costs; and

- Dues and licenses.

Staff Benefits

As with physician benefits, the benefits provided to the nonphysician staff may not be consistent with market norms for employee benefits. Most small medical practices provide below-market benefits to their employees in comparison to larger groups and those operated by corporate entities. Since the typical buyer-employer entity in the current marketplace is a larger group or corporate entity, adjusting these benefits to a market level may be necessary for practice net earnings to be stated on a normalized basis. As discussed in Part I, some practices provide above-market benefits, primarily in the area of retirement benefits. These benefits are typically above industry norms when the physicians in the group are near retirement age and they have established a rich employer-paid retirement plan. Above-market benefits should generally be reduced to market levels in the same way that below-market benefits are adjusted.

Economic Depreciation and Amortization

The costs of a physician practice should include an allocation for the cost of the capitalized assets used in the practice. Capitalized assets are not expensed when purchased because they have a useful life that goes beyond the year in which they are acquired. Practices will generally depreciate and amortize these assets in their financial statements and tax returns. For purposes of computing net practice earnings, the historical amounts reported for depreciation and amortization may not be relevant indications of the usage costs for these assets. The reason for this disjunction is that financial reporting and tax depreciation methods may not match the true economic life of the assets. Useful lives for tax depreciation, for example, can be much shorter than the expected useful life because they were driven by tax policy. In addition, a practice may have deferred capital expenditures to replace obsolete assets; thus, its depreciation cost is understated. For these reasons, an appraiser should analyze the reported depreciation and amortization amounts along with historical capital expenditures to determine normalized depreciation and amortization levels for the practices. These normalized levels should be reflective of the ongoing capital needs of the practice.

Cost of Capital

As discussed in Part I, every business, including a medical practice, has a cost associated with the capital investment that it has in the operating assets of the business. The cost of capital is applicable to for-profit and not-for-profit entities; both require up-front capital investment. A cost of capital should be included in the costs that go into the computation of practice net earnings. The cost of capital is computed using rates of return that are commensurate with the type of operating assets used in the practice. Examples of operating assets include working capital and fixed assets, such as furniture and equipment. (A discussion of intangible assets is included in section "The Cost Approach" below.)

Other Normalization Adjustments

Other facts and circumstances may give rise to other normalization adjustments to the historical revenues and expenses of a physician practice. One potential area for adjustment would relate to non-normative or unique activities or costs for a practice. Another area would be operations, activities, and resource utilization that are not consistent with the typical buyer-employer. As discussed in Part I, hospital and health system ownership and operation of medical practices can introduce a series of extrinsic factors into their economics and operations. These factors may place the practice in an operational setting or context that is atypical or not reflective of market norms. It may be appropriate to adjust for such factors in the determination of normalized historical practice net earnings.

2.8 Optimization Adjustments

Many practices are managed and operated at a suboptimized level. They may use unnecessary levels of staff, space, and other resources such that the cost structure of the practice is higher than it otherwise could be if the practice were managed efficiently and effectively. Operational areas, such as billing and collections, may be poorly performing. Since FMV in the appraisal body of knowledge assumes a hypothetical-typical buyer-employer entity, it may be appropriate to optimize the operations of a practice to be consistent with industry norms. The concept supporting such adjustments is that the typical buyer-employer would be expected to operate the practice in a reasonably efficient manner. Moreover, a well-informed seller would also be aware of the suboptimized level of operations in the practice. Both parties, therefore, would have an expectation that the historical practice net earnings do not represent the potential for the physician or practice. This expectation can be based on how the reasonable operator would run the practice, i.e., based on a reasonable operator standard.

Such adjustments, however, should not be based merely on use of median data from physician compensation and cost surveys. Rather, they should be based on specific analyses relative to the subject practice and its patient base, productivity levels, local market dynamics, and operating profile. The actual facts and circumstances of the practice must be taken into account. The homogenization of practice operations based on the MGMA *Cost Survey* median data as the hypothetical industry norm is not what is contemplated by optimization adjustments that are consistent with the definition of FMV. The reasonable operator standard is not based on a hypothetical practice, but rather on the specific practice as optimized and run as efficiently and effectively as the reasonable operator could realistically achieve.

When looking at areas is which physician practices are not optimized, there are four key areas in which practices can be improved. These areas include the following.

Revenue Cycle Operations

Physician practices often have suboptimized revenue cycles. They do not effectively negotiate with commercial payers or attempt to set charge rates that can maximize their commercial reimbursement levels. Practices may also have ineffective and inaccurate coding and billing practices, leading to claim rejections and delays in getting paid. More frequently, practices do poorly at collection efforts including collecting co-pay and deductible amounts from patients. Revenue cycle issues are a frequently observed phenomenon in both physician and hospital- and health system-owned practices and in large groups as well as solo physicians.

Support Staff Levels

Physician practices can be overstaffed in various areas, including nursing support, front- and back-office functions, and in technicians used in TCS. This overstaffing can be a function of physicians or practice administrators failing to optimize operations or to downsize as needed by changes in a practice. It can also result from physicians requesting special services and tasks from staff that are not consistent with an efficiently run practice. Where a practice-specific assessment indicates a reasonable operator would adjust staffing levels, it may be appropriate to adjust staffing levels for the determination of practice net earnings. It may also be possible that a practice is understaffed because the physician or physician's family members perform support functions without specific compensation from the practice. Cost increases for understaffing should be treated as part of normalization adjustments.

Office Space Utilization and Costs

Unfortunately, physicians are notorious for doing ill-conceived real estate deals. The typical real estate transaction that has gone bad entails physicians buying or leasing more space than is necessary for the effective operation of their practices. It also tends to include excessive costs incurred in building out space. As a result of such actions, physician practices often have real estate occupancy costs in excess of what a reasonable operator would have incurred to run the practice effectively. The potential optimization adjustment in such a situation involves a facts-and-circumstances specific analysis. In general, adjustments should reflect what is actually achievable with respect to office space utilization and costs. Hypothetical assumptions made in the abstract lack reasonableness in relation to the specific arrangement.

Where the physicians are owners of the real estate, it is easier to assume that the buyer-employer can optimize the space utilization. The new employer would be expected to negotiate a new lease with the physician-landlord that is based on square footage that is commensurate with the operational needs of the practice. Yet, this assumption should be practical. The space should be readily divisible so that the new tenant can actually lease a reduced space level. When such delineation and devising is not practical, it may be necessary to assume that the current square footage is what the new employer would lease, unless alternative space can be effectively obtained for the practice. The cost of such alternative space would need to be factored into the costs for practice net earnings. In addition, rental rates should be based on FMV rates consistent with the local market.

Where the physicians are not the landlords for practice office space, the probability of space optimization is reduced. A new employer-tenant may not be able to negotiate new lease terms and may be required to assume the current lease, if the employer elects to keep the practice in the current location. When this is the case, the suboptimized real estate costs of the practice are generally included in the computation of practice net earnings.

Technical Component Service Lines

Many physicians have included technical component service lines in their practices that actually reduce overall practice net earnings. Unfortunately, many physicians only think about TCS in terms of revenue and not net earnings. As a result, they sometimes introduce TCS with high initial investments or fixed costs into their practices without having a sufficient level of volume to make the specific TCS profitable. An appraiser may assume the elimination of such TCS lines as part of the optimization of practice net earnings when such services are not profitable. The basis for this assumption is that the reasonable operator would terminate service lines that are not profitable for the practice. When this assumption is made, the appraiser should remove the revenues and costs associated with the TCS line from the computation of practice net earnings.

2.9 Revenue and Cost Allocations to Individual Physicians in Group Practices

Some employment valuation assignments may require the appraiser to value the compensation of a specific physician who is part of a group practice or to determine compensation individually for physicians in a group. In such engagements, the appraiser may be required to allocate practice net earnings to individual physicians as part of the appraisal process using the framework of earnings-based compensation. An appraisal can use a variety of methods to allocate group practice net earnings to individual physicians. In evaluating allocation methods, an appraiser should consider several issues and factors.

Stark Compliance for TCSNE

The allocation of TCSNE should be consistent with the requirements of the Stark regulations. If it is not, the allocation formula for these earnings should be revised for Stark compliance. A fundamental consideration for Stark compliance is that TCSNE must meet the in-office ancillary exception and the group practice compensation rules. These compensation regulations mandate that TCSNE not be directly related to the volume or value of TCS referrals by individual physicians.

Using Individual Physician Revenues

Most groups track individual physician revenues in terms of charges and collections. Revenues and fees from other services such as hospital call coverage or medical directorships are also typically tracked by individual physicians. Using individual physician revenues may be preferable when computing practice net earnings by physician, when such information is available and reasonably accurate. There are, however, exceptions to this general preference. A required exception for allocating within a group is exclusion of TCS revenues. To be compliant with Stark, compensation from TCS cannot be determined in a way that directly relates to the volume or value of ancillary service referrals. TCS revenues, in general, should be allocated to Stark-compliant pools in which the TCSNE are computed. In the case of a single physician exiting a group, using total revenues may be appropriate, but such use raises the issues discussed above about the use of TCSNE in the practice net earnings of solo employed physicians.

Sometimes, it may be more appropriate to use an allocation of professional component service revenues and other service revenues, rather than the individual revenues by physicians. Many ob/gyn groups often consider their obstetrics-related revenues to be shared commonly among the group due to equal sharing in delivery call coverage for group patients. Revenues may be credited to the individual physicians based on who delivered a baby rather than on the prenatal services provided to an expectant mother. Some groups may also delegate certain patient bases or cases to individual physicians as a matter of overall group productivity optimization. This organizational pattern may yield results in which certain physicians have higher revenues than others. The physicians may contend, however, that this is not a reflection of individual productivity per se, but rather of how the group has sought to allocate work among group physicians.

In summary, there may be cases in which the facts and circumstances warrant an allocation of group revenues rather than use of individual revenues as reported in the group's information systems.

The net effect of using individual physician revenues is that the allocation process becomes a matter of assigning group overhead and costs to individual physicians rather than to group practice net earnings. In these circumstances, the costs allocated should relate to the physicians' professional component services as well as other services provided, excluding TCS. When group revenues are used, the allocation process can become an exercise of allocating group practice net earnings to individual physicians.

Matching Services Provided With Allocation Methods

Allocation of net practice earnings or group revenues and overhead should relate to the services provided by group physicians. There are many allocation methods and techniques for achieving reasonable and equitable allocation outcomes.[12] A few simplified methods include allocations based on productivity measures such as wRVUs or professional collections. Productivity measures would appear to be the most relevant when allocating group practice net earnings. When allocating costs, however, there may be an argument for using a hybrid method that allocates costs on a per full-time-equivalent (FTE) basis and on productivity. The concept behind this type of hybrid allocation is that some resources are fixed and relate to supporting a physician, regardless of productivity. On the other hand, the more productive a physician is, the more resources are utilized in the providing services. In summary, the allocation methods used should have a reasonable relation to the services provided.

Elimination of Ownership Considerations

Allocation methods giving preferences in distributions to shareholders or senior physicians may not relate to the services provided by physicians in the group. Preferential distributions that are not related to physician productivity or physician services are generally reflective of ownership considerations. These considerations do not continue under employment. However, if preferential distributions relate to management or executive services provided by certain senior physicians to the group and these services will continue under employment, it may be appropriate to include additional compensation to these physicians for the specific services provided over and above their clinical services as employees. The value of these services, however, should be factored into the costs used to determine practice net earnings for the group from physician services.

---

12 See Bruce A. Johnson and Deborah Walker Keegan, *Physician Compensation Plans: State-of-the-Art Strategies*, MGMA, 2006, for a comprehensive and in-depth discussion of such methods.

3.0 The Cost Approach

3.1 Key Element of Cost-Based Valuation Methods

The cost approach as applied to service contracts seeks to value the compensation for the subject arrangement by valuing substitutes or alternatives for those services in the marketplace. Cost approach techniques may also attempt to re-create the cost of the same or comparable scope of services to be provided in the subject arrangement as a method for valuing the subject services. This re-creation of the cost of services may involve a buildup of the costs for various resources or subservices that are part of the subject services. Cost approach methods may also seek alternative sources or providers of a service that is comparable to the services being provided in the subject arrangement. Under these methods, the appraiser may gather market data on the cost of comparable or alternative services with the same utility as the subject services.

Another potential indication of the cost for a service is its historical cost, where past compensation for services was based on arm's-length negotiations between parties who are economically independent of each other, not having other business relationships that might influence the consideration in the historical service contract. Under this analysis, the historical cost for a service is a reflection and indication of the market value for the services because it was negotiated at arm's length by independent parities to the arrangement. This past market value may still be a valid indication of the present and future value of the services. Even when the past marketplace is not a good indication of present or future market conditions, the appraiser may be able to adjust past indications of value to reflect current or prospective conditions.

In the case of employment arrangements, one application of the cost approach is to use the historical compensation of the physician as a measure of the cost to re-create the services provided under employment. For this application of the cost approach, however, the physician's historical compensation should be based on a comparable scope of services to that required under employment. If the scope of services is dissimilar, the compensation may not be indicative of the value of the services in the proposed employment arrangement. In certain circumstances, it may be possible for the appraiser to adjust the historical compensation of the physician to place the past scope of services on a comparable basis with those contemplated under employment. The adjustment process entails a segregation or allocation of the historical compensation for the various types of services for which the physician received income in the past. Past compensation may be payment for services such as patient care, hospital call coverage, medical directorships, and owner compensation.

Once the historical compensation has been allocated to the various services provided by the physician in prior periods, the appraiser adjusts the historical compensation for those past services that are consistent with what is required under employment. Historical compensation may also need to be normalized consistent with various market norms related to benefits and operations. It may also be adjusted to eliminate nonrecurring, one-time, or extraordinary items that are not reflective of the physician's normalized or regular services or the economics of those services.

As noted above, use of historical compensation is predicated on this compensation being the result of arm's-length negotiations between independent parties. This condition generally precludes the use of historical compensation for physicians who were employed by hospital and health systems under the cost approach. The regulatory prohibition on the use of data from parties with referral relationships would appear to be applicable to such historical compensation. The existence of the referral relationship places the independence of the parties into question. As a result, the compensation paid to a referral-source by a hospital or health system employer does not generally meet the criteria for arm's-length negotiations that would be necessary for reliance on such compensation as an indication of value under the concept of fair market value for healthcare regulatory purposes.

3.2 The Historical Practice Net Earnings Method

The historical practice net earnings (HPNE) method is a specific valuation technique that applies the concept of earnings-based compensation to the historical economic outcomes of a physician or medical practice. It uses the revenues from physician services less the costs to produce these services from prior periods to establish historical practice net earnings. These past practice net earnings reflect the historical cost to re-create or reproduce the services. As such, they are in indication of the value of the services under the cost approach. The determination of historical practice net earnings should take into account the scope of service and normalization adjustments discussed above. Optimization adjustments may be considered, but many appraisers find it more practical to include such adjustments under the income approach using forecasted practice net earnings. To apply the historical practice net earnings method, the appraiser needs access to the historical financial statements of the practice along with key details and supplemental information about various revenue and cost items.

The decision to use the HPNE method for an employment valuation when data are available is generally a function of the relevance of past compensation to future conditions under employment. If past operating and market conditions are not indicative of the future circumstances, the method may lack relevance. Even when this disconnect between past and future is present, an appraiser may complete the method as part of preparing the forecasted practice net earnings method that looks to future operating and market conditions under employment. A normalized base year is generally required to prepare a forecast of future practice net earnings. The preparation of a normalized base year can serve as a variation of the historical practice net earnings method.

The HPNE method can be applied to multiple prior periods to derive an indication of the value of physician services. A critical question in using multiple prior periods is whether they are indicative of market and operating conditions that will transpire under the proposed employment arrangement. Changes in reimbursement or operations may render prior periods less relevant and applicable to the value of physician services in future periods. Appraisers should use reasonable and supportable judgment in evaluating whether prior periods are relevant and applicable to future periods. Where practical, it may be helpful to prepare the method using multiple periods as a means of looking at trends and developments in the practice that may have a bearing on future periods. Alternatively, an appraiser may review multiple prior periods of financial information to derive a normalized base year level of practice net earnings that is considered to be relevant and applicable to future periods under employment.

3.3 The Adjusted Historical Compensation Method

The adjusted historical compensation (AHC) method is another cost approach method that employs the concept of earnings-based compensation. It uses similar ideas and adjustments as those included in the HPNE method. The starting point for this method, however, is the actual compensation for the physician in prior years rather than the practice income statement. The historical compensation can be based on W-2 earnings and from K-1 earnings in entities treated as partnerships for tax purposes, *but this compensation needs to be reviewed and adjusted.* Beginning with the historical compensation, the method adjusts this income to reflect the scope of services to be provided under employment. The AHC method also uses normalization adjustment to place the historical compensation on a basis that is consistent with an employment arrangement. In general, the same adjustments made for the HPNE method are applicable to this cost approach method. The AHC method can be summarized as follows. The various adjustments listed are not intended to be exhaustive, but rather illustrative of the types of items for which compensation may need to be adjusted.

+ Reported historical compensation

+/- Scope of service adjustments:

  ○ Changes in clinical services;

  ○ Changes in hospital call coverage services;

○ Changes in administrative services;

○ Elimination of owner compensation and distributions;

○ Changes in annual working hours; and

○ Changes in other professional services.

+/- Normalization adjustments:

○ Nonrecurring, nonoperating, and extraordinary revenue and expenses;

○ Physician market-level benefits;

○ Debt proceeds used to fund physician compensation;

○ Prior retained earnings or cash on hand used to fund current-year compensation;

○ Adjustments for related-party costs and expenses to market levels;

○ Cost of capital; and

○ Economic depreciation and amortization.

= Adjusted historical compensation

It should be noted that *the primary use of the AHC method is when historical financial statements are not available for a physician or practice and use of the HPNE method is not available or practical.* This absence of data usually occurs when a physician or number of physicians are seeking to exit their current employment or group practice. The physicians may not have access to such information or may not be able to access it without alerting the current employer to the potential exit. In such cases, the AHC method provides the appraiser with a cost approach technique that takes into account the historical compensation of the subject physician.

Caution and critical scrutiny should be applied when attempting to use the AHC method when limited data are available. The appraiser needs to ascertain what scope of services went into the reported compensation and the compensation formula or method used to pay the physician. Without this information, the appraiser cannot be assured that the scope of services and historical compensation are consistent with those contemplated under the proposed employment arrangement. Lack of information with respect to potential normalization adjustments may also limit the appraiser's ability to ensure comparability. Appraisers should be careful and circumspect in using this method.

3.4 The Cost to Recruit Method

The cost to recruit method seeks to establish the replacement cost for staffing a physician employment arrangement by recruiting a qualified physician to fill the position. The method looks to the compensation that would be necessary for such recruitment. Generally, physician compensation survey data are used as the basis for determining the compensation level that would be necessary to recruit a qualified physician. The appraiser selects certain levels of compensation that are believed to be necessary to attract and recruit a physician with qualifications that are required for the subject employment arrangement. An allowance for recruiter fees and costs may also be considered as part of the cost to recruit. The theory behind this method is that it represents the alternative cost for employing the subject physician. While the method uses physician compensation survey data, it is included under the rubric of the cost approach rather than the market approach because it focuses on the replacement cost of hiring an alternative qualified physician.

In applying this method, there are several issues for appraisers to consider. The first issue is determining what data should be used to establish the compensation level that is necessary to attract a qualified candidate. Generally, three options are available for such data: placement and recruiting survey data, general physician compensation survey data, and individual transactions for recently hired physicians. In general, placement and recruiting survey data should be considered first in establishing a range of compensation for a replacement physician. The reason for this preference is that these data are taken from actual new-hire transactions. It presents data on the actual compensation amounts that induced a physician to enter into a new employment arrangement. Such data should be distinguished from the general survey data; these data are predominately based on physicians in existing employment and shareholder or owner arrangements. The economic outcomes of an established physician can be significantly different than those of a starting physician. Generally, but not always, a newly hired physician will make less than one with an established practice and a significant level of productivity. An employer will typically pay compensation for an unknown level of service from a newly hired physician.

Use of the general survey data should be used to supplement placement and recruiting survey data. Oftentimes, such supplementation is necessary because the number of respondents to the placement data can be small, giving rise to the potential for skewed and unrepresentative results. For certain subspecialties, placement data may not be available. Practically speaking, therefore, general survey data may be the only basis for establishing the compensation for a replacement physician in certain instances.

Once the appropriate market data are selected, the appraiser must use these data to determine the compensation level for the replacement physician. Some of the survey data may have relevant breakdowns that can assist in establishing this compensation level. For example, the placement and recruiting data from MGMA's *Physician Placement Starting Salary Survey* and in the AMGA *Medical Group Compensation and Financial Survey* are segregated between experienced physicians and physician hired out of residency, fellowship, or other training programs. In another example, the general MGMA survey data include compensation by years of experience. Ultimately, however, the appraiser must develop some criteria by which a compensation level is derived from the data for the replacement physician. Attention should also be given to the types of compensation reported in the survey data. Sign-on bonuses and relocation allowances are typical in many new-hire employment arrangements. The appraiser should ensure that the compensation in the survey data is comparable to the compensation assumed for the cost to replace.

Unfortunately, there is a tendency to overuse the median from the general surveys, particularly MGMA, as the universal cost to replace the subject physician. While the gravitation toward the median is understandable, it should not be summarily and universally assumed to be the replacement cost for a new physician. The median means half the data are above this value and the other half are below this value. The median, therefore, should not be misunderstood to be a floor for physician compensation. More importantly, however, the median from the general surveys should not be considered to be the typical compensation level for recruiting a physician because this value is not taken exclusively from newly hired physicians recruited into new positions. Appraisers should use a more informed approach to the survey data than merely assuming the median from the general surveys is the universal compensation floor necessary to recruit a new physician.

3.5 The Locum Tenens Cost Method

Since the cost of locum tenens physicians represents a conceptual alternative to staffing a physician position in a medical practice, its use as an alternative under the cost approach is considered here. In short, use of locum tenens is not a comparable staffing arrangement to the employment of a physician. Locum tenens physicians are intended as temporary staffing to cover services when existing physicians cannot provide them. Because they are used temporarily, the cost of these physicians generally includes a premium and often entails the assumption that the existing practice will bill and collect for services provided by the locum tenens provider. In addition, the cost of locum tenens generally includes a markup for the administrative costs and required return of the locums staffing company. These types of economics and costs are not comparable to an employment arrangement. Thus, use of locum tenens costs as an alternative method under the cost approach is ill-advised at best, and strictly speaking, not comparable from a valuation perspective.

3.6 Evaluating the Use and Relevance of the Cost Approach

In evaluating the potential use of cost approach methods or in assessing the outcomes of cost techniques applied to a subject employment arrangement, it is important to note the relative strengths and weaknesses of the cost approach methods. The advantages of these methods are noteworthy. The HPNE method and the AHC method use the historical performance and actual earned compensation levels of the subject practice or physician in the local market context under independent conditions as the basis for guideline compensation under employment. Local market factors, such as reimbursement, payer mix, and patient demand, are necessarily reflected in the historically earned compensation of the subject, particularly under the HPNE method. Moreover, practice patterns and operating characteristics of the subject are also necessarily reflected in the value indications under the HPNE method. This method is based on the compensation outcomes of these factors on the net earnings of the subject.

The importance of using actual historical compensation outcomes is considerable and significant. Under these methods, the appraiser has a local-market-driven and practice- or physician-specific indication of the value of services that is grounded in actual outcomes and not on an assumed "market" basis using survey data that lack statistical representation of the national, much less a local, market. In very real terms, the HPNE and AHC methods provide specific market indications for the practice or physician in terms of what compensation was, in fact, earned based on arm's-length independent conditions in local service area dynamics. Other methods are not based on this level of realism and factual evidence relative to the subject. Other approaches and methods include levels of speculation, assumptions, projections, and the like. No other valuation methods under the cost approach have this kind of relationship to local market conditions as these two methods.

Moreover, both methods provide indications that reflect the perspective of the seller of the services, i.e., the physician. Since the seller has been receiving this level of compensation for services, it is reasonable for him or her to expect a commensurate level of compensation for those services under employment, unless there are significant changes in market conditions from those in prior periods. In fact, HPNE or adjusted historical compensation reflects the compensation value of the seller's alternative to employment, which is remaining in the current employment or practice arrangement. FMV is intended to reflect the price for services at which both a willing buyer and seller would consummate a transaction. Thus, the alternative price for the same services is highly relevant to determining what the FMV price would be.

The cost to recruit method provides a perspective on one alternative available to the potential buyer-employer through determining the compensation and cost necessary to recruit another physician to provide the services required under the proposed employment arrangement. This alternative cost helps to circumscribe the relevant range of value for these services. All cost approach methods reflect the replacement cost for the services.

The limitations of cost approach methods should be noted as well. These methods are based on past compensation outcomes that resulted from market and operating conditions that may not be indicative of future circumstances. As a result, the cost approach method may not reflect key economic factors and dynamics expected under employment. Past compensation outcomes may not determine future services. The HPNE and AHC methods, moreover, require significant levels of data to be reliably completed. Without this detailed data, the methods may lack the level of precision and accuracy that are part of their appeal. In many valuation assignments, such detailed data are not readily available to allow the appraiser to implement the methods reasonably. In addition, these methods may not be applicable when the subject physician was employed or practicing in an independent or arm's-length arrangement. As more physicians move toward hospital or health system employment, the HPNE and AHC methods will not be available for determining FMV for regulatory purposes. Thus, use of these methods may be limited in many situations.

A major weakness of the cost to recruit method is that it uses general survey data to apply to a specific physician. These general data are not usually reported according to factors that make it easily and accurately comparable to a specific physician. The method provides a general result, rather than a highly specific indication. The cost to get a truly or fully comparable physician can be difficult to determine. Moreover, general survey data may not reflect compensation levels that are relevant for the local service market.

4.0 The Income Approach

4.1 The Income Approach Defined

For valuing service agreements, the income approach may be adapted in terms of the valuation principle of future benefits as the basis for value, but without the conversion to a present value amount. With this adaptation, the income approach can be employed to calculate the future economic benefits to be received by one or both parties to the service agreement.[13] These benefits are then evaluated in terms of investment levels, resources utilized, and services provided in comparison to market rates of return and

---

13 Under this adaptation of the income approach, future economic benefits are not intended to include the value or volume of improper referrals. Rather, the appraiser looks exclusively to the revenues, expenses, resources, and investments related to the specific services and service lines provided for in the agreement.

profitability. Under this reformulation of the income approach, the appraiser seeks to value the services by ensuring that each party receives market returns or margins given the levels of investment, risk, and resource utilization attributable to either party to the service contract.

In the case of employment arrangements, the concept of earnings-based compensation can be used in the application of the income approach. A forecast of the practice net earnings is developed as the value indication for physician compensation under employment. This forecast takes into account future conditions for the practice as well as the specific scope of services contemplated under employment. It projects the anticipated compensation to be received by the employed physicians based on anticipated practice net earnings. Earnings-based compensation under the income approach is forward-looking in its measurement of physician compensation. There are two income approach methods that are used by appraisers for valuing compensation under employment agreements: the forecasted practice net earnings method and the adapted discounted cash flow method.

4.2 The Forecasted Practice Net Earnings Method

The forecasted practice net earnings (FPNE) method is essentially the valuation technique used in the HPNE method except that the periods used for purposes of determining practice net earnings are future rather than historical ones. Essentially, the appraiser uses a forecast of revenues and expenses for the practice to compute net earnings from physician services. The forecast is based on the scope of services required under the subject employment arrangement. The projected net earnings are used as the basis for valuing the services under employment. As with the HPNE method, the expenses of the practice include amounts for the cost of capital, economic depreciation and amortization, and market-level physician benefits. Forecasted revenues and expenses may also include normalization and optimization adjustments and assumptions as discussed in the application of the HPNE method. The projected net earnings can also take into account anticipated changes in the marketplace in terms of future volumes, reimbursement, operations, and services.

One key issue in the application of the FPNE method is what future periods should be used to determine earnings-based compensation. At minimum, the future periods included should coincide with the number of years of the employment agreement covered by the FMV opinion of the appraiser. If the appraiser's FMV analysis is effective for the first two years of the employment agreement, then at least the first two years of the contract should be included in the forecasted periods. Taking an average of the PNE from the years covered by the valuation opinion can be appropriate for establishing the value of the physician services, rather than determining a distinct amount for each discrete period.

The use of periods outside the effective period of the valuation period for purposes of averaging and determining a compensation level during the valuation period can raise some questions, especially if the compensation in the out years is significantly higher than the initial years covered by the valuation opinion. An appraiser might attempt to defend such out-year inclusion if the out years are consistent with the initial term in the subject employment agreement. The argument would be that the typical buyer-employer is looking at compensation over the term of the employment agreement rather than the effective shelf-life of the appraisal. On the other hand, one might question whether a typical buyer-employer would seek to front-load compensation in a longer-term employment arrangement, given potential future changes in the marketplace. The uncertainty of today's physician marketplace in light of healthcare reform and experimentation in reimbursement structures would appear to mitigate against the economic impetus to front-load compensation.

4.3 The Adapted Discounted Cash Flow Method

Another appraisal technique that can be used to establish earnings-based compensation is an adaptation of the discounted cash flow (DCF) method from business valuation.[14] In this application of the DCF method, the appraiser uses a template to solve for the physician compensation level that makes the net present value of the net cash flows from the practice equal to the value of the assets required to operate the practice.[15] Unlike the HPNE method, however, the adapted DCF (A-DCF) method does not include a deduction for the cost of capital. The cost of capital is reflected in the discount rate applied to the future net cash flows from the practice. Depreciation and capital expenditures are included the A-DCF method consistent with standard business valuation practice. The net cash flows can be tax-effected or not tax-effected, with the requirement that the discount rate reflect market rates consistent with the tax-effecting of the net cash flows.

The valuation theory in support of the A-DCF method is that it is another appraisal technique for determining practice net earnings from physician services using future periods. Under this method, practice net earnings are denominated in terms of net

---

14   Todd Sorensen, AVA, of VMG Health introduced me to this adaptation of the DCF method for compensation valuation purposes.

15   In business valuation, the DCF is used to determine the value of the assets of the medical practice. Thus, there would appear to be a "chicken and egg" dilemma in using a DCF for business and compensation valuation purposes. For business valuation, a compensation level is needed to determine the net cash flows from the practice, which in turn provides a value indication for the total assets of the practice. Compensation valuation requires the value of the total assets to determine practice net earnings, and thereby compensation for physician services.

cash flows from the practice, where the costs associated with the total invested capital of the practice are included through capital expenditures and the discount rate. Stated explicitly, the A-DCF method purports to show the compensation level that is available from the practice operations, given the FMV of total invested capital required to own and operate it and a cost of capital that is commensurate with the risk profile of the subject practice. The use of the A-DCF method, as adapted from business valuation practice, separates owner compensation from compensation for physician services by determining the latter after accounting for the former. The A-DCF method can also be seen as an adaptation of the independent investor test using a DCF template.

As with the FPNE method, one key issue in the use of the A-DCF method is what periods should be included in the analysis. A corollary but no less important issue is whether a terminal or liquidation value should be used after the discrete period projections. With regard to the number of years used in discrete period analysis of the DCF, the arguments from the same issue in the FPNE method would appear to apply to the A-DCF method. The employment contract term may extend over a longer horizon than the applicable period for the valuation opinion. One might contend that the term of the employment agreement should coincide with the discrete period analysis. The same issue of front-loading compensation can also arise as a potential objection to the use of periods beyond the effective life of the appraisal.

The question of using a terminal or liquidation value raises a potentially more difficult set of issues, especially if normalized compensation is shown to be higher in the terminal value than in the initial years of the DCF analysis. One potential issue is whether an employment arrangement can be considered to continue into perpetuity, as implied by the use of a terminal value. This question is particularly acute, when the subject employment agreement provides for termination without cause. In addition, the experience of the industry from the 1990s provides a cautionary note to the current expectation that physician employment by hospital and health systems is the new permanent paradigm for physicians. A more supportable approach may be to use a liquidation value at the end of the proposed employment term to reflect the uncertainty of future market conditions over the long run.

4.4 The Importance of Supportable Projections in the Income Approach
As noted in the professional literature related to the use of the income approach in business valuation, it is essential to use a forecast that is grounded in supportable and defensible assumptions. Unrealistic projections undermine the credibility of value conclusions arrived at using the income approach. The same requirements for reasonable and realistic forecasts, projections, and assumptions apply in using the income approach in compensation valuation. An unconvincing and unrealistic pro forma for

practice revenues and expenses yields a questionable indication of value. To avoid this problem, appraisers should perform sufficient research, data gathering, and analysis on the subject practice, its local service market, the subject physician specialty, reimbursement trends, and the larger physician marketplace. This knowledge base should provide the appraiser with a sound basis for determining reasonable and supportable estimations, projections, and assumptions for application of the income approach in valuing physician employment arrangements.

4.5 Determining Asset Values for Use in the Income Approach

Earnings-based compensation includes economic depreciation and amortization on those assets necessary for the operation of the practice. The cost of capital associated with these assets is also included. These costs are included in the computation of practice net earnings because they are essential elements of the cost of providing services. The net earnings from physician services would be overstated if such capital costs were not included in this calculation. Such costs are required in the production of the services. To exclude these costs misstates practice net earnings because the full cost of providing the services cannot be determined without capital costs. For noncapital-intensive physician specialties, capital costs are generally not that material to the calculation. Capital costs can be significant, however, because those specialties utilize significant levels of technology and equipment in the provision of clinical services, particularly TCS. In addition, the recent requirements for electronic medical records systems (EMRs) have resulted in larger technology costs for all physician practices.

In terms of determining the values to use for determining depreciation and amortization as well as a cost of capital, there are key conceptual and practical issues for the appraiser to consider as part of completing income approach methods. The income approach looks forward to future earnings-based compensation that would arise under the proposed employment arrangement. Where the proposed arrangement includes the purchase of the practice, the FMV of the asset values determined in a business appraisal should be used for the determination of economic depreciation and amortization and for the cost of capital. The reason for this use is that the appraisal has identified and valued those assets, both tangible and intangible, that exist in the practice and have value in accordance with the standard of value. These tangible and intangible assets, therefore, are necessary for the operation of the practice. In addition, the appraisal has determined the value that the typical buyer would pay for those assets in acquiring the practice. These asset values must necessarily be used for determining the capital costs of the practice. *One cannot present a congruent and coherent appraisal analysis by indicating that a typical buyer would pay one value to acquire the assets of a practice and then not use those same values to determine the capital costs associated with operating the practice.*

Moreover, one cannot exclude these capital costs from the determination of practice net earnings. The concept of earnings-based compensation as the measure of value for professional services includes those costs necessary for the production of those services. If tangible as well as intangible assets are necessary for the operation of a physician practice, they are necessarily required for the production of physician services. Otherwise, to what end are these assets needed? They would have to be treated as nonoperational to be excluded from the capital costs of operating the practice. One cannot escape the fundamental economic relationship between the costs of operating a business and the operational asset base needed to run the practice. These costs should be factored into the determination of practice net earnings for establishing the value of the professional services provided in a practice. Excluding these costs would represent a mismatching of revenues and expenses related to the service. It would also provide an undue benefit in determining compensation for services: The compensation does not include an adequate allocation of the costs necessary for the provision of the services. Costs would be understated in computing practice net earnings to use as the value of services, if the costs of all capital needed to operate the practice are excluded. Provision of an undue benefit raises the specter of regulatory exposure.

For those acquisition-employment transactions with high tangible and intangible asset values, the net effect of appropriately burdening practice overhead with the costs associated with all operation assets needed in the practice is to lower physician compensation significantly. Whatever business valuation claim one makes in the debate about the priority in the value indications from the cost and income approaches with respect to appraising physician practices, the implication for compensation valuation is clear. If the practice has significant intangible asset value to a typical buyer under the standard of FMV, the costs associated with these assets should be factored into determination of compensation under the income approach based on a forecast of practice net earnings. To claim otherwise is to present an inconsistent and incoherent valuation methodology that uses one set of economic assumptions and analysis for one purpose, i.e., an acquisition, and subsequently uses a completely different approach for determining compensation.

The reason that one cannot use such a bifurcation in fundamental appraisal analysis is that, under any earnings-based method, professional compensation is a function of the net earnings produced by a professional. These net earnings must reflect the costs, including capital costs, associated with the use of practice assets. As discussed previously, the concept of earnings-based compensation actually arose out of the business valuation body of knowledge in looking at the appropriate level of owner compensation for small business, including professional practices. To posit and successfully defend such a bifurcation, one would have to defeat the conceptual framework developed in the appraisal body of knowledge with regard to the determination of owner compensation and the use of the independent investor test as part of that determination, particularly in relation to professional practices.

Now, the appraisal body of knowledge with respect to the owner compensation does afford other techniques for determining the value of owner services, including the use of market-based compensation data. The claim made here is not that earnings-based compensation is the only method for determining the FMV of physician compensation. Rather, the point argued here is that the application of earnings-based compensation techniques should be consistent and congruent. Thus, the use of income approach methods for valuing physician compensation should be based on the FMV of assets established based on a business valuation, where such an appraisal was prepared and is available to the compensation valuation analyst. In the absence of such an appraisal, the analyst should use the best available information on practice assets to establish the capital costs associated with the operation of the practice.

4.6 Evaluating the Use and Relevance of the Income Approach

The use and application of the income approach has several strong points for the valuation of employment arrangements. First, income approach methods are based on forecasts of future market conditions that will exist under the subject arrangement. This feature is important because market conditions can often change significantly, especially in the area of reimbursement. Second, since income approach methods are based on practice net earnings for the subject practice or physician, the value indications derived from these methods can account for local market dynamics. These indications are also based on the practice and operational patterns of the subject. They can entail normalization and optimization assumptions that adjust net earnings to those consistent with a reasonable operator or a typical buyer of physician services. Income approach methods, therefore, can encompass future conditions along with normalized outcomes at a level of specificity not generally available with the cost and market approach methods. Both the cost and market approaches do not consider future conditions, and the market approach generally lacks precision in looking at local market factors and specific practice or physician operating patterns.

The limitations of income approach methods primarily relate to the validity and supportability of the assumptions used in the forecast of revenues and expenses for the subject practice or physician. The indications of value produced by the income approach are only as relevant and valid as the assumptions used in this forecast. Predictions and prognostications necessarily entail some level of uncertainty, even when they are well-researched and -supported. Another critical drawback of income approach methods is that they can be data-intensive. Significant information is required to prepare a base year pro forma for the practice or physician. Additional detailed information is needed to prepare projections going forward from this base year. Without detailed data, the forecast may be unreliable or uncertain with respect to various key assumptions. Limited data may also give rise to forecasts with various assumptions that cannot be readily research, verified, or supported. A highly assumptionized forecast may lack credibility.

Finally, using the income approach on a hospital or health system practice or employed physician may be difficult if the hospital- or health system-affiliated employer has made significant changes to a practice for reasons extrinsic to the operations of the practice. (See Chapter 14, "The Economics of Physician Clinical Services and Compensation," for a discussion of such extrinsic factors.) The hospital or health system may have also converted or moved TCS to HOPD status. Thus, historical data that might be used to prepare a forecast or pro forma for the practice may not reflect economics that are indicative of the typical buyer-employer. It may not be practical or feasible to normalize or adjust the historical financials of a practice to be consistent with the typical buyer-employer.

Chapter 25. Valuing Physician Employment Arrangements for Clinical Services: Valuation Synthesis and Special Issues

CONTENTS

Chapter 25. Valuing Physician Employment Arrangements for Clinical Services: Valuation Synthesis and Special Issues

By Timothy Smith, CPA/ABV

1.0 Valuation Synthesis and Conclusion of Value

1.1 Synthesis Process Overview

Valuation synthesis is the process by which an appraiser evaluates the value indications from various valuation approaches, methods, and techniques and concludes with an opinion of value. The synthesis process can yield a single indication of value or a range of value for the subject being appraised. It is used in various appraisal disciplines, ranging from real estate appraisal to business valuation, where multiple approaches and methods were prepared by the appraiser. No specific formula or methodology governs the synthesis process. Sound and rigorous valuation thinking, however, should direct the synthesis process. Ultimately, the synthesis is a matter of professional judgment. Appraisers are expected to support the final outcome of the process and should be able to articulate the reasons and rationale behind the synthesis.

Many appraisers use formal approaches or systematic techniques for synthesizing various value indications. One popular approach is to weight each indication on a relative percentage basis and compute a weighted average value indication. The percentage weightings assigned to each value indication signify the appraiser's assessment of each indication relative to the others. Weightings are assigned based on the appraiser's judgment as to the relative applicability of the value indication to the subject. Such applicability is evaluated in terms of the relative strengths and weaknesses of the methods and the underlying data used in the methods as well as other factors. Appraisers often favor this approach because it provides a ready-made template and framework for synthesizing the results of multiple methods. The use of weightings, however, is not the only pathway to synthesizing multiple value indications. Other valid approaches include the selection of a specific indication or the use of specific indications to serve as lows or highs for a range of value.

Some appraisers prepare a single value indication for each of the three approaches (cost, market, and income). It should be noted, however, that a single indication of value does not necessarily need to be synthesized for each approach, where multiple valuation methods and techniques were completed for a given approach. An appraiser may decide to evaluate and synthesize the value indications from all methods used in a single comprehensive comparison to assess each method relative to all methods used in the valuation process. Depending on the number of value indications, such a process may be more logical or systematic than synthesizing three indications of value from each approach. Moreover, an appraiser may decide to use different evaluation and synthesis approaches from one valuation to the next based on the facts and circumstances. While such divergence in practice or conventions may be subject to scrutiny, doing so may be more rigorous and sound appraisal practice when done for good reasons. Ultimately, the synthesis process is a matter of professional judgment and analysis. To reiterate, however, an appraiser should be able to articulate the reasons and rationale behind the synthesis process used in the particular valuation assignment.

1.2 General Criteria for the Synthesis Process

Whatever the approach for synthesizing value indications, there are general criteria that can aid in the systematic review of relevant factors and issues in evaluating value indications from different valuation issues. These criteria can apply to methods from all three approaches to value, i.e., cost, market, and income. These criteria can include the following.

The Relative Strengths and Weaknesses of a Method or Technique

An appraiser should go through a process in which the relative strengths and weaknesses of the various methods completed are evaluated in comparison to each other. Generally, this process begins with a conceptual analysis of each method in which the appraiser evaluates each technique from a methodological standpoint. An appraiser may conclude that some methods have greater applicability in encompassing the fundamental economics and market dynamics of a service than others from a conceptual or methodological point of view. Methods can also be assessed relative to a series of economic factors and market dynamics related to the subject employment arrangement. The appraiser weighs the applicability and relevance of the method with reference to the subject services and practice or physician. These factors can include the following:

- Subject physician specialty;

- Scope of services under employment;

- Compensation structure or formula;

- Key contractual terms and duties; and

- Facts and circumstances related to employment.

Examples of how these factors are applied include the following. For a hospital-based physician, practice net earnings methods may be considered less relevant and applicable because the subject physician covers many night or weekend shifts with low volumes or provides services at a hospital with a poor payer mix. In another example, an appraiser may place significant weight on earnings-based compensation methods in appraising an employment agreement where the physician will be employed in-place with a seamless transition for patients. For recruiting a physician into a new market from out of state, an appraiser may conclude that market-approach-based methods are more relevant to the fair market value (FMV) analysis.

The Reliability, Quality, and Quantity of Data Used in the Methods
Data considerations can also play an important role in the synthesis process. Data inputs are a key part of the use of any appraisal method or technique. As a result, valuation methods are dependent on the nature of the data used in their application. To the extent that data are not reliable, questionable, or are lacking in evidence or support, the outcome of those methods using such data is necessarily called into question. The concept of "garbage in, garbage out" applies to the outcomes of valuation methods and their use of data. On the other hand, if clear and well-supported data are used for the implementation of a method, the results of the method should be considered to be relatively strong or supportable from a data-source perspective.

The Relative Degree of Assumptions Used in the Methods
Lack of available or reliable data may necessitate the use of assumptions by the appraiser as part of completing a given valuation method. For purposes of this discussion, assumptions here are defined as inputs to appraisal methods, techniques, or models for which there is not actual data or for which the appraiser lacks certitude or material precision, whether quantitative or qualitative, with respect to the inputs. The issue of

assumptions in the appraisal process can be significant. Certain appraisal methods and techniques require the appraiser to use assumptions. Income approach methods, for example, require projections of future revenues and expenses. An appraiser may also have to make assumptions about what is and is not included in physician compensation survey data when applying market approach techniques. In general, the extent and defensibility of these assumptions can become a key factor in evaluating the value indication of a method or technique. Highly speculative assumptions or assumptions with little independent support or evidence will generally yield less defensible outcomes than those with more support and less speculation.

The Range of Outcomes From the Methods

The relative range in value indications from the various valuation methods prepared can affect the synthesis process. A narrow range may necessitate less comparative evaluation than a broad range of value. When the outcomes are materially disparate, the appraiser will need to complete a more significant comparative assessment of the methods and their divergent indications of value. The appraiser is faced, in such cases, with the necessity of judging between competing ideas, factors, and considerations in arriving at a final conclusion of value.

In addition to these general criteria, specific issues and considerations can go into the assessment and evaluation of methods for each of the three approaches to value. The following sections discuss the specific areas for study and review by appraisers for methods under each approach.

1.3 Evaluating the Outcomes of Market Approach Methods

The examination of value indications from market-approach methods and techniques generally focuses on three key areas: the nature of the market data, the general comparability of the subject to the data, and the measures or criteria used to determine comparability of the subject and market data.

Assessing the Relevance of Market Data

As part of the synthesis process, an appraiser should weigh several factors related to the relevance of the market data that were utilized in the market approach. These factors can include the following:

- *The extent and size of the data set:* In general, smaller data sets and those not taken from diverse respondents may be less indicative of the overall marketplace.

- *The representative scope of the data:* Are the data based on respondents or transactions that are representative of the marketplace or on only certain types of respondents and transactions?

- *The relevance of past market data to future conditions:* Has the market changed materially from the time periods reflected in the market data?

In general, less weight or emphasis is placed on methods using data that are considered to be relatively less comparable and applicable to the subject.

Assessing the Comparability of the Subject to the Market Data

A critical question in evaluating the outcome of market approach methods is the level and extent that the subject practice or physician can be compared to the market data. Do the operating characteristics, fundamental economics, and marketplace dynamics of respondents or of the parties to transactional data parallel those of the subject practice or physician and the proposed employment arrangement? How similar or dissimilar are they? Relatively less similarity between the subject and the data can reduce the relevance and applicability of a market-approach method.

Assessing the Measures or Criteria Used for Establishing Comparability

An appraiser should also weigh the relative importance or priority of the comparability factors, productivity measures, or other criteria used in applying the market data to the subject. Some factors, measures, or criteria may be more determinative than others of compensation in the marketplace for a given type of physician service or physician specialty. In general, such determinants should be given relatively more weight in the synthesis process.

Synthesizing Value Indications From Multiple Surveys

In evaluating indications from different surveys for the same basic measures or factors, several considerations can assist the appraiser in the synthesis process:

- The comparability of the subject to the survey in terms of key respondent profile factors and characteristics.

- The relevance of the data, given the year for which data are reported.

- The methodology used in gathering data for the survey.

- The number of respondents to the survey.

Where an appraiser has concerns about a given survey in terms of the above-noted criteria, the appraiser can consider assigning less weight to the value indications of a survey. The appraiser could also consider not using the survey in the synthesis process. When all of the above factors are relatively equal among surveys except for the number of respondents, many appraisers will weight the indications of value derived from different surveys using the same valuation technique and productivity measure based on the number of respondents. This formulaic approach is viewed as bringing some level of objectivity to the weighting process in that it reflects the relative quantity of data in each survey.

Synthesizing Outcomes From Multiple Methods Into a Single Value Indication

An appraiser may decide to prepare a single indication of value from the outcomes of various market-approach methods and techniques. When a variety of surveys, measures, and methods have been used in the market approach for physician employment compensation, it can helpful to organize the synthesis process in a logical and relational order. Grouping the various indications by commonalities, such as technique or productivity measure, can narrow the range of issues considered in each step of the synthesis process. Such a protocol can simplify the synthesis process and allow the appraiser to be more systematic in addressing key issues. The following represents a suggested sequencing and organization of the synthesis process for multiple market-approach indications of value:

1. Group indications from each survey based on the same valuation technique and productivity measure, e.g., the percentile matching technique based on wRVUs. Evaluate and synthesize the results into a single indication of value.

2. Group the synthesized indications from each technique using the same productivity measure, e.g., all techniques based on wRVUs. Evaluate and synthesize into a single indication of value.

3. Evaluate and synthesize the indications for each productivity measure as the final step in arriving at a value indication for the market approach.

As discussed previously, a single indication of value that is derived from a synthesis of the various value indications from market-approach methods applied to the subject is not required as part of the synthesis process. An appraiser may choose to synthesize the results of all methods used, regardless of the approach, in a single, but comprehensive synthesis.

1.4 Evaluating the Outcomes of Cost Approach Methods

In assessing the relevance and applicability of the cost approach valuation methods for the conclusion of value, there are several issues for the appraiser to consider:

- *How valid, reliable, and accurate are the historical data provided to the appraiser?* Where the historical data used in the historical practice net earnings (HPNE) or adjusted historical compensation (AHC) methods lack important detail or are limited, the value indications from these methods may be held as less relevant and applicable to the subject.

- *How many assumptions were made in application of cost approach methods?* Value indications based on significant levels of assumptions (as defined above) may be more speculative and less defendable than other methods where fewer assumptions are made.

- *Was sufficient data provided such that the historical compensation could be adjusted for scope of service differences between past practice and the proposed employment arrangement?* Difficulties in adjusting for the scope of service can render past compensation less relevant for a proposed scope of services.

- *Is the past scope of services comparable and applicable to the proposed scope of services?* Historical compensation services that lack comparability with future services may not be a valid indication of value for the proposed services.

- *How relevant and applicable are historical operating and market conditions to the future?* Significant changes in the future can make historical compensation less meaningful to a proposed service arrangement.

- *For the cost to recruit method, how extensive are the market data on newly hired physicians and how relevant are these data to employment in the specific marketplace of the subject?*

1.5 Evaluating the Outcomes of Income Approach Methods

Key questions to assess when reviewing value indications from income approach methods can include the following:

- *How valid, accurate, and reliable are the historical data that were used to establish the base year(s) from which the forecast of revenues and expenses was developed?* Limited and questionable historical data can undermine the credibility of the forecast.

- *To what extent can the assumptions and projections in the forecast be supported and defended by independent research and reliable data gathering?* A forecast based on weakly supported assumptions and estimates can reduce the importance of the income approach in the final synthesis of value.

- *How much uncertainty is there with respect to future changes in the operational and market dynamics of the subject practice, physician, or specialty?* A highly uncertain marketplace can limit the applicability of the income approach to the determination of FMV. In such circumstances, less weight may be placed on future expectations in comparison to historical outcomes.

- *How effectively and accurately is the forecast able to model the economics of the proposed scope of services under employment?* When the forecast is limited in its capacity to reflect the key economics and market dynamics of the proposed services, it may have less relevance in establishing the value of the services.

1.6 The Conclusion of Value

The valuation synthesis process ultimately results in a final conclusion of value for the subject arrangement. To summarize the various key points discussed earlier, this final opinion of value can be in the form of a single value indication or a range of value, depending on the professional judgment of the appraiser. There is no generally accepted formula for making the final determination of value in terms of how the appraiser utilizes the various value indications from those appraisal methods applied to the subject. The final determination is based on the professional judgment of the appraisal given the value indications and the overall facts and circumstances related to the subject arrangement. Above all, the appraiser should be able to articulate the reasons that support and defend the final opinion of value.

2.0 Issues in Applying Value Conclusions to Compensation Structures

Depending on how the various valuation methods were applied, it is frequently necessary to convert the conclusion of value into the compensation structure of the proposed employment arrangement. The following sections discuss the issues that can arise when converting conclusions of value into employment compensation structures and potential ways for resolving these issues.

2.1 Converting an Opinion of Value Into a Compensation Formula

Compensation plans for employment arrangements often involve productivity models or the combining of various types of compensation elements, such as base compensation amounts, productivity or incentive bonuses, sign-on bonuses, retention bonuses, or payments for quality outcomes. Compensation may also be segregated by type of service. For example, stipends for hospital call coverage may be paid separately per shift. Since many valuation methods yield indications of value for total compensation, it is frequently necessary to convert, translate, or allocate the concluded opinion of value into these compensation elements.

Matching Compensation to Services Provided

In general, the first step in the conversion or allocation process is to match compensation from the opinion of value to the services provided in terms of the proposed compensation structure. The appraiser takes each component of the compensation plan and determines what services are being paid for by the individual element. If compensation was separately calculated by type of service, then the allocation of the conclusion of value can be rather straight forward. One simply takes the buildup of compensation from the valuation analysis and assigns the value of each element to the corresponding service. Some compensation elements, however, may represent payment for the same services. For these cases, the appraiser will need to assign a portion of the FMV compensation for the service to each element.

In matching compensation for services, it is essential for the appraiser to think through what compensation amounts relate to what services. There is a tendency by some in the physician marketplace to treat certain forms of compensation as additive or incremental to the payment for a type of service when in fact these forms of compensation are simply a part of the payment for the same service. For example, sign-on or retention bonuses generally relate to clinic services or the primary type of service for which a physician is being employed. In most cases, these bonuses should be paid out of the total compensation for clinical services; they should not be paid as incremental compensation to total clinical services compensation. The reason for this treatment is that the bonuses relate back to physician services. In the case of sign-on bonuses, they generally represent an advance form of payment for services. Retention bonuses are payments that incentivize the physician to provide the services over a specified period of time; they relate to the duration of the services. Certain forms of compensation, moreover, can overlap and create potential duplications in payment. Thus, the appraiser must carefully analyze various compensation elements to ensure that any duplications are eliminated (see further discussion below in regards to compensation "stacking").

Part of the analysis involved in allocating the opinion of value also takes into account what services were included or not included in the valuation methods and techniques that are used in the appraisal. For example, was compensation for hospital call coverage or for interpretations of diagnostic imaging for a hospital outpatient facility included in the application of the cost and income approaches? If not, then the value indications from the cost and income approach methods would not relate to these services. On the other hand, if they were included, the values from these methods would represent total compensation for multiple types of services. The compensation attributable to each service would need to be calculated when the compensation plan entailed separate payments for these services.

The question of whether compensation for a given type of service is included in a particular valuation method is the most difficult to address when dealing with the use of physician compensation survey data under the market approach. As discussed in Part III, most of the surveys report total compensation from all sources. They do not generally report compensation by type of service. The appraiser, therefore, has to make a judgment as to whether there is a reasonable basis for assuming that compensation for a particular type of service is included in the reported data. This determination requires a solid understanding of the services, economics, and market trends of physician practices as they relate to key characteristics, such as specialty, practice-setting, and ownership. The appraiser must conjecture and estimate based on what is usual and customary in regards to the survey data used.

It may be sometimes necessary for the appraiser to prepare an individual valuation for a specific service that is paid for separately under a compensation plan. The individual valuation would be needed when the compensation indications from valuation methods reflected total compensation from all services. To determine the FMV compensation for the separate service, the appraiser would have to apportion the total compensation using the individual valuation.

Allocating Total Clinical Service Compensation to Individual Elements
Often, an opinion of FMV total compensation for clinical services will need to be allocated among various individual compensation elements included in the proposed employment arrangement. The key to the allocation process is to ensure that the total compensation from all elements is equal and consistent with the FMV total compensation amount. There may be specific issues, however, that the appraiser needs to address in preparing the allocation among the compensation elements:

Base or Guaranteed Compensation
Many compensation structures provide the physician with a minimum base or guaranteed amount. Generally, this amount should be used as the minimum payment amount to the physician in computing total compensation payable under the proposed arrangement. Base minimum or guaranteed compensation is usually applicable when a physician's compensation formula includes variable or productivity-based elements.

The minimum amount establishes what the physician will be paid regardless of the level of productivity or other variable inputs to the compensation formula. The key valuation issue for such guarantees is whether the appraiser thinks the minimum is consistent with FMV.

Sign-On Bonus

As discussed above, sign-on bonuses should generally be treated as part of total clinical compensation. The value of the sign-on bonus should be deducted from the FMV total compensation in the year paid. Many sign-on bonuses, however, include a payback provision if the contract is terminated prior to the term of agreement or some other specified period. In these cases, the amount of the sign-on bonus may be spread out or amortized over the payback period, consistent with the payback terms in the contract. For example, if a $30,000 bonus is subject to a three-year payback period, then $10,000 per year of the bonus could be included in the annual total compensation amount. The reason for this treatment is that the bonus is not effectively earned in total when paid; it is earned economically as each year of service is completed.

Retention Bonuses

Retention bonuses are the economic equivalent of a sign-on bonus with a payback provision with one deviation: They are paid out over time, rather than up front. The amount of a retention bonus for a given year should be included in the computation of total compensation for the year in question.

Productivity or Incentive Bonus

The total potential amount for a productivity or incentive bonus should be included in the calculation of total compensation for clinical services. For productivity bonuses, the potential should generally be calculated commensurate with the productivity levels used in the valuation analysis to establish the FMV total compensation amount for clinical services.

Conversion Into Productivity Models

The conversion of an FMV analysis into the structure of a productivity-based compensation model can be addressed in two ways. In the first method, the opinion of value for total FMV compensation for clinical services is converted into the compensation rate per unit of measure for productivity. This conversion is calculated by dividing the total FMV compensation amount by the productivity levels used to determine the total FMV compensation. Where different levels of productivity were used in various valuation methods, the appraiser should weight or apply the varying productivity levels consistent with the weighting or application of the value indications from the method used. For the second method, the appraiser computes the compensation rate per unit of productivity for each method and then synthesizes the rates to arrive at a conclusion of value.

2.2 Compensation Stacking

Compensation "stacking" occurs when physicians are hired to provide a variety of services and the proposed compensation for these services is computed based on the cumulatively additive value of each service. In other words, the individual compensation amounts are added up or "stacked" to determine the total compensation under employment.[1] The critical issue arising in such stacking of compensation elements is whether an overpayment for the services occurs when compensation amounts are added together. The overpayment may be the result of duplicative payments for the same service or of payments where the level or scope of service is below that assumed in establishing the compensation. The potential for duplication in compensation typically arises when the compensation for the services is computed individually and then added together for employed physicians. The individual valuations match compensation with the assumed scope of services and duties that are usual and customary for the specific service. Yet, when a physician is employed and required to provide a combination of services, the scope of services can be altered. The purpose of a so-called stacking analysis is to ensure that the potential for such duplication is eliminated. Three key cases can potentially create this kind of compensation duplication.

Employed Physician Providing Medical Director Services

A physician may be employed to provide a medical directorship along with patient care and clinical services. In such a case, the required hours for both clinical and administrative duties should be clarified and delineated consistent with the valuation analysis for each to avoid an overpayment for services. For example, assume the clinical compensation was established assuming a clinical workload of 40 hours per week and the medical directorship compensation was based on 10 hours per week. Further, assume the physician is paid a base salary or a base guaranteed amount. If the employment agreement only requires full-time work without specifying the number of hours or indicates scheduled hours of 40 per week, it is possible that the physician will not provide a level of service that is consistent with the assumed hours in the appraisals used to determine the FMV compensation on a combined basis. The compensation paid may not be consistent with FMV when the level of service provided is below that assumed in the appraisals.

---

1   Edward Richardson, CPA/ABV, aptly coined the term "stacking" to describe this market trend.

Employed Physician Providing Clinical Co-Management Duties

In a recent market development, hospital and health systems are hiring physicians to provide both clinical patient care services in a physician practice setting and hospital clinical co-management or service line management services for a hospital. This particular stacking of services has a significant potential for overcompensation when the employed physician is paid based on a base salary or a base guaranteed amount. If the scope of duties and workload for each type of service is not clarified or delineated, there is the potential for the physician to provide a lower level of work in one service area to the detriment of the other. As a result, the level of work assumed by the valuations for each service may not be met, and therefore, the compensation paid is not consistent with FMV. Since the compensation for these types of hospital management services can be significant, the potential for a material overpayment for services exists when combining these services.

Separate Compensation for Hospital Call Coverage

Perhaps the most ubiquitous case of compensation stacking arises when employed physicians are paid separately for hospital call coverage services. The critical issue in these cases is that the compensation for clinical and call coverage services may be duplicative under certain circumstances. The first instance stems from using the market approach only to establish the base salary or base guaranteed amount for the clinical compensation of an employed physician. The market compensation data may already include payments for hospital call coverage. Thus, when an employer looks to add compensation for call coverage to the clinical compensation, such compensation may be duplicative. To address this potential for double compensation, many appraisers will stipulate that a base salary or guarantee amount includes a normalized level of hospital call coverage. Thus, the physician should only be paid for hospital call coverage shifts worked over and above the normalized level.

A second instance arises when a physician is employed under a productivity or incentive model based on a compensation per wRVU rate. If this model extends to procedures performed while providing hospital call coverage, then the subject physician bears no unfunded care burden associated with providing such coverage. Since hospital call coverage is normally valued including this burden, payment of the typical call coverage stipend amount to such a physician would result in an overpayment for services. The amount paid to the physician for call coverage should be adjusted to eliminate any compensation for unfunded care.

Compensation on Independent Contractor Basis

Another critical issue that arises when stacking services is whether the value of the services was computed on an independent-contractor basis. Most medical directorships and hospital call coverage stipends are valued assuming the services are provided by independent-contractor physicians. As a result, most include an allowance or gross-up amount for employer-paid benefits. When employed physicians provide these services, the compensation should not include this allowance or gross-up amount because the employer already pays for and provides these benefits to the employed physicians.[2]

2.3 Sensitivity Testing of Compensation Plans Over Varying Productivity Levels

In dealing with productivity-based models or productivity bonuses, it may be advisable for the appraiser to complete a sensitivity analysis to evaluate the level of compensation produced by the particular model or bonus formula over a range of productivity levels. The purpose of the analysis is to assess whether the productivity rate or formula should be adjusted at varying levels of productivity. As discussed in Chapter 40, "An Analysis of MGMA's Compensation by Quartile of Production Data: Compensation Rates Decline as Production Increases," the MGMA compensation by quartile of production data indicate that compensation per wRVU or as a percentage of professional collections *declines* as productivity increases. In addition, physician practice can experience step costs as physician productivity ramps up. Because of these factors, an appraiser may want to evaluate the compensation levels at varying productivity levels under the compensation plan in comparison to the outcomes of the valuation methods used to establish the FMV compensation for the subject arrangement. In the sensitivity analysis, the appraiser models compensation under the contractual formula using a range of productivity and then compares the results over the same range of productivity using the valuation methods. The appraiser may recommend changes or adjustments to the FMV compensation amounts and rates based on the results of this analysis.

2.4 Qualitative Analysis and Judgments of Compensation Terms

Appraisers may consider performing qualitative analysis on certain contractual terms and requirements related to compensation and the provision of services in proposed employment arrangements. This analysis focuses on whether the terms are consistent with the definition of FMV, i.e., what arm's-length, independent, and well-informed parties would negotiate apart from referrals. As a corollary assessment, the appraiser may also review whether the terms and requirements of the contract are consistent with the scope of services and service requirements assumed in the valuation. These types of evaluations are not based on numerical models or mathematical techniques. Rather, they are performed on a qualitative analytical basis. The analysis may yield contractual terms or requirements that become opinion qualifications or limiting conditions on the opinion of FMV issued by the appraiser. In the informed judgment of the

---

2   Assuming the employer provides a market level of benefits.

appraiser, the terms and requirements are needed for the employment arrangement to be consistent with FMV.

Examples of such terms and requirements can include the following facts and circumstances.

Productivity Requirement to Maintain Base Compensation

When a physician receives a base salary or a guaranteed minimum amount of compensation, many appraisers require that a minimum level of productivity is maintained for the physician to continue receiving the base amount. Their thinking is that a certain level of productivity is required to support and justify the compensation level paid. Other appraisers think that a physician may be given a guaranteed or minimum amount in the first year or two of a new employment agreement, regardless of productivity outcomes. They base this thinking on the fact that many transition issues can arise in new employment arrangements that can depress the productivity of a physician, but these issues relate to the employer, not the employed physician. As a result, they think that a guarantee for an initial, but limited period is consistent with FMV. They may also require, however, other work measures, such as minimum annual hours and hospital call coverage shifts, as a means to ensure that sufficient work input is provided by the physician to justify the compensation paid.

Required Weekly Hours

An appraiser may require that a physician work a minimum number of weekly clinical or work hours as part of the FMV opinion. This requirement may be a function of the appraiser basing the FMV opinion on historical annual work hours or an assumption regarding normalized work hours for physicians in the marketplace. The requirement for work hours consistent with the hours used or assumed in the valuation analysis should not be overlooked by appraisers. If the FMV opinion was based on a certain level of service or work and the contract does not require the physician to provide this level, the compensation paid for services rendered may be inconsistent with the FMV opinion. The physician may not, in fact, provide the level of service or work assumed in the FMV analysis.

Required Weeks Worked Per Year

In a similar line of reasoning, an appraiser may require that a physician work a required number of weeks per year as part of maintaining the level of duties necessary to support a base salary or compensation amount. The number of weeks is often based on market survey data or on historical levels for the physician, depending on what methods were used in establishing the base amount.

Required Number of Hospital Call Coverage Shifts Per Month

Appraisers will sometimes require that a physician provide a specific minimum level of hospital call coverage or practice call coverage shifts per month as part of the requirements for the FMV compensation amount. Such a requirement would result from assumptions about call coverage made by the appraiser in determining FMV. For example, if a physician historically provided a certain number of shifts per year and the appraiser assumed such coverage in the cost and income approaches along with the accompanying fees from such coverage, the appraiser may require this coverage to continue as part of the FMV opinion. *Appraisers should ensure that scope of service requirements in a subject employment agreement are consistent with the assumptions made in the various valuation techniques used to establish FMV for the arrangement.*

3.0 Special Valuation Issues in Employment Arrangements

3.1 Evaluating the Impact of Benefits on FMV Compensation

Benefits packages can be an important element in the overall compensation package paid to an employed physician. Thus, the benefits afforded to a physician under an employment arrangement should at least be considered conceptually in evaluating the overall compensation level paid to a physician. Data on certain physician benefits are available through the various physician compensation surveys, allowing for a certain level of comparison with market norms. As discussed in the application of each of the approaches, a market level of benefits is assumed to be paid to physicians in employment arrangements. For the market approach, the reported compensation levels in the physician compensation surveys are assumed to be consistent with market norms. Market-level benefits are calculated into the computations of practice net earnings under the cost and income approach methods based on earnings-based compensation.

When a prospective employer provides more or less benefits than this market level, an adjustment to compensation may be needed. The appraiser should consider local market factors as part of determining whether an adjustment is necessary. Health insurance and other similar benefit costs can vary from market to market. (It should be noted that high and low reimbursement markets tend to correlate with high and low health insurance premiums. Higher premiums are what underwrite higher reimbursement.) The size of the employer entity and whether the entity is self-insured can also affect health insurance premiums. When looking at benefits, therefore, it can be more useful to assess the benefits offered rather than their costs in determining market-level benefits. In addition, payroll and other state-mandated employment taxes can also vary by city and state, causing relatively higher or lower costs in comparison to market data on benefits. Finally, for physicians who have historically received more or less than this market-based level of benefits, the benefits paid under employment may play a role in explaining differences in the compensation under the proposed arrangement in comparison to those received in the past.

3.2 Synthetic Employment or Foundation Model Arrangements

As discussed in Chapter 22, "Valuing Physician Employment Arrangements for Clinical Services: An Introduction," so-called synthetic employment or foundation model arrangements are contractual structures in which a physician group provides services on an independent-contractor basis to a hospital or health system physician practice. The physician group is typically responsible for the payment of benefits and professional liability insurance (PLI) for its member physicians and nonphysician providers. As a result, the compensation paid by the practice to the group generally includes an allowance for benefits and PLI. In these arrangements, the benefits are typically established using market data. For PLI, however, it is often difficult to establish a FMV amount for PLI because premiums can be physician-specific based on claims history. In addition, various states have had malpractice crisis or issues in the past that may have adversely affected premium rates. As a result, the actual premiums for the group are frequently used for the PLI allowance. The appraiser, however, may want to review coverage levels to ensure they are reasonable and consistent with market norms.

The compensation paid in synthetic employment deals can be based on productivity-based compensation structures, consistent with regular employment deals. The compensation structure, however, needs to be consistent with healthcare regulatory requirements. The process for determining the rates for the productivity compensation is also consistent with that used in regular employment arrangements, with one exception. The total compensation typically includes amounts for benefits and PLI. Additional sensitivity analysis work may be required to assess the intersection of various productivity levels and the compensation rates vis-à-vis the fixed amounts for benefits and PLI. The rates may need to decline at certain productivity levels, since benefits costs and PLI cost may have been covered at certain threshold levels. On the other hand, an appraiser may conclude that the compensation rate at any level of productivity may be warranted in arrangements where compensation is solely productivity-based. The same rate at higher levels incentivizes the physician to increase productivity over historical outcomes. In addition, the group can have downside risk for covering fixed benefit and PLI costs at lower productivity levels.

3.3 Proposed Changes to a Physician's Practice as Part of Employment

One critical issue that frequently arises in physician employment arrangements is how major changes in the scope of services or operations under employment should affect the determination of FMV compensation. Examples of changes can include those relating to location, service mix, inclusion in commercial contracts, referral patterns from other community physicians, and hospital call coverage at competing hospitals. While each particular change can involve unique considerations related to the facts and circumstances surrounding the change, the general concept followed by experienced appraisers in healthcare valuation is to determine whether the change results from factors related to the specific employer entity or whether they would be made by or would relate to the typical employer. Changes that are a function of the strategies and characteristics of a particular buyer-employer are usually not included in the determination of FMV. Appraisers consider such changes to be reflective of investment or strategic value related to a particular buyer-employer and not FMV. The definition of FMV in the appraisal body of knowledge entails assumptions related to the typical-buyer and seller. This general position, however, is not categorical. The facts and circumstances may warrant consideration of certain changes as being consistent with the definition of FMV.

3.4 Caps on Total Compensation

There is a market trend in which total compensation for a physician is capped at a certain level, often stated in terms of a percentile or a percentage of a percentile from a physician compensation survey. The concept behind these caps is to set an overall limit on the amount of compensation earned by the physician. It appears that regulatory considerations are the impetus behind this trend. Many attorneys and health systems believe that such caps help avoid the potential for regulatory scrutiny with excessive compensation. In addition, these caps may also have operational or business origins, where employers may simply want to limit total compensation. While risk management considerations for regulatory compliance are surely important, it should be noted that, strictly speaking, such total compensation caps do not have their basis in the appraisal body of knowledge. Compensation valuation theory holds that compensation should match the services provided. If a physician provides an array of services and a high volume of services, there is no appraisal reason or economic basis for limiting this compensation at a set total amount, as long as the compensation amounts or rates for each service are established appropriately.

Certainly, the determination of compensation for highly productive physicians should consider the use of stacking and sensitivity analyses to ensure that the compensation is reasonable and consistent with FMV. However, there is no proverbial "Rubicon" level of compensation that serves as a universal or categorical maximum for FMV in terms of standard appraisal methodology. Having made this point from the standpoint of the professional practice of appraisal, there may be sound reasons from a regulatory or compliance risk management standpoint for implementing such caps. Such considerations are important and essential for any healthcare provider in today's regulatory environment.

Chapter 26. Valuing Physician Executive and Administrative Compensation

CONTENTS

Chapter 26. Valuing Physician Executive and Administrative Compensation

By Carol Carden, CPA/ABV, ASA, CFE

1.0 Introduction

Given the movement in the industry toward greater collaboration between hospitals and physicians, hospital executive teams increasingly find themselves in the position of needing greater involvement from physicians in the day-to-day operations of their hospitals and service lines. As a result, physicians are more frequently being employed or engaged on a full- or part-time basis to serve in executive roles or positions that are primarily administrative in nature.

Some examples of these types of positions include:

- Chief medical officer;

- Vice president of medical affairs;

- Chief medical information officer;

- Clinical service line leadership;

- Serving on an executive or operational committee administering a clinical comanagement agreement;

- Director of a service line institute such as a heart and vascular institute;

- Serving as the clinical oncology leader for a hospital with a National Cancer Institute designation;

- Director of the institutional review board or other research-related administrative role; and

- Many others.

In determining the appropriate compensation associated with such positions, a number of factors warrant consideration:

- What are the key skill sets required for the position?

- Does the position require a physician to perform the duties? If so, does it require a physician of a particular specialty?

- What are the time requirements for the requested services?

- Does the position require certifications in addition to being board-certified in a particular specialty?

- How many physicians in the market meet the position requirements?

- Is the position a requirement of a special certification/designation the hospital holds, such as being a Center of Excellence?

- Is the position required by virtue of healthcare regulations, such as those requiring physician supervision of certain clinical services?

2.0 Duties and Structure

The duties required vary widely depending upon the position or need expressed by the hospital. Some possible examples of duties that may be required of a primarily executive/administrative position include:

- Development of clinical protocols;

- Evaluation of clinical staff;

- Input into technology needs of the service line/department;

- Outreach to other physicians regarding services available;

- Outreach to the community regarding services available;

- Analysis and recommendations regarding performance against quality-based indicators;

- Interaction with physicians regarding outcomes improvement (these duties should not include or be interpreted to be peer review services which are a separate hospital function);

- Review of denied claims for opportunities to assist with appeals;

- Assistance with physician credentialing issues;

- Assistance with physician behavioral issues;

- Assistance with positioning the hospital to meet specific clinical criteria for special certifications;

- Assistance remedying deficiencies noted during certification reviews such as those performed by The Joint Commission; and

- Participation in operational or clinical committees included as part of a clinical co-management agreement.

The form of compensation for executive or administrative positions is highly dependent on the hours required. For positions that require at least 20 hours per week (this is really an arbitrary breaking point for purposes of the discussion in this chapter), the compensation is commonly structured as a fixed base compensation with potential bonus (or, more recently, a portion at-risk) related to achieving the goals of the position. For these positions requiring at least a 20-hour-per-week commitment, there is generally not a tracking of hours required of the physician. Alternatively, the compensation could vary if the deliverables/goals of the position are not met, similar to other executive level positions

For positions where the level of commitment is less than 20 hours per week, it is more common to see compensation structured on an hourly basis with a requirement for the physician to submit timesheets documenting the services provided. Many attorneys are more comfortable with such arrangements when timesheets are required. However, it is not uncommon for the timesheet to be identical week-to-week, raising concerns about whether the services were actually provided. If a contract requires timesheets, it is a best practice for the appraiser to review the timesheets. This review will not only help the appraiser evaluate the hours associated with the position, but will also alert the appraiser to any discrepancies between the duties outlined in the contract and those indicated on the timesheet.

In the current environment of healthcare reform, hospitals are increasingly requesting physician assistance in improving their overall clinical quality. Historically, these efforts were met with the ability to earn compensation over and above that available from the provision of the service itself. However, consistent with movements in the industry (primarily in regards to how governmental payers are treating compensation related to improvement of clinical quality), current agreements are more likely to place a portion of the related compensation at risk related to the achievement of quality improvement, rather than making an additional pool of compensation available. Consequently, when specific outcomes goals are set related to administrative positions (whether they be related to clinical issues or administrative deliverables), the current trend is that a portion of the administrative compensation will be at risk pending evaluation of the physician's performance against such metrics.

Therefore, when determining compensation related to a physician executive or administrative position, it is important for the appraiser to have an understanding of whether there is an at-risk element to the proposed agreement. The existence of an at-risk component of compensation factors into the determination of fair market compensation. In this situation, the physician will be at risk of not earning all of the potential compensation and should reasonably have the opportunity to earn some amount of compensation higher than would otherwise be expected to compensate the physician for this additional risk (assuming the physician is able to meet the goals or metrics associated with the agreement).

The theory behind the higher rate to accommodate for an at-risk element is that the physician will not only have to provide the services, but will have to provide them well, in order to earn the higher rate. In providing the services well enough to meet the quality target (the targets should be established such that they are a "stretch" goal and should not typically be achieved 100%), the physician is setting themselves apart from the "typical" services that might be captured in the survey benchmark data. Additionally, depending on how much of the rate is at-risk, if the physician does not earn the entire at-risk portion, they are in jeopardy of committing hours that could be spent in their clinical practice and not earning what would otherwise be deemed fair market compensation related to those hours. To achieve the quality targets should require additional focus and exceptional skill on the part of the physician, thereby justifying a somewhat higher rate of pay.

3.0 Regulatory Considerations

There are no specific OIG advisory opinions related to physician executive or administrative compensation. However, there was guidance contained in the Stark regulations which stated:

> A fair market value hourly rate may be used to compensate physicians for both administrative and clinical work, provided that the rate paid for clinical work is fair market value for the clinical work performed and the rate paid for administrative work is fair market value for the administrative work performed. We note that the fair market value of administrative services may differ from the fair market value of clinical services.[1]

This guidance necessitates that appraisers perform a separate analysis related to physician administrative compensation that is distinct from an analysis for clinical services. That being said, it does not necessitate that the rate paid for administrative positions be different from the clinical rate, but that both rates of pay must be determined in a way that indicates that they are fair market value relative to the economics and characteristics of the services for which the physician is compensated.

Additionally, when determining fair market compensation related to physician administrative positions, it is important to bear in mind the anti-kickback statute (AKS). The AKS prohibits any payments in exchange for referrals. Historically, administrative payments to physicians were scrutinized to ensure the services being acquired were legitimate and not a disguised payment in exchange for referrals. Diligence on the part of the appraiser to ensure a thorough understanding of the duties of any executive or administrative position is well advised.

Finally, the agreement for services should state that the physician is prohibited from providing and billing for professional (i.e., clinical) services during the time when he or she is providing administrative services. This prohibition ensures there is no "double dip" whereby the physician is being paid twice for the same hour of time, an occurrence that would certainly elevate the regulatory risk of the agreement and likely create the perception of an AKS violation. Moreover, a situation in which a physician is providing clinical services while simultaneously being paid for providing administrative services does not meet the appraisal profession's definition of FMV. The hypothetical employer, or buyer of services, is not going to pay an employee who is not doing their job during normal business hours, but is instead running a side business. The employer receives no services in such a situation, and therefore, is not going to pay compensation to the employee.

---

1   *72 F.R.* 51016.

4.0 Valuation Methodology

In determining administrative compensation, the valuation approach most frequently relied upon is the market approach. In applying the market approach in this context, the appraiser will analyze various market indications of compensation levels paid for similar executive or administrative positions. The key issue in applying the market approach is the comparability of the subject arrangement to the market data for similar arrangements. Because there is not typically a revenue or net earnings stream that is directly associated with or attributable to these positions, the income approach is not generally applicable. One might be able to conceive an income approach theoretically that attempted to assess an organization's net earnings with and without a given organizational position. Such an approach, however, would not be practicable and would be subject to significant levels of assumptions.

There are two methods to considering the cost approach for this type of analysis. One way is to analyze market indications of costs for comparable positions; however, application of this method would be dependent upon the market approach. The second way the cost approach could be implemented in this type of situation is to evaluate the historical costs paid for the position (if it had been previously filled by another physician or professional) or, if the physician had served in a similar position for another organization, to consider the historical compensation associated with the similar position. However, for the historical compensation approach to be meaningful, the appraiser would need to undertake a thorough analysis of the responsibilities and market conditions that were present when the historical compensation was being paid. Given the limited application of the cost approach in this context, this chapter will deal with application of the market approach.

In applying the market approach in the determination of physician executive or administrative compensation, a number of industry benchmark sources are available. The more commonly utilized sources of administrative compensation benchmarks are included below, but this list is not intended to be exhaustive of all possible sources of physician administrative compensation.

- Cejka Executive Search and the American College of Physician Executives (ACPE): *Physician Executive Compensation Summary*

- American Medical Group Association (AMGA): *Medical Group Compensation and Financial Survey*

- Sullivan Cotter and Associates (SCA): *Physician Compensation and Productivity Survey*

- Hospital & Healthcare Compensation Service (HCS): *Physician Salary & Benefits Report*

- Medical Group Management Association (MGMA): *Medical Directorship and On-Call Compensation Survey* and *Management Compensation Survey*

- Integrated Healthcare Strategies (IHS): *Medical Director Survey*

Outside of the Cejka/ACPE survey, the other surveys listed provide data on a limited range of administrative positions. For example, the HCS and IHS surveys provide data primarily on hospital-related medical directorships. The MGMA medical directorship survey data represent a mixture of hospital and medical group directorship positions.

Physician recruiting and search firms are another possible source of administrative compensation benchmarks.

Additionally, administrative agreements may have duties that are clinical in nature. In this instance, it is appropriate to consider a clinical rate for the clinical duties blended with the administrative rate for the administrative duties (in accordance with the Stark guidance referenced earlier in this chapter). In addition to the surveys listed previously (some of which contain clinical compensation benchmarks in addition to the administrative information), clinical compensation benchmarks can be found in the following industry sources (again, this is not intended to be an exhaustive list):

- MGMA: *Physician Compensation and Production Survey*

- Towers Watson: *Healthcare Clinical and Professional Compensation Survey Report*

The appraiser's determination of which duties may be clinical in nature as opposed to administrative, may require the input of a professional with a clinical background such as a physician. Additionally, when evaluating the proportion of duties that are clinical in nature, it may be necessary to request time records for a representative period of time to ensure the administrative versus clinical time is properly weighted in your benchmark compensation analysis.

When determining compensation related to a physician executive/administrative position, it is important to use as many sources as can reasonably be expected to provide insight into the fair market value for the physician's services. It is critical when selecting administrative compensation benchmarks to bear in mind the expertise needed for the position rather than the expertise the physician currently has. For example, if determining compensation for a chief medical information officer, it is important to isolate similar physician executive positions that could provide a proxy for fair market compensation. If the physician who will fill the position happens to be a neurosurgeon, that fact does not necessitate use of benchmark data specific to neurosurgery administrative positions as the position does not require the expertise of a neurosurgeon.

Other factors that should be taken into account when evaluating compensation for administrative positions are the size of the organization and the scope of the administrative position. For example, a chief medical officer position for 500-bed hospital is a very different job than a chief medical officer for a 75-bed hospital. Similarly, for multihospital systems, it is important for the appraiser to understand whether the administrative position will have responsibilities across the system, across a region or specific to individual facilities only. Generally speaking, larger organizations or broader scope positions result in responsibilities which are more complex and more highly compensated, all other things being equal. Some of the survey benchmarks have data available specific to size of the organization, in terms of bed size or revenue base, to assist in determining that the appropriate benchmark data is utilized.

Finally, the appraiser should consider the cost of living for the geographic region where the services are being delivered. Unlike clinical services, where the impact of the cost of living may not be apparent due to the impact of the payer mix, administrative compensation is more heavily influenced by cost of living. The American Chamber of Commerce produces a quarterly report that reflects cost of living for various Metropolitan Statistical Areas (MSA) across the U.S. This information is available on line for a nominal fee at www.coli.org.

5.0 Stacking Issues

Stacking of responsibilities comes into play particularly when evaluating a part-time physician administrative position. A stacking analysis involves the process of accumulating all of the disparate components of compensation paid to a physician and ensuring that: 1) there is no overlap of duties and compensation, e.g., the physician is not paid twice for the same block of time or the same set of services, and 2) the totality of the compensation package is still fair market value and commercially reasonable, given the totality of services provided under the arrangement. Therefore, when evaluating a full-time administrative role (assuming there are no other separate agreements with the same physician), stacking is not generally a consideration.

Stacking can become a problem when a physician serves in multiple administrative roles for the same service line or services lines that are very closely related. Stacking can also become a consideration for the hospital when they have multiple facilities in a narrow geographic area and replicate the same administrative position at each location. The relevant stacking issue when this occurs revolves around whether it is commercially reasonable for the hospital to replicate the service at each location.[2] There may be valid reasons for doing so, but if the appraiser is opining on the commercial reasonableness of such an arrangement, documenting the business rational for the duplication becomes a necessary step in the process. Additionally, the appraiser should make inquiries of the hospital to ensure the physician is not being paid compensation for duties required of him or her by virtue of being a member of the medical staff of the facility.

If a stacking analysis becomes necessary, it is important for an appraiser to ensure that the compensation components being stacked are matched as closely as possible to the types of compensation included in the benchmark data to which the stack is being compared. For example, when stacking a medical directorship with clinical compensation (such as when a physician is employed in clinical practice and also serves as a medical director, a very common occurrence), the relevant industry information analyzed in the valuation should include both clinical and administrative compensation.

This situation takes the appraiser into a bit of a gray area. The definition of compensation in the various clinical compensation industry surveys indicate that the direct compensation *may* include compensation related to medical directorships. Unfortunately, the definition applies to the entire survey, not to a specific specialty. Therefore, there is no way to know if the clinical compensation benchmark already incorporates medical director compensation. The appraiser can reasonably draw a couple of conclusions: 1) it is highly unlikely that *all* survey respondents in any given specialty have medical directorships; and, 2) when the survey demographics are comprised of larger-sized physician practices, it is unlikely that all physicians in the group have medical directorships, much less that every group that responded had medical directorships. Therefore, the representation of medical directorship compensation in the survey data is questionable at best. It is a judgment call on the part of the appraiser whether the medical director compensation should be included with clinical compensation to evaluate whether the stacked agreement is still within fair market value and is commercially reasonable.

When evaluating the physician's administrative responsibilities, it is also important to evaluate the time required of the physician to perform the administrative duties relative to his or her other clinical or administrative responsibilities. This evaluation is particularly relevant within the context of commercial reasonableness. For example,

---

2   See Chapter 10, "Commercial Reasonableness: Defining the Concept and Determining Compliance," for a more detailed discussion of this issue.

is it reasonable for a physician who produces clinically at the 90th percentile to also be able and available to serve in an administrative capacity for 15 to 20 hours per week? The answer is not likely. Therefore, the appraiser should question the reasonableness of the hospital engaging this particular physician for additional responsibilities. In the context of stacking, the highly productive clinician is likely to have high compensation before consideration of the additional administrative duties. The totality of the compensation package may therefore rise to the level of being outside the bounds of fair market value and commercially reasonable compensation when additional administrative compensation is layered on, depending, of course, on the facts and circumstances of the specific arrangement.

6.0 Conclusion

A number of resources are available to assist the appraiser in determining fair market value compensation for both full time and part time physician administrative positions. The most important criteria for evaluation by the appraiser, include:

- What skills are necessary to perform the duties?

- Do the duties overlap with any other responsibilities of the physician?

- Do the duties overlap with any other agreements the hospital has in place with other physicians?

- Are the time requirements of the position reasonable relative to the other clinical/administrative responsibilities of the physician?

W. Lyle Oelrich Jr., MHA, FACHE, CMPE, contributed to this chapter.

Chapter 27. Valuing Hospital Call Coverage Arrangements: An Introduction

CONTENTS

Chapter 27. Valuing Hospital Call Coverage Arrangements: An Introduction

By Gregory D. Anderson, CPA/ABV, CVA

1.0 Introduction

Emergencies happen, and not just between 8:00 a.m. and 5:00 p.m. A hospital emergency department (ED) cannot operate without highly skilled emergency physicians, trained to quickly assess a variety of often life-threatening traumas and acute illnesses and take immediate action to resuscitate and stabilize patients. Yet, continued care of patients after stabilization often requires physicians with training in specialized care. In many cases, it is not practical for hospitals to retain specialists in every necessary specialty on a 24/7 basis. Therefore, hospitals have specialists to provide on-call coverage.

Medicare, the primary payer of many hospitals, does not set requirements on the frequency of on-call coverage by a hospital's medical staff. However, the Emergency Medical Treatment and Active Labor Act of 1986 (EMTALA), as more fully described later in this chapter, requires hospitals to provide certain medical care to persons requesting emergency care, including medical screening, stabilization, and appropriate transport if the hospital is not capable of treating the emergency condition. EMTALA places an additional compliance burden on hospitals to ensure specialist physician coverage in the emergency department. State laws often also require hospitals to maintain a comprehensive list of specialists available to respond to ED call within 30 minutes or less to qualify for state trauma designation.

In years past, the medical staff by-laws of a hospital dictated that active medical staff "take ED call" as a requirement of their medical staff privileges; however, a trend toward physicians demanding payment for call has become more prevalent in recent years.

Emergency department on-call service differs from physicians providing call to patients of their clinics. In medical practices in which physicians provide ongoing care to their own patients, a physician may be on call for purposes of his or her own patients or for patients of other physicians in the same practice or specialty. Such "practice" call can include coverage for the following situations in which patients require attention from their physician:

- Asking questions of the physician at times after clinic operating hours;

- Requesting a prescription or refill for medication;

- Seeking instructions or follow-up information related to their care that cannot wait until a clinic appointment; or

- Receiving care from their physician in an outpatient or inpatient setting.

Examples of these include an obstetrician in private practice who receives a call during the night to deliver the baby of a patient in labor at a local hospital's labor and delivery unit and a gastroenterologist on call for a clinic responding to a call by one of the group's patients suffering from gastrointestinal bleeding after an inpatient endoscopic procedure earlier that day. However, valuation and practice operations consultants are sometimes asked to establish guidelines for groups wishing to reduce the compensation of, or "tax," physicians who withdraw from or refuse to take practice call. In our example of the obstetrician, a physician in an OB/GYN practice may opt out of obstetric practice and OB clinic call as she nears retirement. These examples of clinic call are important, but differ from ED call, and are not the main focus of this chapter.

1.1 Description of Services Provided

On-call service generally refers to the doctor's availability, which is usually made available regardless of a patient's ability to pay for the service provided by the physician. Sometimes this may only mean responding to telephone calls to provide consultations to the emergency or attending physician; however, calls often result in the physician's in-person response. If care is provided to the patient, the physician also agrees to furnish follow-up care to that patient, again without regard to the patient's ability to pay. This often includes inpatient follow-up care, as well as follow-up visits after the inpatient stay as part of the episode of care. Depending on the nature of the arrangement, the service may require the doctor's physical presence at the facility. Examples of this include anesthesiologists, who are often required to remain on-site in the hospital and cannot take call off-site as others may be permitted to do.

Hospital medical staff by-laws set forth specific requirements for on-call physicians, such as the time when a physician must respond to calls. Some contractual arrangements dictate not only the period of availability required of the physician, but also specify the physician time commitment for clinical services. Examples of this include arrangements similar to locum tenens staffing firm arrangements, in which the physician agrees to a period of coverage, such as 24 hours, of which a maximum number of patient care hours is established (e.g., four hours of direct patient care). Any patient care beyond the maximum contracted amount is charged under the contract at an hourly rate. The billing arrangement may dictate the type of coverage arrangement; on the other hand, the type of coverage arrangement may dictate the billing arrangement. For example, if an on-call arrangement permits the physician to bill his or her professional fees, the on-call payment arrangement is by necessity generally considered a payment for availability and uncompensated care. On the other hand, if a hospital pays a physician a rate that includes compensation for clinical services as well as availability, the hospital will consequently bill for the physician's professional fees and the physician will be unable to bill for the same professional fees.

1.2 Explanation of the Factors Driving the Need for the Service in the Marketplace

Senior physicians in today's market and their predecessors once recognized the importance of emergency department on-call coverage as a community service and as a means for building their practices. Indigent patients, tort system disrepair, declining reimbursement, and payment reforms were not the daily reality for these physicians that they now are. Hospital medical staff by-laws required on-call coverage; thus, physicians once accepted this requirement in the course of practicing medicine, and compensation for taking call was not the hotly contested issue that it is in many facilities today.

The growing trend toward payment for physician on-call services is a function of market factors affecting the need for the service and physician unwillingness to provide the service without separate compensation. These market forces impact physician reimbursement, quality of life, and liability exposure, while hospitals, health systems, and other medical facilities experience increased regulatory requirements and community demands for physician availability in the emergency department.

Uncompensated Care

The uninsured population in the United States has grown in recent years at alarming rates. Between 2007 and 2010, the non-elderly uninsured rose from 43.4 million to 49.1 million.[1] With the growth in the uninsured population, physicians providing emergency

---

1   S. Streeter, et al., "The Uninsured, A Primer." The Kaiser Commission on Medicaid and the Uninsured, ,Oct. 2011, p. 9.

and trauma coverage increasingly provide care to patients who are unable to pay their professional fees. With full expansion of the Medicaid program through the enacted provisions of the Affordable Care Act prior to the Supreme Court decision of June 28, 2012, it was anticipated that 15.9 million fewer Americans would have been uninsured by 2019 due to Medicaid enrollment. However, these estimates have not yet been updated for states that may opt out of the Medicaid expansion. Nevertheless, it is anticipated that the Medicaid expansion will add millions of previously uninsured Americans to the rolls of the Medicaid program, thus lessening to some extent the uncompensated care burden. Millions more will be covered through health insurance exchanges and employer-sponsored plans adopted under the provisions of the ACA.

Tort Climate

Physicians are reluctant to furnish on-call services in an emergency setting because of the risk of malpractice claims. According to the American College of Surgeons, "a significant number of surgeons have been sued by patients first seen in the ED."[2] This stems from a condition of substantial disrepair that remains in many states throughout the United States. According to a professional liability insurance survey by the American Hospital Association, nearly half of all hospitals reported that the professional liability crisis of the last decade resulted in the loss of physicians or reduced ED coverage.[3]

Fewer emergency departments and increasing utilization

A recent study reported in the *Journal of the American Medical Association* found that out of 2,446 hospitals with EDs in non-rural areas in 1990, 1,041 EDs closed by 2009, 66% of which were due to the closure of the entire hospital.[4] While ED closures have been occurring, ED visits have been on the rise. Furthermore, nationwide hospital closures and closures of emergency rooms have placed additional stresses on those that remain, while increasing problems with limited access to care for many Americans result in overutilization of the nation's emergency services. All of these factors place additional stress on the system and on physicians working in hospital EDs, increase the intensity of on-call services, and have negative impacts on payer mix and, consequently, reimbursement for physicians' services.

Quality-of-life for physicians

Physicians see ED call as a detriment to their quality of life, because most ED calls occur on nights and weekends. Call duties also often interfere with the physician's private

---

2 "A Growing Crisis in Patient Access to Emergency Surgical Care." Division of Advocacy and Health Policy, American College of Surgeons, 2006, p. 1.

3 "Medical Liability Reform NOW! 2012 Edition" American Medical Association, 2012, p. 9.

4 R. Hsia, A. Kellermann, and, Y. Shen, "Factors Associated With Closures of Emergency Departments in the United States," *The Journal of the American Medical Association.* Vol. 305, No. 19. May 18, 2011.

practice, thus impacting income or clinic/surgical schedules, requiring more time away from personal or more profitable activities and resulting in greater inconvenience. Thus, a material element of physicians' demand for ED call compensation is related to their availability, which is identified with the lifestyle burden that is a significant cause of physician dissatisfaction with ED call.

Physician shortages

Physician shortages can result from a variety of factors, including an aging population, a lack of new specialists expected to enter the practice of medicine after completing educational requirements, desirability of location, and general economic factors affecting the ability of many communities to recruit and retain quality physicians. Moreover, other factors can result in a decrease in the number of physicians in the call rotation, amplifying the difficulty and stress of those physicians who remain:

- Increasing subspecialization of physicians has caused many physicians to limit the patients treated while on-call;

- Increasing numbers of physicians dropping out of call rotation because of age, lack of compensation, a desire for equity among physicians, and rigorous schedules have exacerbated an already growing problem.

Observing this market dynamic in a community can be sobering for a hospital administrator. What begins as a request for on-call compensation by a single physician quickly escalates into broad and costly demands by many specialties, further spreading to other facilities in the market. Threats by physicians to relinquish medical staff privileges and drop out of the call rotation unless the hospital concedes to requests for higher payments are coupled with hospital concerns about regulatory compliance and fiscal responsibility. These serve to create an environment of distrust and emotionally charged tensions.

1.3 Analysis of the Fundamental Economics of the Service

As noted above, most ED on-call arrangements are between hospitals and specialist physicians. For 82% of physicians receiving additional compensation for on-call services, according to the Medical Group Management Association (MGMA), the physician in the contract retains the fees for professional services generated when on call.[5] In these situations, the hospital does not bill and collect the professional fee, but receives reimbursement for hospital services. In some ED on-call arrangements, the hospital or a

---

5   *MGMA Medical Directorship and On-Call Compensation Survey, 2012 Report Based on 2011 Data.* Medical Group Management Association, p. 96.

hospital-affiliated practice entity employs the physician taking call. These arrangements are often "stacked" atop the physician employment arrangement, as will be more fully discussed below. In these situations, the hospital bills and collects for the physician's professional services. Yet, even in these situations, the economics to the physician may vary depending on the compensation structure of his or her employment arrangement. In an example discussed below, whether an uninsured or underinsured patient pays for the ED visit or subsequent care may financially impact a hospital-employed physician whose compensation is based on a percentage of collections or net accrual basis revenue.

When the independent physician is responsible for billing and collecting professional fees, the ability of patients to pay for the physician's services economically affects the physician. For example, a patient without insurance first seen in the ED may not have the wherewithal to pay for the hospital or physician services, yet EMTALA or the hospital's charity care policies may require treatment of the patient. Because of the obligation to treat the patient, the physician may receive little or no payment for the services furnished to that patient, not only in the ED, but also for follow-up care in the hospital and in the physician's clinic. This uncompensated care burden is one of the factors that motivate physicians to approach hospitals for compensation for taking call.

In other arrangements, such as those in which the hospital contracting for ED call coverage employs the physician, the compensation arrangement between the hospital and physician is a determinant in the economic impact. For example, the payer mix of the ED or the patient's ability to pay for the ED visit or follow-up care financially impacts physicians on a fixed salary that are contracted for ED call coverage. Additionally, uncompensated care does not affect physicians paid on an incentive arrangement not driven by collected revenues, such as work RVU-based incentive, a per-encounter incentive, or a percentage of charges. On the other hand, patient collections and payer mix issues indeed affect physicians paid on collected revenue, accrual basis net revenue incentives, or practice net earnings; therefore, the financial ramifications of ED call coverage to the physician are important in the analysis of call coverage arrangements. Arrangements in which employed physicians are at risk for uncompensated care often include separate payments from the hospital-employer to the physician-employee in the form of compensation to account for the financial effect of uncompensated care on the compensation of the physician in the employment compensation arrangement. In employment arrangements in which the employed physician is not impacted as a result of uncompensated care, hospital arrangements under normal circumstances should not pay additional compensation for uncompensated care.

An additional financial impact is the compensation associated with the burden of physician availability. Once felt an obligation of active medical staff, many physicians now see on-call coverage as an excessive burden, creating inconvenience on the physician, the physician's family, and the physician's practice and other income-producing activities. For this reason, most doctors taking ED call demand payment for their availability to the hospital. The amount of payment should depend on the degree of the burden, as will be more fully described in later.

More complex arrangements with group coverage also often involve uncompensated care and availability. These arrangements are often comprised of payments by the covered hospital to the physician group to sustain the group for the broader coverage furnished by the group, including physicians and nonphysician providers. Many of these arrangements require the providers to be on-site at the facility during certain hours of the week. These broad coverage arrangements may include coverage by practices such as anesthesia groups, emergency physician groups, hospitalist groups, and specialist practices. These arrangements are often comprised of other duties as well, including administrative responsibilities, and may include clinical services of the providers.

2.0 Contractual Terms and Duties

To comply with the terms of the personal service arrangements exception[6] under the Stark law and the provisions of the anti-kickback statute safe harbor for personal services and management contracts,[7] it is advisable that ED call coverage arrangements be set out in writing and signed by the parties. Applicable Stark exceptions and anti-kickback safe harbors also prescribe other terms of the arrangements, such as the requirement under the Stark exception applicable to personal service arrangements that the term of the arrangement be at least one year. These and other requirements must be carefully adhered to for arrangements to be found compliant with the terms of the applicable Stark law exceptions and anti-kickback safe harbors.

2.1 Typical Terms and Duties Found in ED Call Coverage Agreements

Among the terms found in ED call coverage agreements are those that set forth the duties and responsibilities of both physicians providing ED on-call coverage and the facilities contracting for the physician coverage. Duties of the physician often include the on-call coverage itself, restrictions on physician availability, response time in minutes, compliance with medical staff by-laws, and rules for documentation of the services provided. Hospital responsibilities often include the furnishing of facilities and equipment, personnel and support services, and supplies. The agreements also spell

---

6   42 CFR §411.357(d).
7   42 CFR §1001.952(d).

out other important obligations of the parties, including the qualifications required for physicians that participate in the call rotation, rules of professional conduct by the physicians, responsibility for billing and collection of professional and facility fees, ownership of patient records, nonsolicitation of hospital personnel, minimum coverage requirements for professional liability insurance, CME responsibility, compensation provisions, and responsibility for taxes. Of course, the contract also spells out the term and termination of the agreement itself. Below are some of the more common methods found in structuring coverage and compensation arrangements in ED on-call agreements.

2.2 Common Structuring of Coverage and Compensation Arrangements

Of great importance in the design of ED on-call arrangements is the structure of the coverage arrangement, since several variations on the concept of ED coverage exist. For example, the basic on-call arrangement provides for physician coverage of the ED by requiring the physician to respond to paging within a specified period while on call, and the physician bears the burden of being available to respond as needed, while suffering the economic implications of uninsured or underinsured patients that may be presented to the ED while the physician is on call. However, other variants also exist, which require the agreement between hospital and physician to clearly specify the duties and responsibilities of both parties. Likewise, compensation arrangements vary with the myriad of on-call structures. The value of the payment also varies, depending on the financial impact to the physician of burdens such as restrictions on availability and the degree of uncompensated care.

Restricted and unrestricted arrangements

As with many physician contractual arrangements, the type of on-call or physician coverage arrangement may vary dramatically from one contract to the next. In some cases, the physician specialty may drive the type of arrangement. For example, anesthesiologists in a hospital setting are often required to remain in the OR during specified weekday and weekend shifts. This allows for anesthesia coverage for scheduled and unscheduled surgical cases throughout the shift. In other cases, the needs of the facility may dictate the requirements for physician coverage. Consider the example of the cardiovascular surgeon, required by the hospital to remain on-site in a hospital's cardiac catheterization lab during normal operating hours to provide backup services to the cardiologists and their patients in the facility.

Unrestricted Call

In an unrestricted call arrangement, the physician is not restricted physically to the facility, but is obligated to respond timely in accordance with medical staff by-laws, state trauma rules, or other contractual arrangements. This is essentially known as "beeper" call, with the physician carrying a pager or cell phone to ensure timely contact. Most arrangements require the physician to respond within 30 minutes. This arrangement is fairly common among a wide range of specialists who provide coverage to a hospital's emergency department and can include primary (first responder) call and secondary (backup) call.

Restricted call

In a restricted coverage arrangement, the physician is physically restricted to the facility during the restricted coverage period. This can apply to many different specialties, although hospital-based specialists are among the most commonly utilized in these agreements.

Blended arrangements

When circumstances dictate, facilities may contract with physicians for an arrangement that includes more than one type of on-call coverage or service. These may take on the form of arrangements that include both unrestricted and restricted coverage during a specified period or a blending of on-call and other personal services, such as clinical or administrative services.

Blended unrestricted call and restricted coverage

In some situations, the physician will have periods of both unrestricted and restricted call during the same shift. An example of this would include coverage in which a physician is required to be on-site for a 12-hour shift, immediately followed by a 12-hour shift of unrestricted call.

Blended call with clinical service

In certain circumstances, the physician will have periods of unrestricted and/or restricted call, combined with clinical duties and responsibilities. In this arrangement, the physician is also contracted to provide patient care, wherein the employer or contracting entity bills for the physician's professional fees. Locum tenens firms often offer these arrangements to hospitals, mixing unrestricted call with two to eight hours of patient care within a 24-hour shift. Another example would be a primary care physician who is contracted to work in a weekend community clinic for six hours on Saturday afternoons and remain on unrestricted call for the duration of the weekend.

Blended call with administrative service

In an administrative service arrangement, the physician furnishes administrative or management services, such as a medical directorship, which is often combined with restricted/unrestricted arrangements, such as those found in an outsourcing of a hospital-based physician service. An example of this would be the outsourcing to a physician-owned emergency medicine group practice for ED physician and midlevel provider coverage, including medical direction of the ED, restricted coverage (wherein the physician group bills for its professional fees), and unrestricted call.

2.3 Typical compensation structures and terms

The structure of the physician coverage arrangement and the professional fee billing arrangements affects the payment mechanism for ED on-call coverage. For example, when the hospital bills and collects for the physician professional fee, the concept of payment for uncompensated care is not applicable to the physician payment arrangement. In another example, consider the difference in rates for a physician's administrative service as opposed to paying a physician only for being available to respond to calls when there is no uncompensated care burden. These types of design features must be considered when structuring payment arrangements for ED call pay.

Payments for physician on-call coverage consist of rates for unrestricted and restricted coverage, clinical services, administrative duties, and blended rates (such as per diem rates that include an assumed clinical time). Payment arrangements are most often based on hourly, shift, daily, monthly, or annual rates, although variations can be found. Among the more creative arrangements include the following:

- Hospital A only pays for shortage specialty ED coverage, such as when the physician is required to cover a call rotation vacated by a departing or retiring physician;

- Hospital B only pays physicians who are excused from ED call coverage duties by virtue of the medical staff by-laws, such as those who are exempt from call based on age; and

- Hospital C only pays for excessive call, basing the payment on the number of days in excess of a threshold number, such as 10 per month.

Hourly, daily, weekly, monthly, annual, or shift rates

Approximately half of all compensation arrangements involving call coverage contracts include time- or shift-based payments. Although rates may not be purely hourly rates, shift or per diem rates are often based on hourly values applied to the length of the shift or period covered. According to the MGMA 2012 report, the most common method among both hospital/IDS-owned practices and physician-owned practices for on-call compensation, other than no compensation at all (reported by 39.31% of respondents), is daily stipend rates, reported by 29.17% of respondents. Annual, shift, and hourly stipend rates follow next, at 10.04%, 7.51%, and 6.11%, respectively, with weekly and monthly rates reported least frequently.[8]

Activation Fee

An activity-based payment, or activation fee, usually a flat fee, is initiated when the physician is actually called in while on call. This is often combined with unrestricted call payments. An example of this can be found in a psychiatry weekend coverage arrangement, in which the physician was paid a fixed rate for weekend unrestricted coverage and an additional $200 if the physician was called in during the weekend.

Fee-for-Service

Fee-for-service (FFS) arrangements are similar to activation fee arrangements in that a physician is paid for a specific clinical service, except that in the FFS arrangement, the physician is paid a fee—set in advance—that varies depending upon the type of service, much the same as FFS payments a provider would receive from government and third-party payers. Often, physicians must submit a "claim" or similar request for payment to the facility to receive payment for the service, in a manner similar to a payer claim. Aside from hospitals that utilize this method, some state-sponsored trauma networks employ this approach to pay physicians for uncompensated trauma care. The key to the success of this method, and a very important compliance requirement, is that physicians receive no other payment for the same service.

Subsidy and collection guarantee arrangements

Fixed monthly or annual stipends may be necessary to bring physician or group compensation amounts in line with the market for services furnished, especially with respect to low- or no-pay care (often effective with groups dramatically impacted by the hospital's payer mix). Particularly when the physician bills for the professional fee, this is usually in an amount needed to ensure that net physician compensation is representative of the market and often based on market reimbursement levels. Another example is the malpractice insurance premium subsidy, which serves as a means for providing limited relief toward premium costs incurred by medical staff. Additional examples include payments based on relative value units (RVUs) for uncompensated services and subsidized fee-for-service arrangements in which the physician assigns his benefit under Medicare, Medicaid, or third-party payer to the hospital and the hospital bills and collects the professional fee and remits a market-value fee-for-service payment or payment per RVU to the physician.

---

8   Id., p. 81.

Deferred Compensation

Another trend in on-call compensation involves the deferral of pay until the occurrence of a specified event or certain period, such as milestone tenure on the medical staff or for participation in the on-call rotation. This method has proven effective in some circumstances in promoting physician longevity.

2.4 Other Relevant Terms in Typical Service Agreements

Restrictions on ED physician on-call coverage as addressed in the terms of the service agreement are important to the value of the payment. As will be more fully discussed in the valuation methodology section of this chapter, restrictions have implications on the value of the on-call coverage furnished by the provider.

3.0 Regulatory Compliance Issues and Considerations

The proliferation of health care regulations affecting physician compensation arrangements and the variety of physician on-call arrangements in the market lead to a significant and looming compliance risk for parties to on-call and coverage agreements, particularly when remuneration is exchanged. This necessitates consideration of whether the arrangements are within FMV constraints and the applicable statutory and regulatory exceptions and safe harbors. Of particular importance are Stark law, the federal anti-kickback statute, and, for tax-exempt organizations, IRS reasonable compensation requirements. Compliance with state-level self-referral and kickback legislation are also of vital importance. These broad healthcare regulations are addressed in detail elsewhere in this book.

3.1 Specific Regulatory Pronouncements

Aside from the broader regulatory prohibitions under the Stark law and the federal anti-kickback statute, other laws and anti-fraud pronouncements have implications for physician on-call arrangements. These include advisory opinions from the Office of Inspector General of the Department of Health and Human Services specific to on-call arrangements and the EMTALA.

OIG Advisory Opinion 07-10

On Sept. 20, 2007, the Office of Inspector General (OIG) of the Department of Health and Human Services issued Advisory Opinion 07-10[9] in response to a request for an opinion as to whether a physician on-call and uncompensated care arrangement constituted grounds for imposition of sanctions related to acts in violation of the federal anti-kickback statute. This advisory opinion provides useful insight into the mindset

---

9   www.oig.hhs.gov/fraud/docs/advisoryopinions/2007/AdvOpn07-10A.pdf.

of the OIG as it relates to the risk that payments for physician on-call coverage could result in illegal remuneration and safeguards that the OIG believes reduce the risk that remuneration is intended to generate referrals of items or services reimbursable by federal health care programs.

In the text of the advisory opinion, the OIG commented on the increasing compensation of physicians for hospital emergency department on-call coverage and the existence of legitimate reasons for such arrangements, including compliance with EMTALA, physician shortages, and access to trauma care. The OIG noted the risk that: 1) physicians may demand payment for on-call coverage when neither the services provided nor market conditions warrant payment; or 2) hospitals may misuse payments to entice physicians to generate additional business for the hospital. The OIG further commented that covert kickbacks might take the form of payments in excess of FMV or payments for services not actually provided. Problematic compensation structures noted in the advisory opinion include payments that do not represent bona fide lost income, payments when no identifiable services are provided, aggregate payments that exceed the practice's regular medical practice income, and payments for physician services when the physician actually receives separate reimbursement from insurers or patients (essentially double-paying the physician).

The OIG noted that the requestor engaged an independent consultant to advise it on the reasonableness of the per diem rates paid under the arrangement, the report on which was provided to the OIG. The consultant's analysis incorporated both public and private data on pay rates at dozens of medical facilities, resulting in a set of benchmarks used by the consultant to opine on the FMV of the payment arrangements. The advisory opinion also noted other features that the OIG considered useful in minimizing the risk of fraud and abuse.

In the advisory opinion, the OIG concluded that it would not subject the requestor to administrative sanctions under the Social Security Act, although it noted that the opinion should not be construed as a requirement for a medical center or other facility to pay for on-call coverage.

OIG Advisory Opinion 09-05
In Advisory Opinion 09-05, issued by the OIG on May 14, 2009, and posted May 21, 2009,[10] the OIG addressed a hospital's proposed arrangement with physicians for call coverage services. Advisory Opinion 09-05 stated that the OIG would not impose administrative sanctions regarding the analyzed arrangement, wherein physicians were to receive a

---

10 www.oig.hhs.gov/fraud/docs/advisoryopinions/2009/AdvOpn09-05.pdf.

flat fee for services provided to patients who were indigent, uninsured, and not eligible for state insurance programs.

The OIG acknowledged hospitals' difficulty obtaining appropriate call coverage as a result of limited physician availability due to burden of call and a large number of indigent patients. The hospital reported to the OIG that it experienced three weeks each month without coverage by the specialty group, resulting in outsourced emergency care pursuant to transfer agreements and protocols with other hospitals. The hospital noted that, while its physicians historically took call "out of a sense of duty to their profession, that sentiment is no longer shared by all; rather the physicians commonly view on-call coverage as an unwanted obligation, jeopardizing the hospital's ability to serve patients."

To be eligible to receive payment under the proposed arrangement, a physician had to be an active member of the hospital's medical staff, sign an agreement with the hospital to participate in the on-call policies of the hospital, follow the hospital's claims request process for payment, and participate in the organized on-call schedule. To receive payment, participating physicians were required to submit a claim request form to the hospital and waive all billing and collection rights against any third-party payer or the patient for services rendered. Compensation would be made in accordance with a fixed fee schedule, with rates for emergency consultations, admissions, surgical procedures performed on patients admitted from the ED, and endoscopy procedures performed on patients admitted from the ED. The hospital certified all such fixed fees to be within a range of fair market value.

The OIG acknowledged that, in many cases, valid reasons exist for call coverage arrangements, including: compliance with EMTALA, which places responsibility on hospitals offering emergency services and applies regardless of the patient's ability to pay; the lack of certain physician specialists within a hospital's service area; and access to sufficient and nearby trauma services for local individuals.

The OIG noted that the analyzed arrangement presents a low risk of fraud and abuse based on components of the arrangement that appear to support the certification that the payment amounts are within the range of fair market value for services rendered, without regard to referrals or other business generated between the parties. Such components include the following:

- Payments only for professional services provided;

- No "lost opportunity" payments;

- Payments only for actual services provided in the emergency department; and

- Payments only for uninsured patients, which eliminate the risk of a physician being paid twice for the same services.

EMTALA

Congress created EMTALA in 1986 to ensure access to care for emergency medical conditions, regardless of an individual's ability to pay. Sections 1866 and 1867 of the Social Security Act impose the requirements of EMTALA on hospitals and critical access hospitals that offer emergency services by imposing civil monetary penalties on hospitals and physicians for failure to appropriately screen or stabilize a patient needing emergency care or negligently transferring a patient. Section 1866 of the Social Security Act requires that hospitals maintain a listing of on-call physicians to provide treatment to stabilize a patient with an emergency medical condition; however, EMTALA does not specify how frequently a hospital's on-call physicians are expected to be available. Having specialists, particularly surgical specialists, available to a hospital's emergency room is crucial, particularly in light of EMTALA. Under EMTALA, if an individual comes to the emergency department and a request is made for examination or treatment of a medical condition, then an appropriate medical screening examination must be provided to that individual. If upon examination, a determination is made that the individual has an emergency condition, the hospital must provide necessary stabilizing treatment or provide for an appropriate transfer. There is no requirement under EMTALA that hospitals provide full-time, on-call coverage by a specialist or provide a predetermined coverage ratio; however, relevant factors, such as the number of physicians on staff, other demands on the physicians, the frequency for which on-call physician services are required, and the hospital's response plan to situations in which a physician is unable to respond to call, are all used in determining the hospital's ED call schedule. EMTALA requires that hospitals maintain a list of physicians who are on call to provide stabilizing treatment; beyond that, hospitals have considerable flexibility in how call coverage is provided.

3.2 Impact of Regulatory Guidance on Scope of Services

Clearly, EMTALA has the most far-reaching implications on the scope of services included in physician on-call arrangements entered into by hospitals. In the preamble to the September 2003 final rule, CMS notes, "Some physicians have in the past expressed a desire to refuse to be included on a hospital's on-call list but nevertheless take calls selectively. These physicians might, for example, respond to calls for patients with whom they or a colleague at the hospital have established a doctor-patient relationship, while declining calls from other patients, including those whose ability to pay may be in question. Such a practice would clearly be a violation of EMTALA."[11] Because the final rule did not make call coverage an obligation for physicians, hospitals have lost some leverage in requiring specialists to take call, a situation that has contributed, at least in part, to the growing demand for on-call compensation.

Some facilities establish call coverage arrangements to mirror the arrangements identified in the OIG advisory opinions. Others incorporate certain safeguards identified in the advisory opinions, while some emulate safeguards to reduce the risk that the OIG would impose administrative sanctions under examination. From Advisory Opinion 07-10, the OIG identified certain safeguards, which are often considered in the scope of agreements for physician ED on-call arrangements. These include tailoring the per diem rate to cover substantial, quantifiable services; documenting the existence of a legitimate unmet need for on-call coverage and uncompensated care; and instituting features that minimize risks, such as selectively rewarding the highest referring physicians and cherry-picking. Likewise, from Advisory Opinion 09-05, some facilities employ a claims-based payment for ED call arrangements, paying the physician for otherwise uncompensated services using a fair market value fixed fee for services rendered when on call, with safeguards in place to ensure that the physician is not double-paid for the same service. Other safeguards addressed in 09-05 and often in on-call arrangements are processes that ensure that physician compensation does not represent payment for lost opportunity, such as the amount the physician would have otherwise earned in private practice if not for the ED call coverage arrangement, and payments only for the actual professional services the physician personally performed.

3.3 Impact of Regulatory Guidance on Appraisal Process

Appraisers need to clearly understand healthcare laws, regulations, and specific regulatory guidance before undertaking a valuation of call coverage payment arrangements. The Stark law is implicated when the on-call physician and the hospital have a prohibited referral relationship, defined as when the physician has a financial relationship and the ability to refer designated health services to the hospital. The anti-kickback statute is implicated when the physician receives remuneration that could be intended as an inducement to refer federal healthcare program beneficiaries. EMTALA implications to the hospital are important because the law places requirements on the hospital to provide coverage in the ED, yet the law provides for no similar requirements for physicians. IRS reasonable compensation requirements for exempt organizations place risk of intermediate sanctions on both physician and organization managers who participate in excess private benefit transactions, while also placing the burden of maintaining exempt status on the organization. State self-referral and anti-kickback laws must also be

---

11 68 *F.R.* (Sept. 9, 2003), p. 53255.

considered as applicable. These rules make it imperative that the appraiser understand the distinctions of regulatory fair market value definitions and restrictions on regulatory standards such as the volume-or-value and set-in-advance rules as applicable to payment arrangements when involved in valuing on-call arrangements.

Likewise, if called upon to opine on the commercial reasonableness of an ED on-call arrangement, valuation practitioners must understand the regulatory definitions of commercial reasonableness and be able to clearly differentiate between it and fair market value, understanding the distinctions in inquiry and analysis that exists between the two terms.

Specific issues related to the regulatory definition of FMV and use of data sources

In the last few years, some organizations that produce physician compensation surveys have published compensation survey data related to physician on-call arrangements. This information has proven useful in showing market trends in hospital compensation of physicians for furnishing on-call coverage. However, some feel that since parties with which physicians have referral relationships report most, if not all, of the data, the data presented in survey reports is "tainted." Depending on how this information is used, they feel it renders the information of little value in light of the regulatory definitions of fair market value. Similarly, ad hoc surveys of local and regional hospital payments of physicians for on-call coverage may be viewed in the same way, because the physicians who receive compensation for on-call services represent referral sources for the hospitals paying for the call coverage.[12]

Effect on valuation methodology

Appraisers of ED on-call coverage payment arrangements have devised means of ensuring that payments reported in widely available surveys do not render conclusions of value invalid through the inclusion of tainted data. This is accomplished in myriad ways, such as by using rates derived from payments outside the healthcare industry, by testing survey data using physician specialties not ordinarily considered referral sources, and by using nonphysician on-call rates in the healthcare industry.

4.0 Valuation Methodology

The methods of valuation can be generally categorized into one of three broad approaches: cost-based, income-based, and market-based. These broad approaches are driven by the fundamental economic principles identified above. The cost-based

---

12   For a complete analysis of this issue, see Chapter 8, "To Use or Not to Use: An Appraisal Analysis of the Stark Prohibition on Market Data From Parties in a Position to Refer."

approach considers the value of an arrangement based on the cost of an equally desirable substitute,[13] the income-based approach considers the economic benefit stream associated with the subject arrangement, and the market-based approach considers amounts paid for similar arrangements by similar parties (i.e., alternatives).

On-call and coverage arrangements diverge broadly in terms of economics because some result in generation of professional fee revenues, while others represent compensation for provider availability and reimbursement for what the clinician may not be otherwise able to receive from patients and payers. This variety of economic features results in varying approaches to the valuation of compensation arrangements. Although not in abundance, given the proliferation of on-call arrangements, much more data is available for these arrangements in the last decade than was previously available. Published survey products have increased the availability of this information, and valuation firms have also built their own proprietary databases of these arrangements.

The relevance and applicability of each valuation method to the final conclusion of value can vary depending on the circumstances and the analyst's considered judgment. Valuation analysts often equate this synthesis process to a funnel, with various valuation methods entering the top of the funnel, which itself represents the reconciliation and synthesis of the various methods under each of the three broad approaches, subsequently yielding a conclusion of value at the bottom.

The various valuation approaches and methods that can be applied to hospital call coverage arrangements are discussed in detail in Chapter 28, "Valuing Hospital Call Coverage Arrangements: Appraisal Methods."

5.0 Stacking and Contractual Adaptation Issues

As more fully described elsewhere in this guide, "stacking" involves the incorporation of multiple compensation arrangements for duties and responsibilities covered under one or more agreements between employer/employee and contracting parties. For example, in the context of ED on-call coverage, a hospital may employ a physician under a physician employment agreement, with compensation arrangements that are comprised of a base-plus-incentive for the clinical patient care services of the physician. At the same time, the hospital may also have a separate contract or a separate provision in the physician employment agreement that provides for separate ED call coverage, for which the physician is paid in addition to the base-plus-incentive arrangement described

---

13   Shannon Pratt and Alina Niculita, *Valuing a Business, The Analysis and Appraisal of Closely Held Companies*, fifth edition, McGraw-Hill, p. 358.

above. This on-call payment arrangement may be as simple as payment for excessive call, such as a per diem payment of $800 for each 24-hour shift of coverage furnished by the physician in the hospital's ED. However, when added to the clinical base and incentive compensation earned by the physician, the aggregate compensation may rise to a level that may call into question the fair market value of the aggregate compensation.

5.1 Potential for Stacking

Stacking ED on-call payment arrangements is indeed possible, but depends on the nature of the arrangements. In a hypothetical example of a hospital and independent contractor physicians in private practice, this may not be an issue if all arrangements between the hospital and the physicians are individually at fair market value. These may include nonduplicative medical directorships, midlevel provider preceptorships, ED on-call arrangements, and similar contracts. The likelihood of stacking on-call pay also exists with employment when the physician is employed by the hospital, integrated delivery system, foundation, or a member of the academic medical center faculty practice plan. These arrangements often already include some degree of base or fixed compensation and may include incentive compensation that pays the doctor regardless of a patient's ability to pay, thus creating the risk that rule-of-thumb amounts for ED on-call pay may be duplicative or result in a "stacked" arrangement that could call into question fair market value in the aggregate. It is incumbent upon the valuation analyst to inquire about all contractual arrangements between the hospital and physician to ensure that the aggregate of these arrangements, including the incentive provisions, do not result in overpayment.

5.2 Converting Valuation Conclusions Into a Compensation Structure

Among the challenges in opining on fair market value of on-call arrangements is the translation of an opinion of a value conclusion into a rate that parties to the on-call coverage agreement and their legal counsel can use in an actual payment arrangement. As is all too common, the parties may agree on a payment arrangement that may not fit the mold of the traditional 24-hour shift rate, which may necessitate some type of conversion from the concluded value to the rate that will be made part of the contract. The most common means of accomplishing this conversion is through the use of a common denominator, such as hours, to convert the rate from the conclusion of value to the contracted rate. Below are some simple, hypothetical examples of how such conversions may be accomplished:

- Mr. Appraiser renders an opinion on a fair market value rate for Specialty X of $240 per 24-hour shift of unrestricted on-call pay. However, the contract between Hospital and Dr. John Doe provides for a 14-hour shift from 5 p.m. to 7 a.m. on weekdays. To make his opinion useful for counsel for Hospital, Mr.

Appraiser converts his opinion based on the rate of $10 per hour ($240/24) to $140 for a 14-hour shift.

- Likewise, Mr. Appraiser is asked to give his opinion as to the value of a 63-hour weekend shift of unrestricted call (from 5 p.m. on Friday to 8 a.m. on Monday). Mr. Appraiser determines that no premium rate is applicable for weekend call. Therefore, using a similar formula, Mr. Appraiser arrives at a conclusion of value for the weekend of $630.

- Counsel for Hospital contacts Mr. Appraiser and asks for a flat monthly rate for on-call pay for 1-in-2 coverage. If Dr. Doe does not provide ED on-call coverage personally, he will be required to obtain coverage at his own personal cost. Mr. Appraiser, through conversations with the administration of Hospital, determines that this involves an average of 15 weekday shifts and 2 weekend shifts. Based on the above shift rates and the number of shifts to be covered, Mr. Appraiser determines the monthly value to be $4,860 (15 weekday shifts at $240, plus 2 weekend shifts at $630).

More complex examples can be found in practice, such as in the following hypothetical:

Hospital B contracts with Dr. Smith to provide weekend coverage at an outpatient psychiatric clinic. This coverage arrangement involves all-day coverage on Saturday that includes an 8-hour clinic. Mr. Valuator relied on methodology that placed sole reliance on rates obtained from locum tenens firm quotes for the full-day coverage. Mr. Valuator concluded, after adjusting for locums agency profit, that the locums rate of $2,000 per day of coverage, which included up to 4 hours of on-site coverage, at a rate of $200 per hour for more than 4 hours of coverage, was fair market value. Mr. Valuator determined that Saturday coverage to be paid according to the contract would be $2,800 ($2,000 per diem rate, plus $200 per hour for 4 additional hours for the 8-hour clinic).

Because the facts and circumstances of the on-call arrangement dictate the form of the conclusion of value the valuation analyst will render, the need to communicate with legal counsel and, if possible, obtain copies of the agreement, letter of intent, or terms sheet is vitally important to arrive at a point value or range of values that will be useful to the ultimate users of the value conclusion.

5.3 Other Special Topics or Issues

In the post-reform environment at the time of writing, the Supreme Court of the United States has rendered a decision to effectively allow states to decide whether to follow the provisions of the ACA as they relate to the expansion of the Medicare program. Some states may decide to expand their Medicaid programs to cover nearly all individuals with income levels up to 138% of the federal poverty level, while other states may decide to not expand their Medicaid programs. In states that adopt Medicaid expansion, there may be a significant impact on the payer mix in hospital EDs, as well as a reduction in the number of hospital ED visits. This could result in reduced uncompensated care for physicians providing on-call coverage in the ED, because fewer visits and fewer indigent patients could equate to fewer no-pay patients. While physicians will still be faced with the inconveniences of responding to calls in the middle of the night, the financial burden of call may be somewhat lessened in those states.

In states rejecting the notion of Medicaid expansion, there may still be some relief for hospitals from the high cost of on-call payments. Given the survival in the high court of the individual mandate and with the advent of health insurance exchanges and expansion of employer-sponsored plans, there may be an uptick in covered individuals, which could likewise result in fewer ED visits and fewer uninsured in the ED, again reducing the uncompensated care burden for on-call doctors.

Without a doubt, controlling healthcare cost growth will have a significant impact, likely downward, on future physician payment for on-call coverage in the ED.

Chapter 28. Valuing Hospital Call Coverage Arrangements: Appraisal Methods

CONTENTS

Chapter 28. Valuing Hospital Call Coverage Arrangements: Appraisal Methods

By Gregory D. Anderson, CPA/ABV, CVA

1.0 Introduction

On-call and coverage arrangements diverge broadly in terms of economics because some result in generation of professional fee revenues, while others represent compensation for provider availability and reimbursement for what the clinician may not be otherwise able to receive from patients and payers. This variety of economic features results in varying approaches to the valuation of hospital call coverage arrangements. This chapter will provide an overview of how the various valuation approaches and methods apply to the key types of payment structures encountered in the marketplace. These types include the following:

- Time-based structures: hourly, daily, weekly, annual, or shift rates;

- Activation payments;

- Fee-for-service payments;

- Subsidy arrangements; and

- Deferred compensation.

Application of the market, cost, and income approaches will be discussed for each type, along with discussion of various appraisal methods and techniques available under each approach. The chapter will also discuss important considerations in the valuation synthesis process for each type of compensation structure.

2.0 Valuing Time-Based Payment Structures: Hourly, Daily, Weekly, Monthly, Annual, or Shift Rates

As discussed in Chapter 27, "Valuing Hospital Call Coverage Arrangements: An Introduction," approximately half of all compensation arrangements involving ED call coverage contracts include *hourly, daily, weekly, monthly, annual, or shift rates (time-based)* payments. Despite the fact that all such time-based payments are not based solely on hourly rates, shift or per diem rates are often based on hourly values applied to the length of the shift or period covered, thus an important step involves the conversion of data from the basis of measure as provided in the market data to a common denominator that can be applied to the subject arrangement (i.e., converting from an hourly survey-reported rate to a per diem rate applicable to the subject on-call contract). Methodology under the cost-, income-, and market-based approaches for assessing the fair market value of *time-based rates are available, yet their relative reliability and applicability to the subject arrangement must be considered.*

2.1 Using the Market-Based Approach

With the market-based approach, a wide array of information is available to the appraiser to assist in the valuation of time-based compensation arrangements using market methodology. The key to the effective use of this information is the awareness of available tools and experience and their most appropriate use.

The economics of time-based on-call arrangements are focused on the payment by a hospital to a covering physician as compensation for the physician's service as on call to the ED. When the physician bills and collects for the professional fee, the compensation is most often comprised of pay for the physician's availability and reimbursement for the uncompensated care he or she furnishes to the hospital's patients, whether in the ED, during an inpatient stay subsequent to admission from the ED, or through follow-up care after the ED visit. This economic "make up" of the time-based arrangement generally lends itself to the widespread use of methods under the market-based approach because many "comparable" arrangements exist and can be identified as similar or dissimilar and adjusted accordingly.

The criteria for applying the market-based approach to time-based on-call payment arrangements are as follows:

- Do similar arrangements between similar parties for similar services exist in the marketplace?

- Who bills and collects for the physician professional fees for patients first seen in the ED, including follow-up care?

- Can the comparability of the subject arrangement to the market "comparables" in terms of length of coverage be readily determined (i.e., shift length)?

- Can the comparability of the subject arrangement to market data in terms of restrictions of coverage be readily determined (i.e., restricted coverage versus unrestricted call)?

- Can specific nuances applicable to the subject arrangement be identified based on the information available about the comparable data and, if so, can adjustments be made to account for such differences:

  ○ Trauma or nontrauma coverage?

  ○ Physician specialty?

  ○ Intensity of coverage?

  ○ Frequency of coverage?

  ○ Payer mix?

  ○ Uncompensated care impact?

- If it is impractical to assess the comparability of the subject arrangement to market data in terms of intensity (i.e., difficulty of a call shift in terms of numbers of calls and personal visits to the ED in response to calls, length of time spent at the hospital once called in, surgical cases per night on call, etc.), and frequency (i.e., call rotation—shifts per month), can adjustments be made to reflect such variations?

- If it is impractical to assess the comparability of the subject arrangement to market data in terms of uncompensated care, can adjustments be made to reflect such variations?

Under the market-based approach, the analyst performs market research, such as that described in the methodology sections below, of on-call compensation rates. The explicit use of published on-call rates is beyond the scope of this chapter, but a comprehensive analysis should take into account the type of facility (i.e., trauma, nontrauma, etc.), per diem or hourly rates, restricted or unrestricted rates, and other information that may be pertinent to the arrangement. As described above, the rates obtained through this research are then adjusted to consider the impact of the frequency and intensity of on-call coverage, as well as whether concurrent call (i.e., providing simultaneous ED call at more than one facility, often with the physician receiving on-call pay from multiple facilities) is provided under the contractual arrangements.

A discussion follows regarding several methods commonly applied as part of the market-based approach to the valuation of time-based on-call pay.

Market-Based Approach: Direct and Indirect Use of Published Survey Data

Methodology under the market-based approach enjoys broad acceptance in the valuation community and among in-house financial analysts performing valuation analysis. Some of the data most often referred to in the internal and external valuation of time-based on-call arrangements are taken from published on-call compensation surveys. In its most basic form, the direct analysis of published data involves research of time-based payment norms reported by similar facilities (i.e., trauma centers) for similar physician specialties. The more sophisticated analysis performed by valuation firms includes the indirect use of published on-call compensation survey data, adjusting the survey information to account for factors such as frequency, intensity, payer mix, subspecialization, geographic disparities, and other factors deemed appropriate. Among outside valuators with the knowledge bases, algorithms, and scoring tools to normalize the value of availability by considering these factors, adjustments are made to account for the distinction that exists in value that should be attributed to more or less burdensome call shifts.

Market-Based Approach: Adjusted Clinical Survey Method

The valuation analyst using this methodology begins with specialty-specific clinical compensation from published physician compensation surveys and applies a factor to convert clinical compensation to an on-call rate. Many valuators who have developed a knowledge base of on-call payment rates have become experienced with the nuances of factors such as the intensity and frequency associated with physician on-call coverage, allowing them, through the use of algorithms, to make adjustments to the value of availability associated with these factors. Such adjustments are important to the distinction that exists in value that should be attributed to call shifts when one is more burdensome. Others have developed proprietary methods that consider the relationships that exist between specialists' on-call rates and clinical compensation rates and use an averaging process to arrive at a weighted average relationship that is applied to clinical rates to compute on-call compensation values. In some cases, to mitigate the risk that survey data might be tainted by referral relationships (opinions of the federal government on this issue as published in preambles to two Stark law rules will be discussed in greater detail below) between physicians and the hospitals that pay them to take ED call, some of these methods weight specialist rates that are considered nonreferring specialists.

Once the factor is determined and applied to annual clinical compensation, the adjusted rate is then converted to the time-based rate needed for the valuation.

Some appraisers differ on the classification of this method as cost-based or market-based, with valid rationale supporting both positions. Valuation consultants that place this method under the cost rather than market approach do so because it builds up the rate using various elements and is, therefore, not directly based on market data for on-call coverage compensation.

A Method That Values Only Availability

To determine the value of physician availability only, one method considers the relationship of on-call compensation to clinical compensation for allied health professionals and applies that same relationship to the subject physician specialty. This method does not contemplate the value of uncompensated care because it considers the compensation of allied health professionals, such as nurses, who are paid only for their availability to respond to call.

Market-Based Approach: Ad Hoc Surveying Methods

Formal or informal surveys of local and regional markets by healthcare providers or valuation firms also represent sources of market information on ED on-call payment rates. This is generally only reliable when used in conjunction with other methods because the small respondent volume and referral relationships risk tainting the results (again, as will be more fully discussed later in this chapter, the discussions of tainted relationships in the Stark preamble make the sole use of this method problematic). Data may also be received from respondents in a variety of forms and rates, and information received must be carefully vetted to ensure comparability as to the specific nature of the arrangement, shift length, physician specialty, facility, and other factors.

Market-Based Approach: Proprietary or Comparable Arrangement Database Methods

Valuation firms develop databases of comparable payment arrangements over years of exposure to on-call agreements and use this data to test the reasonableness of the results achieved through the application of other methodology. This information is generally classified in a way that permits sorting on many fields, so arrangements most closely approximating the subject arrangement can be identified.

Market-Based Approach: Methods That Consider Other Documented Offers

Valid, written rejected prior offers and offers by competitors are deployed as valuation methodology, although these are not widely regarded as stand-alone methods capable of producing a conclusion of value without using other mainstream methodology in tandem with these offers. In other cases, these documents are used to "build the file" of documentation maintained by hospital management or counsel in support of the on-call payment arrangement, which also includes other support for the contract, such as the valuation analysis itself. Again, ensuring specific comparability is central to the process, because a misstep can result in a dramatically incorrect conclusion and significant risk for the parties. Furthermore, care should be taken to avoid oral representations, because these are nearly always inaccurate in some manner of detail that compromises the comparability to the subject arrangement.

Issues in the Use of Market Data

Data is critical to the successful use of methods comprising the market-based approach. In recent years, published surveys have greatly improved in terms of numbers of respondents, information presented, and cross-tabulation of data. Among the most widely recognized published survey products are the MGMA and SCA on-call surveys, as follows:

- SCA *Physician On-Call Pay Survey Report.* This SCA survey contains data from nearly 200 healthcare organizations, approximately half of which are trauma centers. Actual on-call pay rates are reported for approximately 40 physician specialties, including midlevel providers.

- MGMA *Medical Directorship and On-Call Compensation Survey.* This MGMA survey contains information on nearly 4,000 on-call providers in over 300 medical organizations.

Clinical compensation, used in indirect methods to determine cost information and proportion of on-call pay to clinical compensation, can be derived from published surveys of physician compensation, such as the following, which are described elsewhere in this book:

- MGMA *Physician Compensation and Production Survey;*[1]

- *Medical Group Compensation and Financial Survey;*[2] and

- *Physician Compensation and Productivity Survey Report.*[3]

---

1   Medical Group Management Association, Englewood, Colo.
2   American Medical Group Association, Alexandria, Va.
3   Sullivan, Cotter and Associates Inc., Southfield, Mich.

Downsides to the increasing usefulness and popularity of published surveys are the misuse and misinterpretation of the information. Such erroneous uses or abuses include cherry-picking of data to get the desired answer, sole reliance on data from a single survey, miscalculation of rates, improper use of per diem or trauma center rates, or incorrect use of statistical levels from respondent data.

Furthermore, of concern to legal counsel in some circles has been the use of market data whose respondents are hospitals with which the contracted physicians are referral sources. This would have the effect of precluding the use of ad hoc surveys to gather data from a particular local or regional market or on-call surveys made up only of respondent hospitals with compensation arrangements with referral sources. This concern results in part from statements by the Centers for Medicare and Medicaid Services (CMS) in the preambles to the Stark final rulemaking. For example, in the Stark II Phase I Final Rule, CMS noted the following:

> In other cases, all the comparables or market data may involve transactions between entities that are in a position to refer or generate other business. For example, in some markets, physician-owned equipment lessors have driven out competitive third-party lessors of similar equipment. In such situations, we would look to alternative valuation methodologies, including, but not limited to, cost plus reasonable rate of return on investment in leases of comparable medical equipment from disinterested lessors.[4]

Furthermore, in the Stark II Phase II Interim Final Rule, CMS noted the following:

> For example, the methodology must exclude valuations where the parties to the transactions are at arm's length but in a position to refer to one another.[5]

However, this position has softened among counsel when the market-based approach is used in concert with other methodology to arrive at a conclusion of value.

Is Median Always FMV?

Believing that FMV is always at least 50th percentile is like rejecting the notion that half the population has an IQ below the median.

---

[4]   66 *F.R.* (Jan. 4, 2001), 944.
[5]   69 *F.R.* (March 26, 2004), 16107.

2.2 Using the Cost-Based Approach

The methodology under the cost-based approach, when an equally desirable substitute is available, is applied through the use of the cost of the equally desirable substitute as a proxy for fair market value. Equally desirable substitutes in the case of ED on-call service include employment of the on-call specialists by the hospital and contracting with locum tenens firms to supply the needed ED coverage. Additionally, the cost-based approach is effective in building up component parts of an arrangement, which will be more fully described later in building up to the cost of unrestricted call by aggregating the value of availability and uncompensated care to arrive at the total value of the service arrangement. In not all cases, however, will equally desirable substitutes or the ability to build up the cost of the service be readily available. In sum, the cost-based approach is best applied when there are other equally desirable substitutes to the subject arrangement; without such, the cost-based approach will likely take a lesser role in the valuation than those of the other approaches.

The criteria for the application of the cost-based approach include determination of whether a substitute represents a viable alternative to the subject arrangement, whether the economic value of the substitute can be readily and accurately measured, and whether any differences between the subject arrangement and the substitute can be appropriately accounted for with economic adjustments. Once these criteria are satisfied and economic adjustments are applied, the adjusted substitute value can be used as a proxy for fair market value. For example, if a locum tenens firm represents the equally desirable substitute and the rate is appropriately adjusted to convert the rate to represent a proxy for the fair market value of the subject arrangement, such as an unrestricted on-call rate, the adjusted rate can then be considered as the result of the cost-based approach.

The criteria for applying the cost-based approach are as follows:

- Is an equally desirable substitute available?

- Does the substitute represent a viable alternative to the subject arrangement (i.e., is the alternative arrangement permissible under healthcare regulatory and billing restrictions)?

- Can the economic value of the substitute be readily and accurately measured?

- Can any differences between the subject arrangement and the substitute be appropriately accounted for with economic adjustments?

An Equally Desirable Substitute?

Often, we describe locum tenens arrangements as a means for determining a proxy for fair market value under the cost-based approach. In so doing, one must consider whether the locums alternative is truly viable because locums arrangements are, by design, short-term in nature and may not represent a viable substitute for a one-year on-call contract.

Cost-Based Approach: Build-Up Method

The build-up method allows the valuation analyst to aggregate the various components of value associated with the time-based rate, including the components of value associated with availability and uncompensated care. For example, the analyst may use an availability-only hourly rate to determine the value of physician on-call availability, such as one might see in the compensation of allied health professionals furnishing coverage when no element of uncompensated care exists. To the availability amount, the valuation analyst adds an aggregate time-based rate for uncompensated care, such as through the use of historical data on write-offs incurred from ED visits and related care, which is then converted to the appropriate time-based rate, such as by dividing annual ED bad debts by the number of shifts. The aggregate time-based rate includes both the availability and uncompensated care values as determined through the use of separate methods.

Cost-Based Approach: Avoided Net Employment Cost Method

Another method in use for determining the value of time-based on-call payment arrangements is applied by calculating the avoided cost to the hospital of employing a similar specialist to provide similar on-call coverage. This has the risk of being highly speculative, in that it involves estimating the professional fee revenues, overhead, physician compensation, and benefits associated with employment, with a goal of arriving at the avoided net cost of employing a specialist to provide the requisite coverage. Additional speculation is warranted when the valuation analyst further analyzes the costs associated with the recruitment of a specialist into the service area to provide the hypothetical on-call coverage. The aggregate cost is then converted to the time-based element for purposes of the valuation. This method closely resembles the income-based methodology used in subsidy valuation for hospital-based specialists as will be more fully discussed later.

Data sources for the cost-based approach begin with similar data to the market-based approach when using build-up methodology. For example, when employing the cost-based approach to build up availability and uncompensated care rates, the analyst will use survey information similar to that under the direct and indirect published survey methodology to establish values for the component parts of the build-up method. With the use of locum tenens quotes to arrive at a proxy amount, the analyst will often rely on locums firm quotes and other information on how these firms profit from their service offerings. Finally, gathering data for the net value associated with employment involves the gathering of hospital or market information regarding revenues and overhead of the subject specialty, as well as quotes from physician staffing firms as to the costs of recruiting specialist physicians into the subject service area.

2.3 Using the Income-Based Approach

Methodology under the income-based approach can also be effective in the valuation of ED on-call valuation arrangements in many circumstances. In traditional ED on-call arrangements, the income-based approach is arguably less applicable, but other applications of this approach are regarded as effective in the valuation of on-call payment arrangements when the income from the "buyer" and "seller" perspectives can be readily and legally measured. Consider a typical arrangement for unrestricted ED call coverage by a surgical specialist—one in which the physician's compensation is comprised of both payment for availability and uncompensated care. The hospital contractor receives no stream of economic benefit under the contract because the physician availability itself produces no revenue for the hospital nor does the uncompensated professional services generated by the physician (and the physician cannot legally receive credit for the inpatient hospital service revenue stream of the hospital, if any, generated by the ED visit). Measuring the stream of economic benefits to the hospital as "buyer" under the on-call arrangement is not a practical measure of physician value to the hospital. Thus, methods under the income-based approach from the buyer's perspective to valuation are of little applicability in establishing the fair market value of on-call pay in a time-based on-call arrangement. In the hands of the "seller" of the service (i.e., the physician contracted to furnish ED on-call coverage), the income-based approach may have little usefulness in arriving at a proxy for fair market value in a time-based on-call analysis. Conceptually, assigning value based on the earnings stream of the physician may be a consideration; however, caution must be observed in application, as the OIG warns against payments based on "lost opportunity" in Advisory Opinions 07-10 and 09-05.

The criteria for applying the income-based approach are as follows:

- Can the arrangement be reasonably or legally measured in terms of a stream of economic benefits?

- Can the economic benefit stream be readily adjusted to reflect an appropriate basis of accounting and an appropriate level of economic reality?

- Can the economic benefit stream be accurately adjusted to reflect fair market value given the facts and circumstances applicable to the arrangement?

Income-Based Approach: Buyer-Based Method

For time-based methodology, methodology that computes the value of on-call compensation under the income-based approach is of little practical use to the analyst because the arrangement itself is not capable of producing a stream of economic benefits for the buyer of the service (i.e., the hospital contracting for the on-call service in the ED). As a valuation method for time-based analysis, the approach is seldom employed; however, it may have value if it is part of another arrangement that generates professional fees, such as in a hospital-based specialty coverage arrangement, which will be more fully described below.

Income-Based Approach: Seller-Based Method

In the hands of the physician in a time-based on-call arrangement, arguably little can be drawn from the assessment of a stream of economic benefit to the "seller," except that the physician's income stream results from compensation for on-call services, which under limited circumstances, could be related to the physician's compensation from similar on-call services. For example, the use of historical physician on-call compensation from a similar facility may be given consideration as a reasonableness test, but cannot be used as a primary valuation method.

2.4 Valuation Synthesis

In making conclusions from the information derived from the various methods employed, no method can be considered as an absolute. To produce a sound conclusion, the analyst should consider results of methods deemed most reliable for indicating fair market value and exclude results deemed less reliable. Whether more or less reliable, methods can nevertheless serve as reasonableness tests on the results of the other methods. It is not unexpected that the conclusions determined by the various methods will not be in exact agreement. The analyst must use objectivity and informed judgment in determining the aggregate significance of the methodologies upon which reliance is placed. Described in the funnel analogy above, the synthesis process yields a valuation conclusion that considers the results of the valuation analyst's professional judgment and the reliance placed on the methods employed. The result may be stated in a point value or a range representing the upper and lower ends of the fair market value conclusion.

3.0 Valuing Activation Payment Structures

Activation payments represent compensation paid to physicians for furnishing services while on call. Thus, the valuation of these payment arrangements is most often centered on the valuation of clinical services and uncompensated care, as opposed to the value of availability.

In valuing activation payments, methods under all three broad valuation approaches can be useful to the analyst. As with valuation of most on-call arrangements, a critical piece of the analysis is the understanding of the economics of the billing of physician professional fees. Inquiry surrounding the contractual provisions and adaptation of those provisions in the execution of the on-call arrangement are important to understand which party to the agreement bills and collects the professional fee, which, in turn, has significant repercussions for the analysis to be performed.

Following are representative methods under each of the three broad approaches applicable to valuing activation payment arrangements.

3.1 Using the Market-Based Approach

Activation payments represent a useful method of compensating physicians for on-call service, yet the data on these arrangements does not share the widespread availability enjoyed by time-based arrangements. However, because activation payments represent compensation for the physician's clinical service, other forms of market data, such as survey data on clinical compensation, are available and can be converted into useful information for the valuation analysis.

What cannot be overlooked is the need to understand the professional fee billing and collection arrangements because this drives the market data that the valuator will incorporate into the analysis. For example, in the case of an employed physician who is paid an activation fee when the employer bills and collects the professional fee, the payment to the physician may simply be a payment for clinical patient care.

On the other hand, in an independent contractor relationship in which the physician is responsible for billing and collecting the professional fee, the activation fee is payment for the physician's uncompensated patient care service because the physician is only paid when "activated." Many contracts account for the other "availability" element with a separate compensation rate for availability only when the physician is not activated. Once the physician is activated and encounters a patient in the ED, if the physician bills and collects the professional fee, any stipend associated with the activation must therefore be limited to the uncompensated care burden. Clearly, these dictate that the valuation analyst research distinctly different market information when performing the market-based approach.

The criteria for applying the market-based approach to time-based on-call payment arrangements are as follows:

- Do similar arrangements between similar parties for similar services exist in the marketplace?

- Who bills and collects for the physician professional fees for patients first seen in the ED, including follow-up care?

- If the physician is an employee of the hospital and the hospital bills and collects the professional fee, is the physician at risk for uncompensated care (i.e., on an incentive model based on collections)?

- Can the comparability of the subject arrangement to the market "comparables" in terms of length of coverage be readily determined (i.e., shift length)?

- If it is impractical to assess the comparability of the subject arrangement to market data in terms of uncompensated care, can adjustments be made to reflect such variations?

Under the market-based approach, the analyst performs market research, such as those described in the methodology sections below, on activation fee rates. A discussion follows regarding several methods commonly applied as part of the market-based approach to valuation of time-based on-call pay.

Market-Based Approach: Adjusted Clinical Survey Method

Applicable when a physician's compensation is for clinical patient care (i.e., when the hospital bills and collects the professional fee), the application of this methodology involves researching as many applicable surveys as possible, with the surveys weighted based on factors such as relevance of the survey data, sufficiency of respondent size, age of the survey report, etc. Dividing the weighted average by 2,080 hours gives the analyst an hourly rate, which can then be multiplied by the number of hours (i.e., average number of hours per activation) of service furnished by the physician when activated.

3.2 Using the Cost-Based Approach

Cost-Based Approach: Avoided Net Locum Tenens Cost Method

In an activation fee arrangement, the buyer of the service (i.e., hospital) has alternatives to the arrangement that often include contracting with a locum tenens firm for the service. When using a locum tenens rate as a proxy for fair market value, the analyst uses rate quotes from firms and adjusts them to convert to the period covered by the activation fee. Such adjustments include the isolation of activation coverage from charges for physician availability if included in the stated rate and removal of agency profit from the stated rate.

3.3 Using the Income-Based Approach

Income-Based Approach: Seller-Based Method

In the income-based approach, accounting for the economics from the seller's vantage point represents a means for determining fair market value. Using this method, the analyst gathers data on the services performed, the frequency of each service, the reimbursement by major payer class, and the payer mix. From there, the analyst determines what a hypothetical seller would receive at market-based reimbursement rates, net of contractual adjustments. When an independent contractor physician is paid an activation fee, it is not a payment for availability because the physician is only paid when "activated," so the revenue a hypothetical seller would receive under the income approach must be adjusted by the income actually received during the activation to estimate the uncompensated care furnished to patients. The analyst then adjusts for the costs a hypothetical seller of the service would incur in generating that fee revenue, such as overhead associated with billing for the service. The result is an amount representing net available income to the seller of the service. The payment represents uncompensated care only—thus, the hypothetical "all-in" number, which includes physician benefits and malpractice premiums the independent physician will bear from the uncompensated care payment.

3.4 Valuation Synthesis

Depending on the billing and collection of professional fees, the analyst will gravitate to one or more methods that are appropriate given the economics of the activation fee arrangement. When a hospital employs the physician and bills for the professional fees, the analyst will likely employ the market-based method of valuing physician clinical patient care during the activation period. As a reasonableness test, the analyst will look to the market for activation fees with similar billing arrangements. Under the cost-based approach, the analyst will employ a locum tenens firm method, if available. With the income-based approach, it is unlikely that the analyst will identify an applicable method that can produce a reliable conclusion for this type of arrangement. It is likely that most, if not all, reliance will be weighted toward the market-based methodology for valuing physician availability under these circumstances.

When the physician is an independent contractor and bills for the professional fees produced during activation, valuation under the market-based approach would look to similar activation arrangements in the marketplace that base pay only on uncompensated care. Under the cost-based approach, it is unlikely that the analyst will find reasonable methodology to account only for uncompensated care. In the income-based approach, the analyst can apply the seller-based analysis of uncompensated care as described above, which will likely receive the greatest weight in the analyst's synthesis.

4.0 Valuing Fee-for-Service Payment Structures

Hospitals sometimes enter into fee-for-service (FFS) payment arrangements with physicians, a payment method in which a physician files a "claim" with the hospital for the services furnished to patients first seen in the ED while on call. It is generally understood in this payment methodology that the physician will assign to the hospital the right to bill and collect the professional fees and will give up the right to any payer or patient compensation for these services because the hospital's compensation will represent 100% of the physician's compensation for service. Methodology for valuing these arrangements can be applied under the market-based, cost-based, and income-based approaches.

As with other payment arrangements not based on time, FFS payments represent an acceptable method of compensating physicians for on-call service, yet market data is not presented in a comparable fashion because of the wide variety of services performed and the relatively few number of FFS payment arrangements in relation to time-based arrangements. However, as was shown above in the case of activation payments, because FFS payments represent compensation for the clinical service, survey data can be converted into useful information for the valuation analysis.

4.1 Using the Market-Based Approach

Market-Based Approach: Guideline Contract Method

When fewer types of cases or services are performed in the ED, guideline contracts may give an indication of the rates paid per case in a FFS model; however, the more likely scenario involves a wide variety of cases or services. In these situations, a weighted average level of compensation relative to a static benchmark can be determined and used as a reasonableness test for the FFS payment arrangement. Consider guideline contracts that pay FFS rates per service performed for patients first seen in the ED while the physicians are on-call. The analyst gathers data regarding the Current Procedural Terminology (CPT)[6] codes and the payment for each as provided for under the guideline on-call contracts. If sufficient numbers of these contracts can be located with enough detail, the analyst determines that for a particular service, the median FFS compensation

---

6   American Medical Association, Chicago.

paid to physicians is 105% of the applicable Medicare Physician Fee Schedule (MPFS). After scoring the arrangement for factors the analyst believes accounts for the nuances of the subject arrangement, the analyst can build a level of expectation as to the percentage (or range of percentages) of MPFS that are reasonable for that service. This same analysis can then be applied to each service identified.

4.2 Using the Cost-Based Approach

Cost-Based Approach: Fully Loaded Physician Compensation Method

An analysis of physician compensation for FFS payment methods may employ a build-up of physician compensation, benefits, and applicable overhead associated with the furnishing of the service to ED patients. This analysis involves identifying the service to be furnished and determining the applicable CPT code and an approximation of the physician cash compensation using market data such as compensation per work RVU. Compensation-per-work-RVU data can be gathered from surveys such as those published by MGMA and AMGA. Depending on the nature of the hospital-physician relationship, the analyst may add malpractice premium and physician benefit costs (i.e., to convert to an independent contractor rate). For office-based services, it may be necessary to include an estimate of office overhead for which the physician should be reimbursed under the FFS model. As with the cash compensation, these amounts must be converted to the same basis of measurement (i.e., per work RVU) to maintain consistency. The result is a fully loaded physician cost per service, which becomes the basis under this method for a fair market value result in the FFS model.

4.3 Using the Income-Based Approach

Income-Based Approach: Reimbursement Method

The analysis may also employ methods that estimate the hypothetical seller's reimbursement associated with the physician's service as a proxy for fair market value compensation. Using this methodology, the analyst estimates professional fee reimbursement for the service furnished to patients first seen in the ED by the on-call physician, from which the estimated cost of billing and collecting the professional fee is deducted to arrive at the net amount available to the physician from which compensation, malpractice premium costs, and benefits may be paid (i.e., an independent contractor rate). It is important that the appropriate baseline for revenues be established as dictated by the site of service (e.g., in-facility reimbursement for services performed in a facility setting). For office-based services, an estimate of office overhead must also be deducted to arrive at the net realizable value. To estimate revenue for the FFS model, the analyst identifies each service to be furnished, determines the applicable CPT code, and determines an approximation of the physician professional fee net revenue using methods of estimation that may include market data on collections per work RVU, a market-based multiple of RBRVS, or historical collections per service.

4.4 Valuation Synthesis

The analyst will have as most reasonable methods those under the income and cost approaches because these are generally more realistic in terms of application, except when on-call physicians perform only a few types of cases or procedures. Between the cost and income methodology, the latter may tend to garner greater reliance because it models reimbursement at the CPT level. An average or range involving the two methods may be considered appropriate in the judgment of the analyst.

5.0 Valuing Subsidy Payment Structures

Subsidy arrangements or collections guarantees are among the more vexing and complex methods for determining fair market value of compensation. Methodology under the income-, cost-, and market-based approaches exist for assessing the fair market value of subsidy arrangements, although, as described below, some are more effective than others as tools in the fair market value assessment process. *Below are summaries of several methods under the three broad approaches to valuing time-based arrangements.*

The economics of subsidies and collections guarantees are centered primarily on reimbursement by the contracting hospital to the physician group for foregone income resulting from uncompensated care provided by the practice due to the hospital's payer mix and charity care policies. The physician or group practice bills and collects the professional fee, and the compensation is designed to make the physician or group whole, given the low collections associated with coverage of the hospital's ED and related inpatient stays subsequent to admission from the ED or through follow-up care after the ED visit. This economic "make up" generally lends itself to cost- and income-based approaches.

5.1 Using the Market-Based Approach

Subsidy and collections guarantee payment arrangements vary widely among contracts because of the nature of the payment, the differences in reimbursement patterns, overhead structure of the contracted practice, and physician compensation and benefits, among many other variables.

Market-Based Approach: Average Subsidy Per FTE Physician Method

Some very generic market information can be found among various sources in the marketplace, including average subsidy amount per FTE physician and other metrics; however, these are seldom considered reliable enough to serve as stand-alone methods.

Such rules of thumb may be given consideration as reasonableness tests or used in conjunction with other methodology, albeit weighted according to the relative ambiguity of the market data. Although not the subject of this chapter, hospital-based physician subsidies are more often the subject of measurement in terms of average subsidy per FTE, with published data available on average subsidy per FTE physician for ER physicians, hospitalists, and anesthesiologists.

5.2 Using the Cost-Based Approach

Methods that follow the cost-based approach are particularly applicable because they represent alternative arrangements available to the contracting hospital to the subject subsidy or collections guarantee arrangement. These methods are effective in that they address the built-up costs that comprise the available substitutes, in some cases similar to a make-or-buy decision. To be considered accurate, these methods must capture all applicable costs associated with the alternate arrangement, as well as address the hypothetical revenues that the hospital would receive, if any, as a result of deploying the alternate arrangement. The appropriate criteria to be considered under such methods include the following:

- Can the revenues associated with the alternate arrangement be accurately estimated?

- Can substantially all overhead cost categories associated with the alternate arrangement be appropriately identified, and all such costs appropriately included and estimated?

- If the financial statements from which costs are derived contain one-time or unusual expenses, can normalizing adjustments be made and substantiated to reflect the economic reality of overhead associated with the arrangement?

- Because physician compensation and benefits are a significant component of any alternate arrangement, can physician compensation be measured relative to the value of the physician contribution to the alternate arrangement (i.e., physician personal productivity), and can physician benefits be reasonably estimated?

Under the cost-based approach, the analyst determines whether the criteria above can be reasonably met and to what extent sufficient, competent information is available to accurately perform the analysis. A discussion follows regarding two methods commonly applied as part of the cost-based approach to the valuation of subsidies or collections guarantees as compensation for on-call coverage.

Cost-Based Approach: Avoided Net Employment Cost Method

Determination of the value of subsidy on-call payment arrangements can be made by calculating the avoided cost to the hospital of owning a practice within which it employs a similar specialist to provide similar on-call coverage. This risks being highly speculative, in that it involves estimating the professional fee revenues, overhead, and physician compensation and benefits associated with employment, with a goal of arriving at the avoided net loss of employing a specialist to provide the required coverage. Additional costs may be incurred associated with the recruitment of a specialist into the service area to provide the hypothetical on-call coverage, the analysis of which adds increased speculation. The hypothetical net loss from operating the practice is the proxy for fair market value of the subject on-call subsidy arrangement for purposes of the valuation. Data sources for the cost-based approach begin with financial statement and production data of the physician practice, along with market research on payer reimbursement. As described above, when employing the cost-based approach to build up availability and uncompensated care rates, the analyst will often turn to published survey data similar to that under the direct and indirect published survey methodology to establish values for the physician compensation components of the methodology.

Cost-Based Approach: Avoided Net Locum Tenens Cost Method

With the use of locum tenens quotes to arrive at a proxy amount, the analyst will often rely on locums firm quotes and other information on how these firms profit from their service offerings. Additionally, gathering data for the net value associated with this method involves gathering hospital or market information regarding revenues of the subject specialty. When using a locum tenens rate as a proxy for fair market value, the analyst uses rate quotes from firms and adjusts them to convert to the period covered by the subject arrangement. Such adjustments include the removal of agency profit from the stated rate.

5.3 Using the Income-Based Approach

Income-Based Approach: Seller-Based Method

One method of assessing the value of the subject arrangement using the income-based approach accounts for the economics of the physician practice from the "seller's" point of reference. When applying this methodology, the analyst gathers financial statement data of the contracted practice and studies reimbursement experienced by the practice based on payer mix for services associated with ED visits. Given the level of services performed, frequency of service, intensity, reimbursement, and other factors, the analyst models normalized physician on-call compensation and makes appropriate adjustments, if any. The analyst then applies normalizing adjustments to the costs a hypothetical seller of the service would incur in generating fee revenue from ED services, inpatient services, and follow-up outpatient care. The result is an amount representing net deficit of available income to the seller of the service, representing the net financial statement impact associated with uncompensated care, or a hypothetical "all-in" number, which includes physician benefits and malpractice premiums the independent physician will bear from the uncompensated care payment.

5.4 Valuation Synthesis

To produce a defensible conclusion of value for subsidy or income guarantee arrangements, the analyst will consider results of methods deemed most reliable for indicating fair market value and exclude results deemed less reliable. Whether more or less reliable, methods can nevertheless serve as reasonableness tests on the results of the other methods. It is expected that the conclusions drawn from methods under the cost- and income-based approaches will not be in exact agreement; however, objectivity and informed judgment will determine the level of significance placed on each method. As with other methods described in the preceding sections of this chapter, the result may be stated in a point value or a range representing the upper and lower ends of the fair market value conclusion.

Summary of Payment Models and Selected Valuation Approaches and Methods			
	Market-Based Approach	**Cost-Based Approach**	**Income-Based Approach**
Hourly, daily, weekly, monthly, annual, or shift rates	- Direct and indirect use of published survey data method - Adjusted clinical survey method - Ad hoc surveying methods - Proprietary or comparable arrangement database methods - Methods that consider other documented offers	- Build-up method - Avoided net employment cost method	- Buyer-based method - Seller-based method
Activation payments	- Adjusted clinical survey method	- Avoided net locum tenens cost method	- Seller-based method
Fee-for-service method	- Guideline contract method	- Fully loaded physician compensation method	- Reimbursement method
Subsidy or collection guarantees	- Average subsidy per FTE physician method	- Avoided net employment cost method - Avoided net locum tenens cost method	- Seller-based method

6.0 Valuing Deferred Compensation Structures

The deferred payment arrangement is not, in and of itself, a distinct payment arrangement with a unique economic footprint. Instead, it is simply the deferral of compensation earned by the on-call physician using methods such as those described above to accrue the balance owed to the physician for furnishing the on-call service. The actual payment of the balance earned by the physician is conditioned on the passage of time or the achievement of a milestone such as previously described. Hence, fair market value methodology applicable to the accrual of earned on-call pay follows the theories described in this chapter.

7.0 Summary

For ease of comparison across various payment techniques and valuation approaches and methods, the table provides a concise summary of the information presented above, both for ease of reference and for purposes of comparing and contrasting methods across payment models.

Chapter 29. Valuing Physician Medical Directorships for Hospitals and Other Healthcare Facilities

CONTENTS

Chapter 29. Valuing Physician Medical Directorships for Hospitals and Other Healthcare Facilities

By Andrea M. Ferrari, JD, MPH, and Timothy Smith, CPA/ABV

1.0 Introduction

A wide variety of healthcare providers, including hospitals, long-term care facilities, and pharmaceutical and device manufacturers, routinely engage physicians to provide administrative services. These arrangements are most commonly termed "medical directorships," although other descriptions, such as "thought leader arrangement," are common as well. Although medical directorships have been a staple of the healthcare industry for many years, regulatory activity over the last several years has increased the attention being given to these types of arrangements.

This chapter discusses the various—and sometimes complex—issues that should be considered when valuing medical directorships in the current regulatory environment. It covers topics in the following order:

1. Identifying and analyzing the scope of services covered by a medical directorship arrangement.

2. Legal and regulatory issues to consider when determining compensation for medical directorships. Selecting and applying the appropriate valuation methodology to determine the fair market value (FMV) of medical director services.

3. Arriving at an FMV range based on consideration of all relevant facts and circumstances.

2.0 Understanding the Types of Services Provided by a Physician Medical Director

The type, level, and extent of services provided are key factors for establishing a defensible opinion of value for a service contract. Another key factor is the qualifications that are required to perform the services. The starting point for valuing medical directorship services is, therefore, cataloging and analyzing both the scope of services and the qualifications necessary for providing such services.

Many types of arrangements fall into the category of medical directorships. These arrangements do not always come with a label that clearly identifies the arrangement as a medical directorship. A medical directorship arrangement may be inked on a generic form agreement that is titled "Professional Services Agreement" or may be a component of a complex management services arrangement, employment arrangement, or other service arrangement. Likewise, arrangements that are labeled "Medical Director" or "Medical Directorship" do not always fit an easily definable mold. The duties that are required under these arrangements vary widely and are increasingly a mix of administrative, and sometimes clinical, duties that may require various special qualifications.

Given that medical directorship arrangements are diverse, comparison of medical directorship arrangements for purposes of either identification or valuation is not an easy task. That being said, most medical directorship arrangements share at least a few common characteristics. To identify and appropriately appraise a medical directorship arrangement, a valuator should understand the typical as well as distinguishing characteristics of the subject arrangement.

2.1 Medical Directorships Frequently Involve Specialized Physician Services

In basic terms, a medical directorship is an arrangement by which a physician is engaged to provide leadership, oversight, and/or planning services for a clinical program or department. Generally, medical directorship services consist of duties that are most appropriately performed by a physician and often, by a physician of a particular specialty. Many medical director duties require the professional training, experience, and peer-to-peer communication skills that only a physician (or in some cases, a physician of a particular specialty) is likely to possess. Examples of common medical directorship duties are:

- Developing, leading, and managing quality and efficiency initiatives for a particular clinical unit, department, or program, including developing clinical quality assessment and improvement programs; providing direct oversight of the care that is provided to patients by the clinical practitioners in the department or program; and selecting, procuring, and directly providing clinical education for practitioners in the department or program.

- Identifying clinical equipment needs and selecting appropriate equipment to purchase to meet those needs and to ensure that the department or program is able to maximize the quality, efficiency, and safety of care.

- Communicating and securing buy-in for operational initiatives from clinical staff that are reluctant to take directives from nonphysician managers.

The training, knowledge, and peer-to-peer communication capability of a physician are assets—if not requirements—in effectively performing these types of tasks. As such, general training as a physician is a requisite qualification for almost all medical directorships.

Training and experience in a particular medical or surgical specialty or subspecialty is an additional qualification for some types of medical directorships. For example, an internal medicine physician who does not regularly perform or participate in cardiac surgeries would not reasonably be expected to develop clinical quality assessment and improvement programs, to anticipate the equipment and staffing needs, or to secure clinical practitioner buy-in for operational initiatives in a cardiovascular surgery program. In short, there are a number of reasons why training and advanced practice experience in a specific medical or surgical specialty or subspecialty may be required to perform the duties of a specific medical director position. A valuator should be tuned in to these when assigning value to a particular set of duties.

2.2 Understanding the Duties to Be Performed by the Medical Director

A valuator should carefully assess the nature of medical directorship duties when assigning value to those duties, including asking the fundamental questions of Who? What? When? Where? and How? Although the details of a specific arrangement may warrant that specific, pointed questions be asked by the valuator, questions may generally be similar to those posed here:

- Who will perform the duties required by the arrangement?

  › Do the duties require the expertise of a physician?

  › Do the duties require the expertise of a physician of a particular specialty (e.g., pediatrics, cardiology, neurology, or surgery)?

- ○ Do the duties require the expertise of a physician of a particular subspecialty (e.g., pediatric cardiology, stroke, or sports medicine)?

- ○ Do the duties require the expertise of a physician with highly specialized training, experience, or expertise (e.g., joint replacement, fetal surgery, or neuroradiology)?

- What are the specific duties to be performed under the arrangement?

    - ○ Is the physician providing oversight of a department or program?

    - ○ Is the physician developing or administering quality assessment or improvement programs for a particular department or program?

    - ○ Is the physician assessing need for, selecting, developing, and personally delivering education programs for staff in a department or program?

    - ○ Is the physician selecting, purchasing, testing, or developing protocols for the use of new equipment or supplies in a department or program?

    - ○ Is the physician performing other duties related to leadership, oversight, or planning of specific services, departments, facilities or clinical units?

- When are the duties to be performed?

    - ○ What is the term of the agreement under which the duties are to be performed?

    - ○ What is the specific schedule or time interval over which the duties are to be performed (e.g., a fixed or maximum number of hours per month, year, or week)?

    - ○ Can the duties be performed during regular work hours (i.e., Monday through Friday during regular business hours)?

    - ○ Does the physician have a greater or lesser burden as a result of the schedule (or lack thereof) for performing the duties?

- Where will the duties be performed?

> What is the geographic region where the services and related duties will be performed?

> In which facility or service location will the physician perform the duties?

> What is the specific service center or unit within a facility where the physician will perform the duties?

- How will the physician be compensated for performing the duties?

  > Will payment be hourly, based on hours worked and documented?

  > Will payment be a fixed fee or salary?

  > If compensation is with a fixed fee or salary payment, the valuator should discern whether the payment is based on one of the following:

    - The estimated time (hours) required to perform the duties.

    - The completion of discrete tasks or work products that have a measurable and discernible value.

    - Other measurable and discernible measures of value.

Detailed answers to the questions of Who? What? When? Where? and How? assist the valuator to identify the scope and level of contemplated medical director services. The valuator may use this information to determine the value of these services with greater accuracy and precision.

2.3 Medical Director Compensation: Hourly Rate or Fixed Fee Arrangements

Medical director services are often provided through independent contractor agreements that provide for hourly compensation based on time worked and documented. However, some medical directorships are components of other agreements, such as employment agreements, management arrangements, or other agreements under which compensation is fixed and paid at regular intervals (e.g., weekly, monthly, or yearly). When a physician is compensated for medical director duties with a fixed fee, the appraiser must carefully consider: 1) the nature of the administrative duties that the physician performs, 2) the range of reasonable hourly compensation for performing such duties, and 3) the hours that are reasonably required and likely to be spent actually performing such duties. A more detailed discussion of valuation considerations for fixed fee arrangements is provided later in this chapter.

3.0 Regulatory Issues to Consider When Valuing Medical Directorships

An understanding of the regulatory environment that is the backdrop for most requests for medical directorship valuations is important before undertaking one. Generally, when healthcare providers request the valuation of medical directorship agreements, at least one purpose in doing so (and, typically, an important purpose) is to establish FMV for the services being provided and thereby, ensure that the arrangement will not implicate Medicare fraud and abuse laws, such as the Stark and anti-kickback statutes. The definition of "fair market value" as it relates to the Stark and anti-kickback statutes is somewhat different from the definition that most valuators know. Therefore, it is generally advisable that valuators have some understanding of the regulatory issues that are implicated by a medical directorship.

The laws and regulations that may have bearing on a medical directorship are complex and may differ from one arrangement to another. As such, valuators are advised to consult with the client or the client's legal counsel to ensure an appropriate understanding of the applicable legal and regulatory issues prior to undertaking the valuation of medical director services. Regulatory guidance given by a client or client's counsel should not interfere with the appraiser's independent judgment but rather should be a helpful aid for determining the scope of work for the appraisal assignment by, for example, identifying the appropriate definition of value for the appraiser. We generally think that it is good practice for valuators to disclose and discuss the regulatory considerations that influenced the appraisal somewhere in the report, usually in the context of discussing the scope of work for the assignment.

There are two major categories of laws and regulations that may be implicated by medical directorships:

- The federal anti-kickback statute and its related regulations and advisory opinions (AKS).

- The Stark law and its related regulations and government guidance (Stark).

A third category of laws and regulations may be implicated when an entity has not-for-profit status. This category includes provisions of the Internal Revenue Code that prohibit private inurement in transactions with tax-exempt entities (tax regulations). Since the implications of tax regulations for tax-exempt entities is often similar to and superseded by concerns related to Stark and AKS, we are not providing a detailed discussion of the tax regulations in this chapter.

3.1 The Anti-Kickback Statute

AKS prohibits individuals from knowingly and willfully offering, paying, soliciting, or receiving any remuneration, in cash or in kind, to induce referrals of items or services that are covered by a federally funded healthcare program, such as Medicare or Medicaid. The courts have interpreted AKS to prohibit any arrangement for which it is established that even *one* purpose is to induce referrals of healthcare items or services.[1] Medical directorship arrangements may implicate AKS if the physician is in a position to order or recommend goods or services that are offered by the party engaging the physician, the goods or services are covered by a federally funded healthcare program, and the compensation paid to the physician under the arrangement exceeds the FMV of the services that are provided by the physician or of the services that are legitimately needed to accomplish the purposes of the arrangement (other than generation of referrals). The Office of the Inspector General of the United States Department of Health and Human Services (OIG), which is the entity that is responsible for monitoring enforcement of AKS, has created certain "safe harbors" for activities that pose a low risk for abuse and overuse of federal healthcare funds. To fit within a safe harbor, an arrangement must meet all the requirements that have been set forth by OIG. The safe harbor that is potentially applicable to most medical directorship arrangements is the one for personal services and management contracts, which has the following requirements:

- The arrangement is set out in writing and is for a term of at least one year.

- The agreement covers all of the services to be provided during the term of the agreement.

- The agreement specifies the services to be rendered and if services are to be provided on a periodic, sporadic, or part-time basis, the agreement specifies the schedule of intervals, their precise length, and the exact charge for such intervals.

- The aggregate compensation that is to be paid over the term of the agreement is set in advance, consistent with FMV in arm's-length transactions, and not determined in a manner that takes into account the volume or value of any referrals or business otherwise generated between the parties that is covered by Medicare or a state healthcare program.

- The services performed under the agreement do not involve the promotion or counseling of an activity or business arrangement that violates any state or federal law.

---

1 *United States v. Kats*, 871 F.2d 105 (9th Cir. 1989); *United States v. Greber*, 760 F.2d 68 (3d Cir.), cert. denied, 474 U.S. 988 (1985).

- The aggregate services do not exceed those that are reasonably necessary to accomplish the commercially reasonable business purpose of the agreement.

- Most requests for valuation of medical directorship services are, at least in part, to allow the parties to establish compliance with requirements for the safe harbor for personal services and management contracts.

3.2 The Stark Law and Regulations

As discussed in Chapter 6, "The Federal Statutes that Make Healthcare Valuation Unique,", Stark prohibits a physician's referral to an entity for a designated health service (DHS) when the physician or a member of the physician's immediate family has a financial relationship with the entity (such as a compensation arrangement), *unless* the arrangement meets one of several enumerated exceptions.

The Stark exceptions include an exception for personal services arrangements, which may be applicable to medical directorship arrangements if the following requirements are met:

- The arrangement is set out in writing, is signed by the parties, and specifies the services covered by the arrangement.

- The arrangement covers all of the services to be furnished by the physician under the arrangement.

- The aggregate services do not exceed those that are reasonable and necessary for the legitimate business purposes of the arrangement.

- The term of the arrangement is for at least one year.

- The compensation to be paid under the arrangement is set in advance, does not exceed FMV, and is not determined in a manner that takes into account the volume or value of any referrals or other business generated between the parties.

- The services to be furnished under the arrangement do not involve the counseling or promotion of a business arrangement or other activity that violates AKS or any state or federal law.

The reader will note that the criteria for the Stark exception for personal services arrangements and the AKS safe harbor for personal services and management contracts are similar. In particular, both the Stark exception and the AKS safe harbor require that compensation does not exceed FMV, and is not determined in a manner that takes into consideration that volume or value of any referrals or other business generated between the parties.

Over the years and through various phases of the Stark regulations, the government has provided a fair amount of guidance and commentary regarding the meaning of FMV for purposes of complying with Stark, including explicitly noting that its definition for purposes of meeting a Stark exception may differ from the one commonly understood by appraisers.[2] One critical difference arises from Stark regulatory text that states that FMV compensation is compensation that is consistent with the compensation that would result from bargaining between parties who are not otherwise in a position to generate business for each other. This difference warrants attention by valuators because it may necessitate limits on the use of a market approach when valuing medical directorship arrangements. An opinion of value for medical directorship compensation should not be based in whole or substantial part on market comparable transactions unless it is clearly known that the market-comparable transactions are not between providers of DHS and referral-source physicians. Valuators should also consider the possibility that a high prevalence of medical directorship arrangements between entities that are in a position to refer or otherwise generate business for each other may "taint" nearly all medical director survey data, thereby undermining the market approach as a valid valuation methodology for medical directorships. For a complete discussion of this issue, see Chapter 8, "To Use of Not to Use: An Appraisal Analysis of the Stark Prohibition on Market Data from Parties in a Position to Refer."

In Stark regulations issued in September 2007 (the "Stark Phase III regulations") the government distinguished between clinical and administrative work by physicians and stated:

> A fair market value hourly rate may be used to compensate physicians for both administrative and clinical work, provided that the rate paid for clinical work is fair market value for the clinical work performed and the rate paid for administrative work is fair market value for the administrative work performed. We note that the fair market value of administrative services may differ from the fair market value of clinical services.[3]

Given this guidance, an appraiser who is engaged to provide an opinion of value for medical directorship services should probably take care to distinguish between clinical and administrative duties when assigning value to the services to that the physician will provide in the arrangement. Although most medical directorships consist wholly

---

2   CMS has stated: "... the definition of "fair market value" in the [Stark] statute ... is qualified in ways that do not necessarily comport with the usage of the term in standard valuation techniques and methodologies. For example, the methodology must exclude valuations where the parties to the transactions are at arm's length but in a position to refer to one another." 69 F.R. 16107 (March 24, 2004).

3   72 F.R. 51016.

---

of administrative services, we are increasingly seeing arrangements that are labeled "medical director" arrangements but consist of a mix of clinical and administrative duties. Often, the proposed compensation in these hybrid arrangements is somewhat higher than in traditional (wholly administrative) medical director arrangements. Such compensation may be appropriate based on proper consideration of the existence and proportion of clinical duties in the services to be performed and the fact that market rates for clinical services compensation often range higher than market rates for administrative services compensation.[4]

3.3 Commercial Reasonableness

We also note that, for arrangements that are intended to fit the Stark exception for personal services arrangements and/or the AKS safe harbor for personal services and management contracts, the requirement that the aggregate services do not exceed those necessary for the "commercially reasonable" purposes of the arrangement may have implications for an appraisal of the FMV of such services. Although not specifically defined anywhere in Stark or AKS, government commentary suggests that, in the context of a medical directorship, the term "commercially reasonable" describes an arrangement that would make commercial sense if entered into by a reasonable entity of similar type and size to the engaging party and a reasonable physician of similar scope and specialty to the engaged physician, even if there were no potential business referrals between such parties.[5] Generally, an entity will not, in the absence of a potential referral relationship, provide compensation for performance of services that are:

- Already sufficiently performed by another party (i.e., redundant services, unless there is a legitimate reason for redundancy).

- Services for which the performing physician already receives compensation from another source (i.e., for which the physician is already "made whole").

- Services that add no value to the entity's operations.

- Services that are to be performed during physician time that an entity has already "purchased" (i.e., medical director services that are performed during hours when a physician is being paid hourly to be onsite at the hospital to provide clinical care but has downtime in the clinical schedule).

---

4   Based on comparisons of hourly rates derived from the general physician compensation surveys to hourly rates in compensation surveys for administrative services.

5   This definition is based on text set forth in the preamble to the Stark II Phase II regulations at 69 *F.R.* 16093 (March 26, 2004). It is also consistent with guidance provided in the "OIG Supplemental Compliance Program Guidance for Hospitals" at 70 *F.R.* 4866 (Jan. 31, 2005).

As such, the value of certain service components should be carved out of an appraisal and the market data used to determine value should be adjusted to ensure that the appraiser's conclusion of value excludes any services that may be in excess of those that are reasonably needed to achieve the commercially reasonable business purposes of the arrangement.

4.0 The Market Approach

Use of the market approach in valuing medical directorship arrangements necessitates that the appraiser identify and understand the scope of services provided in both the subject arrangement and the market comparables. Without such information, the appraiser may incorrectly treat as comparable certain service arrangements that are materially different as to the services provided and the qualifications required to perform them. As a result, the appraiser may arrive at a conclusion of value that is based on a materially dissimilar mix of services or qualifications. In addition, the specific facts and circumstances of the service arrangement, such as the geographic locality and other characteristics of the local market in which the services are being provided, should be carefully analyzed and factored into the valuation, to whatever extent that such information is available. The specific facts and circumstances of an arrangement are crucial considerations when identifying appropriate market comparables, and identifying appropriate market comparables is a key step in valuing the services using a market approach.

4.1 Applying the Market Approach

When utilizing the market approach to value medical director services, the appraiser performs market research to accumulate information on medical director arrangements, including the scope of services provided, the required qualifications of the physician director, and the level of compensation paid. There are multiple sources of data relating to physician compensation in the marketplace. These include the general physician compensation surveys described below. Few sources of published survey data are specific to physician compensation for specialized services such as medical directorships.[6] One potential source of market data for medical directorship compensation is the *Medical Director Survey*, which is published annually by Integrated Healthcare Strategies. The *Medical Director Survey* reports data for a comprehensive list of specialty

---

6   We have elected to treat medical director compensation surveys under the rubric of the market approach and the more general physician compensation surveys (e.g., MGMA, AMGA, SCA, and so on) under the cost approach. Some appraisers conversely place use of the general compensation surveys under the market approach and directorship surveys under the cost approach. Either categorization system has merit and validity. Regardless of how one categorizes the use of the surveys under an approach to value, the analytic and regulatory difficulties discussed in this section apply to the use of such surveys.

medical directorships. It sorts the universe of medical directorships into a large number of specialty categories and reports compensation levels by hospital size. Other medical director surveys, such as one published by MGMA, may also be available to a valuator.

4.2 Key Issues and Limitations of the Market Approach

Valuators should be aware of several issues and limitations that may be encountered in using medical director compensation surveys or other medical director data. These sources generally do not present compensation survey results in ways that allow identification of the specific duties or services that are related to the compensation. As a result, comparisons between the subject medical directorship and those referenced in the published data may be difficult. In addition, labels and descriptors that are assigned to the categories of medical directorships for which data are reported in surveys often lack precision and uniform definition. Therefore, a valuator should use caution in making comparisons based solely on such labels and descriptors.

Since the essence of the market approach is using comparable transactions from the marketplace to establish the value of the subject arrangement, sole or unqualified use of medical director surveys or other published data to establish the FMV of medical director services is problematic. Differences in details distinguish medical directorships, even though agreements may appear to be similar on the surface. Significant differences in the who, what, when, where and how of the medical director's duties may have a material impact on the comparability of services and an appropriate outcome for the valuation analysis. The valuation of medical directorships is not a "one size fits all" analysis. Unless sufficient appropriate information is available for the appraiser to determine comparability, survey results reported in a general or summary manner may not be adequate for establishing the value of medical director services. As stated previously, FMV is ultimately a function of the specific facts and circumstances of the arrangement being analyzed.

As also noted previously in this chapter, much of the available market data concerning medical directorships comes from physicians and healthcare providers who have referral relationships that may implicate Stark or AKS. Hence, the available market data may be tainted by the potential for referrals between the parties and as such, may not be an appropriate benchmark data for determining FMV, even when comparability among arrangements is established. Simply put, some market data points may not represent arm's-length transactions.

Compensation paid in medical directorship arrangements that are *not* between parties in a position to make or receive referrals or other business for each other are less likely to be tainted. Accordingly, to the extent available, data concerning compensation paid by (as an example) an automotive manufacturing company to a physician who oversees the company's cardiovascular health program for its employees may be a reliable supporting benchmark for valuation of a hospital-based cardiovascular health medical directorship, assuming that the duties of the medical director in the company and hospital-based programs are comparable.

When utilizing the market approach, comparability issues may arise when service contracts for medical director duties are included in larger service arrangements between the parties. Increasingly, we observe situations in which a candidate for a medical directorship is party to other existing or contemplated compensated service agreements with the contracting healthcare entity. The existing or contemplated arrangements may include other services in addition to medical director services. When this situation occurs, the appraiser must be attuned to possible overlapping duties in the various arrangements to which the physician and healthcare entity are parties. If appropriate, the appraiser should demonstrate that the physician is not compensated for the same duties through the various arrangements, since multiple payments for a single set of duties may result in compensation that is in excess of FMV for the overall bundle of services.

5.0 The Cost Approach

The cost approach as applied to service contracts values the compensation for the subject arrangement by looking at the value of alternatives for those services in the marketplace. As applied to medical directorship arrangements, the cost approach arrives at an opinion of value based on consideration of the engaging entity's costs to secure similar benefits by an alternative means to the medical directorship arrangement. For example, the cost approach may entail consideration of the cost of employing one or more physicians to perform the duties that are otherwise to be performed under the medical directorship agreement. As a practical matter, a valuator should consider that most medical directorships are structured as independent-contractor arrangements because the duties of the medical director require variable and often limited hours. As such, securing medical director services through an employment arrangement is generally less practical than through an independent contractor arrangement.

5.1 Applying the Cost Approach

The valuator may look to physician compensation levels in the marketplace to establish the alternative cost to procuring the physician services provided in medical directorship arrangements. There are several reliable and readily available sources of survey data for physician compensation in the marketplace. These sources include:

1. American Medical Group Association, *Medical Group Compensation and Financial Survey.*

2. Hospital & Healthcare Compensation Service, *Physician Salary Survey Report* and *Hospital Salary & Benefits Report.*

3. Medical Group Management Association, *Physician Compensation and Production Survey.*

4. Sullivan, Cotter and Associates Inc., *Physician Compensation and Productivity Survey Report.*

5. Towers Watson Data Services, *Health Care Clinical and Professional Compensation Survey Report—U.S.*

It is important that appraisers understand how these various physician compensation surveys gather and report financial information. Such knowledge is needed for the valid use of the survey data to determine physician compensation rates. An appraiser will need to address four critical issues when using the survey data to establish the FMV of physician compensation as it may apply to medical directorship duties. These issues include:

1. The distinction between clinical services and administrative services and any corresponding differentiation in compensation levels for clinical versus administrative work.

2. The distinction between compensation for physician services and business owner compensation.

3. The value of annual hours worked (for purposes of computing an hourly rate for physician services).

4. Adjustments of employment compensation to achieve hourly rates that are applicable to independent contractor services.

The appraiser's analysis and resolution of these critical issues will have a material effect on the valuation opinion.

5.2 Compensation for Clinical Versus Administrative Services

As noted previously in this chapter, the government has indicated that it recognizes a distinction in FMV compensation for a physician's clinical and administrative services. Given that most valuations of medical directorship arrangements are, at least in part, to assist in compliance with government regulations, a valuator should be mindful of the distinction between clinical and administrative duties when assigning value to the duties to be performed in a particular medical directorship arrangement. The salient point is that, generally, the value of clinical work is somewhat greater than the value of administrative work because, generally, clinical work involves a higher degree of complexity and risk than administrative work. Indeed, clinical work may involve responsibility for the immediate health and well-being of patients and in some specialties and cases, the literal difference between life and death. Although administrative duties may require a skill set that is unique to physicians of a particular specialty, these functions and duties do not generally entail the same level of complexity or risk as clinical services. Since medical directorships have historically entailed primarily *administrative* duties, FMV for medical director duties is, on an hourly basis, generally less than the hourly rate that comparably qualified physicians would receive for their clinical services. We note, however, that recent trends suggest a move toward more hybrid arrangements (i.e., arrangements that require a mix of clinical and administrative duties by the physician). These hybrid arrangements may be presented to the valuator with the label of a medical directorship, but with proposed compensation that is higher than may have been paid under similarly termed arrangements in the past. As such, valuators should carefully assess the duties that are required by new medical directorship agreements to determine and appropriately factor into the valuation the existence and relative proportion of clinical versus administrative functions.

Some argue that there should not be a difference in compensation between administrative and clinical work because there is an "opportunity cost" to a physician's time. Opportunity cost proponents argue against the government's purported position that administrative services have a different value than clinical work. They contend that physicians may not agree to provide services for an outside entity for lower hourly compensation than they would expect to receive performing services in their own office. Moreover, the compensation received for clinical services is the best indicator of the value of a physician's time. Regardless of the merits of these arguments, valuation opinions that are prepared for healthcare regulatory compliance purposes should address the distinction between clinical and administrative services and provide support and defense for the value indications that were ultimately selected by the valuator.

We note that physician compensation surveys generally report compensation from all sources. The primary source of income for a physician who is not in an academic setting or a purely administrative role is clinical services. As a result, the compensation values that are reported in most published surveys are most representative of clinical compensation. If a valuator takes the position that administrative services should be compensated at a lower rate than clinical services, he or she should consider whether survey compensation data should be adjusted to account for the administrative nature of the medical directorship duties and whether lower percentiles are the appropriate reference points from the survey data.

5.3 Compensation for Physician Services Versus Other Forms of Compensation

Publishers of physician compensation surveys gather and publish data from a variety of physicians who practice in a variety of settings. The surveys report compensation information in varying levels of detail. However, the key compensation measures generally reflect total compensation received by the physician from all sources, including compensation that may not relate to services provided directly or personally by the physician. Income received from ancillary services, employment of physician extenders, leasing of space or equipment, or sharing in group practice earnings may be included in the reported compensation values. In other words, business owner compensation may skew the values reported by the surveys, as may other forms of nonclinical income, such as on-call pay stipends, medical directorship payments, and expert testimony fees.

The valuator should consider whether compensation survey data should be selected or adjusted to weed out the effect of compensation not related to directly performed physician services. Although there are obvious practical difficulties in doing this, a reasoned attempt is preferable to using data from the surveys in an uncritical, unqualified manner, which may lead to an overstatement of the value of physician time.

5.4 The Annual Hours for Use in Computing Hourly Physician Compensation Rates

When using published survey data that relate to annual physician compensation, a valuator must frequently translate the annual values to hourly amounts. This requires selection of an appropriate denominator for division of the annual values. As a matter of convention, many valuators select 2,000 or 2,080 hours as an approximation of annual physician work hours. Unfortunately, however, there is little publicly available survey data on physician work hours. The valuator's assumption of "standard" annual hours may have the greatest valuation impact with respect to physicians' earning compensation at the highest percentiles, as physicians earning compensation that is consistent with the highest compensation levels may be working high numbers of annual hours.

5.5 Adjustment of Hourly Physician Compensation to an Independent-Contractor Basis

Because most medical directors serve as independent contractors to healthcare facilities, many appraisers argue that the hourly rates derived from physician compensation surveys should be adjusted to account for the value of benefits. The theory supporting this adjustment is that independent contractors across all industries are generally paid at higher rates than employees to account for the fact that independent contractors incur costs that employees do not, such as payment of health and liability insurance premiums.

6.0 The Income Approach

Given the regulatory context for most valuations of medical directorship arrangements, use of the income approach may be limited or impracticable. An appraiser might attempt the approach by borrowing the with-and-without competition technique commonly used in business valuation to arrive at the value of a covenant not to compete. Under such a method, the appraiser would attempt to place a value on medical director services by showing the decrement in net cash flow to the healthcare entity by not contracting with a medical director. Isolating the specific amount of future benefits attributable to contracting with a medical director, however, is a difficult task. In addition, the appraiser would need to prepare projections of revenues and expenses related to the entity or service line in question. The cost of preparing such a pro forma statement appears to outweigh its benefit. Applying the income approach to the other party to the arrangement, i.e., the physician, would require the appraiser to assess the future benefits to the physician in terms of market rates of compensation for physician services. This evaluation returns the appraiser to the analyses of the market and cost approaches. In general, the income approach appears to be the least relevant and applicable of the three approaches available for valuing medical director services.

7.0 Formulation of the Opinion of Value

After completing the applicable approaches to value, the valuator engages in an evaluation and reconciliation process to determine the FMV of the subject arrangement for medical director services. This process is ultimately based on the independent and professional judgment of the valuator. Greater or lesser weight may be assigned to the results of any particular valuation method or technique based on a variety of considerations, such as the reliability of data, extent of comparability, scope of information, regulatory guidance, and facts and circumstances unique to the subject arrangement. The opinion of value may be stated as a specific dollar amount or a range. Whatever the conclusion of value, the appraiser should be prepared to support and defend the conclusion based on the relevant information and sound valuation methodology.

8.0 Evaluating the Method of Compensation: Hourly Versus Fixed Fee Arrangements

Medical directorships may be independent contractor arrangements or employment relationships. In either case, the method of compensation for medical director services is most often hourly and paid in accordance with the number of hours actually worked and recorded by the physician. The alternative compensation structure is a fixed fee paid in weekly, monthly, or other time intervals, or upon the achievement of certain milestones or the completion of certain tasks.

Regardless of whether an arrangement provides for hourly or fixed fee payments, all payments should be based on a FMV hourly rate. Accordingly, to evaluate fixed fee payments, the valuator should determine the hours reasonably required to perform the required services and calculate an effective hourly rate. Unfortunately, there is rarely appropriate benchmark data to allow estimation of the time requirements for specific medical directorship duties; thus, the valuator must rely upon his or her best judgment, the client's representations, or the requirements specified in the arrangement.

To appraise and validate the FMV of an arrangement involving a fixed fee payment for medical director services, a valuator should be able to compare the compensation derived from the arrangement to benchmark data from the marketplace. To permit such comparisons, values must be in comparable units (i.e., they must have the same denominator). If all compensation values are reduced to and expressed in terms of dollars *per hour*, the valuator can readily make comparisons to benchmark data as required to validate an appraisal using market data.

When asked to value a medical director arrangement that provides for fixed fee payments, the valuator may tie the fixed fee payment to an hourly rate using the following four-step process:

1. As specifically as possible, identify the duties that the medical director is required to perform.

2. Determine (from benchmark data) reasonable hourly compensation for performing such duties.

3. Determine the hours that are reasonably necessary to perform the duties, based on any available benchmark data, client representations, or the valuator's independent judgment, or determine the hours that are specifically required by the contract.

4. Multiply the reasonable hourly compensation for performing the duties by the hours that are reasonably necessary or that will actually be required to perform the duties.

After applying this four-step process, the fixed fee should reflect reasonable hourly compensation for the duties, based on a reasonable estimate of the time to be spent performing the duties.

9.0 Conclusion

Valuing medical directorship arrangements requires careful consideration and analysis of the applicable facts and circumstances, including the nature of the services and the qualifications necessary to perform them, the available market data to perform valuation analysis using one of the three accepted valuation approaches, the regulatory context for the valuation request, and the applicable definition and considerations for determining FMV and any unique aspects of the arrangement that warrant adjustment of the valuation approach or reference data. The valuator should take care to validate the conclusion of value by comparing it to marketplace benchmarks and ensuring that the conclusion of value seems reasonable and defensible in light of general marketplace practices.

Chapter 30. Valuing Physician-Hospital Service Line and Clinical Co-Management Arrangements

CONTENTS

Chapter 30. Valuing Physician-Hospital Service Line and Clinical Co-Management Arrangements

By Gregory D. Anderson, CPA/ABV, CVA, and Scott Safriet, MBA, AVA

1.0 Origin of the Co-Management Arrangement

Even before health care reform took center stage, most healthcare organizations found themselves caught in an era of increasing competition, changing reimbursement structures, and shifting operational paradigms. Benchmarks and key clinical performance indicators have taken on even greater importance as carrot-and-stick reforms in government reimbursement now join existing pay-for-performance initiatives in the private payer community. Technological advances allowing less invasive interventions and improved outcomes offer the promise of revolutionizing the way medicine is practiced. These market forces demand a shift in the healthcare industry toward collaborative care and aligned incentives, yet collaborative relationships among healthcare providers trigger compliance and business strategies that have not yet been fully played out in the marketplace and the healthcare regulatory environment. These market forces and compliance risks lead physicians and hospitals to create relationships that concentrate on patient outcomes, safety, and satisfaction, while yielding incentives that reward positive behavioral changes by both parties.

1.1 Increasing Competition

"Hospitals and physicians care for the same patients. Both feel squeezed by stagnating payment, rising expenses, proliferating regulations, and rising consumer expectations."[1] Hospitals also face pressures from consumers for the latest technology, shortages of hospital personnel, increased regulation, rising cost of liability premiums, and the

---

1   Cohn, "Making Hospital-Physician Collaboration Work," Healthcare Financial Management Association, October 2005

obligation for providing care to the uninsured.[2] Yet, the American Hospital Association recognizes that "the integration of clinical care across providers, across settings, and over time" is needed to reduce fragmentation in healthcare delivery and improve the quality and efficiency of care.[3]

1.2 Changing Landscape of Where Services Are Performed

Advances in technology have transformed the delivery of health care in more ways than could have been imagined just a few decades ago. Many procedures that were exclusively performed in an inpatient setting are now furnished in hospital outpatient settings, specialty hospitals, and ambulatory surgery centers, significantly altering the landscape in the industry and raising the element of competition between physicians and hospitals. These surgical and diagnostic facilities represent viable alternatives to acute care hospitals, as patient and physician convenience, cost, and comfort lure insured patients away, leaving hospitals with an ever increasing mix of indigent and low-pay patients. In increasing numbers, hospitals are entering into clinical co-management arrangements (CCMAs) with physicians who once operated competing facilities (e.g., in most instances, a hospital acquires a physician-owned entity, integrates it into the hospital infrastructure, and considers a CCMA with the physician owners). The competitive environment and reimbursement reforms led hospitals to place even more emphasis on achieving better outcomes, higher patient satisfaction scores, and more cost-effective care. Capitalizing on the physician clinical expertise is invaluable to hospitals in reaching these objectives.

1.3 Difficulty in Securing Robust Medical Directorships

Healthcare regulatory enforcement activity by the federal government continues to spotlight medical directorships as highly susceptible to abuse, with examples of arrangements alleged to be disguised payments for referrals of federal healthcare program beneficiaries. Many of these suspect arrangements lack substantiation of duties and fail to implement appropriate systems for tracking and documenting hours worked in providing these services. Further, because commercial reasonableness has received much attention in fraud and abuse enforcement of late, many hospitals and their healthcare legal counsel are rightfully scrutinizing traditional medical directorships.

1.4 Need for Increased Efficiencies and Quality in Patient Care

In response to American's costly, sometimes unsafe, and often inefficient healthcare system, momentum built for a shift to a pay-for-performance (P4P) system that correlated

---

2   "Improving Health Care: A Dose of Competition," U.S. Department of Justice and the Federal Trade Commission, July 2004

3   Am. Hosp. Ass'n., *Aligning Hospital and Physician Interests: Broadening the Concept of Gainsharing to Allow Care Improvement Incentives*, 2005

financial rewards with improved outcomes in patient care. The Centers for Medicare and Medicaid Services (CMS) and many commercial payers implemented pay-for-performance programs that promoted quality patient care through financial rewards. These pay-for-performance programs each include the following elements:

- A set of targets or objectives that define what will be evaluated;

- Measures and performance standards for establishing the target criteria; and

- At-risk financial rewards and a method for allocating payments among individuals who meet or exceed the target criteria.[4]

Furthermore, the core measures of pay-for-performance programs were often quite similar in that they were driven by evidence-based medicine and intended to increase the quality of care and reduce costs by reducing readmissions and limiting medical errors.[5] However, pay-for-performance programs often varied in their development, design, and financial rewards. By the beginning of 2008, 160 pay-for-performance programs had been implemented in the United States,[6] and in March 2010, the United States passed the Patient Protection and Affordable Care Act (PPACA), establishing several healthcare delivery system reforms intended to increase quality and patient satisfaction, and reduce costs. Reform provisions focused on reducing hospital-acquired infections and preventable 30-day readmissions, as well as implementing hospital value-based purchasing and bundled payments, and established accountable care organizations (ACOs).[7] However, although the final rule on ACOs was released in November 2011, the full impact of ACOs on the delivery of health care is yet to be determined because many have not embraced this as the primary vehicle through which integrated care will be delivered in the future. What the ACO rules have shown the industry is that other viable means of delivering collaborative care, such as medical home models or vertically integrated care models, may thrive as long as physicians and hospitals work together toward the common triple-aim of quality gains, cost savings, and better outcomes.

---

4   Congressional Research Service, *Pay-for-Performance in Health Care.*
5   Rosenthal, M., Fernandopulle, R., Song, H., & Landon, B. (2004, March/April). "Paying For Quality: Providers' Incentives for Quality Improvement". *Health Affairs*, pp. 127-141.
6   Francois, S. de Brantes, MBA and B. Guy D'Andrea, MBA. "Physicians Respond to Pay-for-Performance Incentives: Larger Incentives Yield Greater Participation." (2009) *The American Journal of Managed Care.* Vol. 15, No. 5. Pg 305 – 310.
7   Clarke, Richard L. "Impact of Healthcare Reform: A Conversation With HFMA's Dick Clarke." Healthcare Financial Management Association. March 31, 2010.

1.5 Government and Payer Recognition of Core Measures of Quality

Common measures of quality performance allow physicians to receive feedback and tie performance to financial and other incentives through P4P and public quality reporting. Several types of systems have gained traction in the past few years, particularly with the introduction of quality-reporting initiatives by professional organizations, accrediting agencies, and the Medicare Physician Quality Reporting System (PQRS, former PQRI) that provided in 2011 a 1% physician quality reporting incentive to physician groups based on their total Medicare Part B allowed charges. These programs contribute to physicians' acknowledgement that other stakeholders have the right to monitor their behavior and hold them accountable.[8]

1.6 Opportunities for Increased Hospital-Physician Alignment

Long-standing hospital-physician integration strategies that remain in the current market include direct employment of physicians by hospitals, development of clinically integrated hospital and physician entities, formation of community health information networks, and various hybrids and permutations of provider integration strategies. Physician engagement is essential for many cultural and behavioral changes to be successful at the hospital level. Compensation under these plans is increasingly tied to success with varying measurements that align financial incentives among the provider groups.

It is within this environment of interrelated priorities that the CCMA has emerged as an increasingly popular option. In fact, the realization that hospitals and physicians need to work together to achieve desired outcomes has fueled the rapid increase in the number and structural diversity of CCMAs because they represent an effective way to integrate hospital and physician management of clinical services and generally exist between physicians and hospitals. Physicians in a CCMA provide management services to a hospital that go beyond traditional medical director roles, and the CCMA involves physicians as participants in the day-to-day management of the hospital's clinical service line operations. The primary advantage of the CCMA is the significant operational input of the physicians and the alignment of physician and hospital interests to achieve improvements in the overall efficiency and quality of patient care.

---

8   Pham and Ginsburg, *Unhealthy Trends: The Future of Physician Services*, Health Affairs 26(6):1586-1598, November/December 2007

2.0 Structure of Co-Management Arrangements

2.1 Rationale for Formation

Competition. As described above, competitive market forces are primary drivers in the creation of the CCMA. Below is a hypothetical example of a community hospital's struggle to remain competitive by aligning with physicians:

> Healthy Regional Hospital (one of two hospitals in its community) and one of the local cardiology groups reached an impasse when the cardiology group announced its intent to open a cardiac catheterization lab (cath lab) in its own clinic facility. When the cath lab became operational, Healthy Regional saw a substantial decline in commercial patients in its own cath lab, and revenues immediately began a sharp downward trend. As tensions grew, the cardiology group began demanding payment for emergency department call coverage and one of the cardiologists, the medical director for cardiology at Healthy Regional, elected not to renew his administrative contract.

> Healthy Regional's new CEO entered into discussions with the cardiology group to form a CCMA. This endeavor would be a joint venture, which would acquire and operate the cardiologists' cath lab and enter into a management agreement with Healthy Regional to manage the its entire cardiology service line (i.e., inclusive of the cath lab) in the creation of a cardiovascular center of excellence. The end result was an immediate change in the competitive landscape in the community for cardiac care and an integration of the hospital and cardiology group in the operation of the joint venture CCMA.

Alignment with payer interests and participation in payer incentive programs. Many payers, including Congress, the Medicare Payment Advisory Commission (MedPAC) and CMS, all recognize the benefits to patients and the healthcare system as a whole through enhanced quality care, better outcomes, and more efficient care.

CMS has implemented various projects over the years to promote quality and efficiency by rewarding healthcare providers and suppliers for the quality of care they provide by tying a portion of Medicare payments to performance on quality indicators. These projects included demonstration and quality reporting programs applied in settings such as physician practices, ambulatory care facilities, hospitals, nursing homes, home health agencies, and dialysis facilities. CMS's goal has been to transform Medicare from a passive payer to an active purchaser of quality health care for its beneficiaries.

In 2010, section 3001 of PPACA established a budget-neutral hospital valued-based purchasing (VBP) program to compensate hospitals for performance against certain quality measures. The program is scheduled to begin in fiscal year 2013, applicable to payments for discharges occurring on or after Oct. 1, 2012. The hospital VBP program generally applies to acute-care prospective payment system hospitals with certain exceptions for hospitals and those with few applicable measures. The quality measures used in the hospital VBP program will be similar to those used in the Medicare pay-for-reporting program. The hospital VBP program will receive its funding from a reduction in Medicare severity diagnosis-related group (MS-DRG) inpatient prospective payment system (IPPS) reimbursement to hospitals to which the hospital VBP program applies. VBP incentive payments will be made with respect to discharges occurring during fiscal year 2013, and the quality measures will include those applicable to the following conditions:

- Acute myocardial infarction;

- Heart failure;

- Pneumonia;

- Surgeries, as measured by the surgical care improvement project; and

- Healthcare-associated infections, as measured by the HHS Action Plan to Prevent Healthcare-Associated Infections.[9]

Additionally, measures of patients' satisfaction with the level of care will be measured.

The following continues the hypothetical example of Healthy Regional Hospital and its cardiology CCMA:

> In addition to a robust set of day-to-day management services, Healthy Regional and its cardiology group partner developed a set of quality measurements that paralleled those of a significant local payer. The payer's program resulted in bonuses to the hospital for attainment of the payer's targets in quality care. The CCMA agreement for Healthy Regional's cardiac service line included financial incentives for reaching these quality measures, which effectively aligned the interests of the joint venture and the hospital with those of the payer.

---

9   Department of Health and Human Services, "HHS Action Plan to Prevent Healthcare-Associated Infections: Incentives and Oversight," www.hhs.gov/ash/initiatives/hai/incentives.html.

Consolidate medical directorship duties. With physicians as partners in clinical quality, the CCMA affords hospitals with opportunities to develop more robust duties and responsibilities for physician administrative positions over the managed service line. CCMA agreements provide for significant enhancements in administrative requirements for clinicians, to which a portion of the compensation is related (often referred to as the base management fee), and often allows for a consolidation of multiple, and sometimes duplicative, directorships. The hypothetical example of Healthy Regional's CCMA continues below:

> In developing the CCMA, Healthy Regional's legal counsel recommended termination of the hospital's separate cardiology and cath lab medical directorship agreements, in favor of inclusion of the duties of both in the administrative responsibilities of the CCMA. The previous medical directorship agreements contained no requirements for contemporaneous documentation of physician administrative time and were paid in fixed monthly amounts, representing a significant compliance risk. Legal counsel also recommended additional requirements related to physician participation in quality assurance meetings, attendance at quality assurance training conferences and additional duties as medical staff liaison to address quality concerns with staff physicians. As will be discussed in detail further in this chapter, such medical director duties were "folded into" the CCMA and paid out of the negotiated management fee.

Consolidate other physician duties. With broader ties to physicians in hospital service line management, hospitals can use CCMAs to address other service deficiencies and staffing needs. The Healthy Regional Hospital example continues as follows:

> Prior to the CCMA joint venture, a rift developed between the hospital and cardiology group, and the hospital found itself in a position of seeking sporadic (and expensive) emergency department on-call coverage for the specialty of cardiology. Through negotiations with the cardiology group to enter into the CCMA with the hospital, Healthy Regional was able to gain physician commitment to cover emergency call on a 24-hours-a-day, 7-days-a-week, 365-days-a-year basis. This embedded call arrangement saved Healthy Regional nearly $200,000 in annual call coverage compensation paid to other local physicians and physician staffing companies, resulting in dependable cardiology coverage and improved patient quality outcomes.

2.2 Applicable Specialties

CCMAs apply to many physician specialties, particularly when there is a relationship between the physician's administrative and clinical skills and the success of the hospital in meeting quality measures within the related service line. Some of the more common specialties, in no particular order, include the following:

- Cardiology /cardiovascular surgery;

- Orthopedic surgery;

- General surgery;

- Oncology;

- Neurosciences; and

- Gastroenterology.

2.3 Ownership

In some circumstances, CCMAs are formed and operated as joint ventures between hospitals and physicians in what is commonly known as the joint venture or equity model CCMA. While typically done on a 50-50 basis, it is not uncommon to see many different variations. For example, while a hospital may want to have good alignment with its physicians, it may still want to retain ultimate control, and therefore, a 60-40 split (i.e., in favor of hospital) may be the preferred outcome. The impact of this issue will be discussed in more detail later in this chapter. Because some CCMAs have ownership in healthcare facilities (e.g., cath lab or outpatient imaging center), these are also structured as joint ventures, although usually with a significant requirement for capital infusion to accommodate the acquisition and operation of the outpatient facility, and subject to applicable fair market value analysis.

Another variant of the CCMA is the contractual model CCMA, which is, in the vast majority of cases, owned by individual physicians, physician groups, or combinations of the two. The contractual model CCMA is generally thought of as less capital intensive and less structurally complex than an equity model CCMA; however, despite some misinformation, contractual model CCMAs are generally no more or no less favorable to physicians than equity model CCMAs, as will be described more fully later in this chapter.

2.4 Organizational Structure

The CCMA entity is typically established as a limited liability company. This entity enters into a management services arrangement with the hospital for purposes of managing the hospital's designated service line. In general, the equity model CCMA can be somewhat more complex than the contractual model CCMA because the introduction of joint venture partners and multiple classes of ownership can result in a complicated legal structure of the entity.

2.5 Regulatory Compliance

Designing a CCMA requires the guidance of experienced healthcare legal counsel to avoid missteps that could cause the venture to run afoul of federal and state healthcare laws and regulations that govern hospital and physician relationships. Although not discussed in depth in this chapter, compliance with the terms of applicable exceptions to the Stark physician self-referral legislation is critical, as well as applicable anti-kickback statute safe harbors, such as the one for personal services and management contracts. Such violations are also often "bootstrapped" with federal false claims act penalties, which can significantly increase the government's claims. Additionally, because some CCMAs focus on efficiency, care should be taken to avoid incentives that induce physicians to reduce or limit services to Medicare or Medicaid beneficiaries, or hospitals and physicians face civil monetary penalties. Tax-exempt hospitals, as parties to CCMAs, should also be careful to avoid private inurement or excessive private benefit. Intermediate sanctions penalties allow the IRS to levy excise taxes against organization managers and parties to a transaction, thus requiring that tax-exempt hospitals focus on payment of reasonable compensation to physicians.

2.6 Fee Structure—Base Plus Incentive

CCMAs ordinarily maintain management service agreements with the hospital for the service line management, with a multistage compensation structure. The first stage is base compensation associated with the day-to-day medical direction, management, and administrative duties and responsibilities under the contract, and such services are paid for out of the base management fee, as further discussed in our chapter. While this level of compensation is often paid out on a flat "monthly" basis (with an annual true-up based on the percent completion of the assigned management services), more hospitals are electing to inject an additional degree of conservatism into their arrangements by electing to administer the base management fee in the form of an hourly rate applied to the documented hours spent by the physicians furnishing the administrative services. This amount generally does not vary depending on the performance of the manager or the success in meeting the quality objectives of the arrangement. However, it is important to note that should a hospital elect to disburse the base management fee on an hourly basis, the hospital also needs to ensure that it carefully tracks the performance of the management services, as payout of the entire base management fee (whether paid on a flat fee or hourly basis) is only appropriate if the management services have been performed in their entirety.

The second component of compensation is the P4P incentive compensation, which is based on the attainment of clinical quality objectives and other factors such as patient satisfaction and budgetary compliance. P4P incentives are calculated and paid in a variety of ways, the more common of which will be described below.

2.7 Incentive Metrics and Pay-for-Performance

Core measures developed by CMS, the Joint Commission, and third-party payers are often referred to as organizations develop quality standards for incentive pay under CCMAs.

Exhibit 1 summarizes core measures from CMS and the Joint Commission for heart failure:

Exhibit 1. Heart Failure Core Measures	
Medicare Short Name	**Description**
Discharge instructions	Heart failure patients discharged home with written instructions or education material given to the patient or caregiver at discharge or during the hospital stay addressing all of the following: activity level, diet, discharge medications, follow-up appointment, weight monitoring, and what to do if symptoms worsen.
Evaluation of LVS function	Heart failure patients with documentation in the hospital record that left ventricular systolic (LVS) function was evaluated before arrival, during hospitalization, or is planned for after discharge.
ACEI or ARB for LVSD	Heart failure patients with left ventricular systolic dysfunction (LVSD) and without both angiontensin converting enzyme inhibitor (ACEI) and angiontensin receptor blocker (ARB) contraindications who are prescribed an ACEI or ARB at hospital discharge. For purposes of this measure, LVSD is defined as chart documentation of a left ventricular ejection fraction (LVEF) less than 40% or a narrative of left ventricular systolic (LVS) function consistent with moderate or severe systolic dysfunction.
Adult smoking cessation advice and counseling	Heart failure patients with a history of smoking cigarettes, who are giving smoking cessation advice or counseling during the hospital stay. For purposes of this measure, a smoker is defined as someone who has smoked cigarettes anytime during the year prior to hospital arrival.

Quality measures like those above for heart failure are used as measurements in CCMAs to assess the level of quality attained through the management of the hospital service line. For example, a cardiac CCMA would likely measure quality for AMI, heart failure, and cardiac artery bypass graft (CABG), comparing the actual quality scores with expected or target scores. In the case of the Discharge Instructions core measure, the quality score is a fraction, the numerator of which is the number of patients discharged home that were given discharge instructions or educational materials that included all of the required instructions (i.e., activity level, diet, discharge medications, follow-up appointment, weight monitoring, and what to do if symptoms worsen) and the denominator of which is the total number of heart failure patients discharged home.

One of the key distinctions between a CCMA and a traditional management agreement is the P4P component, which provides for incentive compensation to the manager of an incentive above and beyond the base compensation. The incentive compensation component is often based on attainment of quality scores such as the one described above for heart failure. In the example of discharge instructions to heart failure patients, 78% may be the target score for discharge instructions. Reaching or exceeding this level would result in incentive bonus credit or payment to the CCMA manager. CCMAs vary in the application of bonus methodology, as some examples include specific amounts of bonus payment upon attainment of target scores or credit in the form of points to the manager, which are accumulated for purposes of determining payment under the CCMA incentive bonus formula.

3.0 Valuation Method

In the context of a CCMA, determining the FMV of management fees is critical not only for compliance with existing laws, but is also important to the ultimate success of the project. Therefore, before any hospital undertakes the implementation of a co-management arrangement, it is critical to determine the FMV of the management fee, including both the base and incentive components (these two components were discussed earlier in the chapter), to maintain compliance with existing laws and regulations.[10]

3.1 Overview of Valuation Methodology for CCMAs

Several methods exist for determining value in a compensation arrangement. The justification for the use of a particular method or methods will often be dictated by the facts and circumstances of the contractual arrangement. These methods of valuation can be generally categorized into three broad approaches: cost-based, income-based, and market-based. Within the each valuation approach, one or more methods exist for determining value, with the relevance and applicability of each depending on the circumstances and the analyst's judgment.

In considering the value of payments under a CCMA, it is important to consider the value of the individual components of compensation (base compensation and incentive compensation), as well as aggregate compensation under the arrangement. A key consideration that must not be overlooked is that the methodology (and application thereof) that considers the fair market value of the individual components of compensation may differ from methodology that considers the value of aggregate compensation. The valuator should consider the merits and applicability of all three valuation approaches in developing an appropriate FMV range.

---

10 In addition, it should be noted that according to Rev. Proc. 97-13, certain not-for-profit entities with public bond financed property may also face additional Internal Revenue Service scrutiny regarding the split of the management fee. The authors would recommend that any hospital considering a co-management arrangement involve outside counsel in the process.

3.2 Income-Based Approach

Valuation of a CCMA under the income-based approach considers the economic benefits enjoyed by the hospital from the management services furnished by the manager.

Revenues earned by achieving or reporting quality target attainment under governmental and private payer programs result in bonus reimbursement, and income from these programs represent a "proxy" for the fair market value of the attainment of quality metrics within the boundaries of the CCMA. In many cases, these quality, outcomes, and efficiency measures mirror or closely resemble those of the CCMA and therefore represent an income stream associated with the same quality variables with which the CCMA measures its own success. Payers often use a point structure to determine the level of qualifying reimbursement, and scoring information can be made available by the payer to the hospital for use in determining hospital reimbursement and value of the incentive program. For example, some states' Blue Cross programs offer hospital performance or quality improvement programs, based on quality, efficiency, safety, and outcomes. When these measures can be attributed to the service line managed under the CCMA, they represent a stream of economic benefit directly associated with the attainment of quality and other metrics that can sometimes be closely associated with those of the CCMA and therefore represent a proxy for the value of CCMA quality attainment. The authors believe that not all CCMA valuations present opportunities for valuation in such a manner for a number of reasons. First, payer incentive programs may not be directly measurable in a way that can be related to the management services furnished by the manager in a CCMA. Second, payer incentive programs may not facilitate direct correlation to a specific service line, such as that of an oncology program managed under an oncology CCMA.

3.3 Cost-Based Approach

Discussion of applicable service lines. While the income approach certainly has applicability in many instances, the two more prevalent valuation approaches utilized in the marketplace appear to be the cost and market approaches. In considering the cost approach (or "replacement cost" methodology), a possible alternative to the implementation of an agreement is a hospital's opportunity to engage (either as employees or as independent contractors) various medical directors to manage its identified service line offerings.

However, in this approach, it is important to note that the exact number of required work hours typically cannot reasonably be determined in advance. Furthermore, most management arrangements we have observed in the marketplace are not based upon actual underlying time to establish the management fee. Notwithstanding the foregoing, however, we believe that an approach wherein a valuator reviews benchmark data for hypothetical medical directorship positions is reasonable in establishing an alternative means to determine the FMV of the management services.

As an example, if a valuator was engaged to determine the FMV of a cardiovascular co-management arrangement, such service line offerings for consideration would likely include, but not be limited to: medical cardiology, interventional cardiology, cardio and thoracic surgery, cardiac rehabilitation, cardiac intensive care, and outpatient programs and services. Giving consideration to the number of medical directors that might reasonably be required to provide physician management to hospital's service lines, the valuator could then consider the following key factors:

- What is the projected net revenue of the service line? Since most co-management arrangements are implemented for the management of existing service line offerings, looking at the most recent 12-month period of historical collections would be advisable. Alternatively, if the service line in question is a new division of a hospital, for example, a cardiovascular center of excellence, relying on the hospital's annual projected net revenue for purposes of an analysis would be acceptable..

- How diverse are the service offerings? The diversity of service offerings in combination with the complexity of clinical operations and the volume of procedures, including both inpatient and outpatient services, requires significant coordination among numerous physicians, associated hospital services, and a myriad of operational details. For example, for hospital-specific reasons, a proposed orthopedic co-management arrangement might *exclude* outpatient rehabilitation services. In this instance, all other things being equal, the resulting range from methodology employed under the cost approach would likely be less than an arrangement that was all encompassing.

- How many subservice lines are contemplated? For example, in a cardiovascular services CCMA, the analysis is likely more complicated (and thus, the upper end of supportable FMV likely higher) if the arrangement includes general cardiology, interventional cardiology, cardiovascular surgery, and electrophysiology, as compared to a CCMA that solely contemplates invasive cardiology.

Determination of comparable positions. Once the scope of the service line is discussed and agreed upon, the determination of the particular physicians and the corresponding amount of time required to provide medical director services is dependent upon a variety of factors including (1) the size of the hospital, (2) the complexity of services being provided, and (3) the annual number of procedures performed. In consideration of these factors, the initial step would be to develop an expectation for the number of medical director positions that could have reasonably been supported in the absence of the co-management arrangement. The valuation analyst can either develop this guidance based on his or her own experience and informed judgment with similar arrangements or can engage the services of an independent staffing expert (most typically, an independent physician with previous department head experience). By evaluating the applicable service lines through probative inquiry and comparison to comparative data from similar facilities, the valuator should be in a good position to identify the relevant medical director positions, ensuring that there is no overlap and redundancy in the identification of such positions.

For example, as referenced above, if the valuator were analyzing a co-management arrangement for a comprehensive cardiovascular center of excellence, by evaluating each potential service line component, it would not be unreasonable to conclude that Exhibit 2 contains the six part-time medical director positions that might have been engaged. Such positions would have been engaged on an independent contractor basis, in the absence of a co-management arrangement, to manage daily operations and provide needed oversight to hospital's service line.

Exhibit 2. Identified Service Line Medical Directorships
Medical cardiology
Interventional/invasive cardiology
Cardiovascular and cardiothoracic surgery
Cardiac rehabilitation and recovery
Cardiac intensive care (CCU)
Outpatient programs and services

Determination of appropriate compensation rate. To determine the appropriate compensation for each identified medical director position, it is important to note that compensation earned by a physician in his or her specialty practice of medicine may not be directly comparable to the compensation for medical directorship duties. However, the valuator should recognize that with regard to a medical director position, a hospital would need to identify not only an appropriately experienced clinician, but also an individual with the skills and experience necessary to perform required administrative duties. At this point in the analysis, the valuator should also give recognition to the size of the hospital. For example, a 500-bed trauma facility, given its size and focus, would likely need the support for a more diverse community of both inpatients and outpatients than a 150-bed regional hospital. The implication here is that there is likely support for higher compensation and allowable monthly hours for the 500-bed trauma facility arrangement.

Given the above, the valuator should review available compensation levels expected to be earned by a physician in his or her specialty practice of medicine as a reasonable starting point.[11] However, in most instances, such compensation values are likely *not* comparable to the FMV of compensation for medical directorship duties as described above. As stated above, in valuing administrative positions, a FMV analysis is not intended to establish an "opportunity cost" related to professional services. Therefore, to develop the most appropriate compensation range, the valuator should review and consider available, published sources of administrative compensation data, such as publicly available administrative compensation surveys. In developing compensation ranges, as *general* guidance, we believe the valuator should consider benchmark compensation values up to 90th percentile values, as physicians with the ability to operate a significant clinical practice, coupled with the time-consuming administrative responsibilities of the CCMA, generally command compensation in ranges higher than those experienced in a more traditional medical directorship role. However, as will be discussed below in detail, depending on the specific facts and circumstances of the arrangement, it may be reasonable to limit the upper end of the compensation range to the 75th percentile (e.g., in those instances where there are multiple medical director positions, relatively low program revenue, and so on).

Determination of appropriate hours. Once a compensation range is identified, the next step in the cost approach would be to identify the applicable hours attributable to each identified position. For ease of calculation, the typical convention would be to identify an annual number of hours. This number would then be multiplied by the hourly compensation range identified above to determine the annual compensation attributable to the position. To identify the appropriate range of expected monthly hours, the valuator should consider the following questions:

- How large is the hospital's service line to be managed (as measured by net revenue)?

---

11   A good resource for cash compensation values can be obtained from the *MGMA Physician Compensation and Production Survey* because it is a commonly used benchmark percentile in the determination of appropriate FMV compensation values.

- How large is the hospital, as measured by licensed bed count?

- Are both inpatient and outpatient services included in the arrangement?

- Does the co-management arrangement contemplate the management of a single campus or multiple campuses?[12]

As with the development of the compensation range, the valuator should review and consider available, published sources of administrative data regarding ranges of hours for respective administrative positions. This is an area where a significant amount of analysis and valuator judgment should come into play. Based on a review of the particular aspects of the arrangement (i.e., scope of the subservice lines, whether inpatient and outpatient services are included, whether there are multiple sites of services, and so on), the determination of annual hours will likely range between the 25th and 75th percentiles However, as with the derivation of the hourly compensation, specific facts and circumstances might warrant exceeding this upper range in certain instances. For example, using a hypothetical cardiovascular center of excellence, co-management arrangements relate to unique cardiovascular surgery services in that these services are also provided to a hospital's patients that are transferred in from smaller regional hospitals where such services are not provided. In recognition of the added complexity of this relationship between hospitals, it may have been reasonable to utilize benchmark data for the 90th percentile to determine the number of hours required by the applicable cardiovascular surgery medical director positions.

Once these two market data points are identified, this data would then be used in conjunction with the appropriate staffing breakdown as detailed from Exhibit 2 to determine the total FMV range as determined under a cost approach. Exhibit 3 provides a simple summary of a hypothetical analysis used to determine the FMV range, under a cost approach, associated with the management of a hospital's cardiovascular center of excellence.

3.4 Market-Based Approach

The market approach to valuation provides an effective methodology to determine a FMV range while eliminating the constraints of a time-based analysis as required under a cost approach. However, the uniqueness of each co-management arrangement precludes *direct* market comparisons of the subject arrangement to other arrangements in the

---

12 In the authors' experience, it is not uncommon to see co-management arrangements covering multiple campuses for a hospital, particularly if certain services (i.e., rehabilitation) are handled in a distinct location. This dynamic increases the complexity of the management arrangement and would likely warrant an adjustment to the hourly and rate ranges.

Exhibit 3. Summary of Cost Approach					
		50th Percentile		90th Percentile	
Service Offering	Hours Worked Per Year	Hourly Rate	Annual Compensation[1]	Hourly Rate	Annual Compensation
Medical cardiology	215	$134	$28,810	$174	$37,410
Interventional and invasive cardiology	150	$141	$21,150	$184	$27,600
Cardiovascular and cardiothoracic surgery	856	$186	$159,216	$256	$219,136
Cardiac rehabilitation and recovery	174	$150	$26,100	$173	$30,102
Cardiac intensive care (CCU)	220	$164	$36,080	$200	$44,000
Outpatient programs and services	220	$164	$36,080	$200	$44,000
TOTAL	1,835		≈ $308,000		≈ $402,000

marketplace. Therefore, a critical part of the valuation process involves breaking down the co-management arrangement into its individual components. Once individual tasks, objectives, and performance metrics are identified, the arrangement can be compared to other arrangements with similar elements. *In the case of co-management arrangements, in the authors' experience, similar tasks and objectives might be found in ASC arrangements, which are readily available in the marketplace.* By comparing specific elements item by item, the valuator is able to assess the relative worth of each metric, and determine the presence or absence of each metric in comparison to the comparable arrangements. *For example, metrics can be focused around tasks, objectives, or performance outcomes.* Then, with reasonable objectivity, the valuator is able to assess the overall relative value of the identified arrangement by comparing it to other available market arrangements.

Identification of services performed. To compare the management services to be provided by a manager against market comparables where the management fees are known (e.g., a review of ASC management agreements), the valuator can consider the creation of a "scoring grid," whereby a weighting factor and point value are assigned to each specific identified task contemplated under the arrangement. The services to be included in the arrangement can usually be found in the draft agreement provided by counsel (usually as an exhibit to the body of the agreement), but often such services are also either contained within the body of the agreement or not addressed in detail at all. In these latter two examples, the valuator should be certain to have a detailed discussion with counsel with regard to the detail and "breadth" of the contemplated management services because the accurate identification of the specific services to be performed is the main driver within the market approach. For example, will the management company simply "assist" with the credentialing function by coordinating the necessary paperwork or will the management company be responsible for handling the credentialing function? Once these services are identified, the valuator will have a grid comprised of up to 40 specific services. This comprehensive listing of services that are typically provided by management companies will be a "baseline" listing from which the valuator can then begin to make a series of "normalizing" adjustments to the available management fee percentages in developing a range applicable to the agreement.

Identification of baseline market comparables. One common type of management arrangement whereby significant market data are available involves the management of ambulatory surgery centers (ASC) by professional management companies. Generally, ASC management companies provide comprehensive management services, with recognition that the services do not include those that typically require the involvement of physicians. The authors believe that ASC agreements are essentially comparable to CCMAs.[13]

Some companies survey ASCs for operating statistics, and this information is readily available. Data on public ASC operating companies, such as AmSurg Inc. (AMSG), and available data from transactions involving privately held companies, such as Symbion Inc., may provide additional information, Additionally, the valuator can conduct a survey of identified national or regional ASC management companies, identifying the management fee ranges, stated as a percentage of collections (or net revenue). In the authors' experience, management fees range from approximately 3% to 6% of collections; however, the vast majority of such arrangements involve the existence of a full-time on-site manager who is compensated by the ASC, thereby effectively raising the total management fees to levels higher than 6%. If there is not enough available marketplace data on such arrangements, the valuator can also attempt to identify other management arrangements involving programs such as substance abuse, respiratory therapy, and physical therapy.[14] In considering the applicability of these arrangements to the agreement, however, the valuator should be careful to ensure that such arrangements do not include clinical staffing services because they would report a higher-than-expected management fee and result in a skewed analysis. As a result, a review of such arrangements may be helpful from a comparison perspective but may not be as reliable as information gleaned from more "typical" management company arrangements.

---

13 In terms of the underlying services in each type of agreement.
14 Such arrangements may not be based upon designated percentages of net revenue. As such, to ensure an accurate comparison, it will be essential for the valuator to convert each arrangement to a percentage of net revenue equivalent basis to facilitate comparisons.

Adjustments given scope of services. Armed with the data developed in steps 1 and 2 above, the valuator is now in a position to utilize the developed "grid" to evaluate and score each task under the agreement. Some aspects to consider in the creation of a grid would be the following:

- Task importance—Develop a point system that values the complexity and anticipated time commitment required by each identified task, possibly ranging from 1 to 5. For example, "arranging for the purchase of liability insurance, paid for by the hospital" is a much complicated and time-intensive task compared to "developing community relationships that result in a satisfied referral base." As such, the scoring grid should be able to effectively distinguish between the two, and in this example, the latter task may be scored a "5," whereas the former task may be scored as a "3."

- Task—In management agreements, it is common to see tasks identified in an agreement that are meant to be more "supportive" in nature as compared to the management company having sole responsibility for the task. As referenced in the hypothetical example above, will the management company simply assist with the credentialing function by coordinating the necessary paperwork or will it be responsible for handling the credentialing function? The grid should be able to delineate between the two because the former task is certainly more limited in nature.

- Weighting factor—A weighting factor is recommended to be developed and applied to each task based on the above identified categories. As an example, a limited task may receive a weighting of 1, whereas a full task may receive a weighting of 3. Similarly, those tasks not included in the proposed agreement would receive a weighting of 0.

As a result of the above calculations, the analysis will yield a total point value, calculated as the sum of the various point values assigned in the above *task importance* section. In addition, the grid would have produced a weighted point value, which would be the product of each specific point value, multiplied by the identified weighting factor. As an example, if there were 30 tasks, resulting in a total score of 110 possible points, the weighted score might have totaled 80 points, resulting in a final score of 73% (i.e., 80 divided by 110). To determine a comparable value for the management services, the results of the above-described scoring grid (i.e., 73%), would be applied to the identified market range for management fees. In this example, the result would be a *preliminary* fee range for the management services, under a market approach, of from 2.2%[15] to 4.4%[16] of net revenue.

Adjustments given revenue size. *Depending on the specific facts and circumstances of the arrangement, the valuator should also give consideration to the application of a discount of the preliminary range.*

- While this may not appear to be intuitive, it is logical for a number of reasons. First, although the management services contemplated by the co-management agreement are likely comprehensive in nature, the hospital likely has the ability to rely upon many aspects of its infrastructure.[17] *This is a significant point to consider, in that it reduces the hospital's required degree of dependence upon the management company.* Second, in most instances, the revenue size of a service line subject to a co-management agreement is significantly higher than the typical ASC that is subject to an outside management arrangement, thereby warranting a lower fee as a percentage of net revenue.[18] Third, research indicates that as revenue sizes grow, there is an increased likelihood that a management organization would discount its normal management fees in recognition of the fact that it is able to achieve certain economies in the arrangement. Furthermore, once net revenue exceeds a certain threshold, the correlation between net revenue and the cost to manage the services is significantly reduced.

Therefore, in recognition of this disconnect and to apply a certain degree of conservatism to the analysis, the valuator should consider the application of a discount to the initially calculated fee range. In the authors' experience, a reasonable range of discounts would be from 10% to 30%.

3.5 Reconciliation of the Approaches

In considering the outcomes of the valuation approaches, the authors believe the market approach is generally preferable in valuing management services. However, the market approach can be subject to certain limitations since, as discussed above, there are no directly comparable market values. The income approach contains some element of speculation in the projection of LOS and readmission impact and may sometimes

---

15 0.03 times 73%
16 0.06 times 73%
17 Even if the agreement is not a traditional co-management agreement (i.e., it is not uncommon to have such management companies solely owned by the physicians), the authors believe that the participating hospital will still be in a position to leverage aspects of its infrastructure.
18 In the authors' general experience, the "typical" revenue size of a co-managed service line might be in the $30 million-to-$70 million range, whereas the typical ASC has revenues in the range of $10 million or less.

yield inconclusive results; therefore, the valuation analyst must weigh these factors in determining the degree of reliance placed upon these methods. With respect to the cost approach, the build-up of the medical director time requirements does not necessarily value the services that will be contributed by a hospital partner in the management company. As such, a common approach would be to give each methodology equal weighting and take a simple average of the calculated values. In other instances, however, there may be a need to provide a double weighting of one approach or the other, in recognition of additional arrangement dynamics. As an example, if the valuator were analyzing a relatively "light" management arrangement (i.e., a small service line such as ENT at a regional hospital), given the relatively scaled down services contemplated under that type of arrangement, an equal weighting may not necessarily accurately capture the essence of the arrangement.[19] In this instance, the valuator might elect to normalize the valuation by giving a *double weighting* to the results of the cost approach.

3.6 Valuing the Total Fee

Given the typical compensation structure of co-management arrangements, the fair market value range needs to encompass the total management fee (i.e., both the base management fee *and* the incentive management fee). In addition, each co-management arrangement is unique and reflects specific market and operational factors, which are singular to the specific setting. Therefore, the authors believe the FMV should address the *total* management fee, providing the hospital with the opportunity to establish the proportion of the management fee payable as a base management fee versus the incentive management fee (which will be based upon achievement of the predetermined measures). That said, although this practice allows the hospital to have significant discretion in establishing the relative value of the base management fee as compared to the incentive management fee, certain regulatory and market-based constraints should be observed. In particular, regulatory considerations may affect the maximum percentage of the total fee that can be incentive based.[20]

However, within those constraints, it is not likely beneficial to set the incentive management fee too low as a percentage of the total management fee (since such an overemphasis on the base fee would seem to diminish the ideals of achieving the pre-established performance objectives). As general guidance, the authors believe that the

---

19 In other words, the results of the market approach would likely understate the value of the services being provided by sole virtue of its reliance on the net revenue of the service line.

20 According to Rev. Proc. 97-13, certain not-for-profit entities with public bond financed property must ensure that the incentive portion of the management fee is not set too high as compared to the base fee, depending on the length of the contract term and other terms of the arrangement. Therefore, parties considering such arrangements are advised to seek the advice of experienced legal counsel prior to entering into any such arrangements.

base management fee should generally be no higher than 60% and no lower than 25% of the total management fee. These constraints are based upon observations in the marketplace of similar arrangements and, in the authors' opinion, preserve the general intent of the hospital with respect to the desired outcome of the co-managed services.

4.0 Issues Affecting the FMV Analysis

Once the FMV range of the management agreement is identified, it is important that the valuator recognizes that each management arrangement is generally unique, and as with most arrangements, these unique attributes can have a significant impact on the resulting FMV of the arrangement. This section of the chapter will focus on some of the common areas for discussion amongst the parties, each of which should be thoroughly explored by the valuator.

4.1 The Use of Medical Director Positions

A very commonly used practice within co-management arrangements is to utilize medical directorships for select physician participants. While the intent of the arrangements typically is to have the management company perform all of the management services, it is not uncommon to find that certain of the management services are intended to be provided through a medical director arrangement provided by a qualified physician associated with the management company. While this is an acceptable practice, the valuator should ensure the following:

- Such medical director arrangements are to be paid as an expense from the identified base portion of management fee. Since the FMV build-up of the management fee as discussed above in the cost approach section already contemplates the use of such positions, paying for them outside of the management fee would be considered redundant. However, there are instances in which such positions would be allowed in a manner consistent with FMV, such as when the medical directorship was for a specific subset service line, which was now going to be carved out from the management company (e.g., in a cardiac co-management arrangement, the parties might agree to carve cardiac rehabilitation out of the arrangement). In this instance, the valuator should ensure that the net revenue provided for the analysis specifically excludes any revenue attributable to the cardiac rehabilitation so as to not allow for redundancy of payment.

- If all parties agree on the treatment of revenues and positions, it is important that the valuator ensure that such medical director arrangements will be for a number of monthly hours and rate that is *consistent with FMV*. As an example, and as a good rule of thumb, the valuator should ensure that the proposed hours and rate are equal to or below the upper end of the values provided in Table 3 (of course tailored to the specific analysis in question).

- Since the intent of a co-management arrangement is that there are no "passive investors," the valuator should also give consideration to the magnitude of the total monies being allocated toward medical directorships. As discussed above, the base management fee is meant to compensate the management company for handling the day-to-day management services, which are expected to be handled in a proportional manner to each party's ownership. Therefore, assuming a 50-50 ownership (as is typical), it would not be reasonable to have a disproportionate share of the base management fee paid out as medical directorships. While there is latitude in the ultimate percentage "ceiling" that can be approved, another good rule of thumb is that *no more than* 25% of the base fee should be allocated to medical director positions. By doing so, the valuator can avoid any possible interpretation that this management company is simply a vehicle under which a hospital intends to distribute monies to the physicians while allowing them to perform less than the required share of the overall duties. This is especially critical when the medical directorships are going to be with physician owners.

4.2 Provision/Purchase of Administrative Services

It is not uncommon in many arrangements for the management company, whether jointly owned or not, to need certain administrative services. In the case of a physician-owned management company, given the "loose" structure of the arrangement and since there is no need for dedicated building space and staff, the physician owners simply do have the requisite infrastructure necessary to manage their operation. Such needed administrative support services may include, but not be limited to, the following: accounting, financial statement preparation, tax return preparation, payroll processing, and legal support and clerical support. In most instances, the hospital is more than willing to provide such services to the management company. By doing so, however, the hospital has just unintentionally (or intentionally as the case may be) created a fair market value implication by providing additional services that have a defined market worth. The valuator should ensure that such services are independently negotiated and implemented at a rate that is FMV between the parties.[21]

---

21 In many instances, the valuator is not asked to analyze and determine the FMV of such services. It is therefore acceptable to rely on the party's representation and to list such a governing assumption in the valuation report, i.e., that any such services will be subject to an appropriate FMV analysis.

4.3 Ensuring Equitable Division of Responsibilities

As has been stated numerous times throughout this chapter, the co-management structure is intended to be a vehicle that ensures that hospital and physician members both actively participate in the provision of the management services (i.e., there are no passive investors in a management company). Furthermore, a key representation in most management company analyses is that the resulting division of responsibilities within the management company (i.e., the management contribution of each party related to providing the management services) will be in approximate proportion to the ownership percentages determined. However, under most arrangements, assuming a 50-50 ownership structure, it would be virtually impossible to ensure that all of the required duties are handled on an exact 50-50 basis. That said, if the parties each own 50% of the management company and will thus receive 50% of the management fee, the valuator should ensure that (1) each party takes an active role in the management duties and (2) each party will manage efforts in approximate proportion to their ownership.

4.4 Ensuring No Overlap of Responsibilities

Similar to the discussion above related to a medical director position, a service line administrator is often engaged to perform services in conjunction with a CCMA. As with the medical director, if the service line administrator is responsible for performing tasks similar to those required of the co-management company, then the administrator must be compensated as an expense from the base management fee. Notwithstanding, in an increasing number of management arrangements, the administrator is an employee of the hospital and is responsible for overseeing the hospital's interests in terms of service line management (i.e., purely providing oversight), rather than *actually providing* any of the management services. In these cases, since the administrator does not have any responsibility for actually performing any of the specified management services, there is no duplication of activities, and therefore, the administrator would not be required to be compensated from the base management fee.

As an additional example, in arrangements that are structured as straight "management arrangements," (i.e., there is no hospital ownership in the management company, only physician owners), it is very common for an operational committee to be established, with the members comprised of both management company (i.e., physician) and hospital participants. In this case, the committee would typically meet monthly to review operational issues and other issues related to the service line and the management arrangement. While this is acceptable from an operational and structural standpoint, from a FMV standpoint, it is key to ensure that any hospital appointed members of the committee do not perform any of the management services that are the sole responsibility of the management company as set forth in the applicable agreement (i.e., any hospital appointed members function solely in an oversight capacity).

5.0 Summary

The emergence of incentive-based models for the delivery of healthcare services has contributed to the development of a broad range of new opportunities for hospital and physician partnerships. One of the most common forms of these partnerships involves the establishment of a physician-owned or hospital and physician-owned co-management company for the purpose of managing a specific hospital service line. This type of arrangement offers significant value propositions to patients, who have improved access to needed services; to hospitals, which realize improved patient satisfaction, operational efficiencies, financial controls, and enhanced clinical quality; and to physicians, who are incented to effectively and efficiently manage the service line and facilitate the achievement of identified performance-based metrics.

However, the uniqueness of each co-management arrangement precludes direct market comparisons of the subject arrangement to other arrangements in the marketplace. Therefore, a critical part of the valuation process involves breaking down the co-management arrangement into its individual components. Once individual tasks, objectives, and performance metrics are identified, the arrangement can be compared to other arrangements with similar elements and analyzed by completing a build-up of comparable positions that would be required in the absence of such an arrangement. Regardless of the approach undertaken, determining the fair market value of these types of management agreements is of paramount importance, and by incorporating the above elements into a valuation repertoire, one can be assured that a thorough analysis will result.

6.0 Bibliography

Specifications Manual for National Hospital Quality Measures, The Joint Commission and Centers for Medicare and Medicaid Services

Callender, Arianne N. et al., "Corporate Responsibility and Health Care Quality: A Resource for Health Care Boards of Directors", Office of Inspector General

oig.hhs.gov/fraud/docs/complianceguidance/CorporateResponsibilityFinal%209-4-07.pdf. (September 2007).

Lindenauer, Peter K. et al., "Public Reporting and Pay for Performance in Hospital Quality Improvement" *New England Journal of Medicine* Vol. 356, no. 5 (February 2007): 486-96.

Rosenthal, Meredith B. et al., "Paying For Quality: Providers' Incentives for Quality Improvement" *Health Affairs* Vol. 23, no. 2. (March /April 2004): 127.

Williams, Jeni. "Making the Grade With Pay for Performance: 7 Lessons From Best-Performing Hospitals" *Healthcare Financial Management* (December 2006): 79.

"Improving Acute Myocardial Infarction Reliability and Outcomes", Institute for Healthcare Improvement http://www.ihi.org. [Internet accessed on Jan. 24, 2008].

"Keeping 'Pay' in Pay-For-Performance ("P4P") for Anesthesiologists: A Strategic Analysis of the Opportunities and Threats to Anesthesia Related to the Emerging P4P Trend" Smith Anderson Blount Dorsett Mitchell & Jernigan, LLP (September 2005).

"Testimony Before House of Representatives Committee on Ways and Means, Subcommittee on Health: Promoting Quality and Efficiency of Care for Medicare Beneficiaries" Pacific Business Group on Health www.pbgh.org (March 2005).

Chapter 31. Valuing Physician Services as Part of Global and Bundled Payment Structures

CONTENTS

Chapter 31. Valuing Physician Services as Part of Global and Bundled Payment Structures

By William Lyle Oelrich Jr., MHA, FACHE, CMPE

1.0 Introduction

Bundled payments are sometimes referred to as global payments, perhaps given the payment methodology's intent to serve as "total" reimbursement to the providers involved in the service (i.e., both the professional and technical aspects). Technically speaking, however, "global payments" refer to the entirety of reimbursement *specific to an individual service* at the CPT[1]/HCPCS[2] level, while "bundled payments" refer to the entirety of reimbursement *for the group of services included within an episode of care.* As such, "bundled payments" reflect those *for all forms of providers and all phases of care, including physician, facility-based, and post-acute care services.* While other similarities and differences exist (see Exhibit 1), an understanding of global payments effectively assists in valuing physician services within a bundled payment system.

1.1 Global Payments

Under the Medicare-based reimbursement model, which many other payers also follow, a global payment for any given service is predominantly based upon the total number of relative value units (RVUs) that the CPT/HCPCS code assigns to the respective physician service. These RVUs are comprised of three separate components:

---

1 www.ama-assn.org/ama/pub/physician-resources/solutions-managing-your-practice/coding-billing-insurance/cpt/about-cpt.page?. Current Procedural Terminology (CPT) is a classification system for medical procedures and services; both public and private health insurance programs use it.

2 www.cms.gov/Medicare/Coding/MedHCPCSGenInfo/index.html?redirect=/MedHCPCSGenInfo/. Healthcare Common Procedure Coding System (HCPCS) is a code set created by the Centers for Medicare & Medicaid Services (CMS) to be used for medical coding. HCPCS consists of two levels; Level I encompasses the CPT codes, and Level II covers items such as services, supplies, and products (i.e. ambulance, prosthetics, etc.).

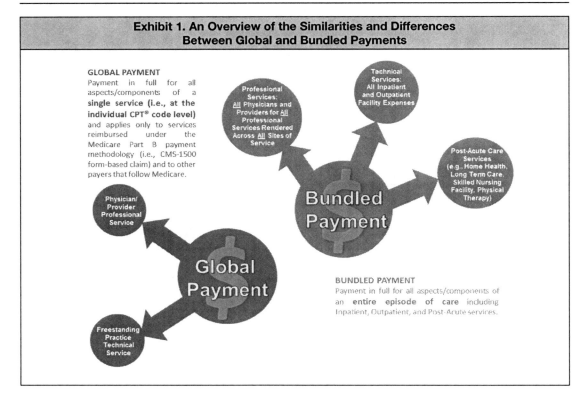

Exhibit 1. An Overview of the Similarities and Differences Between Global and Bundled Payments

- Work—the costs associated with how much provider time and effort is required;

- Practice expense—expenses pertaining to overhead, staffing, equipment, etc.; and

- Malpractice—the associated level of provider malpractice risk.

Assessed collectively, these components form the value of each RVU applicable to a specific service.

Medicare—as well as those payers who follow the Medicare model for their reimbursement methodologies—assigns a payment rate to each service based upon the total RVUs multiplied by an annual conversion factor (CF). In valuing physician services, it is important to understand the RVUs and the CF for the period under valuation, given that they can change annually. For example, adjustments can be made to a RVU value to reflect changes in the cost to provide the service. Further, the CF value is often revised in response to a federal requirement to maintain budget neutrality for the Medicare program (i.e., a function of the sustainable growth rate provision).[3]

---

3 www.cms.gov/Regulations-and-Guidance/Guidance/Transmittals/downloads/R1015OTN.pdf. Change request 7737 (budget).

In terms of assigning RVU value, Medicare sets the RVUs for a service at a level that reflects a national standard for performing a service, based on the technical skill and the effort of a provider. It then uses three geographic practice cost index (GPCI) adjustment factors (one for each RVU component) for each Medicare payment locality to reflect whether the cost associated with that RVU component is higher or lower than the national level, with the GPCI value intended to reflect the degree of variation.[4] For example, the practice expense RVU values for 2012 services rendered and/or billed in West Virginia are adjusted to 0.828 of the national value to reflect lower-than-average costs, resulting in lower-than-average reimbursement.[5] Comparatively, for 2012 services rendered/billed in San Francisco, the practice expense RVUs are adjusted to 1.360 of the national value to reflect higher-than-average costs, resulting in higher-than-average reimbursement.[6] The same GPCI impact concept holds true for the professional liability insurance RVU; however, while also true for the work RVU, federal regulation currently holds the work RVU GPCI adjustment factor "floor" at 1.000 (i.e., work RVUs cannot be adjusted below the national value).[7] In light of these various adjustments, it is essential to understand when (i.e., the calendar year) and where (i.e., the payment locality) the services are rendered and/or billed when valuing or projecting "global" revenue.

In addition, Medicare assigns an indicator code to each CPT/HCPCS code to reflect whether the individual service is considered and reimbursed as wholly professional ("PC only"), wholly technical ("TC only"), or as having aspects of both ("PC/TC" or "global").[8] For most global diagnostic testing services, Medicare allows the service to be billed using the established CPT/HCPCS code in two ways:

- A single claim billed globally: The billing provider is eligible to receive payment for both the PC and TC aspects (i.e., bears the responsibility and expense of both) by submitting the single CPT/HCPCS code unmodified; and

- Two separate claims, one for the PC (assigned CPT/HCPCS appended with modifier -26) and a second for the TC (assigned CPT/HCPCS appended with modifier -TC).

---

4   www.cms.gov/PhysicianFeeSched/01_overview.asp. Medicare Physician Fee Schedule: Payment System Fact Sheet Series.

5   CMS_1524 Addendum E. Final Version 2012 Geographic Practice Cost Index (GPCIs) by State and Medicare Locality.

6   CMS_1524 Addendum E. Final Version 2012 Geographic Practice Cost Index (GPCIs) by State and Medicare Locality.

7   Middle Class Tax Relief and Job Creation Act of 2012 extension of the Temporary Payroll Tax Cut Continuation Act of 2011. Feb. 22, 2012.

8   See the Appendix to Chapter 15, "Practice Aid: Navigating the Medicare Physician Fee Schedule" for further discussion of this indicator code.

Certain CPT/HCPCS codes for global diagnostic testing procedures, however, do not use the above-noted coding and modifier framework. This alternative framework uses separate CPT/HCPCS codes for the global, PC, and TC portions of the service. In other words, one cannot append a "-26" (i.e., PC) or "-TC" modifier to the "global" CPT/HCPCS code and expect component-based payment. In these instances, a different, distinct CPT/ HCPCS exists to separately bill for the individual PC or TC component.[9]

Physician practice revenues are often a mix of PC only, TC only, and global payments. Thus, it is often necessary to understand and separately value the professional versus technical revenue when valuing physician compensation, whether in whole or in part. To do this, one can look to the individual CPT/HCPCS codes billed by the practice for the period under valuation. For services assigned as PC only and TC only, the revenue "split" is not complicated, because 100% of the revenue is one or the other. To determine the PC and TC proportion of global services, one can use the proportion or ratio of the "locality-specific" Medicare reimbursement rates for the PC only and TC only versions of the service (i.e., the "-26" and "-TC" modified versions) to the values assigned to the global service.

Another series of CPT/HCPCS codes dealing with physician services can be thought of as "global." These codes relate to various surgical procedures in which preoperative, intraoperative, and postoperative components are involved in the surgical procedure. The relative proportions of the RVUs for each component are specified in the Medicare Physician Fee Schedule Relative Value File.[10] In addition, baby deliveries are generally treated as global procedures, with components related to the antepartum care, delivery, and postpartum care considered within a single CPT/HCPCS code based on the type of delivery (vaginal, cesarean, etc.).[11] Different, distinct CPT/HCPCS codes exist for "delivery only" services, "delivery and antepartum only" services, or "delivery and postpartum only" services.

In summary, understanding the reimbursement aspects of global payments at the individual CPT/HCPCS service level is fundamental to knowing how to value physician services within a bundled payment. This understanding includes being able to identify the applicable year and locality associated with RVU values as well as the PC versus TC reimbursement rates. Each of these elements, and their application to valuing bundled payments, will be further described below.

---

9   Ibid.
10   Ibid.
11   American Medical Association, CPT 2012.

1.2 Bundled Payments

A bundled payment is a single comprehensive payment made to cover the reimbursements for *all providers* involved in an *episode of care*.[12] This payment covers the hospital, the physician, and any other providers (i.e., home health, nursing home, and other types of post-acute care) associated with the services rendered. On the wide spectrum of reimbursement methods, bundled payments fall in the gap between fee-for-service payments (individual reimbursements per service provided) and capitation (set payments per patient regardless of services rendered). In fact, bundled payments can be structured as fee-for-service with a withhold or as prospective payments based on historical reimbursement. Nevertheless, use of a single, comprehensive payment per episode of care places providers at risk and makes them jointly accountable for the resource management and costs associated with the treatment of each beneficiary.

The growing interest in bundled payments as an alternative reimbursement model has been borne out of the desire to create a model that leads to a greater alignment of incentives between providers. Bundled payment models also provide a structure that incentivizes better outcomes of care with respect to both quality and efficiency, as opposed to the current fee-for-service system, which is designed primarily to reward providers for the volume of care rendered.

Because bundled payments provide a single payment for an entire episode of care, bundled payments help to resolve these issues by requiring physicians to carefully consider what services are truly necessary and appropriate before providing them to a patient. Furthermore, because the payment is to be split among all providers involved, bundled payments help to glue the fragmented healthcare system together by providing incentives for physicians to coordinate care and services across the entire episode of care.

As both government and private payers continue to show a growing interest in this type of model, the need to begin analyzing the valuation methods pertaining to these models will become important. In addition, the use of experienced valuation professionals will be vital to ensure these alternative payment structures for physicians and hospitals fit within the federal and state legal confines.

1.3 The Bundled Payment for Care Improvement Initiative

For many of the reasons previously cited, the Centers for Medicare & Medicaid Services (CMS) has recognized the need for bundled payments and has initiated a pilot program,

---

12 www.ama-assn.org/resources/doc/psa/payment-options.pdf#page=87.

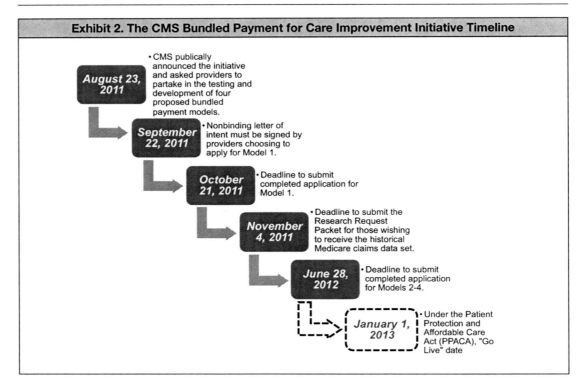

Exhibit 2. The CMS Bundled Payment for Care Improvement Initiative Timeline

The Bundled Payment for Care Improvement Initiative.[13] This initiative was announced on Aug. 23, 2011, and a timeline of its progression is outlined in Exhibit 2.

Although there have been several delays in the process, at the time of publication, CMS remains on track to meet the "Go Live" date. Applications for participation were submitted and an announcement about whom the awardees will be is anticipated in September or October 2012. As such, ample time should exist for awardees to negotiate final contracts with CMS and decide whether they will accept any modifications to their proposals before Jan. 1, 2013.

The CMS pilot is a three-year commitment if an organization is chosen as an awardee. Although CMS has made no formal announcement, many in the industry anticipate that there may be a second round of participation in this, or a similar, CMS bundled pilot prior to the end of this three-year period. Many such bundling models continue to appear across the country from private payers. While currently the number of actual pilot programs in the private payer arena has not been quantified, they are becoming more common, with increasingly rapid growth anticipated for these payment models.

---

13 http://www.innovations.cms.gov/Files/fact-sheet/Bundled-Payment-Fact-Sheet.pdf.

Ultimately, the goal of Medicare's bundled payment initiative is reducing overall payments while improving the levels of quality and patient satisfaction associated with beneficiary treatment. By achieving this goal, CMS believes the bundled payment pilot program could serve as one model of future Medicare reimbursement. Additionally, the opportunity for meaningful gainsharing (i.e., sharing savings achieved in care model redesign with all providers) and the competencies learned from bundled payments will deliver the opportunity for providers to prepare for value-based contracting in the future.[14] While some of these models will be based on historical cost savings, others may use formulas that are more complicated. Therefore, a comprehensive discussion of the various cost savings models and how these savings will be calculated is outside the scope of this valuation chapter.

Under The Bundled Payment for Care Improvement Initiative, participants may apply for four different bundled payment models, three of which are retrospective payment models (Models 1-3) and one that is prospective (Model 4). Exhibit 3 shows the CMS summary of the four models.

2.0 Regulatory Compliance Issues and Considerations

It should be recognized that there are a number of regulatory compliance issues and considerations associated with bundled payments. While a detailed review and explanation of these concepts is outside the scope of this discussion, a brief overview is helpful when contemplating various valuation issues (presented later herein).

2.1 Withholding Care

The Office of Inspector General (OIG) is concerned bundled payments may lead physicians to withhold necessary care from Medicare patients.[15] If an episode of care is treated with fewer services, the opportunity for gainsharing as a result of remaining below the cost target may be greater. This may put the patient at risk of receiving less than necessary care. To address this issue, most bundled payment pilots (both federal and commercial) require continually improved clinical outcomes in the face of cost reductions to ensure appropriate evidence-based care for all patients.

---

14 www.cms.gov/Medicare/Medicare-Fee-for-Service-Payment/PhysicianFeedbackProgram/index.html. According to Section 3007 of the Affordable Care Act, as of 2017, Medicare's value-based-payment modifier will be applied to all physicians. This modifier ties the quality and cost of healthcare to the Medicare Physician Fee Schedule payment formula to incentivize value rather than volume when providing healthcare services.

15 www.mintz.com/newsletter/2011/Advisories/1368-0911-NAT-HL/web.htm.

		MODEL 2 – Inpatient Stay Plus Post-Discharge Services		
MODEL FEATURE	**MODEL 1 – Inpatient Stay Only**		**MODEL 3 – Post-Discharge Services Only**	**MODEL 4 – Inpatient Stay Only**
Eligible Awardees	Physician group practices Acute care hospitals paid under the IPPS Health systems Physician-hospital organizations Conveners of participating health care providers	Physician group practices Acute care hospitals paid under the IPPS Health systems Physician-hospital organizations Post-acute providers Conveners of participating health care providers	Physician group practices Acute care hospitals paid under the IPPS Health systems Long-term care hospitals Inpatient Rehabilitation facilities Skilled nursing facilities Home health agency Physician-hospital organizations Conveners of participating health care providers	Physician group practices Acute care hospitals paid under the IPPS Health systems Physician-hospital organizations Conveners of participating health care providers
Payment of Bundle and Target Price	Discounted IPPS payment; no separate target price	Retrospective comparison of target price and actual FFS payments	Retrospective comparison of target price and actual FFS payments	Prospectively set payment
Clinical Conditions Targeted	All MS-DRGs	Applicants to propose based on MS-DRG for inpatient hospital stay	Applicants to propose based on MS-DRG for inpatient hospital stay	Applicants to propose based on MS-DRG for inpatient hospital stay
Types of Services Included in Bundle	Inpatient hospital services	Inpatient hospital and physician services Related post-acute care services Related readmissions Other services defined in the bundle	Post-acute care services Related readmissions Other services defined in the bundle	Inpatient hospital and physician services Related readmissions

Exhibit 3. An Overview of CMS Bundled Payment for Care Improvement Initiative[*]

(continued on next page)

MODEL FEATURE	MODEL 1 – Inpatient Stay Only	MODEL 2 – Inpatient Stay Plus Post-Discharge Services	MODEL 3 – Post-Discharge Services Only	MODEL 4 – Inpatient Stay Only
Exhibit 3. An Overview of CMS Bundled Payment for Care Improvement Initiative* (cont.)				
Expected Discount Provided to Medicare	To be proposed by applicant; CMS requires minimum discounts increasing from 0% in first 6 mos. to 2% in Year 3	To be proposed by applicant; CMS requires minimum discount of 3% for 30-89 days post-discharge episode; 2% for 90 days or longer episode	To be proposed by applicant	To be proposed by applicant; subject to minimum discount of 3%; larger discount for MS-DRGs in ACE demonstration
Payment From CMS to Providers	Acute care hospital: IPPS payment less pre-determined discount Physician: Traditional fee schedule payment (not included in episode or subject to discount)	Traditional fee-for-service payment to all providers and suppliers, subject to reconciliation with predetermined target price	Traditional fee-for-service payment to all providers and suppliers, subject to reconciliation with predetermined target price	Prospectively established bundled payment to admitting hospital; hospitals distribute payments from bundled payment
Quality Measures	All Hospital IQR measures and additional measures to be proposed by applicants	To be proposed by applicants, but CMS will ultimately establish a standardized set of measures that will be aligned to the greatest extent possible with measures in other CMS programs		

* www.innovations.cms.gov/Files/fact-sheet/Bundled-Payment-Fact-Sheet.pdf.

2.2 The Gainsharing Civil Monetary Penalties Law

While gainsharing has historically been viewed as unfavorable, OIG Advisory Opinion No. 08-16 opened the door for the possibility of gainsharing between hospitals and physicians.[16] Key conditions from this advisory opinion, as well as subsequent advisory opinions, suggest the OIG may allow gainsharing when conditions such as these are met:

- Transparency to all parties involved and/or vested in some manner;

---

16 oig.hhs.gov/fraud/docs/advisoryopinions/2008/AdvOpn08-16A.pdf.

- Protection against reductions in care;

- Written disclosures to patients;

- Reasonable compensation; and

- Per-capita distributions (i.e., even distribution of cost savings among the number of physicians in the practice).

It is important to note that The Bundled Payment for Care Improvement Initiative provides a waiver that allows gainsharing in the context of the pilot program.

2.3 The Anti-Kickback and Stark Laws

Stark Laws

The Stark laws monitor physicians partaking in self-referral for Medicare and Medicaid patients, where self-referral is defined as the action of a physician referring a patient to a particular medical facility in which he or she has a financial interest.[17] This raises a concern due to the increased coordination of care resulting from bundled payments because physicians may be inclined to self-refer to more fully benefit from the gainsharing possibilities tied to bundled payments.

Anti-Kickback Statute

Under the anti-kickback statute, anyone who knowingly and willfully receives or pays anything of value to influence the referral of federal healthcare business (i.e., Medicare and Medicaid) is committing a felony and may be held accountable for violation of the law.[18] Under bundled payments, the anti-kickback statute may be of concern, unless a waiver is granted similar to the one involving The Bundled Payment for Care Improvement Initiative.

2.4 Corporate Practice of Medicine

Some states preclude hospitals from employing physicians for outpatient care to prevent conflicts of interest between the corporation and the patient.[19] This may be an issue when coordinating post-acute care for patients, because the bundled payment is intended to cover services provided both during and after the acute care service. Notably, employment of physicians, if done well, can lead to alignment of both clinical and financial incentives for health systems and physicians that currently may not exist. At times, it

---

17 www.starklaw.org.
18 oig.hhs.gov/fraud/docs/safeharborregulations/safefs.htm.
19 www.irs.gov/pub/irs-tege/eotopicf00.pdf.

can be easier to coordinate care in a scenario in which participants are employed and thus operate "on the same team" (i.e., including the same EMR, same clinical pathways, same support staff, and same clinical/performance expectations).

2.5 Other Regulatory Issues

Other regulatory issues involving bundled payments may include the following:[20]

- *Fee splitting:* Laws may prohibit the splitting of fees with others for referring patients. These laws vary from state to state;

- *Joint price negotiation:* There is concern that price fixing may occur among competitors, constituting civil/criminal penalties; and

- *State laws:* These may include state insurance/risk regulation, state tax considerations, and certificates of need.

As can be seen, there are myriad compliance (or potential compliance) issues that any bundled payment initiative must clear. Nevertheless, a general understanding of these regulations prepares the valuation professional to render an opinion in the context of a dynamic healthcare regulatory environment.

3.0 Valuation Methods

Three generally accepted approaches are commonly used to value any type of asset, contract, or business, which are summarized as follows and discussed elsewhere herein:[21]

1. *Asset (cost) approach:* Based on the anticipated cost to re-create, replace, or replicate the asset or service. This approach is predominantly based upon the principle of substitution (i.e., the premise that a prudent individual will pay no more for a property or service than he or she would pay to acquire a substitute with the same utility).

2. *Income approach:* Based on the economic benefits anticipated from the asset or service. The income approach projects future cash flows that will be generated and then discounts them back to present value to account for the time value of money and the risk associated with actually achieving those projections.

3. *Market approach:* Based on transaction data involving similar assets or services.

---

20 "Bundled Payments: An Overview of the Antitrust, Regulatory, Contracting and State Law Issues," presentation, www.dwt.com.

21 For a complete discussion of the approaches to value in compensation valuation, see Chapter 2, "Defining FMV and the Market, Cost, and Income Approaches in Compensation Valuation."

Additionally, multiple methods fall under one or more of the above generally accepted valuation approaches. The appropriateness of utilizing one or more valuation methods will generally depend upon the facts and circumstances of the asset or service being valued. However, generally speaking, multiple methods should be utilized to the extent possible and the results reconciled for purposes of determining the final determination of fair market value.[22]

3.1 Valuation of Global Payments

Understanding how to value global payments can assist appraisers in a number of different valuation assignments. For example, if a hospital bills globally (i.e., for both the PC and TC services) for a specific procedure to be performed on its premises but subcontracts the professional interpretation to a physician, it will want to understand the fair market value compensation it can pay to the physician solely for the professional interpretation.

In instances such as this, valuing global payments can include approaches such as a compensation per wRVU approach and/or a percentage of collections split for the applicable services (i.e., PC/TC) rendered. For these reasons, having a thorough understanding of CPT/HCPCS codes, wRVUs, and PC/TC reimbursement (as described earlier) is an important foundation to valuing global and bundled payments. Nevertheless, these valuation methods can be considered a blend of the cost and market approach. For example, under the compensation per wRVU method, the number of wRVUs specific to the services rendered may be applied using a situation-specific compensation per wRVU rate that depends on the clinical specialty involved. Exhibit 4 provides an example of how a compensation-per-wRVU calculation may work using sample CPT codes.

Other common productivity metrics that can be substituted in place of wRVUs include total RVUs, professional collections, and patient encounters, to name a few. However, care should be given in establishing any production-based model, particularly to ensure that such a model is based on a formula that is set in advance and would not be contingent upon the volume or value of referrals. Valuation analysts typically benchmark multiple productivity metrics to multiple surveys, with the ultimate goal to align compensation and productivity. In addition, the valuator should also consider other key factors such as physician supply and demand issues, community need, payer mix, and current trends in compensation.

---

22 For a discussion on the use of multiple valuation methods, see Chapter 3, "Using Multiple Methods as a Prudent Practice in Compensation Valuation."

Exhibit 4. Compensation Per wRVU Example

CPT Code	Frequency	Number of wRVUs[1]	Frequency-Adjusted wRVUs	Compensation Based upon wRVUs[2]
A	B	C	D = B*C	E = D*$50
XX263	400	3.14	1,256	$ 62,800
XX300	400	0.62	248	$ 12,400
XX435	400	13.00	5,200	$ 260,000
XX778	400	11.32	4,528	$ 226,400
Total	1,600		11,232	$ 561,600

[1] Based upon Medicare National Physician Fee Schedule Relative Value File.

[2] Based on benchmark compensation per wRVU.

Another comparable method for determining physician compensation within global payments is by analyzing the reimbursement for professional services rendered (i.e., fee-for-service collections). The analyst begins by identifying the specific CPT codes within the services performed, the corresponding Medicare reimbursement rate, and the frequency of each CPT code. In this instance, depending upon the circumstances, the overall calculated Medicare reimbursement can be adjusted to reflect the actual payer mix and/or reimbursement assumptions specific to a payer class. Exhibit 5 provides an example of this analysis.

3.2 Valuation of Bundled Payments

The Bundled Payment for Care Improvement Initiative is in its infancy. Without significant precedent, most experts agree that determining how to fairly divide and distribute a bundled payment, whether structured as fee-for-service with a withhold or as a prospective payment based on historical costs, is a notable challenge. Nonetheless, several current fee-for-service provider payment mechanisms, as well as non-Medicare bundled payment payer initiatives, are in progress. These initiatives offer insight into how to value the physician services within bundled payments.

Exhibit 5. Fee-for-Service Analysis Example

Description	Medicare Reimbursement[1]	Medicare[2]	Medicaid[3]	Commercial[4]	Self Pay[5]	Total Payer-Mix Adjusted Reimbursement
A	B	C=(B*40%)*100%	D=(B*10%)*85%	E=(B*40%)*120%	F=(B*10%)*50%	G=SUM(C:F)
CPT Code XXXX1	$ 2,500.00	$ 1,000.00	$ 212.50	$ 1,200.00	$ 125.00	$ 2,537.50
CPT Code XXXX2	$ 2,000.00	$ 800.00	$ 170.00	$ 960.00	$ 100.00	$ 2,030.00
CPT Code XXXX3	$ 3,000.00	$ 1,200.00	$ 255.00	$ 1,440.00	$ 150.00	$ 3,045.00
CPT Code XXXX4	$ 2,750.00	$ 1,100.00	$ 233.75	$ 1,320.00	$ 137.50	$ 2,791.25

[1] Based upon published Medicare reimbursement for the specific locality.

[2] Medicare as representing 40% of the payer mix and reimbursing at 100% of the Medicare reimbursement rates.

[3] Medicaid as representing 10% of the payer mix and reimbursing at 85% of the Medicare reimbursement rates.

[4] Commercial as representing 40% of the payer mix and reimbursing at 120% of the Medicare reimbursement rates.

[5] Self Pay as representing 10% of the payer mix and reimbursing at 50% of the Medicare reimbursement rates.

Some current non-Medicare bundled payment initiatives begin by making physicians "whole" for their time and work effort (i.e., a fee-for-service approach). Therefore, certain valuation methods represent appropriate approaches when assessing fair market value compensation for physician services provided in a bundled payment setting. These valuation methods may include evaluation of the following:

- Professional/technical/global payments;

- Physician wRVUs;

- Collections per wRVU;

- Compensation per wRVU; and

- Historical reimbursement levels by CPT code.

As previously described, these types of metrics provide valuators guidance in assessing appropriate and fair market value compensation associated with bundled payments.

When assessing and performing such approaches, several fact- and circumstance-specific issues may arise. These issues include, but are not limited to, the following:

- As a consideration in the cost approach, the appraiser should consider what services the physicians should have performed using a recommended standard of care (i.e., an agreed-upon list of services to treat a specific condition), regardless of what services the rendering physician actually provided. In other words, while many bundled payment initiatives seek to make physicians whole for their time and work effort, only the physician time and work effort that is considered within the standard of care should be paid. Nevertheless, in a similar yet perhaps counterintuitive fashion, it is also important to understand that, under a bundled payment methodology, a desired behavior may frequently be the appropriate delivery of more coordinated care or even less care (i.e., fewer professional services rendered appropriately may ultimately lead to a greater value).

- When examining historical utilization and reimbursement for a bundled episode of care, some utilization data provided by individual payers may aggregate all physician services (i.e., the surgeon, emergency room physician, consulting physician, etc.) together. For example, if a patient is having a hip replacement, the orthopedic surgeon performing the surgery may consult another physician if the patient has a complication. In this way, the historical data provided by the payer may have all physician services lumped together. To understand how the aggregate reimbursement for physician services should be split among the physicians who rendered care, it is important to understand what services are typically required during the course of an episode of care. Several discussions with physicians, hospital management, and/or the appropriate billing representative coupled with an understanding of anatomy and procedures may be necessary to ascertain this information.

While many bundled payment initiatives strive to make the physician "whole" for his or her time and work effort, the industry is quickly developing into one that places compensation at risk for the achievement of quality care. Most bundled payment models for physicians will likely include an up-front fee-for-service discount, since the ultimate payment may be less if the quality metrics are not met. For example, if a quality metric is established at 100% compliance (which also represents the standard of care in this case) and the physicians are currently achieving 97% compliance, to incentivize the physicians to improve performance, the agency contracting for the bundled payments may place 5% of the physician's time and work effort at risk for achieving these standards. By structuring the agreement this way, the contracting entity ensures quality goals are met and physicians provide no less than the necessary services for successful outcomes. In contrast, all other factors being the same, as the physicians test the reasonableness of a proposed discount, they may seek to ensure the amount of compensation at risk is proportional to the difficulty of accomplishing the quality objectives. Ultimately, each payer and provider will work together to develop these metrics, their corresponding standards, and the amount of compensation at risk.

In addition to a "fee-for-service" and "at-risk" compensation components, the value of cost savings will be a key element of the valuation of bundled payments. Assuming Medicare's Bundled Payment for Care Improvement Initiative is successful in expanding the concept of shared savings within an episode of care in a legal and compliant manner, dividing the costs savings among the various providers brings up a number of valuation issues, including but not limited to, the following:

- Who has the greatest costs (and subsequently the most risk) in a cost savings model associated with an episode of care? An examination of a typical bundled payment for an episode of care indicates that a large percentage of costs reside within the hospital setting. These costs can include, among others, items such as implants and/or medical devices. For this reason, the hospital is generally paid a larger percentage of the bundled payment and all other factors being the same, since hospitals have the most at risk in this model, they should obtain the majority of the cost savings. The sharing of savings, however, is not always linear and can be affected by multiple other factors as discussed more fully in the questions that follow.

- Who stands to serve as the "change agent" in making cost savings a reality? Historically, hospitals have been challenged to cut costs in certain areas (i.e., the costs of medical devices and/or implants costs). This type of behavior change frequently requires significant physician leadership in partnership with hospital executives. Therefore, considering what impact an individual party can make to any cost savings may also be an appropriate factor when determining how to split the cost savings.

- What was the source of the cost savings and how long will it last? The source of cost savings can be indicative of whether a contracting agent can expect to receive a one-time cost savings or continuous savings over multiple years. Under a typical cost savings model, most cost savings occur within the first three years after implementing any changes to a cost structure. Therefore, the contracting parties may stand to share in these savings in Years 1 through 3, but in Years 4 and 5 (assuming a five-year agreement is in place), the cost savings may be minimal. Evaluating total compensation over the term of the agreement may also be an important fair market value compensation consideration.

- How much time did the physician spend improving or managing costs? If a physician can spend relatively little time yet lead efforts to command significant cost savings, does it make sense for the physician to be compensated significant dollars in return for his or her time?

- What total dollars are at risk for achievement and how difficult is it to accomplish the savings? In some areas, hospitals have been looking for new and creative ways to cut costs for years. While there are a number or reasons why it has been difficult to accomplish these savings, if a hospital stands to improve its profitability significantly, it may also be more willing to share these cost savings with other bundled payment participants.

While valuing bundled payments will depend on the specific structure of the arrangement, undoubtedly the consideration of the physician's time and effort (i.e., fee-for-service), a payment "at risk" for quality metrics, and the potential for "cost savings" *(under a legally permissible arrangement)* will likely play a part in determining fair market value compensation for bundled payments. Therefore, understanding how to value these different components (as well as their aggregate compensation) is important. Of these three components, determining how to split any cost savings in an objective, transparent, and prospectively determined way may be the most difficult. By understanding global payments and asking the questions identified above (as well as others specific to your transaction), deriving fair market value compensation should become easier.

Edited and Contributed by:

Mark W. Browne, MD, MMM, FACPE, CPE

Michael T. Harvey, MBA, CPA/ABV/CFF, CFE

Katelynd A. McElhany, MS candidate (2013)

Chapter 32. Valuing Physician Compensation in the Life Sciences

CONTENTS

Chapter 32. Valuing Physician Compensation in the Life Sciences

By Ann S. Brandt, Ph.D.

1.0 Introduction

The "life sciences industry," as it is frequently termed, encompasses a broad range of healthcare-related industries, including the pharmaceutical, medical device, medical supplies, medical equipment, and biotechnology industries. Two practices that are common in these industries are (i) contracting with physicians to provide speaking, consulting, and or research services and (ii) licensing various forms of intellectual property (IP) from physicians. Because physicians can also be referral sources for the products and services sold by companies in these industries, transactions between life science companies (LSCs) and physicians are subject to federal healthcare regulations that seek to prohibit payments for referrals of healthcare services and products. Such regulations require arrangements between referral-source physicians and LSCs to be commercially reasonable and consistent with fair market value. In recent years, federal regulators have significantly stepped up enforcement actions within the life sciences industry, and this industry is now experiencing the same fair market value compliance scrutiny that the hospital sector experienced over the past two decades. Most recently, under the Physician Payments Sunshine Act, which was included as Section 6002 of the Patient Protection and Affordable Care Act of 2010 (ACA), manufacturers of drugs, biological products, medical devices, and medical supplies must track and report to the U.S. Department of Health and Human Services (HHS) all payments and other transfers of value that they provide to physicians and teaching hospitals. This will be a yearly reporting requirement, commencing March 31, 2013. However, payment tracking by such companies commenced Jan. 1, 2012.[1] As a result, companies in the life sciences industry are seeking to employ widely recognized valuation approaches to ensure compliance and are increasingly turning to appraisal professionals for valuations of services provided by physicians.

This chapter will address issues in determining fair market value within the life sciences industry. It provides an overview of the regulatory context for this industry and an introduction to the service arrangements that are commonly entered into by LSCs and physicians. The chapter discusses key valuation issues and considerations to be addressed by the healthcare appraisal profession in appraising life sciences compensation arrangements.

2.0 Service Arrangements in the Life Sciences Industry

In valuing the compensation provided under a service arrangement, it is essential for the appraiser to understand the nature and scope of the services provided under the subject arrangement. The types, level, and extent of services provided are key factors in arriving at the compensation paid under a service contract. Another critical element in determining the compensation is the required qualifications of the service provider. This relationship between the services provided and amount of compensation should be self-evident to appraisers, who establish appraisal fees routinely with clients based on the scope of the particular appraisal assignment. The level and extent of valuation services coupled with the qualifications of the appraisers providing those services generally determine the fees. In a similar manner, the scope of services and the required qualifications of the individual providing those services are fundamental factors in determining the compensation for service arrangements between physicians and LSCs. The beginning point for valuing such service arrangements, therefore, is cataloging and analyzing the scope of services and the qualifications necessary for providing these services.

In general, physicians provide three types of services in the life sciences industry: consulting, research, and speaking and education (which will be considered as a subset of consulting services within this chapter). LSCs seek such services because experienced physicians offer a level of expertise that often cannot be duplicated by any other group of professionals. As a result, physician (i) input into product design and development, (ii) insight into market requirements, and (iii) expertise in the use of products and services

---

1   The law applies to cash and noncash items received by physicians for consulting, speaking engagements, advisory board services, travel, food, gifts, research, royalty payments, clinical research, and other transfers of value designated by the secretary of HHS. Physician investment interests and ownership (other than publicly traded securities and mutual funds) must also be reported.

are invaluable to LSCs. Within the life sciences industry, physicians with varying levels of expertise and experience can provide these types of services, ranging from local-level practitioners to internationally acclaimed "thought leaders." Thus, establishing the fair market value of consulting, research, or speaking and educational services provided by varying "levels" of physicians is a central issue for healthcare valuation in the life sciences.

From a regulatory standpoint, the government's concern with these types of service arrangements focuses on whether they are being used as a vehicle to induce physicians to purchase or prescribe a given LSC's products. Therefore, regulators have been focusing their attention on various types of service arrangements to determine whether they are tied to prescribing practices or to usage patterns involving the company's products. Of obvious importance in this scrutiny is whether the fees for these services appear to be in excess of fair market value for actual services rendered. Similarly, medical device companies are being targeted for investigation when there is doubt as to the legitimate need for the particular consulting services or when there is a lack of documentation of the services rendered.

2.1 Types of Consulting Services

LSCs contract with physicians to provide an array of consulting services related to the products offered by such companies. These consulting services include:

- Product development;

- Product design;

- Product research activities;

- Advisory services;

- Marketing; and

- Physician education and training.

Such consulting services are provided to LSCs that market drugs and medications, medical devices, medical instruments and equipment, and medical supplies. In today's marketplace, LSCs engage legions of physician consultants and advisors to conduct research and development as well as marketing activities on behalf of their products. Payments to these physician advisors and consultants, which often total millions of dollars per year, have become routine expenses for LSCs.

Why do LSCs contract with so many physicians to provide such consulting services? As noted previously, experienced physicians offer a level of expertise that often cannot be duplicated by any other group of professionals. Their knowledge and experience in treating patients with diseases, illnesses, and sundry healthcare problems is vital to the effective use of life sciences products in the healthcare marketplace. This knowledge base can be tapped to provide important considerations in the development and marketing of products that improve patient care and disease treatment. Such first-hand knowledge of patient care is not always readily available in database or informational formats. It is also essential for marketing such products to the primary decision makers in the healthcare arena—physicians.

Physicians must be very knowledgeable about the drugs and devices they recommend to their patients. Thus, physician education is of paramount importance to the marketing and distribution of these products. This need for education is especially necessary for new drugs and devices that are introduced in the marketplace. Physicians and other healthcare providers need to be educated about the unique properties and medical efficacy of these newer, potentially more effective (and often more costly) products. Yet, physicians may have little time to meet with manufacturers' representatives, who are often forced to compete with patients for the physician's limited time.

In an effort to inform physicians about newly developed products, it is common practice for pharmaceutical companies to engage the services of a broad range of physicians to serve as advisors and consultants to other physicians practicing medicine in their targeted markets. Marketplace trends indicate that physicians are more willing to listen to and change their prescribing patterns after obtaining information regarding the relative benefits of new products from other well-credentialed physicians. With respect to medical device companies, physician input is required to ensure that products are designed, implanted, and used appropriately. LSCs have found that physician consulting services are a necessary and integral part of the product development and marketing life cycle.

The scope of services in consulting arrangements can vary widely within the life sciences industry. In valuing consulting arrangements, it is essential to analyze the specific duties and responsibilities provided by a physician consultant to an LSC under a proposed service agreement. A useful framework for identifying and evaluating the scope of services includes the following considerations:

- Number of hours associated with each duty and responsibility;

- The specific duties and responsibilities of the position;

- The complexity of each duty and responsibility;

- Level of physician expertise required for the duties;

- Specific objectives and deliverables; and

- Potential impact of thought leader on organizational and product success, in terms of visibility and credibility within the medical community or particular physician specialty.

The physician qualifications for consulting arrangements will also vary. Since LSCs generally seek higher credentialed and experienced physicians for consulting services, it is critical to identify, analyze, and categorize qualifications that are required of the physicians who will provide consulting services under an arrangement. These qualifications typically include:

- Educational credentials and specialized training;

- Professional certifications;

- Leadership experience;

- Academic appointments;

- Research experience and funding history;

- Invited presentations;

- Publication history; and

- Other professional leadership activities and reputation in the healthcare community.

In the life sciences industry, it is not uncommon to observe interdependencies between the duties and responsibilities and the qualification requirements of a consulting arrangement. Basic consulting services, for example, may not require the skill and experience of a uniquely qualified or specialized physician or a physician with high visibility and credibility within the medical community or a physician specialty. More advanced responsibilities and services, on the other hand, may only be performed by physicians with specific qualifications and credentials, as well as peer acknowledgement of a certain degree of expertise. Such interdependencies can become important considerations in determining the fair market value compensation for consulting services in the life sciences industry.

2.2 Types of Research Services

In addition to consulting arrangements with physicians, LSCs frequently enter into compensated arrangements with physicians involving clinical trials or research studies. Clinical trials (or studies) are treatment protocols that are coordinated by pharmaceutical companies, biotechnology companies, or medical device manufacturers (commonly referred to as "sponsors") to obtain clinical data involving the use of its drugs or devices in the course of actual patient treatments. Clinical trials are classified as Phase I, II, III, or IV. Briefly described, Phase I and II trials are early-stage studies that are intended to establish the safety and the apparent efficacy of a new drug or device that is not yet FDA-approved. Phase III clinical trials involve much larger groups of human subjects, and the results of Phase III testing are used by sponsors in support of their applications for FDA approval. Phase IV studies entail additional research that is conducted on a post-FDA-approval basis. Sometimes referred to as "market studies," Phase IV trials are intended to establish additional information concerning a drug that may, for example, lead to new indications or improvements in dosing guidelines.

These studies often involve compensation agreements by and among the sponsors, physicians, and other third parties, such as hospitals or ambulatory treatment facilities. As these types of trials involve compensation payable to parties who are in a position to refer to one another, compliance with the fair market value standard is required to demonstrate compliance with applicable federal and state healthcare regulations.

The clinical trials process is complex, and each trial requires the designation of a physician who serves as the principal investigator (PI) of the trial. There are a number of compensable arrangements inherent in clinical trials that must be consistent with fair market value. First, the overall financial arrangement between the sponsor and the PI must be consistent with fair market value. Typically, fees paid by a sponsor to a PI are based upon a study budget and include a fixed payment and a variable payment based upon the number of patients. The fixed payment includes compensation for overall initiation of the study, as well as costs that may be assessed by third parties. For example, clinical studies involving hospital care must generally be approved by the hospital's governing body called the institutional review board, or the IRB. The *per-patient* fees can range from $1,000 per patient or less to $25,000 per patient or more. From the *per-patient* fees, the PI may be responsible for purchasing certain services from third parties, such as diagnostic imaging studies from a hospital or an imaging center. In some cases, the study budget may also contemplate payment to a study participant (i.e., a patient).

Thus, when analyzing the services provided under a research arrangement between a sponsor and a PI, an appraiser may want to give consideration to the PI's overall duties and responsibilities in terms of the following categories:

- The intellectual process of identifying desired clinical trials in which to participate;

- The investment in one or more research nurses and required research infrastructure and resources; and

- The assumption of the overall responsibility and liability for the conduct of such trials.

Identifying responsibilities of the PI in terms of these three major functions allows the appraiser to evaluate the level and scope of services provided in the subject clinical study arrangement.

In determining the value of research services in the life sciences industry, it is important to note that clinical studies frequently require services beyond a physician's time and expertise. Other resources of a physician's practice may be used to perform the research, including nursing staff, space, medical records, equipment, and supplies. In certain circumstances, the conduct of clinical trials may be more comparable to an ancillary service as opposed to a professional service when evaluating the use of physician practice resources. A physician practice may assume certain levels of liability under the terms of some research arrangements. Such liability may require changes in malpractice or other types of liability coverage. In general, research services contrast with consulting services in that the latter typically entail only the provision of a physician's time and expertise, rather than the assembled or turnkey resources of a physician practice.

As described above, many clinical studies reflect financial arrangements negotiated between sponsors and PIs. In other instances, organizations, such as hospitals, may be the party that attracts and negotiates the financial arrangement with the sponsor. Since a PI is still required for the study, a hospital may engage and compensate a physician to serve as the PI. Under this type of arrangement, the PI's services and involvement are significantly different than if the PI assumed the full risk for the study. Accordingly, the valuation methodology used in this case should focus on the more value of the physician's personally performed services.

3.0 Regulatory Issues in the Life Sciences Industry

Physicians who provide services to LSCs may also be referral sources for the healthcare goods and services provided by LSCs. They may be in a position to purchase or prescribe the products marketed by LSCs with whom they have compensation arrangements. As a result of this potential referral relationship, transactions and arrangements between physicians and LSCs may be subject to both federal and state healthcare laws and regulations. These healthcare laws and regulations, among other things, prohibit providers of certain healthcare goods and services from paying for referrals for these goods and services, particularly if the provider entities derive revenue from federal healthcare programs. Therefore, whenever such entities wish to enter into transactions or arrangements for other legitimate goods and services, the requirement that the compensation paid must be consistent with fair market value is a fundamental regulatory tool for ensuring that such exchanges do not entail payments for referrals among the parties. LSCs frequently engage appraisal firms to establish fair market value in these arrangements for regulatory compliance purposes.

Generally, three major areas of federal healthcare laws and regulations govern compensation arrangements with referral-source physicians in the life sciences industry:

- The Patient Protection and Affordable Care Act of 2010 (PPACA);

- The federal anti-kickback statute and related regulations and advisory opinions (collectively, FAKS); and

- The Stark law and accompanying Stark regulations (Stark).

3.1 PPACA

The Patient Protection and Affordable Care Act,[2] signed into law on March 23, 2010, includes provisions from the Physician Payment Sunshine Act (the Sunshine Act).[3] Following the enactment of PPACA, H.R. 4872, the Health Care and Education Reconciliation Act of 2010, was enacted into law on March 30, 2010, "reconciling" and revising portions of PPACA.

The Sunshine Act requires "applicable manufacturers," which are manufacturers of a "covered drug, device, biological, or medical supply," to report annually certain "payments or other transfers of value" provided to a "covered recipient." "Covered drug, device, biological, or medical supply" is defined as a product "for which payment is

---

2   H.R. 3590.
3   The Sunshine Act was introduced in 2009 by Senators Charles Grassley (R-Iowa) and Herb Kohl (D-Wis.).

available under [Social Security Act] title XVIII or a state plan under title XIX or XXI (or a waiver of such plan)." "Covered recipients" are defined as physicians and teaching hospitals. The first report from applicable manufacturers is due to the secretary of Health and Human Services (the Secretary) by March 31, 2013.[4]

For each payment or transfer of value, the manufacturer must report the following information:

- Name, business address, specialty, and Medicare billing number for the covered recipient;

- Amount of the payment or transfer of value;

- Date of the payment or transfer of value;

- Description of the form of the payment (e.g., cash, cash equivalents, in-kind items or services, stock, stock options, other ownerships interests, and dividends);

- Description of the nature of the payment (e.g., consulting fees, compensation for services other than consulting, honoraria, gifts, entertainment, food, travel, education, research, charitable contributions, royalties, licenses, ownership or investment interests, direct compensation for serving as faculty or as a speaker for a medical education program and grants);

- Name of the covered drug, device, biological, or medical supply, if the payment or other transfer of value related to marketing, education, or research of a covered drug, device, biological, or medical supply; and

- Any other categories of information required by the secretary.

The Sunshine Act excludes from the definition of "payment or other transfer of value" anything with a value of less than $10. However, items under $10 may not be excluded from reporting if the aggregate amount to a covered recipient exceeds $100 per calendar year. Furthermore, after providing opportunity for review, the secretary must make the

---

4   At the time of this publication, the final rule has not yet been published, and CMS noted that a final rule will not be published in time for applicable manufacturers and applicable GPOs to begin collecting the information required in Section 1128G of the act on Jan. 1, 2012, as indicated in the statute. Therefore, CMS *will not* require applicable manufacturers and applicable GPOs to begin collecting the required information until after the publication of the final rule.

reported information publicly available in a searchable format by Sept. 30, 2013, and on June 30 of each year thereafter.

The Sunshine Act provides civil monetary penalties for noncompliance. Manufacturers that fail to report "in a timely manner in accordance with rules or regulations" are subject to a civil monetary penalty of $1,000 to $10,000 for each payment or other transfer of value not reported as required. The limit on this provision for each annual submission is $150,000. Similarly, manufacturers that "knowingly"[5] fail to report "in a timely manner in accordance with rules or regulations" are subject to a civil monetary penalty of $10,000 to $100,000 for each payment or other transfer of value with an annual maximum of $1 million.[6] Manufacturers also may be subject to other penalties for noncompliance

3.2 FAKS

The federal anti-kickback statute[7] provides that *anyone who knowingly and willfully pays or receives anything of value to influence the referral of business, which is reimbursable in whole or in part by a federal healthcare program, can be charged with criminal penalties, civil monetary sanctions, and even exclusion from federal healthcare programs.*[8] Prosecution under FAKS requires the government to prove that the parties possessed the intent to induce referrals at the time they entered into the arrangement. As a practical matter, the requirement to prove intent often limits prosecution and enforcement actions under FAKS. FAKS provides for certain safe harbors and outlines requirements that help establish that a given arrangement is not structured to be payment for referrals. One critical requirement is that the compensation paid in an arrangement with a referral source for other legitimate goods or services must be at fair market value. It is important to note, however, that under FAKS, an arrangement is illegal even if only one of the intended purposes of the arrangement is to generate referrals between the parties. Such an arrangement violates the statute regardless of whether the compensation paid is fair market value.[9]

There have been several recent well-publicized enforcement actions for alleged illegal conduct under FAKS for consulting arrangements within the life sciences industry, some of which are discussed below. Many pharmaceutical companies and medical

---

5   "Knowingly" is defined as "a person, with respect to information, [who] (i) has actual knowledge of the information; (ii) acts in deliberate ignorance of the truth or falsity of the information; or (iii) acts in reckless disregard of the truth or falsity of the information, and no proof of specific intent to defraud is required."
6   Manufacturers also may be subject to other penalties for noncompliance.
7   42 U.S.C. §1320a-7b.
8   Section 1128B(b) of the act (42 U.S.C. 1320a-7b(b))(2003).
9   *United States v. Kats*, 871 F.2d 105 (9th Cir. 1989); *United States v. Greber*, 760 F.2d 68 (3d Cir.), cert. denied, 474 U.S. 988 (1985).

device companies have settled the allegations by entering into a deferred prosecution agreement[10] (DPA) with the U.S. Department of Justice and simultaneously executing a corporate integrity agreement (CIA) with the Office of Inspector General (OIG). DPAs and CIAs are intended to cause the offending organization to develop a plan of self-improvement and self-monitoring, coupled with independent outside review to insure that the risk of future violations is minimized. One element of a number of DPAs and CIAs that have been executed with the government is the requirement that independent third-party fair market value analyses be performed for all physician compensation arrangements over a certain dollar value threshold. (In the recent case of five of the country's largest medical device companies, this threshold was identified to be compensation exceeding $500 per hour.) These specific requirements imposed by certain DPAs and CIAs signal the government's concern when physicians receive "high" rates of compensation. The following section presents highlights from some of these enforcement actions.

In July, 2006, Medtronic signed a DPA with the U.S. Department of Justice in which it agreed to pay $40 million to the United States and participating states to settle allegations stemming from two qui tam lawsuits.[11] These lawsuits, which were brought under the federal False Claims Act (FCA), allege that Medtronic made illegal payments to physicians to promote its spinal products in violation of the federal healthcare program anti-kickback statute. The alleged illegal payments included (i) consulting and royalty agreements for which little or no work was performed and (ii) all-expenses-paid trips to lavish venues. In addition to the $40 million payment, Medtronic was required to enter into a five-year CIA with the OIG.

In another well-publicized case, to resolve allegations under the FCA, four major medical device manufacturers[12] entered into civil settlement agreements with the government for a combined total of $311 million. The government alleged that the companies provided financial incentives to physicians, including consulting agreements and lavish trips, to persuade physicians to use their joint replacement products. The government alleged that by offering illegal inducements, the identified companies violated the FCA by causing hospitals to seek and obtain reimbursement from Medicare. To avoid criminal prosecution, each of the identified companies entered into an 18-month DPA with the Department of Justice, under which they agreed to multiple remedies, including

---

10 In some cases, the Department of Justice will enter into a "nonprosecution agreement" instead of a DPA, which differs in that the case cannot be later reopened if the agreement is breached by the defendant. This article refers to both types of agreements as DPAs.

11 Qui tam lawsuits are initiated by a third party on behalf of the government. These actions are generally brought by whistleblowers under the federal False Claims Act.

12 *Biomet Inc., DePuy Orthopedics Inc., Smith & Nephew Inc., Zimmer Inc.*

the posting on their Web sites of the names of consultants, along with the amount of payments to these consultants. In addition, each of the identified companies entered into a five-year CIA with the OIG.

Another case involves a physician who accepted kickbacks from a medical device company in return for using the company's products. Even though criminal prosecutors have rarely directly targeted physicians, a physician who accepts a kickback in return for using a product can be as culpable as the company that provided the kickback. Dr. Patrick Chan, a neurologist in Arkansas, paid a $1.5 million civil settlement in January 2008 and pled guilty to soliciting and accepting kickbacks from Blackstone Medical. The kickbacks included gifts and payments for sham consulting agreements and fake research studies.

In another recent case, Lincare Holdings, a provider of respiratory care, infusion therapy, and medical equipment to patients in the home, paid $10 million and entered into a five-year CIA for allegedly providing kickback payments to physicians in the form of sporting and entertainment tickets, rounds of golf, golf equipment, fishing trips, meals, office expenses, and medical equipment, all of which were intended to induce the physicians to refer patients to the company. The government also alleged that Lincare provided kickbacks in the form of purported consulting arrangements that had no basis or foundation for payment. In addition, the government alleged that Lincare violated the Stark .law by accepting referrals from parties to the consulting agreements.

3.3 Stark

The federal physician self-referral ban (commonly referred to as the Stark law[13]) prohibits referrals by a physician or an immediate family member[14] to an entity for "designated health services"[15] if the physician has a financial relationship with the entity receiving the referral. Within the framework of the Stark law, (i) the physician may not make a referral to the entity for the furnishing of designated health services for which payment may be made under Medicare or Medicaid and (ii) the entity may not bill for designated health services furnished pursuant to such referral. A physician who has a financial relationship with an entity cannot make a referral to the entity for the furnishing of

---

13 The physician Self-Referral Law (the Stark law) is codified at 42 U.S.C.S. §1395nn.
14 The term "immediate family member" includes a husband or wife, birth or adoptive parent, child or sibling, father-in-law, mother-in-law, brother in-law, sister-in-law, grandparent, or grandchild.
15 Designated health services include: radiology and other imaging services (MRI, CT, and ultrasound); physical therapy; occupational therapy; radiation therapy; durable medical equipment; parenteral and enteral nutrients, equipment, and supplies; prosthetics, orthotics, and prosthetic devices and supplies; home health services; outpatient prescription drugs; and inpatient and outpatient hospital services. *Note that this listing of designated health services is not intended to be exhaustive, as the government has expanded the list on several occasions.*

designated health services unless it is demonstrated that the financial arrangement qualified for one of the identified exceptions.[16]

Two areas of the Stark regulations have a direct impact on valuing physician compensation arrangements in the life sciences industry. The first is the prohibition on using market data from parties in a position to refer for establishing FMV.[17] Applying this prohibition to the valuation of service arrangements may have critical consequences. Market information based on surveying existing compensation arrangements within the life sciences industry may be problematic for several reasons, including: (1) existing compensation arrangements may not be within FMV, and therefore, the data itself may be tainted; and (2) data between referral-source physicians and LSCs should be identified and excluded from the determination of fair market value for Stark compliance purposes. As a result, appraisers should consider the source of the market data used to establish fair market value for compensation arrangements in the life sciences industry.

The second is the Stark distinction between administrative and clinical services. In the Stark regulations issued in September 2007 (the Stark Phase III regulations), CMS made an important distinction between the clinical and administrative work provided by physicians and the determination of fair market value for physician services. In its commentary to responses, CMS stated:

> A fair market value hourly rate may be used to compensate physicians for both administrative and clinical work, provided that the rate paid for clinical work is fair market value for the clinical work performed and the rate paid for administrative work is fair market value for the administrative work performed. We note that the fair market value of administrative services may differ from the fair market value of clinical services.[18]

Given this guidance, an appraiser who is engaged to value a service arrangement for Stark compliance purposes should consider the distinction between clinical and administrative duties when appraising the physician services.

---

16 Stark exceptions can be either statutory or regulatory, and exceptions exist for personal services provided by physicians (e.g., LSC consulting arrangements) and for other goods and services provided by physician (e.g., IP license arrangements); the key features of both exceptions are that the compensation must be consistent with fair market value.

17 For a complete discussion of this prohibition, see Chapter 8, "To Use or Not to Use: An Appraisal Analysis of the Stark Prohibition on Market Data From Parties in a Position to Refer."

18 72 *F.R.* 51016.

4.0 The Market Approach

In utilizing the market approach to value physician service arrangements in the life sciences industry, the appraiser performs market research to accumulate information on comparable arrangements, including the scope of services provided, the required qualifications of the physicians providing such services, and the level of compensation paid. Unfortunately, such market information is not readily accessible. Few sources of data are specific to physician compensation for specialized nonclinical services, such as consulting, research, or administration (e.g., medical directorships).[19] By contrast, multiple sources of published data exist relating to physician compensation for clinical services or compensation from all sources, such as the Medical Group Management Association (MGMA), American Medical Group Association (AMGA), or Sullivan, Cotter and Associates Inc. (SCA) physician compensation surveys described in the following section. Appraisers attempting to create such market data "from scratch" may encounter LSCs or physicians who are unwilling to share information about existing service arrangements for confidentiality or proprietary reasons.

Appraisers attempting to accumulate market data on physician consulting and research service arrangements or using published or proprietary sources of market data should be aware of the issues and limitations that may be encountered in using such market information. It is preferable to obtain and use highly detailed market information to establish market comparables for specialized physician services. Differences in the detailed scope of services and the required qualifications for providing those services may have a material impact on the comparability of services and the valuation analysis.

The valuation analyst should use caution in making comparisons when limited information is available on other service arrangements in the marketplace. Unhappily, limited market information may be all that the appraiser is able to obtain on physician consulting and research contracts in the life sciences industry.

A second layer of difficulty may be encountered in using market comparables to establish the value of physician consulting and research services for LSCs. It is highly probable that market information on such services will come from physicians and LSCs who have potential referral relationships that implicate Stark or the FAKS. When, as is

---

19   We have elected to treat use of the general physician compensation surveys (e.g., MGMA, AMGA, SCA, and so on) under the cost approach for purposes of valuing physician consulting and research services in the life sciences industry. Because such surveys are based primarily on clinical services and frequently report compensation from all sources (clinical, administrative, consulting, research, call coverage, business owner, ancillary income, and so on), we would argue that such surveys do not represent pure market data on compensation for specialized services, such as physician consulting and clinical trials, in the life sciences industry. Under the cost approach, however, such general information on physician compensation levels from all sources may be utilized to estimate the cost to re-create such specialized services.

often the case, the valuation is requested for purposes of complying with healthcare laws and regulations, market comparables derived from physicians and providers with referral or potential referral relationships may need to be excluded from consideration. Compensation to physicians under these types of arrangements may be skewed by the potential for referrals between the parties and as such, may not be an appropriate benchmark for fair market value in these types of transactions under the regulatory definition of fair market value. Even when the Stark limitation on the use of market comparables is not part of the valuation assignment scope of work, it may be advisable not to rely solely on market data to establish the fair market value of physician services in the life sciences industry. While some market data points may represent arm's-length transactions, others may not. Sorting out which transactions are independent may not be possible or practicable.

One line of research that may yield potential market comparables for physician consulting services in the life sciences industry is identifying comparable consulting services provided outside of the healthcare context by comparably qualified professionals. Under this valuation technique, the appraiser obtains compensation rates paid to comparably qualified professionals providing comparable services in other nonhealthcare industries and "crosswalks" these rates to the subject arrangement in the life sciences industry. This technique may be derived from an analysis of the consulting services provided by physicians and their qualifications to provide those services. While physicians tend to be among the nation's most highly educated and experienced professionals, the consulting services they provide to LSCs have considerable financial as well as operational implications for these companies. These financial and operational characteristics of physician consulting services can provide a range of comparability with services performed by comparably qualified consultants and specialists in various industries. Compensation rates for attorneys may also provide market guidance. Legal advice and consulting may be comparable in some circumstances to consulting provided by physicians, while legal education and licensing requirements may also provide a certain level of comparability with regard to the educational and licensing qualifications of physicians. Nonetheless, establishing compatibility for valuation purposes may be quite difficult in pursuing this line of research.[20]

5.0 The Cost Approach

As applied to valuing physician services in the life sciences industry, the cost approach seeks to value an arrangement between a LSC and a physician by considering the LSC's

---

20 Editor's note: The SEC filings of publicly held Huron Consulting Group Inc., FTI Consulting Inc., Navigant Consulting Inc. and Charles River Associates (CRA International Inc.) may provide some insight.

costs in the alternative to contracting with a physician. For example, such alternate cost might be based upon the employment of one or more physicians to provide the required services. For research services, the alternative cost may require ownership and operation of a physician practice, including employment of a physician. As a practical matter, however, the appraiser should keep in mind that most consulting or research arrangements in the life sciences industry are structured as independent contractor arrangements. Such consulting or research services require variable and often limited hours. As such, securing these services through an employment or ownership arrangement is generally less practical than through an independent contractor arrangement. Application of the cost approach, therefore, generally represents a hypothetical alternative to obtaining physician services in the life sciences industry.

Because clinical studies may require resources beyond a physician's time and expertise, application of the cost approach to research services involves additional considerations over and above the value of the services provided by an individual physician. Use of the cost approach for research services, therefore, requires a separate analysis for each type of resource used in research studies. Since the value of a physician's time and expertise is a component of both consulting as well as research services, it may be helpful to begin with a discussion of the application of the cost approach to consulting services. Many, if not all, of the issues and considerations in valuing physician consulting services are also applicable to valuing research services in that a physician's time and expertise are critical resources in the latter. Research services include physician services as well as other services and resources.

5.1 Application of the Cost Approach to Valuing Consulting Services

In following the valuation principle of alternatives, an appraiser may look to physician compensation levels in the marketplace, whether from employment or private practice, as a hypothetical basis for the alternative cost to procuring the physician services provided in physician consulting and research arrangements. There are several reliable and readily available sources of survey data for physician compensation in the marketplace. These sources include:

1. Medical Group Management Association (MGMA), *Physician Compensation and Production Survey*. This is an annually published survey that typically reports compensation data from over 2,800 physician practices (predominantly independent physician-owned organizations representing over 59,000 physicians and midlevel providers).

2. Sullivan, Cotter and Associates Inc. (SCA), *Physician Compensation and Productivity Survey Report* (SCA). This is a compendium of data reported by

351 healthcare organizations (including medical centers, group practices, integrated delivery systems, and health maintenance organizations, or HMOs). The 2011 edition represents responses from 58,626 MDs, PhDs, midlevel providers, residents, and medical group executives.

3. Client & Healthcare Compensation Service (HCS), *Physician Salary Survey Report* and *Client Salary & Benefits Report.* The *Physician Salary* report incorporates data from 333 healthcare organizations (including group practice facilities and HMOs). The 2011 edition represents responses from 28,295 physicians. The "Client Salary" report incorporates data from 539 HCS clients, including responses from various client executives, administrators, and nonphysician and midlevel providers.

4. American Medical Group Association (AMGA), *Medical Group Compensation and Financial Survey.* The AMGA report discloses salary survey data obtained from medical groups, (predominantly large multispecialty group practices). Second in size to only the MGMA survey, the AMGA survey is one of the most reliable sources of physician clinical compensation data. The 2011 edition incorporates data from 239 medical groups, predominantly large multispecialty group practices, representing approximately 51,700 physicians and midlevel providers.

5. Towers Watson Data Services (TW), *Health Care Clinical and Professional Compensation Survey Report.* The TW report incorporates data from 368 healthcare organizations representing 652,352 physicians, midlevel providers, and healthcare executives.

It is essential that appraisers understand how these various physician compensation surveys gather and report financial information on physician compensation. Such knowledge is needed for the valid use of the survey data to determine physician compensation rates. An appraiser will need to address five critical issues in using the survey data to establish the fair market value of physician compensation for purposes of medical director services. These issues include:

1. The distinction between clinical services and nonclinical services, such as consulting, research, and administrative, and any corresponding differentiation in compensation levels for clinical versus other specialized work.

2. The relative comparability of physician qualifications as well as job duties and responsibilities in the various surveys relative to the subject consulting arrangement.

3. The distinction between compensation for physician services and business owner compensation.

4. Determining the appropriate level of annual hours worked for purposes of computing an hourly rate for physician services.

5. Adjustment of employment compensation hourly rate to an independent-contractor basis.

The appraiser's analysis and resolution of these critical issues may have a material impact on the valuation opinion for a subject physician service arrangement.

5.2 Compensation for Clinical Versus Administrative Services

At noted in the section on the regulatory context for valuing physician services in the life sciences industry, CMS recently indicated that it recognizes a distinction between clinical and administrative services with regard to physician compensation. According to the regulators, the fair market value for physician clinical services may differ from the fair market value of administrative services provided by a physician for Stark compliance purposes. Appraisers valuing physician consulting and research services for Stark compliance purposes should address this distinction between clinical and administrative duties when determining the fair market value of those services. The salient point to this distinction appears to be that the value of clinical work may be greater or less than the value of nonclinical work in certain instances. On the one hand, clinical services may warrant higher levels of compensation than administrative or other forms of nonclinical services. Under this line of reasoning, clinical work is deemed to involve a higher degree of complexity and risk than administrative or consulting work. Clinical procedures involve the immediate health and well-being of patients and in some specialties and cases, the literal difference between life and death. While consulting services may require a skill set only found in physicians of a given specialty, these functions and duties do not generally entail the same level of complexity or risk as the provision of healthcare services to patients. As a result, the level of compensation paid for administrative or consulting services may be less than the compensation paid for the same amount of time spent performing clinical procedures.

An alternative line of reasoning derived from an opportunity cost analysis argues against the opinion that administrative services should be compensated at a level different from clinical work. It contends that physicians would not agree to provide services at a lower rate because of the opportunity cost for providing administrative or consulting services in comparison to clinical services. Compensation levels for clinical procedures are the indicator of the value of a physician's time. Physicians should be paid at clinical levels for them to agree to provide nonclinical types of services. Otherwise, physicians have no incentive to provide administrative or consulting services.

A third line of reasoning argues that consulting services may entail a higher degree of risk or complexity than a physician encounters in a patient care environment. The risk in product design and development may be greater than a physician experiences in daily practice due to the sheer number of patients that may be affected by flaws in a medical device or instrument. The financial risk inherent in development and marketing plans for some pharmaceuticals and medical equipment can potentially include hundreds of millions of dollars. The services of a physician providing marketing consultations and advice for such products may have a financial impact beyond any malpractice claim or decline in practice profitability resulting from clinical procedures. It is possible, therefore, to determine that levels of physician compensation for consulting services should exceed levels for clinical services.

In considering the idea that the risk and complexity of consulting arrangements for an LSC may exceed that found in a clinical setting, it is interesting to note the terms of recent government settlements with medical device and pharmaceutical manufacturers concerning payments to physician-consultants. While the settlements are not applicable to other companies and their physician-consultant arrangements, they may provide some insight into the areas of concern for healthcare regulators. These settlement agreements reiterated that compensation for such arrangements must be within fair market value, and further, certain settlements require the manufacturers to seek *independent third-party opinions* to establish fair market value for any physician-consultant compensation in excess of $500 per hour.[21] In a striking contrast, Hospital Corporation of America's (HCA) corporate integrity agreement from December 2000 required that it obtain an independent third-party opinion for any physician compensation in excess of $150 per hour. Such disparities in hourly rates may be an indication that regulators perceive a difference in the consulting services provided in the life sciences industry in contrast to physician services provided to hospital systems. It would be problematic, however, to cite these disparate rates as establishing the range of fair market value for physician services.

Whatever position an appraiser takes on the issue of clinical and consulting and administrative compensation, appraisal opinions prepared for Stark compliance purposes should address the distinction and provide support and defense for the position taken

---

21 See article titled "Artificial-Joint Makers Settle Kickback Case," *New York Times*, Sept. 28, 2007, and the agreements between the U.S. Department of Justice and Biomet, DePuy Orthopedics, Zimmer Holdings, Stryker Orthopedics, and Smith and Nephew.

on the issue. Failure to consider this question may constitute an inadequate scope of work for such appraisal assignments. In addition, appraisers may be given regulatory guidance by the client and the client's legal counsel that determines the approach to be taken by the appraiser in valuing consulting services. In such cases, the appraiser should document this regulatory guidance as part of definition of value applicable to the assignment.

The approach taken in comparing compensation for clinical and administrative work is critical in determining how physician compensation survey information is used in valuing physician consulting and research services. Physician compensation surveys generally report compensation from all sources. The primary source of income for a physician outside of an academic practice setting or a purely administrative role is clinical services. As a result, the compensation in most of the published surveys primarily represents clinical compensation. If an appraiser takes the position that administrative services should be compensated at a lower rate than clinical services, he or she may need to adjust the survey compensation levels or choose the lower percentiles from the survey to derive hourly physician compensation rates applicable to medical director services. On the other hand, appraisers who argue in favor of the opportunity cost basis for valuing nonclinical services will tend to use compensation levels from the published surveys without such adjustment or consideration of the lower percentiles.

5.3 Relative Comparability of Qualifications and Responsibilities in Using Survey Data

As noted in detail above, the published physician compensation surveys generally represent compensation from clinical services. These services are essentially different from consulting services provided to LSCs. Because the economics of clinical services differ from that of consulting services, the compensation levels indicated by the published surveys may not be an exact indicator of fair market value for consulting arrangements in the life sciences industry. In using these surveys to establish general levels of physician compensation, however, an appraiser may find that certain surveys contain physician respondents whose qualifications and current job functions are relatively more comparable to those of physician consultants to LSCs than the respondents of other surveys. For example, an appraiser may determine that physicians in an academic practice setting may be relatively more comparable to physician-consultants than physicians in private practice. In such a case, the appraiser may weight compensation levels from one or more surveys, and even one or more job descriptions within a survey, more heavily than others for purposes of establishing a general range of physician compensation to use as a guideline for consulting services.

5.4 Compensation for Physician Services Versus Business-Owner Compensation

The various published physician compensation surveys gather and publish data from a variety of physicians who practice in diverse settings. The surveys report compensation information in varying levels of detail corresponding to these diverse practice settings. The key compensation measures, however, tend to report total compensation received by the physician from all sources. This reporting of compensation from all sources may obscure the fact that certain forms of compensation received by the physician may not relate to services provided directly or personally by the physician. Income received from ancillaries, employment of midlevel providers or physician extenders, leasing of space or equipment, or sharing in group practice earnings may relate more to ownership of a medical practice rather to physician services. In other words, business-owner compensation is often reported along with compensation from physician services in the physician compensation tables in published surveys. Other forms of nonclinical income such as on-call pay stipends, medical directorship payments, expert testimony fees, and other forms may also be included in the physician compensation tables.

Appraisers seeking to find market information on the value of physician services may need to adjust reported compensation levels to eliminate forms of compensation not related to physician services, such as business-owner compensation. Quantifying these amounts, however, may be extremely difficult. Analysis of various financial, production, and operational metrics, ratios, and benchmarks reported in the surveys may be required for the appraiser to attempt to adjust for business-owner compensation that is included in the survey-reported physician compensation tables. While there are clear practical difficulties to addressing this issue, appraisers valuing physician consulting and research services should be aware of disparate forms of income or compensation that are included in the published surveys and make adjustments to the valuation analysis where they deem appropriate and practicable.

5.5 The Annual Hours for Use in Computing Hourly Physician Compensation Rates

In using published survey data on physician compensation to arrive at hourly rates for valuing physician services, appraisers must select the number of annual hours to be used as the divisor for the published annual compensation amounts. Many appraisers use 2,000 or 2,080 hours as the best approximation of typical hours worked by physicians. While this convention may be appropriate and valid, appraisers should be aware of the reported levels of annual physician work hours as provided by certain surveys. For those surveys that do report physician work-hour levels, reported levels may indicate a continuum of annual hours worked that deviates from the standard 40-hour workweek less 10 holidays (i.e., 2,000 hours). Indicated hours may be below or above the typical annual hours. The assumption of standard annual hours may have the greatest valuation impact when an appraiser uses the upper percentiles of the reported compensation levels to determine an hourly rate. In reality, physicians at these higher compensation levels may be working more annual hours than assumed in the standard rates for annual hours worked. As a result, appraisers may need to perform additional research and analysis using survey information to arrive at the appropriate amount of annual hours used for determine hourly physician compensation rates when relying on the upper percentiles of the compensation surveys.

5.6 Adjustment of Hourly Physician Compensation to an Independent-Contractor Basis

Because most physicians providing consulting or research services to LSCs are independent contractors, many appraisers argue that the hourly rates derived from physician compensation surveys should be grossed-up to include a provision for benefits. The theory supporting such gross-up is that independent contractors across all industries are generally paid at higher rates than employees. Such premium rates are intended to cover benefits and other costs incurred by contractors providing services. In the area of physician services, it is argued that one can observe such premiums in the rates paid to locum tenens physicians. Appraisers who value physician consulting and research services should be aware of this issue and provide the support and defense in the appraisal report for the position taken.

5.7 Application of the Cost Approach to Valuing Research Services

In addition to valuing the physician component included in research services, an appraiser using the cost approach must attempt to value the cost of the additional resources employed in providing such services to LSCs. Such resources may include nursing and other practice staff, equipment, supplies, space, and various services. How does the appraiser establish the appropriate cost basis for such resources? Generally, there are two sources for such cost information: 1) the subject physician practice that will provide the research services and 2) market information obtained through the research efforts of the appraiser. In practice, an appraiser may experience difficulties in obtaining cost information from either source. Such data may not be available or obtainable in a feasible or cost-effective manner.

Yet, there is an important conceptual issue that the appraiser must address in choosing between the two sources of cost information. If the standard of value for the appraisal assignment is fair market value, the appraiser must determine whether specific cost information from the subject physician practice represents the cost to the hypothetical willing buyer and seller in a service arrangement. Many appraisers would argue that only normalized or market-based costs should be used in the buildup method. Using the actual costs of the subject service provider may be more consistent with investment value than fair market value because it takes into account the cost structure and economies of a particular seller rather than the hypothetical-typical seller of such services in the marketplace.

Arriving at the appropriate cost basis of resources is only one difficulty in applying the cost approach to valuing research services. Since some of these resources are utilized partially or on a limited basis in performing clinical studies, the appraiser must determine an appropriate allocation or apportionment basis in the cost buildup analysis. Such allocations can be difficult or cumbersome to compute. Appraisers may need to exercise judgment in such calculations with a view to the materiality and cost and benefit of complex allocation formulas. Such judgment may also be necessary in determining the level of detail that is necessary for identifying and valuing the various resources used to provide clinical research studies to LSCs.

6.0 The Income Approach

For valuing physician consulting and research services in the life sciences industry, use of the income approach may be limited or impracticable. Evaluating future benefits under these service arrangements requires the appraiser to access market rates of compensation for physician services and other resources employed in clinical studies. This evaluation returns the appraiser to the analyses of the market or cost approaches. In general, the income approach appears to be the least relevant and applicable of the three approaches available for valuing consulting and research services.

7.0 Formulation of the Opinion of Value

After completing the applicable approaches to value, the appraiser engages in an evaluation and reconciliation process to determine the fair market value of the subject arrangement for consulting or research services. This process is ultimately based on the independent and professional judgment of the appraiser. Weight may be given to a greater or lesser degree to the results of any particular valuation method or technique based on a variety of considerations, such as the reliability of data, extent of comparability, scope of information, regulatory guidance, and facts and circumstances unique to the subject arrangement. The opinion of value may be stated as a specific dollar amount or a range. Whatever the conclusion of value determined, the appraiser should be prepared to support and defend the conclusion based on the relevant information and sound valuation methodology.

Chapter 33. Valuing Intellectual Property Licensing Arrangements Within the Life Sciences Industry

CONTENTS

Chapter 33. Valuing Intellectual Property Licensing Arrangements Within the Life Sciences Industry

By Jason Ruchaber, CFA, ASA

1.0 Introduction

The pharmaceutical industry was one of the first industries in the United States to routinely use licensing programs as a means for identifying and commercializing new drugs. Prior to the rapid advances made over the last 30 to 40 years in computing and the development of sophisticated methods for mapping chemical paths, the process of finding and developing new drugs was arduous and exceptionally expensive, and the probability of successfully commercializing new pharmaceutical applications was extremely low. To combat these hurdles, pharmaceutical companies began licensing the right to screen the chemical libraries of industrial companies for pharmacological properties. This proved to be highly effective in reducing the cost of up-front research and development and allowed existing discoveries to be further exploited through commercialization in previously unconsidered applications.

Today, intellectual capital has become a central focus of business strategy across all industries, and licensing activity for patents alone is estimated to account for more than $100 billion in revenue for U.S. firms. The healthcare industry continues to play a key role in this market. In the medical devices sector of the life sciences industry, it is not uncommon to find physicians who own patents that are licensed to medical device companies. Other types of healthcare entities may also license various forms of intellectual property from physicians. Thus, an understanding of the basic tenets of IP licensing is critical for appraisal professionals providing valuation services in the life sciences.

2.0 Overview of IP Licensing Arrangements

2.1 Definition of Licensing

Licensing is the act of granting another person or entity the right to make use of a particular asset in a specific context or application for a specific length of time and within a specific geographical area. A license does not typically carry the full rights of ownership, and therefore, license agreements must be defined narrowly to prevent conflicts of interest between the owner of the asset (licensor) and the user of the asset (the licensee). This is particularly important when the licensor is exploiting the asset in other commercial uses such as in its own products or through additional licenses.

Why do owners of property find it advantageous to enter licensing arrangements? The basic conceptual framework of the license is to create a symbiotic relationship whereby both the owner of the property and the licensee share in the commercial success of the end product. An example of this type of situation might include an inventor who does not have the resources to successfully commercialize the invention or an owner of property who does not have the necessary expertise to commercialize the product in a new area.

2.2 Asset Types

A licensing arrangement can be entered into for virtually any type of asset, but licensing activity generally centers on intellectual property, such as patents, trademarks, copyrights, and technologies.

Patents

The United States Patent & Trademark Office (USPTO) is the governing body that issues patents and trademarks in the United States. The USPTO defines a patent as "the right to exclude others from making, using, offering for sale, or selling" the invention in the United States or "importing" the invention into the United States. Patent grants have a finite life typically defined as 20 years from the original date of the patent application. There are three distinct types of patents:

1. *Utility patents*—granted for "the invention or discovery of a new and useful process, machine, article of manufacture, or composition of matter or any new and useful improvement thereof."

2. *Design patents*—granted for the invention of a "new, original, and ornamental design for an article of manufacture."

3. *Plant patents*—granted "to anyone who invents or discovers and asexually reproduces any distinct and new variety of plant."

4. Within the life sciences industry, most patents fall under the category of utility patents and include chemical compounds, medical devices, and medical equipment.

Trademarks

Trademarks, or service marks, were established by the Lanham Act, and are described by the USPTO as "a word, name, symbol, or device that is used in trade with goods to indicate the source of the goods and to distinguish them from the goods of others. A service mark is the same as a trademark except that it identifies and distinguishes the source of a service rather than a product." Trademarks need not be registered to enjoy protection under the act; however, most commercially used trademarks are registered with the USPTO. Trademarks registered after November 1989 are valid for a period of 10 years and may be renewed for successive 10-year periods. Nearly every branded product with name recognition enjoys protection under the Lanham Act, but the most commonly observed trademarks in the life sciences are name-brand pharmaceuticals and medical devices.

Copyrights

A copyright is a form of protection for original works of authorship (literary, artistic, musical, and so on) established by the Copyright Act of 1976. A copyright generally establishes the exclusive right to print, publish, reproduce, perform in public, and create derivative works of the material. In the United States, copyrights are issued and registered with Copyright Office of the Library of Congress and have a term equal to the lifetime of the author plus 50 years. In some instances, the copyright may be valid for a period of 75 years from the date of first publication. Within the life sciences industry, copyrights may include medical texts, manuals, research papers, articles, diagrams, photos, and the like.

3.0 Royalties

Compensation under a licensing agreement typically includes the payment of a royalty by the licensee to the owner-licensor for the use of the property. Royalties can take many forms but are most frequently set as an up-front lump-sum, an annual fee, a percentage of revenue on products sold, a dollar amount per unit sold, or a combination thereof. Royalties paid on ongoing revenue or units of sales are referred to as running royalties. It is also common to see royalty arrangements whereby an annual minimum and annual maximum fee applies, the royalty rate decreases with volumes in a stair-step pattern, or royalties decline over time. These types of arrangements are appealing to licensees, because they attempt to match the economic life of the licensed asset with the commercial success of the end product.

Royalty rates vary significantly from one licensing arrangement to the next, and many factors must be considered when attempting to establish a reasonable royalty rate within the context of a specific licensing agreement. Frequently there is no single right answer, and royalty rates for seemingly similar technologies may vary widely. In the landmark case *Georgia Pacific Corporation v. United States Plywood Corp.*,[1] the court set out 15 factors that parties to a hypothetical negotiation would likely consider in determining a reasonable royalty. Though the case dealt specifically with reasonable royalties within the context of patent infringement damages, the context the court used was a hypothetical royalty arrangement that would have been negotiated had the parties negotiated immediately prior to the infringement. This is very similar to the hypothetical negotiation contemplated in the definition of fair market value,[2] and the factors the court used are applicable in assessing reasonable royalties for licenses outside the construct of patent infringement.

The 15 factors identified by the court are listed (in generic form to remove the patent infringement context) and briefly discussed below:

1. The royalty rates received by the owner of the property in other licensing arrangements for the same property, proving or tending to prove an established royalty.

   Existing licensing arrangements for the subject property would tend to establish a reasonable royalty rate. However, it is important to consider relevance of prior licenses within the context of the contemplated license. Differences in the terms of the license (such as Factor 3 below), the remaining life of the property (such as Factor 7 below), and other factors presented in this list may limit the relevance of prior agreements.

2. The royalty rates paid by the licensee for the use of other property rights comparable to the property (for which a license is being contemplated).

   Established rates paid by the licensee for similar properties in agreements with comparable terms may serve to establish the reasonable royalty rate. As with Factor 1, however, terms of the license agreements should be carefully examined for comparability to the contemplated arrangement.

3. The nature and scope of the license, as exclusive or nonexclusive; or as restricted or nonrestricted in terms of territory or with respect to whom the manufactured product may be sold.

---

1   *Georgia Pacific Corporation v. United States Plywood Corp.*, 318 F. Supp. 1116, 166 U.S.P.Q. 235, May 28, 1970.\
2   Fair market value is defined in the *International Glossary of Business Valuation Terms* as "the price, expressed in terms of cash equivalents, at which property would change hands between a hypothetical willing and able buyer and a hypothetical willing and able seller, acting at arm's length in an open and unrestricted market, when neither is under compulsion to buy or sell and when both have reasonable knowledge of the relevant facts."

Exclusivity—A license granting an exclusive right to use a property would generally demand a higher royalty rate than one that is nonexclusive (i.e., allows additional licenses to be granted).

Geography—The geographical limitations of the license grant will influence the appropriate royalty rate. A worldwide license would typically demand a higher royalty rate than a license limiting use to a specific territory or boundary.

Use—The use of the license may influence the royalty rate. A license granting unrestricted use of a property would generally demand a much higher royalty rate than one that is defined narrowly—for example, a chemical compound to be used only in drug-coated stents.

4. The licensor's established policy on licensing, either by not licensing to others the use of the property to maintain a monopoly or by granting licenses under special conditions.

An owner who is highly protective of his or her property rights or has an established policy of not licensing its properties may justify a higher royalty rate. Such a rate would be necessary to induce the owner to deviate from his or her established policy. This is especially pertinent in infringement cases but may be less so in the normal course of establishing a reasonable royalty rate between two willing parties. The absence of a history of licensing or policy restricting licensing should not be used as justification for a higher royalty rate in and of itself.

5. The commercial relationship between the licensor and licensee, such as whether they are competitors in the same territory in the same line of business or whether they are inventor and promoter.

License agreements between competitors tend to justify higher royalty rates than those of noncompetitors. Even when the license is structured to limit the use of the product or if the product's application is in a market where there is no competitive threat, licensors are reluctant to allow competitors to gain information or profits that would advance their competitive position.

6. The effect of selling the licensed property in promoting sales of other products of the licensee, the existing value of the invention to the licensor as a generator of sales of his nonpatented items, and the extent of such derivative (or convoyed) sales.

Licenses that allow the licensee to gain sales in other nonlicensed products tend to justify higher royalty rates. For example, Bausch and Lomb may pay a higher royalty for new contact lens technology if it believes sales of the licensed product will lead to gains in sales of related products, such as saline solution, and so on. Higher royalty rates may also be justified if the license agreement allows the licensee to gain access to new commercial channels, new customers, appeal to a new population demographic, or augment its current commercial presence.

7. The economic or functional life of the property (i.e., expiration date of a patent) and the term of the license.

   A product nearing the end of its life cycle will generally demand a lower royalty rate due to economic obsolescence, increased competition, and design around considerations. This may also be true for new technologies that are expected to have a short, useful life.

   In some instances, the license is written as a perpetual license. This might be seen in the context of a trademark license agreement, where the name brand is expected to continue indefinitely. In these situations, additional analysis may be required to evaluate the life of the economic benefit associated with the licensed property.

8. The established profitability of the property or products embodying the property, its commercial success, and its current popularity.

   It follows logic that royalty rates for highly popular and profitable products are also high. As the popularity and profitability of the product diminishes, so does the appropriate royalty rate.

9. The utility and advantages of the subject property over the old modes or devices, if any, that had been used previously for achieving similar results.

   Products that have significant advantages over currently existing technologies justify higher royalty rates. This is due to the simple fact that products with significant utility advantages also enjoy significant profit advantages.

10. The nature of the subject property, the character of the commercial embodiment of it as owned and produced by the licensor, and the benefits to others who have used the invention.

11. The extent to which the infringer has made use of the subject property and any evidence probative of the value of that use. (*Outside the context of infringement, the intended use of the subject property may be a substitute.*)

12. The portion of the profit or of the selling price that may be customary in the particular business or in comparable businesses to allow for the use of the subject property or comparable properties.

A common rule of thumb, referred to as the Goldscheider rule,[3] suggests that a reasonable royalty represents 25% of the preprofit expected to be made through the use of the licensed asset. Many databases can also be used to search for comparable license transactions within a given industry. In some cases, these databases can provide insight into the royalty rates being paid for similar properties. However, these should be referenced cautiously, because a truly comparable license transaction may be difficult to identify and overgeneralization may miss many of the nuances of the particular license arrangement.

13. The portion of the realizable profit that should be credited to the invention as distinguished from other elements of the end product, such as the manufacturing process, business risks, or significant features or improvements added by the infringer.

Understanding the relative contribution of the licensed property to the overall utility of the end product may be helpful to the determination of a reasonable royalty. A license arrangement whereby both parties contribute technologies that equally support the end product may justify a profit split of 50-50. An example of this might be an owner of a medical laser device licensing sophisticated positioning and tracking software to control the movement of the laser.

14. The opinion of qualified experts.

Frequently professionals in the licensing industry will have experience and expertise that can be helpful in establishing the reasonable royalty.

15. The amount that a licensor and a licensee would have agreed upon if both had been reasonably and voluntarily trying to reach an agreement; that is, the amount that a prudent licensee—who desired, as a business proposition, to obtain a license to manufacture and sell a particular article embodying the subject property—would have been willing to pay as a royalty and still be able to make a reasonable profit and the amount that would have been acceptable by a prudent patentee who was willing to grant a license.

---

3   Robert Goldscheider is a specialist and recognized authority on licensing. His calculations performed in the 1950s laid the groundwork for the "25% rule" now frequently referred to as the Goldscheider rule.

Though this list is fairly comprehensive, additional factors should be considered in determining a reasonable royalty rate. These may include cost to design around the subject property (re-creating the asset versus licensing) and availability and preponderance of nonprotected alternatives. It stands to reason that a licensee would not reasonably pay a royalty rate in excess of the cost to design or develop its own property with the same functionality (assuming it was possible to do so). Royalty rates will also be limited by the availability of acceptable alternatives. A licensee may prefer to have the subject property but will not likely pay a high royalty rate if there are acceptable alternatives with the same or similar attributes available for license at a lower rate.

4.0 Valuation of Royalty Agreements

In some instances, it may be necessary to determine the value of a license agreement. Situations when this might be necessary include purchase price allocations, formation of a new entity (such as a joint venture) where the license agreement is assigned by one of the parties as its initial contribution, bankruptcy, termination of a licensing agreement, or sale of the licensing rights, among others. Though a complete discussion of valuation methodologies is beyond the scope of this chapter, the following is a high-level overview of some of the more common methodologies to valuation and key considerations therein.

4.1 Income Approach

Any income-producing asset can be valued with respect to its income-generating capacity. Because royalty agreements have a fairly predictable royalty stream and a finite life, an income approach to valuation is generally used. Under the simplest variation of this approach, expected future royalties over the remaining life of the agreement are discounted to their present value using a risk-adjusted rate of return or discount rate. This rate of return is set at a level commensurate with the risk of realizing the

Calculating the Value of a Royalty Agreement			
	Year 1	Year 2	Year 3
Expected Product Revenue (000s)	$1,000.0	$1,000.0	$1,000.0
Royalty Rate	10%	10%	10%
Royalty Income	100.0	100.0	100.0
Taxes @ 40%	(40.0)	(40.0)	(40.0)
After Tax Royalty Income	60.0	60.0	60.0
Present Value Factor @ 25%	0.500	0.640	0.512
Present Value of Royalty Income	48.0	38.4	30.7
Value of Royalty Agreement (sum of above)	$117.1		

projected royalty stream. Uncertain royalty streams will have a higher discount rate, and reasonably certain royalty streams will have a lower discount rate.

To demonstrate the mechanics of this approach, assume a royalty arrangement calling for a royalty rate of 10% on sales of a specific product payable at year end over the next three years. Assume further that sales of the product are expected to total $1 million in each of the next three years. Based on the risk profile of the projected sales, a qualified appraiser has determined that a 25% rate of return is appropriate.

In the table, the present value factor is calculated as $1/(1 + \text{rate of return})^{(\text{time})}$, where time equals the number of years in the future (i.e., Year 2 = $1/(1.25)^2$). Excluding consideration of any additional factors, the value of the royalty agreement in this example is $117,100. As suggested, this is an oversimplified example, and each royalty agreement must be valued in context, giving proper consideration to all elements that contribute to value.

4.2 Market Approach

The market approach is premised on the idea that the value of an asset can be estimated by drawing reference to the prices paid for other assets with similar characteristics. The challenge to this approach and especially with intellectual property assets, is finding truly comparable assets. Transactional data related to the prices paid for licensing agreements are somewhat limited, and even when a sufficient volume of data are available, it is highly unlikely that the underlying license agreement contains substantially all of the provisions of the subject agreement or an underlying asset of substantially the same nature.

4.3 Cost (or Asset) Approach

The cost approach is rooted in the concept of replication. Value under this approach is estimated with reference to the actual cost to create the asset or by estimating the cost of reproduction or replacement of the asset. For license agreements, the cost approach has limited application because the primary cost consideration pertains to the underlying asset subject to the license, not the license itself. Additionally, the rights associated with a license are generally less than those associated with full ownership of an asset, and the cost approach may significantly overstate value. However, there are circumstances when the value of the license may be determined in this manner. The question the appraiser must ask is: "But for the license, what would it cost the licensee to develop its own noninfringing alternative to the licensed asset?" Assuming a noninfringing alternative is feasible, the appraiser would then attempt to estimate the indirect costs (man-hours, overhead costs, and so on), direct costs (materials, equipment, lab costs, and so on), and the opportunity costs (time to re-create the asset versus licensing it now).

5.0 Special Considerations

In addition to the normal complexities of intellectual property valuation, the regulatory environment of the healthcare industry poses additional challenges. This is especially true when the intellectual property is owned by physicians. As discussed in prior chapters of this book, financial arrangements with physicians who are in a position to refer are subject to additional constraints not typically present with other intellectual property licensing or sale transactions.

First and foremost, the payment to a physician cannot generally take into consideration the value or volume of referrals from that physician. Because of this, a physician licensor may be precluded from receiving payment of a running royalty or license fee based on a split of incremental profit. Though these types of arrangements are customary in intellectual property licensing, license payments to physicians must generally be paid as a fixed fee.

Transactions involving physicians may also be subject to a test of commercial reasonableness. Even when fair market value for the intellectual property can be established, the appraiser may need to consider whether or not the licensor/purchaser has a legitimate commercial need to enter the transaction. Care must be taken to consider readily available alternatives to the subject intellectual property. Additionally, the appraiser should consider related professional service arrangements that may overlap with the license. An example of such an overlap could include a co-management arrangement with a provision for the development of protocols and procedures while simultaneously licensing established protocols and procedures from the same group. A similar overlap could be present with key opinion leader (KOL) compensation and a subsequent (and related) royalty on sales of the related medical device.

As with all other areas of healthcare valuation, appraisers should not only possesses the requisite valuation and finance training, but also maintain an adequate understanding of the regulatory environment governing these transactions.

6.0 Bibliography

Anson, Weston. *Intellectual Property Valuation Primer* [draft]. Available on www.lesi.org.

Goldscheider, Robert, ed., Licensing Executive Society International, *The LESI Guide to Licensing Best Practices, Strategic Issues and Contemporary Realities*, May 2002.

Porter, Mills and Weinstein, "Industry Norms and Reasonable Royalty Rate Determination," March 2008, available on www.lesi.org.

Reilly, Schweihs. *Valuing Intangible Assets*. McGraw-Hill, 1999.

Smith, Parr. *Valuation of Intellectual Property and Intangible Assets*, 3rd Edition. Wiley, March 31, 2000.

Sullivan and Fradkin, "A Primer on Benchmarking a Licensing Operation," September 2001, available on www.lesi.org.

Wendt, Jeffrey, "Medical Devices: New License Issues for Single Use Devices," *les Nouvelles*. September 2003.

Chapter 34. Valuing Management
Services Arrangements

CONTENTS

Chapter 34. Valuing Management Services Arrangements

By Robert Mundy, CPA, ABV, CVA, and Tynan P. Olechny, MBA, MPH, AVA

1.0 Introduction

Management services arrangements in healthcare have been in existence for decades. These arrangements provide hospitals, ambulatory surgery centers, and physician practices with operational and functional services, including management, human resources, accounting, billing, staffing, and information technology, among others. They offer healthcare providers a viable solution for obtaining necessary business services from companies who have expertise, cost-effectiveness, and economies of scale. The three most common situations in which healthcare providers might look to third-party entities for management services are:

1. When the provider determines that outsourcing certain management functions will result in the best optimization of its operations;

2. As part of an acquisition or joint venture, when the manager purchases an ownership interest in the provider entity or becomes a partner with the provider; or

3. When one provider entity seeks to affiliate with another healthcare provider by integrating some level of operations or by one party providing expertise and infrastructure to the other.

While each of these three fact patterns is different and can result from different market forces, there is a commonality in the *types* of services provided by the manager entity to the other party. The list of specific management services and functions performed does vary from arrangement to arrangement, but one can observe similar types of services across arrangements in the healthcare industry.

This chapter discusses the types of management services found in the healthcare marketplace. It addresses the valuation of these services with a focus on how the appraiser can analyze the key economics and legal terms of management service arrangements. It will also discuss how the commercial reasonableness of these arrangements can be evaluated and assessed as part of the valuation process.

2.0 Management Services Defined

Management services or "purchased services," as they are also referred to in the industry, include those geared toward strengthening the business aspects of an operation. It is not uncommon for healthcare entities, such as hospitals, ambulatory surgery centers, and physician practices, to engage outside organizations to provide medical and/or administrative services that they have neither the time nor the expertise to perform. Organizations that opt to outsource management services often recognize that it would be difficult for them to replicate such services internally in a cost-effective and efficient manner. Management services can include nonclinical operational needs, such as contract negotiations, legal and financial services, risk management, billing, human resources support, and operations management. Such transactions to provide management services can occur between "like" provider entities, such as a hospital providing management services to another hospital or between different types of providers, such as a physician practice and a hospital or health system where the practice may provide back-office practice support (such as billing and collections) to a hospital-owned medical practice. In this case, the physician practice may be more adept at performing such services given its expertise in managing a physician practice's revenue cycle. Finally, management services arrangements can occur between providers and third parties, such as an ambulatory surgical center and a third-party manager whose business is specifically to perform such activities.

More recent variations on the provision of management services include co-management or service line management arrangements whereby hospitals and physicians collaboratively manage and operate a particular hospital service line or program, such as orthopedics, cardiology, or oncology. While historically management services transactions have focused on the performance of administrative and/or operational tasks, co-management arrangements often include both clinical and administrative activities. In recent years, both hospitals and physicians have enjoyed the benefits of such co-management arrangements due to their facilitation of the parties exploring a shared vision. Fundamentally, these arrangements create a specific mechanism for hospitals and physicians to be formally aligned in the pursuit of improved patient care and a more effective delivery model. For instance, such arrangements can fulfill goals of improved program outcomes, enhanced association between hospitals and physicians, operational excellence, and the development of an effective decision-making structure for the service line. As such, clinical co-management arrangements represent one vehicle for achieving hospital-physician integration.

Despite the varying organizations that outsource administrative, operational, and/or clinical management services, a menu of services is available that is applicable to most organizations and management services arrangements found in the marketplace. Examples of typical administrative, operational, management, and clinical tasks are included in the exhibit. It is important to note that not all management companies offer the same types of services. For example, AmSurg, a publicly traded company that develops and operates ambulatory surgery centers in partnership with physicians, offers strategic and operational services, including information technology, marketing, recruitment, business operations, compliance, contracting, facilities management, human resources, and materials management. Another ambulatory surgery management company, Ambulatory Healthcare Strategies, LLC, provides financial oversight, regulatory/accreditation and oversight, interim administration, information technology,

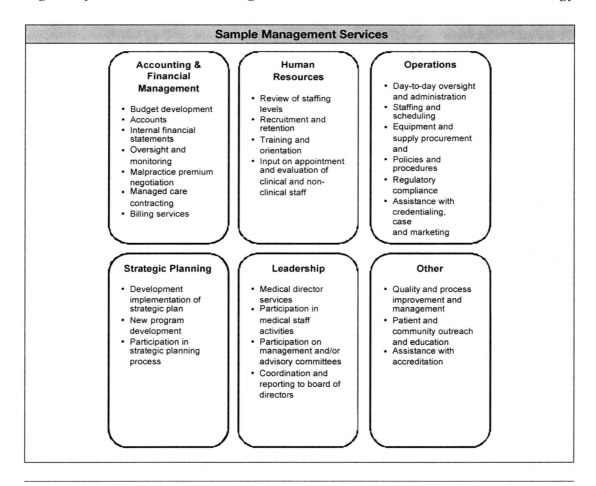

Sample Management Services

Accounting & Financial Management
- Budget development
- Accounts
- Internal financial statements
- Oversight and monitoring
- Malpractice premium negotiation
- Managed care contracting
- Billing services

Human Resources
- Review of staffing levels
- Recruitment and retention
- Training and orientation
- Input on appointment and evaluation of clinical and non-clinical staff

Operations
- Day-to-day oversight and administration
- Staffing and scheduling
- Equipment and supply procurement and
- Policies and procedures
- Regulatory compliance
- Assistance with credentialing, case and marketing

Strategic Planning
- Development implementation of strategic plan
- New program development
- Participation in strategic planning process

Leadership
- Medical director services
- Participation in medical staff activities
- Participation on management and/or advisory committees
- Coordination and reporting to board of directors

Other
- Quality and process improvement and management
- Patient and community outreach and education
- Assistance with accreditation

marketing, billing, and consulting. Careful review and understanding of the service offerings included in the arrangement is critical to the valuation as later described in this chapter.

Traditionally, compensation for the completion of administrative and/or operational tasks has consisted of reimbursement for the costs of providing the service plus a profit factor. While payment of fixed fees for providing the identified services is one alternative, compensation for certain types of services, such as billing, are often paid as a percentage of net patient revenue or a "markup" percentage on cost in the case of employee leasing.

Until recently, management arrangements have not included compensation for the achievement of defined quality outcomes, clinical metrics, or operational and financial outcomes. In fact, the introduction of such incentive payments in arrangements that were previously compensated based on fixed fees only has become more common. For example, the growing popularity of clinical co-management arrangements between hospitals and physician groups, which place the burden of responsibility to manage certain services on multiple parties, has introduced payment mechanisms that are both fixed, based on certain predefined services to be provided, and "at risk," based on the achievement of defined quality outcomes and metrics. Similarly, ambulatory surgery center management companies have also introduced incentive payments for achievement of defined quality metrics, such as reducing infection rates and operational and financial outcomes, including achieving on-time starts, managing costs, and attaining employee and patient satisfaction.

3.0 Critical Factors in Valuing Management Services

Prior to valuing management services, parties to the arrangement need to take multiple steps for an appraiser to effectively opine on the transaction. It is not unusual for an appraiser to receive a request to value such services, yet the details of the arrangement have yet to be fully defined. Ideally the following items should have been considered prior to a request for valuation.

3.1 Identification of the Scope of Services and Areas of Need

It is essential that the parties involved have adequately and accurately defined the services that are needed and will be provided. Specifically, the entity seeking management services needs to have determined whether it requires administrative and operational services only or whether it desires to incorporate clinical responsibilities as well. For example, the parties to the arrangement may wish to incorporate quality incentives whereby the achievement of defined metrics, such as adherence to delineated clinical pathways or attainment of patient satisfaction goals, results in additional compensation. Doing so impacts the thought process an appraiser employs and how he or she sets about valuing the transaction.

3.2 Legal Structure Determination

Comprehension of a transaction's legal structure is an important step in understanding the overall transaction. For example, the provision of management services to a hospital's employed physician group by a private medical practice may take the shape of a direct contract between the practice and the hospital or between the hospital and a management company that was formed to execute management services to multiple parties. An ambulatory surgery center that purchases services from an ASC management company may have a direct contract with that company.

3.3 Presence of a Legal Agreement

It is critical that a legal agreement specifically outline the management services to be provided to the appraiser. The agreement should identify the duties and responsibilities of the management company, the provision of terms and termination of the agreement, and the compensation to be paid to the management company. In addition to other pertinent data, this is an essential piece of the appraiser's puzzle in valuing management services. Typically, appraisers receive draft agreements and are asked to opine on the proposed compensation for associated duties prior to finalization of contracts between the parties. Appraisers will, however, request an executed copy for their files once the valuation is finalized. Since healthcare transactions are becoming increasingly complex and no two management arrangements are alike, upon review of a legal agreement, an appraiser will ensure that he or she clearly understands the terms and conditions of the agreement, including compensation, and that the services to be provided are distinctly defined. Without this information, an appraiser is unable to ascertain the value of the arrangement.

3.4 Fair Market Value Assessment of Management Services and Fees

Given the myriad of healthcare regulatory considerations associated with healthcare valuations, including management services, it is imperative that organizations engage an appraiser who has experience with healthcare regulations and valuation principles related to healthcare. Appraisers who are unfamiliar with healthcare transactions may often overlook vital considerations, such as whether the management arrangement is the only agreement that the two parties have with each other. To ensure an entity is not paid twice for the same services, an appraiser needs to understand what, if any, other arrangements are in place and the duties, responsibilities, and compensation associated with these arrangements. Other agreements to consider include clinical staffing or professional services agreements, call coverage agreements, medical directorship agreements, and physician lease or leaseback agreements. Often, legal counsel will engage an appraiser to conduct the valuation to obtain the benefit associated with attorney-client privilege. Further, the parties to the arrangement might also consider requesting the appraiser to opine on commercial reasonableness of the transaction. The compensation paid for the identified management services may be at fair market value; however, they may not make commercial sense if entered into in the absence of the value or volume of referrals. As indicated later in this chapter, the commercial reasonableness and fair market value of these transactions may vary widely depending upon the types of services to be included.

4.0 Valuation Methodology

The determination of the fair market value of a management arrangement is critical for compliance with existing laws and regulations. Similar to a business valuation, management arrangements can be valued based on three approaches: the cost approach, the market approach, and the income approach.

One way to view the application of the approaches in valuing management services arrangements is the "build or buy" decision analysis. In other words, would it be more cost-effective to perform these services internally or outsource the provision of the services? A prudent business owner will compare the internal costs of providing a service to the price that an outside party would charge to provide the same service and make a decision based on which scenario would likely produce the most efficiency. When valuing a management arrangement, the cost approach is the "build" perspective, while the market approach is the "buy" perspective. The income approach can then be used to analyze the reasonableness of the management fee determined under the cost or market approaches.

One of the most important aspects to consider in determining the fair market value of management services is the amount of risk that the management company assumes. The same risk/return concept in business valuation theory applies to management service valuation as well. Generally, the more risk that the management company assumes, the higher the return or fair market value of the management services will be. The amount of risk the management company assumes should always be taken into account under any of the valuation approaches employed.

Another aspect to consider is the method of payment for the management fee. It is not uncommon for a management fee to be paid as a base fee plus incentive payments for meeting various operational or financial metrics. As the total management fee becomes more weighted to incentive payments, the management company takes on more risk, since more of the management fee is tied to performance. Therefore, the appraiser needs to assess the total management fee (base plus any incentives) in light of the fact that a greater portion of the management fee is "at risk."

This interplay of risk and return needs to be at the forefront of the appraisal process because it will have a direct bearing on the fair market value of the management services. The appraiser should always consider whether certain terms of the management agreement either increase or decrease the risk the management company is assuming and adjust the fair market value of the services accordingly.

4.1 Cost Approach

Under the cost approach, the costs of providing the contemplated management services are analyzed to determine a value indication as if the services were performed internally. This approach is also referred to as the replacement cost method. To apply this method, the appraiser needs to gain an understanding of the scope of management services, determine the level of staffing and resources necessary to perform the services, and develop estimates of the costs of the required staffing and resources.

Gain an understanding of the scope of services.
To properly value any type of asset or service, an appraiser needs to have an understanding of what is being valued. There are typically not any "standard" management agreements because each agreement has its own unique set of considerations and services. Therefore, it is imperative to understand the nature of the management services because this will ultimately drive the determination of fair market value. Most management agreements contain a listing of the services under consideration either in the body of the agreement or as an exhibit to the agreement. However, if the agreement is vague, the appraiser should interview the hospital's legal counsel, for example, to ensure an accurate understanding of the management services. It is also advisable to include in the appraisal report a listing of any client representations as to the meaning, application, and implementation of contract terms and conditions that are not stated clearly in the agreement. The practice of including these client representations affords protection to the appraiser. It also serves to communicate to the report reader what the appraiser's full understanding of the agreement was so that the conclusion of value can be placed in the context of this expanded understanding.

Careful consideration should be paid to the wording in the agreement of the services to be provided. For instance, some agreements might call for the management company to "assist with the billing and collection function," while other agreements might require the performance of the billing and collection function. There is considerable difference in both the scope and cost of services for these two scenarios because assisting with the billing and collection function does not necessarily require the management company itself to perform billing and collection. In any event, the appraiser needs to have a thorough understanding of the services that the management company is required to perform.

Determine the appropriate level of staffing and resources.

After gaining an understanding of the scope of services to be provided under the management agreement, the next step is to determine the appropriate level of staffing and resources necessary to provide the management services. This is the most difficult step of the cost approach because it typically requires the most judgment from the appraiser. The following are some of the key factors to consider:

- *What is the nature of the company being managed?* Managing a physician practice, as opposed to a hospital outpatient department or ambulatory surgery center, will require different expertise and resources from the management company. Therefore, it is important to consider the nature of the company that will be managed.

- *What are the historical and projected volumes and revenues of the company to be managed?* The volumes and revenues of the company that is being managed will impact the level of management services required. As the volumes and revenues of the company increase, more resources will generally be required of the management company, and therefore, the costs of providing the management services will increase.

- *How complex are the services to be provided?* Does the management agreement require the management company to manage all aspects of the company's operations or just provide specific administrative services? The level of complexity in the services to be provided will affect the fair market value of the management services.

- *How diverse or comprehensive are the services to be provided?* Obviously, a management agreement that requires the management company to perform more comprehensive services will require more costs and resources than a management agreement with a limited scope of services. Some management agreements require a whole host of administrative services, such as accounting, human resources, financial statement preparation, information technology, payroll processing, or billing and collection. More costs and resources will be necessary as the diversity of the management services increases.

Determine Costs of Providing the Services.

After determining the appropriate level of staffing and resources to provide the services, the next step is to determine the costs to provide the services. For the required staffing, various salary surveys should be analyzed to determine appropriate compensation amounts. Many management agreements include both clinical and administrative duties. The appraiser should recognize that compensation for a physician practicing in his or her medical specialty may not appropriately reflect the fair market value for administrative duties performed by the physician. Therefore, the appraiser should consider various published data sources of physician administrative compensation. After determining appropriate compensation levels for the provided services, the staffing costs should include the employer portion of payroll taxes and employee benefits expenses as applicable.

Once the appropriate staffing costs are determined, reasonable markups of the costs should be included to reflect the risk that the management company is assuming by employing the required staff. To determine reasonable markup rates, the appraiser should consider margins earned by staffing companies.

Many management agreements include other services that require resources in addition to staffing, such as providing equipment or facility space. In determining the fair market value of providing these services, the appraiser needs to consider the level of risk assumed by the management company. For instance, consider a management agreement that requires the management company to sublease office space to the company. If the sublease agreement has a shorter term than the management company's master lease, then a markup could be applied to the sublease rate to account for the risk the management company is assuming due to the longer master lease term. Unless the appraiser has experience or qualifications in real estate appraisal, the determination of appropriate markups or fair market value rent should be outsourced to a qualified real estate appraiser. A similar requirement for qualifications applies to the valuation of equipment. Obviously, reasonable markups will be dependent upon the specific facts and circumstances, but the important concept to remember is that the markup should reflect the level of risk the management company is assuming.

Once the costs and appropriate markups are calculated for the management services, these amounts are then totaled to arrive at a fair market value indication under the cost approach.

4.2 Market Approach

The market approach is rooted in the economic principle of competition: In a free market, the supply and demand forces will drive the price of business assets to equilibrium.

Buyers will not pay more for products or services than the price available to other buyers in the market, and sellers will not accept less than the price paid to other sellers in the market.

Unfortunately, management agreements are typically unique in nature, and direct market comparisons are often difficult to locate. Therefore, in applying the market approach, the appraiser should try to identify market data with similar components or risk profiles as the subject management agreement and apply appropriate adjustments for comparability.

One good source of market comparable data is ambulatory surgery center (ASC) management companies. Management arrangements are prevalent in the ASC industry, and numerous ASC management companies are providing management services. Because these arrangements typically require comprehensive management services without the involvement of physicians, they can be a good data source for valuing management arrangements. However, caution should be exercised in applying the market data for ASC management companies because these arrangements often include the provision of clinical staff, which could skew the management fee if the subject management agreement does not include clinical services. Also, many ASC management companies assist in the development of an ASC, take a minority ownership position in the ASC, and then provide ongoing management services to the ASC. In some of these circumstances, the ASC management company might take a reduced management fee in exchange for its ownership interest. Therefore, when applying market data from ASC management companies, the appraiser should attempt to gain an understanding of how the management fee is calculated and the nature and scope of management services provided by the ASC management company to ensure comparability to the subject management agreement.

Also, the appraiser should consider data from publicly traded companies that provide management services. In many cases, these companies provide services in addition to management, so the appraiser should consider the relative weight and comparability of the management services provided by these companies when comparing to the subject management services. Some publicly traded companies, such as Insperity Inc. (formerly Administaff) and Barrett Business Services Inc., provide various human resource management services. Others, such as Team Health Holdings Inc., provide a wide range of professional staffing and administrative services to the healthcare industry.

After identifying market comparable data, the appraiser should analyze the data and make adjustments for comparability to the subject management agreement. The relative importance of the tasks in the subject management agreement should be weighed against the market comparable data. For example, if a primary component of the management agreement is the provision of financial-related services, such as financial statement preparation, billing and collecting, accounting, etc., then market data for financial management services should be accorded more weight. Also, the risk and responsibility that the management company is assuming should be compared to the market comparable data. As previously mentioned, many publicly traded management companies perform services in addition to management services, so a management agreement that consists primarily of "support" services may not be entirely comparable.

In addition, adjustments should be considered based on the relative level of revenues for the market comparable data. While many market data points fall within a range of 4% to 6% of revenues, it is dangerous to assume automatically that the subject management fee should fall within this range. As the level of revenue increases, certain economies of scale can be reached, and therefore, the management fee as a percentage of the revenue should decrease. Conversely, for a startup company, the management fee as a percentage of revenue might appropriately exceed this range due to a low level of revenue. The appraiser should consider the revenue size of the market comparable data to determine whether the management fee as a percentage of revenue is an appropriate fit for the subject management fee.

4.3 Income Approach

To apply the income approach, the appraiser determines the value of the economic benefits that would accrue to either side of the management services arrangement. The benefits, however, are evaluated differently from the perspective of the hypothetical buyer and the seller of the services. To analyze the seller's benefits, the appraiser considers the profit level of the management company, given the calculated management fee. This is accomplished by subtracting the estimated costs that the management company would incur to provide the services from the calculated management fee. This profit or margin level is then compared with market-based rates using guideline companies with comparable risk and operating profiles. The income approach analysis can also be completed using levels of investment and rates of return. If the management company is not assuming significant risk or the nature of the management services are more supportive in nature, then the profit margin of the management company should be relatively lower. Conversely, if the management company is assuming greater risk and responsibility, then the management company's profit margin should be relatively higher. In other words, the amount of the management fee should appropriately reflect the level of risk that the management company is assuming.

The economic benefits to the buyer, on the other hand, can be evaluated by determining the value of the benefits that would accrue to the managed organization from the services the manager provides. It can be difficult, however, to quantify the benefit or improved earnings resulting from the arrangement. The appraiser would need to *isolate* this financial impact to those results achieved by the management company's efforts, as opposed to those produced by the managed entity based on its own efforts. This difficulty creates a practical limitation on the use of the income approach in many arrangements. Alternatively, the appraiser can evaluate the total earnings, margins, and returns of the managed organization, given its purchase of the management services. This evaluation is based on comparison with market rates of earnings, margins, and returns, given the risk and operation profile of the managed company. Depending on the size and complexity of the managed company, this alternative method of analysis for the buyer can also have practical limitations.

5.0 Commercial Reasonableness

In addition to determining the fair market value of a management agreement, an appraiser is sometimes asked to opine on the commercial reasonableness of the agreement. This is particularly necessary when the management services involve physicians that are in or potentially could be in a referral relationship with the hospital.

In developing an opinion related to the commercial reasonableness for management agreements, several factors should be considered, including: (1) the legitimate business purpose of the arrangement; (2) the appropriateness of the management services; (3) the necessity of any specialized expertise, if applicable; and (4) the oversight and monitoring of the arrangement. For each of these factors, several questions should be considered to evaluate the commercial reasonableness of the arrangement.

Legitimate business purpose
- Does the proposed arrangement represent a reasonable necessity for the operation of the managed entity?

- Is the management agreement necessary to further a legitimate business purpose of the managed entity?

Appropriateness of the management services
- Are the particular duties of the management company clearly defined?

- Are the management services a necessary addition to the managed entity's current managerial or administrative staff?

Necessity of specialized expertise

- Does the management agreement require the services of physicians or other specialized staff?

- If so, does the management company possess the requisite expertise and experience to perform the management services?

Oversight and monitoring of the agreement

- Is there a written agreement that clearly defines the terms of the arrangement?

- Does the managed entity engage in routine monitoring efforts to ensure that the required services are actually performed?

- If the management agreement includes incentive payments, are there sufficient protocols in place to effectively track and measure any incentive metrics?

In addition, the return on investment for the management company should be compared to the level of risk assumed by the management company to determine commercial reasonableness. Each arrangement will have its own unique facts and circumstances, and an appraiser must consider all relevant factors to opine on commercial reasonableness.

6.0 Conclusion

Management services arrangements are widely used in the healthcare industry by a variety of providers in different settings and relationships. While the types of services found in the marketplace are generally similar, each arrangement can involve a unique bundle of services. Moreover, the compensation structures involved in these arrangements can entail varying levels of risk and return for the entity providing the services. It is essential, therefore, that appraisals of management services focus on analyzing the precise bundle of services included in the underlying arrangement and on the economics of the compensation structure. In determining the fair market value of management services, the risks and responsibilities of the management company should be appropriately identified and reflected in the fair market management fee. In addition, healthcare laws and regulations require any financial arrangement between providers of healthcare services and referral sources for those services to be both consistent with fair market value and commercially reasonable. Therefore, a sound fair market value and commercial reasonableness opinion is imperative for healthcare regulatory compliance considerations.

Part V.
Advanced Issues and Specialized Topics
in Healthcare Compensation Valuations

Chapter 35. Next Generation Clinical Co-Management Agreements: The Challenges of Valuing Value

CONTENTS

Chapter 35. Next Generation Clinical Co-Management Agreements: The Challenges of Valuing Value

By Mark Browne, M.D., David McMillan, CPA, and Burl Stamp, FACHE

"Price is what you pay. Value is what you get." – Warren Buffet

1.0 Introduction

Although there is no doubt the healthcare industry is journeying ever closer to a model based on the value, not the quantity, of care delivered, the path to get there is at best a confusing one. The idea of aligned incentives between hospitals and physicians is an easy one to agree with, but a very difficult one to implement in reality. The clinical co-management model (CCM) is one tactic used by many health systems to begin to aligning the existing disparate financial incentives for hospitals and physicians. Valuation experts are often called upon to provide opinions of value related to the compensation paid to the participating physicians. To comply with federal regulations, participants in these models must ensure that compensation received by physicians is at fair market value (FMV) to prevent overpayment to physicians based on the value or volume of referrals.

To properly evaluate the FMV compensation associated with CCMs, valuators must have a thorough understanding of the components of a co-management agreement and must provide analytics supporting the basis of their valuation. This can be difficult given that many of the "value-based" concepts underpinning these agreements (such as specialty-specific quality and outcomes metrics):

- Are highly subjective;

- Are not yet recognized in a definitive manner within the available regulatory guidance; and,

- Do not correlate easily to widely circulated benchmark materials.

In addition to these challenges, valuators are now faced with second-generation CCMs whose scope of services managed, number of facilities managed, and scope of geographic regions served are expanding. For example, hospitals and health systems are exploring concepts such as:

- Whole-hospital clinical co-management agreements;

- Multiple facility or single service line co-management agreements; and

- Multiple facility or multiple service line co-management agreements.

The emergence of these newer, more expansive models, understanding their construct, and evaluating various valuation issues they present are the topics of conversation among hospitals, physicians, attorneys, healthcare leaders, consultants, and valuators. To explore the unique valuation challenges associated with these second-generation CCMs, it is imperative to first ensure an understanding of the construct and valuation principles underpinning traditional models.

2.0 Understanding Traditional Co-Management Models

Significant attention and professional guidance have been given to the valuation challenges and approaches related to CCMs. Our purpose is not to present a comprehensive overview of the valuation issues inherent in the determination of FMV compensation associated with these more traditional models. However, a brief narrative on the subject is included below to provide appropriate context for the reader when considering the implications of second-generation CCMs.

Historically, co-management agreements have been designed around a single, hospital-based service line. Common service lines considered include orthopedics, cardiology, and neurosurgery. When valuing the compensation associated with CCMs, the approaches utilized by the valuator are consistent with the valuation approaches used for any form of compensation methodology: the income approach, the cost approach, and the market approach.

- Income approach—This approach measures the economic benefit accruing to the contracting organization (typically a hospital or health system) as a result of the management services rendered by the parties to the CCM. Additionally, the income approach may attempt to also measure the economic benefit accruing to the contracting organization from the achievement of certain quality or outcome metrics. Measuring the economic benefits of these services or outcomes, however, involves certain potential risks, such as the implication of valuing volume or referrals, and the perception that the agreements might result in compensation to physicians that is generated more directly from the energies of existing hospital management functions. Despite those concerns, many valuators continue to employ this approach when valuing the compensation associated with CCMs.

- Valuing the economic benefits accruing to the hospital from the achievement of quality and outcome metrics prior to the implementation of the Centers for Medicare and Medicaid Services (CMS) value-based purchasing program (VBP) and other similar reimbursement structures sponsored by private insurers was, at best, subjective. However, the emergence of these defined VBP programs provides today's valuator with discernible economic risks and benefits associated with these metrics. While this clarity is certainly helpful, the introduction of metrics that are increasingly difficult to measure and report, as discussed below, introduce new challenges to the valuator when employing the income approach.

- Cost approach—This approach evaluates the alternative to the proposed structure, i.e., what it would cost the hospital to hire or provide for the management and other services within the CCM. As with all approaches, the valuator must ensure a thorough understanding of the components of the CCM agreement to properly evaluate the merits and usefulness of this approach. Often, due to the inability to match desired services with internal resources, this approach requires significant judgment by the valuator. When making these judgments and assumptions, the valuator may have to access expertise from experts in clinical and operational matters to have an appropriate degree of understanding of the issues and factors contributing to the application of this approach. As a result, the use of multiple approaches, when applicable, will provide a more comprehensive basis for the opinion of value related to the compensation component of the CCM.

- Market approach—A powerful tool in the valuator's arsenal is the ability of the valuator to draw upon experience with other CCM arrangements and analyses. Having an experienced valuation team adds significant value for the hospital seeking assistance. While each CCM is unique in its construct and purpose, various components within the CCM often have characteristics and specific elements common to other CCMs. Once the valuator has gained a thorough understanding of the components of the CCM, he or she can then draw upon his or her experience with other, similar components in assigning an indication of value using this approach.

Ultimately, the valuator's opinion of value will likely be the result of a combination of multiple approaches and judgment.

Traditional CCMs often result in compensation being awarded for the defined services (fixed fee) and the ability to earn additional compensation based on the achievement of predetermined metrics (variable fee). Evaluating the valuation issues presented by these traditional models include:

- Defining the fixed fee component—Careful consideration should be given to the construct of this component of compensation. Hospitals and physicians should collaborate to define these services, whose purposes are to improve the quality of care provided and improve the outcomes of the patients treated. Simply assigning traditional medical directorship services, which are often administrative in nature, is not a substitute for the work and analysis necessary to define the services and duties that will positively impact the care provided to patients.

That is not to say, however, that administrative functions have no place in a co-management agreement. Many co-management agreements include management functions performed by physicians and nonphysician personnel. These functions can be important toward the goals of improved care. However, the valuator must be cognizant of Stark regulations that expressly limit compensation paid to physicians for administrative functions to administrative rates. Having qualified clinical professionals, such as physicians, nurses, and other experienced operational executives, evaluate the duties outlined in the fixed fee component of the co-management agreement is critical to ensure the valuator understands the basis for opining upon this portion of the compensation.

- Defining the variable ("at risk") fee component—The more substantive challenge facing those designing and valuing traditional co-management models is the definition of the metrics and parameters of the components composing the variable compensation portion of the agreement. These components typically consist of quality and outcome metrics, performance metrics, and satisfaction metrics. Regulatory bodies such as the Centers for Medicare and Medicaid Services (CMS) and the Office of Inspector General (OIG) have provided guidance on the construct and measurement of these components. Such guidance should be carefully evaluated by qualified legal counsel when constructing the co-management agreement. Valuators must have an understanding of these regulations, because the valuator's ability to ensure there is a basis for measuring these metrics is dependent upon such. Despite these efforts, however, the healthcare industry continues to refine its ability to track and measure many quality measurements. As a result, there is not always unanimity among participants as to how these metrics are measured.

- Defining the structure to house the co-management functions—Typically, the traditional co-management companies have been structured in one of three ways:

  ◦ As a contract between a hospital and physicians;

  ◦ Within a joint venture company owned by physician-participants and the hospital; or,

  ◦ Within a joint venture company owned by physician participants.

When housed within a joint venture company, the valuator is often called upon to value equity interests in the company often associated with changes in ownership.

3.0 Next Generation Co-Management Models

As organizations continue the simultaneous journeys of new care model development, many are searching for ways to further build on the foundation of existing clinical co-management arrangements. Leveraging the investments made in the infrastructure, operational improvement, and relationships necessary for these existing co-managements arrangements can provide a framework for systems to move closer to the ultimate goal of consistent high quality care delivery rewarded through a value-based payment system. To that end, health systems that have clinical co-management agreements in place are beginning to move toward more complex, integrated types of arrangements as a vehicle to ease the transition to a fully value-based model of care.

These new arrangements often share the same basic tenets of traditional co-management agreements, i.e., a structure that includes an hourly rate for management-related activities and a variable or at-risk component. However, in the more contemporary clinical co-management models, variables constituting the at-risk component emphasize activities related to quality, outcomes, and efficiency.

4.0 New Model Structures

In response to these new challenges, hospitals, healthcare systems, and their physician partners have developed new CCM models whose scope and reach extend beyond the traditional structure. Whole-hospital agreements, multihospital service line agreements, and other model constructs continue to emerge. The scope of services or expanded geographies can present unique challenges to the valuator. Of particular concern to the valuator, when multiple service lines or geographies are involved, is the need to perform additional analyses and due diligence to gain an understanding of the multiplicity of agreements outside the scope of the CCM that may exist. Call arrangements, medical directorships, consulting agreements and other similar contracts must all be considered for the evaluator to accurately estimate the cost of services (application of the cost approach) and the resulting compensation.[1]

While many of the mechanics of compensation (fixed base compensation and variable compensation earned through the achievement of predetermined metrics) are expanded in these second-generation models, the concepts remain fairly similar to traditional CCM models. The challenges faced by the valuators are often associated with the expanded clinical metrics and quality standards incorporated in the models and the leadership and governance structures that can have an impact on roles, responsibilities, and compensation.

5.0 Second-Generation Quality and Outcome Metrics

The traditional co-management model design is quite effective in managing costs and improving quality within the hospital but does little to address issues beyond the acute care continuum such as readmission, outpatient imaging, rehabilitative care, or other clinical issues presented by patients outside of the service line. These other clinical issues, such as diabetes, heart failure, and so on, have a significant impact on the total cost and quality of care delivered. Additionally the traditional co-management models have been limited as to the type of quality metrics typically defined and measured as part of an arrangement. Many hospitals are limited in the quality of data that are readily available for use in these arrangements. As a result, many of the co-management agreements previously executed have reverted to the frequent use of process metrics as opposed to true outcome-based metrics. Measures of performance in this type of model begin to evolve from process-based measures to more sophisticated outcome types of metrics. Measures within the specific service line are transformed to focus

---

1   Although not considered within the scope of this discussion, these expanded models and the potential for a multiplicity of agreements may present commercial reasonableness issues and concerns. A thorough evaluation of commercial reasonableness is an important consideration for valuators, consultants, counsel, and providers when contemplating the compliance standards to be addressed.

more on clinical performance (i.e., infection rates and complication rates) as well as incorporating more subjective measures, such as patient and physician satisfaction. Also in these newer models, a larger percentage of total compensation is placed at risk for performance on quality metrics, typically in the 25%-to-30% range and sometimes as high as 50%.[2]

| Exhibit 1. Examples of Process and Outcome Metrics ||
Process Metrics	Outcome Metrics
Did the heart attack patient receive an aspirin?	Mortality rate for heart attack
Did the congestive heart failure patient receive discharge instructions?	Percentage of patients with congestive heart failure readmitted within 30 days of hospital discharge

The valuator's ability to effectively apply the income, cost and market approaches with respect to quality and outcome metrics was often limited in the past because the economic return to the hospital resulting from the achievement of these metrics was limited. As providers have increasingly provided enhanced reimbursement for proven improvements in quality (or, conversely, penalties to reimbursement for quality or outcome deficiencies), the ability of the valuator to confidently utilize the income approach has improved. Of particular note, the initiation of the value-based payment program by CMS provides significant guidance for measuring the potential economic return to hospitals resulting from increased quality and enhanced outcomes. Contemporary valuators should understand the basic tenets and construct of CMS's value-based reimbursement system because this methodology will likely be prevalent, in some form or fashion, within many privately sponsored value-based reimbursement programs.

5.1 Understanding CMS's Value-Based Program Construct

As the name suggests, the new VBP regulations are designed to reward those healthcare institutions that offer superior *value* to Medicare patients. The VBP program provides a structured mechanism to level the playing field across healthcare institutions that deliver varying levels of quality. Simply, institutions providing measurably higher quality can justify higher cost and reimbursement, while institutions with lower scores on quality metrics should be paid less to balance the value equation. It is important for staff and physicians at all levels of the organization to understand this dynamic and why paying attention to VBP factors is so critical.

---

2   At-risk or variable compensation amounts may be subject to certain limitations depending upon factors such as the presence of tax-exempt debt within the financing structure of the participating hospital or health system. For example, IRS Revenue Procedure 97-13 outlines certain safe harbors that apply to agreements of this type to ensure that the tax-exempt entity does not use bond-financed assets for private business. Valuators and consultants should work closely with tax professionals and counsel when defining the compensation structure for these newer models.

Exhibit 2. FY2012 Metrics

- Fibronolytic therapy received within 30 minutes
- Primary PCI received within 90 minutes
- Discharge instructions for CHF
- Blood cultures performed in Emergency Department for pneumonia
- Initial antibiotic selection for Community Acquired Pneumonia

- Prophylactic antibiotic received within one hour prior to incision
- Surgery patients with appropriate selection of prophylactic antibiotics
- Surgery patients with appropriate discontinuation of prophylactic antibiotics
- Cardiac surgery patient with controlled post-operative serum glucose

- Surgery patients with recommended venous thromboembolism prophylaxis ordered
- Surgery patients who received appropriate venous thromboembolism prophylaxis before and after surgery
- Appropriate beta blocker use in surgical patients

- Communication with Nurses
- Communication with Doctors
- Hospital Staff Responsiveness

- Pain Management
- Communication about Medicine
- Hospital Cleanliness & Quietness

- Discharge Information
- Overall Hospital Rating

While the new value-based purchasing methodology was designed to be revenue- or cost-neutral in aggregate, the funding and incentive payment design forces individual winners and losers. Approximately 50% of participating hospitals will lose money, while the other half will benefit from higher reimbursement for Medicare services. This is particularly important to consider in the context of valuing compensation associated with these next-generation CCMs; achieving the ability to earn reimbursement in the CMS value-based program is not necessarily solely dependent upon achieving certain scores but is also dependent upon how a particular hospital or organization scores *relative to other hospitals and organizations*. This concept is not often found in the CCM construct. The ability to earn compensation relative to the achievement of quality and outcome metrics is usually defined. As value-based reimbursement systems evolve, valuators need to be aware of these market forces when applying the market approach to compensation considerations.

5.2 Paying for the Value-Based Program

To fund incentive payments, base diagnosis-related group (DRG) rates for hospitals reimbursed under the prospective payment system (PPS) will be reduced by 1% beginning Oct. 1, 2012 (see Exhibit 3). For each of the next four years, rates will drop an additional 0.25% until payments are reduced a full 2% in fiscal year 2017.

Although DRG rates are being cut, remember that the regulations today require that all reduced reimbursement—estimated to be approximately $850 million in the first year of the program—be redistributed to providers. CMS estimates that the mean redistributed value-based incentive payments will range from 48% to 155% of an institutions' reduction in DRG reimbursement.

Exhibit 3. Reduction Timeline

July 1, 2011 – March 31, 2012	August 1, 2012	October 1, 2012	November 1, 2012	October 1, 2016
Initial Performance Period • 17 clinical process of care measures • 8 HCAPS measures	Announcement of estimated amount of payment	Medicare discharges reimbursed according to VBP	Exact amount of VBP incentive earned announced to hospitals	

0% Reduction	1% Reduction	2% Reduction

5.3 Value-Based Program Metrics—Scoring and Awarding Reimbursement

The metrics that matter under the new value-based purchasing program are grouped into two broad categories that should be very familiar to hospitals. Clinical Processes of Care Measures were first introduced on CMS's Hospital Compare Web site (www.hospitalcompare.hhs.gov) in 2005 and Hospital Consumer Assessment of Healthcare Providers and Systems (H-CAHPS) measures of patient experience followed in 2007. The 12 process of care measures determine 70% of a hospital's incentive score, with the H-CAHPS survey results accounting for 30%. CMS has committed to additional new measures being available on the Hospital Compare Web site for at least one year before they are added to the incentive formula under VBP.

For both clinical processes of care and H-CAHPS measures, there are two ways for a hospital to earn its performance score in a range from 0 to 10 points: 1) by hitting achievement targets based on its performance as compared to all hospitals across the country or 2) by improving results compared against its own performance during the benchmark period.

Achievement scores are awarded for each individual care process and H-CAHPS measure on an incremental scale from a "threshold" up to the "benchmark" for that performance component, where:

- Threshold = median (50th percentile) of all participating hospitals' performance during baseline period (July 2009 to March 2010) and

- Benchmark = mean of the top 10% of all hospitals' performance during the baseline period.

Improvement scores are awarded on a similar scale, but the organization's lower threshold is set at its own actual performance on each dimension during the baseline period. The improvement score methodology makes it possible for a hospital to receive points when it is making progress on a clinical process or H-CAHPS measure even when its score is still below the median for all hospitals.

In Exhibit 4, this hospital scored 0.43 during the baseline period on one of the VBP dimensions. Its score improved significantly during the 2012 performance period, to 0.82, putting it above the achievement threshold of 0.65 on this measure. Its achievement score on this measure would be approximately 7.2 and rounded to 7. But note that its improvement score would be slightly higher and rounded up to 8. On this measure, it would be awarded the higher improvement score.

For clinical processes of care and H-CAHPS measures, CMS will calculate both the achievement and improvement score and give the hospital the higher of the two scores, rounded to the nearest whole number (see Exhibit 4).

For the patient experience component of value-based purchasing, CMS also wants to reward hospitals for achieving consistency across the various H-CAHPS dimensions. The consistency score, which will comprise 20% of the total H-CAHPS score, will be awarded in a range of 0 to 20 points if a hospital makes improvement across all eight components. If a hospital's scores on all eight of the H-CAHPS dimensions are above the achievement threshold, it will receive the maximum, 20 points.

Actual incentive payments will be calculated at the end of each CMS fiscal year using a hospital's individual scores as compared to performance scores of all other participating hospitals. Again, CMS estimates that the mean redistributed value-based incentive payments will range from 48% to 155% of an institutions' reduction in DRG reimbursement.

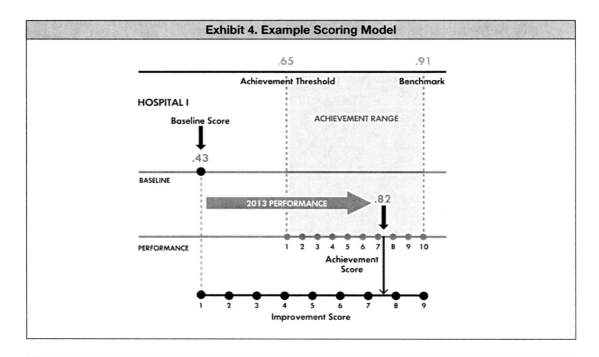

Exhibit 4. Example Scoring Model

As demonstrated above, there is much to learn from CMS's example for hospitals in the design and implementation of contemporary CCM models. An experienced valuator, well-versed in contemporary reimbursement models, will be a valuable member of the team, working to define and implement these next-generation models.

Because CMS is the single largest payer in healthcare, the quality metrics utilized in its value-based program deserve careful consideration and study. However, providers and payers are continually developing new and unique ways to measure quality and outcome metrics, and these concepts are continually finding their way into CCMs.

One such concept being incorporated is that of the "trigger metric." In this model, physicians must overcome a defined performance hurdle (i.e., top decile performance in all relevant core measures) to access any quality-related bonus at all, independent of their performance on the other defined quality metrics. No compensation is directly tied to the achievement of the trigger metric. It is simply the minimum threshold necessary to participate in any quality-related compensation. This model is closely aligned with models currently being employed by CMS in its shared savings program (ACOs) as well as the bundled payment initiative pilot. Structuring the quality portion of co-management agreements in this way allows physicians and hospitals to mutually define clinical priorities and begins to align incentives, leading to a greater focus for all in achieving the desired quality and efficiency outcomes.

Another contemporary quality metric being considered in contemporary CCMs is the composite metric. In this type of metric, efficiency or cost components are married with clinical outcome metrics into a single composite score. This type of metric is frequently used as a trigger metric to remove it from any direct association with the value or volume of referrals. This type of metric must obviously be carefully designed to be compliant with Stark and anti-kickback statutes but can lead to significant improvements in both cost and quality if well-designed.

A third quality concept differentiating this type of alignment model from traditional models is the introduction of shared quality metrics. In this model, "all ships rise, and all ships sink" together. In other words, if all physicians in each individual service line agreement do not achieve the goal outlined by the shared quality metrics, no physician is rewarded for his or her individual performance. Incentive compensation is only rewarded if all physicians in each arrangement achieve a defined goal. This style of metric can be used at the individual service line level as well as at a higher governance level, such as the clinical coordination integration listed above. A good example of a metric to be used in this way is patient satisfaction measures. Each service line will have different satisfaction-related opportunities to address, but it is a measure that is common to all service lines and has direct impact for the system as well.

As the valuator is charged with the task of assigning value to the compensation associated with these new and more comprehensive metrics, he or she may be faced with metrics to measure and value that are unique to the situation being studied, for which other examples (market approaches) are not readily available. To assign an economic "value" to the "value" provided by the accomplishments of these newer, more comprehensive metrics, the valuator must have access to significant expertise in healthcare operations and to qualified clinical resources that can provide expertise and perspective to the activities that may result in compensation to council members. Once again, coordination across a multidisciplinary team of professionals, including the valuator, is required to properly measure the value of compensation and services associated with these newer models of care. Valuators must be actively seeking these resources if they are to continue serving the healthcare industry associated with newer care delivery models. Those who recognize the necessity of such a multidisciplinary approach will be in high demand and will provide a defensible, value-added service for their clients. Those who do not prepare themselves nor recognize the need for these resources may ultimately place both themselves and the clients they serve at risk with regards to defending the compensation associated with these models as being consistent with the standard of FMV.

6.0 Clinical Leadership and Governance

As mentioned previously, historical agreements of this type have typically been focused on a single service line. Model participants are now exploring new designs to begin to address care across the continuum of care. One way this is being accomplished is through the creation of a multidisciplinary clinical advisory or integration council (see Exhibit 5). As it relates to clinical co-management models, this council might be the contracting or governing body for agreements for multiple service lines (necessitating the inclusion of multiple specialties among the council's membership.) Alternatively, this group may function as a complementary committee focused on coordinating the efforts of existing clinical co-management agreements. In this capacity, the council provides oversight to ensure consistent, standardized care delivery across multiple specialties.

This council may also manage other types of agreements (i.e., professional services agreements) to ensure consistency of a value-based design of all physician and hospital arrangements across a system. Physicians on this committee are chosen specifically for their ability to lead and manage care across the continuum and are not necessarily chosen on a representative basis. In other words, they need not be a representative from each existing co-management agreement on the council for it to be a successful model. Physicians invited to participate in the council may also have defined requirements for participation that lead to a more integrated care delivery system. As an example, one system with this type of arrangement requires the physicians to actively participate as members of the statewide Healthcare Information Exchange to assure the necessary collection and analysis of data for value-based payment models.

Physicians serving on this council may receive compensation for their service. While providing hourly compensation is an option, the nature and purpose of these councils are often more in keeping with an at-risk or performance-based compensation construct. To the extent council members may also be a party to other, specialty-specific co-management agreements or contracts, the construct of the council compensation must take into account the risk of compensating a physician member twice for the same achievement of value. The valuator must be particularly attuned to the compensation methodology and the complex flow of funds that can accompany these types of relationships.

Comprehensive approaches to value-based healthcare, such as the council described above, present attorneys, consultants, providers, and valuators with new and often unexplored issues for clarification. While the maintenance of independence is fundamental to the valuator's professional standards, models such as this present the valuator with an even greater need to coordinate and collaborate with other experts to render a defensible opinion of value. Thus, we find that the goal of coordinating care in the clinical aspects of healthcare also requires enhanced coordination among the professionals assigned with designing, valuing, and operating those same models.

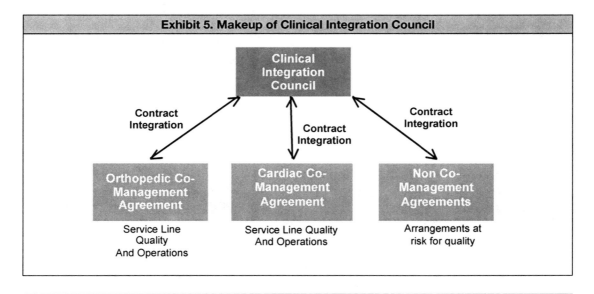

Exhibit 5. Makeup of Clinical Integration Council

7.0 Conclusion

As mentioned at the outset, the road to value-based models of care is not yet fully defined, and we will certainly take many different paths to get there. For those organizations that have clinical CCMs in place, transitioning to this next-generation style of model will create an excellent place to learn about value-based reimbursement, allow your organization to work within this type of model and identify any gaps in abilities or resources, and will ultimately provide a vehicle to help navigate toward a more fully developed value-based model of care, no matter which model it may be. Making certain the experts employed by organizations to assist in the construct of these models (such as attorneys, consultants, and valuators) are aware and capable of working in a multidisciplinary setting will be crucial to the hospital's or health system's ability to manage the complex compliance and risk issues that accompany these models.

Chapter 36. Evaluating RVU-Based Compensation Arrangements

CONTENTS

Chapter 36. Evaluating RVU-Based Compensation Arrangements

By Mark O. Dietrich, CPA/ABV, and Gregory D. Anderson, CPA/ABV, CVA

1.0 Introduction

Compensation arrangements based on relative value units (RVUs) are increasingly popular for compensating physicians. Where collected revenue-based systems—historically common in group practice, for example—reflect the individual physician's underlying payer mix, RVU systems are payer-mix neutral. A RVU system[1] is therefore attractive to a physician employed by a hospital that treats patients regardless of their ability to pay. However, RVU systems may be tainted by payer mix and other market conditions, requiring that the analyst understand and examine the effects of this issue when using compensation survey data to establish fair market value incentive compensation based on RVUs.

2.0 RVU Measurement Systems

Several RVU measurement systems are associated with physician billing codes (current procedural terminology, or CPT™), but the most commonly used is the resource-based relative value scale (RBRVS), which is also used by the Medicare program for establishing its physician fee schedule (MPFS). The RBRVS allocates RVUs to each procedure or service in the CPT™ based upon the amount of physician work, the cost of delivering the service, and the cost of malpractice insurance associated with the service. These RVUs are then multiplied by an amount known as a conversion

---

1   It is important to note that most compensation systems focus on the physician work RVU component (wRVU), which is but one component of the RBRVS measuring of total RVU values; the other two are practice expense and malpractice insurance cost. This allows for measurement of physician productivity using a tool that essentially measures those areas of productivity that are under the control of the physician.

factor and adjusted for geographic differences (the GPCI) to arrive at the fee for the service.

RBRVS has its weaknesses. The Medicare conversion factor suffers from a statutory construct, which attempts to peg overall Medicare physician spending to an annual limit that would seem to make that measurement unit meaningless in the present environment. Sitting at around $38 per RVU before geographic adjustment, the rate has been virtually flat for many years and does not maintain pace with inflation, which the Medicare Payment Advisory Commission (MedPAC) estimates at approximately 3% per annum in physician practices. Nonetheless, the vast majority of physicians continue to accept Medicare patients, suggesting, at least to government agencies such as MedPAC, that payment rate has some relevance in assessing value. RBRVS is also subject to government manipulation that manifests itself in instability. For example, legislative intervention into the formula used to account for the practice expense formula and statutory five-year adjustments to the physician work component of the RVU affect how RBRVS impacts physician payment.

Payment rates per RVU vary significantly from region to region, as well as from payer contract to contract. Providers and, particularly, provider-systems with negotiating strength may have payment rates per RVU well in excess of their competitors. Evaluating reasonable compensation for a physician therefore requires knowledge of the specific contract rates being paid for that physician's services, as well as knowledge of the underlying payer mix. Consider the following example of how contract rates and payer mix impact physician compensation:

Exhibit 1. How Contract Rates and Payer Mix Affect Compensation				
Payer Mix	**40%**	**10%**	**60%**	
Payer	**Medicare**	**Best**	**Non-Medicare Avg. Including Best**	**Weighted Average**
Total RVUs	10,000	10,000	10,000	10,000
Rate	$38	$55	$48	$44
Collections	380,000	550,000	480,000	440,000
Practice Expenses	250,000	250,000	250,000	250,000
Physician Income	130,000	300,000	230,000	190,000
Compensation per total RVU	13	30	23	19

Note: Payer mix weights are used to determine the weighted average rate per RVU. Each column indicates what the physician would have earned if 100% of the services provided were for each of the payer columns shown. For purposes of the example, assume that none of the total RVUs include Stark or other prohibited incentives.

3.0 Example

In the example, the physician is earning $190,000 per year on collected revenue of $440,000. The physician's earnings would vary from $130,000 if the practice were entirely Medicare to $300,000 if it was entirely "market-best," a difference of 230%. The key observation to be taken from the example is that because expenses are fixed for a given volume of services in each scenario, all of the additional revenue from better contracts drops to the bottom line as physician compensation. That in turn suggests that "reasonable compensation" for 10,000 RVUs of services could range from $130,000 to $300,000, depending upon the mix and strength of the underlying payer contracts.

Lest that seem unrealistic on its face, consider the view from the physician working in a private practice holding only "market-best" contracts. Certainly, he or she would not be willing to work for $130,000 per year seeing only Medicare patients. Similarly, a physician employed by a hospital or integrated delivery system (IDS) with strong contracts for physician services would expect to be compensated at a commensurate rate, rather than have the employing institution retain the excess as profit. Similarly, it is unlikely that the managed care companies and other payers would be paying premium rates per RVU, unless market conditions warranted it and made it necessary to attract physician providers into their networks.

The non-Medicare average value per RVU of $48 is an initial reference point for what "market" value for physician services is in this particular circumstance, assuming the weighted average conversion factor, as described in the following paragraph. The Medicare conversion factor is not negotiated but is rather a legislatively imposed *force majeure* disconnected from market forces. As such, it has limited worth in assessing "market" value.

The compensation reported in survey data such as that of the Medical Group Management Association will reflect the "weighted average" compensation or rate per RVU of only those entities participating in the survey. In the example, this compensation would be $190,000. The actual rate per RVU in a given practice may be more or less than the survey result. If practices participating in the survey have a better payer and rate mix than all practices in a given area, the compensation will be higher and conversely, if the participating practices have poorer rates, the survey compensation will be less.

This type of analysis is critical in assessing the fair market value of compensation for hospitals employing physicians. In many markets, integrated provider networks that include both physicians and hospitals succeed in obtaining superior reimbursement from payers, which in turn results in superior compensation. The contracts may be a function of enhanced clinical quality from integration, market-based negotiating leverage, reduced administrative costs to payers due to single-signature contracting, or shifting of contract administration. Traditional analysis focusing solely on compensation surveys to determine fair market value may well fall short of the market value of services based upon actual negotiated contracts for providers with a strong market position.

Returning to Exhibit 1, assume that an IDS has managed care and other payer agreements that result in the following Payer Distribution and Revenue for a physician practice.

In this case, the actual contracts in place generate physician compensation of $216,000 as compared to the "market" compensation described in the first example of $190,000, or about 14% greater. Solely relying on the survey result would seem to understate what is "reasonable compensation" for a physician employed in this particular provider entity. The determination of what is reasonable requires the valuation analyst and the employing provider to have keen insight into market conditions to arrive at an appropriate conclusion.

An appropriate alternative to sole reliance on survey data is to measure the value of compensation per RVU based on data from the practice on revenues and RVUs produced by major payer or payer group. Some analysts will benchmark the physician practice on a more global scale, analyzing collections per RVU to get an overall sense of favorable or unfavorable payer arrangements when the practice is compared against survey data. After this initial "litmus test" is interpreted, exploration of data by payer group, drilling down to compensation per RVU as in Exhibit 2, can give an indication as to whether and to what extent favorable or unfavorable payer contracts impact physician compensation. This, essentially the use of the income-based approach in analyzing

Exhibit 2. Payer Mix				
Payer Mix	**35%**	**30%**	**35%**	**100%**
	Medicare	**Best**	**Other Payers**	**Weighted Average**
Total RVUs	3,500	3,000	3,500	10,000
Rate	$38.00	$55.00	$48.00	$46.60
Collections	133,000	165,000	168,000	466,000
Practice expenses	87,500	75,000	87,500	250,000
Physician income	45,500	90,000	80,500	216,000
Compensation per total RVU	13.00	30.00	23.00	21.60
Note: Exhibit 2 differs from the first in that the payer mix has been applied to the total RVUs of services performed to arrive at the actual compensation earned based upon the given payer mix.				

physician compensation value, supplements the market-based approach conclusions derived from an interpretation of raw survey data.

What becomes clear to the analyst is that simple reliance on single survey data is not enough to yield a completely defensible conclusion of value for compensation under a RVU arrangement. Use of as many independently published surveys and as many different valuation methods as are reasonably available is certainly a prudent practice for those with the responsibility for determining compensation that must be defended as fair market value. Not only should the use of RVUs be considered, but other physician productivity benchmarks (i.e., encounters and visits for primary care and surgical cases for surgeons) may also be appropriate.

4.0 Conclusion

Finally, as an observation, physician practice acquisition value is often considered simultaneously with an employment decision and reasonable compensation analysis. In the practice valuation model, it is *not* appropriate to consider payer contracts held by a *particular* purchasing provider entity unless such contracts are common to the universe of potential purchasing entities in the market. This is because such an adjustment would be inconsistent with fair market value's requirement for *"any* willing buyer."

In contrast, compensation is a function of who employs you and what your services are worth at the time they are performed. From the standpoint of the hypothetical seller of services—i.e., the employed physician—being employed at a rate less than what the market is paying his or her employer currently for the physician's services would be inconsistent with the expected result in arm's-length negotiation where reasonable knowledge is present. Thus, a physician practice may have a low value because there is little profit once the physician receives reasonable compensation for services based upon the practice's existing contracts. However, the physician may be better compensated in the future because his or her new employer holds better payer contracts.

Chapter 37. How Reimbursement and Physician Compensation Vary by Market

CONTENTS

Chapter 37. How Reimbursement and Physician Compensation Vary by Market

By Timothy Smith, CPA/ABV

1.0 Introduction

This chapter uses data findings from a recent study on commercial reimbursement rates around the country to analyze the impact of reimbursement on physician compensation. These findings show wide variation in commercial rates across and within those markets included in the study. Since these rates are reported as a percentage of Medicare, the data from the study is readily adaptable for financial modeling of collections and compensation in each of these markets. This modeling enables analysis of variations in reimbursement on physician compensation with a view toward improved use of physician compensation survey data and valuation analysis in determining fair market value (FMV). This chapter summarizes the study, its findings, and the related modeling for physician reimbursement and compensation.

More importantly, this chapter explores the implications of this modeling for establishing FMV compensation levels for physicians. What will be shown is that commercial reimbursement is one of the key drivers of physician compensation. Since commercial rates vary, however, compensation valuation (CV) analysts need to re-examine and adjust many assumptions about survey data and its application in valuation methods. This chapter points to the use of alternative appraisal methods and techniques that are not part of the prevailing paradigm for valuing physician compensation arrangements for clinical services.

2.0 Wide Variation in Physician Reimbursement Across and Within Markets

2.1 The HSC Study

A recent study by the Center for Studying Health System Change (HSC) indicates a wide range of commercial reimbursement rates across and within various local markets in the United States.[1] The study selected eight markets for research because they were thought to have a wide range of payment rates, based on government studies. HSC was able to obtain data from the four main commercial payers—Aetna, United Healthcare, Cigna, and Blue Cross/Blue Shield—on reimbursement rates for each market. This data included various types of reimbursement, including inpatient, outpatient, and physician services. The payers provided commercial reimbursement rates to HSC as a percentage of Medicare rates. For physician reimbursement, rates were provided for the standard fee schedule and for practices from selected specialties that had negotiated higher rates than the standard fee schedule with the commercial payers. Based on this information, HSC was able to compile the data into key findings about commercial rates in each market.

2.2 Findings of the HSC Study

Exhibit 1 presents a summary of the study's findings for physician reimbursement. It shows commercial rates, as a percentage of Medicare, for the standard fee schedule and the 75th percentile rate for specific practices in selected specialties by market. The data from this study shows a wide variation in commercial payer rates across and within markets, particularly by specialty. The data indicates that groups with bargaining power are able to negotiate significantly higher rates than the standard fee schedule.

Some of the commercial rates are surprising, given the relatively higher cost of living in markets such as Los Angeles or San Francisco. For many observers, Milwaukee or rural Wisconsin would not have been the expected winners for the highest rates according to the standard fee schedule in the markets studied.

2.3 The Study's Analysis of Causes for Variations in Commercial Rates

The study noted that local market dynamics play a significant role in the reimbursement levels paid to physicians. Commercial payers establish a standard fee schedule. This schedule is often based on the framework of the Medicare Physician Fee Schedule (MPFS) and its resource-based relative value system (RBRVS). It also reflects the network goals of the insurer along with local physician supply considerations. Groups with leverage in the marketplace, however, are generally able to negotiate rates that

---

1   See *Wide Variation in Hospital and Physician Payment Rates Evidence of Provider Market Power*, Research Brief, No. 16, November 2010. Center for Studying Health System Change. www.hschange.org.

		75th Percentile Rates					
Market	Standard Rates	Internal Medicine / Family Medicine	Cardiology	Orthopedics	Anesthesiology	Radiology	Oncology - Physician Services
Cleveland	101%	112%	155%	124%	251%	166%	138%
Indianapolis	110	117	156	140	217	147	138
Los Angeles	92	-	-	-	177	-	-
Miami	82	89	110	101	-	134	116
Milwaukee	166	175	223	212	-	238	204
Richmond, VA	112	128	145	144	-	153	132
San Francisco	108	-	-	-	177	-	-
Rural Wisconsin	176	169	234	195	-	240	195

Exhibit 1. Commercial Rates as a Percentage of Medicare

are higher than the standard fee schedule. Small practices with little bargaining power are typically faced with accepting the standard fee schedule or not participating in the network or insurance plan. Unique factors within a local market accounted for variation across markets. For example, HSC specifically noted the large concentration of hospital-employed physicians as a significant factor in the high commercial rates observed in the Milwaukee market. Differences within a particular market were a function of the leverage that particular practices had relative to each other within that market.

3.0 Physician Reimbursement and Compensation Modeling Based on the HSC Study Findings

3.1 The Purpose of Developing the Reimbursement and Compensation Model

Revenue levels can have a significant impact on the earnings available in a practice for physician compensation. Dietrich and Anderson first noted the impact of commercial reimbursement on physician compensation in a critical analysis published in *Health Lawyers Weekly* in November 2008.[2] Their analysis, based on their first-hand experience in the market, showed how commercial rates can significantly affect compensation on a per-wRVU (work relative value unit) basis. To test and evaluate their seminal work further, the HSC data was used to develop a comparative model for a hypothetical cardiology group. The purpose of the model was to show the impact of varying commercial reimbursement rates on physician compensation. To isolate the impact of reimbursement, other factors that might impact compensation were held constant. Examples of these other factors include payer mix, service mix, nonclinical revenues, and overhead.

---

2   Mark O. Dietrich, CPA/ABV, and Gregory D. Anderson, CPA/ABV, CVA, "Evaluating RVU-Based Compensation Arrangements," *Health Lawyers Weekly*, Nov. 14, 2008. Note: This article is included in this guide as Chapter 36.

Since there is material variation in Medicare rates, the model also reflects the variation in Medicare reimbursement from market to market. Significant variations in the practice expense geographic practice cost index (GPCI) and the malpractice GPCI produce notable differences in revenues for Medicare.

3.2 Modeling Physician Reimbursement

The model was based on the 2010 relative value units (RVUs) for an actual nine-physician cardiology group. These RVUs were used to compute reimbursement with Medicare rates. The work, practice expense, and malpractice RVUs were multiplied by the appropriate GPCIs for each market and then by the Medicare conversion factor to compute the total revenue for the group on a Medicare reimbursement basis.[3] A simplified payer mix of 46% Medicare and 54% commercial was assumed. Reimbursement of HCPCS Level II codes were held constant over all markets. Commercial reimbursement was calculated using the data provided in the HSC study, including the standard fee schedule rates and the 75th percentile rates, noted as "Premium." A national average was added to the eight markets included in the study. The rates for the national average were based on figures reported by Medicare and an assumed commercial reimbursement ratio of 125% of Medicare.[4] Exhibit 2 shows the revenue rates per wRVU for Medicare, commercial, and a blended rate based on the payer mix assumption for the model.

Exhibit 2. Revenue Per wRVU				
Market / Rate Level	Market Commercial to Medicare Ratio	Medicare Revenue per wRVU	Commercial Revenue per wRVU	Blended Revenue per wRVU
Milwaukee, WI - Premium	223%	$73.57	$164.06	$122.44
Milwaukee, WI - Standard	166%	$73.57	$122.13	$99.79
Cleveland, OH - Premium	155%	$76.04	$117.86	$98.62
San Francisco, CA - Standard	108%	$93.50	$100.98	$97.54
Indianapolis, IN - Premium	156%	$74.07	$115.55	$96.47
Richmond, VA - Premium	145%	$74.68	$108.29	$92.83
Miami, FL - Premium	110%	$85.46	$94.01	$90.07
National Average	125%	$76.70	$95.88	$87.05
Los Angeles, CA - Standard	92%	$85.97	$79.09	$82.26
Richmond, VA - Standard	112%	$74.68	$83.64	$79.52
Indianapolis, IN - Standard	110%	$74.07	$81.48	$78.07
Miami, FL - Standard	82%	$85.46	$70.08	$77.15
Cleveland, OH - Standard	101%	$76.04	$76.80	$76.45

3   Rural Wisconsin was not included in the model for simplicity reasons. The larger point of the model is demonstrated by the urban/suburban markets that were included.

4   *Report to the Congress: Medicare Payment Policy*, MedPAC, March 15, 2011, p. 8. Medicare pays approximately 80% of private insurer rates.

3.3 Modeling Physician Compensation

To isolate the potential impact of the differences in reimbursement on physician compensation, the model was expanded to include an estimate of compensation based on a standard cost assumption applied to all markets. The computation included overhead and physician benefits using the median practice cost and physician benefits per full-time equivalent (FTE) physician from the *2011 MGMA Cost Survey* for cardiology practices. Physician compensation was computed as available earnings in the practice after deducting for overhead and physician benefits. The compensation results of the model are presented in Exhibit 3.

3.4 Compensation Factors Not Addressed by the Model

As noted earlier, this reimbursement and compensation model was designed to isolate the impact of reimbursement on physician compensation. To do this, other factors that affect compensation were held constant in the model. Some of these key factors include the following:

1. Payer mix;

2. Service mix, including the level of technical component services or ancillaries;

3. Other revenue sources, including on-call pay, clinical co-management fees, and diagnostic interpretation contracts; and

Market / Rate Level	Market Commercial to Medicare Ratio	Revenue per wRVU	Compensation per wRVU	Compensation to Revenue %
Milwaukee, WI - Premium	223%	$122.44	$80.40	65.7%
Milwaukee, WI - Standard	166%	$99.79	$57.75	57.9%
Cleveland, OH - Premium	155%	$98.62	$56.58	57.4%
San Francisco, CA - Standard	108%	$97.54	$55.50	56.9%
Indianapolis, IN - Premium	156%	$96.47	$54.43	56.4%
Richmond, VA - Premium	145%	$92.83	$50.79	54.7%
Miami, FL - Premium	110%	$90.07	$48.03	53.3%
National Average	125%	$87.05	$45.01	51.7%
Los Angeles, CA - Standard	92%	$82.26	$40.22	48.9%
Richmond, VA - Standard	112%	$79.52	$37.48	47.1%
Indianapolis, IN - Standard	110%	$78.07	$36.03	46.1%
Miami, FL - Standard	82%	$77.15	$35.11	45.5%
Cleveland, OH - Standard	101%	$76.45	$34.41	45.0%

Exhibit 3. Compensation for Hypothetical Cardiology Group

4. Cost variables, including geographic differences in cost rates and utilization efficiencies for practice staffing, office space, equipment, and other practice resources.

These items can have a significant effect on net practice earnings available for physician compensation. Consequently, if one were to examine actual practices in the various markets used in the model, one would expect to observe compensation outcomes that would differ from those in the model. The differences would result from the relative degree to which these other factors would impact physician compensation. What is clear from the model, however, is that reimbursement is one of the main drivers of physician compensation levels in a market.

4.0 Implications of the HSC Study and Compensation Modeling

4.1 While wRVUs for Physicians May Be Equal, Reimbursement Is Not

As illustrated in Exhibit 2, reimbursement can vary significantly across and within markets, with commercial rates yielding the greatest differences in comparison to Medicare. The model indicates that reimbursement for the same level of wRVU productivity can vary widely from market to market and from practice to practice within a market based solely on the impact of commercial and Medicare rates. While physician productivity can remain constant in terms of wRVUs, physicians collect different amounts across and within markets for the same level of productivity. These collections set the limits for physician compensation. It should be noted that the model confirms the conclusions of Dietrich and Anderson in 2008.

4.2 Reimbursement Has a Material Impact on Physician Compensation

The model also indicates that the level of reimbursement paid in the marketplace for clinical services directly affects physician compensation. In general, the higher the level of reimbursement, the greater the level of net practice earnings that are available for payment to physicians as compensation, and vice versa. For physician-owned practices, the impact of local market reimbursement is self-adjusting. Physicians are only able to pay themselves based on available net practice earnings, unless they wish to go into debt. For practices owned by other types of providers or entities, such as health systems, physician compensation may not be negatively affected because the owners choose to *subsidize* compensation at a level that is not set commensurate with local market dynamics. Conversely, physician compensation may be artificially depressed because it is not allowed to rise to the level of local market reimbursement. A physician employer who does not pay at rates consistent with the local marketplace is likely to lose physicians to private practice or other employers who pay better. *Whether in terms of pay levels, practice losses, or recruiting issues, reimbursement plays a fundamental role in the economics of physician compensation.*

4.3 Implications for the Use of Survey Data

Two implications can be deduced from the HSC study and the model relative to the use of survey data in compensation-setting practices, including the determination of FMV. The first is that the survey data is not reported at a relevant geographic level. It is not reported by local market. The only geographic indicators for the data in the surveys are usually regional or state. These groupings, however, may not be meaningful. For example, Milwaukee, rural Wisconsin, Indianapolis, and Cleveland are all included in MGMA's Midwest region. Yet, one can see a broad range of reimbursement across and within these markets. The idea that regional data reflects the particular local market would not appear to be the case if these markets were included in the respondents. A similar point can be made with regard to state data. Compare the rates for Los Angeles and San Francisco in the HSC study. There are substantial differences in the standard fees in these Southern and Northern California markets. While not included in the HSC study, a similar disparity in commercial reimbursement exists in the Houston and Dallas/Fort Worth markets. Dallas/Fort Worth rates are substantially higher.[5] To adapt the famous political dictum that "all politics is local" to healthcare reimbursement, one can say that "all reimbursement is local."[6] Consequently, the geographic assortment of survey data may not produce applicable data for a given local market.

The second implication is that *a potential bias may exist in the survey data due to the fact that the survey respondents are overwhelmingly from large groups or large employers.* The physician compensation surveys, especially MGMA and AMGA, tend to be composed of physicians from large groups or organizations.[7] Such groups tend to have greater bargaining power within local markets, as discussed in the HSC study. Thus, the surveys are most likely representative of groups with significant bargaining power. When this is the case, the physician compensation for such groups would tend to reflect higher rates of reimbursement than may be achievable by smaller groups in the marketplace. Since large groups are only a small percentage of the physician marketplace, smaller groups and lower reimbursement levels would be the expected norm in most markets. Thus, the tendency of the surveys may be to reflect premium market compensation.

---

5   Based on discussions with knowledgeable individuals in these markets and the author's experience in valuing practices in these markets.

6   My co-editor, Mark O. Dietrich, is the author of this adaptation of former House Speaker "Tip" O'Neill's famous political dictum.

7   For a complete discussion of this point, see Chapter 38, "Comparing the Surveys to the Physician Marketplace: Implications for Valuation Analysis."

This premium compensation can be illustrated by the difference in compensation per wRVU between the standard fee and premium rates in the model.

4.4 Implications for Valuation Methods and Analysis

A few key implications for CV practice come out of the reimbursement and compensation model. As will be noted, many of these implications run counter to current trends in valuation and compensation-setting practices. Yet, they are consistent with the development of better understanding and application of data and valuation methods that is to be expected in the evolution of any appraisal discipline.

Favoring Professional Collections Over wRVUs for Physician Productivity

The first implication is that wRVUs alone are generally an inadequate determinant of compensation, given the impact of local market reimbursement dynamics. Many valuation consultants focus their compensation analysis on using wRVUs as the sole or primary measure for determining FMV compensation. A typical method is the "percentile matching technique" that uses survey data to match the percentile benchmarking of a subject physician's wRVUs with the corresponding percentile of compensation. The model, however, would indicate that this technique could produce false indications of market-based compensation: The compensation at a given percentile may result from higher reimbursement in a market rather than higher wRVU productivity. Indeed, statistical analysis indicates there is a weak correlation between wRVUs and compensation in the MGMA data.[8] A better application of the percentile matching technique would be to use professional collections as the measure of productivity. The metric of professional collections combines wRVUs along with payer mix and local market reimbursement factors, making it a more meaningful indicator of the value of physician productivity in a given marketplace.

Avoiding the Use of Specific Percentiles as FMV Guidelines

Some consultants will use the median compensation per wRVU rate as the definitive indication of FMV for any given physician in any market. Others will go further and opine that the 75th percentile compensation per wRVU rate is *always* consistent with FMV. Using the model, both of these opinions are examined in Exhibits 4 and 5. These exhibits are based on the use of the 2011 MGMA rates for the invasive-interventional cardiology subspecialty. In addition, the 2011 MGMA median wRVUs of 9,524 for this subspecialty were used for estimating the financial impact of the conversion rates on the practice in total.[9]

---

8   For a complete discussion of this issue, see Chapter 39, "An Analysis of the Relationship Between Productivity and Compensation in the MGMA Data and Its Implications for Valuation and Compensation-Setting Practices."

9   The "total practice impact" is calculated as follows: variance per wRVU × 9,524 wRVUs × 9 physicians.

Exhibit 4. Compensation Based on MGMA Median

Market / Rate Level	Model Compensation per wRVU	MGMA Median Compensation per wRVU	Variance per wRVU	Total Practice Impact
Milwaukee, WI - Premium	$80.40	$52.41	$27.99	$2,399,017
Milwaukee, WI - Standard	$57.75	$52.41	$5.34	$457,549
Cleveland, OH - Premium	$56.58	$52.41	$4.17	$357,262
San Francisco, CA - Standard	$55.50	$52.41	$3.09	$264,688
Indianapolis, IN - Premium	$54.43	$52.41	$2.02	$172,972
Richmond, VA - Premium	$50.79	$52.41	($1.62)	($139,034)
Miami, FL - Premium	$48.03	$52.41	($4.38)	($375,610)
National Average	$45.01	$52.41	($7.40)	($634,472)
Los Angeles, CA - Standard	$40.22	$52.41	($12.19)	($1,045,052)
Richmond, VA - Standard	$37.48	$52.41	($14.93)	($1,279,914)
Indianapolis, IN - Standard	$36.03	$52.41	($16.38)	($1,404,202)
Miami, FL - Standard	$35.11	$52.41	($17.30)	($1,483,061)
Cleveland, OH - Standard	$34.41	$52.41	($18.00)	($1,543,062)

Exhibit 5. Compensation Based on MGMA 75th Percentile

Market / Rate Level	Model Compensation per wRVU	MGMA 75th Percentile Compensation per wRVU	Variance per wRVU	Total Practice Impact
Milwaukee, WI - Premium	$80.40	$65.41	$14.99	$1,284,709
Milwaukee, WI - Standard	$57.75	$65.41	($7.66)	($656,759)
Cleveland, OH - Premium	$56.58	$65.41	($8.83)	($757,046)
San Francisco, CA - Standard	$55.50	$65.41	($9.91)	($849,620)
Indianapolis, IN - Premium	$54.43	$65.41	($10.98)	($941,336)
Richmond, VA - Premium	$50.79	$65.41	($14.62)	($1,253,342)
Miami, FL - Premium	$48.03	$65.41	($17.38)	($1,489,918)
National Average	$45.01	$65.41	($20.40)	($1,748,780)
Los Angeles, CA - Standard	$40.22	$65.41	($25.19)	($2,159,360)
Richmond, VA - Standard	$37.48	$65.41	($27.93)	($2,394,222)
Indianapolis, IN - Standard	$36.03	$65.41	($29.38)	($2,518,510)
Miami, FL - Standard	$35.11	$65.41	($30.30)	($2,597,369)
Cleveland, OH - Standard	$34.41	$65.41	($31.00)	($2,657,370)

Application of the model indicates that use of both the median and 75th percentile compensation per wRVU rates creates significant losses for the hypothetical practice in many of the markets from the HSC study. As would be expected, the median rate produces losses in fewer markets and these losses are less in total than what is observed by using the 75th percentile value. Since the model only addresses reimbursement and not the other key economic factors, the real-world application of a specific conversion rate would vary from the numbers shown in Exhibits 4 and 5. Nonetheless, the model shows the imprecision and inadequacy of summarily using this or that percentile as the universal indication of FMV across the country. Compensation per wRVU is an outcome; it is a calculated rate that results from the combination of many factors. Selecting a given rate as the universal value for FMV is overly simplistic and insufficient for rigorous appraisal analysis.

Some try to argue that physicians have alternatives, including going to other markets and making the median rate, or even higher. They claim that the prevailing market rate for compensation is the median rate. There are some statistical difficulties, however, with this claim. First, the data does not support this assertion. The surveys show a wide variation in compensation per wRVU rates. Statistically speaking, the median is defined as the middle value of the data set. Relatively half the data is below this value, and half is above it. For a specific value figure to be the predominant rate, one would need the mode, not the median. If everyone were paid the median rate, it would reposition the statistical median to a rate higher than the initial median, based on the relative dispersion of the data above this value. More importantly, universal application of the median rate would create material losses in many markets. Not all employers will offer rates that sustain such losses. For those who do, one has to wonder how long such employers, such as hospitals and health systems, would be able to sustain these losses on their physician practices in using the median rate.

As for the view that the 75th percentile compensation per wRVU is FMV for any physician, the model exposes the high degree of inaccuracy of such a claim. This idea lacks support from a rigorous appraisal perspective and would appear to create material losses in many markets for employers who adopt this take on FMV.

Another reason to avoid the creation of losses in physician practices through overly simplistic survey use is the healthcare regulatory risk. A recent Medicare compliance alert indicates that regulators may scrutinize losses on physician practices in terms of commercial reasonableness.[10] It should also be noted that the Stark regulations list location as one of the factors to be considered in determining FMV for regulatory compliance purposes.[11] Clearly, reimbursement varies by location, and the model has shown its impact on physician compensation.

---

10 "In New Angle on Stark Cases, Government Hits Hospitals for Lack of Physician Profit," *Report on Medicare Compliance*, Volume 21, Number 25, July 9, 2012. Atlantic Information Services, Inc. www.AISHealth.com.

11 69 *F.R.* 16107 and 72 *F.R.* 51015-16.

Focus on Earnings-Based Compensation

One of the critical takeaways from the model for appraisal practice is that the use of earnings-based compensation (EBC) can bring greater precision and accuracy than survey-based compensation for determining FMV. EBC uses the net earnings from providing professional services as the basis for establishing compensation for a professional.[12] It is calculated by using the net revenues received from services rendered and deducting the costs incurred to generate the services. EBC has been the historically predominant paradigm for physician compensation, and it is the one framework that ensures practices do not operate significantly in the red. In addition, it is widely used in tax practice for determining reasonable compensation for professionals in corporate entities.[13] EBC is preferred because it takes into account local market reimbursement dynamics, along with the other key economic factors that impact practice net earnings available for physician compensation. To apply EBC in appraisal practice, the analyst uses cost and income approach methods to value a subject physician compensation arrangement.

The Big Picture: Avoid Exclusive and Uncritical Use of Survey Data

Perhaps the most general implication of the HSC study and the model discussed here is that valuation and compensation-setting practices should avoid using survey data without careful study. The wide availability of market survey data for physician compensation has made it relatively simple to obtain and apply such data for compensation purposes. It is also easy to fall into the trap of making assumptions about the surveys without adequate examination of the data. As more research and information on compensation data emerge, the complexity inherent in physician compensation becomes more apparent. This complexity warrants not only more research and analysis, but also more sophisticated economic models that can apply survey data with greater precision and relevance to the fundamental factors that drive physician compensation. One simple solution to avoid the uncritical use of survey data is not to rely on it exclusively for valuation work. Using the market approach in conjunction with the income and cost approach based on EBC can bring reasonableness and reality to appraisals. The triangulation of the three approaches can provide greater accuracy and rigor to the determination of FMV for healthcare regulatory purposes.

---

12 See Chapter 24, "Valuing Physician Employment Arrangements for Clinical Services: Cost and Income-Based Methods," for an in-depth discussion of this concept.

13 See Chapter 12, "Reasonable Compensation for Tax Purposes." See also Kevin Yeanoplos and Ron Seigneur, *Reasonable Compensation: Application and Analysis for Appraisal, Tax, and Management Purposes.* Business Valuation Resources, LLC (BVR), 2010, pp. 8-10.

Chapter 38. Comparing the Surveys to the Physician Marketplace: Implications for Valuation Analysis

CONTENTS

Chapter 38. Comparing the Surveys to the Physician Marketplace: Implications for Valuation Analysis

By Timothy Smith, CPA/ABV

1.0 Introduction

It is important to understand the respondent base to the physician compensation surveys and the extent to which the surveys do and do not reflect the marketplace for physician services. Since the comparability of the subject arrangement to the market data is the key to the application of the market approach, a valuation analyst needs to assess market data before using it. Many CV practitioners and consultants assume that the various physician compensation surveys are representative of the physician marketplace. They apply data without comparative analysis. Yet, the reality is that the surveys are not necessarily representative of the physician marketplace that is applicable for a subject compensation arrangement. The surveys tend to portray segments of the market, and these segments can have different economics and compensation dynamics. The surveys, moreover, can be especially imprecise in mirroring local market conditions. The purpose of this chapter, therefore, is to examine key areas in which the surveys may be limited in their comparability to subject arrangements for physician services.

2.0 Comparison of Survey Respondents to the Physician Marketplace

2.1 How Survey Data Is Compiled

A key consideration in reviewing data from the major physician compensation surveys is that they are not based on statistically valid sampling techniques of physicians in the marketplace. Rather, the surveys are generally produced by trade groups, such as the Medical Group Management Association (MGMA) or the American Medical Group Association (AMGA), that obtain data from their members. They are also published by survey organizations that solicit information from selected healthcare systems and physician groups. Each survey tends to reflect its members or similar types of physician practice organizations or settings. As a result, the physician compensation surveys tend to represent various segments of the physician marketplace; they individually do not reflect the marketplace as a whole.

2.2 A Representative Picture of the Physician Marketplace

Before looking at the various segments of the physician marketplace represented by the surveys, it is helpful to have an understanding of the physician practice landscape in the United States. A nationally representative survey of clinically active physicians is the *Community Tracking Study Physician Survey* compiled by the Center for Studying Health System Change (HSC). This survey has been prepared periodically over the last 15 years. Exhibits 1 and 2 present a summary of the survey results, providing a reasonable picture of the physician practice marketplace. Exhibit 1 shows the distribution of physicians by practice-setting and the percentage of physicians in each type of practice. Exhibit 2 shows the relative percentage of physicians who are owners in their practices in comparison to those employed or practicing as independent contractors.

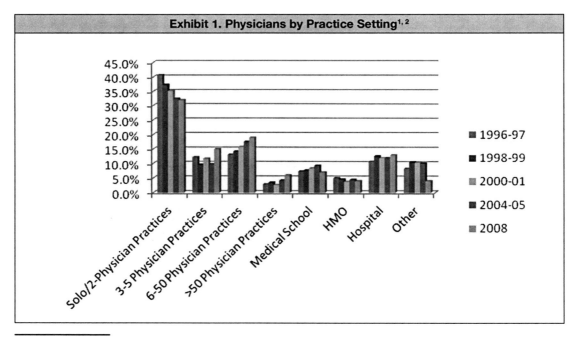

Exhibit 1. Physicians by Practice Setting[1,2]

---

1 Table prepared from *Physicians Moving to Mid-Sized, Single-Specialty Practices, Tracking Report No. 18*, August 2007, and *A Snapshot of U.S. Physicians: Key Findings From the 2008 Health Tracking Physician Survey*, Data Bulletin No. 35, September 2009. See www.hschange.org. While the 2008 study summary indicates that changes in administration of the survey make it not comparable to prior years, the findings for 2008 are included along with prior years for presentation and discussion purposes. This table is intended to provide a broad perspective of the physician marketplace.

2 Per the HSC studies, the hospital category includes hospital-based and office-based physicians employed by hospitals.

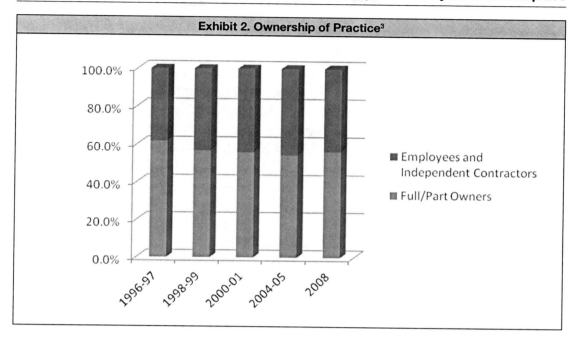

Exhibit 2. Ownership of Practice[3]

The data presented above from the HSC studies do not reflect the recent wave of physician practice acquisition and employment transactions by hospitals and health systems. One will expect the physician ownership percentage of practices to decline significantly in future surveys. In addition, we may see changes in group size as a result of the hospital employment trend and the move toward medical homes and accountable care organizations under the recent healthcare reform legislation. Nonetheless, the picture of the physician marketplace from the HSC studies indicates that the vast majority of physicians practice in groups of less than 50 physicians, with nearly one-third practicing in solo to two-physician groups.

2.3 Profiles of Survey Respondents

This picture of the physician practice landscape contrasts with the respondent profiles from some of the major physician compensation surveys. The following sections provide overviews of the respondent profiles of MGMA, AMGA, and SCA to illustrate the potential for organizational bias in the survey data.[4]

---

3 Table prepared from *Physicians Moving to Mid-Sized, Single-Specialty Practices, Tracking Report No. 18*, August 2007, and *A Snapshot of U.S. Physicians: Key Findings From the 2008 Health Tracking Physician Survey*, Data Bulletin No. 35, September 2009. See www.hschange.org.

4 MGMA, AMGA, and SCA were selected because they are widely used in the marketplace and are the major surveys that include both compensation and productivity data. Matching compensation and productivity is a key valuation method used in the market approach.

MGMA Data

For the 2010 and 2011 surveys, approximately 63% of the respondent physicians or providers included in the MGMA survey come from physician practices of more than 50 FTE physicians. Approximately 55% of the providers came from groups with total medical revenues in excess of $50 million, while about 72% of providers come from groups with over $20 million in such revenues. Approximately 73% of providers come from multispecialty groups. For 2011, 41% of providers came from physician-owned groups, while in 2010, 46% were from physician-owned groups. The percentage of providers from hospital or integrated delivery system-owned groups was 43% in 2010 and 47% in 2011.[5]

AMGA Data

Per AMGA's participant profile summary for the 2010 and 2011 surveys, 97% to 99% of the physicians included in the survey come from multispecialty groups, and 89% to 91% of these physicians are in groups of 100 physicians or more. Physician ownership of groups included in the survey was 40% to 43%, while health system and hospital practices comprised 48% to 51%.[6]

SCA Data

The participant data for SCA indicate that approximately 59% of responding organizations in 2010 were from the category of hospital or medical center, while the 2009 percentage for this category was 65%. In 2010, 42% of the participating organizations were teaching institutions. Such institutions constituted 45% of respondents in 2009.[7] The average and median number of employed physicians from survey participants in 2010 was 178 and 54, respectively, and 177 and 80 in 2009.[8]

2.4 Key Market Segments Represented by the Surveys

In comparing the physician practice setting data from the HSC study to the respondent profiles of these major surveys, it is apparent that the surveys are not necessarily reflective of practice patterns found in the United States for most physicians in terms of group size. *The surveys tend to be overrepresented by large groups.* Physicians have historically practiced in small practices, not the large multispecialty groups that tend to dominate surveys such as MGMA and AMGA. In addition, many CV appraisal assignments will involve small practices or solo physicians. Thus, the survey data may

---

5   See Tables 8, 9, 13, and 23 from the *Demographics—Medical Practice* section of the MGMA surveys for 2010 and 2011.
6   See Table 4 and Figure 2 from the *Participant Profile* section of the 2010 and 2011 surveys.
7   Note: SCA has multiple response categories in its respondent profile. Thus, teaching institutions may also be included in the category of hospital or medical center.
8   See Section I. "Characteristics of Survey Participants" from the 2009 and 2010 surveys.

not be fully comparable to the subject arrangement in terms of group size or practice setting.

With respect to practice ownership, some of the surveys, such as MGMA and AMGA, appear to be more representative of the ownership found in the marketplace, in terms of physician ownership. SCA appears to be more representative of hospital or medical center-affiliated groups and significantly reflective of teaching institutions. If the subject arrangement involves private practice physicians, survey data that is indicative of academic-related compensation may not be fully comparable for valuation purposes.

3.0 Geographical Representation in the Surveys

3.1 Common Use of Regional or State Data to Reflect the Local Market

Some users of the physician compensation surveys tend to assume that national market survey data is readily applicable or comparable to their local market. They simply use national data without further adjustment or analysis for establishing fair market value (FMV) compensation. Implicit in such use is the idea that local market conditions are not material to the valuation analysis. For those that do recognize the impact of local market conditions on physician compensation, regional or state data are often used as a better approximation of local market conditions. Regional data are particularly used since such data are usually available with significant respondent sizes. Moreover, the surveys often publish summaries indicating material differences in regional compensation. Users frequently take these regional analyses and trends to be applicable to their local market.

3.2 The Surveys May Not Be Geographically Representative

In examining the use of regional or state data to mirror local markets, it should first be noted that the physician compensation surveys may have limited geographical diversity or may not be reflective of the distribution of physicians in the United States. Review of the number of respondents by state for a given specialty often indicates that certain states will have few to no respondents. In some cases, moreover, respondents may be concentrated in a handful of states. It is possible that in such cases, the respondents for a given state may come from a few groups to a single group. Minimal to no state representation should also be noted with respect to the regional data presented in the survey. While a state may be included in a given region for geographical categorization, there may be no data for that state in the regional reporting. As a result, regional data may not include data from the state or locale of the subject arrangement. In addition, state data may not include respondents from the location of the subject. Regional and state data, therefore, may not be indicative of local market dynamics for physician compensation.

3.3 Compensation Can Vary Significantly Within a Region, State, or Local Market

In Chapter 37, "How Reimbursement and Physician Compensation Vary by Market," the findings of a recent commercial reimbursement study were discussed. This study noted wide differences in reimbursement across and within markets for commercial payers.[9] As further discussed in Chapter 37, these findings were included in a model for a hypothetical cardiology group, showing the impact on compensation for these variations in commercial reimbursement. This model showed a wide distribution in the effective compensation levels for these markets as a result of commercial reimbursement differences. Dietrich and Anderson prepared a similar analysis in 2008, noting the significant impact that commercial reimbursement rates can have on physician compensation.[10] One key observation from the study and model discussed in Chapter 37 is that compensation levels can be highly divergent within a region and a state, as demonstrated for the markets included in the study. For example, there is a significant variance between reimbursement levels in certain Northern California markets from Southern California.[11] Another example is Texas. There is a material difference in physician reimbursement between Houston and the Dallas-Fort Worth area.[12] These variations indicate that regional and state data may not be representative of a specific local market within that region or state. The markets reflected in the survey data represent those of the respondents. Since the respondents are not included based on statistically valid sampling techniques and since the surveys do not report data by individual market, it is indeterminate as to what markets are represented in the survey data.

In addition, wide variations within a market are possible with respect to commercial payer rates. The HSC study indicated that premium rates were achievable by groups with bargaining power based on size and specialty. Consequently, survey data may reflect the relative degree of the respondents' leverage with commercial payers in a market, rather than representing the market as a whole or what is applicable to a subject physician or practice.

---

9   See *Wide Variation in Hospital and Physician Payment Rates Evidence of Provider Market Power*, Research Brief, No. 16, November 2010. Center for Studying Health System Change. www.hschange.org.

10   Mark O. Dietrich, CPA/ABV, and Gregory D. Anderson, CPA/ABV, CVA, "Evaluating RVU-Based Compensation Arrangements," *Health Lawyers Weekly*, Nov. 14, 2008,

11   As indicated in the HSC data and based on the author's experience.

12   Based on the author's experience in both markets and on information provided by parties with significant knowledge of these markets.

4.0 Implications for Compensation Valuation Practice

4.1 Survey Data Reflects the Dynamics of the Respondents, Not the Local Market

There are two important implications from these reimbursement studies for appraisers using physician compensation survey data. First, it is unlikely that the survey data can be applied with any meaningful degree of precision to reflect the dynamics of any one particular market. Variations across the country, region, or even within a state may not allow a reasonable level of specificity to a given market.[13] Moreover differences within a market in terms of provider leverage with commercial plans can also affect physician reimbursement and compensation levels. Local market dynamics ultimately drive the range of compensation available in a market, and the survey does not report data in a way that allows for its precise application to a subject arrangement.

4.2 A Bias Toward Premium Market Compensation in the Survey Data

A potential bias may exist in the survey data due to the fact that the survey respondents are overwhelmingly from large groups, mostly multispecialty groups. Such groups tend to have greater bargaining power within local markets. Thus, the surveys are most likely representative of groups with significant bargaining power. Where this is the case, the physician compensation for such groups would tend to reflect higher rates of reimbursement than may be achievable by smaller groups in the marketplace. Since large groups are only a small percentage of the physician marketplace, smaller groups and lower reimbursement levels would be the expected norm in most markets. Thus, the tendency of the surveys may be to reflect premium market compensation.

For physician employment arrangements, some argue that the hypothetical employer is a health system, and these larger employers are able to negotiate higher commercial reimbursement rates. Thus, the premium compensation of the surveys is comparable to the subject arrangement. One should expect small practices to receive better reimbursement under the "hypothetical" employer. While the claim that health systems with disproportionate market leverage achieve improved commercial reimbursement is true in many cases, it is not necessarily true in all cases. Evidence is clearly lacking to support the notion of "all" health systems achieving higher reimbursement. In fact, insurers will often provide higher reimbursement to small competitors to maintain market balance. A health system may have the critical mass of physicians necessary to warrant significant bargaining power with commercial plans. Alternatively, a health system may not be willing or able to use hospital inpatient and outpatient reimbursement levels

---

13 See Mark O. Dietrich, CPA/ABV, "Healthcare Market Structure and Its Implication for Valuation of Privately Held Provider Entities—An Empirical Analysis," *The BVR/AHLA Guide to Healthcare Valuation*, 3rd edition, Chapter 3, for a detailed analysis of the impact of local market conditions.

as leverage for physician fee improvements. Some systems may even lack the requisite acumen to negotiate skillfully on the physician fee schedule. Thus, it is not fully clear that a hypothetical employer would always be expected to receive premium compensation. Even if this were the case, one would still need to conclude that the premium compensation in the surveys is relevant to the marketplace for the subject arrangement.

4.3 Conclusion: Use Survey Data Carefully and Critically

This potential bias toward premium compensation, together with the inability to reflect local market conditions adequately, should give pause to appraisers using the survey data to establish physician compensation levels in service arrangements. The appraiser should consider the ambiguities and uncertainties of the market data with respect to local market dynamics. In addition, the appraiser should consider whether the survey data tend to reflect premium compensation levels that may not be applicable for a given subject physician or practice. In short, the valuation analyst needs to avoid uncritical use of the surveys, assuming that the data definitively represents the market for the subject arrangement.

Use of the market surveys for valuation purposes carries with it imprecision and limitations that relate to the issue of the comparability of the survey data to specific subject physician and compensation arrangement. Acknowledging the relative limitations of the surveys for valuing physician compensation is not necessarily an impediment to the use of the approach. Rather, such considerations serve as a cautionary finding relative to the *exclusive* and *uncritical* use of market survey data in establishing physician compensation.

In addition, recognition of these issues should affect the interpretation, assessment, and weighting of the outcomes from valuation techniques that rely on the compensation survey market data. It also signals the need for serious consideration of the cost and income approaches in the valuation process. Comparing the indications of value under the market approach with the results of cost and income approaches mitigates the inherent imprecision that arises from use of the market data for establishing physician compensation.

Practical considerations should also be noted relative to the market approach and physician compensation survey data. One reason for continuing to use market survey data, however imperfect or unrepresentative such data are relative to the entirety of the physician marketplace, is that the physician compensation surveys are the only readily and publicly available source of market data to use in the valuation process. Practically speaking, the market approach would not be available to appraisers in most cases were it not for the market survey data. It should also be noted that, in certain cases, no other methods and data may be available to an appraiser, save the market approach based on the compensation surveys.

When used, however, the market approach should be applied with awareness relative to its limitations. Moreover, the potential for imprecision in the market survey data may not be applicable in every valuation assignment. Rather, certain characteristics of the survey data can make their application to specific compensation arrangements limited and qualified.

Chapter 39. An Analysis of the Relationship Between Productivity and Compensation in the MGMA Data and Its Implications for Valuation and Compensation-Setting Practices

CONTENTS

Chapter 39. An Analysis of the Relationship Between Productivity and Compensation in the MGMA Data and Its Implications for Valuation and Compensation-Setting Practices

By Timothy Smith, CPA/ABV

1.0 Introduction

In today's marketplace, productivity is one of the primary measures for determining compensation in physician employment arrangements with hospitals and health systems. Compensation in these arrangements is often set based on the concept of productivity-matched compensation: A physician's compensation level should correspond with his or her level of productivity. The most commonly used measure of physician productivity in such employment arrangements is work relative value units (wRVUs). Frequently, wRVUs are used to establish compensation for hospital- or health system-employed physicians using one of two valuation techniques based on data from the physician compensation surveys. These techniques include the "percentile matching technique," also known as the "linear interpolation method," and a second technique that selects a compensation-per-wRVU rate from the physician compensation surveys as a guide-line fair market value (FMV) rate and applies this rate to the subject physician's wRVU productivity. Many look to the median rate as the universal standard for FMV, while others claim that the 75th percentile rate is the upper boundary of FMV. Other prac-titioners will also use professional collections as a measure of productivity and apply the percentile matching technique or a survey-based compensation-to-collections ratio to establish FMV compensation.

Implicit in these valuation and compensation-setting techniques is the assumption of a fundamental economic relationship between compensation and productivity in the survey data. This assumption is that a physician's productivity is the *key, if not sole,* predictor or driver of compensation, particularly wRVUs. Using this single driver, one can readily establish FMV compensation using compensation surveys alone. As noted, some analysts will also include professional collections as a second determinant and use both measures to compute FMV compensation. Either way, these survey-based valuation methods, based on the concept of productivity-matched compensation, pre-suppose that productivity is *the* critical factor in physician compensation. When only a market approach is completed in a compensation valuation (CV) assignment using these techniques, the entire conclusion of value is based on this fundamental assumption about the relationship in the survey data between productivity and compensation.

The purpose of this chapter is to examine this assumption using the statistical tool of a linear regression line analysis based on multiple-year data from MGMA's *Physician Compensation and Production Survey*. This chapter will present findings from a five-year study of a sample of 28 different physician specialties, covering the broad groupings of primary care, medical, surgical, and hospital-based specialties. These findings do not necessarily show that productivity is highly predictive of compensation in the MGMA data, particularly predictions based on wRVUs. Professional collections, however, are more predictive of compensation for selected surgical specialties in certain years. This chapter discusses the implications of the study for valuation and compensation-setting practices, noting the imprecision and inaccuracy that can result from *uncritical* or even exclusive use of popular compensation models based on the concept of productivity-matched compensation and survey data. While the findings presented in this chapter raise additional issues related to the causes and factors affecting the relationship of productivity and compensation in the survey data, these additional questions are be-yond the scope of this chapter. *The analysis in this chapter is focused on evaluating whether the unqualified or exclusive use of these models based on survey data is warranted for valuation and compensation-setting practices in hospital/health system employment arrangements.*

2.0 Study Methodology: Use of MGMA's 'Physician Pay-to-Production Plotter' Tool

MGMA's CD-ROM version of the *Physician Compensation and Productivity Survey*, also known as the "Interactive Report" version of the survey, includes a linear regression line analysis tool. This tool, labeled as the "Physician Pay-to-Production Plotter" under the "Analysis" menu option, allows a user to view a scatter-plot diagram of the actual data points for compensation and a selected productivity measure by physician specialty. The two productivity measures include wRVUs and professional collections. The tool also provides the user with a linear regression line analysis, including a regression line formula and the "R-squared" value for the line, which is a measure of the level of the linear correlation in the two variables. Features of the tool include options to select various subsets of the data based on various respondent characteristics, such as the level of total medical revenue for the reporting group or geographic location. It is important to note that the data set on which the tool is based includes only those respondents that report both compensation and the applicable productivity measure. This tool has been included in the interactive CD-ROM version of the survey for the past several years.

This tool was used to compute the R-squared values for 28 selected specialties from the 2008 to 2012 surveys. These specialties were selected to provide a range with varying mixes of services, settings, and economics. They include the following, along with how they have been classified by specialty group:

Primary care
- Family practice (without OB);

- Pediatrics: general; and

- Internal medicine: general.

Medical specialties
- Cardiology: EP;

- Cardiology: invasive-interventional;

- Cardiology: noninvasive;

- Gastroenterology;

- Hematology/oncology;

- Nephrology;

- Neurology;

- Psychiatry;

- Pulmonary medicine; and

- Radiation oncology.

Surgical specialties
- Ophthalmology;

- OB/GYN: general;[1]

- OB/GYN: GYN only;

- Orthopedic surgery: general;

- Surgery: cardiovascular;

- Surgery: general;

- Surgery: neurological;

- Surgery: plastic;

- Surgery: vascular;

- Otorhinolaryngology (ENT); and

- Urology.

Hospital-Based
- Critical care/intensivist;

- Emergency medicine;

- Hospitalist: internal medicine; and

- Radiology: diagnostic-noninvasive.

For those not familiar with linear regression (or for those who have intentionally for-gotten about that college statistics course!), regression line analysis seeks to find the

---

1   The categorization of "OB/GYN: general" is certainly a topic for which many positions can be taken. For example, OB/GYN doctors function as primary care physicians for many female patients. Apart from C-sections, deliveries are not necessarily the same as surgical procedures. At the same time, OB/GYN physicians do perform various gynecological-related surgeries. Thus, I have included them with surgical specialties, noting this categorization is consistent with how the American Medical Group Association (AMGA) classifies the specialty in its survey. I thank Dana Boatman with HealthCare Appraisers, a long-time practice manager (including for an OB/GYN practice), for assisting me with classifications for this study.

formula that best predicts one variable in terms of another variable. This mathematical formula or model can then be evaluated relative to the actual data. One measure of how well the model tracks with the actual data is R-squared. This statistical metric can be used to assess the relative linear correlation between two variables in a given data set. R-squared represents the proportion of the variation in one variable that can be explained by the variation in another variable. It is a measure of the ability of a given linear model reflected in the data to predict future outcomes. For example, when a regression line analysis is used and indicates an R-squared value of 0.60, one can generally say that the independnent variable explains 60% of the variation in dependent variable. A general benchmark for evaluating such correlation is 0.50.[2] Values above this benchmark typically indicate relatively higher levels of predictability by the regression line formula, and values below pointing to relatively lower levels. Since a value of 1.0 represents perfect predictability, the general point is that the lower an R-squared value is from 1.0, the relatively weaker the level of predictability in the two variables (at least for the given data set).

The exhibits present the findings of the study using MGMA's Physician Pay-to-Production Plotter over the five-year period for the sampled specialties. Exhibits 1 and 2 present the weighted average of the R-squared values for each specialty group by year. Exhibit 1 presents the weighted averages for compensation to professional collections, while Exhibit 2 presents the rates for compensation to wRVUs. Weightings for each specialty group were based on the number of respondents for each specialty.[3] The total number of respondents included in the sampled specialties encompassed approximately 65% to 68% of all respondents for compensation and professional collections and about 73% to 76% of all respondents for compensation and wRVUs. It is important to note that surveys such as MGMA, while representing the best data available, are not random samples, but rather are based on voluntary response. Thus, using regression on the survey data to determine the predictive value of productivity on compensation could be affected by the uncertainty of exactly how representative the data set is of the entire pool of applicable physicians in each specialty.[4]

Four broad trends become readily apparent when looking at Exhibits 1 and 2:

1. Only the weighted average for the surgical specialties based on professional collections reaches an R-squared value of 0.50 or greater, and it only does so for some of the years in the sample period. In general, outside of these years,

---

2   That an R-squared value is less than 0.50 does not necessarily mean that there is not a statistically significant correlation in the data, since this judgment must be based on the characteristics of the subject data set.

3   The number of respondents is based on those reported in Tables 8.1 and 22.1.

4   See Chapter 38, "Comparing the Surveys to the Physician Marketplace: Implications for Valuation Analysis," for further discussion of this issue.

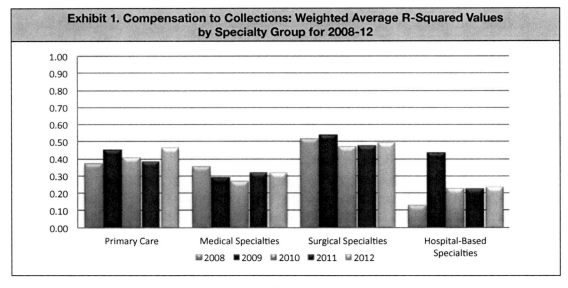

Exhibit 1. Compensation to Collections: Weighted Average R-Squared Values by Specialty Group for 2008-12

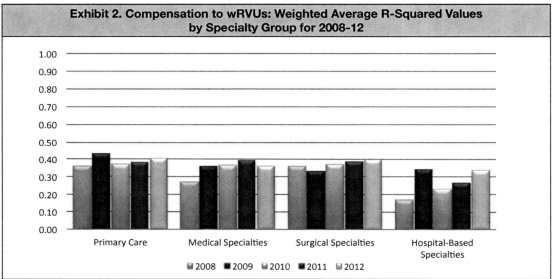

Exhibit 2. Compensation to wRVUs: Weighted Average R-Squared Values by Specialty Group for 2008-12

one does not see values exceeding 0.50 for any specialty group using either productivity measure.

2. The strongest general trend of predictability is found in the surgical specialties based on professional collections, with primary care running second.

3. Excluding hospital-based specialties, the weighted average values for most specialties using wRVUs are in the 0.30 to 0.40 range. A wider range for professional collections is apparent, encompassing about 0.30 to 0.50.

4. Hospital-based specialties show the lowest overall levels of predictability, coupled with the most inconsistent year-to-year trending of all specialty groups.

The broad trend from the sample is that the linear measure of predictability between productivity, especially for wRVUs, and compensation is not as high as many would suppose. *Yet, there is some correlation in the two productivity metrics relative to compensation.*

Exhibits 3, 4, 5, and 6 present the average R-squared values for wRVUs and collections for each specialty group by year.

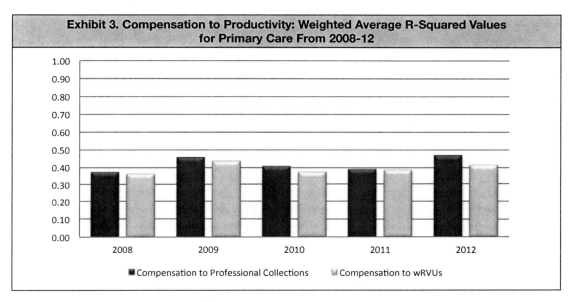

Exhibit 3. Compensation to Productivity: Weighted Average R-Squared Values for Primary Care From 2008-12

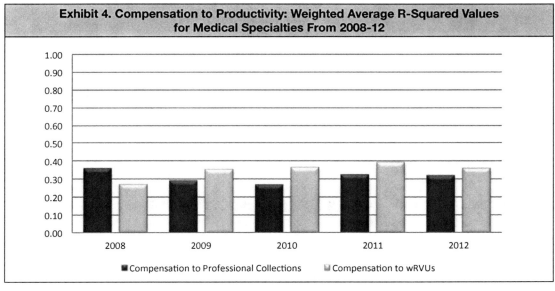

Exhibit 4. Compensation to Productivity: Weighted Average R-Squared Values for Medical Specialties From 2008-12

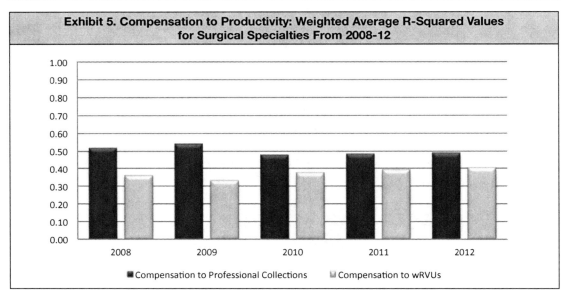

Exhibit 5. Compensation to Productivity: Weighted Average R-Squared Values for Surgical Specialties From 2008-12

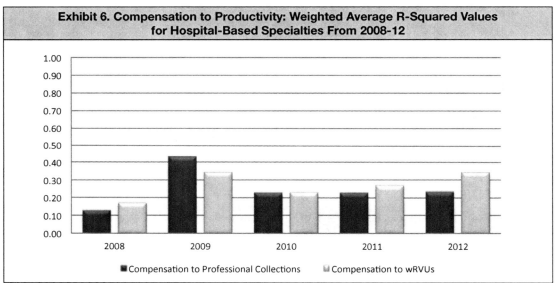

Exhibit 6. Compensation to Productivity: Weighted Average R-Squared Values for Hospital-Based Specialties From 2008-12

Certain additional general trends can be observed in Exhibits 3, 4, 5, and 6:

1. Primary care shows the greatest level of overall consistency using both wRVUs and collections from year to year.

2. For the medical specialties, wRVUs are more predictive than professional collections of compensation.

3. The surgical specialties show stronger predictability with collections than with wRVUs.

4. The trending for hospital-based specialties shows somewhat greater predictability based on wRVUs, especially in 2012.

Exhibits 7, 8, and 9 show the R-squared values for specific physician specialties. They are presented to give the reader a sampling of some of the distinct patterns found in the R-squared values over time. Exhibit 7 illustrates the relatively higher level of predictability between professional collections and compensation for the surgical specialties.

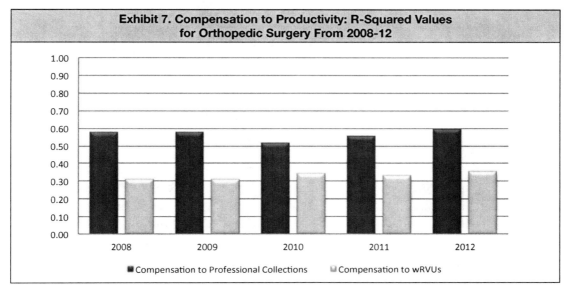

Exhibit 7. Compensation to Productivity: R-Squared Values for Orthopedic Surgery From 2008-12

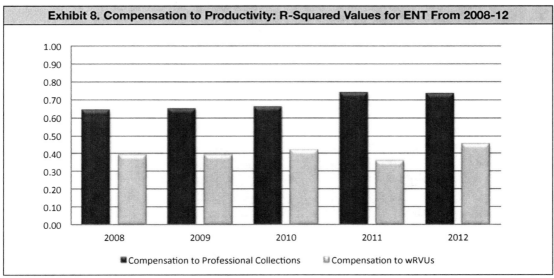

Exhibit 8. Compensation to Productivity: R-Squared Values for ENT From 2008-12

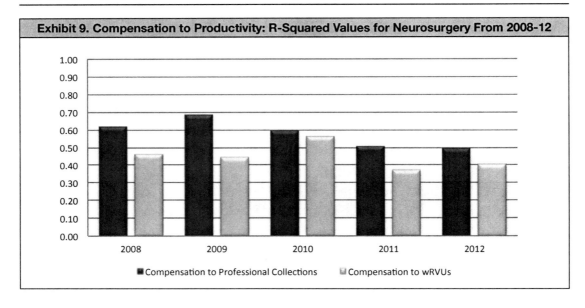

Exhibit 9. Compensation to Productivity: R-Squared Values for Neurosurgery From 2008-12

Exhibits 10, 11, 12, and 13 show some of the inconsistency in the R-squared data over time. Many of the specialties presented for Exhibits 10, 11, 12, and 13 include those that are hospital-based. As discussed in Chapter 13, "An Introduction to Physician Services and Specialties," hospital-based specialties tend to provide services on a shift basis, regardless of patient volumes or collections. Thus, one would *not* expect a high level of predictability between productivity, defined as wRVUs or collections, and compensation for these specialties. They have been included here, however, to illustrate different R-squared values that were observed as part of the study.

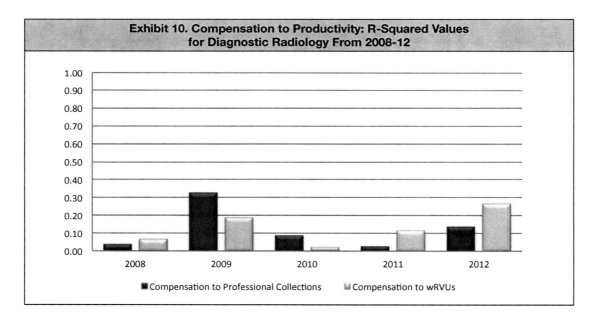

Exhibit 10. Compensation to Productivity: R-Squared Values for Diagnostic Radiology From 2008-12

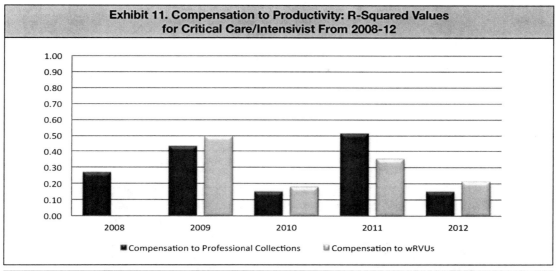

Exhibit 11. Compensation to Productivity: R-Squared Values for Critical Care/Intensivist From 2008-12

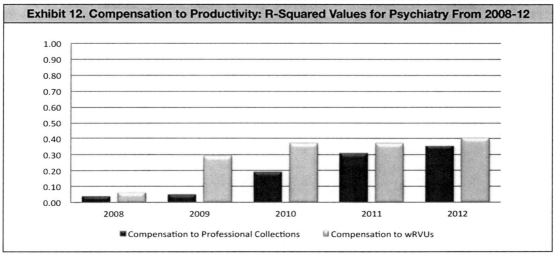

Exhibit 12. Compensation to Productivity: R-Squared Values for Psychiatry From 2008-12

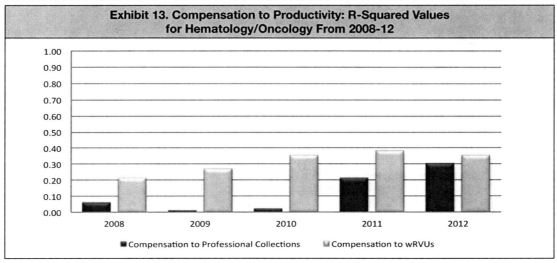

Exhibit 13. Compensation to Productivity: R-Squared Values for Hematology/Oncology From 2008-12

Exhibits 14, 15, and 16 include the three subspecialties of cardiology that are included in the study.

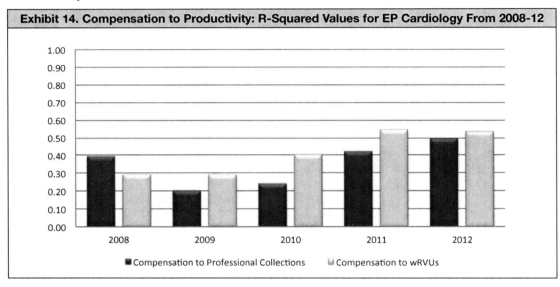

Exhibit 14. Compensation to Productivity: R-Squared Values for EP Cardiology From 2008-12

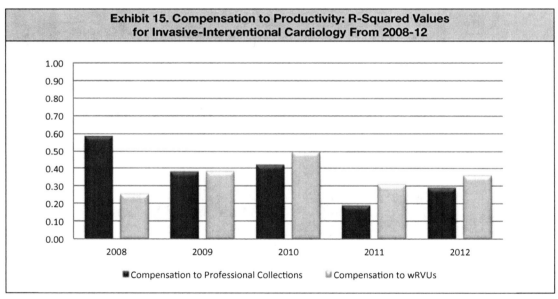

Exhibit 15. Compensation to Productivity: R-Squared Values for Invasive-Interventional Cardiology From 2008-12

3.0 Analysis and Implications of the Study Findings

3.1 Year-to-Year Changes in Respondents

One takeaway from reviewing the exhibits by individual specialty is that, while there may be broad trends in the averages for a specialty group, there can also be a wide variation in R-squared rates from year to year for an individual specialty. One potential cause for such variations is the different respondents for a given year in the survey data.

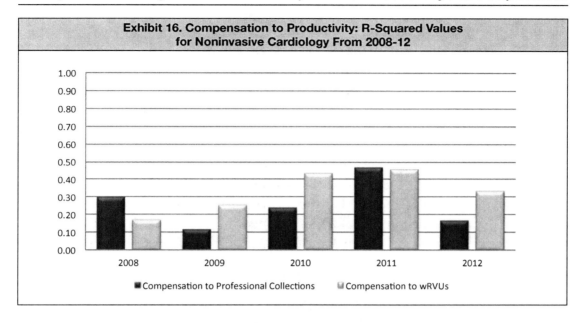

Exhibit 16. Compensation to Productivity: R-Squared Values for Noninvasive Cardiology From 2008-12

MGMA notes the difficulty in making precise year-to-year comparisons using its survey data due to the change in respondents annually. In the Appendix section of the survey, under the heading "Limitations in the Data," MGMA notes: "Additionally, note that the respondent sample varies from year to year. Therefore, conclusions about longitudinal trends or year-to-year fluctuations in summary statistics may not be appropriate."[5] An important implication of the varying respondents each year is that unique factors may affect the data from one year to the next. Consequently, relationships in the data, such as those between productivity and compensation, may not be consistent over time at the expected rates or formulas observed in prior years.

3.2 How Representative Is the Level of Predictability for All Compensation Respondents?

Another key note is that, strictly speaking, the linear predictive relationships in the data indicated by the R-squared values relate to the specific data set analyzed by the regression line tool. As discussed earlier in the chapter, the data set used in the tool is a subset of the data for which compensation is reported in the survey. One cannot say with metaphysical certitude that the R-squared value for the subset would be the same value if productivity data for all compensation respondents were analyzed in a regression line. Speaking with statistical precision, the relationships and level of predictability between productivity and compensation for all respondents in the survey is not known. One can argue that if the subset is a representative sample of all respondents, then the R-squared value would be representative as well. Since the data in MGMA is not based on statistical sampling methods, however, one cannot say with complete

---

5   2012 *Physician Compensation and Production Survey*, p. 284.

certainty that the subset is representative. Yet, one may be able to look at the percentage of total respondents included in the subset. One can conjecture that the more significant the proportion of total respondents included in the subset including productivity, the more the subset would be expected to be comparable to all respondents. In summary, however, the R-squared values should be specifically associated with the subset of data used in the tool.

3.3 Broad Trends in a Specialty Group May Not Be Reflected in an Individual Specialty

While broad trends can be observed at the level of the specialty group, they may not be reflective of the level of predictability in an individual specialty included in the sample. One can see this distinction in looking at the medical specialties. The group trend is not necessarily reflected in the level for a given cardiology subspecialty or for hematology/oncology. Of course, this difference results from the group trend being based on a weighted average from the sampled specialties. Such differences, however, point to the unique factors that can impact compensation and productivity levels in the data for a given specialty. A broad trend or general tendency in the data may not always apply to all segments of the data. Caution and reliance on actual data rather than on assumptions about the data or on highly simplistic views of the data are required when using data effectively and accurately for statistical analysis purposes.

3.4 A Single Variable May Be Insufficient to Account for a Physician's Compensation Level

The most important implication from this regression line analysis study is that a single productivity measure may be insufficient to account for the totality of a physician's compensation level for most specialties in the MGMA survey data. The actual data does not appear to warrant use of a simple, direct, and linear formula or model for setting compensation or predicting what a physician should be paid, given his or her production, in all specialties.[6] The marketplace represented by the survey data is complex and varied with regard to compensation levels, thereby limiting one's ability to predict accurately compensation based on a physician's productivity level. *For a productivity metric such as wRVUs to be the sole and exclusive factor or predictor in determining FMV compensation using survey data based on a direct or linear model, the R-squared values would need to be higher than those observed in this study.* Now, in some specialties in certain years, professional collections comes much closer to being the single fundamental driver of physician compensation in a direct, linear manner. R-squared values exceeding 0.60 and even 0.70 were observed in certain surgical specialties in some years, whereas values based on wRVUs, by contrast, only exceeded a 0.50 level, with 0.57 as the highest observed value, in a much more limited number of years and specialties.

---

6   It may be possible that nonlinear model would yield higher levels of correlation in the underlying variables.

The idea that a single variable, especially one such as wRVUs, may not be adequate to account *fully* for compensation in a simple or direct model is consistent with the fundamental economics of physician services and practices.[7] Many variables can affect these economics, not just personal production. One critical factor is the level of reimbursement in the physician's local market, along with payer mix. Both are not accounted for in using only wRVUs.[8] Other factors can include the following:

1. The level of technical component services net earnings;

2. Net earnings from the use of nonphysician providers;

3. Compensation from various nonclinical services, such as call coverage, medical directorship, clinical co-management, and research;

4. Compensation from clinical services not accounted for through traditional billing, such as professional interpretations of diagnostic testing performed for third parties;

5. Cost structure and cost efficiency;

6. Group practice compensation models that distribute group earnings using nonproduction formulas; and

7. Hospital-employed or hospital-controlled practices where physicians are paid salaries or base compensation that is not consistent with productivity or where data shows consistently higher levels of compensation relative to productivity.

On the factor noted in Item 6, one should not ignore the impact of group compensation models. The vast majority of physicians in the MGMA survey come from large groups, primarily multispecialty groups.[9] Such groups often have net earnings pools that can come from a variety of sources not related to a physician's individual productivity, such as group ancillaries, equal or nonproduction-based formulas for sharing of group earnings, and even ownership in various types of healthcare facilities or side ventures. Group practices can produce a lot of "noise" in how compensation is distributed relative to the productivity of the individual physicians.

---

7   For a complete discussion of these economics, see Chapter 13, "An Introduction to Physician Services and Specialties" and Chapter 14, "The Economics of Physician Clinical Services and Compensation."

8   See Chapter 37, "How Reimbursement and Compensation Vary by Market," for an in-depth analysis of the reimbursement impact.

9   See Chapter 38, "Comparing the Surveys to the Physician Marketplace: Implications for Valuation Analysis," for more discussion on the profiles of respondents to MGMA.

Now, a fair question is how broadly can one interpret and apply a study based on a sample of 28 specialties to other specialties. Three factors go far in saying that this sample is fairly representative of other specialties in the MGMA data. First, the sampled specialties entail approximately two-thirds of all respondents for compensation and professional collections and about three-quarters of respondents for compensation and wRVUs, as noted previously. Second, the specialties included in the sample represent most of the major specialties in the marketplace. Third, the lack of high levels of linear predictability is observed, especially for wRVUs, across divergent specialties over multiple years. The one exception to this observation is the level of professional collections for certain surgical specialties in certain years. Given the regression line outcomes across the 28 specialties sampled and given the variety of specialties in the sample, it would be hard to imagine that the economics and dynamics of other specialties would be substantially different.

Undoubtedly, there is some correlation between productivity and compensation, and this correlation may be significant for some specialties. Further, lack of linear predictability may not close the door to the possibility that productivity data can be used to predict compensation with a nonlinear formula.[10] Yet, the key question is whether such levels of correlation warrant the use of simplistic productivity models as the sole or exclusive basis of establishing FMV compensation. More factors may be needed to predict compensation in the MGMA data.

4.0 Implications for Valuation and Compensation-Setting Practices

4.1 Avoid the Use of Simplistic and Imprecise Models for Determining Compensation

In reviewing the study on the level of correlation in the MGMA data, what should be apparent is that simplistic models such as the PMT generally lack the kind of rigorous statistical support that is necessary for a method to be used *exclusively* for determining compensation. The PMT is based on assumptions about the level of direct or linear predictability in the data between productivity and compensation that is just not substantiated by the data itself.[11] This lack of warrant from the data is particularly true in

---

10 As noted in chapter 40, "An Analysis of MGMA's Compensation by Quartile of Production Data: Compensation Rates Decline as Production Increases," MGMA has indicated for several years that as productivity increases, compensation increases, but productivity ratios (compensation per wRVU, and compensation to collections ratio) tend to decrease. This phenomenon is fairly uniform across many specialties and several years, leading one to surmise the potential for a curvilinear relationship (leveling off at higher productivity levels).

11 This does not necessarily mean productivity and compensation are not correlated in some fashion, only that linear regression is not, by itself, able to reveal the true relationship, if any, between the metrics. This may be because no relationship exists, or because the relationship is non-linear, or it may be that the surveys simply have too much noise in the data set, making it hard for any statistical analysis to reveal any statistical signal,

the case of wRVUs. Historically, there have been cases where the linear relationship between professional collections and compensation has been high enough to justify significant reliance on the PMT for valuation purposes. In general, however, the notion that compensation and productivity directly relate as presupposed by the method is not supported by a linear regression line model. This is not to say that the technique should not be used altogether. Rather, appraisers and those involved in compensation setting should use it knowing its limitations and imprecision. *Exclusive use of the method is what is problematic for determining FMV compensation.*

One may similarly critique the compensation method that selects a compensation-per-wRVU rate from survey data based on productivity benchmarking. If productivity is not a primary determinant of total compensation, how can one suppose that it is a primary driver of the compensation rate? If the wRVU productivity and compensation are not highly related in a linear manner, the compensation-per-wRVU rate and productivity are not highly related. The idea that the 75th percentile compensation per wRVU rate is matched to the 75th percentile productivity for purposes of establishing FMV compensation makes little sense in light of this linear regression statistical analysis. As discussed at length in Chapter 40, "An Analysis of MGMA's Compensation by Quartile of Production Data: Compensation Rates Decline as Production Increases," the data actually tends toward an inverse relationship. Moreover, such matching produces total compensation levels that exceed those of the survey, as discussed in Chapter 41, "Analyzing Physician Compensation per wRVU: Why Benchmarking Data Is Only the Beginning."

4.2 Analyze the Data Before Using It and Assuming Any Relationships in It

As a general matter, the assumption that compensation and productivity correlate is not an unreasonable concept relative to the economics of physician services.[12] Productivity is a foundational metric for physician services. *The issue, however, is the degree to which productivity drives compensation in a simple and direct manner.* Regression line analysis of the MGMA survey data does not indicate that it is as direct and simple as many suppose. Consequently, there are lessons here for valuing physician compensation: It is essential to analyze and study data before using the data. Assuming relationships exist in the data without sufficient analysis can lead to inaccuracy and questionable results. *A related implication of the study is that annual review and analysis of survey data is a prudent*

---

if one truly does exist (as many observers have theorized).

12   Editor Dietrich's Note: At least in my experience, there is a strong correlation in private (nonhospital-controlled) practices between compensation and collected production. This points to the importance of using historical (prehospital employment) compensation and productivity as a primary measure of fair market value in transactions involving newly employed physicians as well as making use of the MGMA's breakdown of data for compensation and productivity for Partner/Shareholder in Practice for All Practices in comparison with that by Legal Organization (Business Corporation Versus Not-for-Profit Corp./Foundation).

practice. As shown in the R-squared values over the years in the study, the data may contain unique characteristics in a given year based on the respondents. These may not continue over time. Thus, one should verify trends and models every year, rather than continuing to apply an economic analysis developed in a prior year with the assumption that the prior year's analysis will hold in subsequent years.

4.3 Use the MGMA's Regression Line Formula

MGMA's Physician Pay-to-Production Plotter Tool from the interactive CD-ROM provides a regression line formula as part of the standard output for the tool. If you want a statistically valid method for applying the MGMA survey data for a given year based on productivity metrics, use this formula. This formula is based on the actual data for the specialty for that year. While a regression line formula is not perfect, as expressed by the R-squared value for the formula, it is certainly more reliable than the PMT or matching the compensation rate to productivity.[13]

4.4 Use the Cost and Income Approaches

The concept of earnings-based compensation does not have the shortcomings and limitations of productivity-based compensation using survey data. Earnings-based compensation takes into account the factors that affect the economics of physician services and practices at a comprehensive level. It is not based on assumptions about data, but is built around the actual market conditions and operating profile of the subject physician or practice. It uses real-time historical data to develop a sophisticated and multifactored analysis of physician compensation.[14] Physician productivity is certainly an element, but it is not the sole variable affecting the determination of value for compensation. Certainly, cost and income approaches require more data, work, and effort to complete, but the results reflect higher degrees of precision and accuracy relative to the full array of economic variables.

As a practical matter, the cost and income approaches can be used along with survey-based methods to provide a rigorous analysis as well as a basis for comparability between a subject and the market survey data. Physicians and clients naturally want to benchmark the subject compensation to peer data. Use of all three approaches allows the appraiser to explain why survey data may relate to the local market conditions and operating profile of a subject physician. In reconciling the different compensation indications from the approaches, the appraiser is required to analyze the subject relative to

---

13   It is possible that a nonlinear analysis could yield even greater predictability and precision in using productivity to establish compensation. Unfortunately, such a tool is not currently available for use with the MGMA survey data.

14   Where such data is available. One can develop an income approach based on assumptions and estimates, but its reliability then comes into question, due to the extent of such assumptions.

the market data. This process helps to identify those differences between the subject and the market data. For a complete discussion of the concept of earnings-based compensation and the use of the cost and income approaches, see Chapter 24, "Valuing Physician Employment Arrangements: Cost and Income-Base Valuation Methods."

5.0 Conclusion

This chapter has presented a study showing that the linearly predictive relationship in the MGMA data between productivity and compensation is not as strong as many have assumed. Whether measured by wRVUs or professional collections, the broad trends in the data indicate that the level of predictability may not be strong enough to support valuation and compensation-setting practices exclusively based on individual physician productivity models that relate productivity and compensation using simple linear models. The only exception to this general finding is found in certain surgical specialties using professional collections. The R-squared values for wRVUs were rarely above a value of 0.50 in the specialties sampled. What this study points to is the need for more statistically rigorous and sound techniques for establishing the FMV compensation level for physicians using survey data. Many of the currently popular methods appear inadequate for appraisal purposes. The study also indicates that users of survey data should complete annual reviews of the data and compensation-related modeling, since the variability in respondents from year to year can afford changing outcomes in the data. A final key takeaway from the study is the need to use the cost and income approaches to achieve greater precision and accuracy in setting physician compensation.

As noted in the introduction, a review of the findings raises additional questions that were not discussed relative to the focus of this chapter on the use of certain survey-based valuation methods. These questions relate to: 1) why one observes a relatively low linear predictability between productivity and compensation in the survey data, when many observers reasonably conjecture that some kind of correlation likely exists; 2) why some specialties show significantly more or less predictability than other specialties, and 3) whether nonlinear models may yield higher levels of predictability (which, if correct, might help to explain the relative difficulty of linear predictability). In Section 3.4, a series of factors were listed that could potentially explain the variability of correlation in the data among specialties. Further study and analysis is needed to begin to understand and explain this variability. Given the wide use of survey data to establish FMV compensation, such study is essential for the appraisal profession to develop more accurate and reliable tools for use in valuing physician employment arrangements.

Chapter 40. An Analysis of MGMA's Compensation by Quartile of Production Data: Compensaton Rates Decline as Production Increases

CONTENTS

Chapter 40. An Analysis of MGMA's Compensation by Quartile of Production Data: Compensation Rates Decline as Production Increases

By Timothy Smith, CPA/ABV, and Albert D. Hutzler, JD, MBA, AVA

1.0 Introduction

With the most recent cycle of hospital-physician alignment, compensation plans for employed physicians have increasingly turned to structures based on work relative value units (wRVUs). Under these plans, physicians are paid at a set rate per wRVU, which is also called a "conversion factor" or "conversion rate." Use of compensation-per-wRVU models has naturally raised the issue of how a fair market value (FMV) conversion factor should be determined. The determination of these FMV rates is one of today's hottest and most controversial topics in the emerging appraisal discipline of compensation valuation (CV). Since the use of physician compensation surveys is ubiquitous, the marketplace has turned to the surveys as a source of FMV conversion rates. Some of the surveys report market data on compensation per wRVU using the standard format of presenting the data by major percentiles, e.g., the 25th, 50th, 75th, and 90th percentiles. This reporting convention has led to some important misconceptions about the data and, in turn, has set the stage for picking and choosing among the survey rates as the basis for determining FMV.

Several popular ideas have developed about how FMV conversion factors should be selected. One school of thought suggests that the median, as the middle value, is the best estimate of FMV. Another group argues that the compensation per wRVU rate should match the subject physician's wRVU benchmarking level. If a physician's annual wRVUs measure at the 75th percentile of the survey data, the physician should be paid the 75th percentile compensation per wRVU rate. Still others criticize the exclusive focus on survey data and point toward cost and income approach methods as the preferred way to determine compensation on a per-wRVU basis.

In recent years, MGMA has entered the "conversion factor wars" with an analysis of its own data on the matter. The purpose of this chapter is to assess MGMA's so-called "compensation by quartile of production data" and analyze its implications for valuation and compensation-setting practices.

2.0 MGMA's Compensation by Quartile of Production Data

2.1 Yearly Analysis Presented in the *Physician Compensation and Production Survey*

In the past few years, MGMA has published certain studies that examine the compensation per wRVU rate of physicians based on their quartile of wRVU production. These studies are included in the "Key Findings" section of its *Physician Compensation and Production Survey*. The studies are based on MGMA's analysis of its compensation and wRVU production data. For those respondents who report both compensation and wRVU data, MGMA computes a median rate for each quartile of production. It does this by first grouping the respondents into quartiles based on their wRVU productivity levels, whereby the first quartile is comprised of the physicians in the first to the 25th percentiles and the fourth quartile is made up of those physicians whose wRVUs exceed the 75th percentile. MGMA then computes the compensation per wRVU rate for each physician in a given quartile and determines the median rate for the quartile.

MGMA observes a unique pattern in this data. The median compensation per wRVU rate per quartile generally decreases as productivity increases. Physicians in the fourth or top quartile of productivity generally make less per unit of productivity than those in lower quartiles, although their total compensation is higher. In other words, the compensation per wRVU rate is inversely related to the level of productivity. Along with its written analysis of this phenomenon, MGMA usually publishes data for one to two selected specialties in its annual survey to illustrate the pattern.

2.2 Data Presented at the 2010 Annual MGMA Conference

At its 2010 national conference, MGMA provided the participants with data on compensation per wRVU by quartile of production for eight different specialties. This data is presented in Exhibit 1. Also presented in Exhibit 1 are the overall medians for these specialties from the 2010 survey, along with the calculated ratio of the quartile medians to the overall median.[1]

---

1   We note that the overall median is determined from the identical data pool because the MGMA reported data for compensation per wRVU is based on values that it calculates for each respondent that reports both compensation and wRVUs in the survey.

	Quartile Median				Overall	Ratio of Quartile to Overall Median			
	1st	2nd	3rd	4th	Median	1st	2nd	3rd	4th
Cardiology: Noninvasive	$69.74	$56.72	$53.84	$47.82	$53.54	130.3%	105.9%	100.6%	89.3%
Family Practice (without OB)	45.76	39.43	36.79	36.44	39.13	116.9	100.8	94.0	93.1
Gastroenterology	57.37	56.10	53.40	49.28	53.93	106.4	104.0	99.0	91.4
Internal Medicine: General	48.91	41.85	41.67	39.08	42.50	115.1	98.5	98.1	92.0
Obstetrics/Gynecology: General	49.55	42.77	41.96	41.08	43.54	113.8	98.2	96.4	94.3
Orthopedic Surgery: General	67.78	59.74	58.11	55.90	60.05	112.9	99.5	96.8	93.1
Pediatrics: General	43.64	38.74	37.66	36.81	38.90	112.2	99.6	96.8	94.6
Surgery: General	58.79	49.72	49.00	45.24	50.10	117.3	99.2	97.8	90.3

Exhibit 1. 2010 Compensation Per wRVU Data by Quartile of Production

To further analyze this data, the ratio of the quartile medians to the overall median is presented graphically in Exhibit 2.

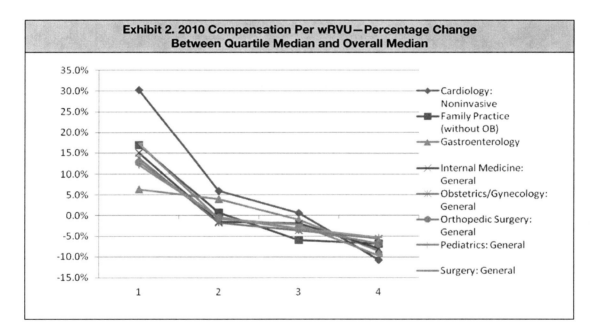

Exhibit 2. 2010 Compensation Per wRVU—Percentage Change Between Quartile Median and Overall Median

2.3 Expanded Data Based on wRVUs and Professional Collections

Through special order, data was obtained from MGMA that tracked median compensation rates by quartile of production for professional collections based on 2010 data for these same eight specialties. This data was obtained to determine whether a similar inverse relationship existed for the compensation-to-collections ratio. To further analyze the relationship between compensation and productivity rates, the median compensation rates by quartile were obtained for these specialties for both wRVUs and professional collections based on 2011 data. Similar to Exhibit 2, this quartile-based data was compared to the overall median rate and graphed in Exhibits 3 to 5.

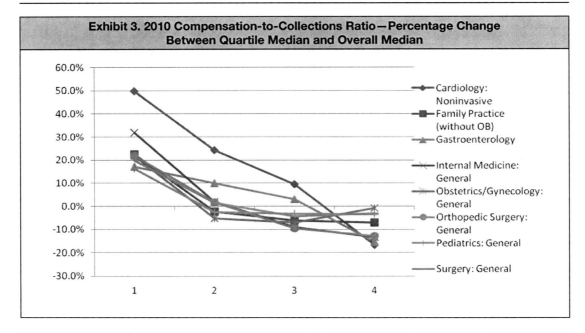

Exhibit 3. 2010 Compensation-to-Collections Ratio—Percentage Change Between Quartile Median and Overall Median

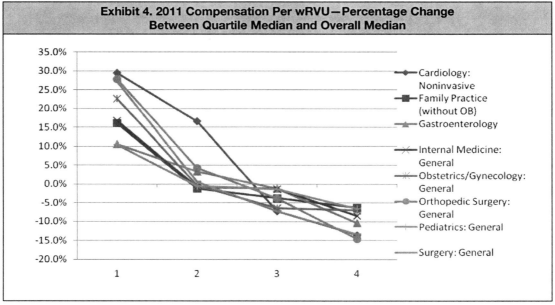

Exhibit 4. 2011 Compensation Per wRVU—Percentage Change Between Quartile Median and Overall Median

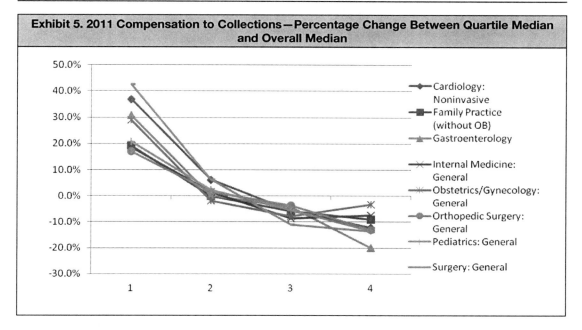

Exhibit 5. 2011 Compensation to Collections—Percentage Change Between Quartile Median and Overall Median

3.0 Analysis of the Data

3.1 How Compensation Rates Are Calculated in the Survey Data

First, it bears explanation that the survey respondents do not report the wRVU conversion rates. MGMA calculates them, based on compensation and productivity data reported. Thus, for example, while all respondents report compensation, only a subset of those respondents report wRVUs or professional collections information. MGMA uses that subset to calculate the productivity ratios (i.e., the compensation per wRVU rate and the compensation-to-collections ratio). Ratios are calculated for each respondent independently, and then the set of ratio data is reported by percentiles.

Given the way the survey data is developed, there is not necessarily any relationship between respondents at a given percentile of productivity (e.g., reported wRVUs) and the same percentile of the corresponding *compensation ratio*. In other words, physicians who produce at the 75th percentile of wRVUs are not necessarily the same physicians who earn at the 75th percentile of compensation per wRVU. In terms of how these conversion factors are computed, there is not a statistical correlation between the percentile rankings for productivity and the compensation ratios. Indeed, MGMA's data on median compensation rates by quartile of production, as shown in Exhibits 3, 4, and 5, indicates that, in general, the higher rates are correlated with lower productivity levels.

3.2 The Significant and Recurring Pattern in the Data

What is fascinating about the data presented in Exhibits 1 to 5 is the similar patterns in the relationship between the median by quartile to the overall reported median. This *general* pattern is observed not only for compensation rates per wRVU over a two-year period, but also for the compensation-to-collections ratio over a two-year period. For both types of compensation ratios or conversion factors, a comparable pattern was observed in which the ratio was higher for physicians in the first quartile of production than the reported overall median and then declined throughout the remaining three quartiles of production. A wider variation in the percentage of change between the quartile median and the overall median is observed, however, in the compensation-to-collections ratio. Another striking feature is that the pattern is seen across various types of specialties. *Given the recurrence of the declining relationship over multiple specialties and years and for two distinct compensation rates, this pattern cannot be summarily dismissed as a data anomaly or random outcome. The data shows an overall inverse relationship between productivity and the compensation rate per unit of productivity.*

3.3 What the Data Does Not Indicate

While the data indicates a general inverse relationship relative to the entire data set, one should not interpret the data in an unqualified or overgeneralized manner. The compensation by quartile of production data reports the median for the quartile. A median implies that data points are higher and lower than the middle point in the data set. Thus, MGMA's data indicates that physicians are making more or less than the median for the quartile. As a result, the median rates for each quartile should not be taken as a precise value that is categorically applicable to each and every physician in the quartile. There is wider variability in the rates for all respondents within a quartile of production than is indicated by sole consideration of the median rate. *Nonetheless, the decline in medians across the quartiles indicates that rates overall are lower as production increases.* To measure the exact range of rates within the quartile, one would need the mean, standard deviation, and rates for various percentiles by quartile. Additional data and further study would be needed to separate the noise in the data from the actual signal and to form stronger conclusions as to the range of rates within a given quartile of production and the overall relationship between the productivity and conversion rate metrics.

3.4 The Usefulness of the Data

The appeal and strength of the compensation by quartile of production technique is that it is based on the actual correlation of compensation and productivity within the data. As discussed earlier in this chapter, to calculate the median by quartile of production, MGMA segregates individual respondents into quartiles based on their production and then computes the compensation to productivity rate for the respondents in each quartile to derive a median for the quartile. These compensation rates are based on the actual compensation of respondents within a quartile of production. They are not based on assumptions made about the data. This attribute makes the data useful for valuation and compensation-setting purposes.

Such actual correlation in the data contrasts with many popular ideas about how compensation, productivity, and compensation ratios relate in the data. A prime example is the concept discussed previously that the reported compensation rate correlates with benchmarked percentile of production for a subject physician. The notion that a physician who produces at the 75th percentile for wRVUs should be paid at the 75th percentile compensation per wRVU rate is an assumption made about the data and its underlying economics. The economic concept on which this assumption is based is that highly productive physicians are able to leverage their fixed costs so that their cost per wRVU is relatively low, resulting in higher conversion rates. At first glance, this would appear to be a reasonable assumption about the dynamics of conversion rates found in the surveys. As shown by the data on compensation by quartile of production, however, this assumption is simply incorrect as a categorical or universal trend. Production and compensation are, in general, inversely related.[2]

Another contrasting example of data use includes the so-called percentile matching technique or linear interpolation method, which uses compensation and productivity data from the surveys. This valuation technique assumes that the compensation at a given percentile correlates with the production at the same percentile in the survey data. In other words, a physician whose production is at the 65th percentile should be compensated at the 65th percentile.[3] This percentile matching is an assumption about the data. The actual correlation level between compensation and productivity is not strong, especially for wRVUs, based on *regression line analysis* performed on the actual MGMA data.[4,5] The MGMA data on compensation by quartile of production is not subject to the limitation that its rates are based on assumptions, rather than actual correlations in the data.

---

2   This general inverse relationship does not preclude the possibility that an individual physician producing at the 75th percentile could be paid at the 75th percentile conversion rate. It does, however, vacate the assumption that they should always correlate.

3   For a complete discussion of the percentile matching technique, see Chapter 23, "Valuing Physician Employment Arrangements for Clinical Services: Market-Based Valuation Methods."

4   See Chapter 39, "An Analysis of the Relationship Between Productivity and Compensation in the MGMA Data and Its Implications for Valuation and Compensation-Setting Practices," for further analysis of the correlation between compensation and production in the MGMA survey data based on linear regression.

5   However, we note that while linear correlation is not strong, the data for compensation per wRVU by quartile suggests that the actual relationship between compensation and productivity may be described by a curvilinear shape that levels off slightly at higher productivity values. Testing that conjecture would require application of statistical transformation techniques to the raw data, which to the authors' knowledge, has never been attempted.

3.5 Possible Explanations for the Declining Pattern of the Data

This declining pattern is undoubtedly striking and counterintuitive to many in the healthcare industry. As discussed, one can readily suppose that the compensation per wRVU rate, for example, would increase as wRVUs increase, because the fixed costs of a physician would be spread over a larger volume level, thereby increasing the margin per wRVU. While a complete explanation would require more in-depth analysis of the data and potentially the need for additional data on the respondents, two characteristics observed in the physician practice marketplace may be conjectured to provide some explanation for this declining compensation rate per unit of productivity phenomenon. First, many physicians are paid using base salaries or base compensation amounts that may not correlate with their productivity. Newly hired physicians, for example, may take a few years to ramp up their productivity to a level commensurate with the compensation level at which they are paid. Physicians in smaller population areas and lower patient volumes may be paid at rates more commensurate with larger markets and higher patient demand to retain them in the community. It is also possible that some physicians are in groups with highly favorable commercial payer contracts and payer mixes, whereby they are able to attain relatively higher revenue levels per wRVU with lower volume levels, resulting in higher compensation per wRVU. Finally, some survey respondents may devote a significant percentage of their time to nonclinical activity, such as administrative, teaching, or research services, thereby reducing their wRVUs and increasing their effective compensation per wRVU rate.

Another potential explanation is that key physician practice costs are not fixed over the horizon of the 25th to 90th percentiles of productivity. Rather, practice costs relate to volumes in a step-cost manner. Practice expenses, such as staffing and space, remain fixed up to a certain level of volume at which the practice must expand its facilities and staffing to accommodate the increased patient demand. Such expansion of resources may be not achievable or practicable in small increments, e.g., hiring a 0.25 FTE for a specific function or leasing an extra 500 square feet of adjacent space. MGMA studies of highly productive practices over the years have frequently noted higher costs per unit of service in many of these practices, pointing to the "stair step" characteristics of many practice costs.[6] Apparently, the highest producers need more staff and assistance to enable them to produce so highly. In effect, the economic "law of diminishing returns" begins to take over. While various causes may be conjectured to explain this phenomenon, further study and analysis with the data are surely warranted.

---

6   We thank our colleague Dana Boatman at HealthCare Appraisers, who was previously a long-time practice manager and MGMA member, for pointing out this insight.

4.0 Implications for Valuation and Compensation-Setting Practices

4.1 The Creation of a New Survey-Based Valuation Method

MGMA's data on compensation by quartile of production has allowed for the development of a new valuation method under the market approach. This new method is the "compensation by quartile of production technique" (CQPT). This technique uses certain median compensation-to-productivity rates by quartile of production for a given physician specialty to determine a guideline compensation level for valuation purposes. The CQPT is applied as follows. First a physician's productivity level is benchmarked to the appropriate quartile of production based on the survey data for the relevant productivity measure. Next, the applicable median compensation-to-productivity rate for the quartile of production is multiplied by the physician's productivity level to compute a guideline level of compensation. In general, physician wRVU and professional collections are used as the measure of productivity for this technique.[7]

4.2 The Need for More Statistically Valid Models in Using Survey Data

One takeaway from MGMA's data is that many seemingly reasonable assumptions about the economics of physician compensation may, in fact, be off the mark. One such example is the previously noted idea that fixed overhead in a practice yields higher compensation rates per wRVU for highly productive physicians. As noted, this idea appears consistent with standard textbook analysis of fixed costs relative to volume: the higher the volume, the lower the cost per unit. The MGMA data, however, does not validate this analysis as applied to physician practices at a general level. What this lack of validation indicates is that our understanding of practice economics relative to volume, overhead, and physician compensation in the survey data may be incomplete or inadequate. The dynamics of physician compensation and productivity, as reported in the surveys, may be more complex than current models are able to accommodate. Many of the current models and assumptions appear to be imprecise and inaccurate in their general application. Consequently, new valuation models with better statistical validity and complexity need to be developed to apply survey data to subject compensation arrangements. Unfortunately, the surveys do not currently provide data at a level and in formats that would readily allow for the development of many such models.

4.3 Evaluating Total Compensation as a Prudent Practice

One helpful tool for evaluating the application and modeling of survey data to a subject arrangement is completing a total compensation analysis. In this analysis, the appraiser

---

7   For a complete discussion of the CQPT, see Chapter 23, "Valuing Physician Employment Arrangements for Clinical Services: Market-Based Valuation Methods."

takes the concluded FMV conversion rate and calculates the total compensation over the expected range of productivity for the subject. The total compensation is then evaluated relative to productivity and other criteria. Returning to the example of using the 75th percentile rate for 75th percentile productivity, a total compensation analysis would generally highlight the difficulties with such a model or at least the need for the appraiser to perform additional work. The total compensation produced by this formula would frequently be well in excess of the 75th percentile, and on occasion, even the 90th percentile. To justify this level of total compensation, the appraiser would need to complete additional analyses and valuation methods that would support and justify the elevated level of compensation, relative to the level of productivity.[8]

4.4 Use of Tiered Compensation Per wRVU Rates

One nuance to the MGMA data for compensation by quartile of production is that the declining rates represent the effective or average rate for the total wRVUs produced by the physician. Recall that conversion factors are a calculated rate based on a mathematic formula: total compensation divided by total wRVUs. That the effective or average rate should generally be lower for higher levels of production does not preclude the use of relatively high rates in a compensation formula or structure for an employed physician. It is possible to have a compensation structure that is consistent with FMV and contains a conversion rate that increases as productivity increases. Of course, the only way to accomplish this is to start with relatively low conversion rates for lower productivity outcomes, but it can be done. As noted in the prior section, it is important to test compensation models at various productivity levels to ensure that compensation remains consistent with FMV at all possible productivity levels.

4.5 Consider the Use of Earnings-Based Compensation in the Cost and Income Approaches

Use of earnings-based compensation (EBC) can be highly effective in bringing greater precision and accuracy to the determination of FMV conversion rates. EBC uses the net earnings from providing professional services as the basis for establishing compensation for a professional.[9] It is calculated by using the net revenues received from services rendered and deducting the costs incurred to generate the services. EBC has been the historically predominate paradigm for physician compensation, and it is the one framework that ensures practices do not operate significantly in the red. In addition, it is widely used in tax practice for determining reasonable compensation for professionals

---

8   This is not to say that there are no cases where FMV compensation is the numerical equivalent of the 75th percentile conversion rate multiplied by the 75th percentile for wRVUs. Rather, the appraisal analysis supporting such a conclusion of value would not be based on the supposition that the conversion rate should match the productivity level.

9   See Chapter 24, "Valuing Physician Employment Arrangements for Clinical Services: Cost and Income-Based Valuation Methods," for an in-depth discussion of this concept.

---

in corporate entities.[10] The benefit of using EBC is that it takes into account the key economic factors that impact practice net earnings available for physician compensation, including productivity, reimbursement, service mix, payer mix, and overhead. Moreover, it addresses these factors relative to the specific facts and circumstances of the subject physician and arrangement. To apply EBC in appraisal practice, the analyst uses cost and income approach methods to value a subject physician compensation arrangement.[11]

5.0 Conclusion

In summary, conversion rates can be an excellent way to set physician compensation, but they require careful application to ensure there is no overpayment, especially for the most productive physicians. The task is often made more difficult by incorrect assumptions about the data, rather than statistically valid models that are validated by the data. One such assumption is the idea that compensation rates should rise with productivity. Careful attention must be paid to the use and application of survey data in setting compensation for physicians. Appraisers, consultants, and employers should consider a variety of methods and techniques when establishing compensation for physicians. There are complexities to the data that marketplace participants do not yet fully understand. Rather than exclusively relying on assumptions about the data, it is better to utilize many tools in the compensation-setting process. By doing so, one can mitigate the impact of assumptions that turn out to be inaccurate upon further study. While making assumptions about data is often a necessity in appraisal practice, valuation analysts need to be wary of exclusive or overreliance on such assumptions when other data and tools are available.

---

10   See Kevin Yeanoplos and Ron Seigneur, *Reasonable Compensation: Application and Analysis for Appraisal, Tax, and Management Purposes*, 2010. Business Valuation Resources, LLC, pp. 8-10.

11   We note that the EBC may have additional tax considerations, especially for nonprofit entities. For a complete discussion of the tax implications of compensation valuation methods for tax-exempt entities, see Chapter 12, "Reasonable Compensation for Tax Purposes."

Chapter 41. Analyzing Physician Compensation Per wRVU: Why Benchmark Data Is Only the Beginning

CONTENTS

Chapter 41. Analyzing Physician Compensation Per wRVU: Why Benchmark Data Is Only the Beginning

By Martin D. Brown, CPA/ABV

1.0 Introduction

In recent years, a measure of physician work effort known as physician work relative value units (wRVU) has become increasingly important as a productivity determinant in a physician's compensation. For example, in 2010, wRVUs were used as the primary determinant of compensation in 60% of all production-compensation arrangements for participants in AMGA's physician compensation survey as compared to 40% in 2005.[1,2] This trend includes the popular production-based compensation model that determines compensation based on a conversion rate per physician wRVU, by which the physician is paid a fixed dollar amount per wRVU produced. While such a model is common (and perhaps growing with the recent wave of hospital and health system employment of physicians), it is important to have an understanding of the underlying benchmark data considered as well as an awareness of potential pitfalls to properly determine a conversion rate per wRVU that yields fair market value and commercially reasonable compensation.

Specifically, the conversion factor or rate per wRVU remains a critical issue in certain production-based models because that particular variable can drive aggregate annual compensation. To determine an appropriate rate per wRVU, many in the healthcare marketplace turn to physician compensation surveys. Some of these benchmarking surveys report compensation per wRVU conversion rates as well as data specific to

---

1   *2006 Medical Group Compensation and Financial Survey.* American Medical Group Association, RSM McGladrey, 2006, p. 16 .

2   *2011 Medical Group Compensation and Financial Survey.* American Medical Group Association, RSM McGladrey, 2011, p. 26.

annual compensation and wRVU levels, thus allowing one to calculate a compensation-to-wRVU relationship. This chapter cautions users of survey data against the use of any compensation per wRVU rate that is not critically examined. Such use can result in total compensation levels that are not commercially reasonable and/or are inconsistent with fair market value.

2.0 Defining Reported and Calculated Compensation Per wRVU Rates

In determining an appropriate conversion rate per wRVU that yields fair market value compensation, valuation professionals generally take into consideration physician benchmark data. The Stark regulations, moreover, have indicated that "reference to multiple, objective, independently published salary surveys remains a prudent practice for evaluating fair market value."[3] These physician benchmarking surveys, which are based on data reported by varying types of practices, including those owned by hospitals/health systems, are commonly used to evaluate physician compensation, collections, productivity, and benefits. These benchmark surveys include data specific to *reported* compensation per wRVU as well as metrics necessary for *calculated* compensation per wRVU.[4]

2.1 *Reported* Compensation Per wRVU

Reported compensation per wRVU refers to the actual compensation per wRVU as reported in the survey data. Many of the benchmark surveys collect and report data on the actual compensation per wRVU rates paid to respondent physicians in the survey. For illustration purposes, we have included an example in Exhibit 1 of *reported* compensation per wRVU at various percentiles similar to that reported in several national benchmark surveys for the specialty of family practice (without OB).[5]

Exhibit 1. Reported Compensation Per wRVU, Family Practice (Without OB)				
Description	25th Percentile	Median	75th Percentile	90th Percentile
Compensation per wRVU, Rounded	$ 35.00	$ 39.90	$ 47.40	$ 57.90

---

3   72 F.R.171/Wednesday, Sept. 5, 2007/Rules and Regulations.

4   In recent years, the majority (approximately half or more) of national benchmark survey respondents have been physicians employed by health systems (i.e., in contrast to those in private practice). For example, in the Medical Group Management Association (MGMA) *2012 Physician Compensation and Production Survey*, hospital and integrated delivery system respondents represented approximately 49% of providers. However, over the last few years, national benchmark surveys (including MGMA) have represented a higher percentage of hospital-employed respondents.

5   Tables herein include combined survey results from the MGMA, the American Medical Group Association (AMGA), and Sullivan Cotter and Associates (Sullivan Cotter).

Notably, as reflected in Exhibit 1, reported compensation per wRVU rises across increasing percentiles. Because this metric is reported in isolation by physicians responding to the surveys, it mirrors that of statistics compiled and reported on a percentile basis. Further discussion regarding this increase, and its applicability to determining fair market value compensation, is discussed below.

2.2 *Calculated* Compensation Per wRVU

In contrast to *reported* data, appraisers can also assess compensation per wRVU on a *calculated* basis. Such calculation represents annual compensation divided by annual wRVUs across respective percentiles reported in benchmark surveys. By reviewing *calculated* compensation per wRVU benchmark data, valuators are able to evaluate the manner in which annual compensation and wRVU production correlate across various percentiles. In short, calculated conversion factors explain the range of reported compensation, given the range of reported wRVUs. Additionally, appraisers can also compare the *calculated* results with a review of *reported* data to determine appropriate conversion rates for use in productivity-based physician compensation models. To calculate compensation per wRVU results using data reported in survey benchmarks, appraisers divide the reported annual compensation at a particular percentile by annual production of wRVUs reported at the same percentile. For illustrative purposes, an example of *calculated* compensation per wRVU at various percentiles utilizing compiled data from several national surveys for the specialty of family practice (without OB) is included in Exhibit 2.

Exhibit 2. Calculated Compensation Per wRVU, Family Practice (Without OB)					
Description	25th Percentile	Median	75th Percentile	90th Percentile	Formula
Compensation	$161,000	$187,000	$223,000	$268,000	A
wRVUs	4,040	4,870	5,830	6,940	B
Compensation per wRVU, Rounded	$39.90	$38.40	$38.30	$38.60	C = A/B

As demonstrated in Exhibit 2, *calculated* compensation per wRVU tends to be more consistent across all percentiles and more closely aligns with the median of the *reported* compensation per wRVU. This phenomenon is generally observed on both an individual survey basis and with calculations utilizing the results of compiled survey data (i.e., as illustrated in Exhibit 2). The significance of this alignment and how best to utilize the results for production-based physician compensation will be further discussed later in this chapter. However, at this time, it is important to note that because *calculated* compensation per wRVU is determined by using two separately reported variables (i.e., annual compensation and annual wRVUs), the survey respondents may not precisely correspond. For example, the respondents who report compensation at the 25th percentile may not be the same respondents who report wRVUs at the 25th percentile. This is typical due to the fact that survey respondents reporting annual wRVUs represent a subset of those reporting annual compensation. Despite this fact, a review of *calculated* compensation per wRVU remains helpful in determining fair market value compensation, as well as in assessing the significance of the *reported* compensation per wRVU results.

3.0 Potential Pitfalls

3.1 *Reported* Compensation Per wRVU

Given the broad range of results among the data on *reported* compensation per wRVU, a critical issue arises as to how to utilize this data appropriately in appraisal work. Using it in isolation or without critical analysis could result in disproportionate outcomes that are based on misleading assumptions about presumed relationships in the data. For instance, 90th percentile *reported* compensation per wRVU may be the result of significant compensation from ancillary or other nonclinical services that do not generate any physician wRVUs. Therefore, these services can equate to higher physician compensation, but may not reflect higher levels of physician wRVU-based productivity. In addition, agreements can exist that include high guaranteed compensation and lower levels of productivity, resulting in significantly higher rates of *reported* compensation per wRVU. A prime example of this results from newly recruited physicians in a practice who have guaranteed compensation and comparatively low productivity. Alternatively, 25th percentile *reported* compensation per wRVU may be the result of a physician's reinvestment in a practice or higher benefits in lieu of compensation. For example, a physician in private practice may often pay discretionary expenses (e.g., personal meals, entertainment, or auto expenses) through the practice, instead of receiving these benefits through direct compensation.

In summary, reported compensation per wRVU may reflect factual considerations specific to the individual survey respondents, particularly at low and high percentiles, which may not be comparable to the relevant facts and circumstances for the subject arrangement being valued. Thus, the use and application of these rates (particularly those with large standard deviations) may be inappropriate if not comparable to the subject arrangement.[6]

---

6   For an analysis of how local market reimbursement levels affect physician compensation, see Chapter 37, "How Reimbursement and Physician Compensation Vary by Market."

Additionally, physicians producing annual wRVUs at the 75th percentile are not generally compensated at the *reported* wRVU conversion rate for the 75th percentile. Instead, annual compensation and physician wRVUs tend to correlate with the approximate equivalent annual benchmark on a percentile basis, i.e., annual physician wRVUs at the 75th percentile generally correspond with annual compensation at the 75th percentile, when using the calculated compensation per wRVU rate. Exhibit 3 demonstrates the potential results of using a conversion rate above *reported* median data.

Exhibit 3. Compensation Per wRVU Comparison, Family Practice (Without OB)					
Description	25th Percentile	Median	75th Percentile	90th Percentile	Formula
Benchmark Annual Compensation[1]	$161,000	$187,000	$223,000	$268,000	A
Reported Compensation per wRVU[2]	$35.00	$39.90	$47.40	$57.90	B
Annual wRVUs[2]	4,040	4,870	5,830	6,940	C
Resulting Annual Compensation	**$141,400**	**$194,313**	**$276,342**	**$401,826**	D = B*C
Variance	*$19,600*	*($7,313)*	*($53,342)*	*($133,826)*	*E=A-D*
Calculated Compensation per wRVU[1]	$39.90	$38.40	$38.30	$38.60	F
Annual wRVUs[1]	4,040	4,870	5,830	6,940	G
Resulting Annual Compensation	**$161,196**	**$187,008**	**$223,289**	**$267,884**	H = F*G
Variance	*($196)*	*($8)*	*($289)*	*$116*	*I = A-H*

[1] Per **Exhibit 2**

[2] Per **Exhibit 1**

As represented in Exhibit 3 and by way of example, *reported* compensation per wRVU at the *75th percentile* of $47.40 multiplied by *75th percentile* annual wRVUs of 5,830 results in an annual compensation of $276,342, which is in excess of the annual compensation in the *90th percentile* (or $268,000 per Exhibit 2). In comparison, a *calculated* compensation per wRVU of $38.30 at the 75th percentile multiplied by 5,830 yields $223,289, which is equivalent to the annual compensation in the 75th percentile benchmark. This calculation reveals that the use of *reported* compensation per wRVU exceeds the median and may not provide a clear basis for correlation between *annual* compensation and productivity.

3.2 *Calculated* Compensation Per wRVU

While reported compensation per wRVU values have their drawbacks, *calculated* conversion rates are also not without limitations. While *calculated* compensation per wRVU rates provide a more narrow range of results, which demonstrate a smaller statistical variance across percentiles, it is important to consider other relevant factors to ultimately determine an appropriate compensation per wRVU value that yields fair market value compensation. For example, it is important to note that because the results of *calculated* compensation per wRVU are derived from two variables reported in benchmark surveys (i.e., annual compensation and annual wRVUs), the results at key intervals across reported percentiles may yield differing rates and outcomes. For instance, 25th percentile annual compensation divided by 25th percentile annual wRVUs may result in a higher calculated compensation per wRVU amount than the results of the same calculation using data reported at the 90th percentile. In fact, the correlation between the two variables often results in an inverse relationship between productivity and compensation. In other words, as productivity levels rise, the compensation rate per *calculated* wRVU often decreases.[7] These limitations, as well as the correlation between annual production and compensation, should also be considered when evaluating *calculated* compensation per wRVU.

4.0 Key Takeaways

It is important to note that *calculated* compensation per wRVU results often approximate the *reported* median compensation per wRVU, a result that is observable across numerous physician specialties and surveys. *Calculated* and *reported* median compensation per wRVU values generally provide a more accurate baseline for determining annual compensation commensurate with a respective production level when using survey data under the market approach. However, due to the narrow scope of these figures, it is important not to rely solely upon this benchmark data, but also to consider and analyze the unique factors and circumstances associated with any potential arrangement. Specifically, the valuation professional should also take into consideration the purpose and goals of the arrangement within the context of its business objectives, community, practice overhead, patient population, payment rates of insurers in the community, and other key factors to properly apply a wRVU conversion factor.[8] Moreover, when appropriate, the cost and income approaches should be utilized in the valuation analysis. As physician production-based compensation agreements become more prevalent, it is crucial to be mindful of the aforementioned facts and potential drawbacks to determine compensation per wRVU rates that yield fair market value compensation.

In addition, a physician's aggregate annual compensation resulting from a compensation-per-wRVU arrangement remains an important indication of the reasonableness of the determined compensation per wRVU. Therefore, to properly gauge the reasonableness of compensation per wRVU amounts, it is essential to compare the total compensation results to respective levels of total compensation data from national benchmark surveys. Specifically, the compensation levels reported by similar physicians in national benchmark surveys provide an important baseline at which to begin assessing the

---

7   This declining phenomenon is also observed in MGMA's data that reports compensation by quartile of production. See Chapter 40, "An Analysis of MGMA's Compensation by Quartile of Production Data: Compensation Rates Decline as Production Increases" for an in-depth analysis of this phenomenon.

8   See Chapter 36, "Evaluating RVU-Based Compensation Arrangements."

reasonableness of a particular wRVU conversion factor. In summary, while compensation per wRVU provides a tool to incentivize physician productivity and efficiency, this rate in itself may not necessarily result in fair market value. Instead, the selected conversion rate should facilitate a commensurate relationship between overall annual physician production and compensation to ensure fair market value results.

Contributed to and edited by:
M. Allison Carty, JD, MBA
Lauren E. Davis, MBA, ASA, CFE
W. Lyle Oelrich, Jr. MHA, FACHE, CMPE

Chapter 42. Choosing the Best Survey for a Physician Compensation Market Study

CONTENTS

Chapter 42. Choosing the Best Survey for a Physician Compensation Market Study

By Darcy Devine, MBA, AIBA, AVA, and Briana Gordon, MBA

1.0 Introduction

When using compensation surveys to value physician services, the appraiser should be aware of what resources are available and be able to evaluate the quality and applicability of the data they contain. Compensation benchmarking appears simple on the surface, but given the proliferation of physician compensation surveys, the task can be complicated.

There are at least four key questions to ask when performing a market compensation study:

1. What type of work is the physician to perform?

2. What type of practice is he or she joining?

3. What type of physician is needed for the job?

4. What type of arrangement is being offered?

Appraisers should also be aware of survey-specific issues that may limit (or add to) the value of physician compensation data contained within a report. Knowing the answers to the four questions and being aware of these issues will help the appraiser choose the right compensation survey and use the most comparable data.

2.0 What Type of Work Is the Physician to Perform?

Physician compensation surveys often divide physician work into (at least) two primary categories: clinical and administrative. This is an important distinction because a physician's clinical time and administrative time may have different values, as noted by the Centers for Medicare & Medicaid Services (CMS) in the Stark II regulations.

> A fair market value hourly rate may be used to compensate physicians for both administrative and clinical work, provided that the rate paid for clinical work is fair market value for the clinical work performed and the rate paid for administrative work is fair market value for the administrative work performed. We note that the fair market value of administrative services may differ from the fair market value of clinical services.[1]

2.1 Clinical Work

Clinical work fits into the classic physician job description. The large majority of active physicians are clinicians, diagnosing and treating injuries and illnesses in patients. A clinical physician's duties may include examining patients, interpreting diagnostic tests, performing operations, and prescribing medications. Clinical physicians are often categorized by specialty to identify those providers with advanced knowledge, skills, and experience in a particular clinical area for the benefit of consumers, colleagues, payers, and the general public. In most situations, patients or their insurance providers pay physicians for their professional services. Many compensation surveys show that, compared to their administrative, research, or teaching counterparts, clinical physicians earn higher levels of compensation because they generate revenue for a practice or other employer.

The Medical Group Management Association's (MGMA) *Physician Compensation and Production Survey* is an annual survey that focuses on compensation paid to physicians for their clinical work. The 2012 edition of the survey reports data on 116 physician specialties. According to the "Demographics" section, 77% of providers were identified as being engaged in full-time clinical work (i.e., 1.0 FTE clinical). Another 11% were identified as 0.9 to 0.99 FTE clinical physicians.

2.2 Administrative Work

Administrative work for physicians is a newer concept. In an administrative role, a physician may be responsible for the performance of a business or business unit, such as a hospital service line. He or she is expected to draw upon a medical background to help manage finances and/or operations. These administrative roles often require specific clinical training and experience on the part of the physician. This expertise is necessary to provide leadership, oversight, medical guidance, and quality assurance for certain

---

1   Stark Preamble: 72 *F.R.* (Sept. 5, 2007), p. 51015-51016.

clinical operations. Administrative physicians are often categorized by title. Common administrative titles are medical director, chief medical officer, and division chief.

Administrative work does not directly generate patient revenue. Certain administrative positions are mandated by CMS and other regulatory bodies and are necessary for some facilities (e.g., hospice and sleep centers) to generate income. However, since administrative services are not directly paid for by patients or payers, they may not command the same compensation as direct clinical care.

The American College of Physician Executives (ACPE) publishes the *Physician Executive Compensation Survey*, a biannual survey focused on compensation paid to physicians in administrative roles. The 2011 results show that the 1,985 ACPE members reporting to the survey spent 69% of their professional time on administrative responsibilities, 29% on clinical duties, and 2% on research. Eighty-seven percent of the respondents were responsible for administrative management, defined as setting organization policy and compliance, strategic planning, marketing, setting physician compensation, and/ or addressing reimbursement issues. The allocation of time to administrative duties versus clinical duties varied among the 18 executive titles represented in the survey.

2.3 Specific Types of Clinical/Administrative Work

Physician compensation surveys sometimes narrow their focus, reporting data on a specific type of clinical or administrative work. These surveys may focus on the value of work that just a small subset of physicians performs. For example, relatively few physicians hold paid medical directorships; however, there are surveys that focus exclusively on administrative compensation paid to different types of medical directors.

Using Clinical Benchmarks to Value Administrative Services

There is often an opportunity cost factor for clinical physicians who provide administrative services. A physician serving on a hospital committee, working on budgets, or reviewing a strategic plan cannot at the same time see patients, perform operations, or provide other revenue-generating clinical services. One strategy to encourage physicians to provide administrative services is to pay them at a rate that offsets the lost clinical revenues and profits. To help ensure the comparability of clinical compensation data with administrative services, the appraiser should make certain that (1) the administrative services require a physician who is currently in clinical practice; and (2) the physician's specialty is crucial to the provision of the services (e.g., an interventional cardiologist may be necessary for a catheterization medical directorship). The appraiser should always be mindful of guidance provided in the Stark laws regarding the potential difference in value between clinical and administrative work.

These surveys may delve into rates of pay for various types of medical directorships, distinguishing between medical directors in different specialties or departments, often with wide-ranging scopes of responsibilities and duties.

Surveys may also focus on the value of services that, while provided by many physicians, may require only a small fraction of a physician's professional time. In recent years, it has become more common for hospitals to pay physicians for their on-call services. Call coverage generally requires less effort from a physician and is, therefore, paid at a much lower rate (on an equated hourly basis) than standard clinical work. Call coverage surveys focus on the nuances of call coverage that affect value—for instance, whether the physician is required to remain on-site (restricted versus unrestricted call)—so that the benchmark data can be applied in a more meaningful way to the situation at hand.

3.0 What Type of Practice Is the Physician Joining?

Compensation may vary significantly between physicians in different practice settings. According to the Bureau of Labor Statistics' *Occupational Outlook Handbook*, physicians and surgeons held about 691,000 jobs in 2010. Many still practice in private offices or clinics as solo practitioners or as part of a group practice; however, physicians are increasingly working for different types of healthcare organizations. A long list of organizations, such as hospitals, transitional care facilities (e.g. hospices, home health, and rehabilitation facilities), and insurance companies, require physician services. The supply and demand of physicians in the United States is in a state of disequilibrium, causing all physician employers to pay more—and more often—for their physician workforce. Given the increased number of practice settings and the growing competition for practitioners, physician compensation surveys often distinguish between where physician services are performed. In some cases, the practice setting will impact the rate that is paid. Whether it will be appropriate to narrow the scope to setting-specific benchmark data will depend on the facts and circumstances of the situation at hand.

3.1 Group Type

The "practice setting" distinction may mean a classification between physicians in private practice as either solo practitioners or physicians in group practices. Group practices can be large or small and single-specialty or multispecialty. These differences can impact overall compensation rates. For example, primary care salaries may receive a boost in multispecialty practices, whereas certain specialties may show slightly lower overall rates of pay in the same type of setting. Surveys by certain physician practice organizations, most notably the American Medical Group Association (AMGA), receive responses primarily from large group practices. More than 89% of physicians

The Solo Practitioner

Solo practitioners may not be adequately represented in some of the better-known physician compensation surveys. Probably the biggest reason is that these surveys are published by organizations, such as the MGMA or AMGA, that require membership fees to join. In addition to cost, the time and effort to submit data to the surveys are also prohibitive to solo physicians. Sources for salary data earned by these types of practitioners may include resources other than the well-known physician compensation surveys. Such resources include wage data published by the Bureau of Labor Statistics (BLS) and the online resource Medscape.com. The *BLS National Compensation Survey* provides data on occupational wages for localities, broad geographic regions, and the nation (www.bls. gov/bls/blswage.htm). The sampling universe for the survey is about 6.7 million nonfarm establishments that file unemployment insurance reports. Medscape's 2012 version of the *Physician Compensation Report* is a collection of compensation data on 24,216 physicians in 25 specialties across the United States. Data for this survey was solicited from physicians in all types of work situations (employed, owner, independent contractor, and partner) (www.medscape.com/sites/public/physician-comp/2012).

represented in the 2012 edition of the AMGA *Medical Group Compensation and Financial Survey* were in group practices with more than 100 physicians, as compared to only 51% of providers who were in groups with more than 100 FTE physicians in the 2012 MGMA report.[2] Nearly all (99.7%) of the providers in the AMGA survey were practicing in multispecialty groups, while only 74% of providers in the MGMA survey represented multispecialty groups.

3.2 Practice Ownership

Users of physician compensation surveys should be aware of the changing landscape and the move toward the hospital-owned physician practice. Appraisers should note that surveys that were predominantly composed of private practice data in the past (such as the MGMA survey) now reflect a much higher percentage of hospital-employed physician data. Some survey respondents include a majority of hospital-owned practices. For example, in the Hospital & Healthcare Compensation Service's (HHCS) 2012 edition of its *Physician Salary & Benefits Report*, 86.47% of the 303 participants were hospitals and only 13.53% were group practices. Towers Watson Data Services (Towers Watson) also publishes a salary survey, the *Health Care Clinical and Professional Compensation Survey Report*, which includes physicians who are predominantly practicing in hospital-owned organizations.

---

2   Additionally, in terms of groups responding to the MGMA survey, the median group size was four physicians.

3.3 Academic Practices

Academic medicine physicians work in—or in close affiliation with—medical schools, teaching hospitals, and/or faculty practice plans. Their time is often divided, spent in clinical care, research, and teaching activities. In general, compensation for physicians in the academic setting is often lower than that of private practitioners in the same specialty because academic physicians do not focus entirely on clinical work. There are numerous sources for academic physician compensation, including the Association of American Medical Colleges (AAMC) *Report on Medical School Faculty Salaries*, which reports total income attributable to teaching, patient care, or research for full-time medical school faculty. Organizations such as MGMA and HHCS also publish compensation surveys or sections dedicated to academic physician data.

4.0 What Type of Physician Is Needed for the Job?

4.1 Specialty

Clinical specialty is typically the most significant factor that determines the value of a physician's services. In fact, compensation benchmarks that are not broken down by specialty are largely irrelevant. (This is mostly seen in broader salary surveys that delve into other healthcare occupations.) As the healthcare benchmarking industry evolves, reported compensation data continues to be refined into further nuanced subspecialties. MGMA, for instance, currently publishes compensation data for three ophthalmology subspecialties. In other surveys, a very general grouping of highly distinctive—and diversely compensated—specialties is reported. In its *Health Care Clinical and Professional Compensation Survey Report*, for example, Towers Watson presents compensation data for over 170 healthcare occupations. Physicians are categorized into large groupings such as "surgeon," with the major surgical specialties not broken out.

In many cases, choosing a survey with subspecialty breakdowns will be crucial to identifying an appropriate rate of pay. A physician with highly specialized training will often earn significantly more than physicians in the same general specialty. When benchmarking a maternal-fetal medicine physician's compensation, for instance, it would be important to use comparables specific to this subspecialty. According to the MGMA data, OB/GYNs in maternal-fetal medicine earn roughly 50% more than OB/GYNs in general practice. At other times, the inherent limits of more specific benchmarks, such as a smaller sample size or a lack of detailed information, may bring into question the usefulness of the data. In certain surveys, some subspecialties may only have the median compensation data point reported (if the specialty is reported at all).

There are some subtle factors to consider when choosing the appropriate specialty for a market study. First, survey respondents self-report their specialties. MGMA indicates that a provider should be classified in the specialty or subspecialty in which he spends 50% of his professional time or more. AMGA cites that more than 70% of a physician's time should be spent in a specialized field. Second, as the number of recognized physician specialties increases, new specialties are broken out in the survey data each year. If several years' worth of survey data is used, a physician's specialty category may change from year to year.

Also, specialty and subspecialty naming conventions vary among surveys. Cardiology, for example, has many subspecialties that can be referenced in different ways. The MGMA, AMGA, Sullivan Cotter & Associates (Sullivan Cotter), HHCS, and Towers Watson report on the identified categories of cardiologists shown in the exhibit in their compensation surveys:

Categories of Cardiologists According to Survey				
MGMA	**AMGA**	**Sullivan Cotter**	**HHCS**	**Towers Watson**
	Cardiology– General	General Cardiology		Cardiology
Cardiology: Invasive	Cardiology–Cath Lab	Invasive- Interventional Cardiology	Cardiology- Invasive	
Cardiology: Invasive- Interventional				
Cardiology: Noninvasive	Cardiology–Echo Lab/Nuclear	Noninvasive Cardiology	Noninvasive Cardiology	
		Cardiac Imaging		
Cardiology: Electrophysiology	Cardiology– Electrophysiology Pacemaker	Electrophysiology		
		Transplant Cardiology		

Benchmarking the subject against the right subspecialties in cardiology (and other specialties) is crucial because subspecialists can have very different practices and generate very different levels of revenue. Compensation may vary accordingly. As seen in the exhibit, marrying up the subspecialty data that is reported in multiple surveys can also be difficult. If using multiple data sources, it makes sense to choose surveys that narrow down the data in a similar fashion.

4.2 Training/Certification

In some specialties, certification will affect compensation. For example, the *2011 National Emergency Medicine Salary Survey Clinical Results* report, published jointly by the American College of Emergency Physicians (ACEP) and Daniel Stern & Associates, shows that the differential between the median compensation rates for board certified and non-board-certified emergency medicine physicians is approximately 11%.

Experience

Almost every physician compensation survey publishes historical compensation data. When a practice responds to a survey questionnaire, it will have limited access to information on historical compensation for new hires. Survey users should be aware of the methodology used by the data compilers in dealing with incomplete data—well-known compensation surveys from organizations such as the MGMA will exclude data for physicians who have been with an organization for less than 12 months, while other less-formal surveys may annualize data. For physicians in new practices, the survey user may want to consider seeking a unique resource and examine published data specific to a physician's years in practice. The AMGA (in its *Medical Group Compensation and Financial Survey*) and the MGMA (in its *Physician Placement Starting Salary Survey*), for example, publish starting base salary data for experienced recruits, as well as for physicians just out of training. Many recruiting firms now publish surveys showing annual guarantees paid to new recruits.

4.3 Highly Compensated Physicians

Surveys generally do not report data over the 90th percentile, so be aware that the published upper-range benchmarks may not be applicable for physicians of national prominence, for example. In the CD-ROM version of MGMA's *Physician Compensation and Production Survey* (called the Interactive Report), there is a tool called the "Physician Pay to Production Plotter," which allows users to graph a physician's work RVUs and compensation against the plotted data points of survey respondents for the same specialty. A fascinating byproduct of this tool is that users are able to view the respondent data that falls outside of the 10th percentile-to-90th percentile range. While some data points are clearly outliers, the MGMA tool gives a more complete picture of the annual compensation spectrum for many specialties.

5.0 What Type of Arrangement Is Being Offered?

5.1 Pay Structure

The pay structure for an arrangement can also dictate which physician compensation benchmarks serve as the best comparables. Among medical director surveys, different compensation components are reported. Integrated Healthcare Strategies' (IHS) *Medical Director Survey* reports compensation paid specifically for medical director duties, expressed either as an hourly rate or an annual stipend that is for generally part-time work provided in addition to a physician's clinical practice. Sullivan Cotter's *Physician Compensation and Productivity Survey*, on the other hand, provides total annual compensation data for medical directors, which includes all administrative, clinical, and other miscellaneous income, such as call pay. If a hospital is contracting with a medical director on a part-time basis, the IHS survey may be most applicable; however, for cases in which the hospital is employing the physician and the appraiser is looking at overall compensation, the Sullivan Cotter survey will likely provide a more complete picture.

5.2 Independent Contractor/Employment

Whether services will be provided on an independent contractor basis or under an employment arrangement can also impact the selection of market benchmarks. When a physician provides services as an independent contractor, the private practice generally bears the responsibility for all employment-related expenses (including benefits, malpractice, employer-responsible taxes, etc.). In some cases, it is appropriate, then, to adjust compensation benchmarks to reflect the true expense to a group of providing the service. This may mean that a 10%, 15%, or 20% increase to compensation data may be warranted. Many of the major compensation surveys report benchmarks related to the cost of physician benefits, which can be used to make this adjustment. Keep in mind, however, that adjusting some benchmarks may not be appropriate and that not all independent contractor agreements warrant adjustment.

5.3 Part-Time Employment

To determine the value of part-time work, appraisers sometimes use a pro rata share of full-time compensation data. It is not uncommon for an appraiser to divide annual compensation by a denominator of 2,000 or 2,080 to determine hourly rates or to multiply annual compensation by a full-time equivalency factor (i.e., multiply full-time compensation by 0.5 for a physician working half time) to determine the value of less than full-time work.[3] However, there are also resources available that focus on part-time pay. The MGMA survey, for example, provides data on total annual compensation paid to physicians who work less than the number of hours considered to be a normal workweek.

5.4 Fringe Benefits

"Total compensation" data reported in the major compensation surveys excludes the value of employee benefits such as payroll taxes, retirement plan contributions, and

---

3 The Stark safe harbor (see insert) references a denominator of 2,000 hours per year. A standard 40-hour workweek requires 2,080 hours of service.

health and life insurance premiums paid by the employer. These costs can be quite significant, running 10% to 20% of a physician's annual compensation, in some cases. Variance in benefit packages can also be significant. Whereas hospital-employed physicians typically receive benefits consistent with corporate or large organizations, private practice physicians have more flexibility in determining the benefits they elect to receive from their practices.[4] These elections frequently result in lower benefits being paid in comparison to those that hospital-employed physicians generally receive. Professionals providing services as independent contractors generally do not receive benefits under these arrangements, so the treatment of these expenses must be considered when benchmarking compensation arrangements.

A number of compensation surveys explore the benefits paid to physicians. MGMA, in its physician compensation survey, separately reports statistics for retirement plan contributions paid on behalf of physicians by their practices or employers. Merritt Hawkins publishes an annual *Review of Physician Recruiting Incentives,* which offers an in-depth view of the benefits and incentives being offered to recruited physicians. HHCS, which has primarily hospital respondents, also publishes detailed physician benefits data in its report, ranging from information on the types of insurance offered to the average premiums amounts paid by policy type.

6.0 Other Considerations When Choosing a Compensation Survey

In addition to answering the previously posed questions, appraisers should be wary of additional factors during the survey selection process.

6.1 Source

Understanding the differences among the various physician compensation resources is crucial to appropriately applying the data they report. The type of group conducting the survey, for instance, will affect the results received. For instance, a professional society for a medical or surgical specialty may draw responses from a different pool than would a larger, association-based survey with a more diverse group of respondents. Interestingly, some publishers, such as the AMGA, outsource the data collection and survey publication process. Sullivan Cotter and Associates actually conducted AMGA's 2012 survey and informed respondents that the data may be used in Sullivan Cotter reports as well.

---

4   For the benefit plan to be nontaxable, however, the plan must meet certain tax-related requirements.

6.2 Respondent Pool

Generally there is a trade-off between the specificity of data and the number of respondents. What makes an acceptable respondent size will be a judgment call and will depend on the position or type of service being assessed. Call pay benchmarks for spine surgery will have fewer data points than general orthopedic call, but the spine benchmark may more accurately reflect call coverage for spine surgery. Frequently, the greatest challenge in the use of physician benchmarking resources is the very limited amount of data included in many of the published statistics, bringing into question whether the survey represents the prevailing market. For many medical director positions, for example, even the largest market surveys report data for many positions that reflect information from fewer than 10 respondents.

6.3 Timeliness

The timeliness of a survey—including both the frequency of reports and the lag time from the reporting period to the publish date—can impact the relevancy of the data to a current arrangement. Many professional societies only conduct their salary surveys every few years and may take up to a year to publish the results. The publication dates on certain surveys may vary from year to year, which can cause issues for the appraiser trying to perform market studies at the same time each year.

6.4 Comparability

The appraiser must understand the differences in the way data is presented from survey to survey. Annual compensation benchmarks include different compensation components, so turning to the back of the survey to review the definitions is an important step in correctly applying the data. In its total annual compensation benchmark, MGMA includes all direct compensation amounts (W-2, 1099, K-1, and profit distributions) to the physician. Alternatively, for its total direct compensation benchmark, the AMGA excludes signing bonuses and any compensation the physician receives for "moonlighting" duties (defined as services provided outside of the physician's specialty/department, normal clinical hours, or outside of the medical group's compensation plan). Certain surveys report separate benchmarks for base pay and total annual earnings.

Different resources also report different percentile tiers; while most surveys provide the 25th, median, 75th, and 90th percentile benchmarks in the hard copy version of their annual salary survey, AMGA publishes the 20th, median, 80th, and 90th percentiles. The electronic version of the MGMA survey reports all percentage points from the 10th to the 90th. Benchmarking resources also often provide regional slices of data; however, different regional definitions are used (e.g., Southeast versus a general Southern grouping.)

Sullivan Cotter reports compensation data for each specialty for up to four position levels, to include staff physicians, program directors, medical director/division chiefs, and department chairs. It is important to note that the Sullivan Cotter survey does not have any combined benchmark data to show the collective representation of all position levels. Once again, there is a trade-off between specificity of data (i.e., the most applicable position benchmark) and the reliability of the data (i.e., the resulting smaller sample size and difficulty in comparing to differently defined benchmarks).

Summary of the (Former) Stark Safe Harbor

In the Centers for Medicare & Medicaid Services' (CMS) Phase II regulations of the Stark Law (also known as the "Physician Self-Referral Law"), the government initially provided two "safe harbor" methodologies for calculating fair market value compensation for physician services. One of these approaches allowed hospitals to use the average of the 50th percentile national compensation benchmarks for physicians in the same specialty. This annual average was divided by 2,000 to determine a safe harbor hourly rate. Data was required to be drawn from at least four of the six identified physician salary surveys, which included:

Sullivan, Cotter and Associates Inc.—*Physician Compensation and Productivity Survey*;

Hay Group—*Physicians Compensation Survey*;

Hospital and Healthcare Compensation Services—*Physician Salary Survey Report*;

Medical Group Management Association—*Physician Compensation and Productivity Survey*;

ECS Watson Wyatt—*Hospital and Health Care Management Compensation Report*; and

William M. Mercer—*Integrated Health Networks Compensation Survey*.

After being issued, concerns arose in the industry regarding applying a blanket approach to determining fair market value physician compensation. Comments noted in CMS's repeal of the safe harbor methodologies in its Phase III final ruling included: lack of flexibility in the approach; inaccessibility of survey data (organizations not responding to certain surveys were not authorized to purchase the data); significant expense; long-term availability (at least one of the listed surveys no longer existed at the time of the ruling); datedness of some of the data; exclusion of several major national surveys from the list; and the requirement for the use of the national averages.

6.5 Accessibility

Certain surveys are cost-prohibitive. Several of the well-known physician compensation surveys cost thousands of dollars. In many cases, it simply does not make financial sense for a smaller organization to purchase a comprehensive set of published market benchmarks year after year. Moreover, some survey publishers will not sell their reports to individuals or organizations that are not a member, client, or survey participant. For these reasons, an appraiser may choose to simply rely on one primary resource or to rely on surveys that are freely available.

6.6 Credibility

Certain surveys are well-known within the industry and are heavily relied upon. A long history and track record, as well as large sample sizes, make certain surveys the "go-to" resources. Surveys that were identified in the former Stark Law safe harbor for calculating the fair market value of physician services gained notoriety for being reliable—even though at least one of the surveys identified was no longer being published when the safe harbor policy was released. (See the insert.)

Another indication that a survey is trustworthy is that it adheres to Department of Justice (DOJ) guidelines related to benchmark data. In response to lawsuits brought against healthcare organizations that directly shared salary data with competitors, in 1996, the DOJ and the Federal Trade Commission (FTC) issued the "Statements of Antitrust Enforcement Policy in Healthcare" to provide guidelines for compiling compensation survey data. Listed as an "antitrust safety zone," these guidelines were intended to safeguard against collusion or reduced competition in the market. The agencies would not challenge an organization's participation in compensation surveys that met the following criteria:

1. The survey data is managed by an independent third-party (such as a trade association, academic institution, or consulting group);

2. The information reported by participants is at least three months old;

3. A reported benchmark reflects data from no fewer than five respondents, and no one responding entity's data can represent more than 25% of the data for a particular statistic; and

4. Data must be aggregated in such a way that particular respondents or providers would not be identifiable.[5]

---

5   www.justice.gov/atr/public/guidelines/1791.htm.

Given the large number of physician compensation surveys available to appraisers, it is important to understand the differences between the reports and assess their value. Following are the basic recommended steps for a physician compensation market study.

7.0 Best Practices

- Determine what percentage of survey respondents' time is spent in clinical, administrative, and/or other roles. Make sure that the allocation is consistent with the professional time for the position or services under review.

- Consider survey data that focuses on the specific type of clinical or administrative service the subject is providing (emergency call coverage, for example).

- Examine the published data to determine what impact, if any, the practice setting has on market compensation rates. Group type, practice ownership, and academic-versus-nonacademic distinctions can weigh significantly on benchmarks.

- Know how much time your physician spends providing primary or specialty care. Check his or her training, experience, and certifications to ensure correct categorization. Read the compensation survey's glossary to ensure that the correct medical specialty is used to benchmark compensation. Be very careful when using multiple surveys to ensure that specialty definitions match from survey to survey.

- Be sure to weigh the potential trade-off between a smaller sample of data and greater specificity of the data.

- Ensure that the type of arrangement has been considered when choosing a market comparable. Using an hourly benchmark rate if the arrangement is hourly or a benchmark specific to part-time compensation in a part-time employment arrangement only makes sense.

- Consideration of source, methodology, sample size, timeliness, comparability, accessibility, and credibility issues are extremely important.

A summary of selected compensation surveys that are currently available is included in the appendix to this chapter.

APPENDIX: Summary of Compensation Surveys

Survey	n	Type	Website
MGMA Physician Compensation and Production Survey	2,913 medical practices	118 clinical specialties	mgma.com
MGMA Physician Placement Starting Salary	749 medical groups	118 clinical specialties	mgma.com
MGMA Management Survey	1,287 medical practices	57 management positions	mgma.com
MGMA Medical Directorship and On-Call Compensation Survey	264 medical practices	100 clinical specialties	mgma.com
AMGA Medical Group Compensation and Financial Survey	239 medical groups	194 clinical specialties and administrative positions	amga.org
Sullivan Cotter Physician Compensation and Productivity Survey Report	424 organizations	212 clinical specialties and administrative positions	sullivancotter.com
Sullivan Cotter Physician On-Call Pay Survey Report	189 organizations	40 clinical specialties	sullivancotter.com
Towers Watson Clinical and Professional Compensation	372 organizations	177 clinical positions	towerswatson.com
Towers Watson Executive and Management Compensation	355 organizations	167 administrative positions	towerswatson.com
ACEP/Daniel Stern National EM Clinical Salary Survey	1,308 physicians	1,308 emergency department physicians	danielstern.com
Merritt Hawkins Review of Physician Recruiting Incentives	2,667 physician placements	86 clinical specialties	merritthawkins.com
IHS Medical Director Survey	159 organizations	92 medical directorships	integratedhealthcarestrategies.com
HHCS Physician Salary and Benefits Report	303 facilities	45 clinical specialties and residencies	hhcsinc.com
ACPE Cejka Physician Executive Compensation Survey	1,985 physician executives	18 administrative positions	acpe.org
Medscape Physician Compensation Report	24,216 physicians	25 clinical specialties	medscape.com/ sites/public/ physician-comp
AAMC Report on Medical School Faculty Salaries	134 medical schools	academic medical specialties	aamc.org
Bureau of Labor Statistics Occupational Employment Statistics	800 occupations	9 physician specialty groupings	bls.gov/oes

How to Read This Book, for Various Types of Users

A book of this size and depth must meet the needs of many different types and levels of readers. Professionals working directly in the field and negotiating with physicians have different information needs from those encountering the subject for the first time, or from those with more experience in healthcare compensation valuation, or from attorneys. To help different reader groups navigate the content of the guide efficiently, we have developed readings of selected chapters that meet the primary information needs of each group. The chapter selections will provide readers with content that is germane to their own use. By focusing on these chapters, users can begin to apply the wealth of knowledge and information available in this guide.

Foundational Chapters for the Practice of Compensation Valuation in Healthcare

Chapter 1, Introduction to the New Appraisal Discipline of Compensation Valuation

Chapter 2, Defining FMV and the Market, Cost, and Income Approaches in Compensation Valuation

Chapter 3, Using Multiple Methods as a Prudent Practice in Compensation Valuation

Chapter 4, On the Informed Use of the Market Data in Compensation Valuation

Chapter 5, Elements of a Compensation Valuation Appraisal Report

Chapter 6, The Federal Statutes That Make Healthcare Valuations Unique: An Introduction to the Anti-Kickback Statute and the Stark Law

Chapter 7, Complying With the Healthcare Definition of FMV in Appraisal Practice

Chapter 8, To Use or Not to Use: An Appraisal Analysis of the Stark Prohibition on Market Data From Parties in a Position to Refer

Chapter 9, BV, CV, and the Relationship Between Fair Market Value and Commercial Reasonableness

Introductory and Overview Chapters for Newcomers to Healthcare and Healthcare Compensation Valuation

Chapter 20, Physician Compensation and Financial Statement Benchmarks: Using MGMA Data

Chapter 21, Benchmarking Practice Performance

Chapter 36, Evaluating RVU-Based Compensation Arrangements

Chapter 37, How Reimbursement and Physician Compensation Vary by Market

Advanced Readings for Experienced Professionals

Chapter 3, Using Multiple Methods as a Prudent Practice in Compensation Valuation

Chapter 7, Complying With the Healthcare Definition of FMV in Appraisal Practice

Chapter 9, BV, CV, and the Relationship Between Fair Market Value and Commercial Reasonableness

Chapter 10, Commercial Reasonableness: Defining Practical Concepts and Determining

Chapter 12, Reasonable Compensation for Physicians Under the Internal Revenue Code

Chapter 36, Evaluating RVU-Based Compensation Arrangements

Chapter 37, How Reimbursement and Physician Compensation Vary by Market

Chapter 38, Comparing the Surveys to the Physician Marketplace: Implications for Valuation Analysis

Chapter 39, An Analysis of the Relationship Between Productivity and Compensation in the MGMA Data and Its Implications for Valuation and Compensation-Setting Practices

Chapter 40, An Analysis of MGMA's Compensation by Quartile of Production Data: Compensation Rates Decline as Production Increases

Readings for Attorneys Who Review Compensation Valuations

Chapter 1, Introduction to the New Appraisal Discipline of Compensation Valuation

Chapter 3, Using Multiple Methods as a Prudent Practice in Compensation Valuation

Chapter 5, Elements of a Compensation Valuation Appraisal Report

Chapter 7, Complying With the Healthcare Definition of FMV in Appraisal Practice

Chapter 8, To Use or Not to Use: An Appraisal Analysis of the Stark Prohibition on Market Data From Parties in a Position to Refer

Chapter 9, BV, CV, and the Relationship Between Fair Market Value and Commercial Reasonableness

Chapter 10, Commercial Reasonableness: Defining Practical Concepts and Determining Compliance in Healthcare Transactions for Physician Services

Chapter 11, Valuation Issues Affecting Tax-Exempt Healthcare Organizations

Chapter 12, Reasonable Compensation for Physicians Under the Internal Revenue Code

Chapter 37, How Reimbursement and Physician Compensation Vary by Market

Readings for Individuals Involved in Compensation-Setting with Physicians

Chapter 4, On the Informed Use of the Market Data in Compensation Valuation

Chapter 12, Reasonable Compensation for Physicians Under the Internal Revenue Code

Chapter 13, An Introduction to Physician Services and Specialties

Chapter 14, The Economics of Physician Clinical Services and Compensation

Chapter 17, Critical Condition—A Coding Analysis for a Physician Practice Valuation

Chapter 18, Understanding and Using the Technical and Professional Component of Ancillary Revenue When Valuing Medical Practices

Chapter 19, Quality Performance and Valuation: What's the Connection?

Chapter 20, Physician Compensation and Financial Statement Benchmarks: Using MGMA Data

Chapter 21, Benchmarking Practice Performance

Chapter 36, Evaluating RVU-Based Compensation Arrangements

Chapter 37, How Reimbursement and Physician Compensation Vary by Market

Chapter 38, Comparing the Surveys to the Physician Marketplace: Implications for Valuation Analysis

Chapter 39, An Analysis of the Relationship Between Productivity and Compensation in the MGMA Data and Its Implications for Valuation and Compensation-Setting Practices

Chapter 40, An Analysis of MGMA's Compensation by Quartile of Production Data: Compensation Rates Decline as Production Increases

Chapter 41, Analyzing Physician Compensation Per wRVU: Why Benchmark Data Is Only the Beginning

Chapter 42, Choosing the Best Survey for Your Physician Compensation Market Study

About the Authors

Gregory D. Anderson, CPA/ABV, CVA, is a partner in the Health Care Practice Group of HORNE LLP, a CPA and business advisory firm headquartered in the southeastern United States. He concentrates his practice in the design and valuation of hospital-physician employment and other compensation arrangements; income distribution plans of physician group practices; and valuation of medical practices, hospitals, and other healthcare facilities. He serves as the firm's healthcare valuation services director and writes and lectures on fair market value, physician compensation, and Stark law matters. He is the co-author with Mark Dietrich of *The Financial Professional's Guide to Healthcare Reform* (John Wiley & Sons, 2012), a contributing author to *The BVR/AHLA Guide to Healthcare Valuation* (3rd edition, 2012), and co-author of "Physician On-Call and Coverage Arrangements: History, Present, and Future" in *Health Law Handbook* (Thomson Reuters/West, 2010). He also co-authored *Valuation of a Medical Practice* (Wiley, 1999).

Ann S. Brandt, Ph.D., is a partner at Healthcare Appraisers Inc. Dr. Brandt specializes in valuing compensation arrangements that may have Stark and anti-kickback implications. Working primarily with pharmaceutical companies, medical device companies, and hospitals, Dr. Brandt leads the firm's life sciences service line. She has specific expertise in valuing compensation and arrangements for healthcare professionals and key opinion leaders as well as clinical trials and principal investigator arrangements. In addition, she has extensive experience in providing valuation and consulting services related to co-management and physician management arrangements. Dr. Brandt has more than 25 years of healthcare experience as a clinician, consultant, strategist, marketer, and professor. She has a Ph.D. in psychology and applied statistics.

Martin D. Brown, CPA/ABV, is managing principal of consulting services for PYA and has 27 years of experience in healthcare. He has performed a multitude of projects for health systems as well as for small and large physician groups related to compensation plans, hospital-physician alignment, fair market value compensation valuations, clinic profitability and overhead analyses, financial oversight, Stark II analyses, strategic planning, physician billing, and business office reviews. Marty has performed well over 200 business valuations in his career in many different industries, including healthcare, construction, manufacturing, and professional services. Marty has also testified as an expert witness in numerous litigation support engagements related to business valuation matters, damage estimates, noncompete agreements, accounting and regulatory matters, and certificates of need.

Mark W. Browne, M.D. is a principal with PYA and has nearly 20 years of experience as a practicing physician, healthcare executive, and consultant. Building on his background from the exam room to the C-suite, Mark has developed expertise in clinical quality, value-based payments, and design of new care delivery models in physician services and compensation, clinical quality, and contemporary practice models. He earned a Doctor of Medicine degree from Wright State University and a Master of Medical Management from Carnegie Mellon University.

Carol W. Carden, CPA/ABV, ASA, CFE, is a principal with PYA and provides business valuation and related consulting services to a wide variety of business organizations, primarily in the healthcare industry. Carol's primary areas of expertise are in finance, valuation, managed care, and revenue cycle operations for healthcare organizations. She has performed appraisals of businesses and securities for a wide variety of purposes such as mergers, acquisitions, joint ventures, management service agreements, and other intangible assets. She is also a nationally recognized speaker and writer on healthcare valuation topics. In addition to being a certified public accountant, she has also earned the Accredited in Business Valuation (ABV) credential from the American Institute of Certified Public Accountants, the Accredited Senior Appraiser (ASA) credential from the American Society of Appraisers, and the Certified Fraud Examiner (CFE) credential from the Association of Certified Fraud Examiners. She is the Chair of the Business Valuation Committee for the AICPA, was chair of the 2010 National AICPA Business Valuation Conference and was on the planning committee for the 2011 AICPA National Healthcare Conference.

Frank Cohen, CMPA is the senior analyst of MIT Solutions Inc. in Clearwater, Fla., and is the creator of the CMPA software. He specializes in data mining and statistical modeling for medical practices and is the author of *A Practical Guide to Reengineering the Medical Practice, The Physician CEO, Coding for the Non Coder, Mastering RBRVS, The Complete Guide to E/M Utilization,* and numerous articles, studies, and seminars. He is a certified Black Belt in Six Sigma and a certified Master Black Belt in Lean Six Sigma.

Darcy Devine, MBA, AIBA, AVA, is a principal with PYA and specializes in the valuation of healthcare assets and physician services, focusing on physician and hospital transactions and financial arrangements. She provides valuation and consulting services to law firms, hospitals, health systems, and physician organizations throughout the country. She holds a Bachelor of Business Administration, with a concentration in finance, from Goizueta School of Business at Emory University and a Master of Business Administration from the University of Georgia.

Mark O. Dietrich, CPA/ABV, is editor, technical editor, and contributing author to the American Health Lawyers' Association/Business Valuation Resources *Guide to Healthcare Valuation, 3rd Edition* (2012), editor and principal author of Business Valuation Resources' *Guide to Physician Practice Valuation* (2nd Edition, due in 2012), and co-author with Gregory Anderson, CPA, CVA, of *The Financial Professional's Guide to Healthcare Reform*, published by John Wiley & Sons. Mark is also author of the *Medical Practice Valuation Guidebook* and co-author of PPC's *Guide to Healthcare Consulting*, along with more than 100 articles on valuation, taxation, managed care, and the healthcare regulatory environment. Mark's career experience includes serving as partner-in-charge of the annual audit of an 80-physician tax-exempt faculty group practice, representation of tax-exempt and taxable entities in Internal Revenue Service field audits, participation in the development of a 250-physician independent network and negotiation of its managed care and Medicare Advantage contracts, and more than 200 valuation engagements in the healthcare industry.

David Fein, MBA, is the CEO and president of ValuSource, which for over 20 years has been the leading provider of business valuation software, data and report writers for CPAs, mergers and acquisitions professionals, and business owners. Since 1997, Mr. Fein has partnered with the Medical Group Management Association (MGMA) to develop its interactive survey CD-ROMs, which provide data and benchmarking tools on physicians' compensation, business costs, and coding practices. ValuSource has crucial technology and data for anyone that needs to benchmark or value a medical practice. He has a bachelor's degree in computer science and an MBA.

Gregory S. Feltenberger, MBA, FACMPE, FACHE, CPHIMS, has over 16 years of operational health care experience. Currently, he is the chief of information project management at the Office of the Air Force Surgeon General, Air Force Medical Support Agency, Decision Support Branch in Falls Church, Va. Greg has been a chief information officer, chief of information management, and group practice manager. In addition, Greg completed a 10-month fellowship in survey development, analysis, and performance measurement at the Medical Group Management Association (MGMA). He is a Ph.D. student at Old Dominion University in the health services research program. Greg has a MBA in information systems from Kent State University, a B.A. in specialized studies (summa cum laude), and an associate degree in engineering technology in biomedical equipment technology from Edinboro University of Pennsylvania. He is a fellow in the American College of Medical Practice Executives (ACMPE), the standard-setting and certification body of the MGMA; a fellow in the American College of Healthcare Executives; a certified medical practice executive in the American College of Medical Practice Executives; and a certified professional in healthcare information and management systems in the Healthcare Information and Management Systems Society. Greg is principal and co-founder of SmHart Inc. (www.SmHart.net), an education, training, and organizational improvement consulting firm. Finally, Greg co-authored a book titled, *Benchmarking Success: The Essential Guide for Medical Practices* with David N. Gans, published by the Medical Group Management Association in March 2008.

Andrea M. Ferrari, JD, MPH, is a manager at HealthCare Appraisers. She is a seasoned lawyer and valuation expert. Ms. Ferrari has broad experience structuring, negotiating, reviewing, and executing many types of healthcare transactions, including mergers and acquisitions, hospital-physician joint ventures, physician recruitment arrangements, compensated on-call coverage arrangements, physician employment arrangements, medical director and physician consulting arrangements, clinical trial and research sponsorship agreements, and billing and other service arrangements. Ms. Ferrari is a member of the Florida Bar and is a Florida-licensed healthcare risk manager. She received a Juris Doctor with a certificate of concentration in health law from Boston University School of Law and a Master of Public Health degree with a concentration in Health Law from Boston University School of Medicine/Public Health. She received her Bachelor's degree (economics) from Smith College.

Mark D. Folk is a member of the Health Care Practice Group and a partner in the Corporate Transactions Practice Group at the law firm of Shutts & Bowen, LLP. He has more than 20 years of experience in private practice, focusing on corporate and securities law matters, including extensive experience representing public and private companies in the healthcare industry. He has represented provider entities in structuring contractual arrangements with referral sources, on general fraud and abuse matters and in structuring healthcare receivables securitizations. Mark is a graduate of Harvard College and Stanford Law School.

David N. Gans, MSHA, FACMPE, administers research and development at MGMA-ACMPE and its research affiliate, the MGMA Center for Research in Englewood, Col. He is an educational program speaker, author of a monthly column in *MGMA Connexion*, and he provides technical assistance to the association's staff and members on topic areas of benchmarking, use of survey data, financial management, cost-efficiency, physician compensation and productivity, managerial compensation, the resource-based relative value scale, employee staffing, cost accounting, medical group organization, and emergency preparedness. He is a retired colonel in the United States Army Reserve. Dave earned an undergraduate degree in government at the University of Notre Dame, a master's degree in education from the University of Southern California, and a master's degree in health administration from the University of Colorado. He is a fellow in the American College of Medical Practice Executives and a certified medical practice executive in the American College of Medical Practice Executives.

Briana Gordon, MBA, is a manager with PYA and specializes in the valuation of healthcare services and assets. Her experience includes the development of fair market value and commercial reasonableness opinions for a wide array of healthcare arrangements. Her primary focus is on the review of physician services related to various physician-hospital alignment initiatives, such as physician employment agreements, medical directorships, call coverage arrangements, and clinical co-management agreements. She also regularly assists with the valuation of physician practices and healthcare assets for acquisition and leasing purposes. She holds a Master of Business Administration from Emory University's Goizueta Business School and a Bachelor of Arts from Georgia State University.

Alice G. Gosfield, Esq., is the principal of Alice G. Gosfield & Associates, P.C. in Philadelphia. Her legal career has been restricted to health law with an emphasis on representation of physicians and their group configurations and a focus on noninstitutional reimbursement including Medicare, managed care, fraud and abuse compliance and avoidance, medical staff issues and utilization management, and quality issues. Ms. Gosfield served as chairman of the Board of Directors of the National Committee for Quality Assurance and on four committees of the Institute of Medicine of the National Academy of Sciences. She is the first chairman of the board of PROMETHEUS Payment Inc. and served as president of the American Health Lawyers Association (formerly the National Health Lawyers Association) and chaired its Physician and Physician Organizations Institute. She is a graduate of Barnard College and New York University School of Law.

Ryan Harvey is a consultant in the Southeast region of CBIZ Valuation Group. He is involved with a wide range of assignments, including the valuation of business enterprises, physician compensation, and employment agreements. Prior to joining CBIZ Valuation Group, Mr. Harvey worked at Gentiva Health Services as a tax accountant, where he was primarily involved with state and local tax compliance. Mr. Harvey earned a Bachelor of Science degree in finance from University of Florida.

Albert Hutzler, JD, MBA, AVA, is a partner at HealthCare Appraisers Inc., in Delray Beach, Fla. Mr. Hutzler has nearly 14 years' experience as a financial analyst and nearly 20 years' experience as an attorney, including positions in healthcare law, private equity investment banking, strategic business development, and business affairs. At HealthCare Appraisers, Mr. Hutzler focuses on fair market value analysis of physician arrangements, including on-call arrangements, medical directorships, employment arrangements, and physician recruitment arrangements. Previously, he represented hospitals as an attorney and also worked for a private equity firm evaluating investment opportunities and managing existing holdings. Mr. Hutzler is an Accredited Valuation Analyst (AVA) and holds the degrees of Master of Business Administration (MBA) from the Wharton School and Juris Doctor (JD) from the University of Maryland. He is an active member of the American Health Lawyers Association (AHLA), where he serves as vice chair of the Hospitals and Health Systems Practice Group and served as the first chair of the FMV Affinity Group from 2007 to 2009.

David McMillan, CPA, is a principal with PYA and leads strategic planning exercises, merger and acquisition projects, and provides physician-hospital alignment and advisory services to executives and boards of directors. David's experience includes the design and valuation of many transactions, ranging from compensation arrangements to mergers and acquisitions. He is active in the American Health Lawyers Association, the Healthcare Financial Management Association, and the Society for Healthcare Strategy and Market Development.

Robert M. Mundy, CPA, ABV, CVA, is a senior manager with PYA and has an extensive background in business valuation with experience in healthcare valuation engagements that involve mergers and acquisitions, financial reporting, joint ventures, divestitures, partnership transactions, leasing arrangements, and divorce settlements. His healthcare valuation experience includes general acute care and specialty hospitals, diagnostic imaging centers, ambulatory surgery centers, skilled nursing facilities, assisted living centers, cancer treatment centers, cardiac catheter laboratories, and a variety of physician practices. Robbie co-authored "The Valuation of Hospitals" chapter in Business Valuation Resources' *Guide to Healthcare Valuation*.

W. Lyle Oelrich Jr., MHA, FACHE, CMPE, is a principal with PYA and consults with physician practices and healthcare systems in the areas of fair market value compensation, commercial reasonableness, and contract compliance. He also advises clients relative to physician/hospital economic alignment models and assists physician practices with strategic, financial, and operational issues. Lyle earned a Bachelor of Science in biology from Wake Forest University and a Master of Healthcare Administration from the University of North Carolina. He is a Fellow of the American College of Healthcare Executives and is a Certified Medical Practice Executive of the American College of Medical Practice.

Tynan P. Olechny, MBA, MPH, AVA, is a senior manager with PYA, and her experience includes performing valuations and fair market value analyses of medical practices and ancillary service lines for a variety of physician and hospital transactions. Additionally, her experience includes conducting medical staff development plans, physician need analyses, and market assessments. Tynan has 15 years of healthcare consulting experience and prior to rejoining PYA GatesMoore in 2007, spent several years providing strategic planning expertise to community hospitals/healthcare systems, academic medical centers and physician groups regarding the development of coordinated, comprehensive cancer programs. Ms. Olechny earned a Bachelor of Science in biology from The College of William and Mary prior to earning a Master in Business Administration and a Master in Public Health from Emory University. She is certified as an Accredited Valuation Analyst (AVA) through the National Association of Certified Valuators and Analysts (NACVA).

Robert F. Reilly, MBA, CPA, CMA, CFA, ASA, CBA, is a managing director of Willamette Management Associates. Robert has been the principal analyst on over 2,000 valuations of businesses, business interests, and intellectual properties in virtually every industry and business sector. Robert holds a B.S. in economics and an MBA in finance, both from Columbia University. He is a certified public accountant, certified management accountant, chartered financial analyst, accredited senior appraiser, certified business appraiser, certified review appraiser, and state-certified general real estate appraiser. He is a member of the American Economic Association, National Association of Business Economists, American Society of Appraisers, Institute of Business Appraisers, American Bankruptcy Institute, Institute of Property Taxation, and several other professional organizations.

He is co-author of the following six textbooks: Valuing a Business: The Analysis and Appraisal of Closely Held Companies, The Handbook of Advanced Business Valuation, Valuing Intangible Assets, Valuing Small Businesses and Professional Practices, Valuing Accounting Practices, and Valuing Professional Practices: A Practitioners Approach.

Richard A. Romero, PAHM, AVA, CHFP, is a director with CBIZ Healthcare Valuation. His practice focuses on regulatory compliance, valuation, and litigation support. His previous experience includes strategic and operational consulting, valuation, litigation support, expert witness services, and compliance-related matters. Mr. Romero has experience with various aspects of healthcare, including physician compensation, physician practices, hospitals, specialty hospitals, joint ventures, managed care organizations, billing companies, long-term care, hospice, and others. He has presented nationally and been published on topics involving healthcare, litigation, and valuation. Mr. Romero maintains memberships in several professional healthcare organizations and currently serves on the Advisory Committee for the Healthcare Practice Group of the National Association of Certified Valuation Analysts. Mr. Romero has a Master of Business Administration degree from the University of Florida and Bachelor of Science degree from the University of Tampa. His professional designations include Accredited Valuation Analyst (AVA), Certified Healthcare Financial Professional (CHFP), and Professional, Academy for Healthcare Management (PAHM).

Jason Ruchaber, CFA, ASA, is a partner with HealthCare Appraisers and head of business valuation services in the Colorado office. Mr. Ruchaber has more than 15 years of finance and valuation experience, the last 12 of which have been spent exclusively in business valuation and litigation consulting. Prior to joining HealthCare Appraisers, Mr. Ruchaber was a principal in Cogence Group, P.C., a business valuation and litigation support firm located in Portland, Ore. Mr. Ruchaber has also worked in Standard & Poor's Corporate Value Consulting practice, where he focused on intellectual property valuation and damages calculations. Mr. Ruchaber received a degree in finance from the University of Texas at Austin, has earned the chartered financial analyst (CFA) designation, and is an accredited senior appraiser (ASA). He is a member of the CFA Institute, the Denver Society of Financial Analysts, the American Society of Appraisers, and the Licensing Executives Society International. Mr. Ruchaber is a frequent speaker and author on healthcare valuation topics.

Scott Safriet, MBA, AVA, is a partner at HealthCare Appraisers. He has almost 20 years of broad healthcare experience, the last eight of which have been focused exclusively on healthcare valuation, primarily addressing any type of agreement or compensation arrangement that may have Stark and anti-kickback implications. Mr. Safriet is an accredited valuation analyst (AVA) and holds a Master of Business Administration (MBA) in corporate finance. He is a frequent speaker and author on healthcare valuation topics.

Timothy Smith, CPA/ABV, is the president of Touchstone Valuation, LLC, a valuation consulting firm specializing in the healthcare industry. Tim has over 18 years of experience in the healthcare industry, including more than 14 years at Hospital Corporation of America Inc. (HCA), the nation's largest hospital company. During his tenure at HCA, he worked on hundreds of physician practice acquisition, divestiture, and employment deals. He also completed regulatory compliance reviews on hundreds of appraisals for acquisitions, divestitures, and compensation arrangements. Following his HCA tenure, Tim has worked in the appraisal profession with a focus on physician compensation arrangements. He holds the Accredited in Business Valuation (ABV) certification from the American Institute of Certified Public Accountants (AICPA) and is a licensed CPA in two states. He is co-editor, along with Mark O. Dietrich, of *The BVR/AHLA Guide to Healthcare Industry Compensation and Valuation* (November 2012).

Burl E. Stamp, FACHE, is a principal with PYA and Burl has more than 25 years of healthcare experience in executive roles ranging from strategic planning/business development to hospital administration. He currently is president of PYA/Stamp, an organization that assists healthcare providers and organizations to improve quality, performance, and communications in response to new healthcare reform requirements and incentives.

Kathie L. Wilson, CPA, CVA, maintains a consulting practice, assisting accountants and attorneys in the areas of medical practice accounting and valuation and family law litigation in the San Francisco Bay Area. She holds a Masters in Taxation from Bentley College, a Bachelor of Arts in Business Administration (with an accounting concentration) from the University of Washington, and a certified valuation analyst credential.

CPSIA information can be obtained at www.ICGtesting.com
Printed in the USA
BVOW052147200213

313733BV00010B/379/P

GREYSCALE

BIN TRAVELER FORM

Cut By _Yeferson Benitez_ Qty _14_ Date _____

Scanned By _____ Qty _____ Date _____

Scanned Batch IDs

_____   _____   _____

Notes / Exception

_____

_____

_____

_____

_____